Pro T-SQL 2008 Programmer's Guide

Michael Coles

Apress®

Pro T-SQL 2008 Programmer's Guide

Copyright © 2008 by Michael Coles

ISBN-13 (pbk): 978-1-4302-1001-6

ISBN-13 (electronic): 978-1-4302-1002-3

Printed and bound in the United States of America 9 8 7 6 5 4 3 2 1

Lead Editors: Jonathan Gennick, Tony Campbell
Technical Reviewer: Adam Machanic
Editorial Board: Clay Andres, Steve Anglin, Ewan Buckingham, Tony Campbell, Gary Cornell, Jonathan Gennick, Matthew Moodie, Joseph Ottinger, Jeffrey Pepper, Frank Pohlmann, Ben Renow-Clarke, Dominic Shakeshaft, Matt Wade, Tom Welsh
Project Manager: Kylie Johnston
Copy Editor: Damon Larson
Associate Production Director: Kari Brooks-Copony
Production Editor: Elizabeth Berry
Compositor: Lynn L'Heureux
Proofreaders: Linda Seifert, April Eddy
Indexer: Broccoli Information Management
Artist: Kinetic Publishing Services, LLC
Cover Designer: Kurt Krames
Manufacturing Director: Tom Debolski

Distributed to the book trade worldwide by Springer-Verlag New York, Inc., 233 Spring Street, 6th Floor, New York, NY 10013. Phone 1-800-SPRINGER, fax 201-348-4505, e-mail orders-ny@springer-sbm.com, or visit http://www.springeronline.com.

For information on translations, please contact Apress directly at 2855 Telegraph Avenue, Suite 600, Berkeley, CA 94705. Phone 510-549-5930, fax 510-549-5939, e-mail info@apress.com, or visit http://www.apress.com.

Apress and friends of ED books may be purchased in bulk for academic, corporate, or promotional use. eBook versions and licenses are also available for most titles. For more information, reference our Special Bulk Sales–eBook Licensing web page at http://www.apress.com/info/bulksales.

The source code for this book is available to readers at http://www.apress.com.

For Devoné and Rebecca

Contents at a Glance

Contents

About the Author

■**MICHAEL COLES** is a Microsoft MVP with over a dozen years' experience in SQL database design, T-SQL development, and client-server application programming. He has consulted in a wide range of industries, including the insurance, financial, retail, and manufacturing sectors, among others. Michael's specialty is developing and performance-tuning high-profile SQL Server–based database solutions. He currently works as a consultant for a business intelligence consulting firm. He holds a degree in information technology and multiple Microsoft and other certifications.

Michael has published dozens of technical articles online and in print magazines, including SQL Server Central, ASPToday, and *SQL Server Standard*. Michael is the author of the books *Pro T-SQL 2005 Programmer's Guide* (Apress, 2007) and *Pro SQL Server 2008 XML* (Apress, 2008), and he contributed to *Accelerated SQL Server 2008* (Apress, 2008). His current projects include coauthoring the book *Pro SQL Server 2008 Full-Text Search*.

About the Technical Reviewer

ADAM MACHANIC is a Boston-based independent database consultant, writer, and speaker. He has been involved in dozens of SQL Server implementations for both high-availability OLTP and large-scale data warehouse applications, and has optimized data access layer performance for several data-intensive applications. Adam has written for numerous web sites and magazines, including SQLblog, Simple Talk, Search SQL Server, SQL Server Professional, CoDe, and VSJ. He has also contributed to several books on SQL Server, including *Expert SQL Server 2005 Development* (Apress, 2007) and *Inside SQL Server 2005: Query Tuning and Optimization* (Microsoft Press, 2007). Adam regularly speaks at user groups, community events, and conferences on a variety of SQL Server and .NET-related topics. He is a Microsoft Most Valuable Professional (MVP) for SQL Server and a Microsoft Certified IT Professional (MCITP).

Acknowledgments

I've said it before, and I'll say it again—delivering books like this into your hands takes the coordinated efforts of dozens of people working toward a common goal. There's no way you would be reading these words right now if not for the entire team at Apress. This book is the product of the work of all my Apress teammates.

With that in mind, I would like to start by thanking my editors Tony Campbell and Jonathan Gennick, who pulled this project together and oversaw it from the first page of the dedication to the last page of the index. I would also like to thank the hardest-working project manager ever, Kylie Johnston, who kept everyone on track and on schedule. I want to send a special thank you to my technical reviewer (and one of my favorite SQL authors), Adam Machanic, for keeping me honest and challenging me to "explain, explain, explain!" at every opportunity. I would also like to thank Elizabeth Berry, Damon Larson, Linda Seifert, and April Eddy, the team members who ensured that I expressed myself as clearly and cleanly as possible during the copy edit and proofreading phases. I also want to thank the numerous other team members who spent countless hours laying out pages, manipulating images, and contributing their skills in a variety of ways to bring this book to you.

I would like to thank my family, including my girlfriend, Donna; my mom; Eric; Jennifer; Chris; Desmond; and Deja. I'd also like to thank my aunt Linda and her family for their support.

Most important, thank you to Devoné and Rebecca—my little angels—for keeping a smile on my face.

Finally, I would like to send a special thank you to Steve Jones, Microsoft MVP and entrepreneur extraordinaire of SQL Server Central fame, and Chuck Heinzelman, also an MVP and editor-in-chief of *SQL Server Standard* magazine, for their continued support.

Introduction

I still recall the first "database" application I ever wrote. It was a Turbo Pascal–based application for state government, designed to keep an inventory of tools and hazardous waste materials for a state institution in the late 1980s. I recall running into a lot of issues, including performance, large data storage, extensibility, and data integrity. I mention this only because these are just the types of problems that modern enterprise-class SQL DBMSs are specifically designed to handle. What's more, they abstract away the internal workings (well, most of them anyway) so that you can concentrate more on your data and less on writing code to manipulate it. As an example, a simple sort algorithm that consumed over 100 lines of code in my custom Turbo Pascal "database" application is whittled down to a single ORDER BY clause in SQL.

This abstraction allows you to spend less time worrying about *how things get done* and more time thinking about *what you want to get done*. Although I don't use the term in everyday conversation, I can say that this change in thinking about storage represents a true "paradigm shift." The new version of SQL Server builds on the foundation laid out by previous releases, adding new capabilities and functionality designed to meet the increasing demands of a sophisticated developer base.

This book was originally scheduled to be an update of my *Pro T-SQL 2005 Programmer's Guide* book. The sheer number of new features, however, demanded a nearly complete rewrite. I designed this new book with the goal of helping T-SQL developers get the absolute most out of the exciting new development features and functionality in SQL Server 2008.

Who This Book Is For

This book is intended for SQL Server developers who need to port code from prior versions of SQL Server, and those who want to get the most out of T-SQL on the 2008 release. You should have a working knowledge of SQL, preferably T-SQL on SQL Server 2005 or 2000, as most of the examples in this book are written in T-SQL. In this book, I will cover some of the basics of T-SQL, including some introductory concepts like data domain and three-valued logic—but this is not a beginner's book. I will not be discussing database design, database architecture, normalization, and the most basic of SQL constructs in any kind of detail. Instead I will be focusing most of my discussion on topics of new SQL Server 2008 functionality, which assumes a basic understanding of SQL statements like INSERT and SELECT.

A working knowledge of C# and the .NET Framework is also useful (but not required), as some examples in the book will be written in C#. When C# sample code is provided, it is explained in detail, so an in-depth knowledge of the .NET Framework class library is not required.

How This Book Is Structured

This book was written to address the needs of three types of readers:

- SQL developers who are coming from other platforms to SQL Server 2008

- SQL developers who are moving from prior versions of SQL Server to SQL Server 2008

- DBAs and nondevelopers who need a working knowledge of T-SQL functionality to effectively support SQL Server 2008 instances

For all types of readers, this book is designed to act as a tutorial that describes and demonstrates new T-SQL features with working examples, and as a reference for quickly locating details about specific features. The following sections provide a chapter-by-chapter overview.

Chapter 1

Chapter 1 starts this book off by putting SQL Server 2008's implementation of T-SQL in context, including a short history of T-SQL, a discussion of T-SQL basics, and an overview of T-SQL coding best practices.

Chapter 2

Chapter 2 dives right into the new features of T-SQL on SQL Server 2008, with a discussion of productivity-enhancing features, the new MERGE statement, new data types like geometry and hierarchyid, and grouping sets.

Chapter 3

Chapter 3 gives an overview of the newest generation of tools available to SQL Server developers. Tools discussed include SQL Server Management Studio (SSMS), SQLCMD, Business Intelligence Development Studio (BIDS), and SQL Profiler, among others.

Chapter 4

Chapter 4 introduces T-SQL procedural code, including control-of-flow statements like IF...THEN and WHILE. In this chapter, I also discuss CASE expressions and CASE-derived functions, and provide an in-depth discussion of SQL three-valued logic.

Chapter 5

Chapter 5 discusses the various types of T-SQL user-defined functions available to encapsulate T-SQL logic on the server. I talk about all forms of T-SQL–based user-defined functions, including scalar user-defined functions, inline table-valued functions, and multistatement table-valued functions.

Chapter 6

Chapter 6 covers stored procedures, which allow you to create server-side T-SQL subroutines. In addition to describing how to create and execute stored procedures on SQL Server, I also address a thorny issue for some—the issue of why you might want to use stored procedures.

Chapter 7

Chapter 7 introduces all three types of SQL Server triggers: classic DML triggers, which fire in response to DML statements; DDL triggers, which fire in response to server and database DDL events; and logon triggers, which fire in response to server LOGON events.

Chapter 8

Chapter 8 discusses SQL Server encryption functionality, including the column-level encryption functionality introduced in SQL Server 2005 and the new transparent database encryption (TDE) and extensible key management (EKM) functionality, both introduced in SQL Server 2008.

Chapter 9

Chapter 9 dives into the details of common table expressions (CTEs) and windowing functions in SQL Server 2008, which feature the OVER clause.

Chapter 10

Chapter 10 discusses the advancements made to SQL Server 2008 integrated full-text search (iFTS), including greater integration with the SQL Server query engine and greater transparency by way of new iFTS-specific data management views and functions.

Chapter 11

Chapter 11 provides an in-depth discussion of SQL Server 2008 XML functionality, which carries forward the new features introduced in SQL Server 2005 and improves upon them. I cover several XML-related topics in this chapter, including the xml data type and its built-in methods, the FOR XML clause, and XML indexes.

Chapter 12

Chapter 12 discusses XQuery and XPath support in SQL Server 2008. SQL Server 2008 improves on the XQuery support introduced in SQL Server 2005, including support for the xml data type in XML DML insert statements and the let clause in FLWOR expressions.

Chapter 13

Chapter 13 introduces SQL Server 2008 catalog views, which are the preferred tools for retrieving database and database object metadata. This chapter also discusses dynamic management views and functions, which provide access to server and database state information.

Chapter 14

Chapter 14 is a discussion of SQL Common Language Runtime (SQL CLR) functionality in SQL Server 2008. In this chapter, I discuss and provide examples of SQL CLR stored procedures, user-defined functions, user-defined types, and user-defined aggregates. I also talk about the restrictions that have been removed in SQL CLR support in SQL Server 2008.

Chapter 15

Chapter 15 focuses on client-side support for SQL Server, including ADO.NET-based connectivity and one of Microsoft's newest technology offerings, LINQ to SQL.

Chapter 16

Chapter 16 discusses SQL Server connectivity using middle-tier technologies. Since native HTTP endpoints are deprecated in SQL Server 2008, I discuss them as items that may need to be supported in existing databases but should not be used for new development. I focus instead on possible replacement technologies, such as ADO.NET Data Services and IIS/.NET Web Services.

Chapter 17

Chapter 17 switches the focus back to T-SQL with a discussion of additional SQL Server 2008 features that were carried forward from their initial introduction in SQL Server 2005; features like the INTERSECT and EXCEPT operators, the DML statement OUTPUT clause, and improvements to the TOP clause. I also discuss some additional features and functionality that are new in SQL Server 2008, like new date and time functions and FILESTREAM support.

Chapter 18

Chapter 18 discusses improvements to server-side error handling made possible with the TRY...CATCH block. I also discuss various methods for debugging code, including using the Visual Studio T-SQL debugger. This chapter wraps up with a discussion of dynamic SQL and SQL injection, including the causes of SQL injection and methods you can use to protect your code against this type of attack.

Chapter 19

Chapter 19 provides an overview of performance-tuning SQL Server code. This chapter discusses SQL Server storage, indexing mechanisms, and query plans. I wrap up the chapter with a discussion of my own personal methodology for troubleshooting T-SQL performance issues.

Appendix A

Appendix A provides the answers to the exercise questions that I've included at the end of each chapter.

Appendix B

Appendix B is designed as a quick reference to the XQuery Data Model (XDM) type system.

Appendix C

Appendix C provides a quick reference glossary to several terms, many of which may be new to those using SQL Server for the first time.

Appendix D

Appendix D is a quick reference to the SQLCMD command-line tool, which allows you to execute ad hoc T-SQL statements and batches interactively, or run script files.

Conventions

To help make reading this book a more enjoyable experience, and to help you get as much out of it as possible, I've used the following standardized formatting conventions throughout.

C# code is shown in code font. Note that C# code is case sensitive. Here's an example:

```
while (i < 10)
```

T-SQL source code is also shown in code font, with keywords capitalized. Note that I've lowercased the data types in the T-SQL code to help improve readability. Here's an example:

```
DECLARE @x xml;
```

XML code is shown in code font with attribute and element content in bold for readability. Some code samples and results have been reformatted in the book for easier reading. XML ignores whitespace, so the significant content of the XML has not been altered. Here's an example:

```
<book publisher = "Apress">Pro SQL Server 2008 XML</book>:
```

■**Note** Notes, tips, and warnings are displayed like this, in a special font with solid bars placed over and under the content.

SIDEBARS

Sidebars include additional information relevant to the current discussion and other interesting facts. Sidebars are shown on a gray background.

Prerequisites

This book requires an installation of SQL Server 2008 to run the T-SQL sample code provided. Note that the code in this book has been specifically designed to take advantage of new SQL Server 2008 features, and most of the code samples will not run on prior versions of SQL Server. The code samples presented in the book are designed to be run against the Adventure-Works 2008 sample database, available from the CodePlex web site at `www.codeplex.com/ MSFTDBProdSamples`.

If you are interested in compiling and deploying the .NET code samples (the client code and SQL CLR examples) presented in the book, I highly recommend an installation of Visual Studio 2008. Although you can compile and deploy .NET code from the command line, I've provided instructions for doing so through the Visual Studio Integrated Development Environment (IDE). I find that the IDE provides a much more enjoyable experience.

Some examples, such as the ADO.NET Data Services examples in Chapter 16, require an installation of IIS as well. Other code samples presented in the book may have specific requirements, such as the LINQ samples, which require the .NET Framework 3.5. I've added notes to code samples that have additional requirements like these.

Downloading the Code

The sample code for this book is available in a ZIP file in the Downloads section of the Apress web site at `www.apress.com`. The ZIP file is structured so that each subdirectory contains all the sample code for its corresponding chapter.

Contacting the Author

The Apress team and I have made every effort to ensure that this book is free from errors and defects. Unfortunately, the occasional error does slip past us, despite our best efforts. In the event that you find an error in the book, please let us know! You can submit errors to Apress by visiting `www.apress.com`, locating the book page for this book, and clicking Submit Errata. Alternatively, feel free to drop a line directly to me at `michaelco@optonline.net`.

CHAPTER 1

■■■

Foundations of T-SQL

SQL Server 2008 is the latest release of Microsoft's enterprise-class database management system (DBMS). As the name implies, a DBMS is a tool designed to manage, secure, and provide access to data stored in structured collections within databases. T-SQL is the language that SQL Server speaks. T-SQL provides query and data manipulation functionality, data definition and management capabilities, and security administration tools to SQL Server developers and administrators. To communicate effectively with SQL Server, you must have a solid understanding of the language. In this chapter, we will begin exploring T-SQL on SQL Server 2008.

A Short History of T-SQL

The history of Structured Query Language (SQL), and its direct descendant Transact-SQL (T-SQL), begins with a man. Specifically, it all began in 1970 when Dr. E. F. Codd published his influential paper "A Relational Model of Data for Large Shared Data Banks" in the Communications of the Association for Computing Machinery (ACM). In his seminal paper, Dr. Codd introduced the definitive standard for relational databases. IBM went on to create the first relational database management system, known as System R. They subsequently introduced the Structured English Query Language (SEQUEL, as it was known at the time) to interact with this early database to store, modify, and retrieve data. The name of this early query language was later changed from SEQUEL to the now-common SQL due to a trademark issue.

Fast-forward to 1986 when the American National Standards Institute (ANSI) officially approved the first SQL standard, commonly known as the ANSI SQL-86 standard. Microsoft entered the relational database management system picture a few years later through a joint venture with Sybase and Ashton-Tate (of dBase fame). The original versions of Microsoft SQL Server shared a common code base with the Sybase SQL Server product. This changed with the release of SQL Server 7.0, when Microsoft partially rewrote the code base. Microsoft has since introduced several iterations of SQL Server, including SQL Server 2000, SQL Server 2005, and now SQL Server 2008. In this book, we will focus on SQL Server 2008, which further extends the capabilities of T-SQL beyond what was possible in previous releases.

Imperative vs. Declarative Languages

SQL is different from many common programming languages such as C# and Visual Basic because it is a *declarative language*. To contrast, languages such as C++, Visual Basic, C#, and even assembler language are *imperative languages*. The imperative language model requires

1

the user to determine what the end result should be and also tell the computer step by step how to achieve that result. It's analogous to asking a cab driver to drive you to the airport, and then giving him turn-by-turn directions to get there. Declarative languages, on the other hand, allow you to frame your instructions to the computer in terms of the end result. In this model, you allow the computer to determine the best route to achieve your objective, analogous to just telling the cab driver to take you to the airport and trusting him to know the best route. The declarative model makes a lot of sense when you consider that SQL Server is privy to a lot of "inside information." Just like the cab driver who knows the shortcuts, traffic conditions, and other factors that affect your trip, SQL Server inherently knows several methods to optimize your queries and data manipulation operations.

Consider Listing 1-1, which is a simple C# code snippet that reads in a flat file of names and displays them on the screen.

Listing 1-1. *C# Snippet to Read a Flat File*

```
StreamReader sr = new StreamReader("c:\\Person_Person.txt");
string FirstName = null;
while ((FirstName = sr.ReadLine()) != null) {
    Console.WriteLine(s);
}                       FirstName
sr.Dispose();
```

The example performs the following functions in an orderly fashion:

1. The code explicitly opens the storage for input (in this example, a flat file is used as a "database").

2. It then reads in each record (one record per line), explicitly checking for the end of the file.

3. As it reads the data, the code returns each record for display using `Console.WriteLine()`.

4. And finally, it closes and disposes of the connection to the data file.

Consider what happens when you want to add or delete a name from the flat-file "database." In those cases, you must extend the previous example and add custom routines to explicitly reorganize all the data in the file so that it maintains proper ordering. If you want the names to be listed and retrieved in alphabetical (or any other) order, you must write your own sort routines as well. Any type of additional processing on the data requires that you implement separate procedural routines.

The SQL equivalent of the C# code in Listing 1-1 might look something like Listing 1-2.

Listing 1-2. *SQL Query to Retrieve Names from a Table*

```
SELECT FirstName
FROM Person.Person;
```

■**Tip** Unless otherwise specified, you can run all the T-SQL samples in this book in the AdventureWorks 2008 sample database using SQL Server Management Studio or SQLCMD.

To sort your data, you can simply add an ORDER BY clause to the SELECT query in Listing 1-2. With properly designed and indexed tables, SQL Server can automatically reorganize and index your data for efficient retrieval after you insert, update, or delete rows.

T-SQL includes extensions that allow you to use procedural syntax. In fact, you could rewrite the previous example as a cursor to closely mimic the C# sample code. These extensions should be used with care, however, since trying to force the imperative model on T-SQL effectively overrides SQL Server's built-in optimizations. More often than not, this hurts performance and makes simple projects a lot more complex than they need to be.

One of the great assets of SQL Server is that you can invoke its power, in its native language, from nearly any other programming language. For example, in .NET you can connect and issue SQL queries and T-SQL statements to SQL Server via the System.Data.SqlClient namespace, which I will discuss further in Chapter 15. This gives you the opportunity to combine SQL's declarative syntax with the strict control of an imperative language.

SQL Basics

Before we discuss development in T-SQL, or on any SQL-based platform for that matter, we have to make sure we're speaking the same language. Fortunately for us, SQL can be described accurately using well-defined and time-tested concepts and terminology. We'll begin our discussion of the components of SQL by looking at *statements*.

Statements

To begin with, in SQL we use statements to communicate our requirements to the DBMS. A statement is composed of several parts, as shown in Figure 1-1.

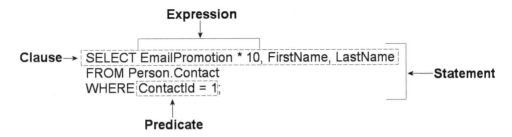

Figure 1-1. *Components of a SQL statement*

As you can see in the figure, SQL statements are composed of one or more *clauses*, some of which may be optional depending on the statement. In the SELECT statement shown, there are three clauses: the SELECT clause, which defines the columns to be returned by the query; the FROM clause, which indicates the source table for the query; and the WHERE clause, which is used to limit the results. Each clause represents a primitive operation in the relational algebra. For instance, in the example, the SELECT clause represents a relational *projection* operation, the FROM clause indicates the *relation*, and the WHERE clause performs a *restriction* operation.

■**Note** The *relational model* of databases is the model formulated by Dr. E. F. Codd. In the relational model, what we know in SQL as *tables* are referred to as *relations*; hence the name. *Relational calculus* and *relational algebra* define the basis of query languages for the relational model in mathematical terms.

ORDER OF EXECUTION

Understanding the logical order in which SQL clauses are applied within a statement or query is important when setting your expectations about results. While vendors are free to physically perform whatever operations, in any order, that they choose to fulfill a query request, the results must be the same as if the operations were applied in a standards-defined order.

The WHERE clause in the example contains a *predicate*, which is a logical expression that evaluates to one of SQL's three possible logical results: true, false, or unknown. In this case, the WHERE clause and the predicate limit the results returned so that they include only rows in which the ContactId column is equal to 1.

The SELECT clause includes an expression that is calculated during statement execution. In the example, the expression EmailPromotion * 10 is used. This expression is calculated for every row of the result set.

SQL THREE-VALUED LOGIC

SQL institutes a logic system that might seem foreign to developers coming from other languages like C++ or Visual Basic (or most other programming languages, for that matter). Most modern computer languages use simple two-valued logic: a Boolean result is either true or false. SQL supports the concept of NULL, which is a placeholder for a missing or unknown value. This results in a more complex three-valued logic (3VL).

Let me give you a quick example to demonstrate. If I asked you the question, "Is *x* less than 10?" your first response might be along the lines of, "How much is *x*?" If I refused to tell you what value *x* stood for, you would have no idea whether *x* was less than, equal to, or greater than 10; so the answer to the question is neither true nor false—it's the third truth value, *unknown*. Now replace *x* with NULL and you have the essence of SQL 3VL. NULL in SQL is just like a variable in an equation when you don't know the variable's value.

No matter what type of comparison you perform with a missing value, or which other values you compare the missing value to, the result is always unknown. I'll continue the discussion of SQL 3VL in Chapter 4.

The core of SQL is defined by statements that perform five major functions: querying data stored in tables, manipulating data stored in tables, managing the structure of tables, controlling access to tables, and managing transactions. All of these subsets of SQL are defined following:

- *Querying*: The SELECT query statement is a complex statement. It has more optional clauses and vendor-specific tweaks than any other statement, bar none. SELECT is concerned simply with retrieving data stored in the database.

- *Data Manipulation Language (DML)*: DML is considered a sublanguage of SQL. It is concerned with manipulating data stored in the database. DML consists of four commonly used statements: INSERT, UPDATE, DELETE, and MERGE. DML also encompasses cursor-related statements. These statements allow you to manipulate the contents of tables and persist the changes to the database.

- *Data Definition Language (DDL)*: DDL is another sublanguage of SQL. The primary purpose of DDL is to create, modify, and remove tables and other objects from the database. DDL consists of variations of the CREATE, ALTER, and DROP statements.

- *Data Control Language (DCL)*: DCL is yet another SQL sublanguage. DCL's goal is to allow you to restrict access to tables and database objects. DCL is composed of various GRANT and REVOKE statements that allow or deny users access to database objects.

- *Transactional Control Language (TCL)*: TCL is the SQL sublanguage that is concerned with initiating and committing or rolling back *transactions*. A transaction is basically an atomic unit of work performed by the server. The BEGIN TRANSACTION, COMMIT, and ROLLBACK statements comprise TCL.

Databases

A SQL Server *instance*—an individual installation of SQL Server with its own ports, logins, and databases—can manage multiple *system databases* and *user databases*. SQL Server has five system databases, as follows:

- resource: The resource database is a read-only system database that contains all system objects. You will not see the resource database in the SQL Server Management Studio (SSMS) Object Explorer window, but the system objects persisted in the resource database will logically appear in every database on the server.

- master: The master database is a server-wide repository for configuration and status information. The master database maintains instance-wide metadata about SQL Server as well as information about all databases installed on the current instance. It is wise to avoid modifying or even accessing the master database directly in most cases. An entire server can be brought to its knees if the master database is corrupted. If you need to access the server configuration and status information, use catalog views instead.

- model: The model database is used as the template from which newly created databases are essentially cloned. Normally, you won't want to change this database in production settings, unless you have a very specific purpose in mind and are extremely knowledgeable about the potential implications of changing the model database.

SSIS Packages

- **msdb**: The msdb database stores system settings and configuration information for various support services, such as SQL Agent and Database Mail. Normally, you will use the supplied stored procedures and views to modify and access this data, rather than modifying it directly.

- **tempdb**: The tempdb database is the main working area for SQL Server. When SQL Server needs to store intermediate results of queries, for instance, they are written to tempdb. Also, when you create temporary tables, they are actually created within tempdb. The tempdb database is reconstructed from scratch every time you restart SQL Server.

Microsoft recommends that you use the system-provided stored procedures and catalog views to modify system objects and system metadata, and let SQL Server manage the system databases itself. You should avoid modifying the contents and structure of the system databases directly.

User databases are created by database administrators (DBAs) and developers on the server. These types of databases are so called because they contain user data. The Adventure-Works 2008 sample database is one example of a user database.

Transaction Logs

Every SQL Server database has its own associated transaction log. The transaction log provides recoverability in the event of failure, and ensures the atomicity of transactions. The transaction log accumulates all changes to the database so that database integrity can be maintained in the event of an error or other problem. Because of this arrangement, all SQL Server databases consist of at least two files: a database file with an .mdf extension and a transaction log with an .ldf extension.

THE ACID TEST

SQL folks, and IT professionals in general, love their acronyms. A common acronym in the SQL world is ACID, which stands for "atomicity, consistency, isolation, durability." These four words form a set of properties that database systems should implement to guarantee reliability of data storage, processing, and manipulation.

- *Atomicity*: All data changes should be transactional in nature. That is, data changes should follow an all-or-nothing pattern. The classic example is a double-entry bookkeeping system in which every debit has an associated credit. Recording a debit-and-credit double-entry in the database is considered one "transaction," or a single unit of work. You cannot record a debit without recording its associated credit, and vice versa. Atomicity ensures that either the entire transaction is performed or none of it is.

- *Consistency*: Only data that is consistent with the rules set up in the database will be stored. Data types and constraints can help enforce consistency within the database. For instance, you cannot insert the name Dolly in an int column. Consistency also applies when dealing with data updates. If two users update the same row of a table at the same time, an inconsistency could occur if one update is only partially complete when the second update begins. The concept of isolation, described following, is designed to deal with this situation.

- *Isolation*: Multiple simultaneous updates to the same data should not interfere with one another. SQL Server includes several locking mechanisms and isolation levels to ensure that two users cannot modify the exact same data at the exact same time, which could put the data in an inconsistent state. Isolation also prevents you from even reading uncommitted data by default.

- *Durability*: Data that passes all the previous tests is committed to the database. The concept of durability ensures that committed data is not lost. The transaction log and data backup and recovery features help to ensure durability.

The transaction log is one of the main tools SQL Server uses to enforce the ACID concept when storing and manipulating data.

Schemas

SQL Server 2008 supports database schemas, which are little more than logical groupings of database objects. The AdventureWorks 2008 sample database, for instance, contains several schemas, such as HumanResources, Person, and Production. These schemas are used to group tables, stored procedures, views, and user-defined functions (UDFs) for management and security purposes.

■**Tip** When you create new database objects, like tables, and don't specify a schema, they are automatically created in the default schema. The default schema is normally dbo, but DBAs may assign different default schemas to different users. Because of this, it's always best to specify the schema name explicitly when creating database objects.

Tables

SQL Server supports several types of objects that can be created within a database. SQL stores and manages data in its primary data structures, tables. A table consists of rows and columns, with data stored at the intersections of these rows and columns. As an example, the AdventureWorks HumanResources.Department table is shown in Figure 1-2.

In the table, each row is associated with columns and each column has certain restrictions placed on its content. These restrictions comprise the *data domain*. The data domain defines all the values a column can contain. At the lowest level, the data domain is based on the data type of the column. For instance, a smallint column can contain any integer values between –32,768 and +32,767.

The data domain of a column can be further constrained through the use of check constraints, triggers, and foreign key constraints. *Check constraints* provide a means of automatically checking that the value of a column is within a certain range or equal to a certain value whenever a row is inserted or updated. *Triggers* can provide similar functionality to check constraints. *Foreign key constraints* allow you to declare a relationship between the columns of one table and the columns of another table. You can use foreign key constraints to restrict the data domain of a column to only include those values that appear in a designated column of another table.

Departmen...	Name	GroupName	ModifiedDate
1	Engineering	Research and Development	1998-06-01 00:00:00.000
2	Tool Design	Research and Development	1998-06-01 00:00:00.000
3	Sales	Sales and Marketing	1998-06-01 00:00:00.000
4	Marketing	Sales and Marketing	1998-06-01 00:00:00.000
5	Purchasing	Inventory Management	1998-06-01 00:00:00.000
6	Research and Development	Research and Development	1998-06-01 00:00:00.000
7	Production	Manufacturing	1998-06-01 00:00:00.000
8	Production Control	Manufacturing	1998-06-01 00:00:00.000
9	Human Resources	Executive General and Ad...	1998-06-01 00:00:00.000
10	Finance	Executive General and Ad...	1998-06-01 00:00:00.000
11	Information Services	Executive General and Ad...	1998-06-01 00:00:00.000
12	Document Control	Quality Assurance	1998-06-01 00:00:00.000
13	Quality Assurance	Quality Assurance	1998-06-01 00:00:00.000
14	Facilities and Maintenance	Executive General and Ad...	1998-06-01 00:00:00.000
15	Shipping and Receiving	Inventory Management	1998-06-01 00:00:00.000
16	Executive	Executive General and Ad...	1998-06-01 00:00:00.000

Figure 1-2. *Representation of the HumanResources.Department table*

RESTRICTING THE DATA DOMAIN: A COMPARISON

In this section, I have given a brief overview of three methods of constraining the data domain for a column—restricting the values that can be contained in the column. Here's a quick comparison of the three methods:

- Foreign key constraints allow SQL Server to perform an automatic check against another table to ensure that the values in a given column exist in the referenced table. If the value you are trying to update or insert in a table does not exist in the referenced table, an error is raised. The foreign key constraint provides a flexible means of altering the data domain, since adding or removing values from the referenced table automatically changes the data domain for the referencing table. Also, foreign key constraints offer an additional feature known as cascading *declarative referential integrity (DRI)*, which automatically updates or deletes rows from a referencing table if an associated row is removed from the referenced table.

- Check constraints provide a simple, efficient, and effective tool for ensuring that the values being inserted or updated in a column are within a given range or a member of a given set of values. Check constraints, however, are not as flexible as foreign key constraints and triggers since the data domain is normally defined using hard-coded constant values.

- Triggers are stored procedures attached to insert, update, or delete events on a table. A trigger provides a flexible solution for constraining data, but it may require more maintenance than the other options since it is essentially a specialized form of stored procedure. Unless they are extremely well designed, triggers have the potential to be much less efficient than the other methods, as well. Triggers to constrain the data domain are generally avoided in modern databases in favor of the other methods. The exception to this is when you are trying to enforce a foreign key constraint across databases, since SQL Server doesn't support cross-database foreign key constraints.

Which method you use to constrain the data domain of your column(s) needs to be determined by your project-specific requirements on a case-by-case basis.

Views

A view is like a virtual table—the data it exposes is not stored in the view object itself. Views are composed of SQL queries that reference tables and other views, but they are referenced just like tables in queries. Views serve two major purposes in SQL Server: they can be used to hide the complexity of queries, and they can be used as a security device to limit the rows and columns of a table that a user can query. Views are expanded, meaning that their logic is incorporated into the execution plan for queries when you use them in queries and DML statements. SQL Server may not be able to use indexes on the base tables when the view is expanded, resulting in less-than-optimal performance when querying views in some situations.

To overcome the query performance issues with views, SQL Server also has the ability to create a special type of view known as an *indexed view*. An indexed view is a view that SQL Server persists to the database like a table. When you create an indexed view, SQL Server allocates storage for it and allows you to query it like any other table. There are, however, restrictions on inserting, updating, and deleting from an indexed view. For instance, you cannot perform data modifications on an indexed view if more than one of the view's base tables will be affected. You also cannot perform data modifications on an indexed view if the view contains aggregate functions or a DISTINCT clause.

You can also create indexes on an indexed view to improve query performance. The downside to an indexed view is increased overhead when you modify data in the view's base tables, since the view must be updated as well.

Indexes

Indexes are SQL Server's mechanisms for optimizing access to data. SQL Server 2008 supports several types of indexes, including the following:

- *Clustered index*: A clustered index is limited to one per table. This type of index defines the ordering of the rows in the table. A clustered index is physically implemented using a b-tree structure with the data stored in the leaf levels of the tree. Clustered indexes order the data in a table in much the same way that a phone book is ordered by last name. A table with a clustered index is referred to as a *clustered table*, while a table with no clustered index is referred to as a *heap*.

- *Nonclustered index*: A nonclustered index is also a b-tree index managed by SQL Server. In a nonclustered index, *index rows* are included in the leaf levels of the b-tree. Because of this, nonclustered indexes have no effect on the ordering of rows in a table. The index rows in the leaf levels of a nonclustered index consist of the following:

  - A nonclustered key value

  - A row locator, which is the clustered index key on a table with a clustered index, or a SQL-generated row ID for a heap

  - Nonkey columns, which are added via the INCLUDE clause of the CREATE INDEX statement

A nonclustered index is analogous to an index in the back of a book.

- *XML index*: SQL Server supports special indexes designed to help efficiently query XML data. See Chapter 11 for more information.

- *Spatial index*: A spatial index is an interesting new indexing structure to support efficient querying of the new geometry and geography data types. See Chapter 2 for more information.

- *Full-text index*: A full-text index (FTI) is a special index designed to efficiently perform full-text searches of data and documents.

Beginning with SQL Server 2005, you can also include nonkey columns in your nonclustered indexes with the INCLUDE clause of the CREATE INDEX statement. The included columns give you the ability to work around SQL Server's index size limitations.

Stored Procedures

SQL Server supports the installation of server-side T-SQL code modules via *stored procedures (SPs)*. It's very common to use SPs as a sort of intermediate layer or custom server-side *application programming interface (API)* that sits between user applications and tables in the database. Stored procedures that are specifically designed to perform queries and DML statements against the tables in a database are commonly referred to as *CRUD (create, read, update, delete)* procedures.

User-Defined Functions

User-defined functions (UDFs) can perform queries and calculations, and return either scalar values or tabular result sets. UDFs have certain restrictions placed on them. For instance, they cannot utilize certain nondeterministic system functions, nor can they perform DML or DDL statements, so they cannot make modifications to the database structure or content. They cannot perform dynamic SQL queries or change the state of the database (i.e., cause side effects).

SQL CLR Assemblies

SQL Server 2008 supports access to Microsoft .NET functionality via the SQL Common Language Runtime (SQL CLR). To access this functionality, you must register compiled .NET SQL CLR assemblies with the server. The assembly exposes its functionality through class methods, which can be accessed via SQL CLR functions, procedures, triggers, user-defined types, and user-defined aggregates. SQL CLR assemblies replace the deprecated SQL Server extended stored procedure (XP) functionality available in prior releases.

■Tip Avoid using XPs on SQL Server 2008. The same functionality provided by XPs can be provided by SQL CLR code. The SQL CLR model is more robust and secure than the XP model. Also keep in mind that the XP library is deprecated and XP functionality may be completely removed in a future version of SQL Server.

Elements of Style

Now that I've given a broad overview of the basics of SQL Server, we'll take a look at some recommended development tips to help with code maintenance. Selecting a particular style and using it consistently helps immensely with both debugging and future maintenance. The following sections contain some general recommendations to make your T-SQL code easy to read, debug, and maintain.

Whitespace

SQL Server ignores extra whitespace between keywords and identifiers in SQL queries and statements. A single statement or query may include extra spaces and tab characters, and can even extend across several lines. You can use this knowledge to great advantage. Consider Listing 1-3, which is adapted from the HumanResources.vEmployee view in the AdventureWorks database.

Listing 1-3. *The HumanResources.vEmployee View from the AdventureWorks Database*

```
SELECT [HumanResources].[Employee].[EmployeeID],[Person].[Contact].[Title],[
Person].[Contact].[FirstName],[Person].[Contact].[MiddleName],[Person].[Cont
act].[LastName],[Person].[Contact].[Suffix],[HumanResources].[Employee].[Tit
le] AS [JobTitle],[Person].[Contact].[Phone],[Person].[Contact].[EmailAddres
s],[Person].[Contact].[EmailPromotion],[Person].[Address].[AddressLine1],[Pe
rson].[Address].[AddressLine2],[Person].[Address].[City],[Person].[StateProv
ince].[Name] AS [StateProvinceName],[Person].[Address].[PostalCode],[Person]
.[CountryRegion].[Name] AS [CountryRegionName],[Person].[Contact].[Additiona
lContactInfo] FROM [HumanResources].[Employee] INNER JOIN [Person].[Contact]
 ON [Person].[Contact].[ContactID] = [HumanResources].[Employee].[ContactID]
 INNER JOIN [HumanResources].[EmployeeAddress] ON [HumanResources].[Employee
].[EmployeeID] = [HumanResources].[EmployeeAddress].[EmployeeID] INNER JOIN
[Person].[Address] ON [HumanResources].[EmployeeAddress].[AddressID] = [Pers
on].[Address].[AddressID] INNER JOIN [Person].[StateProvince] ON [Person].[S
tateProvince].[StateProvinceID] = [Person].[Address].[StateProvinceID] INNER
 JOIN [Person].[CountryRegion] ON [Person].[CountryRegion].[CountryRegionCod
e] = [Person].[StateProvince].[CountryRegionCode]
```

This query will run and return the correct result, but it's very hard to read. You can use whitespace and table aliases to generate a version that is much easier on the eyes, as demonstrated in Listing 1-4.

Listing 1-4. *The HumanResources.vEmployee View Reformatted for Readability*

```
SELECT
    e.EmployeeID,
    c.Title,
    c.FirstName,
    c.MiddleName,
    c.LastName,
    c.Suffix,
    e.Title AS JobTitle,
    c.Phone,
    c.EmailAddress,
    c.EmailPromotion,
    a.AddressLine1,
    a.AddressLine2,
    a.City,
    sp.Name AS StateProvinceName,
    a.PostalCode,
    cr.Name AS CountryRegionName,
    c.AdditionalContactInfo
FROM HumanResources.Employee e
INNER JOIN Person.Contact c
    ON c.ContactID = e.ContactID
INNER JOIN HumanResources.EmployeeAddress ea
    ON e.EmployeeID = ea.EmployeeID
INNER JOIN Person.Address a
    ON ea.AddressID = a.AddressID
INNER JOIN Person.StateProvince sp
    ON sp.StateProvinceID = a.StateProvinceID
INNER JOIN Person.CountryRegion cr
    ON cr.CountryRegionCode = sp.CountryRegionCode;
```

Notice that the ON keywords are indented, associating them visually with the INNER JOIN operators directly before them in the listing. The column names on the lines directly after the SELECT keyword are also indented, associating them visually with the SELECT keyword. This particular style is useful in helping visually break up a query into sections. The personal style you decide upon might differ from this one, but once you have decided on a standard indentation style, be sure to apply it consistently throughout your code.

Code that is easy to read is easier to debug and maintain. The code in Listing 1-4 uses table aliases, plenty of whitespace, and the semicolon (;) terminator marking the end of the SELECT statement to make the code more readable. Although not always required, it is a good idea to get into the habit of using the terminating semicolon in your SQL queries.

Note Semicolons are required terminators for some statements in SQL Server 2008. Instead of trying to remember all the special cases where they are or aren't required, it is a good idea to use the semicolon statement terminator throughout your T-SQL code. You will notice the use of semicolon terminators in all the examples in this book.

Naming Conventions

SQL Server allows you to name your database objects (tables, views, procedures, and so on) using just about any combination of up to 128 characters (116 characters for local temporary table names), as long as you enclose them in double quotes (") or brackets ([ ]). Just because you *can*, however, doesn't necessarily mean you *should*. Many of the allowed characters are hard to differentiate from other similar-looking characters, and some might not port well to other platforms. The following suggestions will help you avoid potential problems:

- Use alphabetic characters (A–Z, a–z, and Unicode Standard 3.2 letters) for the first character of your identifiers. The obvious exceptions are SQL Server variable names that start with the at sign (@), temporary tables and procedures that start with the number sign (#), and global temporary tables and procedures that begin with a double number sign (##).

- Many built-in T-SQL functions and system variables have names that begin with a double at sign (@@), such as @@ERROR and @@IDENTITY. To avoid confusion and possible conflicts, don't use a leading double at sign to name your identifiers.

- Restrict the remaining characters in your identifiers to alphabetic characters (A–Z, a–z, and Unicode Standard 3.2 letters), numeric digits (0–9), and the underscore character (_). The dollar sign ($) character, while allowed, is not advisable.

- Avoid embedded spaces, punctuation marks (other than the underscore character), and other special characters in your identifiers.

- Avoid using SQL Server 2008 reserved keywords as identifiers.

- Limit the length of your identifiers. Thirty-two characters or less is a reasonable limit while not being overly restrictive. Much more than that becomes cumbersome to type and can hurt your code readability.

Finally, to make your code more readable, select a capitalization style for your identifiers and code, and use it consistently. My preference is to fully capitalize T-SQL keywords and use mixed-case and underscore characters to visually "break up" identifiers into easily readable words. Using all capital characters or inconsistently applying mixed case to code and identifiers can make your code illegible and hard to maintain. Consider the example query in Listing 1-5.

Listing 1-5. *All-Capital SELECT Query*

```
SELECT I.CUSTOMERID, C.TITLE, C.FIRSTNAME, C.MIDDLENAME,
    C.LASTNAME, C.SUFFIX, C.PHONE, C.EMAILADDRESS,
    C.EMAILPROMOTION
FROM SALES.INDIVIDUAL I
INNER JOIN PERSON.CONTACT C
    ON C.CONTACTID = I.CONTACTID
INNER JOIN SALES.CUSTOMERADDRESS CA
    ON CA.CUSTOMERID = I.CUSTOMERID;
```

The all-capital version is difficult to read. It's hard to tell the SQL keywords from the column and table names at a glance. Compound words for column and table names are not easily identified. Basically, your eyes have to work a lot harder to read this query than they should, which makes otherwise simple maintenance tasks more difficult. Reformatting the code and identifiers makes this query much easier on the eyes, as Listing 1-6 demonstrates.

Listing 1-6. *Reformatted, Easy-on-the-Eyes Query*

```
SELECT
    i.CustomerID,
    c.Title,
    c.FirstName,
    c.MiddleName,
    c.LastName,
    c.Suffix,
    c.Phone,
    c.EmailAddress,
    c.EmailPromotion
FROM Sales.Individual i
INNER JOIN Person.Contact c
    ON c.ContactID = i.ContactID
INNER JOIN Sales.CustomerAddress ca
    ON ca.CustomerID = i.CustomerID;
```

The use of all capitals for the keywords in the second version makes them stand out from the mixed-case table and column names. Likewise, the mixed-case column and table names make the compound word names easy to recognize. The net effect is that the code is easier to read, which makes it easier to debug and maintain. Consistent use of good formatting habits helps keep trivial changes trivial and makes complex changes easier.

One Entry, One Exit

When writing SPs and UDFs, it's good programming practice to use the "one entry, one exit" rule. SPs and UDFs should have a single entry point and a single exit point (RETURN statement). The following SP retrieves the ContactTypeID number from the AdventureWorks Person. ContactType table for the ContactType name passed into it. If no ContactType exists with the name passed in, a new one is created, and the newly created ContactTypeID is passed back. Listing 1-7 demonstrates this simple procedure with one entry point and several exit points.

Listing 1-7. *Stored Procedure Example with One Entry and Multiple Exits*

```
CREATE PROCEDURE dbo.GetOrAdd_ContactType
(
    @Name NVARCHAR(50),
    @ContactTypeID INT OUTPUT
)
AS   BEGIN   SET NOCOUNT ON;
    DECLARE @Err_Code AS INT;
    SELECT @Err_Code = 0;

    SELECT @ContactTypeID = ContactTypeID
    FROM Person.ContactType
    WHERE [Name] = @Name;

    IF @ContactTypeID IS NOT NULL
        RETURN;                -- Exit 1: if the ContactType exists

    INSERT
    INTO Person.ContactType ([Name], ModifiedDate)
    SELECT @Name, CURRENT_TIMESTAMP;

    SELECT @Err_Code = @@error;
    IF @Err_Code <> 0
        RETURN @Err_Code;    -- Exit 2: if there is an error on INSERT

    SELECT @ContactTypeID = SCOPE_IDENTITY();

    RETURN @Err_Code;        -- Exit 3: after successful INSERT
    END
GO
```

This code has one entry point, but three possible exit points. Figure 1-3 shows a simple flowchart for the paths this code can take.

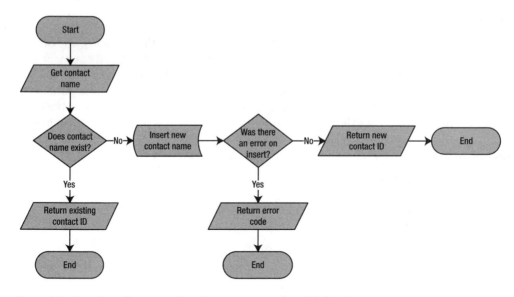

Figure 1-3. *Flowchart for example with one entry and multiple exits*

As you can imagine, maintaining code such as in Listing 1-7 becomes more difficult because the flow of the code has so many possible exit points, each of which must be accounted for when you make modifications to the SP. Listing 1-8 updates Listing 1-7 to give it a single entry point and a single exit point, making the logic easier to follow.

Listing 1-8. *Stored Procedure with One Entry and One Exit*

```
CREATE PROCEDURE dbo.GetOrAdd_ContactType
(
    @Name NVARCHAR(50),
    @ContactTypeID INT OUTPUT
)
AS
    BEGIN
        SET NOCOUNT ON;
    DECLARE @Err_Code AS INT;
    SELECT @Err_Code = 0;

    SELECT @ContactTypeID = ContactTypeID
    FROM Person.ContactType
    WHERE [Name] = @Name;

    IF @ContactTypeID IS NULL
    BEGIN
        INSERT
        INTO Person.ContactType ([Name], ModifiedDate)
        SELECT @Name, CURRENT_TIMESTAMP;
```

```
        SELECT @Err_Code = @@error;
        IF @Err_Code = 0          -- If there's an error, skip next
            SELECT @ContactTypeID = SCOPE_IDENTITY();
    END
    RETURN @Err_Code;    -- Single exit point
    GO
END
```

Figure 1-4 shows the modified flowchart for this new version of the SP.

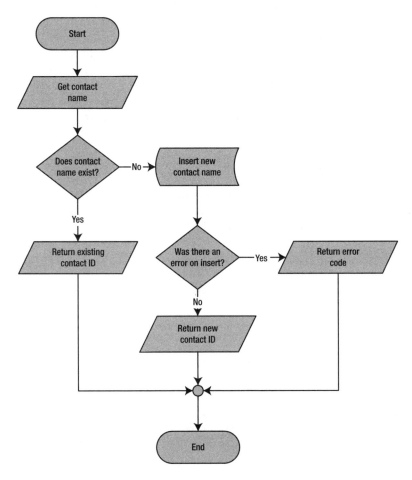

Figure 1-4. *Flowchart for example with one entry and one exit*

The single-entry/single-exit model makes the logic easier to follow, which in turn makes the code easier to manage. This rule also applies to looping structures, which you implement via the WHILE statement in T-SQL. Avoid using the WHILE loop's CONTINUE and BREAK statements and the GOTO statement; these statements lead to old-fashioned, difficult-to-maintain spaghetti code.

Defensive Coding

Defensive coding involves anticipating problems before they occur and mitigating them through good coding practices. The first and foremost lesson of defensive coding is to always check user input. Once you open your system up to users, expect them to do everything in their power to try to break your system. For instance, if you ask users to enter a number between 1 and 10, expect that they'll ignore your directions and key in `; DROP TABLE dbo.syscomments; --` at the first available opportunity. Defensive coding practices dictate that you should check and scrub external inputs. Don't blindly trust anything that comes from an external source.

Another aspect of defensive coding is a clear delineation between exceptions and run-of-the-mill issues. The key is that exceptions are, well, exceptional in nature. Ideally, exceptions should be caused by errors that you can't account for or couldn't reasonably anticipate, like a lost network connection or physical corruption of your application or data storage. Errors that can be reasonably expected, like data entry errors, should be captured before they are raised to the level of exceptions. Keep in mind that exceptions are often resource intensive, expensive operations. If you can avoid an exception by anticipating a particular problem, your application will benefit in both performance and control.

SQL-92 Syntax Outer Joins

Microsoft has been warning us for a long time, and starting with SQL 2005 they finally went and did it. SQL Server 2008, like SQL Server 2005, eliminates the old-style *= and =* outer join operators. Queries like the one in Listing 1-9 won't work with SQL Server 2008.

Listing 1-9. *Query Using Old-Style Join Operators*

```
SELECT o.name
FROM sys.objects o,
     sys.views v
WHERE o.object_id *= v.object_id;
```

SQL responds to this query with one of the most elaborate error messages ever seen in a Microsoft product:

```
SQL2008(SQL2008\Michael): Msg 4147, Level 15, State 1, Line 4
The query uses non-ANSI outer join operators ("*=" or "=*"). To run this query
without modification, please set the compatibility level for current database
to 80, using the SET COMPATIBILITY_LEVEL option of ALTER DATABASE. It is
strongly recommended to rewrite the query using ANSI outer join operators
(LEFT OUTER JOIN, RIGHT OUTER JOIN). In the future versions of SQL Server,
non-ANSI join operators will not be supported even in backward-compatibility
modes.
```

As the error message suggests, you can use the `sp_dbcmptlevel` SP to revert the database compatibility to 80 (SQL Server 2000) as a workaround for this problem. Best practices dictate that you should eliminate the old-style joins from your code as soon as possible. Backward-compatibility mode should be considered a temporary workaround for the old-style join issue, not a permanent fix.

COMPATIBILITY MODE CHANGES

You can use the system SP `sp_dbcmptlevel` to revert various SQL Server behaviors to a version prior to SQL Server 2000. Use a compatibility level of 90 for SQL Server 2005 and 80 for SQL Server 2000. The SP call that converts the AdventureWorks sample database to SQL Server 2000 compatibility mode looks like this:

```
EXEC sp_dbcmptlevel 'AdventureWorks', 90
```

To convert it back to SQL Server 2008 compatibility mode, you would use a statement like this:

```
EXEC sp_dbcmptlevel 'AdventureWorks', 100
```

When you set a database to backward-compatibility mode, you can lose access to some of the new functionality, such as SQL CLR support and SSMS diagrams for that database. Note that previous compatibility levels of 70 for SQL Server 7.0, 65 for SQL Server 6.5, and 60 for SQL Server 6.0 are no longer available in SQL Server 2008. Microsoft has announced that from here on out they will only be supporting two prior versions in backward-compatibility modes, so you can expect SQL Server 2000 compatibility mode to be gone with the next SQL Server release after 2008. You should avoid using backward-compatibility mode unless you have a compelling reason.

The error message also suggests that the old-style join operators will not be supported in future versions, even in backward-compatibility mode. If you have old-style joins in your T-SQL code, the best course of action is to convert them to ISO SQL standard joins as soon as possible. Listing 1-10 updates the previous query to use the current SQL standard.

Listing 1-10. *ISO SQL-92 Standard Join Syntax*

```
SELECT o.name
FROM sys.objects o
LEFT  JOIN sys.views v
    ON o.object_id = v.object_id;
```

Note that you can still use the abbreviated inner join syntax without any problems. The abbreviated inner join syntax looks like Listing 1-11.

Listing 1-11. *Abbreviated Inner Join Syntax*

```
SELECT o.name
FROM sys.objects o,
    sys.views v
WHERE o.object_id = v.object_id;
```

This book uses the ISO SQL-92 standard syntax joins exclusively in code examples.

The SELECT * Statement

Consider the SELECT * style of querying. In a SELECT clause, the asterisk (*) is a shorthand way of specifying that all columns in a table should be returned. Although SELECT * is a handy tool for ad hoc querying of tables during development and debugging, you should normally not use it in a production system. One reason to avoid this method of querying is to minimize the amount of data retrieved with each call. SELECT * retrieves all columns, whether or not they are needed by the higher-level applications. For queries that return a large number of rows, even one or two extraneous columns can waste a lot of resources.

Also, if the underlying table or view is altered, columns might be added to or removed from the returned result set. This can cause errors that are hard to locate and fix. By specifying the column names, your front-end application can be assured that only the required columns are returned by a query, and that errors caused by missing columns will be easier to locate.

As with most things, there are always exceptions—for example, if you are using the FOR XML AUTO clause to generate XML based on the structure and content of your relational data. In this case, SELECT * can be quite useful, since you are relying on FOR XML to automatically generate the node names based on the table and column names in the source tables.

Variable Initialization

When you create SPs, UDFs, or any script that uses T-SQL user variables, you should initialize those variables before the first use. Unlike other programming languages that guarantee that newly declared variables will be initialized to 0 or an empty string (depending on their data types), T-SQL guarantees only that newly declared variables will be initialized to NULL. Consider the code snippet shown in Listing 1-12.

Listing 1-12. *Sample Code Using an Uninitialized Variable*

```
DECLARE @i INT;
SELECT @i = @i + 5;
SELECT @i;
```

The result is NULL, a shock if you were expecting 5. Expecting SQL Server to initialize numeric variables to 0 (like @i in the previous example) or an empty string will result in bugs that can be extremely difficult to locate in your T-SQL code. To avoid these problems, always explicitly initialize your variables after declaration, as demonstrated in Listing 1-13.

Listing 1-13. *Sample Code Using an Initialized Variable*

```
DECLARE @i INT = 0; -- Changed this statement to initialize @i to 0
SELECT @i = @i + 5;
SELECT @i;
```

Summary

This chapter has served as an introduction to T-SQL, including a brief history of SQL and a discussion of the declarative programming style. I started this chapter with a discussion of ISO SQL standard compatibility in SQL Server 2008 and the differences between imperative and declarative languages, of which SQL is the latter. I also introduced many of the basic components of SQL, including databases, tables, views, SPs, and other common database objects. Finally, I provided my personal recommendations for writing SQL code that is easy to debug and maintain. I subscribe to the "eat your own dog food" theory, and throughout this book I will faithfully follow the best practice recommendations that I've asked you to consider.

The next chapter provides an overview of the new and improved tools available out of the box for developers. Specifically, Chapter 2 will discuss the SQLCMD text-based SQL client (originally a replacement for osql), SSMS, SQL Server 2008 Books Online (BOL), and some of the other tools available for making writing, editing, testing, and debugging easier and faster than ever.

EXERCISES

1. Describe the difference between an imperative language and a declarative language.

2. What does the acronym *ACID* stand for?

3. SQL Server 2008 supports five different types of indexes. What are they?

4. Name two of the restrictions on any type of SQL Server UDF.

5. [True/false] In SQL Server, newly declared variables are always assigned the default value 0 for numeric data types and an empty string for character data types.

CHAPTER 2

■■■■

T-SQL 2008 New Features

Every new version of SQL Server comes with several new T-SQL features and enhancements. SQL Server 2008 is no exception. In the newest version of SQL Server, Microsoft has responded to developer requests in a big way. SQL Server 2008 supports brand new developer convenience features like single-statement variable declaration and initialization, new data types to manipulate and query date-based and spatial data, new statements like MERGE that add much-needed functionality to T-SQL, and a whole lot more.

When moving from SQL Server 2000, there will be a slight learning curve, although the basics of T-SQL will still be familiar. SQL Server 2005 developers, on the other hand, will feel right at home when developing for SQL Server 2008. If you wrote your SQL Server 2005 scripts to follow best practices, most will run with minimal, if any, changes. Because of the deprecation of some features, SQL Server 2000 scripts that followed best practices may require slight modification to run on SQL Server 2008. Converting old scripts to run on SQL Server 2008 is just a starting point, though. Once you've made the move to SQL Server 2008, you'll undoubtedly want to take advantage of the new features and functionality to solve common problems. This chapter gives an overview of the exciting new features that SQL Server 2008 adds to T-SQL.

■**Note** You'll find a list of deprecated features in BOL. To locate the list, search for "deprecated SQL 2008" in BOL. The list has deprecated features and their replacements, when available. Although many of these features are currently supported in SQL Server 2008, they will be removed in a future version of the product.

Productivity Enhancements

Taking a cue from languages like C# and Visual Basic, SQL Server 2008 supports many new productivity-enhancing T-SQL features for developers. The first of these new features is single-statement variable declaration and initialization. In the past, developers had to declare new variables in one or more DECLARE statements and assign values to the variables in one or more SET or SELECT statements, as shown in Listing 2-1.

Listing 2-1. *Separate Variable Declaration and Initialization*

```
DECLARE @x int,
  @y int,
  @z int;
```

```
SET @x = 1;
SET @y = 2;
SET @z = 3;
```

With single-statement declaration and initialization, you can combine these two steps into a single statement, as shown in Listing 2-2.

Listing 2-2. *Single-Statement Variable Declaration and Initialization*

```
DECLARE @x int = 1,
  @y int = 2,
  @z int = 3;
```

T-SQL has been further improved with the addition of several C-style assignment operators. For those unfamiliar with C-style languages, many mathematical, logical, and string concatenation operators can be combined with the equal sign (=) to create new assignment operators like += and *=. In C-style languages, these operators are often used to give the compiler optimization hints; in T-SQL, they are simply a convenience for developers. Listing 2-3 demonstrates T-SQL's new C-style assignment operators.

Listing 2-3. *Calculating and Assigning Values with C-Style Assignment*

```
DECLARE @x int = 4,
  @y int = 25,
  @s1 varchar(20) = 'Sql';

SET @x *= @y;
SET @s1 += ' Server';

SELECT @x, @s1;
```

This example declares and assigns values to the int variables @x and @y, and to the varchar variable @s1. It uses the *= operator to assign the value of @x multiplied by @y back to @x. C# programmers will recognize the assignment expression in the statement SET @x *= @y as simple shorthand for SET @x = @x * @y.

The += string concatenation operator is used to append the string ' Server' to the varchar @s1 variable. As before, the assignment statement SET @s1 += ' Server' is shorthand for SET @s1 = @s1 + ' Server'. The results of this simple example are shown in Figure 2-1.

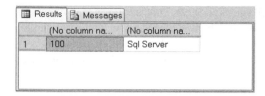

Figure 2-1. *The results of the C-style assignment operator example*

The complete list of T-SQL supported C-style assignment operators is shown in Table 2-1.

Table 2-1. *T-SQL C-Style Assignment Operators*

Operator	Description
+=	Addition with assignment, or string concatenation with assignment
-=	Subtraction with assignment
*=	Multiplication with assignment
/=	Division with assignment
%=	Modulo with assignment
^=	Bitwise exclusive-OR with assignment
|=	Bitwise OR with assignment
&=	Bitwise AND with assignment

Another convenience feature is offered by the new *row constructors*, which allow you to specify multiple rows in the VALUES clause of the INSERT statement. This new feature allows you to specify more than one row of data to be inserted in a single INSERT statement. This is particularly handy when initially populating tables, since you don't have to re-create the entire INSERT statement over and over. Listing 2-4 demonstrates how row constructors can be used to insert three new work shifts into the AdventureWorks HumanResources.Shift table.

Listing 2-4. *Using Row Constructors to Create Three New Work Shifts*

```
INSERT INTO HumanResources.Shift
(
  Name,
  StartTime,
  EndTime
)
VALUES
(
  'Noon Part-time',
  '12:00:00',
  '16:00:00'
),
(
  'Evening Part-time',
  '16:00:00',
  '20:00:00'
),
(
  'Midnight Part-time',
  '00:00:00',
  '04:00:00'
);
```

```
SELECT ShiftID,
  Name,
  StartTime,
  EndTime,
  ModifiedDate
FROM HumanResources.Shift;
```

In previous versions of SQL Server, this would have had to have been written as three separate INSERT statements, each with the columns specified completely; or as an INSERT statement with multiple SELECT queries unioned together with the UNION ALL set operator. As you can see, a row constructor simplifies the code. The result of the INSERT statement that uses a row constructor is shown in Figure 2-2.

Results | Messages

	ShiftID	Name	StartTime	EndTime	ModifiedDate
1	1	Day	1900-01-01 07:00:00.000	1900-01-01 15:00:00.000	1998-06-01 00:00:00.000
2	2	Evening	1900-01-01 15:00:00.000	1900-01-01 23:00:00.000	1998-06-01 00:00:00.000
3	3	Night	1900-01-01 23:00:00.000	1900-01-01 07:00:00.000	1998-06-01 00:00:00.000
4	4	Noon Part-time	1900-01-01 12:00:00.000	1900-01-01 16:00:00.000	2008-01-27 17:05:01.113
5	5	Evening Part-time	1900-01-01 16:00:00.000	1900-01-01 20:00:00.000	2008-01-27 17:05:01.113
6	6	Midnight Part-time	1900-01-01 00:00:00.000	1900-01-01 04:00:00.000	2008-01-27 17:05:01.113

Figure 2-2. *The results of creating three new AdventureWorks work shifts*

The MERGE Statement

Microsoft teased us with the possibility in prerelease Beta versions of SQL Server 2005, but it yanked the MERGE statement out of T-SQL right before the SQL Server 2005 RTM was released. SQL Server 2008 fixes this situation by finally giving us a fully functional MERGE statement. The MERGE statement is a combination statement that can perform INSERT, UPDATE, and DELETE statements based on whether rows that match the selection criteria exist in the target table or not.

Because it is so flexible, the MERGE statement syntax is a bit more complex than other Data Manipulation Language (DML) statements. It definitely takes some getting used to. For the most part, you will see it used as a combination UPDATE/INSERT, or "upsert," statement. You can run the MERGE statement example in Listing 2-5 as a stand-alone sample, or you can run it after running the example in Listing 2-4, which adds three new shifts to the AdventureWorks HumanResources.Shift table. I recommend the latter option.

Listing 2-5. *Using MERGE to Update AdventureWorks Work Shifts*

```
CREATE TABLE #TempShifts
(
  Name varchar(50) NOT NULL,
  StartTime time NOT NULL,
  EndTime time NOT NULL
);
```

```
INSERT INTO #TempShifts
(
  Name,
  StartTime,
  EndTime
)
VALUES
(
  'Morning Part-time',
  '08:00:00',
  '12:00:00'
),
(
  'Evening Part-time ',
  '18:00:00',
  '22:00:00'
),
(
  'Midnight Swing Shift',
  '00:00:00',
  '04:00:00'
);

MERGE HumanResources.Shift AS target
USING #TempShifts AS source
  ON (target.Name = source.Name)
    OR (target.StartTime = source.StartTime
      AND target.EndTime = source.EndTime)
WHEN MATCHED THEN
  UPDATE
    SET
      Name = source.Name,
      StartTime = source.StartTime,
      EndTime = source.EndTime
WHEN TARGET NOT MATCHED THEN
  INSERT
  (
    Name,
    StartTime,
    EndTime
  )
  VALUES
  (
    source.Name,
    source.StartTime,
    source.EndTime
  );
```

```
SELECT ShiftID,
  Name,
  StartTime,
  EndTime,
  ModifiedDate
FROM HumanResources.Shift;
```

```
DROP TABLE #TempShifts;
```

The MERGE sample begins by creating a temporary table into which you insert names and start and end times for three different work shifts:

```
CREATE TABLE #TempShifts
(
  Name varchar(50) NOT NULL,
  StartTime time NOT NULL,
  EndTime time NOT NULL
);
```

```
INSERT INTO #TempShifts
(
  Name,
  StartTime,
  EndTime
)
VALUES
(
  'Morning Part-time',
  '08:00:00',
  '12:00:00'
),
(
  'Evening Part-time ',
  '18:00:00',
  '22:00:00'
),
(
  'Midnight Swing Shift',
  '00:00:00',
  '04:00:00'
);
```

If you've run the example in Listing 2-4, you'll notice that one of the new shifts, Evening Part-time, already exists with a start time of 18:00:00 and an end time of 22:00:00. Another shift, Midnight Part-time, exists for the hours between 00:00:00 and 04:00:00. The Morning Part-time shift does not exist at all.

The interesting part of the code sample is the actual `MERGE` statement itself. This statement begins with the `MERGE` keyword and the target table. Notice that the table name is aliased, which will make it easier to reference later in the `ON` clause.

```
MERGE HumanResources.Shift AS target
```

The `USING` clause specifies the data rows to match against the target table. In this case, I'm matching the rows I created in the `#TempShifts` table against the target `HumanResources.Shift` table. The `USING` clause is very important to get right, since the rows returned by this clause determine the actions taken later in the `MERGE` statement. In this case, I'm simply using the `#TempShifts` table as the source, but you can also use a derived table.

```
USING #TempShifts AS source
```

The `ON` clause determines which rows between the target table and the `USING` clause data rows are matches. This example uses a compound predicate that flags any two rows as matches when they both have either the same `Name` or the same `StartTime` and `EndTime`.

```
ON (target.Name = source.Name)
  OR (target.StartTime = source.StartTime
    AND target.EndTime = source.EndTime)
```

The `WHEN MATCHED` clause performs its action whenever two rows match based on your `ON` clause criteria. The action is specified in the `THEN` clause, and can be either an `UPDATE` or a `DELETE`. This example is using the `UPDATE` clause, which looks like an abbreviated `UPDATE` statement. Notice that the `UPDATE` clause does not specify a target table, since the target table is already specified in the `MERGE` clause at the beginning of the statement.

```
WHEN MATCHED THEN
  UPDATE
    SET Name = source.Name,
      StartTime = source.StartTime,
      EndTime = source.EndTime
```

The `MERGE` statement can have only one `WHEN TARGET NOT MATCHED` clause. This clause can only perform an `INSERT` when a row is found in the `USING` clause source that does not match a row in the target table.

```
WHEN TARGET NOT MATCHED THEN
  INSERT
  (
    Name,
    StartTime,
    EndTime
  )
  VALUES
  (
    source.Name,
    source.StartTime,
    source.EndTime
  );
```

The results of the MERGE statement example in Listing 2-5 are shown in Figure 2-3. Notice that MERGE has updated the Evening Part-time shift so that it is now has a StartTime of 18:00:00 and an EndTime of 22:00:00. Likewise, the Name of the Midnight Part-time shift has been updated to Midnight Swing Shift. Last, a new shift called Morning Part-time has been inserted by the MERGE statement.

	ShiftID	Name	StartTime	EndTime	ModifiedDate
1	1	Day	1900-01-01 07:00:00.000	1900-01-01 15:00:00.000	1998-06-01 00:00:00.000
2	2	Evening	1900-01-01 15:00:00.000	1900-01-01 23:00:00.000	1998-06-01 00:00:00.000
3	3	Night	1900-01-01 23:00:00.000	1900-01-01 07:00:00.000	1998-06-01 00:00:00.000
4	4	Noon Part-time	1900-01-01 12:00:00.000	1900-01-01 16:00:00.000	2008-01-27 17:10:58.233
5	5	Evening Part-time	1900-01-01 18:00:00.000	1900-01-01 22:00:00.000	2008-01-27 17:10:58.233
6	6	Midnight Swing Shift	1900-01-01 00:00:00.000	1900-01-01 04:00:00.000	2008-01-27 17:10:58.233
7	7	Morning Part-time	1900-01-01 08:00:00.000	1900-01-01 12:00:00.000	2008-01-27 17:11:09.760

Figure 2-3. *MERGE statement updates and inserts to HumanResources.Shifts*

DELETING MATCHES AND HANDLING UNMATCHED SOURCE ROWS

The new MERGE statement allows you to specify up to two WHEN MATCHED clauses in your MERGE statement. The actions you can take in a WHEN MATCHED clause are limited to UPDATE and DELETE. You can add AND with a predicate to the WHEN MATCHED clause to differentiate between WHEN MATCHED clauses. To be honest, I doubt that the DELETE functionality will gain the same widespread use that INSERT/UPDATE will receive, but it is one of those features that you'll be glad to have when you actually need it. I will give an example of multiple WHEN MATCHED clauses and DELETE functionality later in this section.

The WHEN TARGET NOT MATCHED clause, as explained previously in this section, is what the MERGE statement uses to insert new rows from the source rows (the USING clause is considered the source) that do not have a match in the target table. The WHEN MATCHED clause performs actions when rows from both the source and target tables match. This covers two of the three possible scenarios when matching source and target rows.

The third scenario, which hasn't been discussed yet, is when a row exists in the target table but does not have a match in the source rows. On occasion, you may need to handle this third possibility. Enter the WHEN SOURCE NOT MATCHED clause. This clause can perform an UPDATE or DELETE of the target table row when a row exists in the source that does not exist in the target table. Also, you can specify at most two WHEN SOURCE NOT MATCHED clauses. If you specify two of these clauses, the first must have an AND clause with a predicate.

The MERGE statement is an important new DML feature, and the second MERGE example demonstrates the MERGE statement DELETE functionality that I mentioned previously in this section. If you've already run the example in Listing 2-5, then your HumanResources.Shift table will contain the data shown in Figure 2-3.

The example in Listing 2-6 builds on Listing 2-5. The lines that are different in this listing are displayed in bold.

Listing 2-6. *Using MERGE to Update, Insert, or Delete Work Shifts*

```
CREATE TABLE #TempShifts
(
  Name varchar(50) NOT NULL,
  StartTime time NOT NULL,
  EndTime time NOT NULL,
  Action varchar(10) NOT NULL
);
GO

INSERT INTO #TempShifts
(
  Name,
  StartTime,
  EndTime,
  Action
)
VALUES
(
  'Morning Part-time',
  '08:00:00',
  '12:00:00',
  'DELETE'
),
(
  'Evening Part-time ',
  '18:00:00',
  '22:00:00',
  'UPDATE'
),
(
  'Midnight Swing Shift',
  '00:00:00',
  '04:00:00',
  'DELETE'
);

MERGE HumanResources.Shift AS target
USING #TempShifts AS source
  ON (target.Name = source.Name)
    OR (target.StartTime = source.StartTime
      AND target.EndTime = source.EndTime)
WHEN MATCHED AND (source.Action = 'Delete') THEN
  DELETE
WHEN MATCHED THEN
  UPDATE SET Name = source.Name,
    StartTime = source.StartTime,
    EndTime = source.EndTime
```

```
WHEN TARGET NOT MATCHED THEN
  INSERT
  (
    Name,
    StartTime,
    EndTime
  )
  VALUES
  (
    source.Name,
    source.StartTime,
    source.EndTime
  );

SELECT ShiftID,
  Name,
  StartTime,
  EndTime,
  ModifiedDate
FROM HumanResources.Shift;
GO

DROP TABLE #TempShifts;
```

This example begins like the previous example: by building a temporary table to hold the new shift information. This time, however, I've added an `Action` column that determines the action to take when a row is matched. If the `Action` is Delete, matched rows are deleted from the target table. If the `Action` is Update (or anything else for that matter), matched rows will be updated.

```
CREATE TABLE #TempShifts
(
  Name varchar(50) NOT NULL,
  StartTime time NOT NULL,
  EndTime time NOT NULL,
  Action varchar(10) NOT NULL
);
GO

INSERT INTO #TempShifts (Name, StartTime, EndTime, Action)
VALUES
  ('Morning Part-time', '08:00:00', '12:00:00', 'DELETE'),
  ('Evening Part-time ', '18:00:00', '22:00:00', 'UPDATE'),
  ('Midnight Swing Shift', '00:00:00', '04:00:00', 'DELETE');
```

The `MERGE` statement begins as before, the only difference being that the `Action` column is also returned by the `USING` source table:

```
MERGE HumanResources.Shift AS target
USING #TempShifts AS source
```

There are now two WHEN MATCHED clauses in the MERGE statement. The first performs a DELETE when the row is matched and the source row Action is Delete. Notice that the DELETE clause is like a thoroughly abbreviated DELETE statement. Unlike the DELETE statement, you don't need to specify a table to delete from, since the target table was already specified at the beginning of the MERGE statement. You also don't need to use a WHERE clause to restrict the rows, since it only deletes the current matched row.

```
WHEN MATCHED AND (source.Action = 'Delete') THEN
  DELETE
```

The second WHEN MATCHED clause captures every matching row that falls through the first WHEN MATCHED clause. It doesn't need an AND clause.

```
WHEN MATCHED THEN
  UPDATE SET Name = source.Name,
    StartTime = source.StartTime,
    EndTime = source.EndTime
```

Finally, the WHEN TARGET NOT MATCHED clause captures and inserts all source rows that don't match the target table:

```
WHEN TARGET NOT MATCHED THEN
  INSERT
  (
    Name,
    StartTime,
    EndTime
  )
  VALUES
  (
    source.Name,
    source.StartTime,
    source.EndTime
  );
```

The results of this MERGE statement example are that the Morning Part-time and Midnight Swing Shift work shifts are deleted. The Evening Part-time shift is updated so that its new StartTime and EndTime are 16:00:00 and 20:00:00, respectively. The results are shown in Figure 2-4.

	ShiftID	Name	StartTime	EndTime	ModifiedDate
1	1	Day	1900-01-01 07:00:00.000	1900-01-01 15:00:00.000	1998-06-01 00:00:00.000
2	2	Evening	1900-01-01 15:00:00.000	1900-01-01 23:00:00.000	1998-06-01 00:00:00.000
3	3	Night	1900-01-01 23:00:00.000	1900-01-01 07:00:00.000	1998-06-01 00:00:00.000
4	4	Noon Part-time	1900-01-01 12:00:00.000	1900-01-01 16:00:00.000	2008-01-27 17:10:58.233
5	5	Evening Part-time	1900-01-01 16:00:00.000	1900-01-01 20:00:00.000	2008-01-27 17:10:58.233

Figure 2-4. *The results of updating and deleting work shifts with MERGE*

The MERGE statement may offer code simplification and performance benefits over other methods of performing the same type of conditional updates, inserts, and deletes. I've actually seen production ETL (extract, transform, load) systems and client-side solutions that resort to performing individual SELECT queries against a table for every row to be inserted, just to determine if the target table contains a match. The client-side solution then decides whether to send a single UPDATE, INSERT, or DELETE statement for each row. For 1,000,000 rows being imported, you're suddenly looking at 2,000,000 total separate SQL statements and 2,000,000 round trips to the server! It's a horrible solution, at best, and often the bottleneck in an otherwise decent ETL process. A proper MERGE statement solution has the potential to eliminate a lot of the pain and performance problems inherent in many custom ETL solutions.

The MERGE statement is poised to figure prominently in both object/relational (O/R) systems for transactional databases and ETL solutions for data warehouses and data marts. In both cases, the MERGE statement may be able to offer both code simplification and potential performance benefits over other common methods of performing conditional row updates, inserts, and deletes.

New Data Types

SQL Server 2008 provides new data types that support storage, manipulation, and querying of new forms of data. Some, like the date data type, which stores a simple date without the time component, have been requested by developers since the heady days of SQL Server 6.5. Others, like the geometry data type, which allows storage and querying of spatial data, have only recently been addressed. All of the new data types add to SQL Server's already rich data typing capabilities. In this section, we will begin by exploring the new SQL Server 2008 data types, and continue the discussion with a review of the SQL Server 2008–supported data types that were first introduced in SQL Server 2005.

Date and Time Data Types

SQL Server has long supported two basic date and time data types: datetime and smalldatetime. These data types have always allowed storage of date and time data combined in a single instance. For years developers have worked around the fact that date and time data could not be stored as separate values, and for years Microsoft has not responded to developer requests for new date and time data types. With the release of SQL Server 2008, the SQL Server team has responded to users in a big way. SQL Server 2008 supports four brand new date and time data types: date, time, datetime2, and datetimeoffset.

The date data type finally allows us to store date-only data without the time component. It can also store a much larger range of dates than the datetime and smalldatetime data types. The date data type can handle dates from January 1, 1 CE (0001-01-01) to December 31, 9999 CE (9999-12-31)—a much wider range than either the datetime or smalldatetime data types. Listing 2-7 shows a simple usage of the date data type, demonstrating that the DATEDIFF function works with the date type just as it does with the datetime data type.

Listing 2-7. *Sample date Data Type Usage*

```
-- August 19, 14 C.E.
DECLARE @d1 date = '0014-08-19';
```

```
-- February 26, 1983
DECLARE @d2 date = '1983-02-26';

SELECT
  @d1 AS Date1,
  @d2 AS Date2,
  DATEDIFF(YEAR, @d1, @d2) AS YearsDifference;
```

The results of this simple example are shown in Figure 2-5.

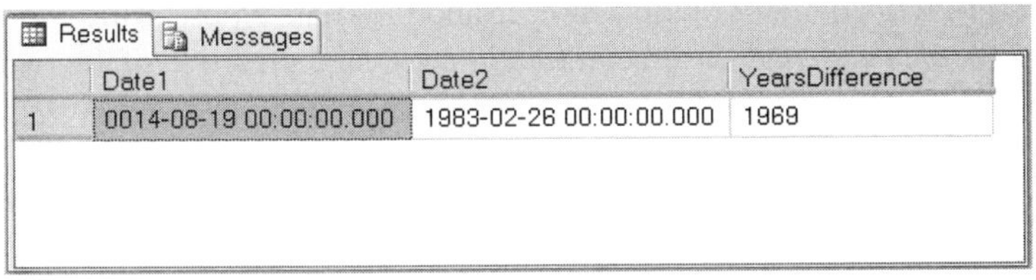

Figure 2-5. *The results of the date data type example*

In contrast to the date data type, the time data type lets you store time-only data. The range for the time data type is defined on a 24-hour clock, from 00:00:00.0000000 through 23:59:59.9999999, with a user-definable fractional second precision of up to seven digits. The default precision, if you don't specify one, is seven digits of fractional second precision. Listing 2-8 demonstrates the time data type in action.

Listing 2-8. *Demonstrating time Data Type Usage*

```
-- 6:25:19.1 AM
DECLARE @start_time time(1) = '06:25:19.1'; -- 1 digit fractional precision

-- 6:25:19.1234567 PM
DECLARE @end_time time = '18:25:19.1234567'; -- default fractional precision

SELECT
  @start_time AS start_time,
  @end_time AS end_time,
  DATEADD(HOUR, 6, @start_time) AS StartTimePlus,
  DATEDIFF(HOUR, @start_time, @end_time) AS EndStartDiff;
```

In Listing 2-8, two data type instances are created. The @start_time variable is explicitly declared with a fractional second precision of one digit. You can specify a fractional second precision of one to seven digits with 100 nanoseconds (ns) accuracy; the fixed fractional precision of the classic datetime data type is three digits with 3.33 milliseconds (ms) accuracy. The default fractional precision for the time data type, if no precision is specified, is seven digits. The @end_time variable in the listing is declared with the default precision. As with the date and datetime data types, the DATEDIFF and DATEADD functions also work with the time data type. The results of Listing 2-8 are shown in Figure 2-6.

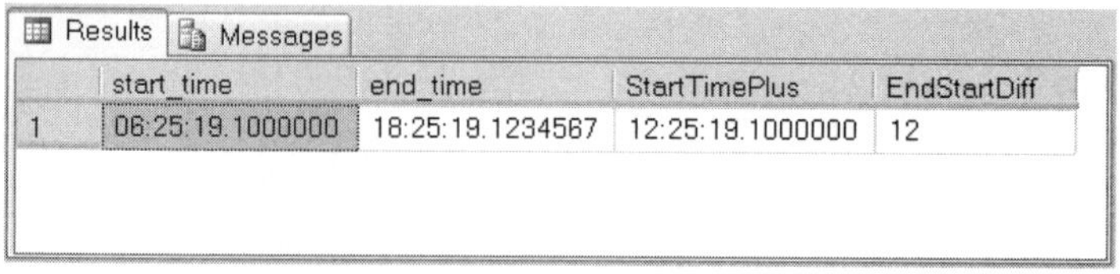

Figure 2-6. *The results of the time data type example*

The cleverly named datetime2 data type is an extension to the standard datetime data type. The datetime2 data type combines the benefits of the new date and time data types, giving you the wider date range of the date data type and the greater fractional second precision of the time data type. Listing 2-9 demonstrates simple declaration and usage of datetime2 variables.

Listing 2-9. *Declaring and Querying datetime2 Variables*

```
DECLARE @start_dt2 datetime2 = '1972-07-06T07:13:28.8230234',
  @end_dt2 datetime2 = '2009-12-14T03:14:13.2349832';

SELECT
  @start_dt2 AS start_dt2,
  @end_dt2 AS end_dt2;
```

The results of Listing 2-9 are shown in Figure 2-7.

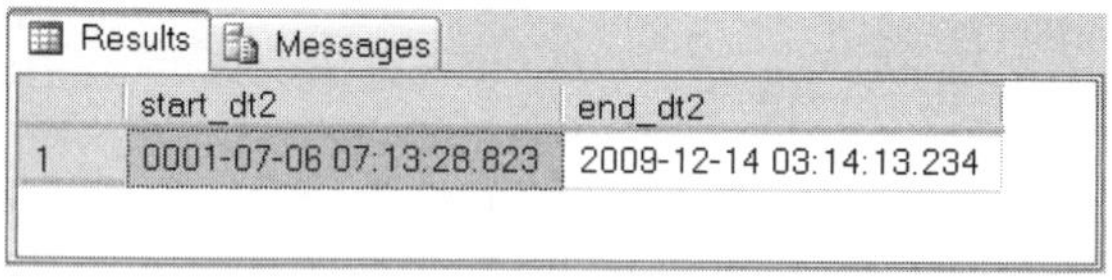

Figure 2-7. *Declaring and selecting datetime2 data type variables*

The new datetimeoffset data type builds on datetime2 by adding the ability to store off-sets relative to the International Telecommunication Union (ITU) standard for Coordinated Universal Time (UTC) with your date and time data. When creating a datetimeoffset instance, you can specify an offset that complies with the ISO 8601 standard, which is in turn based on UTC. Basically, the offset must be specified in the range –14:00 to +14:00. The Z offset identifier is shorthand for the offset designated "zulu," or +00:00. Listing 2-10 shows the datetimeoffset data type in action.

Listing 2-10. *datetimeoffset Data Type Sample*

```
DECLARE @start_dto datetimeoffset = '1492-10-12T13:29:59.9999999-05:00';

SELECT
  @start_dto AS start_dto,
  DATEPART(YEAR, @start_dto) AS start_year;
```

The results of Listing 2-10 are shown in Figure 2-8.

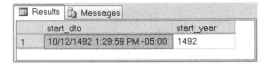

Figure 2-8. *The results of the datetimeoffset sample*

A sampling of possible offsets is shown in Table 2-2. Note that this list is not exhaustive, but demonstrates some common offsets.

Table 2-2. *Common Standard Time Zones*

Time Zone Offset	Name	Locations
–10:00	Hawaii-Aleutian Standard	Alaska (Aleutian Islands), Hawaii
–08:00	Pacific Standard	US West Coast; Los Angeles, CA
–05:00	Eastern Standard	US East Coast; New York, NY
–04:00	Atlantic Standard	Bermuda
+00:00	Coordinated Universal	Dublin, Lisbon
+01:00	Central European	Paris, Berlin, Madrid, Rome
+03:00	Baghdad	Kuwait, Riyadh
+06:00	Indian Standard	India
+09:00	Japan Standard	Japan

UTC AND MILITARY TIME

Some people see the acronym *UTC* and think that it stands for "Universal Time Coordination" or "Universal Time Code." Unfortunately, the world is not so simple. When the ITU standardized Coordinated Universal Time, it was decided that it should have the same acronym in every language. Of course, international agreement could not be reached, with the English-speaking countries demanding the acronym *CUT* and French-speaking countries demanding that *TUC* (*temps universel coordonné*) be used. In the final compromise, the nonsensical *UTC* was adopted as the international standard.

You may notice that I use "military time," or the 24-hour clock, when representing time in the code samples throughout this book. There's a very good reason for that—the 24-hour clock is an ISO international standard. The ISO 8601 standard indicates that time should be represented in computers using the 24-hour clock to prevent ambiguity.

The 24-hour clock begins at 00:00:00, which is midnight or 12 AM. Noon, or 12 PM, is represented as 12:00:00. One second before midnight is 23:59:59, or 11:59:59 PM. In order to convert the 24-hour clock to AM/PM time, simply look at the hours. If the hours are less than 12, then the time is AM. If the hours are equal to 12, you are in the noon hour, which is PM. If the hours are greater than 12, subtract 12 and add PM to your time.

Table 2-3 summarizes the differences between all SQL Server 2008 date and time data types.

Table 2-3. *SQL Server 2008 Date and Time Data Type Comparison*

Data Type	Components	Range	Precision
datetime	Date and time	1753-01-01 to 9999-12-31	Fixed, three fractional second digits, 3.33 ms
smalldatetime	Date and time	1900-01-01 to 2079-06-06	Fixed, 1 minute
date	Date	0001-01-01 to 9999-12-31	Fixed, 1 day
time	Time	00:00:00 to 23:59:59	User-defined, one to seven fractional second digits, 100 ns
datetime2	Date and time	0001-01-01 to 9999-12-31	User-defined, one to seven fractional second digits, 100 ns
datetimeoffset	Date, time, and offset	0001-01-01 9999-12-31	User-defined, one to seven fractional second digits, 100 ns, offset range of −14:00 to +14:00

The hierarchyid Data Type

The new hierarchyid data type offers a new twist on an old model for representing hierarchical data in the database. This new data type offers built-in support for representing your hierarchical data using one of the simplest models available: materialized paths.

REPRESENTING HIERARCHICAL DATA

The representation of hierarchical data in relational databases has long been an area of interest for SQL developers. The most common model of representing hierarchical data with SQL Server is the *adjacency list* model. In this model, each row of a table maintains a reference to its parent row. The following illustration demonstrates how the adjacency list model works in a SQL table.

The AdventureWorks sample database makes use of the adjacency list model in its HumanResources. Employee table, where each employee entry references its manager by ID number. AdventureWorks also uses the adjacency list model in the Production.BillOfMaterials table, where every component references its parent assembly.

The *materialized path* model requires that you store the actual hierarchical path from the root node to the current node. The hierarchical path is similar to a modern file system path, where each folder or directory represents a node in the path. The hierarchyid data type supports generation and indexing of materialized paths for hierarchical data modeling. The following illustration shows how the materialized path might look in SQL.

Path
/a
/a/b
/a/b/c
/a/b/d

It is a relatively simple matter to represent adjacency list model data using materialized paths, as you'll see later in this section in the discussion on converting AdventureWorks adjacency list data to the materialized path model using the hierarchyid data type.

Another model for representing hierarchical data is the *nested sets* model. In this model, every row in the table is considered a set that may contain or be contained by another set. Each row is assigned a pair of numbers defining the lower and upper bounds for the set. The following illustration shows a logical representation of the nested sets model, with the lower and upper bounds for each set shown to the set's left and right. Notice that the sets in the figure are contained within one another logically, the structure from which this model derives its name.

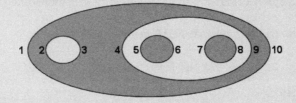

In this section, I'll use the AdventureWorks Production.BillOfMaterials table extensively to demonstrate the adjacency list model, the materialized path model, and the hierarchyid data type. Technically speaking, a bill of materials (BOM), or "parts explosion," is a *directed acyclic graph*. A directed acyclic graph is essentially a generalized tree structure in which some subtrees may be shared by different parts of the tree. Think of a cake recipe, represented as a tree, in which "sugar" can be used multiple times (once in the "cake mix" subtree, once in the "frosting" subtree, and so on). This book is not about graph theory, though, so I'll pass on the technical details and get to the BOM at hand. Although *directed acyclic graph* is the technical term for a true BOM, I'll be representing the AdventureWorks BOMs as materialized path hierarchies using the hierarchyid data type, so you'll see the term *hierarchy* used a lot in this section.

In order to understand the AdventureWorks BOM hierarchies, it's important to understand the relationship between product assemblies and components. Basically, a *product assembly* is composed of one or more *components*. An assembly can become a component for use in other assemblies, defining the recursive relationship. All components with a product assembly of NULL are top-level components, or "root nodes," of each hierarchy. If a hierarchyid data type column is declared a primary key, it can contain only a single hierarchyid root node.

The hierarchyid data type stores hierarchy information as an optimized materialized path, which is a very efficient way to store hierarchical information. The first example converts the AdventureWorks BOMs to materialized path form using the hierarchyid data type. The first step, shown in Listing 2-11, is to create the table that will contain the hierarchyid BOMs. To differentiate it from the Production.BillOfMaterials table, I've called this table Production.HierBillOfMaterials.

Listing 2-11. *Creating the hierarchyid Bill of Materials Table*

```
CREATE TABLE Production.HierBillOfMaterials
(
  BomNode hierarchyid NOT NULL PRIMARY KEY NONCLUSTERED,
  ProductAssemblyID int NULL,
  ComponentID int NULL,
  UnitMeasureCode nchar(3) NULL,
  PerAssemblyQty decimal(8, 2) NULL,
  BomLevel AS BomNode.GetLevel()
);
GO
```

The `Production.HierBillOfMaterials` table consists of the `BomNode` hierarchyid column, which will contain the hierarchical path information for each component. The `ProductAssemblyID`, `ComponentID`, `UnitMeasureCode`, and `PerAssemblyQty` are all pulled from the source tables. `BomLevel` is a calculated column that contains the current level of each `BomNode`. The next step is to convert the adjacency list BOMs to hierarchyid form, which will be used to populate the `Production.HierBillOfMaterials` table. This is demonstrated in Listing 2-12.

Listing 2-12. *Converting AdventureWorks BOMs to hierarchyid Form*

```
WITH BomChildren
(
  ProductAssemblyID,
  ComponentID
)
AS
(
  SELECT
    b1.ProductAssemblyID,
    b1.ComponentID
  FROM Production.BillOfMaterials b1
  GROUP BY
    b1.ProductAssemblyID,
    b1.ComponentID
),
BomPaths
(
  Path,
  ComponentID,
  ProductAssemblyID
)
AS
(
  SELECT
    hierarchyid::GetRoot() AS Path,
    NULL,
    NULL
```

```
    UNION ALL

    SELECT
      CAST
      (
        '/' +
          CAST
          (
            bc.ComponentId AS varchar(30)
          ) +
        '/' AS hierarchyid
      ) AS Path,
      bc.ComponentID,
      bc.ProductAssemblyID
    FROM BomChildren AS bc
    WHERE bc.ProductAssemblyID IS NULL

    UNION ALL

    SELECT
      CAST
      (
        bp.path.ToString() +
          CAST
          (
            bc.ComponentID AS varchar(30)
          ) +
          '/' AS hierarchyid
      ) AS Path,
      bc.ComponentID,
      bc.ProductAssemblyID
    FROM BomChildren AS bc
    INNER JOIN BomPaths AS bp
      ON bc.ProductAssemblyID = bp.ComponentID
)
INSERT INTO Production.HierBillOfMaterials
(
  BomNode,
  ProductAssemblyID,
  ComponentID,
  UnitMeasureCode,
  PerAssemblyQty
)
SELECT
  bp.Path,
  bp.ProductAssemblyID,
  bp.ComponentID,
```

```
  bom.UnitMeasureCode,
  bom.PerAssemblyQty
FROM BomPaths AS bp
LEFT OUTER JOIN Production.BillOfMaterials bom
  ON bp.ComponentID = bom.ComponentID
    AND COALESCE(bp.ProductAssemblyID, -1) = COALESCE(bom.ProductAssemblyID, -1)
WHERE bom.EndDate IS NULL
GROUP BY
  bp.path,
  bp.ProductAssemblyID,
  bp.ComponentID,
  bom.UnitMeasureCode,
  bom.PerAssemblyQty;
GO
```

This statement is a little more complex than the average hierarchyid data example you'll probably run into, since most people currently out there are demonstrating conversion of the simple, single-hierarchy AdventureWorks organizational chart. The AdventureWorks Production.BillOfMaterials table actually contains several individual hierarchies.

I'll step through the code here to show you exactly what's going on in this statement. The first part of the statement is a common table expression (CTE) called BomChildren. It returns all ProductAssemblyID's and ComponentID's from the Production.BillOfMaterials table.

```
WITH BomChildren
(
  ProductAssemblyID,
  ComponentID
)
AS
(
  SELECT
    b1.ProductAssemblyID,
    b1.ComponentID
  FROM Production.BillOfMaterials b1
  GROUP BY
    b1.ProductAssemblyID,
    b1.ComponentID
),
```

While the organizational chart represents a simple top-down hierarchy with a single root node, the BOM is actually composed of dozens of separate hierarchies with no single hierarchyid root node. BomPaths is a recursive CTE that returns the current hierarchyid, ComponentID, and ProductAssemblyID for each row.

```
BomPaths
(
  Path,
  ComponentID,
  ProductAssemblyID
)
```

The anchor query for the CTE is in two parts. The first part returns the root node for the entire hierarchy. In this case, the root just represents a logical grouping of all the BOM's top-level assemblies; it does not represent another product that can be created by mashing together every product in the AdventureWorks catalog.

```
SELECT
  hierarchyid::GetRoot(),
  NULL,
  NULL
```

The second part of the anchor query returns the hierarchyid path to the top-level assemblies. Each top-level assembly has its ComponentId appended to the root path, represented by a leading forward slash (/).

```
SELECT
  CAST
  (
    '/' +
      CAST
      (
        bc.ComponentId AS varchar(30)
      ) +
    '/' AS hierarchyid
  ) AS Path,
  bc.ComponentID,
  bc.ProductAssemblyID
FROM BomChildren AS bc
WHERE bc.ProductAssemblyID IS NULL
```

The recursive part of the CTE recursively appends forward slash–separated ComponentId values to the path to represent each component in any given assembly:

```
SELECT
  CAST
  (
    bp.path.ToString() +
      CAST
      (
        bc.ComponentID AS varchar(30)
      ) +
      '/' AS hierarchyid
  ) AS Path,
  bc.ComponentID,
  bc.ProductAssemblyID
FROM BomChildren AS bc
INNER JOIN BomPaths AS bp
  ON bc.ProductAssemblyID = bp.ComponentID
)
```

The next part of the statement inserts the results of the recursive `BomPaths` CTE into the `Production.HierBillOfMaterials` table. The results of the recursive CTE are joined to the `Production.BillOfMaterials` table for a couple of reasons:

- To ensure that only components currently in use are put into the hierarchy, by making sure that the `EndDate` is `NULL` for each component

- To retrieve the `UnitMeasureCode` and `PerAssemblyQty` columns for each component

I use a `LEFT OUTER JOIN` in this statement instead of an `INNER JOIN` because of the inclusion of the `hierarchyid` root node, which has no matching row in the `Production.BillOfMaterials` table. If you had opted not to include the `hierarchyid` root node, you could turn this join back into an `INNER JOIN`.

```
INSERT INTO Production.HierBillOfMaterials
(
  BomNode,
  ProductAssemblyID,
  ComponentID,
  UnitMeasureCode,
  PerAssemblyQty
)
SELECT
  bp.Path,
  bp.ProductAssemblyID,
  bp.ComponentID,
  bom.UnitMeasureCode,
  bom.PerAssemblyQty
FROM BomPaths AS bp
LEFT OUTER JOIN Production.BillOfMaterials bom
  ON bp.ComponentID = bom.ComponentID
    AND COALESCE(bp.ProductAssemblyID, -1) = COALESCE(bom.ProductAssemblyID, -1)
WHERE bom.EndDate IS NULL
GROUP BY
  bp.path,
  bp.ProductAssemblyID,
  bp.ComponentID,
  bom.UnitMeasureCode,
  bom.PerAssemblyQty;
```

The simple query in Listing 2-13 shows the BOM after conversion to materialized path form with the `hierarchyid` data type, with partial results shown in Figure 2-9.

Listing 2-13. *Viewing the hierarchyid BOMs*

```
SELECT
  BomNode,
  BomNode.ToString(),
  ProductAssemblyID,
```

```
    ComponentID,
    UnitMeasureCode,
    PerAssemblyQty,
    BomLevel
FROM Production.HierBillOfMaterials
ORDER BY BomNode;
GO
```

	BomNode	(No column na...	ProductAssembl...	Component...	UnitMeasureCo...	PerAssembly...	BomLe...
1	0x	/	NULL	NULL	NULL	NULL	0
2	0xEA2EC0	/749/	NULL	749	EA	1.00	1
3	0xEA2EF999F0	/749/519/	749	519	EA	1.00	2
4	0xEA2EF999FE644C	/749/519/497/	519	497	EA	4.00	3
5	0xEA2EF999FE6844	/749/519/528/	519	528	EA	1.00	3
6	0xEA2EF999FE6854	/749/519/530/	519	530	EA	1.00	3
7	0xEA2EF999FEC84C	/749/519/913/	519	913	EA	1.00	3
8	0xEA2EFA3BB0	/749/717/	749	717	EA	1.00	2
9	0xEA2EFA3BBE2E...	/749/717/324/	717	324	EA	2.00	3
10	0xEA2EFA3BBE2E...	/749/717/324/4...	324	486	EA	1.00	4
11	0xEA2EFA3BBE2E...	/749/717/325/	717	325	EA	2.00	3
12	0xEA2EFA3BBE2E...	/749/717/326/	717	326	EA	1.00	3
13	0xEA2EFA3BBE2E...	/749/717/327/	717	327	EA	1.00	3
14	0xEA2EFA3BBE2E...	/749/717/327/4...	327	483	EA	1.00	4
15	0xEA2EFA3BBE46...	/749/717/399/	717	399	EA	1.00	3

Figure 2-9. *Partial results of the hierarchical BOM conversion*

As you can see, the hierarchyid column, BomNode, represents the hierarchy as a compact path in a variable-length binary format. Converting the BomNode column to string format with the ToString() method results in a forward slash–separated path reminiscent of a file path. The BomLevel column uses the GetLevel() method to retrieve the level of each node in the hierarchy. The hierarchyid root node has a BomLevel of 0. The top-level assemblies are on level 1, and their children are on levels 2 and below.

hierarchyid Methods

The hierarchyid data type includes several methods for querying and manipulating hierarchical data. The IsDescendant() method, for instance, can be used to retrieve all descendants of a given node. The example in Listing 2-14 retrieves the descendant nodes of product assembly 749. The results are shown in Figure 2-10.

Listing 2-14. *Retrieving Descendant Nodes of Assembly 749*

```
DECLARE @CurrentNode hierarchyid;

SELECT @CurrentNode = BomNode
FROM Production.HierBillOfMaterials
WHERE ProductAssemblyID = 749;
```

```
SELECT
  BomNode,
  BomNode.ToString(),
  ProductAssemblyID,
  ComponentID,
  UnitMeasureCode,
  PerAssemblyQty,
  BomLevel
FROM Production.HierBillOfMaterials
WHERE @CurrentNode.IsDescendant(BomNode) = 1;
GO
```

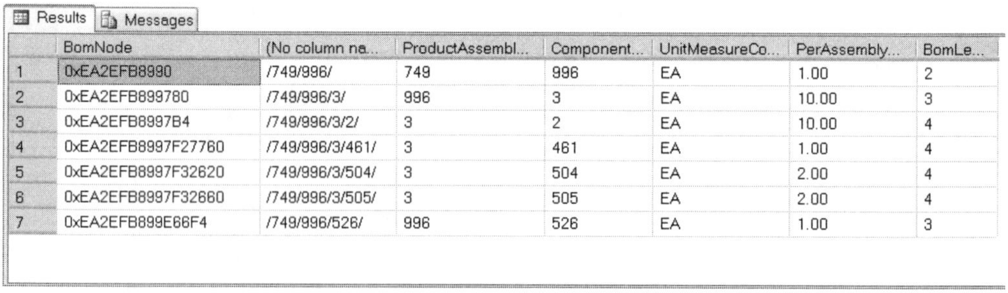

	BomNode	(No column na...	ProductAssembl...	Component...	UnitMeasureCo...	PerAssembly...	BomLe...
1	0xEA2EFB8990	/749/996/	749	996	EA	1.00	2
2	0xEA2EFB899780	/749/996/3/	996	3	EA	10.00	3
3	0xEA2EFB8997B4	/749/996/3/2/	3	2	EA	10.00	4
4	0xEA2EFB8997F27760	/749/996/3/461/	3	461	EA	1.00	4
5	0xEA2EFB8997F32620	/749/996/3/504/	3	504	EA	2.00	4
6	0xEA2EFB8997F32660	/749/996/3/505/	3	505	EA	2.00	4
7	0xEA2EFB899E66F4	/749/996/526/	996	526	EA	1.00	3

Figure 2-10. *Descendant nodes of assembly 749*

Table 2-4 is a quick summary of the hierarchyid data type methods.

Table 2-4. *hierarchyid Data Type Methods*

Method	Description
GetAncestor(*n*)	Retrieves the *n*th ancestor of the hierarchyid node instance.
GetDescendant(*n*)	Retrieves the *n*th descendant of the hierarchyid node instance.
GetLevel()	Gets the level of the hierarchyid node instance in the hierarchy.
GetRoot()	Gets the hierarchyid instance root node; GetRoot() is a static method.
IsDescendant(*node*)	Returns 1 if a specified *node* is a descendant of the hierarchyid instance node.
Parse(*string*)	Converts the given canonical *string*, in forward slash–separated format, to a hierarchyid path.
Reparent(*old_root*, *new_root*)	Reparents a node by moving nodes from *old_root* to *new_root*.
ToString()	Converts a hierarchyid instance to a canonical forward slash–separated string representation.

Spatial Data Types

SQL Server 2008 includes two new data types for storing, querying, and manipulating spatial data. The geometry data type is designed to represent flat-earth, or Euclidean, spatial data per the Open Geospatial Consortium (OGC) standard. The geography data type supports round-earth, or ellipsoidal, spatial data. Figure 2-11 shows a simple two-dimensional flat geometry for a small area, with a point plotted at location (2, 1).

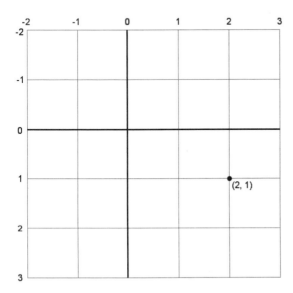

Figure 2-11. *Flat spatial representation*

(X, Y) OR (LATITUDE, LONGITUDE)?

Coordinates in spatial data are generally represented using (x, y) coordinate pairs, as in Figure 2-11. However, we often say "latitude-longitude" when we refer to coordinates. The problem is that latitude is the y axis, while longitude is the x axis. The Well-Known Text format we'll discuss later in this section represents spatial data using (x, y) coordinate pair ordering for the geometry data type. The geography data type, however, uses (lat, long) ordering of coordinate pairs in Well-Known Text format. This means that the order is flipped for geometry, and coordinates are actually represented in (y, x) order. Based on community feedback, the SQL Server team has expressed that changes to the coordinate ordering are being considered.

The spatial data types store representations of spatial data using instance types. There are 12 instance types, all derived from the Geography Markup Language (GML) abstract Geometry type. Of those 12 instance types, only 7 are concrete types that can be instantiated; the other 5 serve as abstract base types from which other types derive. Figure 2-12 shows the spatial instance type hierarchy with the XML-based GML top-level elements.

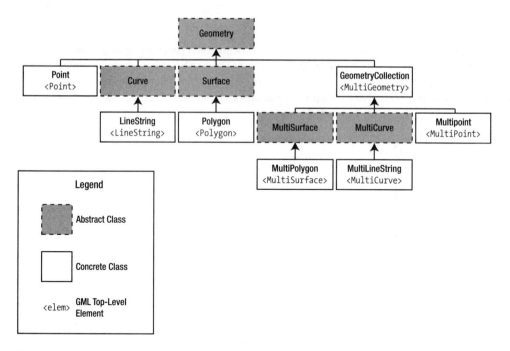

Figure 2-12. *Spatial instance type hierarchy*

The available spatial instance types include the following:

- Point: This object represents a zero-dimensional object representing a single location. The Point requires, at a minimum, a two-dimensional (x, y) coordinate pair, but it may also have an elevation coordinate (z) and an additional user-defined measure. The Point object has no area or length.

- MultiPoint: This type represents a collection of multiple points. It has no area or length.

- LineString: This is a one-dimensional object representing one or more connected line segments. Each segment is defined by a start point and an endpoint, and all segments are connected in such a way that the endpoint of one line segment is the start point for the next line segment. The LineString has length, but no area.

- MultiLineString: This is a one-dimensional object composed of multiple LineString objects. The LineString objects in a MultiLineString do not necessarily have to be connected to one another. The MultiLineString has no area, but it has an associated length, which is the sum of the lengths of all LineString objects in the MultiLineString.

- Polygon: This is a two-dimensional object defined by a sequence of connected points. The Polygon object must have a single exterior bounding ring, which defines the interior region of the Polygon object. In addition, the Polygon may have interior bounding rings, which exclude portions of the area inside the interior bounding ring from the Polygon's area. Polygon objects have a length, which is the length of the exterior bounding ring, and an area, which is the area defined by the exterior bounding ring minus the areas defined by any interior bounding rings.

- MultiPolygon: This is a collection of Polygon objects. Like the Polygon, the MultiPolygon has both length and area.

- GeometryCollection: This is the base class for the "multi" types (e.g., MultiPoint, MultiLine, and MultiPolygon). This class can be instantiated and can contain a collection of any spatial objects.

You can populate spatial data using Well-Known Text (WKT) strings or GML-formatted data. WKT strings are passed into the geometry and geography data types' STGeomFromText() static method and related static methods. Spatial data types can be populated from GML-formatted data with the GeomFromGml() static method. Listing 2-15 shows how to populate a spatial data type with a Polygon instance via a WKT-formatted string. The coordinates in the WKT Polygon are the borders of the state of Wyoming, chosen for its simplicity.

Listing 2-15. *Representing Wyoming As a geometry Object*

```
DECLARE @Wyoming geometry;
SET @Wyoming = geometry::STGeomFromText ('POLYGON
  ( ( -104.053108 41.698246, -104.054993 41.564247,
    -104.053505 41.388107, -104.051201 41.003227,
    -104.933968 40.994305, -105.278259 40.996365,
    -106.202896 41.000111, -106.328545 41.001316,
    -106.864838 40.998489, -107.303436 41.000168,
    -107.918037 41.00341, -109.047638 40.998474,
    -110.001457 40.997646, -110.062477 40.99794,
    -111.050285 40.996635, -111.050911 41.25848,
    -111.050323 41.578648, -111.047951 41.996265,
    -111.046028 42.503323, -111.048447 43.019962,
    -111.04673 43.284813, -111.045998 43.515606,
    -111.049629 43.982632, -111.050789 44.473396,
    -111.050842 44.664562, -111.05265 44.995766,
    -110.428894 44.992348, -110.392006 44.998688,
    -109.994789 45.002853, -109.798653 44.99958,
    -108.624573 44.997643, -108.258568 45.00016,
    -107.893715 44.999813, -106.258644 44.996174,
    -106.020576 44.997227, -105.084465 44.999832,
    -105.04126 45.001091, -104.059349 44.997349,
    -104.058975 44.574368, -104.060547 44.181843,
    -104.059242 44.145844, -104.05899 43.852928,
    -104.057426 43.503738, -104.05867 43.47916,
    -104.05571 43.003094, -104.055725 42.614704,
    -104.053009 41.999851, -104.053108 41.698246) )', 0);
```

Listing 2-15 demonstrates a couple of interesting items, which I previously touched on but would like to reiterate here. The first point is that the coordinates are given in longitude-latitude order. This might be a bit counterintuitive for geospatial beginners, who are used to hearing coordinates referenced as "latitude-longitude" coordinates, but it's easier to grasp once you understand that longitude represents the x axis and latitude represents the y axis.

The second point is that the final coordinate pair, (−104.053108, 41.698246), is the same as the first coordinate pair. This is a requirement for Polygon objects.

You can populate a geography instance similarly using WKT or GML. Listing 2-16 populates a geography instance with the border coordinates for the state of Wyoming using GML.

Listing 2-16. *Using GML to Represent Wyoming As a geography Object*

```
DECLARE @Wyoming geography;
SET @Wyoming = geography::GeomFromGml ('<Polygon
  xmlns="http://www.opengis.net/gml">
  <exterior>
    <LinearRing>
      <posList>
        41.698246 -104.053108 41.999851 -104.053009
        43.003094 -104.05571 43.503738 -104.057426
        44.145844 -104.059242 44.574368 -104.058975
        45.001091 -105.04126 44.997227 -106.020576
        44.999813 -107.893715 44.997643 -108.624573
        45.002853 -109.994789 44.992348 -110.428894
        44.664562 -111.050842 43.982632 -111.049629
        43.284813 -111.04673 42.503323 -111.046028
        41.578648 -111.050323 40.996635 -111.050285
        40.997646 -110.001457 41.00341 -107.918037
        40.998489 -106.864838 41.000111 -106.202896
        40.994305 -104.933968 41.388107 -104.053505
        41.698246 -104.053108
      </posList>
    </LinearRing>
  </exterior>
</Polygon>', 4269);
```

Like the geometry data type, the geography data type has some interesting features. The first thing to notice is that the coordinates are given in latitude-longitude order, the opposite of the geometry object. This complicates matters a bit if you want to reuse the same coordinate data between geometry and geography instances. Another thing to notice is that in GML format, there are no comma separators between coordinate pairs. All coordinates are separated by whitespace characters. GML also requires you to declare the GML namespace http://www.opengis.net/gml.

The coordinate pairs in Listing 2-16 are also listed in reverse order from the geometry instance in Listing 2-15. This is required because the geography data type represents ellipsoidal spatial data. Ellipsoidal data in SQL Server has a couple of restrictions on it: an object must all fit in one hemisphere and it must be expressed with a counterclockwise orientation. These limitations do not apply to the geometry data type. These limitations are discussed further in the *Hemisphere and Orientation* sidebar in this section.

The final thing to notice is that when you create a geometry instance, you must specify a spatial reference identifier (SRID). The SRID used here is 4269, which is the GCS North American Datum 1983 (NAD 83). A *datum* is an associated ellipsoid model of Earth on which the coordinate data is based. I used SRID 4269 because the coordinates used in the example are borrowed from the US Census Bureau's TIGER/Line data, which is in turn based on NAD 83. As you can see, using the geography data type is slightly more involved than using the geometry data type, but it can provide more accurate results and additional functionality for Earth-based geographic information systems (GISs).

HEMISPHERE AND ORIENTATION

The geography data type requires spatial objects to be contained in a single hemisphere—they cannot cross the equator. If you create a Polygon or other object within a geography instance that crosses hemispheres, you'll receive an error message like the following:

```
The specified input does not represent a valid geography instance because it
exceeds a single hemisphere. Each geography instance must fit inside a
single hemisphere. A common reason for this error is that a polygon has the
wrong ring orientation.
```

This restriction is in place primarily to help with complex calculations. SQL Server must project geography instances onto a plane—flatten them out—to perform indexing and other operations like intersection calculations. Limiting geographic objects to a single hemisphere simplifies these calculations from a technical perspective.

You might also receive this error message if you create a Polygon with the wrong ring orientation. So why is ring orientation so important, and what is the "right" ring orientation? To answer these questions, you have to ask yet another question: "What is the inside of a Polygon?" You might instinctively say that the inside of a Polygon is the smallest area enclosed by the coordinates you supply. But you could end up in a situation where your Polygon should be the larger area enclosed by your coordinates. If you created a border around the North Pole, for instance, is your Polygon the area within the border or is it the rest of the Earth minus the North Pole? Your answer to this question determines what the "inside" of the Polygon really is.

The next step is to tell SQL Server where the inside of the Polygon lies. SQL Server's geography instance makes you define your coordinates in counterclockwise order, so the inside of the Polygon is everything that falls on the left-hand side of the lines connecting the coordinates. In the following illustration, the image on the left side is an invalid orientation because the coordinates are defined in a clockwise order. The image on the right side is a valid orientation because its coordinates are defined in a counterclockwise order. If you follow the direction of the arrows on the image, you'll notice that the area on the left-hand side of the arrows is the area "inside" the Polygon. This eliminates any ambiguity from your Polygon definitions.

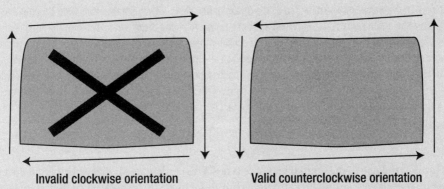

Invalid clockwise orientation   Valid counterclockwise orientation

Keep these restrictions in mind if you decide to use the geography data type in addition to, or instead of, the geometry data type.

Polygon and MultiPolygon are two of the more interesting and complex spatial objects you can create. I like to use the state of Utah as a real-world example of a Polygon object for a couple of reasons. First, the exterior bounding ring for the state is very simple, composed of relatively straight lines. Second, the Great Salt Lake within the state can be used as a highly visible example of an interior bounding ring. Figure 2-13 shows the state of Utah.

The state of Michigan provides an excellent example of a MultiPolygon object. Michigan is composed of two distinct peninsulas, known as the Upper Peninsula and Lower Peninsula, respectively. The two peninsulas are separated by the Straits of Mackinac, which join Lake Michigan to Lake Huron. Figure 2-14 shows the Michigan MultiPolygon.

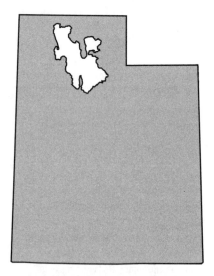

Figure 2-13. *The state of Utah with the Great Salt Lake as an interior bounding ring*

Figure 2-14. *Michigan as a MultiPolygon*

MICHIGAN AND THE GREAT LAKES

Michigan's two peninsulas are separated by the Straits of Mackinac, which is a five-mile-wide channel that joins two of the Great Lakes, Lake Michigan and Lake Huron. Although these two bodies of water are historically referred two as separate lakes, hydrologists consider them to be one contiguous body of water. Hydrology experts sometimes refer to the lakes as a single entity, Lake Michigan-Huron. On the other hand, it makes sense to consider the two lakes as separate from a political point of view, since Lake Michigan is wholly within the borders of the United States, while the border between the United States and Canada divides Lake Huron. For the purposes of this section, the most important fact is that the lakes separate Michigan into two peninsulas, making it a good example of a MultiPolygon.

Through the use of the spatial instance types, you can create spatial objects that cover the entire range from very simple to extremely complex. Once you've created spatial objects, you can use the geometry and geography data type methods on them or create spatial indexes on spatial data type columns to increase calculation efficiency. Listing 2-17 uses the geography data type instance created in Listing 2-16 and the STIntersects() method to report whether the town of Laramie and the Statue of Liberty are located within the borders of Wyoming. The results are shown in Figure 2-15.

Listing 2-17. *Are the Statue of Liberty and Laramie in Wyoming?*

```
DECLARE @Wyoming geography,
  @StatueOfLiberty geography,
  @Laramie geography;

SET @Wyoming = geography::GeomFromGml ('<Polygon
  xmlns="http://www.opengis.net/gml">
  <exterior>
    <LinearRing>
      <posList>
        41.698246 -104.053108 41.999851 -104.053009
        43.003094 -104.05571 43.503738 -104.057426
        44.145844 -104.059242 44.574368 -104.058975
        45.001091 -105.04126 44.997227 -106.020576
        44.999813 -107.893715 44.997643 -108.624573
        45.002853 -109.994789 44.992348 -110.428894
        44.664562 -111.050842 43.982632 -111.049629
        43.284813 -111.04673 42.503323 -111.046028
        41.578648 -111.050323 40.996635 -111.050285
        40.997646 -110.001457 41.00341 -107.918037
        40.998489 -106.864838 41.000111 -106.202896
        40.994305 -104.933968 41.388107 -104.053505
        41.698246 -104.053108
      </posList>
    </LinearRing>
  </exterior>
</Polygon>', 4269);

SET @StatueOfLiberty = geography::GeomFromGml('<Point
  xmlns="http://www.opengis.net/gml">
  <pos>
    40.689124 -74.044483
  </pos>
</Point>', 4269);

SET @Laramie = geography::GeomFromGml('<Point
  xmlns="http://www.opengis.net/gml">
  <pos>
    41.312928 -105.587253
  </pos>
</Point>', 4269);
```

```
SELECT 'Is the Statue of Liberty in Wyoming?',
  CASE @Wyoming.STIntersects(@StatueOfLiberty)
    WHEN 0 THEN 'No'
    ELSE 'Yes'
  END AS Answer
UNION
SELECT 'Is Laramie in Wyoming?',
  CASE @Wyoming.STIntersects(@Laramie)
    WHEN 0 THEN 'No'
    ELSE 'Yes'
  END;
```

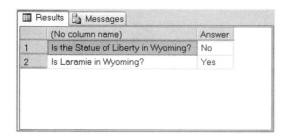

Figure 2-15. *The results of the STIntersection() method example*

SQL Server 2008 also allows you to create spatial indexes that optimize spatial data calculations. Spatial indexes are created by decomposing your spatial data into a b-tree–based grid hierarchy four levels deep. Each level represents a further subdivision of the cells above it in the hierarchy. Figure 2-16 shows a simple example of a decomposed spatial grid hierarchy.

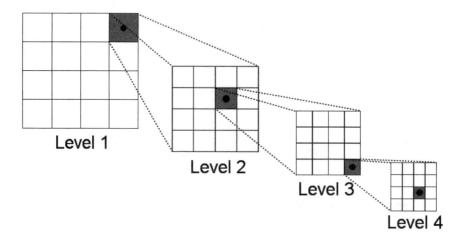

Figure 2-16. *Decomposing space for spatial indexing*

The CREATE SPATIAL INDEX statement allows you to create spatial indexes on spatial data type columns. Listing 2-18 is an example of a CREATE SPATIAL INDEX statement.

Listing 2-18. *Creating a Spatial Index*

```
CREATE SPATIAL INDEX SIX_Location
ON MyTable (SpatialColumn);
```

Spatial indexing is one of the biggest benefits of storing spatial data inside the database. As one astute developer pointed out, "Without spatial indexing, you may as well store your spatial data in flat files."

Grouping Sets

In previous versions of SQL Server, developers were given two GROUP BY extensions to return multiple levels of aggregated data in a single result set on the server—the CUBE and ROLLUP options. Consider Listing 2-19, which demonstrates a simple use of CUBE to add additional summarization rows to the results of a sales-based query. This particular query retrieves the total sales by year and by territory. Partial results are shown in Figure 2-17.

Listing 2-19. *Total Sales by Year by Territory with CUBE*

```
SELECT DATEPART(year, soh.OrderDate) AS SalesYear,
    st.Name AS TerritoryName,
    SUM(soh.SubTotal) AS TotalSales
FROM Sales.SalesOrderHeader soh
INNER JOIN Sales.SalesTerritory st
  ON soh.TerritoryID = st.TerritoryID
WHERE st.CountryRegionCode = 'US'
GROUP BY DATEPART(year, soh.OrderDate),
  st.Name
WITH CUBE
ORDER BY DATEPART(year, soh.OrderDate),
  st.Name;
```

	SalesYear	TerritoryName	TotalSales
1	NULL	NULL	74593068.7848
2	NULL	Central	9564668.9505
3	NULL	Northeast	8388906.1628
4	NULL	Northwest	18825882.9554
5	NULL	Southeast	9566136.1287
6	NULL	Southwest	28247474.5874
7	2001	NULL	8980014.6754
8	2001	Central	1143786.5178
9	2001	Northeast	683106.9723
10	2001	Northwest	2446589.8533
11	2001	Southeast	1744930.8718
12	2001	Southwest	2961600.4602
13	2002	NULL	23717356.6759
14	2002	Central	3183878.2581
15	2002	Northeast	2964092.4615

Figure 2-17. *The results of the CUBE query*

While some developers were able to use CUBE and ROLLUP to great effect for SQL Server–based data analysis and reporting applications, many developers created their own custom methods of generating such summaries, or turned to more powerful analytical tools like SQL Server Analysis Services (SSAS). As you can see in Figure 2-17, the GROUP BY with the CUBE option added aggregates data to the result set, returning all of the following:

- The single row with NULL in both the SalesYear and TerritoryName columns contains the grand total of the TotalSales column entries.

- The rows with NULL in the SalesYear and a valid TerritoryName (Northeast, Northwest, Central, etc.) contain the totals of the TotalSales column entries aggregated by TerritoryName.

- The rows with a valid SalesYear (2001, 2002, etc.) and NULL in the TerritoryName contain the totals of the TotalSales column entries aggregated by SalesYear.

- The rows with both a valid SalesYear and a valid TerritoryName contain the totals of the TotalSales column entries aggregated by both SalesYear and TerritoryName.

SQL Server 2008 offers a much more powerful method of customizing your summarization experience through a new SQL 2008 standard feature called *grouping sets*. The results from Listing 2-19 can be generated with the new GROUPING SETS extension to GROUP BY, as shown in Listing 2-20.

Listing 2-20. *Total Sales by Year by Territory with Grouping Sets*

```
SELECT
    DATEPART(year, soh.OrderDate) AS SalesYear,
    st.Name AS TerritoryName,
    SUM(soh.SubTotal) AS TotalSales
FROM Sales.SalesOrderHeader soh
INNER JOIN Sales.SalesTerritory st
  ON soh.TerritoryID = st.TerritoryID
WHERE st.CountryRegionCode = 'US'
GROUP BY GROUPING SETS
(
  (DATEPART(year, soh.OrderDate), st.Name),
  (DATEPART(YEAR, soh.OrderDate)),
  (st.Name),
  ()
)
ORDER BY
  DATEPART(year, soh.OrderDate),
  st.Name;
```

Each set you wish to group by is included in parentheses after the GROUPING SETS keywords. In this instance, I'm telling the query to group by the OrderDate year and territory name, then by each column separately, and finally by the empty set identified by () (empty parentheses). With grouping sets, you can specify groupings and summarizations that you cannot get with the CUBE or ROLLUP options.

Consider Listing 2-21, which modifies Listing 2-19 from a CUBE query to a ROLLUP query. This option basically eliminates the rows from the CUBE result set where NULL appears in the first column (in this case, the SalesYear column), except for the grand total where NULL appears in both the SalesYear and TerritoryName columns. Partial results of the ROLLUP query are shown in Figure 2-18. This query returns the same results as the previous CUBE query, except that the rows that returned totals by TerritoryName alone are removed.

Listing 2-21. *Total Sales by Year by Territory with ROLLUP*

```
SELECT DATEPART(year, soh.OrderDate) AS SalesYear,
  st.Name AS TerritoryName,
  SUM(soh.SubTotal) AS TotalSales
FROM Sales.SalesOrderHeader soh
INNER JOIN Sales.SalesTerritory st
  ON soh.TerritoryID = st.TerritoryID
WHERE st.CountryRegionCode = 'US'
GROUP BY DATEPART(year, soh.OrderDate),
  st.Name
WITH ROLLUP
ORDER BY DATEPART(year, soh.OrderDate),
  st.Name;
```

	SalesYear	TerritoryName	TotalSales
1	NULL	NULL	74593068.7848
2	2001	NULL	8980014.6754
3	2001	Central	1143786.5178
4	2001	Northeast	683106.9723
5	2001	Northwest	2446589.8533
6	2001	Southeast	1744930.8718
7	2001	Southwest	2961600.4602
8	2002	NULL	23717356.6759
9	2002	Central	3183878.2581
10	2002	Northeast	2964092.4615
11	2002	Northwest	5114650.3647
12	2002	Southeast	3452438.1395
13	2002	Southwest	9002297.4521
14	2003	NULL	27264873.8277
15	2003	Central	3633807.1257

Figure 2-18. *Partial results of the ROLLUP query*

But consider a situation in which, for instance, you want to summarize data, but you want to keep all summary rows where the SalesYear is NULL and eliminate all rows where the TerritoryName is NULL. This is basically the opposite of the ROLLUP option. ROLLUP and CUBE don't provide this option, but you can easily do this with grouping sets, as shown in Listing 2-22 (partial results are shown in Figure 2-19).

Listing 2-22. *Using Grouping Sets to Generate a Customized ROLLUP-Style Result*

```
SELECT
    DATEPART(year, soh.OrderDate) AS SalesYear,
    st.Name AS TerritoryName,
    SUM(soh.SubTotal) AS TotalSales
FROM Sales.SalesOrderHeader soh
INNER JOIN Sales.SalesTerritory st
  ON soh.TerritoryID = st.TerritoryID
WHERE st.CountryRegionCode = 'US'
GROUP BY GROUPING SETS
(
  (DATEPART(year, soh.OrderDate), st.Name),
  (st.Name)
)
ORDER BY
    DATEPART(year, soh.OrderDate),
    st.Name;
```

	SalesYear	TerritoryName	TotalSales
1	NULL	Central	9564668.9505
2	NULL	Northeast	8388906.1628
3	NULL	Northwest	18825882.9554
4	NULL	Southeast	9566136.1287
5	NULL	Southwest	28247474.5874
6	2001	Central	1143786.5178
7	2001	Northeast	683106.9723
8	2001	Northwest	2446589.8533
9	2001	Southeast	1744930.8718
10	2001	Southwest	2961600.4602
11	2002	Central	3183878.2581
12	2002	Northeast	2964092.4615
13	2002	Northwest	5114650.3647
14	2002	Southeast	3452438.1395
15	2002	Southwest	9002297.4521

Figure 2-19. *Partial results of the GROUPING SETS query*

Other New Features

SQL Server 2008 builds upon the functionality set out in SQL Server 2005. SQL Server 2005 included several new T-SQL features, which are implemented and in many cases improved upon in SQL Server 2008. You can expect most SQL Server 2005 T-SQL scripts to run on SQL Server 2005 with little or no change, as long as they are well-written. By "well-written," I'm referring to code that follows best practices for coding, including the following:

- Well-written code should avoid features that have been deprecated in prior releases of SQL Server. This includes previously deprecated features like the old-style outer join operators `*=` and `=*`, the T-SQL `DUMP` and `RESTORE` statements, and system SPs like `sp_addalias` and `sp_dropalias`.

- Well-written code should also avoid undocumented SPs like `sp_executeresultset`.

Many of the previously deprecated features have been discontinued in SQL Server 2008. You should also ensure that your code is up to current coding standards, meaning that it should not require backward-compatibility mode. SQL Server 2008 only supports backward compatibility for the prior two versions of SQL Server (2005 and 2000). Backward compatibility is not a magic bullet. While it provides access to some deprecated features, it does not support them all. Backward-compatibility mode can also restrict your access to some of SQL Server's new features and functionality. Information useful for the upgrade process can be found in BOL under the heading "Upgrade (Database Engine)" (`http://msdn2.microsoft.com/en-us/library/ bb500267(SQL.100).aspx`). The SQL Server 2008 Upgrade Advisor tool is available on the SQL Server 2008 installation media, and should also be available for download from the Microsoft Download Center (`www.microsoft.com/downloads`), although it was not available for download at the time of this writing. The Upgrade Advisor tool is useful for identifying features and configuration settings that might affect your upgrade.

In addition to the features already listed in this chapter, SQL Server 2008 includes new functionality encompassing security, server and database management, performance optimization, and several other enhancements, many of which I will cover in later chapters of this book.

Summary

This chapter has provided an overview of many of SQL Server 2008's new features for T-SQL developers. These include productivity-enhancing features like single-statement variable declaration and initialization, C-style assignment operators, and multirow `VALUES` clauses.

In this chapter, I also discussed the flexible new T-SQL `MERGE` statement, which can perform conditional insert, update, and delete actions all in a single statement. SQL Server 2008 also introduces several new data types, including the `date`, `time`, `datetime2`, and `datetimeoffset` types for representing date and time values, the `hierarchyid` data type for representing hierarchical data, the spatial `geometry` and `geography` data types, and new grouping sets that provide flexible summarization capabilities over the old-style `CUBE` and `ROLLUP` options. Finally, I discussed some of the development issues that could affect an upgrade or migration of existing code.

In Chapter 4, I will cover T-SQL control-of-flow language statements and begin to lay the groundwork for a detailed discussion of SQL Server 2008 SPs, UDFs, and triggers.

EXERCISES

1. [Choose all that apply] SQL Server 2008 provides which of the following new productivity enhancements in the T-SQL language:

   a.   Single-statement variable declaration and initialization

   b.   C-style assignment operators

   c.   Multitable TRUNCATE TABLE statement option

   d.   Row constructors

2. [True/false] The new date data type stores time offset information.

3. What model does the hierarchyid data type use to represent hierarchical data in the database?

4. [Fill in the blank] The ___ data type stores flat-earth spatial data, while the ___ data type stores round-earth spatial data.

5. [Choose one] Which of the following is true of Polygon spatial objects when created in geography data type instances?

   a.   They must have a clockwise orientation.

   b.   They must have a counterclockwise orientation.

   c.   Orientation does not matter.

   d.   They can cross up to two hemispheres.

6. [True/false] You can use grouping sets to perform the same tasks previously performed with the CUBE and ROLLUP operators.

7. [Choose one] A spatial index is which of the following:

   a.   A hash table

   b.   An inverted keyword list

   c.   An n-gram index

   d.   A B-tree grid hierarchy

8. [Fill in the blank] Existing T-SQL scripts should run with minimal changes if you follow ___ ___.

CHAPTER 3

■■■

Tools of the Trade

SQL Server 2008 comes with a wide selection of tools and utilities to make development easier. In this chapter, I will introduce some of the most important tools for SQL Server developers, including SQL Server Management Studio (SSMS) and the SQLCMD utility, Business Intelligence Development Studio (BIDS), SQL Profiler, and SQL Server 2008 Books Online (BOL). I will also introduce supporting tools like SQL Server Integration Services (SSIS), the Bulk Copy Program (BCP), and the AdventureWorks 2008 sample database, which I will use in examples throughout the book. I will also cover some of the SQL Server connectivity features of Visual Studio 2005 and 2008.

SQL Server Management Studio

Back in the heyday of SQL Server 2000, it was common for developers to fire up the Enterprise Manager (EM) and Query Analyzer (QA) GUI database tools in rapid succession every time they sat down to write code. Historically, developer and DBA roles in the DBMS have been highly separated, and with good reason. DBAs have historically brought hardware and software administration and tuning skills, database design optimization experience, and healthy doses of skepticism and security to the table. On the other hand, developers have focused on coding skills, problem solving, system optimization, and debugging. This separation of powers works very well in production systems, but in development environments developers are often responsible for their own database design and management. Sometimes developers are put in charge of their own development server local security!

SQL Server 2000 EM was originally designed as a DBA tool, providing access to the GUI (graphical user interface) administration interface, including security administration, database object creation and management, and server management functionality. QA was designed as a developer tool, the primary GUI tool for the creation, testing, and tuning of queries.

SQL Server 2008 continues the tradition begun with SQL Server 2005 by combining the functionality of both of these GUI tools into a single GUI interface known as SSMS. This makes perfect sense in supporting real-world SQL Server development, where the roles of DBA and developer are often intermingled in development environments.

Many SQL Server developers prefer the GUI administration and development tools to the text-based query tool SQLCMD, and on this front SQL Server 2008 doesn't disappoint. SSMS offers several features that make development and administration work easier, including the following:

- The integrated, functional Object Explorer, which provides the ability to easily view and manage the server, databases, and database objects. The Object Explorer also provides right-click scripting ability for database objects.

- Color coding of scripts, making editing and debugging easier.

- *Intellisense*, which is the long-awaited automatic suggestion feature for SQL scripts. SQL developers have been waiting for this feature that has been a mainstay of Visual Studio development for many years now.

- Context-sensitive help provides F1-accessible help for keywords and code snippets. Just highlight a keyword or other text and press the F1 key—again, like Visual Studio developers have been doing for years.

- Graphical query execution plans are the bread and butter of the query optimization process. They greatly simplify the process of optimizing complex queries, quickly exposing potential bottlenecks in your code.

- Project management and code version control integration have been introduced, including integration with Team Foundation Server (TFS) and Visual SourceSafe version control systems.

- SQLCMD mode allows you to execute SQL scripts using SQLCMD, taking advantage of SQLCMD's additional script capabilities like scripting variables.

SSMS also includes database and server management features, but I'll limit the discussion of this section to some of the most important developer-specific features. Figure 3-1 shows the SSMS interface with an Intellisense example.

■**Note** Connecting to SQL Server 2008 via Enterprise Manager is not supported. SQL Server 2005 SSMS will connect, but requires SQL Server 2005 SP 2 Cumulative Update 5. You will lose some functionality if you connect to SQL Server 2008 instances with the older tools.

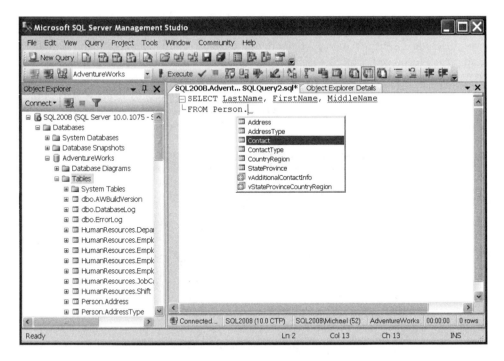

Figure 3-1. *Using Intellisense in SSMS*

SSMS Editing Options

SSMS incorporates and improves on many of the developer features found in QA. You can change the editing options discussed in this section via the Tools ➤ Options menu.

SSMS includes fully customizable script color coding. You can customize the foreground and background colors, font face, size, and style for elements of T-SQL, XML, XSLT, and MDX scripts. Likewise, you can customize just about any feedback that SSMS generates to suit your personal tastes.

You can set other editing options such as word wrap, line number display, indentation, and tabs for different file types based on their associated file extensions. Like its predecessors, SSMS lets you configure your own keyboard shortcuts to execute common T-SQL statements or SPs. You can redefine Alt+F1, Ctrl+F1, and all Ctrl+<number> combinations.

By default, SSMS displays queries using a tabbed window environment. If you prefer the classic multiple-document interface (MDI) window style, you can switch the environment layout to suit your tastes. You can also change the query results' output style from the default grid output to text or file output.

Context-Sensitive Help

To access the context-sensitive help, just highlight the T-SQL or other statement you want help with, and press F1. You can configure Help to use your locally installed copy of SQL Server 2008 BOL, or you can specify that Help search MSDN Online for the most up-to-date BOL information. You can add Help pages to your Help Favorites or go directly to the MSDN Community Forums to ask questions with the click of a button. Figure 3-2 shows the result of calling context-sensitive help for the CREATE CERTIFICATE statement.

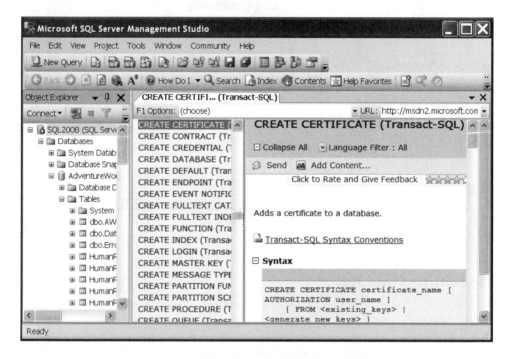

Figure 3-2. *Using SSMS context-sensitive help to find CREATE CERTIFICATE answers*

SSMS Help has several options that allow you to control help functionality and presentation. You can, for example, use the SSMS Integrated Help Viewer, which was shown in Figure 3-2, or you can use the External Help Viewer. The Help Options window is shown in Figure 3-3.

Help Search rounds out the discussion of the help functionality in SSMS. The Help Search function automatically searches several online providers of SQL Server–related information for answers to your questions. Your searches are not restricted to SQL Server keywords or statements; you can search for anything at all, and the Help Search function will scour registered web sites and communities for relevant answers. Figure 3-4 shows the results of using Help Search to find XQuery content and articles.

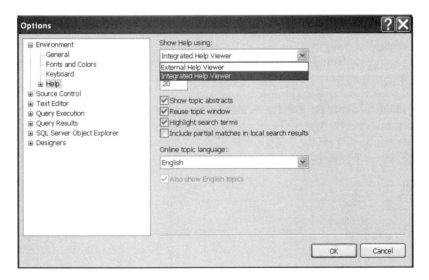

Figure 3-3. *Using the Help Options window to personalize SSMS Help*

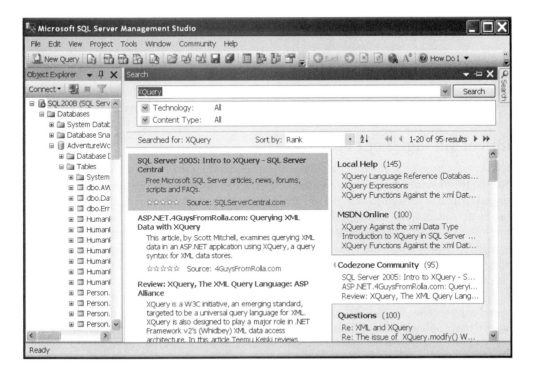

Figure 3-4. *Using Help Search to find help on XQuery*

Graphical Query Execution Plans

SSMS offers graphical query execution plans similar to the plans available in QA. The graphical query execution plan is an excellent tool for optimizing query performance. SSMS allows you to view two types of graphical query execution plans: estimated and actual. The *estimated* query execution plan is SQL Server's cost-based performance estimate of a query. The *actual* execution plan is virtually identical to the estimated execution plan, except that it shows additional information like actual row counts, number of rebinds, and number of rewinds when the query is run. These options are available via the Query menu. Figure 3-5 shows an estimated query execution plan in SSMS.

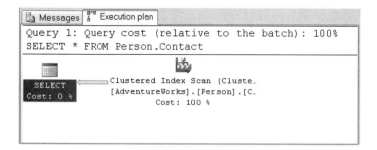

Figure 3-5. *Estimated query execution plan for a simple query*

In addition, you can right-click the Execution Plan window to save the XML version of the graphical query plan to an XML file. SSMS can open these XML query plan files (with the extension .sqlplan) and automatically show you the graphical version. This is extremely useful for remotely troubleshooting performance problems with slow-running queries.

Project Management Features

SSMS incorporates new project management features familiar to Visual Studio developers. SSMS supports solution-based development. It allows you to create solutions that consist of projects, which in turn contain T-SQL scripts, XML files, connection information, and other files. By default, projects and solutions are saved in your My Documents\SQL Server Management Studio\Projects directory. Solution files have the extension .ssmssln, and project files are saved in XML format with the .smssproj extension. SSMS incorporates a Solution Explorer window similar to Visual Studio's Solution Explorer, as shown in Figure 3-6. You can access the Solution Explorer through the View menu.

SSMS can take advantage of source control integration with TFS to help you manage versioning and deployments. To use SSMS's source control integration, you have to set the appropriate source control options in the Options menu. The Options window is shown in Figure 3-7.

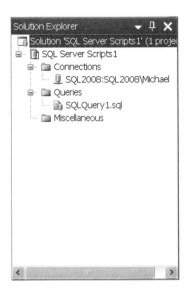

Figure 3-6. *Viewing a solution in the SSMS Solution Explorer*

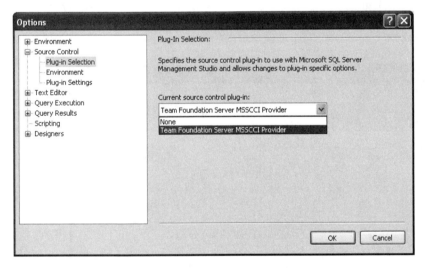

Figure 3-7. *Selecting the TFS MSSCCI provider in the source control options*

■**Note** To use SSMS with TFS, you will need to download and install the appropriate Microsoft Source Code Control Interface (MSSCCI) provider from Microsoft. Go to www.microsoft.com/, search for "MSSCCI," and download either the Visual Studio Team System 2005 or 2008 version of the MSSCCI provider, depending on which version you're using.

After you create a solution and add projects, connections, and SQL scripts, you can add your solution to TFS by right-clicking the solution in the Solution Explorer and selecting Add Solution to Source Control (see Figure 3-8).

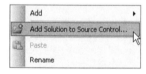

Figure 3-8. *Adding a solution to source control*

To check out items from source control, open a local copy and choose Check Out for Edit. You'll find options for checking out items from source control on the File ➤ Source Control menu. After checking out a solution from TFS, SSMS shows you the pending check-ins, letting you add comments to, or check in, individual files or projects.

The Object Explorer

The SSMS Object Explorer lets you view and manage database and server objects. In the Object Explorer, you can view tables, stored procedures (SPs), user-defined functions (UDFs), HTTP endpoints, users, logins, and just about every other database-specific or server-scoped object. Figure 3-9 shows the Object Explorer in the left-hand pane and the Object Explorer Details tab on the right.

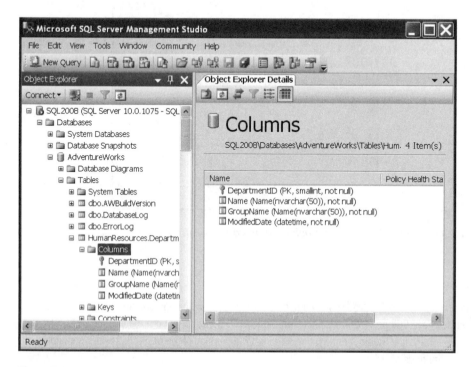

Figure 3-9. *Viewing the Object Explorer and the Object Explorer Details tab*

Most objects in the Object Explorer and the Object Explorer Details tabs have object-specific pop-up context menus. Right-clicking any given object will bring up the menu. Figure 3-10 shows an example pop-up context menu for database tables.

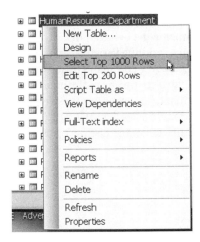

Figure 3-10. *Object Explorer database table pop-up context menu*

The SQL Server 2008 SSMS Object Explorer context menus offer several new options that weren't available in SQL Server 2005. The table context menu, for example, has options for selecting the top 1000 rows, editing the top 200 rows, and policy administration. The additional options available in the new version of the Object Explorer can help ease development and administration.

The SQLCMD Utility

The SQLCMD utility was originally introduced in SQL Server 2005 as an updated replacement for the SQL 2000 `osql` command-line utility. You can use SQLCMD to execute batches of T-SQL statements from script files, individual queries or batches of queries in interactive mode, or individual queries from the command line.

■**Note** Appendix D provides a quick reference to SQLCMD command-line options, scripting variables, and commands. The descriptions in the appendix are based on extensive testing of SQLCMD, and differ in some areas from the descriptions given in BOL.

SQLCMD offers support for a wide variety of command-line switches, making it a flexible utility for one-off batch or scheduled script execution. The following command demonstrates the use of some commonly used command-line options to connect to a SQL Server instance and execute a T-SQL script in the AdventureWorks database. The command uses some of the more common command-line options, including `-S` to specify the server/instance name, `-E` to indicate Windows authentication, `-d` to set the database name, and `-i` to specify the name of a script file to execute. The command-line switches are all case sensitive, so -v is a different option from -V, for instance.

```
sqlcmd -S SQL2008 -E -d AdventureWorks -i "c:\scripts\batch.sql"
```

SQLCMD allows you to use scripting variables that let you use a single script in multiple scenarios. Scripting variables provide a mechanism for customizing the behavior of T-SQL scripts without modifying the scripts' content. You can reference scripting variables that were previously set with the -v command-line switch, the SQLCMD :setvar command (discussed in the next section), or via Windows environment variables. You can also use any of the predefined SQLCMD scripting variables from within your scripts. The format to access any of these types of scripting variables from within your script is the same: $(variable_name). SQLCMD replaces your scripting variables with their respective values during script execution. Listing 3-1 shows some examples of scripting variables in action.

Listing 3-1. *Using Scripting Variables in a SQLCMD Script*

```
-- Windows environment variable
SELECT '$(PATH)';

-- SQLCMD scripting variable
SELECT '$(SQLCMDSERVER)';

-- Command-line scripting variable -v COLVAR= "Name" switch
SELECT $(COLVAR)
FROM Sys.Tables;
```

Because scripting variables are replaced in a script wholesale, some organizations might consider their use a security risk because of the possibility of SQL injection–style attacks. For security reasons, some might choose to use the -x command-line option to turn this feature off.

An example of a SQLCMD scripting variable is the predefined SQLCMDINI scripting variable, which specifies the SQLCMD startup script. The startup script is run every time SQLCMD is run. The startup script is useful for setting scripting variables with the :setvar command, setting initial T-SQL options such as QUOTED_IDENTIFIER or ANSI_PADDING, and performing any necessary database tasks before other scripts are run.

In addition to T-SQL statements, SQLCMD recognizes several commands specific to the application. SQLCMD commands allow you to perform tasks like listing servers and scripting variables, connecting to a server, and setting scripting variables, among others. Except for the batch terminator GO, all SQLCMD commands begin with a colon (:). SQLCMD can also be run interactively. To start an interactive mode session, run SQLCMD with any of the previous options that do not exit immediately on completion.

■**Note** SQLCMD options such as -Q, -i, -Z, and -? exit immediately on completion. You cannot start an interactive SQLCMD session if you specify any of these command-line options.

During an interactive SQLCMD session, you can run T-SQL queries and commands from the SQLCMD prompt. The interactive screen looks similar to Figure 3-11.

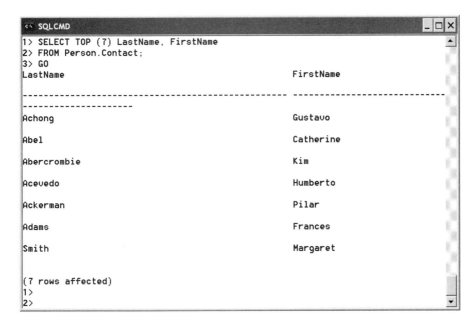

Figure 3-11. *Sample query run from the SQLCMD interactive prompt*

The SQLCMD prompt indicates the current line number of the batch (1>, 2>, etc.). You can enter T-SQL statements or SQLCMD commands at the prompt. T-SQL statements are stored in the statement cache as they are entered; SQLCMD commands are executed immediately. Once you have entered a complete batch of T-SQL statements, use the GO batch terminator to process all the statements in the cache.

Business Intelligence Development Studio

SQL Server 2008 ships with the Visual Studio integrated development environment (IDE) and a set of business intelligence development add-on packages, known collectively as BIDS. BIDS allows you to create and manage projects for SQL Server Analysis Services (SSAS), SQL Server Reporting Services (SSRS), and SQL Server Integration Services (SSIS). Figure 3-12 shows the New Project window, which lists the different types of projects available in BIDS.

■**Tip** If you install Visual Studio on the same server as SQL Server, BIDS gives you additional options based on the Visual Studio components you've installed. With Visual Studio installed, you may see options for projects including Visual Basic, C#, C++.

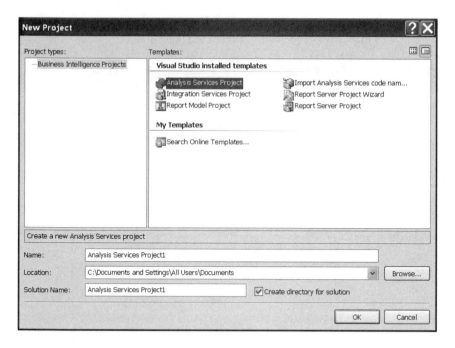

Figure 3-12. *Creating a new project in BIDS*

The BIDS interface makes it easy to create and edit SQL Server business intelligence projects, like the SSIS project shown in Figure 3-13.

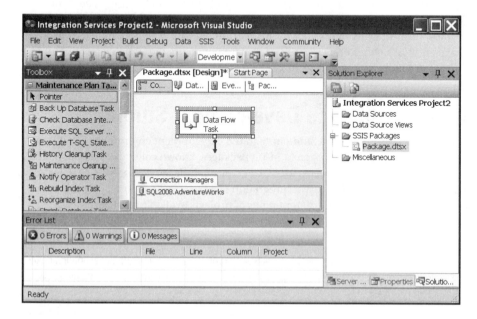

Figure 3-13. *Editing an SSIS project in BIDS*

SQL Profiler

SQL Profiler is the primary tool for analyzing SQL Server performance. If you have a performance problem but aren't sure where the bottleneck lies, SQL Profiler can help you rapidly narrow down the suspects. SQL Profiler works by capturing events that occur on the server and logging them to a trace file. The classes of events that can be captured are exhaustive, covering a wide range of server-side events, including T-SQL and SP preparation and execution, security events, transaction activity, locks, and database resizing.

When you create a new trace, SQL Profiler allows you to select all of the events you wish to audit. Normally, you will narrow this list down as much as possible for both performance and manageability reasons. Figure 3-14 is a sample trace that captures T-SQL-specific events on the server.

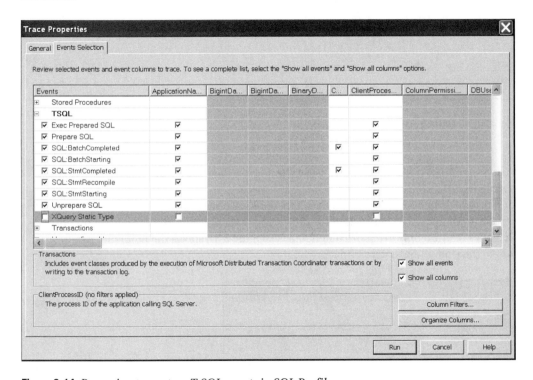

Figure 3-14. *Preparing to capture T-SQL events in SQL Profiler*

Once a trace is configured and running, it captures all of the specified events on the server. A sample trace run using the T-SQL events is shown in Figure 3-15.

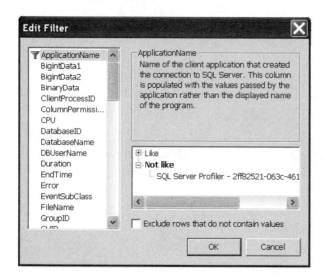

EventClass	ApplicationName	ClientProcessID	DatabaseID	DatabaseName	EventSequence	Gro
SQL:StmtStarting	Microsoft SQ...	728	5	Adventure...	774	
SQL:StmtCompleted	Microsoft SQ...	728	5	Adventure...	775	
SQL:BatchCompleted	Microsoft SQ...	728	5	Adventure...	776	
SQL:BatchStarting	Microsoft SQ...	728	5	Adventure...	777	
SQL:StmtStarting	Microsoft SQ...	728	5	Adventure...	779	
SQL:StmtCompleted	Microsoft SQ...	728	5	Adventure...	780	
SQL:BatchCompleted	Microsoft SQ...	728	5	Adventure...	781	
SQL:BatchStarting	Microsoft SQ...	728	5	Adventure...	782	
SQL:StmtStarting	Microsoft SQ...	728	5	Adventure...	783	
Trace Pause						

```
SELECT *
FROM Person.Contact;
```

Trace is paused.   Ln 30, Col 4   Rows: 31
Connections: 1

Figure 3-15. *Running a trace of T-SQL events*

As you can see in the example, even a simple trace with a relatively small number of events captured can easily become overwhelming, particularly if run against a SQL Server instance with several simultaneous user connections. SQL Profiler offers the Column Filter option, which allows you to eliminate results from your trace. Using filters, you can narrow the results down to include only actions performed by specific applications or users, or those activities relevant only to a particular database. Figure 3-16 shows the Edit Filter window, where trace filter selections are made.

Edit Filter

ApplicationName
  BigintData1
  BigintData2
  BinaryData
  ClientProcessID
  ColumnPermissi...
  CPU
  DatabaseID
  DatabaseName
  DBUserName
  Duration
  EndTime
  Error
  EventSubClass
  FileName
  GroupID

ApplicationName
Name of the client application that created the connection to SQL Server. This column is populated with the values passed by the application rather than the displayed name of the program.

⊞ Like
⊟ Not like
  └ SQL Server Profiler - 2ff82521-063c-461

☐ Exclude rows that do not contain values

OK   Cancel

Figure 3-16. *Editing filters in SQL Profiler*

SQL Profiler offers several additional options, including trace replay and the ability to save trace results to either a file or a database table. SQL Profiler is vital to troubleshooting SQL Server performance and security issues.

SQL Server Integration Services

SSIS was introduced in SQL Server 2005 as the replacement service for SQL Server 7.0 and 2000 Data Transformation Services (DTS). SSIS provides a true ETL tool that allows you to design simple or complex packages to pull data from multiple sources and integrate them into your SQL Server databases. In addition to data transformations, SSIS provides SQL Server–specific tasks that allow you to perform database administration and management functions like updating statistics and rebuilding indexes.

SSIS divides the ETL process into three major parts: control flow, data flow, and event handlers. The *control flow* provides structure to SSIS packages and controls execution via tasks, containers, and precedence constraints. The *data flow* imports data from various sources, transforms it, and stores it in specified destinations. The data flow, from the perspective of the control flow, is just another task. However, the data flow is important enough to require its own detailed design surface within a package. *Event handlers* allow you to perform actions in response to predefined events during the ETL process. Figure 3-17 shows a simple SSIS data flow that imports data from a flat file into a table.

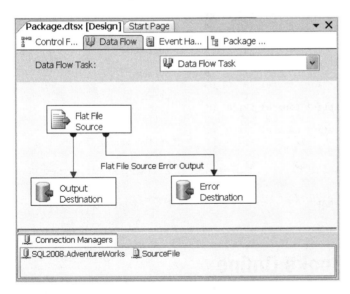

Figure 3-17. *Data flow to import a flat file*

SSIS is a far more advanced ETL tool than DTS, and you will find that it provides significant improvements in features, functionality, and raw power over the old DTS tools.

The Bulk Copy Program

If ETL tools were cars, SSIS might be considered the newest model Cadillac of SQL Server ETL. SSIS's distant cousin, BCP, would be more like an austere 1960's-era Jeep. While not as flashy or feature-rich as SSIS, BCP is small, fast, and can perform simple imports with no hassle. BCP is handy for generating format files for BCP and other bulk import tools, for one-off imports where a full-blown SSIS package would be overkill, for exporting data from database tables to files, and for backward compatibility when you don't have the resources to devote to immediately upgrading old BCP-based ETL processes. Figure 3-18 shows a simple command-line call to BCP to create a BCP format file and a listing of the format file. The format files generated by BCP can be used by BCP, SSIS, and the T-SQL BULK INSERT statement.

```
 C:\WINDOWS\system32\cmd.exe                                          _ □ ×

C:\>bcp AdventureWorks.Person.Contact format nul -SSQL2008 -T -fContact.fmt -c

C:\>copy Contact.fmt con
10.0
15
1        SQLCHAR            0        12       "\t"     1      ContactID
                             ""
2        SQLCHAR            0        3        "\t"     2      NameStyle
                             ""
3        SQLCHAR            0        16       "\t"     3      Title
                   SQL_Latin1_General_CP1_CI_AS
4        SQLCHAR            0        100      "\t"     4      FirstName
                   SQL_Latin1_General_CP1_CI_AS
5        SQLCHAR            0        100      "\t"     5      MiddleName
                   SQL_Latin1_General_CP1_CI_AS
6        SQLCHAR            0        100      "\t"     6      LastName
                   SQL_Latin1_General_CP1_CI_AS
7        SQLCHAR            0        20       "\t"     7      Suffix
                   SQL_Latin1_General_CP1_CI_AS
8        SQLCHAR            0        100      "\t"     8      EmailAddress
                   SQL_Latin1_General_CP1_CI_AS
9        SQLCHAR            0        12       "\t"     9      EmailPromotion
                             ""
10       SQLCHAR            0        50       "\t"     10     Phone
```

Figure 3-18. *Generating a format file with BCP*

SQL Server 2008 Books Online

BOL is the primary reference for T-SQL and SQL Server 2008 programming and administration. You can access a locally installed copy of BOL or you can access it over the Web at Microsoft's web site. I highly recommend installing the local version of BOL on any computer running SQL Server; you never know when you're going to need it for reference when you sit down at a server. Figure 3-19 shows a search of a local copy of BOL.

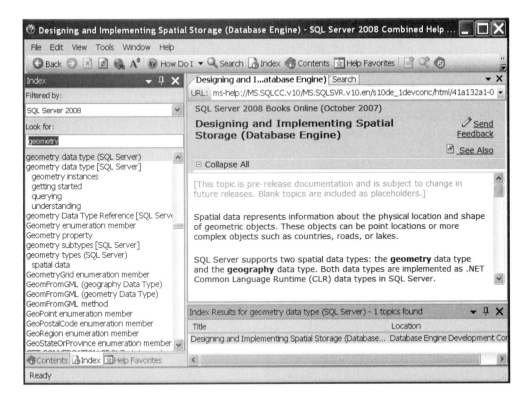

Figure 3-19. *Searching local BOL for information on the geometry data type*

You can get updates for BOL at www.microsoft.com/sql/default.mspx. The online version of SQL Server 2008 BOL is available at http://msdn2.microsoft.com/en-us/library/ bb543165(sql.100).aspx. Also keep in mind that you can search online and local versions of BOL, as well as several other SQL resources, via the Help Search function discussed previously in this chapter.

■**Tip** Microsoft now offers an additional option for obtaining the most up-to-date version of BOL. You can download the latest BOL updates from the Microsoft Update site, at http://update.microsoft.com/ microsoftupdate. Microsoft has announced plans to refresh BOL with updated content more often, and to integrate SQL Server developer and DBA feedback into BOL more quickly.

The AdventureWorks Sample Database

As of SQL Server 2005, Microsoft finally put the good old Northwind sample database to rest. SQL Server 2008 has two main sample databases: the AdventureWorks OLTP and Adventure-Works Data Warehouse databases. In this book, I'll refer to the AdventureWorks OLTP database for most samples. Microsoft now releases SQL Server sample databases through its CodePlex web site. You can download the AdventureWorks databases and associated sample code from www.codeplex.com/MSFTDBProdSamples.

■**Note** I highly recommend that you download the SQL Server AdventureWorks 2008 OLTP database so that you can run the sample code in this book as you go through each chapter.

Summary

SQL Server 2008 includes several of the tools we've come to expect with any SQL Server release. In this chapter, I've provided an overview of several tools that will be important to you as a SQL Server 2008 developer. The tools discussed include the following:

- SSMS, the primary GUI for SQL Server development and administration

- SQLCMD, SSMS's text-based counterpart

- BIDS, which provides a Visual Studio–style designer for creating SSIS, SSAS, and SSRS packages

- SQL Profiler, which supplies event capture and server-side tracing capabilities for analyzing SQL Server performance and auditing security

- SSIS, the primary ETL tool for SQL Server 2008

- BCP, a command line–based bulk import tool

- BOL, the first place to look when trying to locate information about all things SQL Server

- AdventureWorks, the freely available Microsoft-supplied sample database

These topics could easily fill a book by themselves (and many, in fact, have). In the next chapter, I will provide a survey of new SQL Server 2008 features, with contrast to both SQL Server 2005 and SQL Server 2000 functionality.

EXERCISES

1. SSMS is a SQL development and administration GUI tool. What two SQL Server 2000 GUI tools does SSMS replace?

2. [Choose all that apply] SQL Server 2008 SSMS provides which of the following features:

   a. Automatic color-coding of SQL scripts

   b. An integrated Object Explorer for viewing and managing the server, databases, and database objects

   c. Intellisense, which suggests table, object, and function names as you type SQL statements

   d. PDF and PostScript query plans

3. SSIS is considered what type of tool?

4. [True/false] SQLCMD can use command-line options, environment variables, and SQLCMD :setvar commands to set scripting variables.

5. [Choose one] BCP can be used to perform which of the following tasks:

   a. Generating format files for use with SSIS

   b. Importing data into tables without format files

   c. Exporting data from a table to a file

   d. All of the above

6. SQL Profiler allows you to specify the events you wish to capture during a trace. How can you further narrow down the data SQL Profiler reports during a trace?

7. BIDS allows you to create what three types of projects?

CHAPTER 4

■■■

Procedural Code and CASE Expressions

T-SQL has always included support for procedural programming in the form of control-of-flow statements and cursors. One thing that throws developers from other languages off their guard when migrating to SQL is the peculiar three-valued logic (3VL) we enjoy. I will introduce SQL 3VL, which is different from most other programming languages' simple two-valued Boolean logic, in this chapter. I will also discuss T-SQL control-of-flow constructs, which allow you to change the normally sequential order of statement execution. Control-of-flow statements allow you to branch your code logic with statements like `IF...ELSE...`, perform loops with statements like `WHILE`, and perform unconditional jumps with the `GOTO` statement. I will also introduce `CASE` expressions and `CASE`-derived functions that return values based on given comparison criteria in an expression. Finally, I will finish the chapter by explaining a topic closely tied to procedural code: SQL cursors.

Three-Valued Logic

SQL Server 2008, like all ANSI-compatible SQL DBMS products, implements a peculiar form of logic known as 3VL. 3VL is necessary because SQL introduces the concept of `NULL` to serve as a placeholder for values that are not known at the time they are stored in the database. The concept of `NULL` introduces an unknown logical result into SQL's ternary logic system. I will introduce SQL 3VL with a simple set of propositions:

- Consider the proposition "1 is less than 3." The result is logically true because the value of the number 1 is less than the value of the number 3.

- The proposition "5 is equal to 6" is logically false because the value of the number 5 is not equal to the value of the number 6.

- The proposition "X is greater than 10" presents a bit of a problem. The variable X is an algebraic placeholder for an actual value. Unfortunately, I haven't told you what value X stands for at this time. Because you don't know what the value of X is, you can't say the statement is true or false; instead you can say the result is unknown. SQL `NULL` represents an unknown value in the database in much the same way that the variable X represents an unknown value in this proposition, and comparisons with `NULL` produce the same unknown logical result in SQL.

Because NULL represents unknown values in the database, comparing anything with NULL (even other NULLs) produces an unknown logical result. Figure 4-1 is a quick reference for SQL Server 3VL, where p and q represent 3VL result values.

p	q	p AND q	p OR q
TRUE	TRUE	TRUE	TRUE
TRUE	FALSE	FALSE	TRUE
TRUE	UNKNOWN	UNKNOWN	TRUE
FALSE	TRUE	FALSE	TRUE
FALSE	FALSE	FALSE	FALSE
FALSE	UNKNOWN	FALSE	UNKNOWN
UNKNOWN	TRUE	UNKNOWN	TRUE
UNKNOWN	FALSE	FALSE	UNKNOWN
UNKNOWN	UNKNOWN	UNKNOWN	UNKNOWN

p	NOT p
TRUE	FALSE
FALSE	TRUE

Figure 4-1. *SQL 3VL quick reference chart*

As mentioned previously, the unknown logic values shown in the chart are the result of comparisons with NULL. The following predicates, for example, all evaluate to an unknown result:

```
@x = NULL
FirstName <> NULL
PhoneNumber > NULL
```

If you used one of these as the predicate in a WHERE clause of a SELECT statement, the statement would return no rows at all—SELECT with a WHERE clause returns only rows where the WHERE clause predicate evaluates to true; it discards rows for which the WHERE clause is false or unknown. Similarly, the INSERT, UPDATE, and DELETE statements with a WHERE clause only affect rows for which the WHERE clause evaluates to true.

SQL Server provides a proprietary mechanism, the SET ANSI_NULLS OFF option, to allow direct equality comparisons with NULL using the = and <> operators. The only ISO-compliant way to test for NULL is with the IS NULL and IS NOT NULL comparison predicates. I highly recommend that you stick with the ISO-compliant IS NULL and IS NOT NULL predicates for a few reasons:

- Many SQL Server features like computed columns, indexed views, and XML indexes require SET ANSI_NULLS ON at creation time.

- Mixing and matching SET ANSI_NULLS settings within your database can confuse other developers who have to maintain your code. Using ISO-compliant NULL-handling consistently eliminates confusion.

- SET ANSI_NULLS OFF allows direct equality comparisons with NULL, returning true if you compare a column or variable to NULL. It does not return true if you compare NULLs contained in two columns, though, which can be confusing.

- To top it all off, Microsoft has deprecated the SET ANSI_NULLS OFF setting. It will be removed in a future version of SQL Server, so it's a good idea to start future-proofing your code now.

IT'S A CLOSED WORLD, AFTER ALL

The *closed-world assumption (CWA)* is an assumption in logic that the world is "black and white," "true and false," or "ones and zeros." When applied to databases, the CWA basically states that all data stored within the database is true; everything else is false. The CWA presumes that only knowledge of the world that is complete can be stored within a database.

NULL introduces an *open-world assumption (OWA)* into the mix. It allows you to store information in the database that may or may not be true. This means that a SQL database can store incomplete knowledge of the world—a direct violation of the CWA. Many relational management (RM) theorists see this as an inconsistency in the SQL DBMS model. This argument fills many an RM textbook and academic blog, including web sites like Hugh Darwen and C.J. Date's "The Third Manifesto" (www.thethirdmanifesto.com/), so I won't go deeply into the details here. Just realize that many RM experts dislike SQL NULL. As a SQL practitioner in the real world, however, you may discover that NULL is often the best option available to accomplish many tasks.

Control-of-Flow Statements

T-SQL implements procedural language control-of-flow statements, including such constructs as BEGIN...END, IF...ELSE, WHILE, and GOTO. T-SQL's control-of-flow statements provide a framework for developing rich server-side procedural code. Procedural code in T-SQL does come with some caveats, though, which I will discuss in this section.

The BEGIN and END Keywords

T-SQL uses the keywords BEGIN and END to group multiple statements together in a statement block. The BEGIN and END keywords don't alter execution order of the statements they contain, nor do they define an atomic transaction, limit scope, or perform any function other than defining a simple grouping of T-SQL statements.

Unlike other languages, such as C++ or C#, which use braces ({ }) to group statements in logical blocks, T-SQL's BEGIN and END keywords do not define or limit scope. The following sample C# code, for instance, will not even compile:

```
{
    int j = 10;
}
Console.WriteLine (j);
```

C# programmers will automatically recognize that the variable j in the previous code is defined inside braces, limiting its scope and making it accessible only inside the braces. T-SQL's roughly equivalent code, however, does not limit scope in this manner:

```
BEGIN
    DECLARE @j int = 10;
END
PRINT @j;
```

The previous T-SQL code executes with no problem, as long as the DECLARE statement is encountered before the variable is referenced in the PRINT statement. The scope of variables in T-SQL is defined in terms of command batches and database object definitions (such as SPs, UDFs, and triggers). Declaring two or more variables with the same name in one batch or SP will result in errors.

■**Caution** T-SQL's BEGIN and END keywords create a statement block but do not define a scope. Variables declared inside a BEGIN...END block are not limited in scope just to that block, but are scoped to the whole batch, SP, or UDF in which they are defined.

BEGIN...END is useful for creating statement blocks where you want to execute multiple statements based on the results of other control-of-flow statements like IF...ELSE and WHILE. BEGIN...END can also have another added benefit if you're using SSMS 2008 or a good third-party SQL editor like ApexSQL Edit (www.apexsql.com/). In advanced editors like these, BEGIN...END can alert the GUI that a section of code is collapsible, as shown in Figure 4-2. This can speed up development and ease debugging, especially if you're writing complex T-SQL scripts.

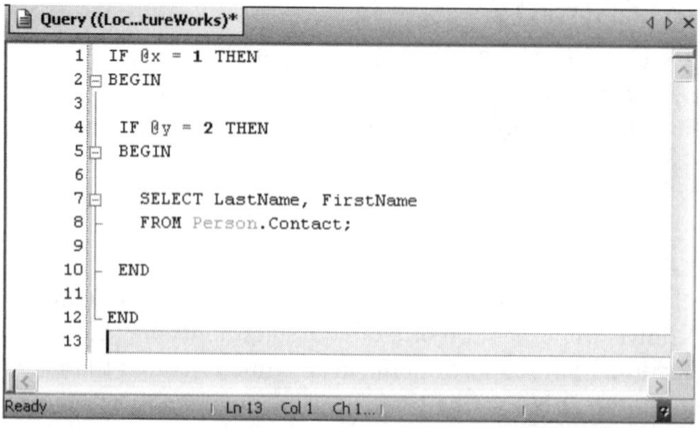

Figure 4-2. *BEGIN...END statement blocks marked collapsible in ApexSQL Edit*

> **Tip** Although it's not required, I like to wrap the body of CREATE PROCEDURE statements with BEGIN...END. This clearly delineates the bodies of the SPs, separating them from other code in the same script.

The IF...ELSE Statement

Like many procedural languages, T-SQL implements conditional execution of code using the simplest of procedural statements: the IF...ELSE construct. The IF statement is followed by a logical predicate. If the predicate evaluates to true, the single SQL statement or statement blocked wrapped in BEGIN...END is executed. If the predicate evaluates to either false or unknown, SQL Server falls through to the ELSE statement and executes the single statement or statement block following ELSE.

> **Tip** A predicate in SQL is an expression that evaluates to one of the logical results true, false, or unknown. Predicates are used in IF...ELSE statements, WHERE clauses, and anywhere that a logical result is needed.

The example in Listing 4-1 performs up to three comparisons to determine whether a variable is equal to a specified value. The second ELSE statement executes if and only if the tests for both true and false conditions fail.

Listing 4-1. *Simple IF...ELSE Example*

```
DECLARE @i int = NULL;
IF @i = 10
    PRINT 'TRUE.';
ELSE IF NOT (@i = 10)
    PRINT 'FALSE.';
ELSE
    PRINT 'UNKNOWN.';
```

Because the variable @i is NULL in the example, SQL Server reports that the result is unknown. If you assign the value 10 to the variable @i, SQL Server will report that the result is true; all other values will report false.

To create a statement block containing multiple T-SQL statements after either the IF statement of the ELSE statement, simply wrap your statements with the T-SQL BEGIN and END keywords discussed in the previous section. The simple example in Listing 4-2 is an IF...ELSE statement with statement blocks. The example uses IF...ELSE to check the value of the variable @direction. If @direction is ASCENDING, a message is printed, and the top ten names, in order of last name, are selected from the Person.Contact table. If @direction is DESCENDING, a different message is printed, and the bottom ten names are selected from the Person. Contact table. Any other value results in a message that @direction was not recognized. The results of Listing 4-2 are shown in Figure 4-3.

Listing 4-2. *IF...ELSE with Statement Blocks*

```
DECLARE @direction NVARCHAR(20) = N'DESCENDING';

IF @direction = N'ASCENDING'
BEGIN
    PRINT 'Start at the top!';

    SELECT TOP (10)
        LastName,
        FirstName,
        MiddleName
    FROM Person.Contact
    ORDER BY LastName ASC;
END
ELSE IF @direction = N'DESCENDING'
BEGIN
    PRINT 'Start at the bottom!';

    SELECT TOP (10)
        LastName,
        FirstName,
        MiddleName
    FROM Person.Contact
    ORDER BY LastName DESC;
END
ELSE
    PRINT '@direction was not recognized!';
```

	LastName	FirstName	MiddleName
1	Zwilling	Michael	J.
2	Zwilling	Michael	J
3	Zukowski	Jake	NULL
4	Zugelder	Judy	N.
5	Zubaty	Carla	J.
6	Zubaty	Patricia	M.
7	Zimprich	Karin	NULL
8	Zimprich	Karin	NULL
9	Zimmerman	Jo	J.
10	Zimmerman	Juanita	J.

Figure 4-3. *The last ten contact names in the AdventureWorks database*

The WHILE, BREAK, and CONTINUE Statements

Looping is a standard feature of procedural languages, and T-SQL provides looping support through the WHILE statement and its associated BREAK and CONTINUE statements. The WHILE loop is immediately followed by a predicate, and WHILE will execute a given SQL statement or statement block bounded by the BEGIN and END keywords as long as the associated predicate evaluates to true. If the predicate evaluates to false or unknown, the code in the WHILE loop will not execute and control will pass to the next statement after the WHILE loop. The WHILE loop in Listing 4-3 is a very simple example that counts from 1 to 10. The result is shown in Figure 4-4.

Listing 4-3. *WHILE Statement Example*

```
DECLARE @i int = 1;
WHILE @i <= 10
BEGIN
    PRINT @i;
    SET @i = @i + 1;
END
```

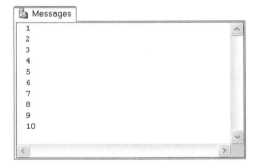

Figure 4-4. *Counting from 1 to 10 with WHILE*

Tip Be sure to update your counter or other flag inside the WHILE loop. The WHILE statement will keep looping until its predicate evaluates to false or unknown. A simple coding mistake could create a nasty infinite loop.

T-SQL also includes two additional keywords that can be used with the WHILE statement: BREAK and CONTINUE. The CONTINUE keyword forces the WHILE loop to immediately jump to the start of the code block, as in the modified example in Listing 4-4.

Listing 4-4. *WHILE...CONTINUE Example*

```
DECLARE @i int = 1;
WHILE @i <= 10
BEGIN
    PRINT @i;
    SET @i = @i + 1;

    CONTINUE; -- Force the WHILE loop to restart

    PRINT 'The CONTINUE keyword ensures that this will never be printed.';

END
```

The BREAK keyword, on the other hand, forces the WHILE loop to terminate immediately. In Listing 4-5, BREAK forces the WHILE loop to exit during the first iteration so that the numbers 2 through 10 are never printed.

Listing 4-5. *WHILE...BREAK Example*

```
DECLARE @i int = 1;
WHILE @i <= 10
BEGIN
    PRINT @i;
    SET @i = @i + 1;

    BREAK; -- Force the WHILE loop to terminate

    PRINT 'The BREAK keyword ensures that this will never be printed.';
END
```

■**Tip** BREAK and CONTINUE can and should be avoided in most cases. It's not uncommon to see a WHILE 1 = 1 statement with a BREAK in the body of the loop. This can always be rewritten, usually very easily, to remove the BREAK statement. Most of the time, the BREAK and CONTINUE keywords introduce additional complexity to your logic and cause more problems than they solve.

The GOTO Statement

Despite Edsger W. Dijkstra's best efforts at warning developers (see Dijkstra's 1968 letter, "Go To Statement Considered Harmful"), T-SQL still has a GOTO statement. The GOTO statement transfers control of your program to a specified label unconditionally. Labels are defined by placing the label identifier on a line followed by a colon (:), as shown in Listing 4-6. This simple example executes its step 1 and uses GOTO to dive straight into step 3, skipping step 2. The results are shown in Figure 4-5.

Listing 4-6. *Simple GOTO Example*

```
PRINT 'Step 1 Begin.';
GOTO Step3_Label;

PRINT 'Step 2 will not be printed.';

Step3_Label:
PRINT 'Step 3 End.';
```

Figure 4-5. *GOTO statement transfers control unconditionally*

The GOTO statement is best avoided, since it can quickly degenerate your programs into unstructured spaghetti code. When you have to write procedural code, you're much better off using structured programming constructs like IF...ELSE and WHILE statements.

The WAITFOR Statement

The WAITFOR statement suspends execution of a transaction, SP, or T-SQL command batch until a specified time is reached, a time interval has elapsed, or a message is received from Service Broker.

■**Note** Service Broker is a SQL Server messaging system. I don't detail Service Broker in this book, but you can find out more about it in *Pro SQL Server 2008 Service Broker*, by Klaus Aschenbrenner and Remus Rusana (Apress, 2008).

The WAITFOR statement has a DELAY option that tells SQL Server to suspend code execution until one of the following criteria is met or a specified time interval has elapsed. The time interval is specified as a valid time string in the format hh:mm:ss. The time interval cannot contain a date portion; it must only include the time, and it can be up to 24 hours. Listing 4-7 is an example of the WAITFOR statement with the DELAY option, which blocks execution of the batch for 3 seconds.

WAITFOR CAVEATS

There are some caveats associated with the WAITFOR statement. In some situations, WAITFOR can cause longer delays than the interval you specify. SQL Server also assigns each WAITFOR statement its own thread, and if SQL Server begins experiencing *thread starvation*, it can randomly stop WAITFOR threads to free up thread resources. If you need to delay execution for an exact amount of time, you can guarantee more consistent results by suspending execution through an external application like SSIS.

In addition to its DELAY and TIME options, you can use WAITFOR with the RECEIVE and GET CONVERSATION GROUP options with Service Broker–enabled applications. When you use WAITFOR with RECEIVE, the statement waits for receipt of one or more messages from a specified queue.

When you use WAITFOR with the GET CONVERSATION GROUP option, it waits for a conversation group identifier of a message. GET CONVERSATION GROUP allows you to retrieve information about a message and lock the conversation group for the conversation containing the message, all before retrieving the message itself.

A detailed description of Service Broker is beyond the scope of this book, but *Accelerated SQL Server 2008*, by Rob Walters et al. (Apress, 2008) gives a good description of Service Broker functionality and options for SQL Server 2008.

Listing 4-7. *WAITFOR Example*

```
PRINT 'Step 1 complete. ';
GO

DECLARE @time_to_pass nvarchar(8);
SELECT @time_to_pass = N'00:00:03';
WAITFOR DELAY @time_to_pass;
PRINT 'Step 2 completed three seconds later. ';
```

You can also use the TIME option with the WAITFOR statement. If you use the TIME option, SQL Server will wait until the appointed time before allowing execution to continue. Datetime variables are allowed, but the date portion is ignored when the TIME option is used.

The RETURN Statement

The RETURN statement exits unconditionally from an SP or command batch. When you use RETURN, you can optionally specify an integer expression as a return value. The RETURN statement returns a given integer expression to the calling routine or batch. If you don't specify an integer expression to return, a value of 0 is returned by default. RETURN is not normally used to return calculated results, except for UDFs, which offer more RETURN options (I will detail these in Chapter 5). For SPs and command batches, the RETURN statement is used almost exclusively to return a success indicator, failure indicator, or error code.

WHAT NUMBER, SUCCESS?

All system SPs return 0 to indicate success, or a nonzero value to indicate failure (unless otherwise documented in BOL). It is considered bad form to use the RETURN statement to return anything other than an integer status code from a script or SP.

UDFs, on the other hand, have their own rules. UDFs have a flexible variation of the RETURN statement, which exits the body of the UDF. In fact, a UDF *requires* the RETURN statement be used to return scalar or tabular results to the caller. You will see UDFs again in detail in Chapter 5.

The TRY...CATCH Statement

The TRY...CATCH statement, first introduced in SQL Server 2005, implements structured error handling for T-SQL. The TRY...CATCH statement provides error handling similar to C++ and the .NET languages. If one of the statements in the TRY block generates an error, control is passed to the CATCH block. Prior to the introduction of TRY...CATCH error handling, the only way to handle server-side errors was through the @@ERROR system function, the RAISERROR statement, and a few system SPs like sp_addmessage.

In order for TRY...CATCH to catch errors, several conditions must be met, including the following:

- The error must have a severity higher than 10, but cannot close the database connection.

- The error cannot be a compilation error at the same level of execution as the TRY...CATCH block, such as a syntax error.

- The error cannot have occurred during a statement-level recompilation (e.g., a name resolution error).

- The error must not have been caused by a broken connection (e.g., KILL statement execution).

- The error must not have been caused by an attention, such as those sent by Microsoft Distributed Transaction Coordinator.

Unlike C++ and .NET structured error handling, T-SQL's TRY...CATCH does not allow you to apply multiple CATCH blocks to a single TRY. The TRY...CATCH statement also prevents the error from being automatically passed on to the calling batch, procedure, or front-end application. You can use the RAISERROR statement to rethrow an error or throw a new error from within a CATCH block, though.

TRY...CATCH blocks can be nested. If a statement in a nested TRY block throws an error, control is passed to its associated CATCH block. If a statement in a nested CATCH block throws an error, control passes to the containing CATCH block. A nested TRY...CATCH block is useful for capturing potential errors in a CATCH block as well.

In addition, SQL Server 2008 enhances error handling by adding several functions for gathering specific error information inside a CATCH block:

- ERROR_NUMBER is the number of the error, which is the same value returned by the @@ERROR function. Unlike @@ERROR, ERROR_NUMBER() is not cleared and reset on each statement executed.

- ERROR_SEVERITY is the error severity level, a number from 0 to 25 that indicates the type of error that occurred. Severity levels between 0 and 10 indicate informational messages, levels between 11 and 16 are user-correctable errors, and levels of 17 and above are more severe and require administrator intervention.

- ERROR_STATE is the error state number, which can be between 1 and 127. The error state number is used to represent information about the source of the error, and can be useful for pinpointing the exact location where an error occurred.

- ERROR_PROCEDURE is the name of the SP or trigger where the error occurred—also very useful for locating the source of an error.

- ERROR_LINE is the number of the line in the routine that generated the error, which is about as close as you can get to the exact location of a given error.

- ERROR_MESSAGE returns the complete error message text, which was unavailable in SQL Server versions prior to SQL Server 2005.

All of these functions are available only within the scope of a CATCH block. If you try to get these values outside of the CATCH block, they will return NULL. Listing 4-8 shows a simple example of a TRY...CATCH block. The sample code generates a severity 16 error when it tries to insert an explicit value into the Person.Contact identity column. The error information is then returned as formatted XML by the FOR XML query. The results are shown in Figure 4-6.

Listing 4-8. *Example of TRY...CATCH Block Error Handling*

```
BEGIN TRY

  INSERT INTO Person.Contact
  (
    ContactID,
    FirstName,
    LastName
  )
  VALUES
  (
    10,
    'Joe',
    'Louis'
  );

END TRY
```

```
BEGIN CATCH

  SELECT
    ERROR_NUMBER() AS "@Number",
    ERROR_STATE() AS "@State",
    ERROR_SEVERITY() AS "@Severity",
    ERROR_MESSAGE() AS "Message",
    ERROR_LINE() AS "Procedure/@Line",
    ERROR_PROCEDURE() AS "Procedure"
  FOR XML PATH('Error');

END CATCH
```

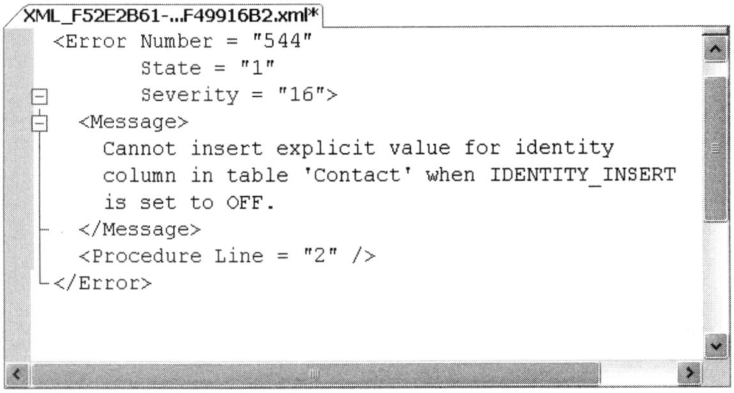

Figure 4-6. *Capturing an error with TRY...CATCH*

■Note XML results, when shown in this book, have been reformatted for easy reading. The content of the results has not been changed, however.

The CASE Expression

The T-SQL CASE function is SQL Server's implementation of the ISO SQL CASE expression. While the previously discussed T-SQL control-of-flow statements allow for conditional execution of SQL statements or statement blocks, the CASE expression allows for set-based conditional processing inside a single query. CASE provides two syntaxes, *simple* and *searched*, which I will discuss in this section.

The Simple CASE Expression

The simple CASE expression returns a result expression based on the value of a given input expression. The simple CASE expression compares the input expression to a series of expressions following WHEN keywords. Once a match is encountered, CASE returns a corresponding result expression following the keyword THEN. If no match is found, the expression following the keyword ELSE is returned, and NULL is returned if no ELSE keyword is supplied.

Consider the example in Listing 4-9, which uses a simple CASE expression to count all the AdventureWorks customers on the West Coast (which I arbitrarily defined as the states of California, Washington, and Oregon). The results are shown in Figure 4-7.

Listing 4-9. *Counting West Coast Customers with a Simple CASE Expression*

```
WITH CustomersByRegion(Region)
AS
(
  SELECT
    CASE sp.StateProvinceCode
      WHEN 'CA' THEN 'West Coast'
      WHEN 'WA' THEN 'West Coast'
      WHEN 'OR' THEN 'West Coast'
      ELSE 'Elsewhere'
    END
  FROM Sales.CustomerAddress a
  INNER JOIN Person.Address p
    ON a.AddressID = p.AddressID
  INNER JOIN Person.StateProvince sp
    ON p.StateProvinceID = p.StateProvinceID
  WHERE sp.CountryRegionCode = 'US'
)
SELECT COUNT(Region) AS NumOfCustomers, Region
FROM CustomersByRegion
GROUP BY Region;
```

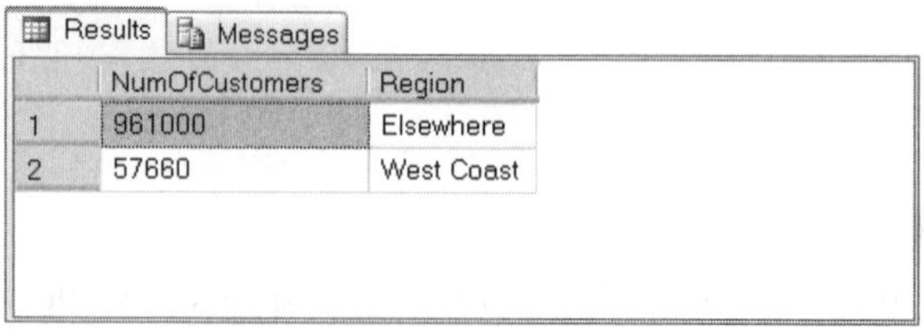

	NumOfCustomers	Region
1	961000	Elsewhere
2	57660	West Coast

Figure 4-7. *Results of the West Coast customer count*

The CASE expression in the subquery compares the StateProvinceCode value to each of the state codes following the WHEN keywords, returning the name West Coast when the StateProvinceCode is equal to CA, WA, or OR. For any other StateProvinceCode in the United States, it returns a value of Elsewhere.

```
SELECT CASE sp.StateProvinceCode
    WHEN 'CA' THEN 'West Coast'
    WHEN 'WA' THEN 'West Coast'
    WHEN 'OR' THEN 'West Coast'
    ELSE 'Elsewhere'
END
```

The remainder of the example simply counts the number of rows returned by the query, grouped by Region.

A SIMPLE CASE OF NULL

The simple CASE expression performs basic equality comparisons between the input expression and the expressions following the WHEN keywords. This means that you cannot use the simple CASE expression to check for NULLs. Recall from the "Three-Valued Logic" section of this chapter that a NULL, when compared to anything, returns unknown. The simple CASE expression only returns the expression following the THEN keyword when the comparison returns true. This means that if you ever try to use NULL in a WHEN expression, the corresponding THEN expression will never be returned. If you need to check for NULL in a CASE expression, use a searched CASE expression with the IS NULL or IS NOT NULL comparison operators.

The Searched CASE Expression

The searched CASE expression provides a mechanism for performing more complex comparisons. The searched CASE evaluates a series of predicates following WHEN keywords until it encounters one that evaluates to true. At that point, it returns the corresponding result expression following the THEN keyword. If none of the predicates evaluates to true, the result following the ELSE keyword is returned. If none of the predicates evaluates to true and ELSE is not supplied, the searched CASE expression returns NULL.

Predicates in the searched CASE expression can take advantage of any valid SQL comparison operators (e.g., <, >, =, LIKE, and IN). The simple CASE expression from Listing 4-9 can be easily expanded to cover multiple geographic regions using the searched CASE expression and the IN logical operator, as shown in Listing 4-10. This example uses a searched CASE expression to group states into West Coast, Pacific, and New England regions. The results are shown in Figure 4-8.

Listing 4-10. *Counting Customers by Region with a Searched CASE Expression*

```
WITH CustomersByRegion(Region)
AS
(
  SELECT
    CASE WHEN sp.StateProvinceCode IN ('CA', 'WA', 'OR') THEN 'West Coast'
      WHEN sp.StateProvinceCode IN ('HI', 'AK') THEN 'Pacific'
      WHEN sp.StateProvinceCode IN ('CT', 'MA', 'ME', 'NH', 'RI', 'VT')
        THEN 'New England'
      ELSE 'Elsewhere'
    END
  FROM Sales.CustomerAddress a
  INNER JOIN Person.Address p
    ON a.AddressID = p.AddressID
  INNER JOIN Person.StateProvince sp
    ON p.StateProvinceID = p.StateProvinceID
  WHERE sp.CountryRegionCode = 'US'
)
SELECT COUNT(*) AS NumOfCustomers, Region
FROM CustomersByRegion
GROUP BY Region;
```

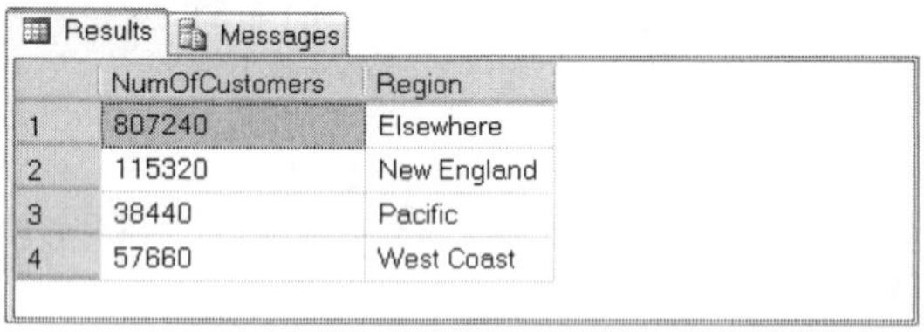

	NumOfCustomers	Region
1	807240	Elsewhere
2	115320	New England
3	38440	Pacific
4	57660	West Coast

Figure 4-8. *Results of the regional customer count*

The searched CASE expression in the example uses the IN operator to return the geographic area that StateProvinceCode is in: California, Washington, and Oregon all return West Coast; Hawaii and Alaska return Pacific; and Connecticut, Massachusetts, Maine, New Hampshire, Rhode Island, and Vermont all return New England. If the StateProvinceCode does not fit in one of these regions, the searched CASE expression will return Elsewhere.

```
SELECT
  CASE WHEN sp.StateProvinceCode IN ('CA', 'WA', 'OR') THEN 'West Coast'
    WHEN sp.StateProvinceCode IN ('HI', 'AK') THEN 'Pacific'
    WHEN sp.StateProvinceCode IN ('CT', 'MA', 'ME', 'NH', 'RI', 'VT')
      THEN 'New England'
    ELSE 'Elsewhere'
  END
```

The balance of the sample code in Listing 4-10 counts the rows returned, grouped by Region. The CASE expression, either simple or searched, can be used in SELECT, UPDATE, INSERT, MERGE, and DELETE statements.

A CASE BY ANY OTHER NAME

Many programming and query languages offer expressions that are analogous to the SQL CASE expression. C++ and C#, for instance, offer the ?: operator, which fulfills the same function as a searched CASE expression. XQuery has its own flavor of if...then...else expression that is also equivalent to the SQL searched CASE.

C# and Visual Basic also supply the switch and Select statements, respectively, which are semianalogous to SQL's simple CASE expression. The main difference, of course, is that SQL's CASE expression simply returns a scalar value, while the C# and Visual Basic statements actually control program flow, allowing you to execute statements based on an expression's value. The similarities and differences between SQL expressions and statements and similar constructs in other languages provide a great starting point for learning the nitty-gritty details of T-SQL.

CASE and Pivot Tables

Many times, business reporting requirements dictate that a result should be returned in pivot table format. Pivot table format simply means that the labels for columns and/or rows are generated from the data contained in rows. Microsoft Access and Excel users have long had the ability to generate pivot tables on their data, and SQL Server 2008 supports the PIVOT and UNPIVOT operators introduced in SQL Server 2005. Back in the days of SQL Server 2000 and before, however, CASE expressions were the only method of generating pivot table–type queries. And even though SQL Server 2008 provides the PIVOT and UNPIVOT operators, truly dynamic pivot tables still require using CASE expressions and dynamic SQL. The static pivot table query shown in Listing 4-11 returns a pivot table–formatted result with the total number of orders for each AdventureWorks sales region in the United States. The results are shown in Figure 4-9.

Listing 4-11. *CASE-Style Pivot Table*

```
SELECT
  t.CountryRegionCode,
  SUM
  (
    CASE WHEN t.Name = 'Northwest' THEN 1
      ELSE 0
    END
  ) AS Northwest,
  SUM
  (
    CASE WHEN t.Name = 'Northeast' THEN 1
      ELSE 0
    END
  ) AS Northeast,
  SUM
  (
```

```
    CASE WHEN t.Name = 'Southwest' THEN 1
      ELSE 0
    END
  ) AS Southwest,
  SUM
  (
    CASE WHEN t.Name = 'Southeast' THEN 1
      ELSE 0
    END
  ) AS Southeast,
  SUM
  (
    CASE WHEN t.Name = 'Central' THEN 1
      ELSE 0
    END
  ) AS Central
FROM Sales.SalesOrderHeader soh
INNER JOIN Sales.SalesTerritory t
  ON soh.TerritoryID = t.TerritoryID
WHERE t.CountryRegionCode = 'US'
GROUP BY t.CountryRegionCode;
```

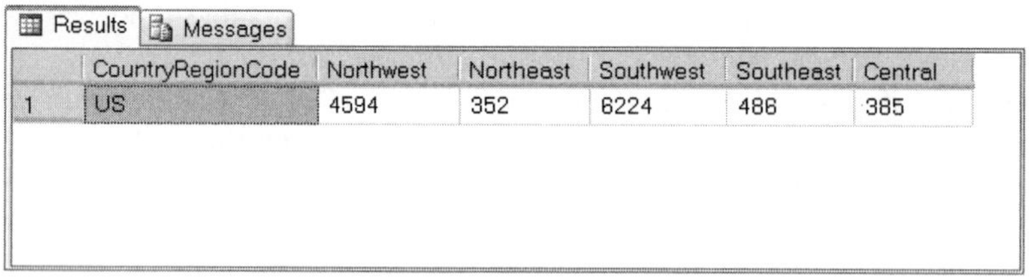

	CountryRegionCode	Northwest	Northeast	Southwest	Southeast	Central
1	US	4594	352	6224	486	385

Figure 4-9. *Number of sales by region in pivot table format*

This type of static pivot table can also be used with the SQL Server 2008 PIVOT operator. The sample code in Listing 4-12 uses the PIVOT operator to generate the same result as the CASE expressions in Listing 4-11.

Listing 4-12. *PIVOT Operator Pivot Table*

```
SELECT
  CountryRegionCode,
  Northwest,
  Northeast,
  Southwest,
  Southeast,
  Central
```

```
FROM
(
  SELECT
    t.CountryRegionCode,
    t.Name
  FROM Sales.SalesOrderHeader soh
  INNER JOIN Sales.SalesTerritory t
    ON soh.TerritoryID = t.TerritoryID
  WHERE t.CountryRegionCode = 'US'
) p
PIVOT
(
  COUNT (Name)
  FOR Name
  IN
  (
    Northwest,
    Northeast,
    Southwest,
    Southeast,
    Central
  )
) AS pvt;
```

On occasion, you might need to run a pivot table–style report where you don't know the column names in advance. This is a dynamic pivot table script that uses a temporary table and dynamic SQL to generate a pivot table, without specifying the column names in advance. Listing 4-13 demonstrates one method of generating dynamic pivot tables in T-SQL. The results are shown in Figure 4-10.

Listing 4-13. *Dynamic Pivot Table Query*

```
-- Declare variables
DECLARE @sql nvarchar(4000);

DECLARE @temp_pivot table
(
  TerritoryID int NOT NULL PRIMARY KEY,
  CountryRegion nvarchar(20) NOT NULL,
  CountryRegionCode nvarchar(3) NOT NULL
);
```

```
-- Get column names from source table rows
INSERT INTO @temp_pivot
(
  TerritoryID,
  CountryRegion,
  CountryRegionCode
)
SELECT
  TerritoryID,
  Name,
  CountryRegionCode
FROM Sales.SalesTerritory
GROUP BY
  TerritoryID,
  Name,
  CountryRegionCode;

-- Generate dynamic SQL query
SET @sql = N'SELECT' +
  SUBSTRING(
  (
    SELECT N', SUM(CASE WHEN t.TerritoryID = ' +
      CAST(TerritoryID AS NVARCHAR(3)) +
      N' THEN 1 ELSE 0 END) AS ' + QUOTENAME(CountryRegion) AS "*"
    FROM @temp_pivot
    FOR XML PATH('')
  ), 2, 4000) +
  N' FROM Sales.SalesOrderHeader soh ' +
  N' INNER JOIN Sales.SalesTerritory t ' +
  N' ON soh.TerritoryID = t.TerritoryID; ' ;

-- Print and execute dynamic SQL
PRINT @sql;

EXEC (@sql);
```

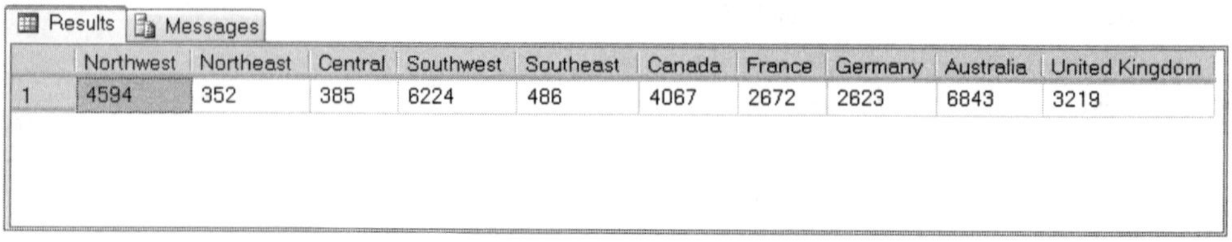

	Northwest	Northeast	Central	Southwest	Southeast	Canada	France	Germany	Australia	United Kingdom
1	4594	352	385	6224	486	4067	2672	2623	6843	3219

Figure 4-10. *Dynamic pivot table result*

The script in Listing 4-13 first declares an `nvarchar` variable that will hold the dynamically generated SQL script and a table variable that will hold all of the column names, which are retrieved from the row values in the source table.

```
-- Declare variables
DECLARE @sql nvarchar(4000);

DECLARE @temp_pivot table
(
  TerritoryID int NOT NULL PRIMARY KEY,
  CountryRegion nvarchar(20) NOT NULL,
  CountryRegionCode nvarchar(3) NOT NULL
);
```

Next, the script grabs a list of distinct territory-specific values from the table and stores them in the `@temp_pivot` table variable. These values from the table will become column names in the pivot table result.

```
-- Get column names from source table rows
INSERT INTO @temp_pivot
(
  TerritoryID,
  CountryRegion,
  CountryRegionCode
)
SELECT DISTINCT
  TerritoryID,
  Name,
  CountryRegionCode
FROM Sales.SalesTerritory;
```

The script then uses `FOR XML PATH` to efficiently generate the dynamic SQL `SELECT` query that contains `CASE` expressions and column names generated dynamically based on the values in the `@temp_pivot` table variable. This `SELECT` query will create the dynamic pivot table result.

```
-- Generate dynamic SQL query
SET @sql = N'SELECT' +
  SUBSTRING(
  (
    SELECT N', SUM(CASE WHEN t.TerritoryID = ' +
      CAST(TerritoryID AS NVARCHAR(3)) +
      N' THEN 1 ELSE 0 END) AS ' + QUOTENAME(CountryRegion) AS "*"
    FROM @temp_pivot
    FOR XML PATH('')
  ), 2, 4000) +
  N' FROM Sales.SalesOrderHeader soh ' +
  N' INNER JOIN Sales.SalesTerritory t ' +
  N' ON soh.TerritoryID = t.TerritoryID; ' ;
```

Finally, the dynamic pivot table query is printed out and executed with the T-SQL PRINT and EXEC statements.

```
-- Print and execute dynamic SQL
PRINT @sql;

EXEC (@sql);
```

Listing 4-14 shows the dynamic SQL pivot table query generated by the code in Listing 4-13.

Listing 4-14. *Autogenerated Dynamic SQL Pivot Table Query*

```
SELECT SUM
(
  CASE WHEN t.TerritoryID = 1 THEN 1
    ELSE 0
  END
) AS [Northwest],
SUM
(
  CASE WHEN t.TerritoryID = 2 THEN 1
    ELSE 0
  END
) AS [Northeast],
SUM
(
  CASE WHEN t.TerritoryID = 3 THEN 1
    ELSE 0
  END
) AS [Central],
SUM
(
  CASE WHEN t.TerritoryID = 4 THEN 1
    ELSE 0
  END
) AS [Southwest],
SUM
(
  CASE WHEN t.TerritoryID = 5 THEN 1
    ELSE 0
  END
) AS [Southeast],
SUM
(
  CASE WHEN t.TerritoryID = 6 THEN 1
    ELSE 0
  END
) AS [Canada],
```

```
SUM
(
  CASE WHEN t.TerritoryID = 7 THEN 1
    ELSE 0
  END
) AS [France],
SUM
(
  CASE WHEN t.TerritoryID = 8 THEN 1
    ELSE 0
  END
) AS [Germany],
SUM
(
  CASE WHEN t.TerritoryID = 9 THEN 1
    ELSE 0
  END
) AS [Australia],
SUM
(
  CASE WHEN t.TerritoryID = 10 THEN 1
    ELSE 0
  END
) AS [United Kingdom]
FROM Sales.SalesOrderHeader soh
INNER JOIN Sales.SalesTerritory t
  ON soh.TerritoryID = t.TerritoryID;
```

■**Caution** Anytime you use dynamic SQL, make sure that you take precautions against *SQL injection*—that is, malicious SQL code being inserted into your SQL statements. In this instance, we're using the QUOTENAME function to quote the column names being dynamically generated to help avoid SQL injection problems. I'll cover dynamic SQL and SQL injection in greater detail in Chapter 18.

COALESCE and NULLIF

The COALESCE function takes a list of expressions as arguments and returns the first non-NULL value from the list. The COALESCE function is defined by ISO as shorthand for the following equivalent searched CASE expression:

```
CASE
    WHEN expression1 IS NOT NULL THEN expression1
    WHEN expression2 IS NOT NULL THEN expression2
    [ ...n ]
END
```

The following COALESCE function example returns the value of MiddleName when MiddleName is not NULL, and the string No Middle Name when MiddleName is NULL:

```
COALESCE (MiddleName, 'No Middle Name')
```

The NULLIF function accepts exactly two arguments. NULLIF returns NULL if the two expressions are equal, and it returns the value of the first expression if the two expressions are not equal. NULLIF is defined by the ISO standard as equivalent to the following searched CASE expression:

```
CASE WHEN expression1 = expression2 THEN NULL
ELSE expression1
END
```

NULLIF is often used in conjunction with COALESCE. Consider Listing 4-15, which combines COALESCE with NULLIF to return the string This is NULL or A if the variable @s is set to the character value A or NULL.

Listing 4-15. *Using COALESCE with NULLIF*

```
DECLARE @s varchar(10);
SELECT @s = 'A';
SELECT COALESCE(NULLIF(@s, 'A'), 'This is NULL or A');
```

T-SQL has long had alternate functionality similar to COALESCE. Specifically, the ISNULL function accepts two parameters and returns NULL if they are equal.

COALESCE OR ISNULL?

The T-SQL functions COALESCE and ISNULL perform similar functions, but which one should you use? COALESCE is more flexible than ISNULL and is compliant with the ISO standard to boot. This means that it is also the more portable option among ISO-compliant systems. COALESCE also implicitly converts the result to the data type with the highest precedence from the list of expressions. ISNULL implicitly converts the result to the data type of the first expression. Finally, COALESCE is a bit less confusing than ISNULL, especially considering that there's already a comparison operator called IS NULL. In general, I recommend using the COALESCE function instead of ISNULL.

Cursors

The word *cursor* comes from the Latin word for *runner*, and that is exactly what a T-SQL cursor does: it "runs" through a result set, returning one row at a time. Many T-SQL programming experts rail against the use of cursors for a variety of reasons—the chief among these include the following:

- Cursors use a lot of overhead, often much more than an equivalent set-based approach.

- Cursors override SQL Server's built-in query optimizations, often making them much slower than an equivalent set-based solution.

Because cursors are procedural in nature, they are often the slowest way to manipulate data in T-SQL. Rather than spend the balance of the chapter ranting against cursor use, however, I'd like to introduce T-SQL cursor functionality and play devil's advocate to point out some areas where cursors provide an adequate solution.

The first such area where I can recommend the use of cursors is in scripts or procedures that perform administrative tasks. In administrative tasks, the following items often hold true:

- Unlike normal data queries and data manipulations that are performed dozens, hundreds, or potentially thousands of times per day, administrative tasks are often performed on a one-off basis or on a regular schedule like once per day.

- Administrative tasks often require calling an SP or executing a procedural code block once for each row when performing administrative tasks based on a table of entries.

- Administrative tasks generally don't need to query or manipulate massive amounts of data to perform their jobs.

- The order of the steps in which administrative tasks are performed and the order of the database objects they touch are often important.

The sample SP in Listing 4-16 is an example of an administrative task performed with a T-SQL cursor. The sample uses a cursor to loop through all indexes on all user tables in the current database. It then creates dynamic SQL statements to rebuild every index whose fragmentation level is above a user-specified threshold. The results are shown in Figure 4-11.

Listing 4-16. *Sample Administrative Task Performed with a Cursor*

```
CREATE PROCEDURE dbo.RebuildIndexes
  @ShowOrRebuild nvarchar(10) = N'show',
  @MaxFrag decimal(20, 2) = 20.0
AS
BEGIN
  -- Declare variables
  SET NOCOUNT ON;

  DECLARE
    @Schema nvarchar(128),
    @Table nvarchar(128),
    @Index nvarchar(128),
    @Sql nvarchar(4000),
    @DatabaseId int,
    @SchemaId int,
    @TableId int,
    @IndexId int;

  -- Create the index list table
  DECLARE @IndexList TABLE
  (
    DatabaseName nvarchar(128) NOT NULL,
    DatabaseId int NOT NULL,
```

```
    SchemaName nvarchar(128) NOT NULL,
    SchemaId int NOT NULL,
    TableName nvarchar(128) NOT NULL,
    TableId int NOT NULL,
    IndexName nvarchar(128),
    IndexId int NOT NULL,
    Fragmentation decimal(20, 2),
    PRIMARY KEY (DatabaseId, SchemaId, TableId, IndexId)
);

-- Populate index list table
INSERT INTO @IndexList
(
  DatabaseName,
  DatabaseId,
  SchemaName,
  SchemaId,
  TableName,
  TableId,
  IndexName,
  IndexId,
  Fragmentation
)
SELECT
  db_name(),
  db_id(),
  s.Name,
  s.schema_id,
  t.Name,
  t.object_id,
  i.Name,
  i.index_id,
  MAX(ip.avg_fragmentation_in_percent)
FROM sys.tables t
INNER JOIN sys.schemas s
  ON t.schema_id = s.schema_id
INNER JOIN sys.indexes i
  ON t.object_id = i.object_id
INNER JOIN sys.dm_db_index_physical_stats (db_id(), NULL, NULL, NULL, NULL) ip
  ON ip.object_id = t.object_id
    AND ip.index_id = i.index_id
WHERE ip.database_id = db_id()
GROUP BY
  s.Name,
  s.schema_id,
```

```
  t.Name,
  t.object_id,
  i.Name,
  i.index_id;

-- If user specified rebuild, use a cursor to loop through all indexes and
-- rebuild them
IF @ShowOrRebuild = N'rebuild'
BEGIN

  -- Declare a cursor to create the dynamic SQL statements
  DECLARE Index_Cursor CURSOR FAST_FORWARD
  FOR SELECT SchemaName, TableName, IndexName
  FROM @IndexList
  WHERE Fragmentation > @MaxFrag
  ORDER BY Fragmentation DESC, TableName ASC, IndexName ASC;

  -- Open the cursor for reading
  OPEN Index_Cursor;

  -- Loop through all the tables in the database
  FETCH NEXT FROM Index_Cursor
  INTO @Schema, @Table, @Index;

  WHILE @@FETCH_STATUS = 0
  BEGIN
    -- Create ALTER INDEX statement to rebuild index
    SET @Sql = N'ALTER INDEX ' +
      QUOTENAME(RTRIM(@Index)) + N' ON ' + QUOTENAME(@Schema) + N'.' +
      QUOTENAME(RTRIM(@Table)) + N' REBUILD WITH (ONLINE = OFF); ';

    PRINT @Sql;

    -- Execute dynamic SQL
    EXEC (@Sql);

    -- Get the next index
    FETCH NEXT FROM Index_Cursor
    INTO @Schema, @Table, @Index;
  END

  -- Close and deallocate the cursor.
  CLOSE Index_Cursor;
  DEALLOCATE Index_Cursor;
```

```
  END

  -- Show results, including old fragmentation and new fragmentation
  -- after index rebuild
  SELECT
    il.DatabaseName,
    il.SchemaName,
    il.TableName,
    il.IndexName,
    il.Fragmentation AS FragmentationStart,
    MAX(
      CAST(ip.avg_fragmentation_in_percent AS DECIMAL(20, 2))
    ) AS FragmentationEnd
  FROM @IndexList il
  INNER JOIN sys.dm_db_index_physical_stats (@DatabaseId, NULL, NULL,
    NULL, NULL) ip
    ON DatabaseId = ip.database_id
      AND TableId = ip.object_id
      AND IndexId = ip.index_id
  GROUP BY
    il.DatabaseName,
    il.SchemaName,
    il.TableName,
    il.IndexName,
    il.Fragmentation
  ORDER BY
    Fragmentation DESC,
    TableName ASC,
    IndexName ASC;

  RETURN;
END
GO

-- Execute index rebuild stored procedure
EXEC dbo.RebuildIndexes N'rebuild', 30;
```

	Databa...	Schema...	TableN...	IndexName	FragmentationStart	FragmentationEnd
1	Advent...	Sales	Store	PXML_Store_Demographics	98.44	0.00
2	Advent...	Sales	StoreC...	PK_StoreContact_CustomerID_Contac...	80.00	60.00
3	Advent...	dbo	Datab...	PK_DatabaseLog_DatabaseLogID	66.67	66.67
4	Advent...	HumanR...	Emplo...	AK_Employee_LoginID	66.67	66.67
5	Advent...	Production	Product	AK_Product_Name	66.67	66.67
6	Advent...	Production	Produc...	AK_ProductDescription_rowguid	66.67	66.67
7	Advent...	Production	Produc...	IX_ProductReview_ProductID_Name	66.67	66.67
8	Advent...	Sales	Specia...	PK_SpecialOfferProduct_SpecialOfferI...	66.67	66.67
9	Advent...	Sales	StoreC...	AK_StoreContact_rowguid	66.67	66.67
10	Advent...	HumanR...	Emplo...	PK_Employee_EmployeeID	57.14	85.71
11	Advent...	Person	Contact	AK_Contact_rowguid	53.85	0.00
12	Advent...	Person	Countr...	PK_CountryRegion_CountryRegionCo...	50.00	50.00
13	Advent...	Sales	Custo...	PK__Customer__A4AE64B800750D23	50.00	75.00
14	Advent...	HumanR...	Emplo...	AK_Employee_NationalIDNumber	50.00	50.00
15	Advent...	Production	Product	AK_Product_ProductNumber	50.00	50.00
16	Advent...	Production	Product	AK_Product_rowguid	50.00	50.00
17	Advent...	Production	Produc...	PK_ProductModelProductDescriptionC...	50.00	75.00

Figure 4-11. *The results of a cursor-based index rebuild in the AdventureWorks database*

The dbo.RebuildIndexes procedure shown in Listing 4-16 populates a table variable with the information necessary to identify all indexes on all tables in the current database. It also uses the sys.dm_db_index_physical_stats catalog function to retrieve initial index fragmentation information.

```
-- Populate index list table
INSERT INTO @IndexList
(
  DatabaseName,
  DatabaseId,
  SchemaName,
  SchemaId,
  TableName,
  TableId,
  IndexName,
  IndexId,
  Fragmentation
)
SELECT
  db_name(),
  db_id(),
  s.Name,
  s.schema_id,
  t.Name,
  t.object_id,
```

```
    i.Name,
    i.index_id,
    MAX(ip.avg_fragmentation_in_percent)
FROM sys.tables t
INNER JOIN sys.schemas s
  ON t.schema_id = s.schema_id
INNER JOIN sys.indexes i
  ON t.object_id = i.object_id
INNER JOIN sys.dm_db_index_physical_stats (db_id(), NULL, NULL, NULL, NULL) ip
  ON ip.object_id = t.object_id
    AND ip.index_id = i.index_id
WHERE ip.database_id = db_id()
GROUP BY
  s.Name,
  s.schema_id,
  t.Name,
  t.object_id,
  i.Name,
  i.index_id;
```

If you specify a rebuild action when you call the procedure, it creates a cursor to loop through the rows of the @IndexList table, but only for indexes with a fragmentation percentage higher than the level that you specified when calling the procedure.

```
-- Declare a cursor to create the dynamic SQL statements
DECLARE Index_Cursor CURSOR FAST_FORWARD
FOR
SELECT
  SchemaName,
  TableName,
  IndexName
FROM @IndexList
WHERE Fragmentation > @MaxFrag
ORDER BY
  Fragmentation DESC,
  TableName ASC,
  IndexName ASC;
```

The procedure then loops through all the indexes in the @IndexList table, creating an ALTER INDEX statement to rebuild each index. Each ALTER INDEX statement is created as dynamic SQL to be printed and executed using the SQL PRINT and EXEC statements.

```
-- Open the cursor for reading
OPEN Index_Cursor;

-- Loop through all the tables in the database
FETCH NEXT FROM Index_Cursor
INTO @Schema, @Table, @Index;
```

```
WHILE @@FETCH_STATUS = 0
BEGIN
  -- Create ALTER INDEX statement to rebuild index
  SET @Sql = N'ALTER INDEX ' +
    QUOTENAME(RTRIM(@Index)) + N' ON ' + QUOTENAME(@Schema) + N'.' +
    QUOTENAME(RTRIM(@Table)) + N' REBUILD WITH (ONLINE = OFF); ';

  PRINT @Sql;

  -- Execute dynamic SQL
  EXEC (@Sql);

  -- Get the next index
  FETCH NEXT FROM Index_Cursor
  INTO @Schema, @Table, @Index;
END

-- Close and deallocate the cursor.
CLOSE Index_Cursor;
DEALLOCATE Index_Cursor;
```

The dynamic SQL statements generated by the procedure look similar to the following:

```
ALTER INDEX [IX_PurchaseOrderHeader_EmployeeID]
ON [Purchasing].[PurchaseOrderHeader] REBUILD WITH (ONLINE = OFF);
```

The balance of the code simply displays the results, including the new fragmentation percentage after the indexes are rebuilt.

NO DBCC?

You'll notice in the sample code in Listing 4-16 that I specifically avoided using database console commands (DBCCs) like DBCC DBREINDEX and DBCC SHOWCONTIG to manage index fragmentation and rebuild the indexes in the database. There's a very good reason for this—these DBCC statements, and many others, are deprecated. Microsoft is planning to do away with many common DBCC statements in favor of catalog views and enhanced T-SQL statement syntax. The DBCC DBREINDEX statement, for instance, is now being replaced by the ALTER INDEX REBUILD syntax, and DBCC SHOWCONTIG is replaced by the sys.dm_db_index_physical_stats catalog function. Keep this in mind when porting code from legacy systems and creating new code.

Another situation where I would advise developers to use cursors is when the solution required is a one-off task, a set-based solution would be very complex, and time is short. Examples include creating complex running sum–type calculations or performing complex data-scrubbing routines on a very limited timeframe. I would not advise using a cursor as a permanent production application solution without exploring all available set-based options, however. Remember that whenever you use a cursor, you override SQL Server's automatic optimizations; and the SQL Server query engine has much better and more current information to optimize operations than you will have access to at any given point in time. Also keep in mind that the tasks you consider extremely complex today will become much easier as SQL's set-based processing becomes second nature to you.

CURSORS, CURSORS EVERYWHERE

Although cursors commonly get a lot of bad press from SQL gurus, there is nothing inherently evil about them. They are just another tool in the toolkit, and should be viewed as such. What is wrong, however, is the ways in which developers abuse them. Generally speaking, and perhaps as much as 90 percent of the time, cursors are absolutely not the best tool for the job when you're writing T-SQL code. Unfortunately, many SQL newbies find set-based logic difficult to grasp at first. Cursors provide a comfort zone for procedural developers because they lend themselves to procedural design patterns.

One of the worst design patterns you can adopt is the "cursors, cursors everywhere" design pattern. Believe it or not, there are people out there who have been writing SQL code for years and have never bothered learning about SQL's set-based processing. These people tend to approach every SQL problem as if it were a C# or Visual Basic problem, and their code tends to reflect it with the "cursors, cursors everywhere" design pattern. And remember, replacing cursor-based code with WHILE loops does not solve the problem. Simulating the behavior of cursors with WHILE loops doesn't solve the design flaw inherent in the cursor-based solution: row-by-row processing of data. WHILE loops might, under some circumstances, perform comparably to cursors; in many situations, however, even a cursor will outperform a WHILE loop.

Another horrible design pattern results from what are actually best practices in other procedural languages. Code reuse is not SQL's strong point (although in SQL Server it is getting slightly better with each new release). Many programmers coming from object-oriented languages that promote heavy code reuse tend to write layers and layers of SPs that call one another. These SPs often have cursors, and cursors within cursors, to feed each layer of procedures. While it does promote code reuse, this design pattern causes severe performance degradation. A commonly used term for this type of design pattern, popularized by SQL professional Jeff Moden, is "row-by-agonizing-row" (or RBAR) processing. This design pattern is high on my top-ten list of ways to abuse SQL Server, and will cause you far more problems than it ever solves. SQL Server 2008 offers a new feature, the *table-valued parameter*, which may help increase manageability and performance of the layered SP design methodology. I'll discuss table-valued parameters in Chapter 6.

SQL Server supports syntax for both ISO standard cursors and T-SQL extended syntax cursors. The ISO standard supports the following cursor options:

- The INSENSITIVE option makes a temporary copy of the cursor result set, and uses that copy to fulfill cursor requests. This means that changes to the underlying tables are not reflected when you request rows from the cursor.

- The SCROLL option allows you to use all cursor fetch options to position the cursor on any row in the cursor result set. The cursor fetch options include FIRST, LAST, NEXT, PRIOR, ABSOLUTE, and RELATIVE. If the SCROLL option is not specified, only the NEXT cursor fetch option is allowed.

- The READ ONLY option in the cursor FOR clause prevents updates to the underlying data through the cursor. In a non–read only cursor, you can update the underlying data with the WHERE CURRENT OF clause in the UPDATE and DELETE statements.

- The UPDATE OF option allows you to specify a list of updatable columns in the cursor's result set. You can specify UPDATE without the OF keyword and its associated column list to allow updates to all columns.

The T-SQL extended syntax provides many more options than the ISO syntax. In addition to supporting read-only cursors (the keyword is READ_ONLY, however), the UPDATE OF option, the SCROLL option, and insensitive cursors (using the STATIC keyword), T-SQL extended syntax cursors support the following options:

- Cursors that are local to the current batch, procedure, or trigger in which they are created via the LOCAL keyword. Cursors that are global to the connection in which they are created can be defined using the GLOBAL keyword.

- The FORWARD_ONLY option, which is the opposite of the SCROLL option, allowing you to only fetch rows from the cursor using the NEXT option.

- The KEYSET option, which specifies that the number and order of rows is fixed at the time the cursor is created. Trying to fetch rows that are subsequently deleted does not succeed, and a @@FETCH_STATUS value of -2 is returned.

- The DYNAMIC option, which specifies a cursor that reflects all data changes made to the rows in its underlying result set. This type of cursor is one of the slowest, since every change to the underlying data must be reflected whenever you scroll to a new row of the result set.

- The FAST_FORWARD option, which specifies a performance-optimized combination forward-only/read-only cursor.

- The SCROLL_LOCKS option, which locks underlying data rows as they are read to ensure that data modifications will succeed. The SCROLL_LOCKS option is mutually exclusive with the FAST_FORWARD and STATIC options.

- The OPTIMISTIC option, which uses timestamps to determine if a row has changed since the cursor was loaded. If a row has changed, the OPTIMISTIC option will not allow the current cursor to update the same row. The OPTIMISTIC option is incompatible with the FAST_FORWARD option.

- The TYPE_WARNING option, which sends a warning if a cursor will be automatically converted from the requested type to another type. This can happen, for instance, if SQL Server needs to convert a forward-only cursor to a static cursor.

■**Note** If you don't specify a cursor as LOCAL or GLOBAL, cursors that are created default to the setting defined by the default to local cursor database setting.

CURSOR COMPARISONS

Cursors come in several flavors, and you could spend a lot of time just trying to figure out which one you need to perform a given task. Most of the time, the cursors you'll need are forward-only/read-only cursors. These cursors are efficient because they move in only one direction and do not need to perform updates on the underlying data. Maximizing cursor efficiency by choosing the right type of cursor for the job is a quick-win strategy that you should keep in mind when you have to resort to a cursor.

Summary

In this chapter, I introduced SQL 3VL, which consists of three logical result values: true, false, and unknown. This is a key concept to understanding SQL development in general, but can be a foreign idea to developers coming from backgrounds in other programming languages. If you're not yet familiar with the 3VL chart, I highly recommend revisiting Figure 4-1. This chart summarizes the logic that governs SQL 3VL.

I also introduced T-SQL's control-of-flow statement offerings, which allow you to branch conditionally and unconditionally within your code, loop, handle exceptions, and force delays within your code. I also covered the two flavors of CASE expression, and some of the more advanced uses of CASE, including dynamic pivot table queries and CASE-based functions like COALESCE and NULLIF.

Finally, I discussed the redheaded stepchild of SQL development, the cursor. Although cursors commonly get a bad rap, there's nothing inherently bad about them; the problem is with how people use them. I focused my discussion of cursors on some common scenarios where they might be considered the best tool for the job, including administrative and complex one-off tasks. Finally, I presented the options available for ISO-compliant cursors and T-SQL extended syntax cursors, both of which are supported by SQL Server 2008.

In the next chapter, I'll begin discussing T-SQL programmability features, starting with an in-depth look at T-SQL UDFs in all their various forms.

EXERCISES

1. [True/false] SQL 3VL supports the logical result values true, false, and unknown.

2. [Choose one] SQL NULL represents which of the following:
    a. An unknown or missing value
    b. The number 0
    c. An empty (zero-length) string
    d. All of the above

3. [True/false] The BEGIN and END keywords delimit a statement block and limit the scope of variables declared within that statement block, like curly braces ({ }) in C#.

4. [Fill in the blank] The ___ keyword forces a WHILE loop to terminate immediately.

5. [True/false] The TRY...CATCH block can catch every possible SQL Server error.

6. [Fill in the blank] SQL CASE expressions come in two forms, ___ and ___.

7. [Choose all that apply] T-SQL supports which of the following cursor options:

   a. Read-only cursors

   b. Forward-only cursors

   c. Backward-only cursors

   d. Write-only cursors

8. Modify the code in Listing 4-13 to generate a pivot table result set that returns the total dollar amount (TotalDue) of orders by region, instead of the count of orders by region.

■ ■ ■

CHAPTER 5

User-Defined Functions

Each new version of SQL Server features improvements to T-SQL that make development easier. SQL Server 2000 introduced (among other things) the concept of user-defined functions (UDFs). Like functions in other programming languages, T-SQL UDFs provide a convenient way for developers to define routines that accept parameters, perform actions based on those parameters, and return data to the caller. T-SQL functions come in three flavors: inline table-valued functions (TVFs), multistatement TVFs, and scalar functions. SQL Server 2008 also supports the ability to create SQL CLR UDFs, which I'll talk about in Chapter 14.

Scalar Functions

Basically, a scalar UDF is a function that accepts zero or more parameters and returns a single scalar value as the result. You're probably already familiar with scalar functions in mathematics, and with T-SQL's built-in scalar functions (e.g., ABS and SUBSTRING). The CREATE FUNCTION statement allows you to create custom scalar functions that behave like the built-in scalar functions.

To demonstrate scalar UDFs, I'll take a trip back in time to high school geometry class. In accordance with the rules passed down from Euclid to Miss Kopp (my high school geometry teacher), this UDF accepts a circle's radius and returns the area of the circle using the formula $area = \pi \cdot r^2$. Listing 5-1 demonstrates this simple scalar UDF.

Listing 5-1. *Simple Scalar UDF*

```
CREATE FUNCTION dbo.CalculateCircleArea (@Radius float = 1.0)
RETURNS float
WITH RETURNS NULL ON NULL INPUT
AS
BEGIN
    RETURN PI() * POWER(@Radius, 2);
END;
```

The first line of the CREATE FUNCTION statement defines the schema and name of the function using a standard SQL Server two-part name (dbo.CalculateCircleArea) and a single required parameter, the radius of the circle (@Radius). The @Radius parameter is defined as a T-SQL float type. The parameter is assigned a default value of 1.0 by the = 1.0 after the parameter declaration.

```
CREATE FUNCTION dbo.CalculateCircleArea (@Radius float = 1.0)
```

The next line contains the RETURNS keyword, which specifies the data type of the result that will be returned by the UDF. In this instance, the RETURNS keyword indicates that the UDF will return a float result.

```
RETURNS float
```

The third line contains additional options following the WITH keyword. In the sample, I use the RETURNS NULL ON NULL INPUT function option for a performance improvement. The RETURNS NULL ON NULL INPUT option is a performance-enhancing option that automatically returns NULL if any of the parameters passed in are NULL. The performance enhancement occurs because SQL Server will not execute the body of the function if a NULL is passed in and this option is specified.

```
WITH RETURNS NULL ON NULL INPUT
```

The AS keyword indicates the start of the function body, which must be enclosed in the T-SQL BEGIN and END keywords. The sample function in Listing 5-1 is very simple, consisting of a single RETURN statement that immediately returns the value of the circle area calculation. The RETURN statement must be the last statement before the END keyword in every scalar UDF.

```
RETURN PI() * POWER(@radius, 2);
```

You can test this simple UDF with a few SELECT statements like the following. The results are shown in Figure 5-1.

```
SELECT dbo.CalculateCircleArea(10);
SELECT dbo.CalculateCircleArea(NULL);
SELECT dbo.CalculateCircleArea(2.5);
```

Figure 5-1. *The results of the sample circle area calculations*

UDF PARAMETERS

UDF parameters operate similarly to, but slightly differently from, stored procedure (SP) parameters. It's important to be aware of the differences. For instance, if you create a UDF that accepts no parameters, you still need to include empty parentheses after the function name—both when creating and invoking the function. Some built-in functions, like the PI() function used in Listing 5-1, which represents the value of the constant π (3.14159265358979), do not take parameters. Notice that when the function is called in the UDF, it is still called with empty parentheses.

Also, when SPs are assigned default values, you can simply leave the parameter off your parameter list completely when calling the procedure. This is not an option with UDFs. To use a UDF default value, you must use the DEFAULT keyword when calling the UDF. To use the default value for the @radius parameter of the example dbo.CalculateCircleArea UDF, you would call the UDF like this:

```
SELECT dbo.CalculateCircleArea (DEFAULT);
```

Finally, SPs have no equivalent to the RETURNS NULL ON NULL INPUT option. You can simulate this functionality to some extent by checking your parameters for NULL immediately on entering the SP, though. I'll discuss SPs in greater detail in Chapter 6.

UDFs provide several creation-time options that allow you to improve performance and security, including the following:

- The ENCRYPTION option can be used to store your UDF in the database in obfuscated format. Note that this is not true encryption, but rather an easily circumvented obfuscation of your code. See the "UDF 'Encryption'" sidebar for more information.

- The SCHEMABINDING option indicates that your UDF will be bound to database objects referenced in the body of the function. With SCHEMABINDING turned on, attempts to change or drop referenced tables and other database objects results in an error. This helps prevent inadvertent changes to tables and other database objects that can break your UDF. Additionally, the SQL Server Database Engine team has published information indicating that SCHEMABINDING can improve the performance of UDFs, even if they don't reference other database objects at all.

- The CALLED ON NULL INPUT option is the opposite of RETURNS NULL ON NULL INPUT. When CALLED ON NULL INPUT is specified, SQL Server executes the body of the function even if one or more parameters are NULL. CALLED ON NULL INPUT is a default option for all scalar-valued functions.

- The EXECUTE AS option manages caller security on UDFs. You can specify that the UDF will be executed as any of the following:

  - CALLER indicates that the UDF should be run under the security context of the user calling the function. This is the default.

  - SELF indicates that the UDF should be run under the security context of the user who created (or altered) the function.

  - OWNER indicates that the UDF should run under the security context of the owner of the UDF (or the owner of the schema containing the UDF).

  - Finally, you can specify that the UDF should run under the security context of a specific user by specifying a username.

> **UDF "ENCRYPTION"**
>
> Using the ENCRYPTION option on UDFs performs a simple obfuscation of your code. It actually does little more than "keep honest people honest," and in reality it tends to be more trouble than it's worth. Many a developer and DBA have spent precious time scouring the Internet for tools to decrypt their database objects because they were convinced the scripts in their source control database were out of sync with the production database. Keep in mind that those same decryption tools are available to anyone with an Internet connection and a browser. If you write commercial database scripts or perform database consulting services, your best (and really only) protection against curious DBAs and developers reverse-engineering and modifying your code is a well-written contract. Keep this in mind when deciding whether to "encrypt" your database objects.

Recursion in Scalar User-Defined Functions

Now that I've covered the basics, I think I'll hang out in math class for a few more minutes to talk about recursion. Like most procedural programming languages that allow function definitions, T-SQL allows recursion in UDFs. There's hardly a better way to demonstrate recursion than the most basic recursive algorithm around: the factorial function.

For those who put factorials out of their minds immediately after graduation, let me give a brief rundown of what they are. A *factorial* is the product of all natural (or counting) numbers less than or equal to n, where $n > 0$. Factorials are represented in mathematics with the *bang* notation: $n!$. As an example, $5! = 1 \cdot 2 \cdot 3 \cdot 4 \cdot 5 = 120$. The simple scalar dbo.CalculateFactorial UDF in Listing 5-2 calculates a factorial recursively for an integer parameter passed into it.

Listing 5-2. *Recursive Scalar UDF*

```
CREATE FUNCTION dbo.CalculateFactorial (@n int = 1)
RETURNS decimal(38, 0)
WITH RETURNS NULL ON NULL INPUT
AS
BEGIN
    RETURN
        (CASE
            WHEN @n <= 0 THEN NULL
            WHEN @n > 1 THEN CAST(@n AS float) * dbo.CalculateFactorial (@n - 1)
            WHEN @n = 1 THEN 1
        END);
END;
```

The first few lines are similar to Listing 5-1. The function accepts a single int parameter and returns a scalar decimal value. The RETURNS NULL ON NULL INPUT option returns NULL immediately if NULL is passed in.

```
CREATE FUNCTION dbo.CalculateFactorial(@n int = 1)
RETURNS decimal(38, 0)
WITH RETURNS NULL ON NULL INPUT
```

I've decided to return a decimal result in this example because of the limitations of the int and bigint types. Specifically, the int type overflows at 13! and bigint bombs out at 21!. In order to put the UDF through its paces, I have to allow it to return results up to 32!, which I'll discuss later in this section. As in Listing 5-1, the body of this UDF is a single RETURN statement, this time with a searched CASE expression.

```
RETURN
    (CASE
        WHEN @n <= 0 THEN NULL
        WHEN @n > 1 THEN CAST(@n AS float) * dbo.CalculateFactorial (@n - 1)
        WHEN @n = 1 THEN 1
    END);
```

The CASE expression checks the value of the UDF parameter, @n. If @n is 0 or negative, dbo.CalculateFactorial returns NULL since the result is undefined. If @n is greater than 1, dbo.CalculateFactorial returns @n * dbo.CalculateFactorial(@n - 1), the recursive part of the UDF. This ensures that the UDF will continue calling itself recursively, multiplying the current value of @n by (@n-1)!.

Finally, when @n reaches 1, the UDF returns 1. This is the part of dbo.CalculateFactorial that actually stops the recursion. Without the check for @n = 1, you could theoretically end up in an infinite recursive loop. In practice, however, SQL Server will save you from yourself by limiting you to a maximum of 32 levels of recursion. Demonstrating the 32-level limit on recursion is why I decided it was important the UDF needed to return results up to 32!. Following are some examples of dbo.CalculateFactorial calls with various parameters, with the results shown in Figure 5-2.

```
SELECT dbo.CalculateFactorial(NULL); -- Returns NULL
SELECT dbo.CalculateFactorial(-1);-- Returns NULL
SELECT dbo.CalculateFactorial(0);   -- Returns NULL
SELECT dbo.CalculateFactorial(5);   -- Returns 120
SELECT dbo.CalculateFactorial(32);-- Returns 263130836933693520000000000000000000
```

As you can see, the dbo.CalculateFactorial function easily handles the 32 levels of recursion required to calculate 32!. If you try to go beyond that limit, you'll get an error message. Executing the following code, which attempts 33 levels of recursion, does not work.

```
SELECT dbo.CalculateFactorial(33);
```

This causes SQL Server to grumble loudly with an error message similar to the following:

```
SQL2008(SQL2008\Michael): Msg 217, Level 16, State 1, Line 1
Maximum stored procedure, function, trigger, or view nesting level
exceeded (limit 32).
```

MORE THAN ONE WAY TO SKIN A CAT

The 32-level recursion limit is a *hard limit*; that is, you can't programmatically change it through server or database settings. This really isn't as bad a limitation as you might think. Very rarely do you actually need to recursively call a UDF more than 32 times, and doing so could result in a severe performance penalty. There's generally more than one way to get the job done, however, and you can work around the 32-level recursion limitation in the dbo.CalculateFactorial function by rewriting it with a WHILE loop or using a recursive common table expression (CTE), as shown here:

```
CREATE FUNCTION dbo.CalculateFactorial (@n int = 1)
RETURNS float
WITH RETURNS NULL ON NULL INPUT
AS
BEGIN
  DECLARE @result float;
  SET @result = NULL;

  IF @n > 0
  BEGIN
    SET @result = 1.0;

    WITH Numbers (num)
    AS
    (
      SELECT 1
      UNION ALL
      SELECT num + 1
      FROM Numbers
      WHERE num < @n
    )
    SELECT @result = @result * num
    FROM Numbers;
  END;
  RETURN @result;
END;
```

This rewrite of the dbo.CalculateFactorial function averts the recursive function call limit by eliminating the recursive function calls. Instead, it pushes the recursion back into the body of the function through the use of a recursive CTE. By default, SQL Server allows up to 100 levels of recursion in a CTE (you can override this with the MAXRECURSION option), greatly expanding your factorial calculation power. With this function, you can easily find out that 33! is 8.68331761881189E+36, or even that 100! is 9.33262154439441E+157. The important idea to take away from this discussion is that while recursive function calls have hard limits on them, you can often work around those limitations using other T-SQL functionality.

Also keep in mind that although I used factorial calculation as a simple example of recursion, this method is considered naive, and there are several more-efficient methods of calculating factorials.

Please note that no cats were harmed during the writing of this book.

Procedural Code in User-Defined Functions

So far, we've talked about simple functions that demonstrate the basic points of scalar UDFs. But in all likelihood, unless we're implementing business logic for a swimming pool installation company, neither you nor I will likely need to spend much time calculating the area of a circle in T-SQL.

A common problem that you have a much greater chance of running into is name-based searching. T-SQL offers tools for exact matching, partial matching, and even limited pattern matching via the LIKE predicate. T-SQL even offers built-in phonetic matching (*sound-alike matching*) through the built-in SOUNDEX function.

Heavy-duty approximate matching, however, usually requires a more advanced tool, like a better phonetic matching algorithm. I'll use one of these algorithms, the New York State Identification and Intelligence System (NYSIIS) algorithm, to demonstrate procedural code in UDFs.

THE SOUNDEX ALGORITHM

The NYSIIS algorithm is an improvement on the Soundex phonetic encoding algorithm, itself nearly 90 years old. The NYSIIS algorithm converts groups of one, two, or three alphabetic characters (known as *n-grams*) in names to a phonetic ("sounds like") approximation. This makes it easier to search for names that have similar pronunciations but different spellings, such as *Smythe* and *Smith*. As mentioned in this section, SQL Server provides a built-in SOUNDEX function, but Soundex provides very poor accuracy and usually results in many false hits. NYSIIS and other modern algorithms provide much better results than Soundex.

To demonstrate procedural code in UDFs, I will implement a UDF that phonetically encodes names using NYSIIS encoding rules. The rules for NYSIIS phonetic encoding are relatively simple, with the majority of the rules requiring simple n-gram substitutions. The following is a complete list of NYSIIS encoding rules:

1. Remove all nonalphabetic characters from the name.

2. The first characters of the name are encoded according to the n-gram substitutions shown in the "Start of Name" table in Figure 5-2. In Figure 5-2, the n-grams shown on the left-hand side of the arrows are replaced with the n-grams on the right-hand side of the arrows during the encoding process.

3. The last characters of the name are encoded according to the n-gram substitutions shown in the "End of Name" table in Figure 5-2.

4. The first character of the encoded value is set to the first character of the name.

5. After the first and last n-grams are encoded, all remaining characters in the name are encoded according to the n-gram substitutions shown in the "Middle of Name" table in Figure 5-2.

6. All side-by-side duplicate characters in the encoded name are reduced to a single character. This means that *AA* is reduced to *A* and *SS* is reduced to *S*.

7. If the last character of the encoded name is *S*, it is removed.

8. If the last characters of the encoded name are *AY*, they are replaced with *Y*.

9. If the last character of the encoded name is *A*, it is removed.

10. The result is truncated to six characters maximum length.

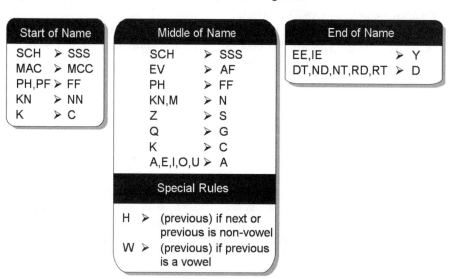

NYSIIS Phonetic Encoding Rules

Figure 5-2. *NYSIIS phonetic encoding rules/character substitutions*

You could use some fairly large CASE expressions to implement these rules, but I've chosen the more flexible option of using a replacement table. This table will contain the majority of the replacement rules in just the three columns, as described here:

- Location: This column tells the UDF whether the rule should be applied to the start, end, or middle of the name.

- NGram: This column is the n-gram, or sequence of characters, that will be encoded. These n-grams correspond to the left-hand side of the arrows in Figure 5-2.

- Replacement: This column represents the replacement value for the corresponding n-gram on the same row. These character sequences correspond to the right-hand side of the arrows in Figure 5-2.

Listing 5-3 is a CREATE TABLE statement that builds the NYSIIS phonetic encoding replacement rules table.

Listing 5-3. *Creating the NYSIIS Replacement Rules Table*

```
-- Create the NYSIIS replacement rules table
CREATE TABLE dbo.NYSIIS_Replacements
   (Location nvarchar(10) NOT NULL,
    NGram nvarchar(10) NOT NULL,
    Replacement nvarchar(10) NOT NULL,
    PRIMARY KEY (Location, NGram));
```

Listing 5-4 is a single INSERT statement that uses the new SQL Server 2008 row constructors to populate all of the NYSIIS replacement rules, as shown in Figure 5-2.

Listing 5-4. *INSERT Statement to Populate NYSIIS Replacement Rules Table*

```
INSERT INTO NYSIIS_Replacements (Location, NGram, Replacement)
VALUES (N'End', N'DT', N'DD'),
    (N'End', N'EE', N'YY'),
    (N'End', N'IE', N'YY'),
    (N'End', N'ND', N'DD'),
    (N'End', N'NT', N'DD'),
    (N'End', N'RD', N'DD'),
    (N'End', N'RT', N'DD'),
    (N'Mid', N'A', N'A'),
    (N'Mid', N'E', N'A'),
    (N'Mid', N'I', N'A'),
    (N'Mid', N'K', N'C'),
    (N'Mid', N'M', N'N'),
    (N'Mid', N'O', N'A'),
    (N'Mid', N'Q', N'G'),
    (N'Mid', N'U', N'A'),
    (N'Mid', N'Z', N'S'),
    (N'Mid', N'AW', N'AA'),
    (N'Mid', N'EV', N'AF'),
    (N'Mid', N'EW', N'AA'),
    (N'Mid', N'IW', N'AA'),
    (N'Mid', N'KN', N'NN'),
    (N'Mid', N'OW', N'AA'),
    (N'Mid', N'PH', N'FF'),
    (N'Mid', N'UW', N'AA'),
    (N'Mid', N'SCH', N'SSS'),
    (N'Start', N'K', N'C'),
    (N'Start', N'KN', N'NN'),
    (N'Start', N'PF', N'FF'),
    (N'Start', N'PH', N'FF'),
    (N'Start', N'MAC', N'MCC'),
    (N'Start', N'SCH', N'SSS');
GO
```

Listing 5-5 is the actual UDF that encodes a string using NYSIIS. This UDF demonstrates the complexity of the control-of-flow logic that can be implemented in a scalar UDF.

Listing 5-5. *Function to Encode Strings Using NYSIIS*

```
CREATE FUNCTION dbo.EncodeNYSIIS
(
  @String nvarchar(100)
)
RETURNS nvarchar(6)
WITH RETURNS NULL ON NULL INPUT
AS
BEGIN
  DECLARE @Result nvarchar(100);
  SET @Result = UPPER(@String);

  -- Step 1: Remove all nonalphabetic characters
  WITH Numbers (Num)
  AS
  (
    SELECT 1

    UNION ALL

    SELECT Num + 1
    FROM Numbers
    WHERE Num < LEN(@Result)
  )
  SELECT @Result = STUFF
    (
      @Result,
      Num,
      1,
      CASE WHEN SUBSTRING(@Result, Num, 1) >= N'A'
          AND SUBSTRING(@Result, Num, 1) <= N'Z'
        THEN SUBSTRING(@Result, Num, 1)
        ELSE N'.'
      END
    )
  FROM Numbers;

  SET @Result = REPLACE(@Result, N'.', N'');

  -- Step 2: Replace the start n-gram
  SELECT TOP (1) @Result = STUFF
```

```
  (
    @Result,
    1,
    LEN(NGram),
    Replacement
  )
FROM dbo.NYSIIS_Replacements
WHERE Location = N'Start'
  AND SUBSTRING(@Result, 1, LEN(NGram)) = NGram
ORDER BY LEN(NGram) DESC;

-- Step 3: Replace the end n-gram
SELECT TOP (1) @Result = STUFF
  (
    @Result,
    LEN(@Result) - LEN(NGram) + 1,
    LEN(NGram),
    Replacement
  )
FROM dbo.NYSIIS_Replacements
WHERE Location = N'End'
  AND SUBSTRING(@Result, LEN(@Result) - LEN(NGram) + 1, LEN(NGram)) = NGram
ORDER BY LEN(NGram) DESC;

-- Step 4: Save the first letter of the name
DECLARE @FirstLetter nchar(1);
SET @FirstLetter = SUBSTRING(@Result, 1, 1);

-- Step 5: Replace all middle n-grams
DECLARE @Replacement nvarchar(10);
DECLARE @i int;
SET @i = 1;
WHILE @i <= LEN(@Result)
BEGIN
  SET @Replacement = NULL;

  -- Grab the middle-of-name replacement n-gram
  SELECT TOP (1) @Replacement = Replacement
  FROM dbo.NYSIIS_Replacements
  WHERE Location = N'Mid'
    AND SUBSTRING(@Result, @i, LEN(NGram)) = NGram
  ORDER BY LEN(NGram) DESC;

  SET @Replacement = COALESCE(@Replacement, SUBSTRING(@Result, @i, 1));
```

```
    -- If we found a replacement, apply it
    SET @Result = STUFF(@Result, @i, LEN(@Replacement), @Replacement)

    -- Move on to the next n-gram
    SET @i = @i + COALESCE(LEN(@Replacement), 1);
END;

-- Replace the first character with the first letter we saved at the start
SET @Result = STUFF(@Result, 1, 1, @FirstLetter);

-- Here we apply our special rules for the 'H' character. Special handling for
-- 'W' characters is taken care of in the replacement rules table
WITH Numbers (Num)
AS
(
  SELECT 2       -- Don't bother with the first character

  UNION ALL

  SELECT Num + 1
  FROM Numbers
  WHERE Num < LEN(@Result)
)
SELECT @Result = STUFF
  (
    @Result,
    Num,
    1,
    CASE SUBSTRING(@Result, Num, 1)
      WHEN N'H' THEN
        CASE WHEN SUBSTRING(@Result, Num + 1, 1)
            NOT IN (N'A', N'E', N'I', N'O', N'U')
          OR SUBSTRING(@Result, Num - 1, 1)
            NOT IN (N'A', N'E', N'I', N'O', N'U')
          THEN SUBSTRING(@Result, Num - 1, 1)
        ELSE N'H'
      END
    ELSE SUBSTRING(@Result, Num, 1)
  END
  )
FROM Numbers;
```

```
-- Step 6: Reduce all side-by-side duplicate characters
-- First replace the first letter of any sequence of two side-by-side
-- duplicate letters with a period
WITH Numbers (Num)
AS
(
    SELECT 1

    UNION ALL

    SELECT Num + 1
    FROM Numbers
    WHERE Num < LEN(@Result)
)
SELECT @Result = STUFF
  (
    @Result,
    Num,
    1,
    CASE SUBSTRING(@Result, Num, 1)
      WHEN SUBSTRING(@Result, Num + 1, 1) THEN N'.'
      ELSE SUBSTRING(@Result, Num, 1)
    END
  )
FROM Numbers;

-- Next replace all periods '.' with an empty string ''
SET @Result = REPLACE(@Result, N'.', N'');

-- Step 7: Remove trailing 'S' characters
WHILE RIGHT(@Result, 1) = N'S' AND LEN(@Result) > 1
  SET @Result = STUFF(@Result, LEN(@Result), 1, N'');

-- Step 8: Remove trailing 'A' characters
WHILE RIGHT(@Result, 1) = N'A' AND LEN(@Result) > 1
  SET @Result = STUFF(@Result, LEN(@Result), 1, N'');

-- Step 9: Replace trailing 'AY' characters with 'Y'
IF RIGHT(@Result, 2) = 'AY'
  SET @Result = STUFF(@Result, LEN(@Result) - 1, 1, N'');

-- Step 10: Truncate result to 6 characters
  RETURN COALESCE(SUBSTRING(@Result, 1, 6), '');
END;
GO
```

The NYSIIS_Replacements table rules reflect most of the NYSIIS rules described by Robert L. Taft in his famous paper "Name Search Techniques." The start and end n-grams are replaced, and then the remaining n-gram rules are applied in a WHILE loop. The special rules for the letter *H* are applied, side-by-side duplicates are removed, special handling of certain trailing characters is performed, and the first six characters of the result are returned.

NUMBERS TABLES

In this example, I use recursive CTEs to dynamically generate virtual numbers tables in a couple of places. A *numbers table* is simply a table of numbers counting up to a specified maximum. The following recursive CTE generates a small numbers table (the numbers 1 through 100):

```
WITH Numbers (Num)
AS
(
  SELECT 1
  UNION ALL

  SELECT Num + 1
  FROM Numbers
  WHERE Num < 100
)
SELECT Num
FROM Numbers;
```

In Listing 5-5, I've used the number of characters in the name to limit the recursion of the CTEs. This speeds up the UDF overall. You can get even more performance gains by creating a permanent numbers table in your database with a clustered index/primary key on it, instead of using CTEs. A numbers table is always handy to have around, doesn't cost you very much to build or maintain, doesn't take up much storage space, and is extremely useful for converting loops and cursors to set-based code. A numbers table is by far one of the handiest and simplest tools you can add to your T-SQL toolkit.

As an example, I used the query in Listing 5-6 to phonetically encode the last names of all contacts in the AdventureWorks database using NYSIIS. Partial results are shown in Figure 5-3.

Listing 5-6. *Using NYSIIS to Phonetically Encode All AdventureWorks Contacts*

```
SELECT LastName,
  dbo.EncodeNYSIIS(LastName) AS NYSIIS
FROM Person.Person
GROUP BY LastName;
```

	LastName	NYSIIS
23	Pal	PAL
24	Nath	NAT
25	Louverdis	LAVARD
26	Kawai	C
27	Lee	LY
28	Whitehead	WATAHA
29	Suri	SAR
30	Gimmi	GAN
31	Grande	GRAND
32	Tullao	TAL
33	Nartker	NARTCA
34	Piaseczny	PASACS
35	Teper	TAPAR
36	Rousey	RASY
37	Hedlund	HADLAD
38	Core	CAR

Figure 5-3. *Partial results of NYSIIS Encoding AdventureWorks Contacts*

Using the dbo.EncodeNYSIIS UDF is relatively simple. Listing 5-7 is a simple example of using the new UDF in the WHERE clause to retrieve all AdventureWorks contacts whose last name is phonetically similar to the name Liu. The results are shown in Figure 5-4.

Listing 5-7. *Retrieving All Contact Phonetic Matches for Liu*

```
SELECT
  BusinessEntityID,
  LastName,
  FirstName,
  MiddleName,
  dbo.EncodeNYSIIS(LastName) AS NYSIIS
FROM Person.Person
WHERE dbo.EncodeNYSIIS(LastName) = dbo.EncodeNYSIIS(N'Liu');
```

	BusinessEntityID	LastName	FirstName	MiddleName	NYSIIS
337	18213	Lu	Todd	D	L
338	4740	Lu	Trisha	NULL	L
339	17505	Lu	Valerie	NULL	L
340	17955	Lu	Vincent	NULL	L
341	12013	Lu	Warren	H	L
342	18106	Lu	Wesley	P	L
343	13352	Lu	Willie	NULL	L
344	12532	Luo	Alejandro	K	L
345	19779	Luo	Alicia	NULL	L
346	12000	Luo	Alisha	NULL	L
347	16643	Luo	Alison	A	L
348	4946	Luo	Alvin	NULL	L

Figure 5-4. *AdventureWorks Contacts with Names Phonetically Similar to Liu*

The example in Listing 5-7 is the naive method of using a UDF. The query engine must apply the UDF to every single row of the source table. In this case, the dbo.EncodeNYSIIS function is applied to the nearly 20,000 last names in the Person.Contact table, resulting in an inefficient query plan and excessive I/O. A more efficient method is to perform the NYSIIS encodings ahead of time—to preencode the names. The preencoding method is demonstrated in Listing 5-8.

Listing 5-8. *Preencoding AdventureWorks Contact Names with NYSIIS*

```
CREATE TABLE Person.ContactNYSIIS
(
  BusinessEntityID int NOT NULL,
  NYSIIS nvarchar(6) NOT NULL,
  PRIMARY KEY(NYSIIS, ContactId)
);
GO


INSERT INTO Person.ContactNYSIIS
(
  BusinessEntityID,
  NYSIIS
)
SELECT
  BusinessEntityID,
  dbo.EncodeNYSIIS(LastName)
FROM Person.Person;
GO
```

Once you have preencoded the data, queries are much more efficient. The query shown in Listing 5-9 uses the table created in Listing 5-8 to return the same results as Listing 5-7—just much more efficiently, since this version doesn't need to encode every row of data for comparison in the WHERE clause at query time.

Listing 5-9. *Efficient NYSIIS Query Using Preencoded Data*

```
SELECT
  cn.BusinessEntityID,
  c.LastName,
  c.FirstName,
  c.MiddleName,
  cn.NYSIIS
FROM Person.ContactNYSIIS cn
INNER JOIN Person.Person c
  ON cn.BusinessEntityID = c.BusinessEntityID
WHERE cn.NYSIIS = dbo.EncodeNYSIIS(N'Liu');
```

To keep the efficiency of the dbo.EncodeNYSIIS UDF-based searches optimized, I highly recommend preencoding your search data. This is especially true in production environments where performance is critical. NYSIIS (and phonetic matching in general) is an extremely useful tool for approximate name-based searches in a variety of applications, such as customer service, business reporting, and law enforcement.

Multistatement Table-Valued Functions

Multistatement TVFs are similar in style to scalar UDFs, but instead of returning a single scalar value, they return their result as a table data type. The declaration is very similar to that of a scalar UDF, with a few important differences:

- The return type following the RETURNS keyword is actually a table variable declaration, with its structure declared immediately following the table variable name.

- The RETURNS NULL ON NULL INPUT and CALLED ON NULL INPUT function options are not valid in a multistatement TVF definition.

- The RETURN statement in the body of the multistatement TVF has no values or variables following it.

Inside the body of the multistatement TVF, you can use the SQL Data Manipulation Language (DML) statements INSERT, UPDATE, MERGE, and DELETE to create and manipulate the return results in the table variable that will be returned as the result.

For the example of a multistatement TVF, I'll create another business application function. Namely, I'm going to create a product pull list for AdventureWorks. This TVF will match the AdventureWorks sales orders stored in the Sales.SalesOrderDetail table against the product inventory in the Production.ProductInventory table. It will effectively create a list for AdventureWorks employees, telling them exactly which inventory bin to go to in order to fill an order. There are some business rules that need to be defined before I write this multistatement TVF:

- In some cases, the number of ordered items might be more than are available in one bin. In that case, the pull list will instruct the employee to grab the product from multiple bins.

- Any partial fills from a bin will be reported on the list.

- Any substitution work (e.g., substituting a different colored item of the same model) will be handled by a separate business process and won't be allowed on this list.

- No zero fills (ordered items for which there is no matching product in inventory) will be reported back on the list.

For purposes of this example, I'll say that there are three customers: Jill, Mike, and Dave. Each of these three customers places an order for exactly five items: number 783, the black Mountain-200 42-inch mountain bike. I'll also say that AdventureWorks has six of this particular inventory item in bin 1, shelf A, location 7, and another four of this particular item in bin 2, shelf B, location 10. Our business rules will create a pull list like the following:

- *Jill's order*: Pull five of item 783 from bin 1, shelf A, location 7; mark the order as a complete fill.

- *Mike's order*: Pull one of item 783 from bin 1, shelf A, location 7; mark the order as a partial fill.

- *Mike's order*: Pull three of item 783 from bin 2, shelf B, location 10; mark the order as a partial fill.

In this example, there are only 9 of the ordered items in inventory, while 15 total items have been ordered (3 customers multiplied by 5 items each). Because of this, Dave's order will be zero-filled—no items will be pulled from inventory to fill his order. Figure 5-5 is designed to help you visualize the sample inventory/order fill scenario I've described up to this point.

Since the inventory is out of item 783 at this point (there were nine items in inventory and all nine were used to fill Jill and Mike's orders), Dave's order will not even be listed on the pull list report. This function doesn't concern itself with product substitutions—for example, completing Mike and Dave's orders with a comparable product such as item ID number 780 (the silver Mountain-200 42-inch mountain bike), if there happens to be some in stock. The business rule for substitutions states that a separate process will handle this aspect of order fulfillment.

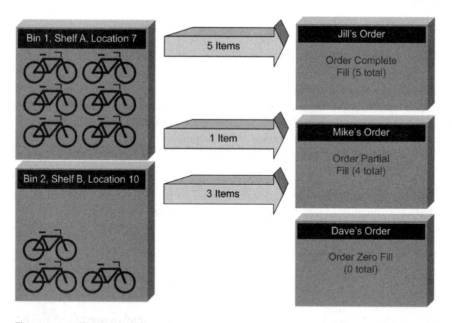

Figure 5-5. *Filling orders from inventory*

Many developers might see this problem as an opportunity to flex their cursor-based coding muscles. If you look at the problem from a procedural point of view, it essentially calls for performing nested loops through AdventureWorks's customer orders and inventory to match them up. However, this code does not require procedural code, and the task can be completed in a set-based fashion using a numbers table, as described in the previous section. A numbers table with numbers from 0 to 30000 is adequate for this task, and the code to create the numbers table is shown in Listing 5-10.

Listing 5-10. *Creating a Numbers Table*

```
-- Create a numbers table to allow the product pull list to be
-- created using set-based logic
CREATE TABLE dbo.Numbers (Num int NOT NULL PRIMARY KEY);
GO

-- Fill the numbers table with numbers from 0 to 30,000
WITH NumCTE (Num)
AS
(
  SELECT 0

  UNION ALL

  SELECT Num + 1
  FROM NumCTE
  WHERE Num < 30000
)
INSERT INTO dbo.Numbers (Num)
SELECT Num
FROM NumCTE
OPTION (MAXRECURSION 0);
GO
```

So, with a better understanding of order fulfillment logic and business rules, Listing 5-11 creates a multistatement TVF to return the product pull list according to the rules provided. As I mentioned, this multistatement TVF uses set-based logic (no cursors or loops) to retrieve the product pull list.

LOOK MA, NO CURSORS!

Many programming problems in business present a procedural loop-based solution on first glance. This applies to problems that you must solve in T-SQL as well. If you look at business problems with a set-based mindset, you'll often find a set-based solution. In the product pull list example, the loop-based process of comparing every row of inventory to the order detail rows is immediately apparent.

However, if you think of the inventory items and order detail items as two sets, then the problem becomes a set-based problem. In this case, the solution is a variation of the classic computer science/mathematics *bin-packing problem*. In the bin-packing problem, you are given a set of bins (in this case orders) in which to place a finite set of items (inventory items in this example). The natural bounds provided are the number of each item in inventory and the number of each item on each order detail line.

By solving this as a set-based problem in T-SQL, you allow SQL Server to optimize the performance of your code based on the most current information available. As I mentioned in Chapter 4, when you use cursors and loops, you take away SQL Server's performance optimization options and you assume the responsibility for performance optimization yourself. I chose to use set-based logic instead of cursors and loops to solve this particular problem. In reality, solving this problem with a set-based solution took only about 30 minutes of my time. A cursor or loop-based solution would have taken just as long or longer, and it wouldn't have been nearly as efficient.

Listing 5-11. *Creating a Product Pull List*

```
CREATE FUNCTION dbo.GetProductPullList()
RETURNS @result table
(
  SalesOrderID int NOT NULL,
  ProductID int NOT NULL,
  LocationID smallint NOT NULL,
  Shelf nvarchar(10) NOT NULL,
  Bin tinyint NOT NULL,
  QuantityInBin smallint NOT NULL,
  QuantityOnOrder smallint NOT NULL,
  QuantityToPull smallint NOT NULL,
  PartialFillFlag nchar(1) NOT NULL,
  PRIMARY KEY (SalesOrderID, ProductID, LocationID, Shelf, Bin)
)
AS
BEGIN
  INSERT INTO @result
  (
    SalesOrderID,
    ProductID,
    LocationID,
    Shelf,
    Bin,
    QuantityInBin,
    QuantityOnOrder,
    QuantityToPull,
    PartialFillFlag
  )
  SELECT
    Order_Details.SalesOrderID,
    Order_Details.ProductID,
    Inventory_Details.LocationID,
    Inventory_Details.Shelf,
    Inventory_Details.Bin,
    Inventory_Details.Quantity,
    Order_Details.OrderQty,
    COUNT(*) AS PullQty,
    CASE WHEN COUNT(*) < Order_Details.OrderQty
      THEN N'Y'
      ELSE N'N'
    END AS PartialFillFlag
  FROM
  (
    SELECT ROW_NUMBER() OVER
```

```
      (
        PARTITION BY p.ProductID
        ORDER BY p.ProductID,
          p.LocationID,
          p.Shelf,
          p.Bin
      ) AS Num,
      p.ProductID,
      p.LocationID,
      p.Shelf,
      p.Bin,
      p.Quantity
    FROM Production.ProductInventory p
    INNER JOIN dbo.Numbers n
      ON n.Num BETWEEN 1 AND Quantity
  ) Inventory_Details
  INNER JOIN
  (
    SELECT ROW_NUMBER() OVER
      (
        PARTITION BY o.ProductID
        ORDER BY o.ProductID,
          o.SalesOrderID
      ) AS Num,
      o.ProductID,
      o.SalesOrderID,
      o.OrderQty
    FROM Sales.SalesOrderDetail o
    INNER JOIN dbo.Numbers n
      ON n.Num BETWEEN 1 AND o.OrderQty
  ) Order_Details
  ON Inventory_Details.ProductID = Order_Details.ProductID
    AND Inventory_Details.Num = Order_Details.Num
  GROUP BY
    Order_Details.SalesOrderID,
    Order_Details.ProductID,
    Inventory_Details.LocationID,
    Inventory_Details.Shelf,
    Inventory_Details.Bin,
    Inventory_Details.Quantity,
    Order_Details.OrderQty;
  RETURN;
END;
GO
```

Retrieving the product pull list involves a simple SELECT query like the following. Partial results are shown in Figure 5-6.

```
SELECT
  SalesOrderID,
  ProductID,
  LocationID,
  Shelf,
  Bin,
  QuantityInBin,
  QuantityOnOrder,
  QuantityToPull,
  PartialFillFlag
FROM dbo.GetProductPullList();
```

	SalesOrderID	ProductID	LocationID	Shelf	Bin	QuantityInBin	QuantityOnOrder	QuantityToPull	PartialFillFlag
4765	46964	793	60	N/A	0	78	4	4	N
4766	46964	794	7	N/A	0	116	2	2	N
4767	46964	795	7	N/A	0	100	2	2	N
4768	46964	796	7	N/A	0	65	4	4	N
4769	46964	797	60	N/A	0	81	5	5	N
4770	46964	798	60	N/A	0	60	3	3	N
4771	46964	799	7	N/A	0	104	4	4	N
4772	46964	800	7	N/A	0	30	6	3	Y
4773	46964	800	60	N/A	0	99	6	3	Y
4774	46964	801	60	N/A	0	78	6	6	N
4775	46964	811	10	E	7	257	4	4	N
4776	46964	813	10	E	9	251	1	1	N
4777	46964	819	5	T	5	409	7	7	N
4778	46964	820	5	T	6	446	9	9	N
4779	46964	822	10	N/A	0	115	4	4	N
4780	46964	826	6	A	11	393	7	7	N

Figure 5-6. *AdventureWorks product pull list (partial)*

One interesting aspect of the multistatement TVF is the actual CREATE FUNCTION keyword and its RETURNS clause, which define the name of the procedure, parameters passed in (if any), and the result set table structure.

```
CREATE FUNCTION dbo.GetProductPullList()
RETURNS @result table
(
  SalesOrderID int NOT NULL,
  ProductID int NOT NULL,
  LocationID smallint NOT NULL,
  Shelf nvarchar(10) NOT NULL,
  Bin tinyint NOT NULL,
```

```
  QuantityInBin smallint NOT NULL,
  QuantityOnOrder smallint NOT NULL,
  QuantityToPull smallint NOT NULL,
  PartialFillFlag nchar(1) NOT NULL,
  PRIMARY KEY (SalesOrderID, ProductID, LocationID, Shelf, Bin)
)
```

You may notice that I've defined a primary key on the table result. This also serves as the clustered index for the result set. Due to limitations in table variables, you can't explicitly specify other indexes on the result set.

The body of the function begins with the INSERT INTO and SELECT clauses that follow:

```
INSERT INTO @result
(
  SalesOrderID,
  ProductID,
  LocationID,
  Shelf,
  Bin,
  QuantityInBin,
  QuantityOnOrder,
  QuantityToPull,
  PartialFillFlag
)
SELECT
  Order_Details.SalesOrderID,
  Order_Details.ProductID,
  Inventory_Details.LocationID,
  Inventory_Details.Shelf,
  Inventory_Details.Bin,
  Inventory_Details.Quantity,
  Order_Details.OrderQty,
  COUNT(*) AS PullQty,
  CASE WHEN COUNT(*) < Order_Details.OrderQty
    THEN N'Y'
    ELSE N'N'
  END AS PartialFillFlag
```

These clauses establish population of the @result table variable. The most important point to notice here is that the return results of this multistatement TVF are created by manipulating the contents of the @result table variable. When the function ends, the @result table variable is returned to the caller. Some other important facts about this portion of the multistatement TVF are that the COUNT(*) AS PullQty aggregate function returns the total number of each item to pull from a given bin to fill a specific order detail row, and the CASE expression returns Y when an order detail item is partially filled from a single bin and N when an order detail item is completely filled from a single bin.

The source for the SELECT query is composed of two subqueries joined together. The first subquery, aliased as Inventory_Details, is shown following. This subquery returns a single row for every item in inventory with information identifying the precise location where the inventory item can be found.

```
(
    SELECT ROW_NUMBER() OVER
      (
        PARTITION BY p.ProductID
        ORDER BY p.ProductID,
          p.LocationID,
          p.Shelf,
          p.Bin
      ) AS Num,
      p.ProductID,
      p.LocationID,
      p.Shelf,
      p.Bin,
      p.Quantity
    FROM Production.ProductInventory p
    INNER JOIN dbo.Numbers n
      ON n.Num BETWEEN 1 AND Quantity
) Inventory_Details
```

Considering the previous example with the customers Jill, Mike, and Dave, if there are nine black Mountain-200 42-inch mountain bikes in inventory, this query returns nine rows, one for each instance of the item in inventory, and each with a unique row number counting from 1.

The Inventory_Details subquery is inner-joined to a second subquery, identified as Order_Details, as shown following:

```
(
    SELECT ROW_NUMBER() OVER
      (
        PARTITION BY o.ProductID
        ORDER BY o.ProductID,
          o.SalesOrderID
      ) AS Num,
      o.ProductID,
      o.SalesOrderID,
      o.OrderQty
    FROM Sales.SalesOrderDetail o
    INNER JOIN dbo.Numbers n
      ON n.Num BETWEEN 1 AND o.OrderQty
) Order_Details
```

This subquery breaks up quantities of items in all order details into individual rows. Again considering the example of Jill, Mike, and Dave, this query will break each of the order details into five rows, one for each item of each order detail. The rows are assigned unique numbers for each product. So in the example, the rows for each black Mountain-200 42-inch mountain bike that our three customers ordered will be numbered individually from 1 to 15.

The rows of both subqueries are joined based on their ProductID numbers and the unique row numbers assigned to each row of each subquery. This effectively assigns one item from the inventory to fill exactly one item in each order. Figure 5-7 is a visualization of the process that I've described here, where the inventory items and order detail items are split into separate rows and the two rowsets are joined together.

Figure 5-7. *Splitting and joining individual inventory and sales detail items*

The SELECT statement also requires a GROUP BY to aggregate the total number of items to be pulled from each bin to fill each order detail, as opposed to returning the raw inventory-to-order detail items on a one-to-one basis.

```
GROUP BY
  Order_Details.SalesOrderID,
  Order_Details.ProductID,
  Inventory_Details.LocationID,
  Inventory_Details.Shelf,
  Inventory_Details.Bin,
  Inventory_Details.Quantity,
  Order_Details.OrderQty;
```

Finally, the RETURN statement returns the @result table back to the caller as the multistatement TVF result. Notice that the RETURN statement in a multistatement TVF isn't followed by an expression or variable as it is in a scalar UDF:

```
RETURN;
```

The table returned by a TVF can be used just like a table in a WHERE clause or a JOIN clause of a SQL SELECT query. Listing 5-12 is a sample query that joins the example TVF to the Production.Product table to get the product names and colors for each product listed in the pull list. Figure 5-8 shows the output of the product pull list joined to the Production.Product table.

Listing 5-12. *Retrieving a Product Pull List with Product Names*

```
SELECT
  p.Name AS ProductName,
  p.ProductNumber,
  p.Color,
  ppl.SalesOrderID,
  ppl.ProductID,
  ppl.LocationID,
  ppl.Shelf,
  ppl.Bin,
  ppl.QuantityInBin,
  ppl.QuantityOnOrder,
  ppl.QuantityToPull,
  ppl.PartialFillFlag
FROM Production.Product p
INNER JOIN dbo.GetProductPullList() ppl
  ON p.ProductID = ppl.ProductID;
```

	ProductName	Produc...	Color	SalesOrde...	Produc...	Locatio...	Sh...	Bin	Qua...	Qu...	Qu...	Parti...
10119	Touring-3000 Blue, ...	BK-T1...	Blue	51165	979	7	N/A	0	86	1	1	N
10120	HL Road Handlebars	HB-R956	NULL	51166	813	20	S	6	260	1	1	N
10121	ML Road Frame-W ...	FR-R7...	Yell...	51168	822	50	N/A	0	153	2	2	N
10122	Classic Vest, M	VE-C3...	Blue	51168	865	7	N/A	0	216	13	11	Y
10123	Water Bottle - 30 oz.	WB-H0...	NULL	51168	870	7	N/A	0	252	3	3	N
10124	Patch Kit/8 Patches	PK-7098	NULL	51168	873	7	N/A	0	180	2	2	N
10125	Racing Socks, M	SO-R8...	White	51168	874	7	N/A	0	252	3	3	N
10126	Racing Socks, L	SO-R8...	White	51168	875	7	N/A	0	288	2	2	N
10127	Short-Sleeve Classi...	SJ-019...	Yell...	51168	881	7	N/A	0	324	13	13	N
10128	LL Road Pedal	PD-R347	Silv...	51168	938	1	E	21	169	8	8	N
10129	ML Road Pedal	PD-R563	Silv...	51168	939	1	E	16	168	3	3	N
10130	Road-350-W Yellow...	BK-R7...	Yell...	51168	976	60	N/A	0	123	4	4	N
10131	Road-750 Black, 48	BK-R1...	Black	51168	998	60	N/A	0	56	10	10	N
10132	Road-750 Black, 52	BK-R1...	Black	51168	999	60	N/A	0	116	2	2	N
10133	Water Bottle - 30 oz.	WB-H0...	NULL	51169	870	7	N/A	0	252	22	22	N
10134	Patch Kit/8 Patches	PK-7098	NULL	51169	873	7	N/A	0	180	5	5	N

Figure 5-8. *Joining the product pull list to the Production.Product table*

Inline Table-Valued Functions

If scalar UDFs and multistatement TVFs aren't enough to get you excited about T-SQL's UDF capabilities, here comes a third form of UDF: the inline TVF. *Inline TVFs* are similar to multi-statement TVFs in that they return a tabular rowset result.

However, where a multistatement TVF can contain multiple SQL statements and control-of-flow statements in the function body, the inline function consists of only a single SELECT query. The inline TVF is literally "inlined" by SQL Server (expanded by the query optimizer as part of the SELECT statement that contains it), much like a view. In fact, because of this behavior, inline TVFs are sometimes referred to as *parameterized views*.

The inline TVF declaration must simply state that the result is a table via the RETURNS clause. The body of the inline TVF consists of a SQL query after a RETURN statement. Since the inline TVF returns the result of a single SELECT query, you don't need to bother with declaring a table variable or defining the return table structure. The structure of the result is implied by the SELECT query that makes up the body of the function.

The sample inline TVF I'll introduce performs a function commonly implemented by developers in T-SQL using control-of-flow statements. Many times, a developer will determine that a function or SP requires that a large or variable number of parameters be passed in to accomplish a particular goal. The ideal situation would be to pass an array as a parameter. T-SQL doesn't provide an "array" data type per se, but you can split a comma-delimited list of strings into a table to simulate an array. This gives you the flexibility of an "array" that you can use in SQL joins.

Tip SQL Server 2008 also allows table-valued parameters, which will be covered in Chapter 6 in the discussion of SPs. Because table-valued parameters have special requirements, they may not be optimal in all situations.

While you could do this using a multistatement TVF and control-of-flow statement such as a WHILE loop, you'll get better performance if you let SQL Server do the heavy lifting with a set-based solution. The sample function will accept a comma-delimited varchar(max) string and return a table with two columns, Num and Element, which are described following:

- The Num column contains a unique number for each element of the array, counting from 1 to the number of elements in the comma-delimited string.

- The Element column contains the substrings extracted from the comma-delimited list.

Listing 5-13 is the full code listing for the comma-separated string-splitting function. This function accepts a single parameter, which is a comma-delimited string like Ronnie,Bobbie,Ricky,Mike. The output is a table-like rowset with each comma-delimited item returned on its own row. To avoid looping and procedural constructs (which are not allowed in an inline TVF), I've used the same Numbers table created previously in Listing 5-10.

Listing 5-13. *Comma-Separated String-Splitting Function*

```
CREATE FUNCTION dbo.GetCommaSplit (@String nvarchar(max))
RETURNS table
AS
RETURN
(
  WITH Splitter (Num, String)
  AS
  (
    SELECT Num, SUBSTRING(@String,
      Num,
      CASE CHARINDEX(N',', @String, Num)
        WHEN 0 THEN LEN(@String) - Num + 1
        ELSE CHARINDEX(N',', @String, Num) - Num
      END
    ) AS String
  FROM dbo.Numbers
  WHERE Num <= LEN(@String)
    AND (SUBSTRING(@String, Num - 1, 1) = N',' OR Num = 0)
  )
```

```
SELECT
    ROW_NUMBER() OVER (ORDER BY Num) AS Num,
    RTRIM(LTRIM(String)) AS Element
  FROM Splitter
  WHERE String <> ''
);
GO
```

The inline TVF name and parameters are defined at the beginning of the CREATE FUNCTION statement. The RETURNS table clause specifies that the function returns a table. Notice that the structure of the table is not defined as it is with a multistatement TVF.

```
CREATE FUNCTION dbo.GetCommaSplit (@String varchar(max))
RETURNS table
```

The body of the inline TVF consists of a single RETURN statement followed by a SELECT query. For this example, I used a CTE called Splitter to perform the actual splitting of the comma-delimited list. The query of the CTE returns each substring from the comma-delimited list. CASE expressions are required to handle two special cases, as follows:

- The first item in the list because it is not preceded by a comma

- The last item in the list because it is not followed by a comma

```
WITH Splitter (Num, String)
AS
(
  SELECT Num, SUBSTRING(@String,
    Num,
    CASE CHARINDEX(N',', @String, Num)
      WHEN 0 THEN LEN(@String) - Num + 1
      ELSE CHARINDEX(N',', @String, Num) - Num
    END
  ) AS String
  FROM dbo.Numbers
  WHERE Num <= LEN(@String)
    AND (SUBSTRING(@String, Num - 1, 1) = N',' OR Num = 0)
)
```

Finally, the query selects each ROW_NUMBER and Element from the CTE as the result to return to the caller. Extra space characters are stripped from the beginning and end of each string returned, and empty strings are ignored.

```
SELECT
    ROW_NUMBER() OVER (ORDER BY Num) AS Num,
    LTRIM(RTRIM(String)) AS Element
  FROM Splitter
  WHERE String <> ''
```

You can use this inline TVF to split up the Jackson family, as shown in Listing 5-14. The results are shown in Figure 5-9.

Listing 5-14. *Splitting Up the Jacksons*

```
SELECT Num, Element
FROM dbo.GetCommaSplit ('Michael,Tito,Jermaine,Marlon,Rebbie,➥
  Jackie,Janet,La Toya,Randy');
```

	Num	Element
1	1	Michael
2	2	Tito
3	3	Jermaine
4	4	Marlon
5	5	Rebbie
6	6	Jackie
7	7	Janet
8	8	La Toya
9	9	Randy

Figure 5-9. *Splitting up the Jacksons*

Or, possibly more usefully, you can use it to pull descriptions for a specific set of Adventure-Works products. A usage like this is good for front-end web page displays or business reports where end users can select multiple items for which they want data returned. Listing 5-15 retrieves product information for a comma-delimited list of AdventureWorks product numbers. The results are shown in Figure 5-10.

Listing 5-15. *Using the fnCommaSplit Function*

```
SELECT n.Num,
  p.Name,
  p.ProductNumber,
  p.Color,
  p.Size,
  p.SizeUnitMeasureCode,
  p.StandardCost,
  p.ListPrice
FROM Production.Product p
INNER JOIN dbo.GetCommaSplit('FR-R38R-52,FR-M94S-52,FR-M94B-44,BK-M68B-38') n
  ON p.ProductNumber = n.Element;
```

	Num	Name	ProductNum...	Color	Size	Size...	StandardC...	ListPrice
1	4	Mountain-200 Black, 38	BK-M68B-38	Black	38	CM	1251.9813	2294.9900
2	3	HL Mountain Frame - Black, 44	FR-M94B-44	Black	44	CM	699.0928	1349.6000
3	2	HL Mountain Frame - Silver, 48	FR-M94S-52	Silver	48	CM	706.8110	1364.5000
4	1	LL Road Frame - Red, 52	FR-R38R-52	Red	52	CM	187.1571	337.2200

Figure 5-10. *Using a comma-delimited list to retrieve product information*

Restrictions on User-Defined Functions

T-SQL imposes some restrictions on UDFs. In this section, I'll discuss these restrictions and some of the reasoning behind them.

Nondeterministic Functions

T-SQL prohibits the use of nondeterministic functions inside of UDFs. A *deterministic* function is one that returns the same value every time when passed a given set of parameters (or no parameters). A *nondeterministic* function can return different results with the same set of parameters passed to it. An example of a deterministic function is ABS, the mathematical absolute value function. Every time—and no matter how many times—you call ABS(-10), the result is always 10. This is the basic idea behind determinism.

On the flip side, there are functions that do not return the same value despite the fact that you pass in the same parameters, or no parameters. Built-in functions such as RAND (without a seed value) and NEWID are nondeterministic because they return a different result every time they are called. One hack that people sometimes use to try to circumvent this restriction is creating a view that invokes the nondeterministic function and selecting from that view inside their UDFs. While this may work to some extent, it is not recommended, as it could fail to produce the desired results or cause a significant performance hit, since SQL won't be able to cache or effectively index the results of nondeterministic functions. Also, if you create a computed column that tries to reference your UDF, the nondeterministic functions you are trying to access via your view can produce unpredictable results. If you need to use nondeterministic functions in your application logic, SPs are probably the better alternative. I'll discuss SPs in Chapter 6.

NONDETERMINISTIC FUNCTIONS IN A UDF

In SQL Server 2000, there were several restrictions on the use of nondeterministic system functions in UDFs. In SQL Server 2008, these restrictions are somewhat relaxed. In SQL Server 2008, you can use the nondeterministic system functions listed in the following table in your UDFs. One thing these system functions have in common is that they don't cause side effects or change the database state when you use them.

Nondeterministic System Functions Allowed in UDFs

@@CONNECTIONS	@@PACK_RECEIVED	@@TOTAL_WRITE
@@CPU_BUSY	@@PACK_SENT	CURRENT_TIMESTAMP
@@DBTS	@@PACKET_ERRORS	GET_TRANSMISSION_STATUS
@@IDLE	@@TIMETICKS	GETDATE
@@IO_BUSY	@@TOTAL_ERRORS	GETUTCDATE
@@MAX_CONNECTIONS	@@TOTAL_READ	

If you want to build an index on a view or computed column that uses a UDF, your UDF has to be deterministic. The requirements to make a UDF deterministic include the following:

- The UDF must be declared using the WITH SCHEMABINDING option. When a UDF is schema-bound, no changes are allowed to any tables or objects that it's dependent on without dropping the UDF first.

- Any functions that you refer to in your UDF must also be deterministic. This means that if you use a nondeterministic system function—such as GETDATE—in your UDF, it will be marked nondeterministic.

- You cannot invoke extended stored procedures (XPs) inside the function. This shouldn't be a problem, since XPs are deprecated and will be removed from a future version of SQL Server.

If your UDF meets all these criteria, you can check to see if SQL Server has marked it deterministic via the OBJECTPROPERTY function, with a query like the following:

```
SELECT OBJECTPROPERTY (OBJECT_ID('dbo.GetCommaSplit'), 'IsDeterministic');
```

The OBJECTPROPERTY function will return 0 if your UDF is nondeterministic and 1 if it is deterministic.

State of the Database

One of the restrictions on UDFs is that they are not allowed to change the state of the database or cause other side effects. This prohibition on side effects in UDFs means that you can't even execute PRINT statements from within a UDF. It also means that while you can query database tables and resources, you can't execute INSERT, UPDATE, MERGE, or DELETE statements against database tables. Some other restrictions include the following:

- You can't create temporary tables within a UDF. You can, however, create and modify table variables within the body of a UDF.

- You cannot execute `CREATE`, `ALTER`, or `DROP` on database tables from within a UDF.

- Dynamic SQL is not allowed within a UDF, although XPs and SQLCLR functions can be called.

- A TVF can return only a single table/result set. If you need to return more than one table/result set, you might be better served by an SP.

MORE ON SIDE EFFECTS

Although XPs and SQL CLR functions can be called from a UDF, Microsoft warns against depending on results returned by XPs and SQL CLR functions that cause side effects. If your XP or SQL CLR function modifies tables, alters the database schema, accesses the file system, changes system settings, or utilizes nondeterministic resources external to the database, you might get unpredictable results from your UDF. If you need to change database state or rely on side effects in your server-side code, consider using a SQL CLR function or a regular SP instead of a UDF.

The prohibition on UDF side effects extends to the SQL Server display and error systems. This means that you cannot use the T-SQL `PRINT` or `RAISERROR` statements within a UDF. The `PRINT` and `RAISERROR` statements are useful in debugging stored procedures and T-SQL code batches, but are unavailable for use in UDFs. One workaround that I often use is to temporarily move the body of my UDF code to an SP while testing. This gives me the ability to use `PRINT` and `RAISERROR` while testing and debugging code in development environments.

Variables and table variables created within UDFs have a well-defined scope and cannot be accessed outside of the UDF. Even if you have a recursive UDF, you cannot access the variables and table variables that were previously declared and assigned values by the calling function. If you need values that were generated by a UDF, you must pass them in as parameters to another UDF call or return them to the caller in the UDF result.

Summary

In this chapter, I discussed the three types of T-SQL UDFs and provided working examples of the different types. Scalar UDFs are analogous to mathematical functions that accept zero or more parameters and return a single scalar value for a result. You can use the standard SQL statements, as well as control-of-flow statements, in a scalar UDF. Multistatement TVFs allow control-of-flow statements as well, but return a table-style result set to the caller. You can use the result set returned by a multistatement TVF in `WHERE` and `JOIN` clauses. Finally, inline TVFs return table-style result sets to the caller as well; however, the body consists of a single `SELECT` query much like a SQL view. In fact, inline TVFs are sometimes referred to as parameterized views.

The type of UDF that you need to accomplish a given task depends on the problem you're trying to solve. For instance, if you need to calculate a single scalar value, a scalar UDF will do the job. On the other hand, if you need to perform complex calculations or manipulations and return a table, a multistatement TVF might be the correct choice.

I also discussed recursion in UDFs, including the 32-level recursion limit. Although 32 levels of recursion is the hard limit, for all practical purposes you should rarely—if ever—hit this limit. If you do find the need for recursion beyond 32 levels, you can replace recursive function calls with CTEs and other T-SQL constructs.

Finally, I talked about determinism and side effects in your UDFs. Specifically, your UDFs cannot cause side effects, and there are specific criteria that must be met in order for SQL Server to mark your UDFs as deterministic. Determinism is an important aspect to UDFs if you plan on using them in indexed views or computed columns.

In the next chapter, we will look at SPs—another tool that allows procedural T-SQL code to be consolidated into server-side units.

EXERCISES

1. [Fill in the blank] SQL Server supports three types of T-SQL UDFs: ___, ___, and ___.

2. [True/false] The RETURNS NULL ON NULL INPUT option is a performance-enhancing option available for use with scalar UDFs.

3. [True/false] The ENCRYPTION option provides a secure option that prevents anyone from reverse-engineering your source code.

4. [Choose all that apply] You are not allowed to do which of the following in a multistatement TVF:

    a. Execute a PRINT statement

    b. Call RAISERROR to generate an exception

    c. Declare a table variable

    d. Create a temporary table

5. The algebraic formula for converting Fahrenheit measurements to the Celsius scale is

    $$C = (F - 32.0) \cdot (5 \div 9)$$

    where F is the measurement in degrees Fahrenheit and C is the measurement in degrees Celsius. Write a deterministic scalar UDF that converts a measurement in degrees Fahrenheit to degrees Celsius. The UDF should accept a single float parameter and return a float result. You can use the OBJECTPROPERTY function to ensure that the UDF is deterministic.

■ ■ ■

CHAPTER 6

Stored Procedures

Stored procedures (SPs) have been a part of T-SQL from the beginning. SPs provide a means for creating server-side subroutines written in T-SQL. This chapter begins with a discussion of what SPs are and why you might want to use them, and continues with a discussion of SP creation and usage, including examples.

Introducing Stored Procedures

SPs are saved collections of one or more T-SQL statements stored on the server as code units. They are analogous to procedures or subroutines in procedural languages like Visual Basic or C#. And just like procedures in procedural languages, SPs give you the ability to effectively extend the language of SQL Server by letting you add named custom subroutines to your databases.

An SP declaration begins with the CREATE PROCEDURE keywords followed by the name of the SP. The name can specify a schema name and procedure name, or just a procedure name. If you don't specify a schema name when creating an SP, SQL Server will create it in the default schema for your login. It's a best practice to always specify the schema name so that your SPs are always created in the proper schema, rather than leaving it up to SQL Server. In a very primitive form of "version control," SQL Server allows you to also indicate a group number after the procedure name. SQL Server allows you to drop groups of procedures with the same name with a single DROP PROCEDURE statement.

Warning The group number option, specified during SP creation, is deprecated and will be removed from a future version of SQL Server. Don't use this option in new development, and start planning to update code that uses this option.

SPs, like the T-SQL user-defined functions (UDFs) discussed in Chapter 5, can accept parameter values from the caller. The parameters are specified in a comma-separated list following the procedure name in the CREATE PROCEDURE statement. Unlike UDFs, when you call an SP, you can specify the parameters in any order, and omit them altogether if you assigned a default value at creation time. You can also specify OUTPUT parameters, which return values back from the procedure. All of this makes SP parameters far more flexible than UDF parameters.

Each parameter is declared as a specific type and can also be declared as OUTPUT or with the VARYING keyword (for cursor parameters only). When calling SPs, you have two choices: you can specify parameters by position or by name. If you specify an unnamed parameter list,

the values are assigned based on position. If you specify named parameters in the format
@parameter = value, they can be in any order. If your parameter specifies a default value in its
declaration, you don't have to pass a value in for that parameter. Unlike UDFs, SPs don't
require the DEFAULT keyword as a placeholder to specify default values. Just leaving a parameter out when you call the SP will apply the default value to that parameter.

Unlike UDFs, which can return results only via the RETURN statement, SPs can communicate with the caller in a variety of ways:

- The RETURN statement of the SP can return an int value to the caller. Unlike UDFs, SPs
  do not require a RETURN statement. If the RETURN statement is left out of the SP, 0 is
  returned by default if no errors were raised during execution.

- SPs don't have the same restrictions on database side effects and determinism as do UDFs.
  SPs can read, write, delete, and update permanent tables. In this way, the caller and SP can
  communicate information to one another through the use of permanent tables.

- When a temporary table is created in an SP, that temporary table is available to any
  SPs called by that SP. Furthermore, they are accessible to any SPs subsequently called
  by those SPs. As an example, if dbo.MyProc1 creates a temporary table named #Temp
  and then calls dbo.MyProc2, dbo.MyProc2 will be able to access #Temp as well. If
  dbo.MyProc2 then calls dbo.MyProc3, dbo.MyProc3 will also have access to the same
  #Temp temporary table. This provides a useful method of passing an entire table of temporary results from one SP to another for further processing.

- Output parameters provide the primary method of retrieving scalar results from an SP.
  Parameters are specified as output parameters with the OUTPUT keyword.

- To return table-type results from an SP, the SP can return one or more result sets. Result
  sets are like virtual tables that can be accessed by the caller. Unlike views, updates to
  these result sets by applications do not change the underlying tables used to generate
  them. Also, unlike TVFs and inline functions that return a single table only, SPs can
  return multiple result sets with a single call.

SP RETURN STATEMENTS

Since the SP RETURN statement can't return tables, character data, decimal numbers, and so on, it is normally
used only to return an int status or error code. This is a good convention to follow, since most developers who
use your SPs will be expecting it. The normal practice, followed by most of SQL Server's system SPs, is to
return a value of 0 to indicate success and a nonzero value or an error code to indicate an error or a failure.

Calling Stored Procedures

You can call an SP without the EXECUTE keyword if it is the first statement in a batch. For
instance, if you have an SP named dbo.MyProc, you can call it like this:

dbo.MyProc;

On the other hand, you can invoke an SP from anywhere in a batch or from another SP with the EXECUTE statement. Calling it like the following will discard the int return value:

EXECUTE dbo.MyProc;

If you need the return value from the SP, you can use the following variation of EXECUTE to assign the return value to an int variable:

EXECUTE @variable = dbo.MyProc;

Listing 6-1 is a simple SP example that accepts an AdventureWorks employee's ID and returns the employee's full name and e-mail address via output parameters.

Listing 6-1. *Retrieving an Employee's Name and E-mail with an SP*

```
CREATE PROCEDURE dbo.GetEmployee (@BusinessEntityID int = 199,
  @Email_Address nvarchar(50) OUTPUT,
  @Full_Name nvarchar(100) OUTPUT)
AS
BEGIN
  -- Retrieve email address and full name from HumanResources.Employee table
  SELECT @Email_Address = ea.EmailAddress,
    @Full_Name = p.FirstName + ' ' + COALESCE(p.MiddleName,'') + ' ' + p.LastName
  FROM HumanResources.Employee e
  INNER JOIN Person.Person p
    ON e.BusinessEntityID = p.BusinessEntityID
  INNER JOIN Person.EmailAddress ea
    ON p.BusinessEntityID = ea.BusinessEntityID
  WHERE e.BusinessEntityID = @BusinessEntityID;

  -- Return a code of 1 when no match is found, 0 for success
  RETURN (
    CASE
      WHEN @Email_Address IS NULL THEN 1
        ELSE 0
      END
  );
END;
GO
```

The SP in the example, dbo.GetEmployee, accepts a business entity ID number as an input parameter and returns the corresponding employee's e-mail address and full name as output parameters. If the business entity ID number passed in is valid, the SP returns 0 as a return value; otherwise 1 is returned. Listing 6-2 shows a sample call to the dbo.GetEmployee SP, with results shown in Figure 6-1.

Listing 6-2. *Calling the dbo.GetEmployee SP*

```
-- Declare variables to hold the result
DECLARE @Email nvarchar(50),
  @Name nvarchar(100),
  @Result int;

-- Call procedure to get employee information
EXECUTE @Result = dbo.GetEmployee 123,
  @Email OUTPUT,
  @Name OUTPUT;

-- Display the results
SELECT @Result AS Result,
  @Email AS Email,
  @Name AS [Name];
```

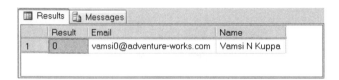

Figure 6-1. *Results of the sample dbo.GetEmployee SP call*

The sample SP call retrieves the information for the employee with ID number 123 in variables, and displays the results in a result set via SELECT. Notice that the OUTPUT keyword in the call to the SP is required after the two output parameters.

■Tip You don't *have* to wrap the body of your SP in a BEGIN...END block as I'm doing in these examples, but I personally think it makes the code more readable. It can also help when using the newest version of SSMS or third-party editors that provide collapsible code blocks, as described in Chapter 2.

As with UDFs, there are additional options you can specify when you create a procedure. The options include the following:

- The ENCRYPTION option obfuscates the SP text and helps prevent unauthorized users from accessing the obfuscated text. This option does for SPs what the UDF ENCRYPTION option does for functions.

- The RECOMPILE option prevents the SQL Server engine from caching the execution plan for the SP, forcing runtime compilation of your SP.

- The EXECUTE AS clause specifies the context that the SP will run under. You can specify CALLER, SELF, OWNER, or a specific username with the EXECUTE AS clause. These options are the same as they are for the UDF EXECUTE AS clause, described in Chapter 5.

Additionally, you can specify FOR REPLICATION to create an SP specifically for replication purposes. An SP created with the FOR REPLICATION option can't be executed on the replication subscriber. FOR REPLICATION can't be used with the RECOMPILE option.

Managing Stored Procedures

T-SQL provides two statements that allow you to modify and delete SPs: the ALTER PROCEDURE and DROP PROCEDURE statements, respectively. ALTER PROCEDURE allows you to modify the code for an SP without first dropping it. The syntax is the same as the CREATE PROCEDURE statement, except that the keywords ALTER PROCEDURE are used in place of CREATE PROCEDURE. ALTER PROCEDURE, like CREATE PROCEDURE, must always be the first statement in a batch.

To delete a procedure from your database, use the DROP PROCEDURE statement. Listing 6-3 shows how to drop the procedure created in Listing 6-1.

Listing 6-3. *Dropping the dbo.GetEmployee SP*

```
DROP PROCEDURE dbo.GetEmployee;
```

You can specify multiple SPs in a single DROP PROCEDURE statement by putting the SP names in a comma-separated list. Note that you cannot specify the database or server name when dropping an SP, and you must be in the database containing the SP in order to drop it. Additionally, as with other database objects, you can grant or deny EXECUTE permissions on an SP through the GRANT and DENY statements.

WHY STORED PROCEDURES?

Debates have raged through the years over the utility of SQL Server SPs. SPs cache and reuse query execution plans, which provided significant performance improvements in SQL Server 6.5 and 7.0. Although SQL Server 2008 SPs offer the same execution plan caching and reuse, the luster of this benefit has faded somewhat. Query optimization, query caching, and reuse of query execution plans for parameterized queries have been in a state of constant improvement since SQL Server 2000. Query optimization has been improved even more in SQL Server 2008. SPs still offer the performance benefit of not having to send large and complex queries over the network, but the primary benefit of query execution plan caching and reuse is not as enticing as it once was.

So why use SPs? Apart from the performance benefit, which is not as big a factor in these days of highly efficient parameterized queries, SPs offer code modularization and security. Creating code modules helps reduce redundant code, eliminating potential maintenance nightmares caused by duplicate code stored in multiple locations. By using SPs, you can deny users the capability to perform direct queries against tables, but still allow them to use SPs to retrieve the relevant data from those tables. SPs also offer the advantage of centralized administration of portions of your database code. Finally, SPs can return multiple result sets with a single procedure call, such as the sp_help system SP demonstrated here (the results are shown in the following illustration):

```
EXECUTE dbo.sp_help;
```

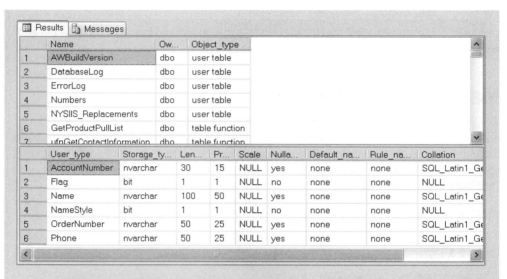

Using SPs, you can effectively build an application programming interface (API) for your database. Creation and adherence to such an API can help ensure consistent access across applications and make development easier for front-end and client-side developers who need to access your database. Some third-party applications, such as certain ETL programs and database drivers, also require SPs.

So what are the arguments against SPs? One major argument tends to be that they tightly couple your code to the DBMS. A code base that is tightly integrated with SQL Server 2008 will be more difficult to port over to another RDBMS (such as Oracle, DB2, or MySQL) in the future. A loosely coupled application, on the other hand, is much easier to port to different SQL DBMSs.

Portability, in turn, has its own problems. Truly portable code can result in databases and applications that are slow and inefficient. To get true portability out of any RDBMS system, you have to take great care to code everything in *plain vanilla* SQL, meaning that a lot of the platform-specific performance-enhancing functionality offered by SQL Server is off limits.

I'm not going to dive too deeply into a discussion of the pluses and minuses of SPs. In the end, the balance between portability and performance needs to be determined by your business needs and corporate IT policies on a per-project basis. Just keep these competing factors in mind when making that decision.

Stored Procedures in Action

A common application of SPs is to create a layer of abstraction for various data query, aggregation, and manipulation functionality. The example SP in Listing 6-4 performs the common business reporting task of calculating a running total. The results are shown in Figure 6-2.

Listing 6-4. *Procedure to Calculate and Retrieve Running Total for Sales*

```
CREATE PROCEDURE dbo.GetSalesRunningTotal (@Year int)
AS
BEGIN
  WITH RunningTotalCTE
  AS
```

```
  (
    SELECT soh.SalesOrderNumber,
      soh.OrderDate,
      soh.TotalDue,
      (
        SELECT SUM(soh1.TotalDue)
        FROM Sales.SalesOrderHeader soh1
        WHERE soh1.SalesOrderNumber <= soh.SalesOrderNumber
      ) AS RunningTotal,
      SUM(soh.TotalDue) OVER () AS GrandTotal
    FROM Sales.SalesOrderHeader soh
    WHERE DATEPART(year, soh.OrderDate) = @Year
    GROUP BY soh.SalesOrderNumber,
      soh.OrderDate,
      soh.TotalDue
  )
  SELECT rt.SalesOrderNumber,
    rt.OrderDate,
    rt.TotalDue,
    rt.RunningTotal,
    (rt.RunningTotal / rt.GrandTotal) * 100 AS PercentTotal
  FROM RunningTotalCTE rt
  ORDER BY rt.SalesOrderNumber;
  RETURN 0;
END;
GO

EXEC dbo.GetSalesRunningTotal @Year = 2001;
GO
```

	SalesOrderNumber	OrderDate	TotalDue	RunningTotal	PercentTotal
1	SO43659	2001-07-01 00:00:00.000	27231.5495	27231.5495	0.19
2	SO43660	2001-07-01 00:00:00.000	1716.1794	28947.7289	0.20
3	SO43661	2001-07-01 00:00:00.000	43561.4424	72509.1713	0.50
4	SO43662	2001-07-01 00:00:00.000	38331.9613	110841.1326	0.77
5	SO43663	2001-07-01 00:00:00.000	556.2026	111397.3352	0.77
6	SO43664	2001-07-01 00:00:00.000	32390.2031	143787.5383	1.00
7	SO43665	2001-07-01 00:00:00.000	19005.2087	162792.747	1.13
8	SO43666	2001-07-01 00:00:00.000	6718.051	169510.798	1.18
9	SO43667	2001-07-01 00:00:00.000	8095.7863	177606.5843	1.23
10	SO43668	2001-07-01 00:00:00.000	47815.6341	225422.2184	1.57
11	SO43669	2001-07-01 00:00:00.000	974.0229	226396.2413	1.58
12	SO43670	2001-07-01 00:00:00.000	8115.6763	234511.9176	1.63
13	SO43671	2001-07-01 00:00:00.000	10784.9873	245296.9049	1.71
14	SO43672	2001-07-01 00:00:00.000	8116.2564	253413.1613	1.76
15	SO43673	2001-07-01 00:00:00.000	4944.3422	258357.5035	1.80

Figure 6-2. *Partial results of the running total calculation for year 2001*

The SP in Listing 6-4 accepts a single `int` parameter indicating the year for which the calculation should be performed:

```
CREATE PROCEDURE dbo.GetSalesRunningTotal (@Year int)
```

Inside the SP, I've used a CTE to return the relevant data for the year specified, including calculations for the running total via a simple scalar subquery and the grand total via a `SUM` calculation with an `OVER` clause:

```
WITH RunningTotalCTE
AS
(
  SELECT soh.SalesOrderNumber,
    soh.OrderDate,
    soh.TotalDue,
    (
      SELECT SUM(soh1.TotalDue)
      FROM Sales.SalesOrderHeader soh1
      WHERE soh1.SalesOrderNumber <= soh.SalesOrderNumber
    ) AS RunningTotal,
    SUM(soh.TotalDue) OVER () AS GrandTotal
  FROM Sales.SalesOrderHeader soh
  WHERE DATEPART(year, soh.OrderDate) = @Year
  GROUP BY soh.SalesOrderNumber,
    soh.OrderDate,
    soh.TotalDue
)
```

The result set is returned by the CTE's outer `SELECT` query, and the SP finishes up with a `RETURN` statement that sends a return code of `0` back to the caller:

```
SELECT rt.SalesOrderNumber,
  rt.OrderDate,
  rt.TotalDue,
  rt.RunningTotal,
  (rt.RunningTotal / rt.GrandTotal) * 100 AS PercentTotal
FROM RunningTotalCTE rt
ORDER BY rt.SalesOrderNumber;
RETURN 0;
```

RUNNING SUMS

The *running sum*, or running total, is a very commonly used business reporting tool. A running sum calculates totals as of certain points in time (usually dollar amounts, and often calculated over days, months, quarters, or years—but not always). In Listing 6-4, the running sum is calculated per order, for each day over the course of a given year.

The running sum generated in the sample gives you a total sales amount as of the date and time when each order is placed. When the first order is placed, the running sum is equal to the amount of that order. When the second order is placed, the running sum is equal to the amount of the first order plus the amount of the second order, and so on. Another closely related and often used calculation is the *running average*, which represents a calculated point-in-time average as opposed to a point-in-time sum.

As an interesting aside, the ISO SQL standard allows you to use the OVER clause with aggregate functions like SUM and AVG. The ISO SQL standard allows the ORDER BY clause to be used with the aggregate function OVER clause, making for extremely efficient and compact running sum calculations. Unfortunately, SQL Server 2008 does not support this particular option, so you will still have to resort to subqueries and other less efficient methods of performing these calculations for now.

For the next example, assume that AdventureWorks management has decided to add a database-driven feature to its web site. The feature they want is a "recommended products list" that will appear when customers add products to their online shopping carts. Of course, the first step to implementing any solution is to clearly define the requirements. The details of the requirements-gathering process are beyond the scope of this book, so I'll work under the assumption that the AdventureWorks business analysts have done their due diligence and reported back the following business rules for this particular function:

- The recommended products list should include additional items on orders that contain the product selected by the customer. As an example, if the product selected by the customer is product ID 773 (the silver Mountain-100 44-inch bike), then items previously bought by other customers in conjunction with this bike—like product ID 712 (the AWC logo cap)—should be recommended.

- Products that are in the same category as the product the customer selected should not be recommended. As an example, if a customer has added a bicycle to an order, other bicycles should not be recommended.

- The recommended product list should never contain more than ten items.

- The default product ID should be 776, the black Mountain-100 42-inch bike.

- The recommended products should be listed in descending order of the total quantity that has been ordered. In other words, the best-selling items will be listed in the recommendations list first.

Listing 6-5 shows the SP that implements all of these business rules to return a list of recommended products based on a given product ID.

Listing 6-5. *Recommended Product List SP*

```
CREATE PROCEDURE dbo.GetProductRecommendations (@ProductID int = 776)
AS
BEGIN
    WITH RecommendedProducts
```

```
    (
      ProductID,
      ProductSubCategoryID,
      TotalQtyOrdered,
      TotalDollarsOrdered
    )
  AS
    (
      SELECT
          od2.ProductID,
          p1.ProductSubCategoryID,
          SUM(od2.OrderQty) AS TotalQtyOrdered,
          SUM(od2.UnitPrice * od2.OrderQty) AS TotalDollarsOrdered
      FROM Sales.SalesOrderDetail od1
      INNER JOIN Sales.SalesOrderDetail od2
          ON od1.SalesOrderID = od2.SalesOrderID
      INNER JOIN Production.Product p1
          ON od2.ProductID = p1.ProductID
      WHERE od1.ProductID = @ProductID
          AND od2.ProductID <> @ProductID
      GROUP BY
          od2.ProductID,
          p1.ProductSubcategoryID
    )
  SELECT TOP(10) ROW_NUMBER() OVER
  (
    ORDER BY rp.TotalQtyOrdered DESC
  ) AS Rank,
      rp.TotalQtyOrdered,
      rp.ProductID,
      rp.TotalDollarsOrdered,
      p.[Name]
  FROM RecommendedProducts rp
  INNER JOIN Production.Product p
      ON rp.ProductID = p.ProductID
  WHERE rp.ProductSubcategoryID <>
      (
          SELECT ProductSubcategoryID
          FROM Production.Product
          WHERE ProductID = @ProductID
      )
  ORDER BY TotalQtyOrdered DESC;
END;
GO
```

The SP begins with a declaration that accepts a single parameter, @ProductID. The default @ProductID is set to 776, per the AdventureWorks management team's rules:

```
CREATE PROCEDURE dbo.GetProductRecommendations (@ProductID int = 776)
```

Next, the CTE that will return the TotalQtyOrdered, ProductID, TotalDollarsOrdered, and ProductSubCategoryID for each product is defined:

```
WITH RecommendedProducts
  (
    ProductID,
    ProductSubCategoryID,
    TotalQtyOrdered,
    TotalDollarsOrdered
  )
```

In the body of the CTE, the Sales.SalesOrderDetail table is joined to itself based on SalesOrderID. A join to the Production.Product table is also included to get each product's SubcategoryID. The point of the self-join is to grab the total quantity ordered (OrderQty) and the total dollars ordered (UnitPrice * OrderQty) for each product.

The query is designed to include only orders that contain the product passed in via @ProductID in the WHERE clause, and it also eliminates results for @ProductID itself from the final results. All of the results are grouped by ProductID and ProductSubcategoryID:

```
  (
    SELECT
        od2.ProductID,
        p1.ProductSubCategoryID,
        SUM(od2.OrderQty) AS TotalQtyOrdered,
        SUM(od2.UnitPrice * od2.OrderQty) AS TotalDollarsOrdered
    FROM Sales.SalesOrderDetail od1
    INNER JOIN Sales.SalesOrderDetail od2
        ON od1.SalesOrderID = od2.SalesOrderID
    INNER JOIN Production.Product p1
        ON od2.ProductID = p1.ProductID
    WHERE od1.ProductID = @ProductID
        AND od2.ProductID <> @ProductID
    GROUP BY
        od2.ProductID,
        p1.ProductSubcategoryID
  )
```

The final part of the CTE excludes products that are in the same category as the item passed in by @ProductID. It then limits the results to the top ten and numbers the results from highest to lowest by TotalQtyOrdered. It also joins on the Production.Product table to get each product's name:

```
SELECT TOP(10) ROW_NUMBER() OVER
(
  ORDER BY rp.TotalQtyOrdered DESC
) AS Rank,
    rp.TotalQtyOrdered,
    rp.ProductID,
    rp.TotalDollarsOrdered,
    p.[Name]
```

```
FROM RecommendedProducts rp
INNER JOIN Production.Product p
    ON rp.ProductID = p.ProductID
WHERE rp.ProductSubcategoryID <>
    (
        SELECT ProductSubcategoryID
        FROM Production.Product
        WHERE ProductID = @ProductID
    )
ORDER BY TotalQtyOrdered DESC;
```

Figure 6-3 shows the result set of a recommended product list for people who bought a silver Mountain-100 44-inch bike (ProductID = 773), as shown in Listing 6-6.

Listing 6-6. *Getting a Recommended Product List*

```
EXECUTE dbo.GetProductRecommendations 773;
```

	Rank	TotalQtyOrde...	ProductID	TotalDollarsOrde...	Name
1	1	878	709	4861.72	Mountain Bike Socks, M
2	2	340	715	9762.4748	Long-Sleeve Logo Jersey, L
3	3	297	712	1538.3157	AWC Logo Cap
4	4	235	711	4743.8275	Sport-100 Helmet, Blue
5	5	201	708	4057.4865	Sport-100 Helmet, Black
6	6	177	707	3573.0105	Sport-100 Helmet, Red
7	7	156	716	4499.1024	Long-Sleeve Logo Jersey, XL
8	8	150	714	4326.06	Long-Sleeve Logo Jersey, M
9	9	148	748	106944.0452	HL Mountain Frame - Silver, 38
10	10	145	741	118711.50	HL Mountain Frame - Silver, 48

Figure 6-3. *Recommended product list for ProductID 773*

Implementing this business logic in an SP provides a layer of abstraction that makes it easier to use from front-end applications. Front-end application programmers don't need to worry about the details of which tables need to be accessed, how they need to be joined, and so on. All your application developers need to know to utilize this logic from the front end is that they need to pass the SP a ProductID number parameter and it will return the relevant information in a well-defined result set.

The same procedure can be reused if you want to use this same logic elsewhere. Also, if you need to change the business logic, it can be done one time, in one place. Consider what happens if the AdventureWorks management decides to make suggestions based on total dollars worth of a product ordered instead of the total quantity ordered. Simply change the ORDER BY clause from the following:

```
ORDER BY TotalQtyOrdered DESC;
```

to the following:

```
ORDER BY TotalDollarsOrdered DESC;
```

This simple change in the procedure does the trick. No additional changes to front-end code or logic are required, and no recompilation and redeployment of code to web server farms is required, since the interface to the SP remains the same.

Recursion in Stored Procedures

Like UDFs, SPs can call themselves recursively. There is a SQL Server–imposed limit of 32 levels of recursion. To demonstrate recursion, I'll solve a very old puzzle.

The Towers of Hanoi puzzle consists of three pegs and a specified number of discs of varying sizes that slide onto the pegs. The puzzle begins with the discs stacked on top of one another, from smallest to largest, all on one peg. The Towers of Hanoi puzzle start position is shown in Figure 6-4.

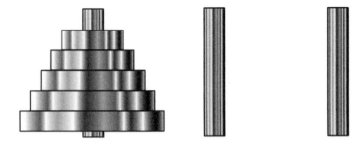

Figure 6-4. *The Towers of Hanoi puzzle start position*

The object of the puzzle is to move all of the discs from the first tower to the third tower. The trick is that you can only move one disc at a time, and no larger disc may be stacked on top of a smaller disc at any time. You can temporarily place discs on the middle tower as necessary, and you can stack any smaller disc on top of a larger disc on any tower. The Towers of Hanoi puzzle is often used as an exercise in computer science courses to demonstrate recursion in procedural languages. This makes it a perfect candidate for a T-SQL solution to demonstrate SP recursion.

My T-SQL implementation of the Towers of Hanoi puzzle will use five discs and display each move as the computer makes it. The complete T-SQL Towers of Hanoi puzzle solution is shown in Listing 6-7.

Listing 6-7. *The Towers of Hanoi Puzzle*

```
-- This stored procedure displays all the discs in the appropriate
-- towers.
CREATE PROCEDURE dbo.ShowTowers
AS
BEGIN

    -- Each disc is displayed like this "===3===" where the number is the disc
    -- and the width of the === signs on either side indicates the width of the
    -- disc.
```

```
-- These CTEs are designed for displaying the discs in proper order on each
-- tower.
WITH FiveNumbers(Num) -- Recursive CTE generates table with numbers 1...5
AS
(
  SELECT 1

  UNION ALL

  SELECT Num + 1
  FROM FiveNumbers
  WHERE Num < 5
),
GetTowerA (Disc)          -- The discs for Tower A
AS
(
  SELECT COALESCE(a.Disc, -1) AS Disc
  FROM FiveNumbers f
  LEFT JOIN #TowerA a
  ON f.Num = a.Disc
),
GetTowerB (Disc)          -- The discs for Tower B
AS
(
  SELECT COALESCE(b.Disc, -1) AS Disc
  FROM FiveNumbers f
  LEFT JOIN #TowerB b
  ON f.Num = b.Disc
),
GetTowerC (Disc)          -- The discs for Tower C
AS
(
  SELECT COALESCE(c.Disc, -1) AS Disc
  FROM FiveNumbers f
  LEFT JOIN #TowerC c
  ON f.Num = c.Disc
)
-- This SELECT query generates the text representation for all three towers
-- and all five discs. FULL OUTER JOIN is used to represent the towers in a
-- side-by-side format.
SELECT CASE a.Disc
    WHEN 5 THEN '  =====5=====  '
    WHEN 4 THEN '   ====4====   '
    WHEN 3 THEN '    ===3===    '
    WHEN 2 THEN '     ==2==     '
    WHEN 1 THEN '      =1=      '
```

```
        ELSE '    |    '
        END AS Tower_A,
      CASE b.Disc
        WHEN 5 THEN '  =====5===== '
        WHEN 4 THEN '   ====4====  '
        WHEN 3 THEN '   ===3===    '
        WHEN 2 THEN '    ==2==     '
        WHEN 1 THEN '     =1=      '
        ELSE '    |    '
        END AS Tower_B,
      CASE c.Disc
        WHEN 5 THEN '  =====5===== '
        WHEN 4 THEN '   ====4====  '
        WHEN 3 THEN '   ===3===    '
        WHEN 2 THEN '    ==2==     '
        WHEN 1 THEN '     =1=      '
        ELSE '    |    '
        END AS Tower_C
    FROM (
      SELECT ROW_NUMBER() OVER(ORDER BY Disc) AS Num,
        COALESCE(Disc, -1) AS Disc
      FROM GetTowerA
    ) a
    FULL OUTER JOIN (
      SELECT ROW_NUMBER() OVER(ORDER BY Disc) AS Num,
        COALESCE(Disc, -1) AS Disc
      FROM GetTowerB
    ) b
      ON a.Num = b.Num
    FULL OUTER JOIN (
      SELECT ROW_NUMBER() OVER(ORDER BY Disc) AS Num,
        COALESCE(Disc, -1) AS Disc
      FROM GetTowerC
    ) c
      ON b.Num = c.Num
    ORDER BY a.Num;
END;
GO


-- This SP moves a single disc from the specified source tower to the
-- specified destination tower.
CREATE PROCEDURE dbo.MoveOneDisc (@Source nchar(1),
  @Dest nchar(1))
AS
BEGIN
  -- @SmallestDisc is the smallest disc on the source tower
  DECLARE @SmallestDisc int = 0;
```

```
-- IF ... ELSE conditional statement gets the smallest disc from the
-- correct source tower
IF @Source = N'A'
BEGIN
  -- This gets the smallest disc from Tower A
  SELECT @SmallestDisc = MIN(Disc)
  FROM #TowerA;

  -- Then delete it from Tower A
  DELETE FROM #TowerA
  WHERE Disc = @SmallestDisc;
END
ELSE IF @Source = N'B'
BEGIN
  -- This gets the smallest disc from Tower B
  SELECT @SmallestDisc = MIN(Disc)
  FROM #TowerB;

  -- Then delete it from Tower B
  DELETE FROM #TowerB
  WHERE Disc = @SmallestDisc;
END
ELSE IF @Source = N'C'
BEGIN
  -- This gets the smallest disc from Tower C
  SELECT @SmallestDisc = MIN(Disc)
  FROM #TowerC;

  -- Then delete it from Tower C
  DELETE FROM #TowerC
  WHERE Disc = @SmallestDisc;
END

-- Show the disc move performed
SELECT N'Moving Disc (' + CAST(COALESCE(@SmallestDisc, 0) AS nchar(1)) +
  N') from Tower ' + @Source + N' to Tower ' + @Dest + ':' AS Description;

-- Perform the move - INSERT the disc from the source tower into the
-- destination tower
IF @Dest = N'A'
  INSERT INTO #TowerA (Disc) VALUES (@SmallestDisc);
ELSE IF @Dest = N'B'
  INSERT INTO #TowerB (Disc) VALUES (@SmallestDisc);
ELSE IF @Dest = N'C'
  INSERT INTO #TowerC (Disc) VALUES (@SmallestDisc);
```

```sql
  -- Show the towers
  EXECUTE dbo.ShowTowers;
END;
GO


-- This SP moves multiple discs recursively
CREATE PROCEDURE dbo.MoveDiscs (@DiscNum int,
  @MoveNum int OUTPUT,
  @Source nchar(1) = N'A',
  @Dest nchar(1) = N'C',
  @Aux nchar(1) = N'B'
)
AS
BEGIN
  -- If the number of discs to move is 0, the solution has been found
  IF @DiscNum = 0
    PRINT N'Done';
  ELSE
  BEGIN
    -- If the number of discs to move is 1, go ahead and move it
    IF @DiscNum = 1
    BEGIN

      -- Increase the move counter by 1
      SELECT @MoveNum += 1;

      -- And finally move one disc from source to destination
      EXEC dbo.MoveOneDisc @Source, @Dest;
    END
    ELSE
    BEGIN
      -- Determine number of discs to move from source to auxiliary tower
      DECLARE @n int = @DiscNum - 1;

      -- Move (@DiscNum - 1) discs from source to auxiliary tower
      EXEC dbo.MoveDiscs @n, @MoveNum OUTPUT, @Source, @Aux, @Dest;

      -- Move 1 disc from source to final destination tower
      EXEC dbo.MoveDiscs 1, @MoveNum OUTPUT, @Source, @Dest, @Aux;

      -- Move (@DiscNum - 1) discs from auxiliary to final destination tower
      EXEC dbo.MoveDiscs @n, @MoveNum OUTPUT, @Aux, @Dest, @Source;
    END;
  END;
END;
GO
```

```
-- This SP creates the three towers and populates Tower A with 5 discs
CREATE PROCEDURE dbo.SolveTowers
AS
BEGIN
  -- SET NOCOUNT ON to eliminate system messages that will clutter up
  -- the Message display
  SET NOCOUNT ON;

  -- Create the three towers: Tower A, Tower B, and Tower C
  CREATE TABLE #TowerA (Disc int PRIMARY KEY NOT NULL);
  CREATE TABLE #TowerB (Disc int PRIMARY KEY NOT NULL);
  CREATE TABLE #TowerC (Disc int PRIMARY KEY NOT NULL);

  -- Populate Tower A with all five discs
  INSERT INTO #TowerA (Disc)
  VALUES (1), (2), (3), (4), (5);

  -- Initialize the move number to 0
  DECLARE @MoveNum int = 0;

  -- Show the initial state of the towers
  EXECUTE dbo.ShowTowers;

  -- Solve the puzzle. Notice you don't need to specify the parameters
  -- with defaults
  EXECUTE dbo.MoveDiscs 5, @MoveNum OUTPUT;

  -- How many moves did it take?
  PRINT N'Solved in ' + CAST (@MoveNum AS nvarchar(10)) + N' moves.';

  -- Drop the temp tables to clean up - always a good idea.
  DROP TABLE #TowerC;
  DROP TABLE #TowerB;
  DROP TABLE #TowerA;

  -- SET NOCOUNT OFF before we exit
  SET NOCOUNT OFF;
END;
GO
```

To solve the puzzle, just run the following statement:

```
-- Solve the puzzle
EXECUTE dbo.SolveTowers;
```

Figure 6-5 is a screenshot of the processing as the discs are moved from tower to tower.

Note The results of Listing 6-7 are best viewed in Results to Text mode. You can put SSMS in Results to Text mode by pressing Ctrl+T while in the Query Editor window. To switch to Results to Grid mode, press Ctrl+D.

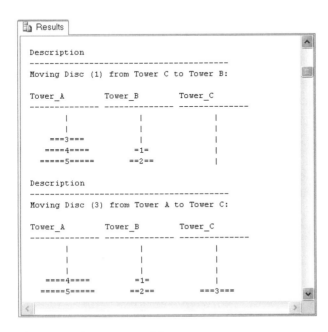

Figure 6-5. *Discs are moved from tower to tower*

The main procedure you call to solve the puzzle is dbo.SolveTowers. This SP creates three temporary tables, named #TowerA, #TowerB, and #TowerC. It then populates #TowerA with five discs and initializes the current move number to 0.

```
-- Create the three towers: Tower A, Tower B, and Tower C
CREATE TABLE #TowerA (Disc int PRIMARY KEY NOT NULL);
CREATE TABLE #TowerB (Disc int PRIMARY KEY NOT NULL);
CREATE TABLE #TowerC (Disc int PRIMARY KEY NOT NULL);

-- Populate Tower A with all five discs
INSERT INTO #TowerA (Disc)
VALUES (1), (2), (3), (4), (5);

-- Initialize the move number to 0
DECLARE @MoveNum INT = 0;
```

Since this SP is the entry point for the entire puzzle-solving program, it displays the start position of the towers and calls dbo.MoveDiscs to get the ball rolling:

```
-- Show the initial state of the towers
EXECUTE dbo.ShowTowers;

-- Solve the puzzle. Notice you don't need to specify the parameters
-- with defaults
EXECUTE dbo.MoveDiscs 5, @MoveNum OUTPUT;
```

When the puzzle is finally solved, control returns back from dbo.MoveDiscs to dbo.SolveTowers, which displays the number of steps it took to complete the puzzle and performs some cleanup work, like dropping the temporary tables.

```
-- How many moves did it take?
PRINT N'Solved in ' + CAST (@MoveNum AS nvarchar(10)) + N' moves.';

-- Drop the temp tables to clean up - always a good idea.
DROP TABLE #TowerC;
DROP TABLE #TowerB;
DROP TABLE #TowerA;

-- SET NOCOUNT OFF before we exit
SET NOCOUNT OFF;
```

■Tip When an SP that created temporary tables ends, the temporary tables are automatically dropped. Because temporary tables are created in the tempdb system database, it's a good idea to get in the habit of explicitly dropping temporary tables. By explicitly dropping temporary tables, you can guarantee that they exist only as long as they are needed, which can help minimize contention in the tempdb database.

The procedure responsible for moving discs from tower to tower recursively is dbo.MoveDiscs. This procedure accepts several parameters, including the number of discs to move (@DiscNum); the number of the current move (@MoveNum); and the names of the source, destination, and auxiliary/intermediate towers. This procedure uses T-SQL procedural IF statements to determine which types of moves are required—single disc moves, recursive multiple-disc moves, or no more moves (when the solution is found). If the solution has been found, the message Done is displayed and control is subsequently passed back to the calling procedure, dbo.SolveTowers.

```
-- If the number of discs to move is 0, the solution has been found
IF @DiscNum = 0
  PRINT N'Done';
ELSE
. . .
RETURN 0;
```

If there is only one disc to move, the move counter is incremented and dbo.MoveOneDisc is called to perform the move:

```
-- If the number of discs to move is 1, go ahead and move it
IF @DiscNum = 1
BEGIN

  -- Increase the move counter by 1
  SELECT @MoveNum += 1;

  -- And finally move one disc from source to destination
  EXEC dbo.MoveOneDisc @Source, @Dest;
END
```

Finally, if there is more than one disc move required, dbo.MoveDiscs calls itself recursively until there are either one or zero discs left to move:

```
ELSE
BEGIN
  -- Determine number of discs to move from source to auxiliary tower
  DECLARE @n INT = @DiscNum - 1;

  -- Move (@DiscNum - 1) discs from source to auxiliary tower
  EXEC dbo.MoveDiscs @n, @MoveNum OUTPUT, @Source, @Aux, @Dest;

  -- Move 1 disc from source to final destination tower
  EXEC dbo.MoveDiscs 1, @MoveNum OUTPUT, @Source, @Dest, @Aux;

  -- Move (@DiscNum - 1) discs from auxiliary to final destination tower
  EXEC dbo.MoveDiscs @n, @MoveNum OUTPUT, @Aux, @Dest, @Source;
END;
```

The basis of the Towers of Hanoi puzzle is the movement of a single disc at a time from tower to tower, so the most basic procedure, dbo.MoveOneDisc, simply moves a disc from the specified source tower to the specified destination tower. Given a source and destination tower as inputs, this procedure first determines the smallest (or top) disc on the source and moves it to the destination table using simple SELECT queries. The smallest disc is then deleted from the source table.

```
-- @SmallestDisc is the smallest disc on the source tower
DECLARE @SmallestDisc int = 0;

-- IF ... ELSE conditional statement gets the smallest disc from the
-- correct source tower
IF @Source = N'A'
BEGIN
  -- This gets the smallest disc from Tower A
  SELECT @SmallestDisc = MIN(Disc)
  FROM #TowerA;
```

```
    -- Then delete it from Tower A
    DELETE FROM #TowerA
    WHERE Disc = @SmallestDisc;
END
. . .
```

Once the smallest disc of the source table is determined, dbo.MoveOneDisc displays the move it is about to perform, and then performs the INSERT to place the disc in the destination tower. Finally, it calls the dbo.ShowTowers procedure to show the current state of the towers and discs.

```
-- Show the disc move performed
SELECT N'Moving Disc (' + CAST(COALESCE(@SmallestDisc, 0) AS nchar(1)) +
  N') from Tower ' + @Source + N' to Tower ' + @Dest + ':' AS Description;

-- Perform the move - INSERT the disc from the source tower into the
-- destination tower
IF @Dest = N'A'
  INSERT INTO #TowerA (Disc) VALUES (@SmallestDisc);
ELSE IF @Dest = N'B'
  INSERT INTO #TowerB (Disc) VALUES (@SmallestDisc);
ELSE IF @Dest = N'C'
  INSERT INTO #TowerC (Disc) VALUES (@SmallestDisc);

-- Show the towers
EXECUTE dbo.ShowTowers;
```

The dbo.ShowTowers procedure doesn't affect processing; it's simply included as a convenience to output a reasonable representation of the towers and discs they contain at any given point during processing.

This implementation of a solver for the Towers of Hanoi puzzle demonstrates several aspects of SPs I've introduced in this chapter, including the following:

- SPs can call themselves recursively. This is demonstrated with the dbo.MoveDiscs procedure, which calls itself until the puzzle is solved.

- When default values are assigned to parameters in an SP declaration, you do not have to specify values for them when you call the procedure. This concept is demonstrated in the dbo.SolveTowers procedure, which calls the dbo.MoveDiscs procedure.

- The scope of temporary tables created in an SP include the procedure in which they are created, as well as any SPs it calls, and any SPs they in turn call. This is demonstrated in dbo.SolveTowers, which creates three temporary tables, and then calls other procedures that access those same temporary tables. The procedures called by dbo.SolveTowers and those called by those procedures (and so on) can also access these same temporary tables.

- The dbo.MoveDiscs SP demonstrates output parameters. This procedure uses an output parameter to update the count of the total number of moves performed after each move.

Table-Valued Parameters

Beginning with SQL Server 2008, developers now have the capability of passing table-valued parameters to SPs and UDFs. Prior to SQL Server 2008, the primary methods of passing multiple rows of data to an SP included the following:

- Converting your multiple rows to an intermediate format like comma-delimited or XML. If you use this method, you have to parse out the parameter into a temporary table, table variable, or subquery to extract the rows from the intermediate format. These conversions to and from intermediate format can be costly, especially when large amounts of data are involved.

- Placing rows in a permanent or temporary table and calling the procedure. This method eliminates conversions to and from the intermediate format, but is not without problems of its own. Managing multiple sets of input rows from multiple simultaneous users can introduce a lot of overhead and additional conversion code that must be managed.

- Passing lots and lots of parameters to the SP. SQL Server SPs can accept up to 2,100 parameters. Conceivably, you could pass several rows of data using thousands of parameters and ignore those parameters you don't need. One big drawback to this method, however, is that it results in complex code that can be extremely difficult to manage.

- Calling procedures multiple times with a single row of data each time. This method is probably the simplest method, resulting in code that is very easy to create and manage. The downside to this method is that querying and manipulating potentially tens of thousands of rows of data or more, one row at a time, can result in a big performance penalty.

SQL Server 2008 table-valued parameters offer a new option. A table-valued parameter allows you to pass rows of data to your SPs and UDFs in tabular format. To create a table-valued parameter you must first create a *table type* that defines your table structure, as shown in Listing 6-8.

Listing 6-8. *Creating a Table Type*

```
CREATE TYPE HumanResources.LastNameTableType
AS TABLE (LastName nvarchar(50) NOT NULL PRIMARY KEY);
GO
```

The CREATE TYPE statement in Listing 6-8 creates a simple table type that represents a table with a single column named LastName, which also serves as the primary key for the table. To use table-valued parameters, you must declare your SP with parameters of the table type. The SP in Listing 6-9 accepts a single table-valued parameter of the HumanResources. LastNameTableType type from Listing 6-8. It then uses the rows in the table-valued parameter in an inner join to restrict the rows returned by the SP.

Listing 6-9. *Simple Procedure Accepting a Table-Valued Parameter*

```
CREATE PROCEDURE HumanResources.GetEmployees
  (@LastNameTable HumanResources.LastNameTableType READONLY)
AS
BEGIN
  SELECT
    p.LastName,
    p.FirstName,
    p.MiddleName,
    e.NationalIDNumber,
    e.Gender,
    e.HireDate
  FROM HumanResources.Employee e
  INNER JOIN Person.Person p
    ON e.BusinessEntityID = p.BusinessEntityID
  INNER JOIN @LastNameTable lnt
    ON p.LastName = lnt.LastName
  ORDER BY
    p.LastName,
    p.FirstName,
    p.MiddleName;
END
GO
```

The `CREATE PROCEDURE` statement in Listing 6-9 declares a single table-valued parameter, `@LastNameTable`, of the `HumanResources.LastNameTableType` created in Listing 6-8.

```
CREATE PROCEDURE HumanResources.GetEmployees
  (@LastNameTable HumanResources.LastNameTableType READONLY)
```

The table-valued parameter is declared `READONLY`, which is mandatory. Although you can query and join to the rows in a table-valued parameter just like a table variable, you cannot manipulate the rows in table-valued parameters with `INSERT`, `UPDATE`, `DELETE`, or `MERGE` statements.

The `HumanResources.GetEmployees` procedure performs a simple query to retrieve the names, national ID number, gender, and hire date for all employees whose last names match any of the last names passed into the SP via the `@LastNameTable` table-valued parameter. As you can see in Listing 6-9, the `SELECT` query performs an inner join against the table-valued parameter to restrict the rows returned:

```
SELECT
  p.LastName,
  p.FirstName,
  p.MiddleName,
  e.NationalIDNumber,
  e.Gender,
  e.HireDate
FROM HumanResources.Employee e
```

```
INNER JOIN Person.Person p
  ON e.BusinessEntityID = p.BusinessEntityID
INNER JOIN @LastNameTable lnt
  ON p.LastName = lnt.LastName
ORDER BY
  p.LastName,
  p.FirstName,
  p.MiddleName;
```

To call a procedure with a table-valued parameter, like the `HumanResources.GetEmployees` SP in Listing 6-9, you need to declare a variable of the same type as the table-valued parameter. Then you populate the variable with rows of data and pass the variable as a parameter to the procedure. Listing 6-10 demonstrates how to call the `HumanResources.GetEmployees` SP with a table-valued parameter. The results are shown in Figure 6-6.

Listing 6-10. *Calling a Procedure with a Table-Valued Parameter*

```
DECLARE @LastNameList HumanResources.LastNameTableType;

INSERT INTO @LastNameList
  (LastName)
VALUES
  (N'Walters'),
  (N'Anderson'),
  (N'Chen'),
  (N'Rettig'),
  (N'Lugo'),
  (N'Zwilling'),
  (N'Johnson');

EXECUTE HumanResources.GetEmployees @LastNameList;
```

	LastName	FirstNa...	MiddleNa...	NationalIDNum...	Gen...	HireDate
1	Anderson	Nancy	A	693325305	F	1999-02-03 00:00:00.000
2	Chen	Hao	O	416679555	M	1999-03-10 00:00:00.000
3	Chen	John	Y	305522471	M	1999-03-13 00:00:00.000
4	Johnson	Barry	K	912265825	M	1998-02-07 00:00:00.000
5	Johnson	David	N	498138869	M	1999-01-03 00:00:00.000
6	Johnson	Willis	T	332040978	M	1999-01-14 00:00:00.000
7	Lugo	Jose	R	788456780	M	1999-03-14 00:00:00.000
8	Rettig	Bjorn	M	420023788	M	1999-02-08 00:00:00.000
9	Walters	Rob	NULL	112457891	M	1998-01-05 00:00:00.000
10	Zwilling	Michael	J	582347317	M	2000-03-26 00:00:00.000

Figure 6-6. *Employees returned by the SP call in Listing 6-10*

In addition to being read-only, the following additional restrictions apply to table-valued parameters:

- As with table variables, you cannot use a table-valued parameter as the target of a SET or SELECT assignment statement.

- Table-valued parameters are scoped just like other parameters and local variables declared within a procedure or function. They are not visible outside of the procedure in which they are declared.

- SQL Server does not maintain column-level statistics for table-valued parameters, which can affect performance if you are passing large numbers of rows of data via table-valued parameters.

You can also pass table-valued parameters to SPs from ADO.NET clients, which I will discuss in Chapter 15.

Temporary Stored Procedures

In addition to normal SPs, T-SQL provides what are known as *temporary SPs*. Temporary SPs are created just like any other SPs; the only difference is that the name must begin with a number sign (#) for a local temporary SP and two number signs (##) for a global temporary SP.

While a normal SP remains in the database and schema it was created in until it is explicitly dropped via the DROP PROCEDURE statement, temporary SPs are dropped automatically. A local temporary SP is visible only to the current session and is dropped when the current session ends. A global temporary SP is visible to all connections and is automatically dropped when the last session using it ends.

Normally you won't use temporary SPs, as they are usually used for specialized solutions like database drivers. Open Database Connectivity (ODBC) drivers, for instance, make use of temporary SPs to implement SQL Server connectivity functions.

Recompilation and Caching

SQL Server has several features that work behind the scenes to optimize your SP performance. The first time you execute an SP, SQL Server compiles it into a query plan, which it then caches. This compilation process invokes a certain amount of overhead, which can be substantial for procedures that are complex or that are run very often. SQL Server uses a complex caching mechanism to store and reuse query plans on subsequent calls to the same SP, in an effort to minimize the impact of SP compilation overhead. In this section, I'll talk about managing query plan recompilation and cached query plan reuse.

Stored Procedure Statistics

SQL Server 2008 provides *dynamic management views (DMVs)* and *dynamic management functions (DMFs)* to expose SP query plan usage and caching information that can be useful for performance tuning and general troubleshooting. Listing 6-11 is a procedure that retrieves and displays several relevant SP statistics from a few different DMVs and DMFs.

Listing 6-11. *Procedure to Retrieve SP Statistics with DMVs and DMFs*

```
CREATE PROCEDURE dbo.GetProcStats (@order varchar(100) = 'use')
AS
BEGIN
  WITH GetQueryStats
  (
    plan_handle,
    total_elapsed_time,
    total_logical_reads,
    total_logical_writes,
    total_physical_reads
  )
  AS
  (
    SELECT
      qs.plan_handle,
      SUM(qs.total_elapsed_time) AS total_elapsed_time,
      SUM(qs.total_logical_reads) AS total_logical_reads,
      SUM(qs.total_logical_writes) AS total_logical_writes,
      SUM(qs.total_physical_reads) AS total_physical_reads
    FROM sys.dm_exec_query_stats qs
    GROUP BY qs.plan_handle
  )
  SELECT
    DB_NAME(st.dbid) AS database_name,
    OBJECT_SCHEMA_NAME(st.objectid, st.dbid) AS schema_name,
    OBJECT_NAME(st.objectid, st.dbid) AS proc_name,
    SUM(cp.usecounts) AS use_counts,
    SUM(cp.size_in_bytes) AS size_in_bytes,
    SUM(qs.total_elapsed_time) AS total_elapsed_time,
    CAST
    (
      SUM(qs.total_elapsed_time) AS decimal(38, 4)
    ) / SUM(cp.usecounts) AS avg_elapsed_time_per_use,
    SUM(qs.total_logical_reads) AS total_logical_reads,
    CAST
    (
      SUM(qs.total_logical_reads) AS decimal(38, 4)
    ) / SUM(cp.usecounts) AS avg_logical_reads_per_use,
    SUM(qs.total_logical_writes) AS total_logical_writes,
    CAST
    (
      SUM(qs.total_logical_writes) AS decimal(38, 4)
    ) / SUM(cp.usecounts) AS avg_logical_writes_per_use,
    SUM(qs.total_physical_reads) AS total_physical_reads,
    CAST
```

```
    (
        SUM(qs.total_physical_reads) AS decimal(38, 4)
    ) / SUM(cp.usecounts) AS avg_physical_reads_per_use,
    st.text
FROM sys.dm_exec_cached_plans cp
CROSS APPLY sys.dm_exec_sql_text(cp.plan_handle) st
INNER JOIN GetQueryStats qs
    ON cp.plan_handle = qs.plan_handle
INNER JOIN sys.procedures p
    ON st.objectid = p.object_id
    WHERE p.type IN ('P', 'PC')
    GROUP BY st.dbid, st.objectid, st.text
    ORDER BY
        CASE @order
            WHEN 'name' THEN OBJECT_NAME(st.objectid)
            WHEN 'size' THEN SUM(cp.size_in_bytes)
            WHEN 'read' THEN SUM(qs.total_logical_reads)
            WHEN 'write' THEN SUM(qs.total_logical_writes)
            ELSE SUM(cp.usecounts)
        END DESC;
END
GO
```

This procedure uses the `sys.dm_exec_cached_plans` and `sys.dm_exec_query_stats` DMVs in conjunction with the `sys.dm_exec_sql_text` DMF to retrieve relevant SP execution information. The `sys.procedures` catalog view is used to limit the results to only SPs (type P). Aggregation is required on most of the statistics since the DMVs and DMFs can return multiple rows, each representing individual statements within SPs. The `dbo.GetProcStats` procedure accepts a single parameter that determines how the result rows are sorted. Setting the `@order` parameter to `size` sorts the results in descending order by the `size_in_bytes` column, while `read` sorts in descending order by the `total_logical_reads` column. Other possible values include `name` and `write`—all other values sort by the default `use_counts` column in descending order.

Tip In this SP, I used a few useful system functions: `DB_NAME` accepts the ID of a database and returns the database name; `OBJECT_SCHEMA_NAME` accepts the ID of an object and a database ID, and returns the name of the schema in which the object resides; and `OBJECT_NAME` accepts the object ID and returns the name of the object itself. These are handy convenience functions, and you can retrieve the same information via SQL Server's catalog views.

Listing 6-12 demonstrates how to call this SP. Sample results are shown in Figure 6-7.

Listing 6-12. *Retrieving SP Statistics*

```
EXEC dbo.GetProcStats @order = 'use';
GO
```

	database_name	schema_name	proc_name	use_counts	size_i...	total_elapsed_time	avg_elapsed_time_per_use	total
1	AdventureWorks...	dbo	ShowTowers	96	540672	448430	4671.145833	1320
2	AdventureWorks...	dbo	MoveOneDisc	93	491520	78246	841.354838	388
3	AdventureWorks...	dbo	GetProcStats	10	245760	2022451	202245.100000	8015
4	AdventureWorks...	HumanReso...	GetEmployees	7	57344	79252	11321.714285	4074
5	AdventureWorks...	dbo	SolveTowers	3	98304	2006	668.666666	44
6	AdventureWorks...	dbo	SolveSodoku	1	565248	65207	65207.000000	694

Figure 6-7. *Partial results of calling the GetProcStats procedure*

SQL Server DMVs and DMFs can be used in this way to answer several questions about your SPs, including the following:

- Which SPs are executed the most?

- Which SPs take the longest to execute?

- Which SPs perform the most logical reads and writes?

The answers to these types of questions can help you quickly locate performance bottle-necks and focus your performance-tuning efforts where they are most needed.

Parameter Sniffing

SQL Server uses a method known as *parameter sniffing* to further optimize SP calls. During compilation or recompilation of an SP, SQL Server captures the parameters used and passes the values along to the optimizer. The optimizer then generates and caches a query plan optimized for those parameters. This can actually cause problems in some cases—for example, when your SP can return wildly varying numbers of rows based on the parameters passed in. Listing 6-13 shows a simple SP that retrieves all products from the Production.Product table with a Name like the @Prefix parameter passed into the SP.

Listing 6-13. *Simple Procedure to Demonstrate Parameter Sniffing*

```
CREATE PROCEDURE Production.GetProductsByName
  @Prefix NVARCHAR(100)
AS
BEGIN
  SELECT
    p.Name,
    p.ProductID
  FROM Production.Product p
  WHERE p.Name LIKE @Prefix;
END
GO
```

Calling this SP with the @Prefix parameter set to % results in a query plan optimized to return 504 rows of data with a nonclustered index scan, as shown in Figure 6-8.

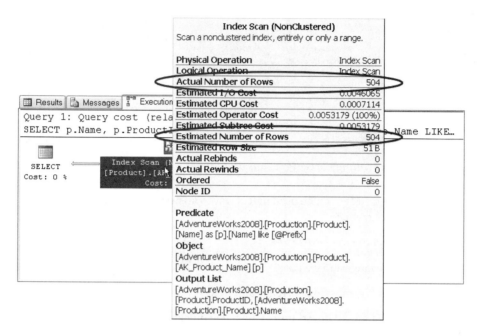

Figure 6-8. *Query plan optimized to return 504 rows*

If you run the Production.GetProductsByName procedure a second time with the @Prefix parameter set to M%, the query plan will show that the plan is still optimized to return 504 estimated rows, although only 102 rows are actually returned by the SP. Figure 6-9 shows the query plan for the second procedure call.

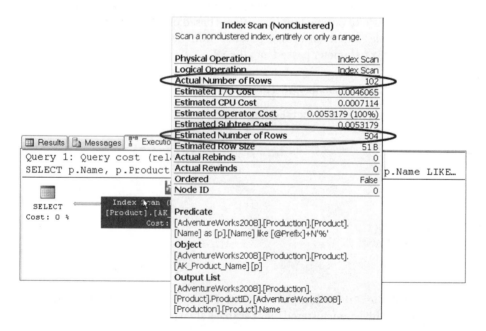

Figure 6-9. *Query plan optimized for the wrong number of rows*

In cases where you expect widely varying numbers of rows to be returned by your SPs, you can override parameter sniffing on a per-procedure basis. Overriding parameter sniffing is simple—just declare a local variable in your SP, assign the parameter value to the variable, and use the variable in place of the parameter in your query. When you override parameter sniffing, SQL Server uses the source table data distribution statistics to estimate the number of rows to return. The theory is that the estimate will be better for a wider variety of possible parameter values. In this case, the estimate will still be considerably off for the extreme case of the 504 rows returned in this example, but it will be much closer and will therefore generate better query plans for other possible parameter values. Listing 6-14 alters the SP in Listing 6-13 to override parameter sniffing. Figure 6-10 shows the results of calling the updated SP with a @Prefix parameter of M%.

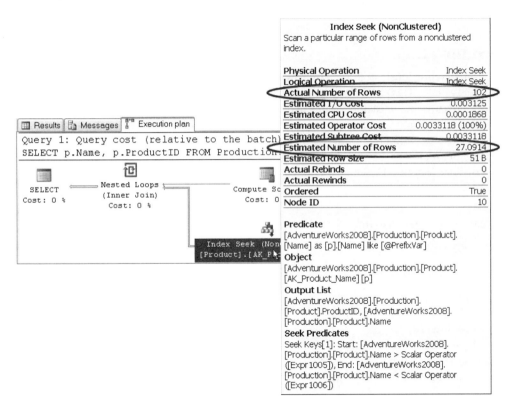

Figure 6-10. *Results of the SP with parameter sniffing overridden*

Listing 6-14. *Overriding Parameter Sniffing in an SP*

```
ALTER PROCEDURE Production.GetProductsByName
  @Prefix NVARCHAR(100)
AS
BEGIN
  DECLARE @PrefixVar NVARCHAR(100) = @Prefix;
```

```
  SELECT
    p.Name,
    p.ProductID
  FROM Production.Product p
  WHERE p.Name LIKE @PrefixVar;
END
GO
```

With parameter sniffing overridden, the query plan for the SP in Listing 6-14 uses the same estimated number of rows, in this case 27.0914, no matter what value you pass in the @Prefix parameter. This results in a query plan that uses a nonclustered index seek—not an index scan—which is a much better query plan for the vast majority of possible parameter values for this particular SP.

Recompilation

As I discussed previously in this chapter, SQL Server optimizes performance by caching compiled query plans. This eliminates the overhead associated with recompiling your query on subsequent runs, but occasionally this feature can cause performance to suffer. When you expect your SP to return widely varying numbers of rows in the result set with each call, the cached query execution plan will only be optimized for the first call. It won't be optimized for subsequent executions. In cases like this, you may decide to force recompilation with each call. Consider Listing 6-15, which is an SP that returns order header information for a given salesperson.

Listing 6-15. *SP to Retrieve Orders by Salesperson*

```
CREATE PROCEDURE Sales.GetSalesBySalesPerson (@SalesPersonId int)
AS
BEGIN
  SELECT
    soh.SalesOrderID,
    soh.OrderDate,
    soh.TotalDue
  FROM Sales.SalesOrderHeader soh
  WHERE soh.SalesPersonID = @SalesPersonId;
END
GO
```

There happens to be a nonclustered index on the SalesPersonID column of the Sales.SalesOrderHeader table, which you might expect to be considered by the optimizer. However, when this SP is executed with the EXECUTE statement in Listing 6-16, the optimizer ignores the nonclustered index, and instead performs a clustered index scan, as shown in Figure 6-11.

Listing 6-16. *Retrieving Sales for Salesperson 277*

```
EXECUTE Sales.GetSalesBySalesPerson 277;
```

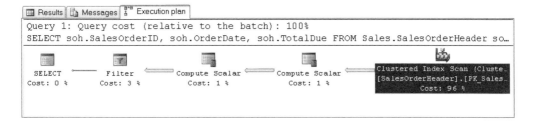

Figure 6-11. *The SP ignores the nonclustered index*

The reason the SP ignores the nonclustered index on the `SalesPersonID` column is because 473 matching rows are returned by the query in the procedure. SQL Server uses a measure called *selectivity*, the ratio of qualifying rows to the total number of rows in the table, as a factor in determining which index, if any, to use. In Listing 6-16, the parameter value 277 represents low selectivity, meaning that there are a large number of rows returned relative to the number of rows in the table. SQL Server favors indexes for highly selective queries, to the point of completely ignoring indexes when the query has low selectivity.

If you subsequently call the SP with the `@SalesPersonId` parameter set to 285, which represents a highly selective value (only 16 rows are returned), query plan caching forces the same clustered index scan, even though it's suboptimal for a highly selective query. Fortunately, SQL Server provides options that allow you to force recompilation at the SP level or the statement level. You can force a recompilation in your SP call by adding the `WITH RECOMPILE` option to your `EXECUTE` statement, as shown in Listing 6-17.

Listing 6-17. *Executing an SP with Recompilation*

```
EXECUTE Sales.GetSalesBySalesPerson 285 WITH RECOMPILE;
```

The `WITH RECOMPILE` option of the `EXECUTE` statement forces a recompilation of your SP when you execute it. This option is useful if your data has significantly changed since the last SP recompilation or if the parameter value you're passing to the procedure represents an atypical value. The query plan for this SP call with the highly selective value 285 is shown in Figure 6-12.

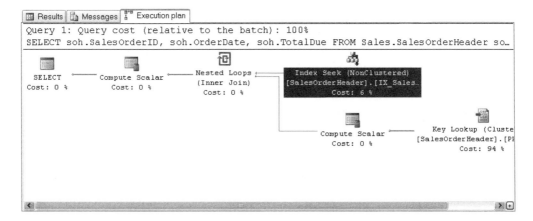

Figure 6-12. *SP query plan optimized for highly selective parameter value*

You can also use the sp_recompile system SP to force an SP to recompile the next time it is run.

If you expect that the values submitted to your SP will vary a lot, and that the "one execution plan for all parameters" model will cause poor performance, you can specify statement-level recompilation by adding OPTION (RECOMPILE) to your statements. The statement-level recompilation also considers the values of local variables during the recompilation process. Listing 6-18 alters the SP created in Listing 6-15 to add statement-level recompilation to the SELECT query.

Listing 6-18. *Adding Statement-Level Recompilation to the SP*

```
ALTER PROCEDURE Sales.GetSalesBySalesPerson (@SalesPersonId int)
AS
BEGIN
  SELECT
    soh.SalesOrderID,
    soh.OrderDate,
    soh.TotalDue
  FROM Sales.SalesOrderHeader soh
  WHERE soh.SalesPersonID = @SalesPersonId
  OPTION (RECOMPILE);
END
GO
```

As an alternative, you can specify procedure-level recompilation by adding the WITH RECOMPILE option to your CREATE PROCEDURE statement. This option is useful if you don't want SQL Server to cache the query plan for the SP. With this option in place, SQL Server recompiles the entire SP every time you run it. This can be useful for procedures containing several statements that need to be recompiled often. Keep in mind, however, that this option is less efficient than a statement-level recompile since the entire SP needs to be recompiled. Because it is less efficient than statement-level recompilation, this option should be used with care.

Summary

SPs are powerful tools for SQL Server development. They provide a flexible method of extending the power of SQL Server by allowing you to create custom server-side subroutines. While some of the performance advantages provided by SPs in older releases of SQL Server are not as pronounced in SQL Server 2008, the ability to modularize server-side code, administer your T-SQL code base in a single location, provide additional security, and ease front-end programming development still make SPs powerful development tools in any T-SQL developer's toolkit.

In this chapter, I introduced key aspects of SP development, including SP creation and management, passing scalar parameters to SPs, and retrieving result sets, output parameters, and return values from SPs. I also demonstrated some advanced topics, including the use of temporary tables to pass tabular data between SPs, writing recursive SPs, and SQL Server 2008's new table-valued parameters.

Finally, I finished the chapter with a discussion of SP optimizations, including SP caching, accessing SP cache statistics through DMVs and DMFs, parameter sniffing, and recompilation options, including statement-level and procedure-level recompilation.

The samples provided in this chapter are designed to demonstrate several aspects of SP functionality in SQL Server 2008. The next chapter introduces further important aspects of T-SQL programming for SQL Server 2008: DML and DDL triggers.

EXERCISES

1. [True/false] The SP RETURN statement can return a scalar value of any data type.

2. The recursion level for SPs is 32 levels, as demonstrated by the following code sample, which errors out after reaching the maximum depth of recursion:

```
CREATE PROCEDURE dbo.FirstProc (@i int)
AS
BEGIN
  PRINT @i;
  SET @i += 1;
  EXEC dbo.FirstProc @i;
END;
GO

EXEC dbo.FirstProc 1;
```

Write a second procedure and modify this one to prove that the recursion limit applies to two SPs that call each other recursively.

3. [Choose one] Table-valued parameters must be declared with which of the following modifiers:
    a.   READWRITE
    b.   WRITEONLY
    c.   RECOMPILE
    d.   READONLY

4. [Choose all that apply] You can use which of the following methods to force SQL Server to recompile an SP:
    a.   The sp_recompile system SP
    b.   The WITH RECOMPILE option
    c.   The FORCE RECOMPILE option
    d.   The DBCC RECOMPILE_ALL_SPS command

CHAPTER 7

■ ■ ■

Triggers

$\mathbf{S}$QL Server provides triggers as a means of executing T-SQL code in response to database object, database, and server events. SQL Server 2008 implements three types of triggers: classic T-SQL Data Manipulation Language (DML) triggers, which fire in response to insert, update, and delete events against tables; Data Definition Language (DDL) triggers, which fire in response to CREATE, ALTER, and DROP statements; and logon triggers, which fire in response to LOGON events. DDL triggers can also fire in response to some system SPs that perform DDL-like operations.

Triggers are a form of specialized SP, closely tied to your data and database objects. In the past, DML triggers were used to enforce various aspects of business logic, such as foreign key and other constraints on data, and other more complex business logic. Cascading declarative referential integrity (DRI) and robust check constraints in T-SQL have supplanted DML triggers in many areas, but they are still useful in their own right. In this chapter, I will discuss how triggers work, how to use them, and when they are most appropriate. I will also discuss DDL triggers and explore their use.

DML Triggers

DML triggers are composed of T-SQL code that is executed (fired) in response to an INSERT, an UPDATE, or a DELETE statement on a table or view. DML triggers are created via the CREATE TRIGGER statement, which allows you to specify the following details about the trigger:

- The name of the trigger, which is the identifier you can use to manage the trigger. You can specify a two-part name for a trigger (schema and trigger name), but the schema must be the same as the schema for the table on which the trigger executes.

- The table or view on which the trigger executes.

- The triggering events, which can be any combination of INSERT, UPDATE, and DELETE. The triggering events indicate the type of events that the trigger fires in response to.

- The AFTER/FOR or INSTEAD OF indicators, which determine whether the trigger is fired after the triggering statement completes or whether the trigger overrides the firing statement.

- Additional options like the ENCRYPTION and EXECUTE AS clauses, which allow you to obfuscate the trigger source code and specify the context that the trigger executes under, respectively.

> ■**Note** DML triggers have some restrictions on their creation that you should keep in mind. For one, DML triggers cannot be defined on temporary tables. Also, DML triggers cannot be declared on table variables. Finally, only INSTEAD OF triggers can be used on views.

In addition to the CREATE TRIGGER statement, SQL Server provides an ALTER TRIGGER statement to modify the definition of a trigger, a DROP TRIGGER statement to remove an existing trigger from the database, and DISABLE TRIGGER and ENABLE TRIGGER statements to disable and enable a trigger, respectively.

When to Use DML Triggers

Way back in the day, using triggers was the best (and in some cases only) way to perform a variety of tasks, such as ensuring cascading DRI, validating data before storing it in tables, auditing changes, and enforcing complex business logic. Newer releases of SQL Server have added functionality that more closely integrates many of these functions into the core database engine. For instance, in most cases, you can use SQL Server's built-in cascading DRI to ensure referential integrity and check constraints for simple validations during insert and update operations. DML triggers are still a good choice when simple auditing tasks or validations with complex business logic are required.

> ■**Note** DRI is not enforced across databases. What this means is that you cannot reference a table in a different database in a DRI/foreign key constraint. Because they can reference objects such as tables and views in other databases, triggers are still a good option when this type of referential integrity enforcement is necessary.

Listing 7-1 shows a very simple trigger that is defined on the HumanResources.Employee table of the AdventureWorks database. The HumanResources.EmployeeUpdateTrigger trigger simply updates the ModifiedDate column of the HumanResources.Employee table with the current date and time whenever a row is updated.

Listing 7-1. *HumanResources.EmployeeUpdateTrigger Code*

```
CREATE TRIGGER HumanResources.EmployeeUpdateTrigger
ON HumanResources.Employee
AFTER UPDATE
NOT FOR REPLICATION
AS
BEGIN
  -- Get number of affected rows
  DECLARE @Count int = @@ROWCOUNT;

  -- Turn off "rows affected" messages
  SET NOCOUNT ON;
```

```
-- Make sure at least one row was affected
IF @Count > 0
BEGIN

  -- Update ModifiedDate for all affected rows
  UPDATE HumanResources.Employee
  SET ModifiedDate = GETDATE()
  WHERE EXISTS
  (
    SELECT 1
    FROM inserted i
    WHERE i.BusinessEntityID = HumanResources.Employee.BusinessEntityID
  );

END;

END;
```

The first part of the CREATE TRIGGER statement defines the name of the trigger and specifies that it will be created on the HumanResources.Department table. The definition also specifies that the trigger will fire after rows are updated, and the NOT FOR REPLICATION keywords prevent replication events from firing the trigger.

```
CREATE TRIGGER HumanResources.EmployeeUpdateTrigger
ON HumanResources.Employee
AFTER UPDATE
NOT FOR REPLICATION
```

The body of the trigger starts by declaring an int variable to temporarily hold the number of rows affected by the UPDATE statement, retrieved from the @@ROWCOUNT system function. Next, the trigger turns off the rows affected messages via the SET NOCOUNT ON statement.

```
-- Get number of affected rows
DECLARE @Count int = @@ROWCOUNT;

-- Turn off "rows affected" messages
SET NOCOUNT ON;
```

■Note Using SET NOCOUNT ON is not strictly required in triggers, but it prevents superfluous rows affected messages from being generated by the trigger. Some older database drivers—and even some more recent ones, such as certain Java Database Connectivity (JDBC) drivers—can get confused by these extra messages, so it's not a bad idea to disable them in the body of your triggers. Any SET statement can be used in the body of a trigger. The statement remains in effect while the trigger executes and reverts to its former setting when the trigger completes.

The trigger then uses an IF statement to ensure that at least one row was affected by the data manipulation statement that fired the trigger. This is an optimization that skips the body of the trigger if no rows were affected.

Whenever any trigger is fired, it is implicitly wrapped in the same transaction as the DML statement that fired it. This has big implications for your database. What it means is that whatever your trigger does, it should do it as quickly and efficiently as possible. The T-SQL statements in your trigger body can potentially create locks in your database, a situation that you want to minimize. It is not unheard of for inefficient triggers to cause blocking problems. It also means that a ROLLBACK TRANSACTION statement in the trigger will roll back DML statements executed in the trigger, as well as the original DML statement that fired the trigger.

Checking @@ROWCOUNT at the start of your trigger helps ensure that your triggers are efficient. If @@ROWCOUNT is 0, it means that no rows were affected by the original DML statement that fired the trigger. This means your trigger has no work to do, and you can skip the body of the trigger. You should also minimize the amount of work done inside the trigger and optimize the operations it has to perform.

```
-- Make sure at least one row was affected
IF @Count > 0
BEGIN
  ...
END;
```

The IF statement contains an UPDATE statement that sets the ModifiedDate column to the current date and time when rows in the table are updated. An important concept of trigger programming is to be sure that you account for multiple row updates. It's not safe to assume that a DML statement will update only a single row of your table. In this trigger, the UPDATE statement uses the EXISTS predicate in the WHERE clause to ensure that ModifiedDate is updated for every row that was affected. It accomplished this by using the inserted virtual table, described in the "The inserted and deleted Virtual Tables" sidebar in this section.

```
-- Update ModifiedDate for all affected rows
UPDATE HumanResources.Employee
SET ModifiedDate = GETDATE()
WHERE EXISTS
(
  SELECT 1
  FROM inserted i
  WHERE i.BusinessEntityID = HumanResources.Employee.BusinessEntityID
);
```

THE INSERTED AND DELETED VIRTUAL TABLES

A DML trigger needs to know which rows were affected by the DML statement that fired it. The inserted and deleted virtual tables fulfill this need. When a trigger fires, SQL Server populates the inserted and deleted virtual tables and makes them available within the body of the trigger. These two virtual tables have the same structure as the affected table and contain the data from all affected rows.

The inserted table contains all rows inserted into the destination table by an INSERT statement. The deleted table contains all rows deleted from the destination table by a DELETE statement. For UPDATE statements, the rows are treated as a DELETE followed by an INSERT, so that the pre-UPDATE-affected rows are stored in the deleted table, while the post-UPDATE-affected rows are stored in the inserted table.

The virtual tables are read-only and cannot be modified directly. The example in Listing 7-1 uses the inserted virtual table to determine which rows were affected by the UPDATE statement that fired the trigger. The trigger updates the ModifiedDate column for every row in the HumanResources.Employee table with a matching row in the inserted table. I'll be using the inserted and deleted virtual tables in other sample code in this section.

Testing the trigger is as simple as using SELECT and UPDATE. The sample in Listing 7-2 changes the marital status of employees with BusinessEntityID numbers 1 and 2 to M (for "married").

Listing 7-2. *Testing HumanResources.EmployeeUpdateTrigger*

```
UPDATE HumanResources.Employee
SET MaritalStatus = 'M'
WHERE BusinessEntityID IN (1, 2);

SELECT BusinessEntityID, NationalIDNumber, MaritalStatus, ModifiedDate
FROM HumanResources.Employee
WHERE BusinessEntityID IN (1, 2);
```

■**Caution** If the RECURSIVE TRIGGERS database option is turned on in the AdventureWorks database, HumanResources.EmployeeUpdateTrigger will error out with a message that the "nesting limit has been exceeded." This is caused by the trigger recursively firing itself after the UPDATE statement in the trigger is executed. Use SET RECURSIVE TRIGGERS OFF to turn off recursive triggers and SET RECURSIVE TRIGGERS ON to turn the option back on.

The results, shown in Figure 7-1, demonstrate that the UPDATE statement fired the trigger and properly updated the ModifiedDate for the two specified rows.

	BusinessEntityID	NationalIDNumber	MaritalStatus	ModifiedDate
1	1	295847284	M	2008-03-22 00:39:48.330
2	2	245797967	M	2008-03-22 00:39:48.330

Figure 7-1. *Updated marital status for two employees*

Auditing with DML Triggers

Another common use for DML triggers is auditing DML actions against tables. The primary purpose of DML auditing is to maintain a record of changes to the data in your database. This might be required for a number of reasons, including regulatory compliance or to fulfill contractual obligations. The first step to implementing DML auditing is to create a table to store your audit information. Listing 7-3 creates just such a table.

■**Tip** SQL Server 2008 provides a new feature known as *Change Data Capture (CDC)*, which provides built-in auditing functionality. The new CDC functionality provides another option for logging DML actions against tables. While CDC functionality is beyond the scope of this book, I recommend looking into this option before deciding which method to use when you need DML logging functionality.

Listing 7-3. *DML Audit Logging Table*

```
CREATE TABLE dbo.DmlActionLog
(
  EntryNum int IDENTITY(1, 1) PRIMARY KEY NOT NULL,
  SchemaName sysname NOT NULL,
  TableName sysname NOT NULL,
  ActionType nvarchar(10) NOT NULL,
  ActionXml xml NOT NULL,
  UserName nvarchar(256) NOT NULL,
  Spid int NOT NULL,
  ActionDateTime datetime NOT NULL DEFAULT (GETDATE())
);
GO
```

The dbo.DmlActionLog table in Listing 7-3 stores information for each DML action performed against a table, including the name of the schema and table against which the DML action was performed, the type of DML action performed, XML-formatted snapshots of the before and after states of the rows affected, and additional information to identify who performed the DML action and when the action was performed. Once the audit logging table is created, it's time to create a trigger to log DML actions. This is shown in Listing 7-4.

Listing 7-4. *DML Audit Logging Trigger*

```
CREATE TRIGGER HumanResources.DepartmentChangeAudit
ON HumanResources.Department
AFTER INSERT, UPDATE, DELETE
NOT FOR REPLICATION
AS
BEGIN
  -- Get number of affected rows
  DECLARE @Count int = @@ROWCOUNT;
```

```sql
-- Make sure at least one row was actually affected
IF (@Count > 0)
BEGIN

  -- Turn off "rows affected" messages
  SET NOCOUNT ON;

  DECLARE @ActionType nvarchar(10);
  DECLARE @ActionXml xml;

  -- Get count of inserted rows
  DECLARE @inserted_count int =
  (
    SELECT COUNT(*)
    FROM inserted
  );

  -- Get count of deleted rows
  DECLARE @deleted_count int =
  (
    SELECT COUNT(*)
    FROM deleted
  );

  -- Determine the type of DML action that fired the trigger
  SELECT @ActionType = CASE
      WHEN (@inserted_count > 0) AND (@deleted_count = 0)
        THEN N'insert'
      WHEN (@inserted_count = 0) AND (@deleted_count > 0)
        THEN N'delete'
      ELSE N'update'
    END;

  -- Use FOR XML AUTO to retrieve before and after snapshots of the changed
  -- data in XML format
  SELECT @ActionXml = COALESCE
  (
    (
      SELECT *
      FROM deleted
      FOR XML AUTO
    ), N'<deleted/>'
  ) + COALESCE
  (
    (
      SELECT *
      FROM inserted
```

```
      FOR XML AUTO
  ), N'<inserted/>'
);

-- Insert a row for the logged action in the audit logging table
INSERT INTO dbo.DmlActionLog
(
  SchemaName,
  TableName,
  ActionType,
  ActionXml,
  UserName,
  Spid,
  ActionDateTime
)
SELECT
  OBJECT_SCHEMA_NAME(@@PROCID, DB_ID()),
  OBJECT_NAME(t.parent_id, DB_ID()),
  @ActionType,
  @ActionXml,
  USER_NAME(),
  @@SPID,
  GETDATE()
FROM sys.triggers t
WHERE t.object_id = @@PROCID;

  END;

END;
GO
```

The trigger in Listing 7-4 is created on the HumanResources.Department table, although it is written in such a way that the body of the trigger contains no code specific to the table it's created on. This means you can easily modify the trigger to work as-is on most tables.

The HumanResources.DepartmentChangeAudit trigger definition begins with the CREATE TRIGGER statement, which names the trigger and creates it on the HumanResources.Department table. It also specifies that the trigger should fire after INSERT, UPDATE, or DELETE statements are performed against the table. Finally, the NOT FOR REPLICATION clause specifies that replication events will not cause the trigger to fire.

```
CREATE TRIGGER HumanResources.DepartmentChangeAudit
ON HumanResources.Department
AFTER INSERT, UPDATE, DELETE
NOT FOR REPLICATION
```

The trigger body begins by getting the number of rows affected by the DML statement with the @@ROWCOUNT function. The trigger skips the remainder of the statements in the body if no rows were affected.

```
-- Get number of affected rows
DECLARE @Count int = @@ROWCOUNT;

-- Make sure at least one row was actually affected
IF (@Count > 0)
BEGIN
  ...
END;
```

If there was at least one row affected by the DML statement that fired the trigger, the statements in the main body of the trigger are executed, beginning with an initialization that turns off extraneous rows affected messages, declares local variables, and gets the count of rows inserted and deleted by the DML statement from the inserted and deleted virtual tables.

```
-- Turn off "rows affected" messages
SET NOCOUNT ON;

DECLARE @ActionType nvarchar(10);
DECLARE @ActionXml xml;

-- Get count of inserted rows
DECLARE @inserted_count int =
(
  SELECT COUNT(*)
  FROM inserted
);

-- Get count of deleted rows
DECLARE @deleted_count int =
(
  SELECT COUNT(*)
  FROM deleted
);
```

Since the trigger is logging the type of DML action that caused it to fire (an insert, a delete, or an update action), it must determine the type programmatically. This can be done by applying the following simple rules to the counts of rows from the inserted and deleted virtual tables:

1. If at least one row was inserted but no rows were deleted, the DML action was an insert.

2. If at least one row was deleted but no rows were inserted, the DML action was a delete.

3. If at least one row was deleted and at least one row was inserted, the DML action was an update.

These rules are applied in the form of a CASE expression, as shown following:

```
-- Determine the type of DML action that fired the trigger
SELECT @ActionType = CASE
    WHEN (@inserted_count > 0) AND (@deleted_count = 0)
      THEN N'insert'
```

```
      WHEN (@inserted_count = 0) AND (@deleted_count > 0)
        THEN N'delete'
      ELSE N'update'
    END;
```

The next step in the trigger uses the SELECT statement's FOR XML AUTO clause to generate XML-formatted before and after snapshots of the affected rows. FOR XML AUTO is useful because it automatically uses the source table name as the XML element name—in this case inserted or deleted. The FOR XML AUTO clause automatically uses the names of the columns in the table as XML attributes for each element. Because the inserted and deleted virtual tables have the same column names as this affected table, you don't have to hard-code column names into the trigger. In the resulting XML, the <deleted> elements represent the before snapshot and the <inserted> elements represent the after snapshot of the affected rows.

```
-- Use FOR XML AUTO to retrieve before and after snapshots of the changed
-- data in XML format
SELECT @ActionXml = COALESCE
(
  (
    SELECT *
    FROM deleted
    FOR XML AUTO
  ), N'<deleted/>'
) + COALESCE
(
  (
    SELECT *
    FROM inserted
    FOR XML AUTO
  ), N'<inserted/>'
);
```

■Tip The DML audit logging trigger was created to be flexible so that you could use it with minimal changes on most tables. However, there are some circumstances where it might require use of additional options or more extensive changes to work with a given table. As an example, if your table contains a varbinary column, you have to use the FOR XML clause's BINARY BASE64 directive.

The final step in the trigger inserts a row representing the logged action into the dbo.DmlActionLog table. Several SQL Server *metadata functions*—like @@PROCID, OBJECT_SCHEMA_NAME, and OBJECT_NAME, as well as the sys.triggers catalog view—are used in the INSERT statement to dynamically identify the current trigger procedure ID, and the schema and table name information dynamically. Again, this means that this information does not need to be hard-coded into the trigger, making it easier to use the trigger on multiple tables with minimal changes.

```
-- Insert a row for the logged action in the audit logging table
INSERT INTO dbo.DmlActionLog
(
  SchemaName,
  TableName,
  ActionType,
  ActionXml,
  UserName,
  Spid,
  ActionDateTime
)
SELECT
  OBJECT_SCHEMA_NAME(@@PROCID, DB_ID()),
  OBJECT_NAME(t.parent_id, DB_ID()),
  @ActionType,
  @ActionXml,
  USER_NAME(),
  @@SPID,
  GETDATE()
FROM sys.triggers t
WHERE t.object_id = @@PROCID;
```

■Tip SQL Server includes several metadata functions, catalog views, and dynamic management views and functions that are useful for dynamically retrieving information about databases, database objects, and the current state of the server. I'll describe more of these useful T-SQL functions and views as they're encountered in later chapters.

You can easily verify the trigger with a few simple DML statements. Listing 7-5 changes the name of the AdventureWorks Information Services department to Information Technology, and then inserts and deletes a Customer Service department. The results are shown in Figure 7-2.

Listing 7-5. *Testing the DML Audit Logging Trigger*

```
UPDATE HumanResources.Department
SET Name = N'Information Technology'
WHERE DepartmentId = 11;

INSERT INTO HumanResources.Department
(
  Name,
  GroupName
)
VALUES
```

```
(
  N'Customer Service',
  N'Sales and Marketing'
);

DELETE
FROM HumanResources.Department
WHERE Name = N'Customer Service';

SELECT
  EntryNum,
  SchemaName,
  TableName,
  ActionType,
  ActionXml,
  UserName,
  Spid,
  ActionDateTime
FROM dbo.DmlActionLog;
```

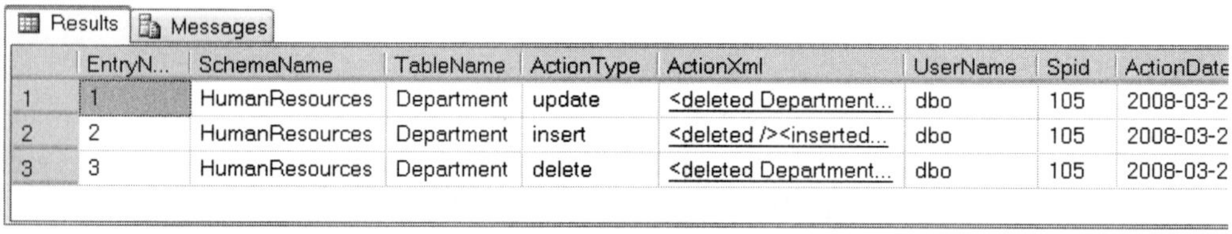

	EntryN...	SchemaName	TableName	ActionType	ActionXml	UserName	Spid	ActionDate
1	1	HumanResources	Department	update	<deleted Department...	dbo	105	2008-03-2
2	2	HumanResources	Department	insert	<deleted /><inserted...	dbo	105	2008-03-2
3	3	HumanResources	Department	delete	<deleted Department...	dbo	105	2008-03-2

Figure 7-2. *Audit logging results*

The FOR XML AUTO–generated ActionXml column data deserves a closer look. As I mentioned earlier in this section, the FOR XML AUTO clause automatically generates element and attribute names based on the source table and source column names. The UPDATE statement in Listing 7-5 generates the ActionXml entry shown in Figure 7-3. Note that I've formatted the XML for easier reading, but I have not changed the content.

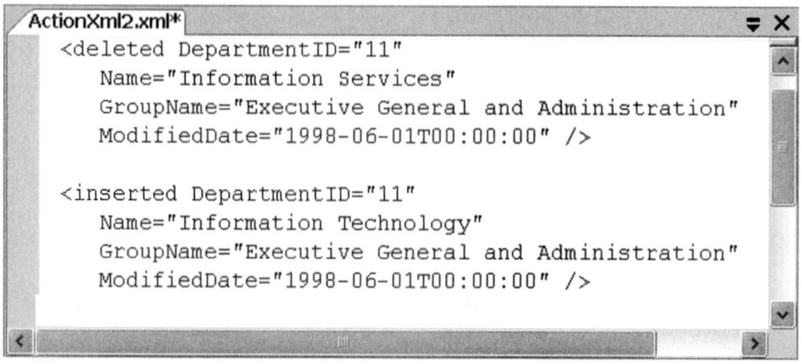

```
ActionXml2.xml*
    <deleted DepartmentID="11"
      Name="Information Services"
      GroupName="Executive General and Administration"
      ModifiedDate="1998-06-01T00:00:00" />

    <inserted DepartmentID="11"
      Name="Information Technology"
      GroupName="Executive General and Administration"
      ModifiedDate="1998-06-01T00:00:00" />
```

Figure 7-3. *The ActionXml entry generated by the UPDATE statement*

SHARING DATA WITH TRIGGERS

A commonly asked question is "How do you pass parameters to triggers?" The short answer is you can't. Because they are automatically fired in response to events, SQL Server triggers provide no means to pass in parameters. If you need to pass additional data to a trigger, you do have a couple of options available, however. The first option is to create a table, which the trigger can then access via SELECT queries. The advantage to this method is that the amount of data your trigger can access is effectively unlimited. A disadvantage is the additional overhead required to query the table within your trigger.

Another option, if you have small amounts of data to share with your triggers, is to use the CONTEXT_INFO function. You can assign up to 128 bytes of varbinary data to the CONTEXT_INFO for the current session through the SET CONTEXT_INFO statement. This statement accepts only a variable or constant value—no other expressions are allowed. After you've set the CONTEXT_INFO for your session, you can access it within your trigger via the CONTEXT_INFO function. The disadvantage of this method is the small amount of data you can store in the CONTEXT_INFO. Keep these methods in mind, as you may one day find that you need to pass information into a trigger from a batch or SP.

Nested and Recursive Triggers

SQL Server supports triggers firing other triggers through the concept of nested triggers. A *nested trigger* is simply a trigger that is fired by the action of another trigger. Triggers can be nested up to 32 levels deep. I would advise against nesting triggers deeply, however, since the additional levels of nesting will affect performance. If you do have triggers nested deeply, you might want to reconsider your trigger design. Nested triggers are turned on by default, but you can turn them off with the sp_configure statement, as shown in Listing 7-6.

Listing 7-6. *Turning Off Nested Triggers*

```
sp_configure 'nested triggers', 0;
GO
RECONFIGURE;
GO
```

Set the nested triggers option to 1 to turn nested triggers back on. Triggers can also be called recursively. There are two types of trigger recursion:

- *Direct recursion*: Occurs when a trigger performs an action that causes it to recursively fire itself.

- *Indirect recursion*: Occurs when a trigger fires another trigger (which can fire another trigger, etc.), which eventually fires the first trigger.

Direct and indirect recursion of triggers applies only to triggers of the same type. As an example, an INSTEAD OF trigger that causes another INSTEAD OF trigger to fire is direct recursion. Even if a different type of trigger is fired between the first and second firing of the same trigger, it is still considered direct recursion. For example, if one or more AFTER triggers are fired between the first and second firings of the same INSTEAD OF trigger, it is still considered direct recursion. Indirect recursion occurs when a trigger of the same type is called between firings of the same trigger.

You can use the `ALTER DATABASE` statement's `SET RECURSIVE_TRIGGERS` option to turn direct recursion of `AFTER` triggers on and off, as shown in Listing 7-7. Turning off direct recursion of `INSTEAD OF` triggers requires that you also set the `nested triggers` option to 0, as shown previously in Listing 7-6.

Listing 7-7. *Turning Off Recursive AFTER Triggers*

```
ALTER DATABASE AdventureWorks
SET RECURSIVE_TRIGGERS OFF;
GO
```

Actions taken with an `INSTEAD OF` trigger will not cause it to fire again. Instead, the `INSTEAD OF` trigger will perform constraint checks and fire any `AFTER` triggers. As an example, if an `INSTEAD OF UPDATE` trigger on a table is fired, and during the course of its execution performs an `UPDATE` statement against the table, the `UPDATE` will not fire the `INSTEAD OF` trigger again. Instead the `UPDATE` statement will initiate constraint check operations and fire `AFTER` triggers on the table.

■**Caution** Nested and recursive triggers should be used with care, since nesting and recursion that's too deep will cause your triggers to throw exceptions. You can use the `TRIGGER_NESTLEVEL` function to determine the current level of recursion from within a trigger.

The UPDATE and COLUMNS_UPDATED Functions

Triggers can take advantage of two system functions, `UPDATE` and `COLUMNS_UPDATED`, to tell you which columns are affected by the `INSERT` or `UPDATE` statement that fires the trigger in the first place. `UPDATE` takes the name of a column as a parameter and returns true if the column is updated or inserted, and false otherwise. `COLUMNS_UPDATED` returns a bit pattern indicating which columns are affected by the `INSERT` or `UPDATE` statement.

The sample trigger in Listing 7-8 demonstrates the use of triggers to enforce business rules. In this example, the trigger uses the `UPDATE` function to determine if the `Size` or `SizeUnitMeasureCode` has been affected by an `INSERT` or `UPDATE` statement. If either of these columns is affected by an `INSERT` or `UPDATE` statement, the trigger checks to see if a recognized `SizeUnitMeasureCode` was used. If so, the trigger converts the `Size` to centimeters. The trigger recognizes several `SizeUnitMeasureCode` values, including centimeters (`CM`), millimeters (`MM`), and inches (`IN`).

Listing 7-8. *Trigger to Enforce Standard Sizes*

```
CREATE TRIGGER Production.ProductEnforceStandardSizes
ON Production.Product
AFTER INSERT, UPDATE
NOT FOR REPLICATION
AS
```

```
BEGIN
  -- Make sure at least one row was affected and either the Size or
  -- SizeUnitMeasureCode column was changed
  IF (@@ROWCOUNT > 0)
    AND (UPDATE(SizeUnitMeasureCode) OR UPDATE(Size))
  BEGIN

    -- Eliminate "rows affected" messages
    SET NOCOUNT ON;

    -- Only accept recognized units of measure or NULL
    IF EXISTS
    (
      SELECT 1
      FROM inserted
      WHERE NOT
      (
        SizeUnitMeasureCode IN (N'M', N'DM', N'CM', N'MM', N'IN')
        OR SizeUnitMeasureCode IS NULL
      )
    )
    BEGIN
      -- If the unit of measure wasn't recognized raise an error and roll back
      -- the transaction
      RAISERROR ('Invalid Size Unit Measure Code.', 10, 127);
      ROLLBACK TRANSACTION;
    END

    ELSE

    BEGIN

      -- If the unit of measure is a recognized unit of measure then set the
      -- SizeUnitMeasureCode to centimeters and perform the Size conversion
      UPDATE Production.Product
      SET SizeUnitMeasureCode =
        CASE
          WHEN SizeUnitMeasureCode IS NULL THEN NULL
          ELSE N'CM'
        END,
        Size = CAST
        (
          CAST
          (
            CASE i.SizeUnitMeasureCode
              WHEN N'M' THEN CAST(i.Size AS float) * 100.0
              WHEN N'DM' THEN CAST(i.Size AS float) * 10.0
```

```
                WHEN N'CM' THEN CAST(i.Size AS float)
                WHEN N'MM' THEN CAST(i.Size AS float) * 0.10
                WHEN N'IN' THEN CAST(i.Size AS float) * 2.54
            END
            AS int
          ) AS nvarchar(5)
        )
      FROM inserted i
      WHERE Production.Product.ProductID = i.ProductID
      AND i.SizeUnitMeasureCode IS NOT NULL;

    END;

  END;

END;
GO
```

The first part of the trigger definition gives the trigger its name,
Production.ProductEnforceStandardSizes, and creates it on the Production.Product
table. It is specified as an AFTER INSERT, UPDATE trigger, and is declared as NOT
FOR REPLICATION.

```
CREATE TRIGGER Production.ProductEnforceStandardSizes
ON Production.Product
AFTER INSERT, UPDATE
NOT FOR REPLICATION
```

The code in the body of the trigger immediately checks @@ROWCOUNT to make sure that at
least one row was affected by the DML statement that fired the trigger, and uses the UPDATE
function to ensure that the Size or SizeUnitMeasureCode columns were affected by the DML
statement:

```
IF (@@ROWCOUNT > 0)
  AND (UPDATE(SizeUnitMeasureCode) OR UPDATE(Size))
BEGIN
  ...
END;
```

Once the trigger has verified that at least one row was affected and the appropriate
columns were modified, the trigger sets NOCOUNT ON to prevent the rows affected messages
from being generated by the trigger. The IF EXISTS statement checks to make sure that valid
unit-of-measure codes are used. If not, the trigger raises an error and rolls back the transaction.

```
-- Eliminate "rows affected" messages
SET NOCOUNT ON;

-- Only accept recognized units of measure or NULL
IF EXISTS
(
```

```
SELECT 1
FROM inserted
WHERE NOT
(
  SizeUnitMeasureCode IN (N'M', N'DM', N'CM', N'MM', N'IN')
  OR SizeUnitMeasureCode IS NULL
)
)
BEGIN
  -- If the unit of measure wasn't recognized raise an error and roll back
  -- the transaction
  RAISERROR ('Invalid Size Unit Measure Code.', 10, 127);
  ROLLBACK TRANSACTION;
END
```

■Tip The ROLLBACK TRANSACTION statement in the trigger rolls back the transaction and prevents further triggers from being fired by the current trigger.

If the unit-of-measure validation is passed, the SizeUnitMeasureCode is set to centimeters and the Size is converted to centimeters for each inserted or updated row.

```
BEGIN

  -- If the unit of measure is a recognized unit of measure then set the
  -- SizeUnitMeasureCode to centimeters and perform the Size conversion
  UPDATE Production.Product
  SET SizeUnitMeasureCode =
    CASE
      WHEN SizeUnitMeasureCode IS NULL THEN NULL
      ELSE N'CM'
    END,
    Size = CAST
    (
      CAST
      (
        CASE i.SizeUnitMeasureCode
          WHEN N'M' THEN CAST(i.Size AS float) * 100.0
          WHEN N'DM' THEN CAST(i.Size AS float) * 10.0
          WHEN N'CM' THEN CAST(i.Size AS float)
          WHEN N'MM' THEN CAST(i.Size AS float) * 0.10
          WHEN N'IN' THEN CAST(i.Size AS float) * 2.54
        END
        AS int
      ) AS nvarchar(5)
    )
```

```
      FROM inserted i
      WHERE Production.Product.ProductID = i.ProductID
      AND i.SizeUnitMeasureCode IS NOT NULL;

    END;
```

This trigger enforces simple business logic by ensuring that standard-size codes are used when updating the `Production.Product` table and converting the `Size` values to centimeters. To test the trigger, you can perform updates of existing rows in the `Production.Product` table. Listing 7-9 updates the sizes of the products with `ProductID` 680 and 780 to 600 millimeters and 22.85 inches, respectively. The results, with the `Size` values automatically converted to centimeters, are shown in Figure 7-4.

Listing 7-9. *Testing the Trigger by Adding a New Product*

```
UPDATE Production.Product
SET Size = N'600',
  SizeUnitMeasureCode = N'MM'
WHERE ProductId = 680;

UPDATE Production.Product
SET Size = N'22.85',
  SizeUnitMeasureCode = N'IN'
WHERE ProductId = 706;

SELECT ProductID,
  Name,
  ProductNumber,
  Size,
  SizeUnitMeasureCode
FROM Production.Product
WHERE ProductID IN (680, 706);
```

	Product...	Name	ProductNumber	Size	SizeUnitMeasureCo...
1	680	HL Road Frame - Black, 58	FR-R92B-58	60	CM
2	706	HL Road Frame - Red, 58	FR-R92R-58	58	CM

Figure 7-4. *The results of the Production.ProductEnforceStandardSizes trigger test*

While the `UPDATE` function accepts a column name and returns true if the column is affected, the `COLUMNS_UPDATED` function accepts no parameters and returns a `varbinary` value with a single bit representing each column. You can use the bitwise AND operator (&) and a bit mask to test which columns are affected. The bits are set from left to right, based on the `ColumnID` number of the columns.

To create a bit mask, you must use 2^0 (1) to represent the first column, 2^1 (2) to represent the second column, and so on. Because COLUMNS_UPDATED returns a varbinary result, the column indicator bits can be spread out over several bytes. To test columns beyond the first eight, like the Size and SizeUnitMeasureCode columns in the example code (columns 11 and 12), you can use the SUBSTRING function to return the second byte of COLUMNS_UPDATED and test the appropriate bits with a bit mask of 12 ($12 = 2^2 + 2^3$). The sample trigger in Listing 7-8 can be modified to use the COLUMNS_UPDATED function, as shown here:

```
IF (@@ROWCOUNT > 0)
  AND (SUBSTRING(COLUMNS_UPDATED(), 2, 1) & 12 <> 0x00)
```

The COLUMNS_UPDATED function will not return correct results if the ColumnID values of the table are changed. If the table is dropped and recreated with columns in a different order, you will need to change the triggers that use COLUMNS_UPDATED to reflect the changes. There may be specialized instances in which you'll be able to take advantage of the COLUMNS_UPDATED functionality, but in general I would advise against using COLUMNS_UPDATED, and instead use the UPDATE function to determine which columns were affected by the DML statement that fired your trigger.

Triggers on Views

Although you cannot create AFTER triggers on views, SQL Server does allow you to create INSTEAD OF triggers on your views. A trigger can be useful for updating views that are otherwise nonupdatable, such as views with multiple base tables or views that contain aggregate functions. INSTEAD OF triggers on views also give you fine-grained control, since you can control which columns of the view are updatable through the trigger. The AdventureWorks database comes with a view named Sales.vSalesPerson, which is formed by joining 11 separate tables together. The INSTEAD OF trigger in Listing 7-10 allows you to update specific columns of two of the base tables used in the view by executing UPDATE statements directly against the view.

Listing 7-10. *INSTEAD OF Trigger on a View*

```
ALTER TRIGGER Sales.vIndividualCustomerUpdate
ON Sales.vIndividualCustomer
INSTEAD OF UPDATE
NOT FOR REPLICATION
AS
BEGIN

  -- First make sure at least one row was affected
  IF (@@ROWCOUNT > 0)
  BEGIN

    -- Turn off "rows affected" messages
    SET NOCOUNT ON;

    -- Initialize a flag to indicate update success
    DECLARE @UpdateSuccessful nchar(1) = N'N';
```

```
-- Check for updatable columns in the first table
IF UPDATE(FirstName) OR UPDATE(MiddleName) OR UPDATE(LastName)
BEGIN

  -- Update columns in the base table
  UPDATE Person.Person
  SET
    FirstName = i.FirstName,
    MiddleName = i.MiddleName,
    LastName = i.LastName
  FROM inserted i
  WHERE i.BusinessEntityID = Person.Person.BusinessEntityID;

  -- Set flag to indicate success
  SET @UpdateSuccessful = N'Y';
END;

-- If updatable columns from the second table were specified, update those
-- columns in the base table
IF UPDATE(EmailAddress)
BEGIN

  -- Update columns in the base table
  UPDATE Person.EmailAddress
  SET EmailAddress = i.EmailAddress
  FROM inserted i
  WHERE i.BusinessEntityID = Person.EmailAddress.BusinessEntityID;

  -- Set flag to indicate success
  SET @UpdateSuccessful = N'Y';
END;

-- If the update was not successful, raise an error and roll back the
-- transaction
IF @UpdateSuccessful = N'N'
  RAISERROR('Must specify updatable columns.', 10, 127);
END;
END;
GO
```

The trigger in Listing 7-10 is created as an INSTEAD OF UPDATE trigger on the Sales.vIndividualCustomer view, as shown following:

```
ALTER TRIGGER Sales.vIndividualCustomerUpdate
ON Sales.vIndividualCustomer
INSTEAD OF UPDATE
NOT FOR REPLICATION
```

As with the previous examples in this chapter, this trigger begins by checking @@ROWCOUNT to ensure that at least one row was updated:

```
-- First make sure at least one row was affected
IF (@@ROWCOUNT > 0)
BEGIN
  ...
END;
```

Once the trigger verifies that one or more rows were affected by the DML statement that fired the trigger, it turns off the rows affected messages and initializes a flag to indicate success or failure of the update operation:

```
-- Turn off "rows affected" messages
SET NOCOUNT ON;

-- Initialize a flag to indicate update success
DECLARE @UpdateSuccessful nchar(1) = N'N';
```

The trigger then checks to see if the columns designated as updatable were affected by the UPDATE statement. If the proper columns were affected by the UPDATE statement, the trigger performs updates on the appropriate base tables for the view. For purposes of this demonstration, the columns that are updatable by the trigger are the FirstName, MiddleName, and LastName columns from the Person.Person table, and the EmailAddress column from the Person. EmailAddress column.

```
-- Check for updatable columns in the first table
IF UPDATE(FirstName) OR UPDATE(MiddleName) OR UPDATE(LastName)
BEGIN

  -- Update columns in the base table
  UPDATE Person.Person
  SET
    FirstName = i.FirstName,
    MiddleName = i.MiddleName,
    LastName = i.LastName
  FROM inserted i
  WHERE i.BusinessEntityID = Person.Person.BusinessEntityID;

  -- Set flag to indicate success
  SET @UpdateSuccessful = N'Y';
END;

-- If updatable columns from the second table were specified, update those
-- columns in the base table
IF UPDATE(EmailAddress)
BEGIN
```

```
    -- Update columns in the base table
    UPDATE Person.EmailAddress
    SET EmailAddress = i.EmailAddress
    FROM inserted i
    WHERE i.BusinessEntityID = Person.EmailAddress.BusinessEntityID;

    -- Set flag to indicate success
    SET @UpdateSuccessful = N'Y';
  END;
```

Finally, if no updatable columns were specified by the UPDATE statement that fired the trigger, an error is raised and the transaction is rolled back:

```
  -- If the update was not successful, raise an error and roll back the
  -- transaction
  IF @UpdateSuccessful = N'N'
    RAISERROR('Must specify updatable columns.', 10, 127);
```

Listing 7-11 demonstrates a simple UPDATE against the Sales.vIndividualCustomer view with the INSTEAD OF trigger from Listing 7-10 created on it. The result is shown in Figure 7-5.

Listing 7-11. *Updating a View Through an INSTEAD OF Trigger*

```
UPDATE Sales.vIndividualCustomer
SET
  FirstName = N'Dave',
  MiddleName = N'Robert',
  EmailAddress = N'dave.robinett@adventure-works.com'
WHERE BusinessEntityID = 1699;
```

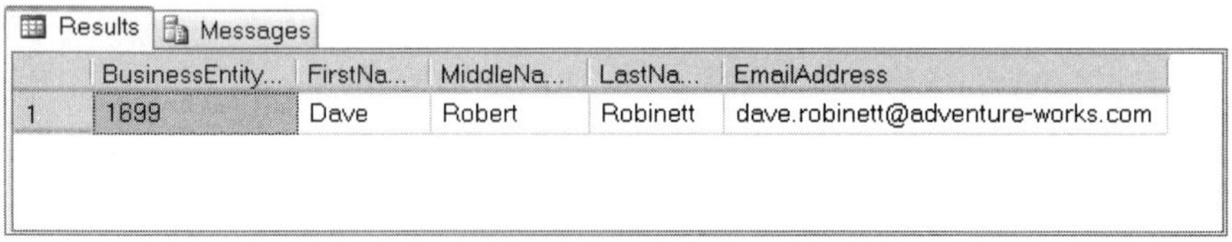

	BusinessEntity...	FirstNa...	MiddleNa...	LastNa...	EmailAddress
1	1699	Dave	Robert	Robinett	dave.robinett@adventure-works.com

Figure 7-5. *The result of the INSTEAD OF trigger view update*

DDL Triggers

Since SQL Server 2005, T-SQL programmers have had the ability to create DDL triggers that fire when DDL events occur within a database or on the server. In this section, I will discuss DDL triggers, the events that fire them, and the purpose. The format of the CREATE TRIGGER statement for DDL triggers is only slightly different from the DML trigger syntax, with the major difference being that you must specify the scope for the trigger, either ALL SERVER or DATABASE. The DATABASE scope causes the DDL trigger to fire if an event of a specified event type or event group occurs within the database in which the trigger was created. ALL SERVER scope causes the DDL trigger to fire if an event of the specified event type or event group occurs anywhere on the current server.

DDL triggers can only be specified as FOR or AFTER (there's no INSTEAD OF–type DDL trigger). The event types that can fire a DDL trigger are largely of the form CREATE, ALTER, DROP, GRANT, DENY, or REVOKE. Some system SPs that perform DDL functions also fire DDL triggers. The ALTER TRIGGER, DROP TRIGGER, DISABLE TRIGGER, and ENABLE TRIGGER statements all work for DDL triggers just as they do for DML triggers.

DDL triggers are useful when you want to prevent changes to your database, perform actions in response to a change in the database, or audit changes to the database. Which DDL statements can fire a DDL trigger depends on the scope of the trigger.

DDL EVENT TYPES AND EVENT GROUPS

DDL triggers can fire in response to a wide variety of event types and event groups, scoped at either the database or server level. The events that fire DDL triggers are largely DDL statements like CREATE and DROP, and DCL (Data Control Language) statements like GRANT and DENY. Event groups form a hierarchical structure of DDL events in logical groupings, like DDL_FUNCTION_EVENTS and DDL_PROCEDURE_EVENTS. Event groups allow you to fire triggers in response to a wide range of DDL events.

BOL has complete listings of all available DDL trigger event types and event groups, so I won't reproduce them fully here. Just keep in mind that you can fire triggers in response to most T-SQL DDL and DCL statements.

With DDL triggers, you can specify either an event type or an event group, the latter of which can encompass multiple events or other event groups. If you specify an event group, any events included within that group, or within the subgroups of that group, will fire the DDL trigger.

■**Note** Creation of a DDL trigger with ALL SERVER scope requires CONTROL SERVER permission on the server. Creating a DDL trigger with DATABASE scope requires ALTER ANY DATABASE DDL TRIGGER permissions.

Once the DDL trigger fires, you can access metadata about the event that fired the trigger with the EVENTDATA function. EVENTDATA returns information such as the time, connection, object name, and type of event that fired the trigger. The results are returned as a SQL Server xml data type instance. Listing 7-12 shows a sample of the type of data returned by the EVENTDATA function.

Listing 7-12. *EVENTDATA Function Sample Data*

```
<EVENT_INSTANCE>
  <EventType>CREATE_TABLE</EventType>
  <PostTime>2008-03-22T21:08:28.527</PostTime>
  <SPID>115</SPID>
```

```
<ServerName>SQL2008</ServerName>
<LoginName>SQL2008\Michael</LoginName>
<UserName>dbo</UserName>
<DatabaseName>AdventureWorks</DatabaseName>
<SchemaName>dbo</SchemaName>
<ObjectName>MyTable</ObjectName>
<ObjectType>TABLE</ObjectType>
<TSQLCommand>
  <SetOptions ANSI_NULLS="ON"
    ANSI_NULL_DEFAULT="ON"
    ANSI_PADDING="ON"
    QUOTED_IDENTIFIER="ON"
    ENCRYPTED="FALSE" />
  <CommandText>
    CREATE TABLE dbo.MyTable (i int);
  </CommandText>
</TSQLCommand>
</EVENT_INSTANCE>
```

You can use the xml data type's value() method to retrieve specific nodes from the result. The sample DDL trigger in Listing 7-13 creates a DDL trigger that fires in response to the CREATE TABLE statement in the AdventureWorks database. It logs the event data to a table named dbo.DdlActionLog.

Listing 7-13. *CREATE TABLE DDL Trigger Example*

```
-- Create a table to log DDL CREATE TABLE actions
CREATE TABLE dbo.DdlActionLog
(
  EntryNum int IDENTITY(1, 1) NOT NULL PRIMARY KEY,
  EventType nvarchar(200) NOT NULL,
  PostTime datetime NOT NULL,
  Spid int NOT NULL,
  LoginName sysname NOT NULL,
  UserName sysname NOT NULL,
  ServerName sysname NOT NULL,
  SchemaName sysname NOT NULL,
  DatabaseName sysname NOT NULL,
  ObjectName sysname NOT NULL,
  ObjectType sysname NOT NULL,
  CommandText nvarchar(max) NOT NULL
);
GO

CREATE TRIGGER AuditCreateTable
ON DATABASE
FOR CREATE_TABLE
AS
```

```
BEGIN
  -- Assign the XML event data to an xml variable
  DECLARE @event_data xml;
  SET @event_data = EVENTDATA();

  -- Shred the XML event data and insert a row in the log table
  INSERT INTO dbo.DdlActionLog
  (
    EventType,
    PostTime,
    Spid,
    LoginName,
    UserName,
    ServerName,
    SchemaName,
    DatabaseName,
    ObjectName,
    ObjectType,
    CommandText
  )
  SELECT
    EventNode.value(N'EventType[1]', N'nvarchar(200)'),
    EventNode.value(N'PostTime[1]', N'datetime'),
    EventNode.value(N'SPID[1]', N'int'),
    EventNode.value(N'LoginName[1]', N'sysname'),
    EventNode.value(N'UserName[1]', N'sysname'),
    EventNode.value(N'ServerName[1]', N'sysname'),
    EventNode.value(N'SchemaName[1]', N'sysname'),
    EventNode.value(N'DatabaseName[1]', N'sysname'),
    EventNode.value(N'ObjectName[1]', N'sysname'),
    EventNode.value(N'ObjectType[1]', N'sysname'),
    EventNode.value(N'(TSQLCommand/CommandText)[1]', 'nvarchar(max)')
  FROM @event_data.nodes('/EVENT_INSTANCE') EventTable(EventNode);

END;
GO
```

The first part of the example in Listing 7-13 creates a simple table to store the event-specific data generated by events that fire the DDL trigger:

```
-- Create a table to log DDL CREATE TABLE actions
CREATE TABLE dbo.DdlActionLog
(
  EntryNum int IDENTITY(1, 1) NOT NULL PRIMARY KEY,
  EventType nvarchar(200) NOT NULL,
  PostTime datetime NOT NULL,
  Spid int NOT NULL,
  LoginName sysname NOT NULL,
```

```
  UserName sysname NOT NULL,
  ServerName sysname NOT NULL,
  SchemaName sysname NOT NULL,
  DatabaseName sysname NOT NULL,
  ObjectName sysname NOT NULL,
  ObjectType sysname NOT NULL,
  CommandText nvarchar(max) NOT NULL
);
GO
```

The DDL trigger definition begins with the name, the scope (DATABASE), and the DDL action that fires the trigger. In this example, the action that fires this trigger is the CREATE TABLE event. Notice that unlike DML triggers, DDL triggers do not belong to schemas and do not have schemas specified in their names.

```
CREATE TRIGGER AuditCreateTable
ON DATABASE
FOR CREATE_TABLE
```

The body of the trigger begins by declaring an xml variable, @event_data. This variable holds the results of the EVENTDATA function for further processing later in the trigger.

```
-- Assign the XML event data to an xml variable
DECLARE @event_data xml;
SET @event_data = EVENTDATA();
```

Next, the trigger uses the nodes() and value() methods of the @event_data xml variable to shred the event data, which is then inserted into the dbo.DdlActionLog table in relational form:

```
-- Shred the XML event data and insert a row in the log table
INSERT INTO dbo.DdlActionLog
(
  EventType,
  PostTime,
  Spid,
  LoginName,
  UserName,
  ServerName,
  SchemaName,
  DatabaseName,
  ObjectName,
  ObjectType,
  CommandText
)
SELECT EventNode.value(N'EventType[1]', N'nvarchar(200)'),
  EventNode.value(N'PostTime[1]', N'datetime'),
  EventNode.value(N'SPID[1]', N'int'),
  EventNode.value(N'LoginName[1]', N'sysname'),
  EventNode.value(N'UserName[1]', N'sysname'),
  EventNode.value(N'ServerName[1]', N'sysname'),
```

```
    EventNode.value(N'SchemaName[1]', N'sysname'),
    EventNode.value(N'DatabaseName[1]', N'sysname'),
    EventNode.value(N'ObjectName[1]', N'sysname'),
    EventNode.value(N'ObjectType[1]', N'sysname'),
    EventNode.value(N'(TSQLCommand/CommandText)[1]', 'nvarchar(max)')
  FROM @event_data.nodes('/EVENT_INSTANCE') EventTable(EventNode);
```

Listing 7-14 demonstrates the DDL trigger by performing a CREATE TABLE statement. Partial results are shown in Figure 7-6.

Listing 7-14. *Testing the DDL Trigger with a CREATE TABLE Statement*

```
CREATE TABLE dbo.MyTable (i int);
GO

SELECT
  EntryNum,
  EventType,
  UserName,
  ObjectName,
  CommandText
FROM DdlActionLog;
GO
```

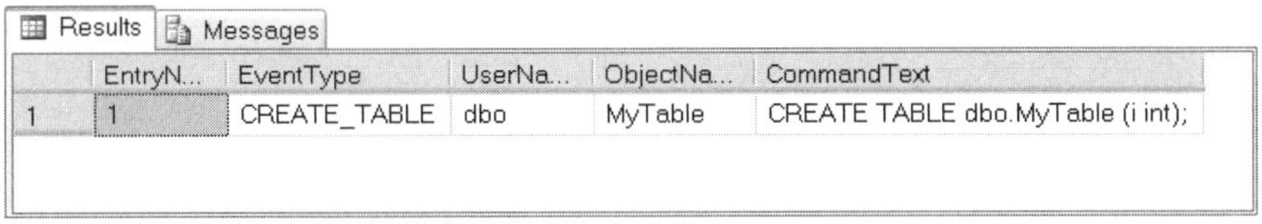

	EntryN...	EventType	UserNa...	ObjectNa...	CommandText
1	1	CREATE_TABLE	dbo	MyTable	CREATE TABLE dbo.MyTable (i int);

Figure 7-6. *DDL audit logging results*

Dropping a DDL trigger is as simple as executing the DROP TRIGGER statement, as shown in Listing 7-15. Notice that the ON DATABASE clause is required in this instance. The reason is that the DDL trigger exists outside the schemas of the database, so you must tell SQL Server whether the trigger exists at the database or server scope.

Listing 7-15. *Dropping a DDL Trigger*

```
DROP TRIGGER AuditCreateTable
ON DATABASE;
GO
```

Logon Triggers

SQL Server offers yet another type of trigger: the logon trigger. *Logon triggers* were first made available in SQL Server 2005 SP 2. These triggers fire in response to a SQL Server LOGON event—

after authentication succeeds, but before the user session is established. You can perform tasks ranging from simple LOGON event auditing to more advanced tasks like restricting the number of simultaneous sessions for a login or denying users the ability to create sessions during certain times.

The code example for this section uses logon triggers to deny a given user the ability to log into SQL Server during a specified time period (e.g., during a resource-intensive nightly batch process). Listing 7-16 begins the logon trigger example by creating a sample login and a table that holds a logon denial schedule. The first entry in this table will be used to deny the sample login the ability to log into SQL Server between the hours of 9:00 and 11:00 PM on Saturday nights.

Listing 7-16. *Creating a Test Login and Logon Denial Schedule*

```
CREATE LOGIN PublicUser
WITH PASSWORD = 'p@$$w0rd';
GO

CREATE TABLE dbo.DenyLogonSchedule
(
  UserId sysname NOT NULL,
  DayOfWeek int NOT NULL,
  TimeStart time NOT NULL,
  TimeEnd time NOT NULL,
  PRIMARY KEY (UserId, DayOfWeek, TimeStart, TimeEnd)
);
GO

INSERT INTO dbo.DenyLogonSchedule
(
  UserId,
  DayOfWeek,
  TimeStart,
  TimeEnd
)
VALUES
(
  'PublicUser',
  7,
  '21:00:00',
  '23:00:00'
);
GO
```

The logon trigger that makes use of this table to deny logons on a schedule is shown in Listing 7-17.

Listing 7-17. *Sample Logon Trigger*

```
CREATE TRIGGER DenyLogons
ON ALL SERVER
WITH EXECUTE AS 'sa'
FOR LOGON
AS
BEGIN
  IF EXISTS
  (
    SELECT 1
    FROM AdventureWorks.dbo.DenyLogonSchedule
    WHERE UserId = ORIGINAL_LOGIN()
      AND DayOfWeek = DATEPART(WeekDay, GETDATE())
      AND CAST(GETDATE() AS TIME) BETWEEN TimeStart AND TimeEnd
  )
  BEGIN
    ROLLBACK TRANSACTION;
  END;
END;
GO
```

■Caution If your logon trigger errors out, you will be unable to log into SQL Server normally. You can still connect using the Dedicated Administrator Connection (DAC), which bypasses logon triggers, however. Make sure that your logon trigger works properly before putting it in production.

The CREATE TRIGGER statement begins much like the other trigger samples I've used to this point, by specifying the name and scope (ALL SERVER). The WITH EXECUTE clause is used to specify that the logon trigger should run under the sa security context, and the FOR LOGON clause indicates that this is actually a logon trigger.

```
CREATE TRIGGER DenyLogons
ON ALL SERVER
WITH EXECUTE AS 'sa'
FOR LOGON
```

The trigger body is fairly simple. It simply checks for the existence of an entry in the AdventureWorks.dbo.DenyLogonSchedule table, indicating that the current user (retrieved with the ORIGINAL_LOGIN function) is denied login based on the current date and time. If there is an entry indicating that the login should be denied, then the ROLLBACK TRANSACTION statement is executed, denying the login.

```
IF EXISTS
(
  SELECT 1
  FROM AdventureWorks.dbo.DenyLogonSchedule
  WHERE UserId = ORIGINAL_LOGIN()
    AND DayOfWeek = DATEPART(WeekDay, GETDATE())
    AND CAST(GETDATE() AS TIME) BETWEEN TimeStart AND TimeEnd
)
BEGIN
  ROLLBACK TRANSACTION;
END;
```

Notice that the three-part name of the table is used in this statement, since the user attempting to log in may be connecting to a different default database. Attempting to log on to SQL Server using the `PublicUser` account on Saturday night between the hours indicated results in an error message like the one shown in Figure 7-7.

■Tip Logon triggers are useful for auditing and restricting logins, but because they only fire after a successful authentication, they cannot be used to log unsuccessful login attempts.

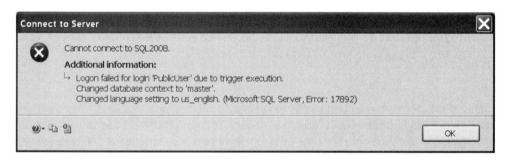

Figure 7-7. *A logon trigger denying a login*

The logon trigger also makes logon information available in XML format within the trigger via the `EVENTDATA` function. An example of the logon information generated by the `LOGON` event is shown in Listing 7-18.

Listing 7-18. *Sample Event Data Generated by a LOGON Event*

```
<EVENT_INSTANCE>
  <EventType>LOGON</EventType>
  <PostTime>2008-03-22T23:18:33.357</PostTime>
  <SPID>110</SPID>
  <ServerName>SQL2008</ServerName>
  <LoginName>PublicUser</LoginName>
```

```
    <LoginType>SQL Login</LoginType>
    <SID>zgPcN6UCBE2j/HYTugOi4A==</SID>
    <ClientHost>&lt;local machine&gt;</ClientHost>
    <IsPooled>0</IsPooled>
</EVENT_INSTANCE>
```

Summary

This chapter discussed triggers, including traditional DML triggers, DDL triggers, and logon triggers. As you've seen, triggers are useful tools for a variety of purposes.

DML triggers are the original form of trigger. Much of the functionality that DML triggers were used for in the past, such as enforcing referential integrity, has been supplanted by newer and more efficient T-SQL functionality over the years, like cascading DRI. DML triggers are useful for auditing DML statements and for enforcing business rules and logic in the database. They can also be used to implement updating for views that are normally not updatable.

In this chapter, I discussed the inserted and deleted virtual tables, which hold copies of the rows being affected by a DML statement. I also discussed the UPDATE and COLUMNS_UPDATED functions in DML triggers, which identify the columns that were affected by the DML state-ment that fired a trigger. Finally, I talked about the differences between AFTER and INSTEAD OF triggers and explained nested triggers and trigger recursion.

DDL triggers, introduced in SQL Server 2005, can be used to audit and restrict database object and server changes. DDL triggers can help provide protection against accidental or mali-cious changes to, or destruction of, database objects. In this chapter, I discussed the EVENTDATA function and how you can use it to audit DDL actions within a database or on the server.

Logon triggers, introduced in SQL Server 2005 SP 2, can likewise be used to audit success-ful logins and restrict logins for various reasons.

In the next chapter, I will discuss the native encryption functionality available in SQL Server 2008.

EXERCISES

1. [True/false] The EVENTDATA function returns information about DDL events within DDL triggers.

2. [True/false] In a DML trigger, the inserted and deleted virtual tables are both populated with rows during an UPDATE event.

3. [Choose all that apply] Which of the following types of triggers does SQL Server 2008 support?

    a. Logon triggers

    b. TCL triggers

    c. DDL triggers

    d. Hierarchy triggers

    e. DML triggers

4. [Fill in the blank] The ___ statement prevents triggers from generating extraneous rows affected messages.

5. [Choose one] The COLUMNS_UPDATED function returns data in which of the following formats?

    a.   A varbinary string with bits set to represent affected columns

    b.   A comma-delimited varchar string with a column ID number for each affected column

    c.   A table consisting of column ID numbers for each affected column

    d.   A table consisting of all rows that were inserted by the DML operation

6. [True/false] @@ROWCOUNT, when used at the beginning of a DML trigger, reflects the number of rows affected by the DML statement that fired the trigger.

7. [True/false] You can create recursive AFTER triggers on views.

CHAPTER 8

■■■

Encryption

SQL Server 2008 supports built-in column- and database-level encryption functionality directly through T-SQL. Column-level encryption allows you to encrypt the data in your database at the column level. Back in the days of SQL Server 2000 (and before), you had to turn to third-party tools or write your own extended stored procedures (XPs) to encrypt sensitive data. Even with these tools in place, subpar implementation of various aspects of the system, such as encryption key management, could leave many systems in a vulnerable state.

SQL Server 2008's encryption model takes advantage of the Windows CryptoAPI to secure your data. With built-in encryption key management and facilities to handle encryption, decryption, and one-way hashing through T-SQL statements, SQL Server 2008 provides useful tools for efficient and secure data encryption. SQL Server 2008 also supports two new encryption options: *transparent data encryption (TDE)* for supporting encryption of an entire database, and *extensible key management (EKM)*, which allows you to use third-party hardware-based encryption key management and encryption acceleration.

In this chapter, I will discuss SQL Server 2008's built-in column-level encryption and decryption functionality, key management capabilities, one-way hashing functions, and the new TDE and EKM functionality.

The Encryption Hierarchy

SQL Server 2008 offers a layered approach to encryption key management by allowing several levels of key-encrypting keys between the top-level master key and the lowest-level data-encrypting keys. SQL Server also allows for encryption by certificates, symmetric keys, and asymmetric keys. The SQL Server 2008 encryption model is hierarchical, as shown in Figure 8-1.

At the top of the SQL Server 2008 encryption hierarchy is the Windows Data Protection API (DPAPI), which is used to protect the granddaddy of all SQL Server 2008 encryption keys: the *service master key (SMK)*. The SMK is automatically generated by SQL Server the first time it is needed to encrypt another key. There is only one SMK per SQL Server instance, and it directly or indirectly secures all keys in the SQL Server encryption key hierarchy on the server.

While each SQL Server instance has only a single SMK, each database can have a *database master key (DMK)*. The DMK is encrypted by the SMK. The DMK is used to encrypt lower-level keys and certificates.

At the bottom of the SQL Server 2008 key hierarchy are the certificates, symmetric keys, and asymmetric keys used to encrypt data.

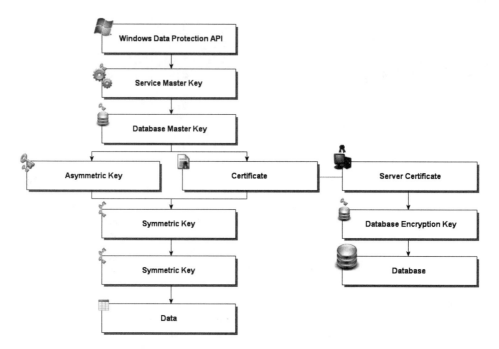

Figure 8-1. *SQL Server 2008 encryption hierarchy*

SQL Server 2008 also introduces the concept of the *server certificate*, which is a certificate created in the master database for the purpose of protecting database encryption keys. *Database encryption keys* are symmetric encryption keys created to encrypt entire databases via TDE.

Service Master Keys

As I mentioned in the previous section, the SMK is automatically generated by SQL Server the first time it is needed. Because the SMK is generated automatically and managed by SQL Server, there are only a couple of administrative tasks you need to perform for this key, namely backing it up and restoring it on a server as necessary. Listing 8-1 demonstrates the BACKUP and RESTORE SERVICE MASTER KEY statements.

Listing 8-1. *BACKUP and RESTORE SMK Examples*

```
-- Back up the SMK to a file
BACKUP SERVICE MASTER KEY TO FILE = 'c:\SQL2008.SMK'
  ENCRYPTION BY PASSWORD = 'p@$$w0rd';

-- Restore the SMK from a file
RESTORE SERVICE MASTER KEY FROM FILE = 'c:\SQL2008.SMK'
  DECRYPTION BY PASSWORD = 'p@$$w0rd';
```

The `BACKUP SERVICE MASTER KEY` statement allows you to back up your SMK to a file. The SMK is encrypted in the file, so the `ENCRYPTION BY PASSWORD` clause of this statement is mandatory.

The `RESTORE SERVICE MASTER KEY` statement restores the SMK from a previously created backup file. The `DECRYPTION BY PASSWORD` clause must specify the same password used to encrypt the file when you created the backup. Backing up and restoring an SMK requires `CONTROL SERVER` permissions.

The `RESTORE SERVICE MASTER KEY` statement can include the optional keyword `FORCE` to force the SMK to restore even if there is a data decryption failure. If you have to use the `FORCE` keyword, you can expect to lose data, so use this option with care and only as a last resort.

■**Tip** After installing SQL Server 2008, you should immediately back up your SMK and store a copy of it in a secure offsite location. If your SMK becomes corrupted or is otherwise compromised, you could lose access to all of your encrypted data if you don't have a backup of the SMK.

In addition to `BACKUP` and `RESTORE` statements, SQL Server provides the `ALTER SERVICE MASTER KEY` statement to allow you to change the SMK for an instance of SQL Server. When SQL Server generates the SMK, it uses the credentials of the SQL Server service account to encrypt the SMK. If you change the SQL Server service account, you can use `ALTER SERVICE MASTER KEY` to update it using the current service account credentials. Alternatively, you can advise SQL Server to secure the SMK using the local machine key, which is managed by the operating system. You can also use `ALTER SERVICE MASTER KEY` to regenerate the SMK completely.

As with the `RESTORE SERVICE MASTER KEY` statement, the `ALTER SERVICE MASTER KEY` statement allows use of the `FORCE` keyword. Normally, if there is a decryption error during the process of altering the SMK, SQL Server will stop the process with an error message. When `FORCE` is used, the SMK is regenerated even at the risk of data loss. Just like the `RESTORE` statement, the `FORCE` option should be used with care, and only as a last resort.

■**Tip** When you regenerate the SMK, all keys that are encrypted by it must be decrypted and reencrypted. This operation can be resource intensive and should be scheduled during off-peak time periods.

Database Master Keys

Each database can have a single DMK, which is used to encrypt certificate private keys and asymmetric key-pair private keys in the current database. The DMK is created with the `CREATE MASTER KEY` statement, as shown in Listing 8-2.

Listing 8-2. *Creating a Master Key*

```
USE AdventureWorks;
GO

CREATE MASTER KEY
  ENCRYPTION BY PASSWORD = 'p@$$w0rd' ;
```

The CREATE MASTER KEY statement creates the DMK and uses triple DES (Data Encryption Standard) to encrypt it with the supplied password. If the password you supply does not meet Windows's password complexity requirements, SQL Server will complain with an error message like the following:

```
Msg 15118, Level 16, State 1, Line 1
Password validation failed. The password does not meet Windows
policy requirements because it is not complex enough.
```

SQL Server 2008 automatically uses the SMK to encrypt a copy of the DMK. When this feature is used, SQL Server can decrypt your DMK when needed without the need to first open the master key. When this feature is not in use, you must issue the OPEN MASTER KEY statement and supply the same password initially used to encrypt the DMK whenever you need to use it. The potential downside to encrypting your DMK with the SMK is that any member of the sysadmin server role can decrypt the DMK. You can use the ALTER MASTER KEY statement to change the method SQL Server uses to decrypt the DMK. Listing 8-3 shows how to turn off encryption by SMK for a DMK.

Listing 8-3. *Turning Off DMK Encryption by the SMK*

```
ALTER MASTER KEY
  DROP ENCRYPTION BY SERVICE MASTER KEY;
```

When the DMK is regenerated, all the keys it protects are decrypted and reencrypted with the new DMK. The FORCE keyword is used to force SQL Server to regenerate the DMK even if there are decryption errors. As with the SMK, the FORCE keyword should be used only as a last resort. You can expect to lose data if you have to use FORCE.

You can also back up and restore a DMK with the BACKUP MASTER KEY and RESTORE MASTER KEY statements. The BACKUP MASTER KEY statement is similar in operation to the BACKUP SERVICE MASTER KEY statement. When you back up the DMK, you must specify the password that SQL Server will use to encrypt the DMK in the output file. When you restore the DMK, you must specify the same password in the DECRYPTION BY PASSWORD clause to decrypt the DMK in the output file. In addition, you must specify an encryption password that SQL Server will use to encrypt the password in the ENCRYPTION BY PASSWORD clause. Listing 8-4 demonstrates backing up and restoring a DMK.

Listing 8-4. *Backing Up and Restoring a DMK*

```
USE AdventureWorks;
GO

-- Back up DMK
BACKUP MASTER KEY
  TO FILE = 'c:\AdventureWorks.DMK'
  ENCRYPTION BY PASSWORD = 'p@$$w0rd';

-- Restore DMK from backup
RESTORE MASTER KEY
  FROM FILE = 'c:\AdventureWorks.DMK'
  DECRYPTION BY PASSWORD = 'p@$$w0rd'
  ENCRYPTION BY PASSWORD = '3rt=d4uy';
```

The FORCE keyword is available for use with the RESTORE MASTER KEY statement, but as with other statements, it should only be used as a last resort, as it could result in unrecoverable encrypted data.

The DROP MASTER KEY statement can be used to remove a DMK from the database. DROP MASTER KEY will not remove a DMK if it is currently being used to encrypt other keys in the database. If you want to drop a DMK that is protecting other keys in the database, the protected keys must be altered to remove their encryption by the DMK first.

Tip Always make backups of your DMKs immediately upon creation and store them in a secure location.

If you choose to disable automatic key management with the ALTER MASTER KEY statement, you will need to use the OPEN MASTER KEY and CLOSE MASTER KEY statements every time you wish to perform encryption and decryption in a database.

OPEN MASTER KEY requires you to supply the same password used to encrypt the DMK in the DECRYPTION BY PASSWORD clause. This password is used to decrypt the DMK, a required step when you are encrypting and decrypting data. When finished using the DMK, issue the CLOSE MASTER KEY statement. If your DMK is encrypted by the SMK, you do not need to use the OPEN MASTER KEY and CLOSE MASTER KEY statements; SQL Server will handle that task for you automatically.

Certificates

Certificates are asymmetric encryption key pairs with additional metadata, such as subject and expiration date, in the X.509 certificate format. Asymmetric encryption is a method of encrypting data using two separate but mathematically related keys. SQL Server 2008 uses the standard public key/private key encryption methodology. You can think of a certificate as a wrapper for an asymmetric encryption public key/private key pair. The CREATE CERTIFICATE statement can be used to either install an existing certificate or create a new certificate on SQL Server. Listing 8-5 shows how to create a new certificate on SQL Server.

Listing 8-5. *Creating a Certificate on SQL Server*

```
CREATE CERTIFICATE TestCertificate
  ENCRYPTION BY PASSWORD = 'p@$$w0rd'
  WITH SUBJECT = 'Adventureworks Test Certificate',
    EXPIRY_DATE = '2026-10-31';
```

The CREATE CERTIFICATE statement includes several options. The only things mandatory are the SQL Server identifier for the certificate immediately following the CREATE CERTIFICATE statement (in this case TestCertificate), and the WITH SUBJECT clause, which sets the certificate subject name. If the ENCRYPTION BY PASSWORD clause is not used when you create a certificate, the certificate's private key is encrypted by the DMK. Additional options available to the CREATE CERTIFICATE statement include START_DATE and EXPIRY_DATE, which set the start and expiration dates for the certificate; and the ACTIVE FOR BEGIN DIALOG clause, which makes the certificate available for use by Service Broker dialogs.

■**Tip** If START_DATE is not specified, the current date is used. If EXPIRY_DATE is omitted, the expiration date is set to one year after the start date.

You can also use the CREATE CERTIFICATE statement to load an existing certificate in a variety of ways, including the following:

- You can use the FROM ASSEMBLY clause to load an existing certificate from a signed assembly already loaded in the database.

- You can use the EXECUTABLE FILE clause to create a certificate from a signed DLL file.

- You can use the FILE clause to create a certificate from an existing Distinguished Encoding Rules (DER) X.509 certificate file.

- You can also use the WITH PRIVATE KEY clause with the FILE or EXECUTABLE FILE options to specify a separate file containing the certificate's private key. When you specify the WITH PRIVATE KEY clause, you can specify the optional DECRYPTION BY PASSWORD and ENCRYPTION BY PASSWORD clauses to specify the password that will be used to decrypt the private key if it is encrypted in the source file, and to secure the private key once it is loaded.

■**Note** SQL Server generates private keys that are 1024 bits in length. If you import a private key from an external source, it must be a multiple of 64 bits, between 384 and 3456 bits in length.

After creating a certificate—as with DMKs and SMKs—you should immediately make a backup and store it in a secure location. Listing 8-6 demonstrates how to make a backup of a certificate.

Listing 8-6. *Backing Up a Certificate*

```
BACKUP CERTIFICATE TestCertificate
  TO FILE = 'c:\TestCertificate.CER'
  WITH PRIVATE KEY
  (
    FILE = 'c:\TestCertificate.PVK',
    ENCRYPTION BY PASSWORD = '7&rt0xp2',
    DECRYPTION BY PASSWORD = 'p@$$w0rd'
  );
```

The BACKUP CERTIFICATE statement in Listing 8-6 backs up the TestCertificate certificate to the c:\TestCertificate.CER file and the certificate's private key to the c:\TestCertificate.PVK file. The DECRYPTION BY PASSWORD clause specifies the password to use to decrypt the certificate, and ENCRYPTION BY PASSWORD gives SQL Server the password to use when encrypting the private key in the file. There is no RESTORE statement for certificates; instead, the CREATE CERTIFICATE statement has all the options necessary to restore a certificate from a backup file. T-SQL also provides an ALTER CERTIFICATE statement that allows you to make changes to an existing certificate.

You can use certificates to encrypt and decrypt data directly with the certificate encryption and decryption functions, EncryptByCert and DecryptByCert. The EncryptByCert function encrypts a given clear text message with a specified certificate. The function accepts an int certificate ID and a plain text value to encrypt. The int certificate ID can be retrieved by passing the certificate name to the Cert_ID function. Listing 8-7 demonstrates this function. EncryptByCert returns a varbinary value up to a maximum of 432 bytes in length (the length of the result depends on the length of the key). The "Limitations of Asymmetric Encryption" sidebar describes some of the limitations of asymmetric encryption on SQL Server, including encryption by certificate.

LIMITATIONS OF ASYMMETRIC ENCRYPTION

Asymmetric encryption has certain limitations that should be noted before you attempt to encrypt data directly with certificates or asymmetric keys. The EncryptByCert function can accept a char, varchar, binary, nchar, nvarchar, or varbinary constant, column name, or variable as clear text to encrypt. Asymmetric encryption, including encryption by certificate, on SQL Server returns a varbinary result, but will not return a result longer than 432 bytes. As mentioned, the maximum length of the result depends on the length of the encryption key used. As an example, with the default private key length of 1024 bits, you can encrypt a varchar plain text message with a maximum length of 117 characters and an nvarchar plain text message with a maximum length of 58 characters. The result in either case is a varbinary result of 128 bytes.

Microsoft recommends that you avoid using asymmetric encryption to encrypt data directly because of the size limitations, and for performance reasons. Symmetric encryption algorithms use shorter keys but operate more quickly than asymmetric encryption algorithms. The SQL Server 2008 encryption key hierarchy provides the best of both worlds—the long key lengths of asymmetric keys protecting the shorter, more efficient symmetric keys. To maximize performance, Microsoft recommends using symmetric encryption to encrypt data and asymmetric encryption to encrypt symmetric keys.

The DecryptByCert function decrypts text previously encrypted by EncryptByCert. The DecryptByCert function accepts an int certificate ID, an encrypted varbinary cipher text message, and an optional certificate password that must match the one used when the certificate was created (if one was specified at creation time). If no certificate password is specified, the DMK is used to decrypt it. Listing 8-7 demonstrates encryption and decryption by certificate for short plain text. The results are shown in Figure 8-2.

Listing 8-7. *Sample Encryption and Decryption by Certificate*

```
-- Create a DMK
CREATE MASTER KEY
  ENCRYPTION BY PASSWORD = 'P@55w0rd';

-- Create a certificate
CREATE CERTIFICATE TestCertificate
  WITH SUBJECT = N'Adventureworks Test Certificate',
  EXPIRY_DATE = '2026-10-31';

-- Create the plain text data to encrypt
DECLARE @plaintext nvarchar(58) =
  N'This is a test string to encrypt';
SELECT 'Plain text = ', @plaintext;

-- Encrypt the plain text by certificate
DECLARE @ciphertext varbinary(128) =
  EncryptByCert(Cert_ID('TestCertificate'), @plaintext);
SELECT 'Cipher text = ', @ciphertext;

-- Decrypt the cipher text by certificate
DECLARE @decryptedtext nvarchar(58) =
  DecryptByCert(Cert_ID('TestCertificate'), @ciphertext);
SELECT 'Decrypted text = ', @decryptedtext;

-- Drop the test certificate
DROP CERTIFICATE TestCertificate;

-- Drop the DMK
DROP MASTER KEY;
```

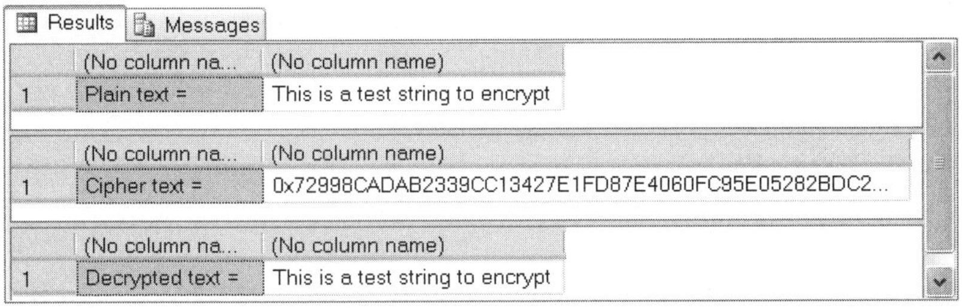

Figure 8-2. *Result of encrypting and decrypting by certificate*

Listing 8-7 first creates a DMK and a test certificate using the CREATE MASTER KEY and CREATE CERTIFICATE statements presented previously in this chapter. It then generates an nvarchar plain text message to encrypt.

```
-- Create a DMK
CREATE MASTER KEY
  ENCRYPTION BY PASSWORD = 'P@55w0rd';

-- Create a certificate
CREATE CERTIFICATE TestCertificate
  WITH SUBJECT = N'Adventureworks Test Certificate',
  EXPIRY_DATE = '2026-10-31';

-- Create the plain text data to encrypt
DECLARE @plaintext nvarchar(58) =
  N'This is a test string to encrypt';
SELECT 'Plain text = ', @plaintext;
```

The sample uses the EncryptByCert function to encrypt the plain text message. The Cert_ID function is used to retrieve the int certificate ID for TestCertificate.

```
-- Encrypt the plain text by certificate
DECLARE @ciphertext varbinary(128) =
  EncryptByCert(Cert_ID('TestCertificate'), @plaintext);
SELECT 'Cipher text = ', @ciphertext;
```

The DecryptByCert function is then used to decrypt the cipher text. Again, the Cert_ID function is used to retrieve the TestCertificate certificate ID.

```
-- Decrypt the cipher text by certificate
DECLARE @decryptedtext nvarchar(58) =
  DecryptByCert(Cert_ID('TestCertificate'), @ciphertext);
SELECT 'Decrypted text = ', @decryptedtext;
```

The balance of the code performs some cleanup, dropping the certificate and DMK:

```
-- Drop the test certificate
DROP CERTIFICATE TestCertificate;

-- Drop the DMK
DROP MASTER KEY;
```

You can also use a certificate to generate a signature for a plain text message. SignByCert accepts a certificate ID, a plain text message, and an optional certificate password. The result is a varbinary string, up to a length of 432 characters (again, the length of the result is determined by the length of the encryption key). When SignByCert is used, the slightest change in the plain text message—even a single character—will result in a completely different signature being generated for the message. This allows you to easily detect whether your plain text has been tampered with. Listing 8-8 uses the SignByCert function to create a signature for a plain text message. The results are shown in Figure 8-3.

Listing 8-8. *Signing a Message with the SignByCert Function*

```
-- Create a DMK
CREATE MASTER KEY ENCRYPTION BY PASSWORD = 'P@55w0rd';

-- Create a certificate
CREATE CERTIFICATE TestCertificate
  WITH SUBJECT = 'Adventureworks Test Certificate',
  EXPIRY_DATE = '2026-10-31';

-- Create message
DECLARE @message nvarchar(4000) = N'Four score and seven years ago our
fathers brought forth on this continent a new nation, conceived in Liberty,
and dedicated to the proposition that all men are created equal.

Now we are engaged in a great civil war, testing whether that nation, or
any nation, so conceived and so dedicated, can long endure. We are met
on a great battle-field of that war. We have come to dedicate a portion
of that field, as a final resting place for those who here gave their
lives that that nation might live. It is altogether fitting and proper
that we should do this.


But, in a larger sense, we can not dedicate–we can not consecrate–we can
not hallow–this ground. The brave men, living and dead, who struggled here,
have consecrated it, far above our poor power to add or detract. The world
will little note, nor long remember what we say here, but it can never
forget what they did here. It is for us the living, rather, to be dedicated
here to the unfinished work which they who fought here have thus far so
nobly advanced. It is rather for us to be here dedicated to the great task
remaining before us–that from these honored dead we take increased devotion
```

to that cause for which they gave the last full measure of devotion–that we
here highly resolve that these dead shall not have died in vain–that this
nation, under God, shall have a new birth of freedom–and that government of
the people, by the people, for the people, shall not perish from the earth.';

```
-- Sign the message by certificate
SELECT SignByCert(Cert_ID(N'TestCertificate'), @message);

-- Drop the certificate
DROP CERTIFICATE TestCertificate;

-- Drop the DMK
DROP MASTER KEY;
```

Figure 8-3. *Signature generated by SignByCert (partial)*

Asymmetric Keys

Asymmetric keys are actually composed of a key pair: a *public key*, which is publicly accessible,
and a *private key*, which is kept secret. The mathematical relationship between the public and
private keys allows for encryption and decryption without revealing the private key. T-SQL
includes statements for creating and managing asymmetric keys.

The CREATE ASYMMETRIC KEY statement allows you to generate an asymmetric key pair or
install an existing key pair on the server, in much the same manner as when creating a certificate. Encryption key length is often used as an indicator of relative encryption strength, and
when you create an asymmetric key on SQL Server, you can specify an RSA key length, as
shown in Table 8-1.

Table 8-1. *Asymmetric Key Algorithms and Limits*

Algorithm	Key Length	Plain Text	Cipher Text	Signature Length
RSA_512	512 bits	53 bytes	64 bytes	64 bytes
RSA_1024	1024 bits	117 bytes	128 bytes	128 bytes
RSA_2048	2048 bits	245 bytes	256 bytes	256 bytes

Listing 8-9 creates an asymmetric key pair on SQL Server 2008.

Listing 8-9. *Creating an Asymmetric Key Pair*

```
CREATE ASYMMETRIC KEY TempAsymmetricKey
  WITH ALGORITHM = RSA_1024;
```

You can alter an existing asymmetric key with the ALTER ASYMMETRIC KEY statement. ALTER ASYMMETRIC KEY offers the following options for managing your asymmetric keys:

- You can use the REMOVE PRIVATE KEY clause to remove the private key from the asymmetric public key/private key pair.

- You can use the WITH PRIVATE KEY clause to change the method used to protect the private key.

- You can change the asymmetric key protection method from DMK encryption to password encryption with the ENCRYPTION BY PASSWORD option.

- You can switch from password protection for your asymmetric key to DMK protection with the DECRYPTION BY PASSWORD clause.

- You can specify both the ENCRYPTION BY PASSWORD and DECRYPTION BY PASSWORD clauses together to change the password used to encrypt the private key.

The DROP ASYMMETRIC KEY statement removes an asymmetric key from the database.

The EncryptByAsymKey and DecryptByAsymKey functions allow you to encrypt and decrypt data with an asymmetric key, in the same way as EncryptByCert and DecryptByCert.

The EncryptByAsymKey function accepts an int asymmetric key ID and plain text to encrypt. The AsymKey_ID function can be used to retrieve an asymmetric key ID by name. DecryptByAsymKey accepts an asymmetric key ID, encrypted cipher text to decrypt, and an optional password to decrypt the asymmetric key. If the password is specified, it must be the same password used to encrypt the asymmetric key at creation time.

■**Tip** The limitations for asymmetric key encryption and decryption on SQL Server are the same as those for certificate encryption and decryption.

Listing 8-10 demonstrates the use of asymmetric key encryption and decryption functions. The results are shown in Figure 8-4.

Listing 8-10. *Encrypting and Decrypting with Asymmetric Keys*

```
-- Create DMK
CREATE MASTER KEY
  ENCRYPTION BY PASSWORD = 'P@55w0rd';

-- Create asymmetric key
CREATE ASYMMETRIC KEY TestAsymmetricKey
  WITH ALGORITHM = RSA_512;
```

```
-- Assign a credit card number to encrypt
DECLARE @CreditCard nvarchar(26) = N'9000 1234 5678 9012';
SELECT @CreditCard;

-- Encrypt the credit card number
DECLARE @EncryptedCreditCard varbinary(64) =
  EncryptByAsymKey(AsymKey_ID(N'TestAsymmetricKey'), @CreditCard);
SELECT @EncryptedCreditCard;

-- Decrypt the encrypted credit card number
DECLARE @DecryptedCreditCard nvarchar(26) =
  DecryptByAsymKey(AsymKey_ID(N'TestAsymmetricKey'), @EncryptedCreditCard);
SELECT @DecryptedCreditCard;

-- Drop asymmetric key
DROP ASYMMETRIC KEY TestAsymmetricKey;

-- Drop DMK
DROP MASTER KEY;
```

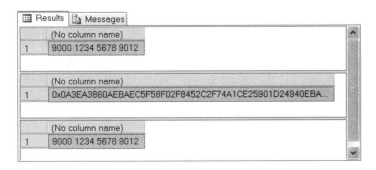

Figure 8-4. *Asymmetric key encryption results*

This example first creates a DMK and an RSA asymmetric key with a 512-bit private key length. Then it creates plain text representing a simple credit card number.

```
-- Create DMK
CREATE MASTER KEY
  ENCRYPTION BY PASSWORD = 'P@55w0rd';

-- Create asymmetric key
CREATE ASYMMETRIC KEY TestAsymmetricKey
  WITH ALGORITHM = RSA_512;

-- Assign a credit card number to encrypt
DECLARE @CreditCard nvarchar(26) = N'9000 1234 5678 9012';
SELECT @CreditCard;
```

The sample then encrypts the credit card number with the `EncryptByAsymKey` function, and decrypts it with the `DecryptByAsymKey` function. Both functions use the `AsymKey_ID` function to retrieve the asymmetric key ID.

```
-- Encrypt the credit card number
DECLARE @EncryptedCreditCard varbinary(64) =
  EncryptByAsymKey(AsymKey_ID(N'TestAsymmetricKey'), @CreditCard);
SELECT @EncryptedCreditCard;

-- Decrypt the encrypted credit card number
DECLARE @DecryptedCreditCard nvarchar(26) =
  DecryptByAsymKey(AsymKey_ID(N'TestAsymmetricKey'), @EncryptedCreditCard);
SELECT @DecryptedCreditCard;
```

The sample finishes up with a little housekeeping; namely dropping the asymmetric key and the DMK created for the example.

```
-- Drop asymmetric key
DROP ASYMMETRIC KEY TestAsymmetricKey;

-- Drop DMK
DROP MASTER KEY;
```

Like certificates, asymmetric keys offer a function to generate digital signatures for plain text. The `SignByAsymKey` function accepts a string up to 8000 bytes in length and returns a varbinary signature for the string. The length of the signature is dependent on the key length, as previously shown in Table 8-1. Listing 8-11 is a simple example of the `SignByAsymKey` function in action. The results are shown in Figure 8-5.

Listing 8-11. *Signing a Message by Asymmetric Key*

```
-- Create DMK
CREATE MASTER KEY
  ENCRYPTION BY PASSWORD = 'P@55w0rd';

-- Create asymmetric key
CREATE ASYMMETRIC KEY TestAsymmetricKey
  WITH ALGORITHM = RSA_512;

-- Create message
DECLARE @message nvarchar(4000) = N'Alas, poor Yorick!';
SELECT @message;

-- Sign message by asymmetric key
SELECT SignByAsymKey(AsymKey_ID(N'TestAsymmetricKey'), @message);

-- Drop asymmetric key
DROP ASYMMETRIC KEY TestAsymmetricKey;
```

```
-- Drop DMK
DROP MASTER KEY;
```

(No column na...
1	Alas, poor Yorick!

(No column name)
1	0x39197F39DD0E671FA4AFE5D2A777724B1F849503DCD587...

Figure 8-5. *Signing a message with an asymmetric key*

ASYMMETRIC KEY "BACKUPS"

SQL Server provides no BACKUP or RESTORE statements for asymmetric keys. For physical backups of your asymmetric keys, you should install the asymmetric keys from an external source like an assembly, an executable file, a strong-name file, or a hardware security module (HSM). You can make backups of the source files containing your asymmetric keys. As an alternative, you can use certificates instead of asymmetric keys. Keep these options in mind when you are planning to take advantage of SQL Server 2008 encryption.

Symmetric Keys

Symmetric keys are at the bottom of the SQL Server encryption key hierarchy. Symmetric encryption algorithms use trivially related keys to both encrypt and decrypt your data. *Trivially related* simply means that the algorithm can use either the same key for both encryption and decryption, or two keys that are mathematically related via a simple transformation to derive one key from the other. Symmetric keys on SQL Server 2008 are specifically designed to support SQL Server's symmetric encryption functionality. The algorithms provided by SQL Server 2008 use a single key for both encryption and decryption. In the SQL Server 2008 encryption model, symmetric keys are encrypted by certificates or asymmetric keys, and they can be used in turn to encrypt other symmetric keys or raw data. The CREATE SYMMETRIC KEY statement allows you to generate symmetric keys, as shown in Listing 8-12.

Listing 8-12. *Creating a Symmetric Key*

```
CREATE SYMMETRIC KEY TestSymmetricKey
  WITH ALGORITHM = AES_128
  ENCRYPTION BY PASSWORD = 'p@55w0rd';
```

The options specified in the CREATE SYMMETRIC KEY statement in Listing 8-12 specify that the symmetric key will be created with the name TestSymmetricKey, it will be protected by the password p@55w0rd, and it will use the Advanced Encryption Standard (AES) algorithm with a 128-bit key (AES_128) to encrypt data.

When creating a symmetric key, you can specify any of several encryption algorithms, including the following:

- AES_128, AES_192, and AES_256 specify the AES block encryption algorithm with a symmetric key length of 128, 192, or 256 bits, and a block size of 128 bits.

- DES specifies the DES block encryption algorithm, which has a symmetric key length of 56 bits and a block size of 64 bits.

- DESX specifies the DES-X block encryption algorithm, which was introduced as a successor to the DES algorithm. DES-X also has a symmetric key length of 56 bits (although because the algorithm includes security augmentations, the effective key length is calculated at around 118 bits) and a block size of 64 bits.

- RC2 specifies the RC2 block encryption algorithm, which has a key size of 128 bits and a block size of 64 bits.

- RC4 and RC4_128 specify the RC4 stream encryption algorithm, which has a key length of 40 or 128 bits. RC4 and RC4_128 are not recommended, as they do not generate random initialization vectors to further obfuscate the cipher text.

The CREATE SYMMETRIC KEY statement also provides additional options that allow you to specify options for symmetric key creation, including the following:

- You can specify a KEY_SOURCE to designate a passphrase to be used as key material from which the symmetric key is derived. If you don't specify a KEY SOURCE, SQL Server generates the symmetric key from random key material.

- The ENCRYPTION BY clause specifies the method used to encrypt this symmetric key in the database. You can specify encryption by a certificate, password, asymmetric key, another symmetric key, or HSM.

- The PROVIDER_KEY_NAME and CREATION_DISPOSITION clauses allow you to use your symmetric key with EKM security.

- The IDENTITY_VALUE clause specifies an identity phrase that is used to generate a GUID to "tag" data encrypted with the key.

TEMPORARY SYMMETRIC KEYS

You can create temporary symmetric keys by prefixing the symmetric key name with a number sign (#). A temporary symmetric key exists only during the current session and is automatically removed when the current session ends. Temporary symmetric keys are not accessible to any sessions outside of the session they are created in. When referencing a temporary symmetric key, the number sign (#) prefix must be used. You can use the same WITH clause options described in this section to specify how the symmetric key should be created. To be honest, I don't really see much use for temporary symmetric keys at this point, although I don't want to discount them totally. After all, someone may find a use for them in the future.

SQL Server also provides the ALTER SYMMETRIC KEY and DROP SYMMETRIC KEY statements for symmetric key management. The ALTER statement allows you to add or remove encryption methods on a symmetric key. As an example, if you created a symmetric key and encrypted it by password but later wished to change it to encryption by certificate, you would issue two ALTER SYMMETRIC KEY statements—the first ALTER statement would specify the ADD ENCRYPTION BY CERTIFICATE clause and the second would specify DROP ENCRYPTION BY PASSWORD, as shown in Listing 8-13.

Listing 8-13. *Changing the Symmetric Key Encryption Method*

```
OPEN SYMMETRIC KEY TestSymmetricKey
  DECRYPTION BY PASSWORD = 'pa55w0rd';

ALTER SYMMETRIC KEY TestSymmetricKey
  ADD ENCRYPTION BY CERTIFICATE TestCertificate;

ALTER SYMMETRIC KEY TestSymmetricKey
  DROP ENCRYPTION BY PASSWORD = 'pa55w0rd';

CLOSE SYMMETRIC KEY TestSymmetricKey;
```

■**Note** Before you alter a symmetric key, you must first open it with the OPEN SYMMETRIC KEY statement.

The DROP SYMMETRIC KEY statement allows you to remove a symmetric key from the database.

Once you create a symmetric key, you can encrypt data with the EncryptByKey and DecryptByKey functions. Listing 8-14 creates a symmetric key and encrypts 100 names with it. Partial results are shown in Figure 8-6.

Listing 8-14. *Encrypting Data with a Symmetric Key*

```
-- Create a temporary table to hold results
CREATE TABLE #TempNames
(
  BusinessEntityID  int PRIMARY KEY,
  FirstName         nvarchar(50),
  MiddleName        nvarchar(50),
  LastName          nvarchar(50),
  EncFirstName      varbinary(200),
  EncMiddleName     varbinary(200),
  EncLastName       varbinary(200)
);

-- Create DMK
CREATE MASTER KEY
  ENCRYPTION BY PASSWORD = 'Test_P@ssw0rd';
```

```
-- Create certificate to protect symmetric key
CREATE CERTIFICATE TestCertificate
  WITH SUBJECT = 'AdventureWorks Test Certificate',
  EXPIRY_DATE = '2026-10-31';

-- Create symmetric key to encrypt data
CREATE SYMMETRIC KEY TestSymmetricKey
  WITH ALGORITHM = AES_128
  ENCRYPTION BY CERTIFICATE TestCertificate;

-- Open symmetric key
OPEN SYMMETRIC KEY TestSymmetricKey
  DECRYPTION BY CERTIFICATE TestCertificate;

-- Populate temp table with 100 encrypted names from the Person.Person table
INSERT
INTO #TempNames
(
  BusinessEntityID,
  EncFirstName,
  EncMiddleName,
  EncLastName
)
SELECT TOP(100) BusinessEntityID,
  EncryptByKey(Key_GUID(N'TestSymmetricKey'), FirstName),
  EncryptByKey(Key_GUID(N'TestSymmetricKey'), MiddleName),
  EncryptByKey(Key_GUID(N'TestSymmetricKey'), LastName)
FROM Person.Person
ORDER BY BusinessEntityID;

-- Update the temp table with decrypted names
UPDATE #TempNames
SET FirstName = DecryptByKey(EncFirstName),
  MiddleName = DecryptByKey(EncMiddleName),
  LastName = DecryptByKey(EncLastName);

-- Show the results
SELECT BusinessEntityID,
  FirstName,
  MiddleName,
  LastName,
  EncFirstName,
  EncMiddleName,
  EncLastName
FROM #TempNames;
```

```
-- Close the symmetric key
CLOSE SYMMETRIC KEY TestSymmetricKey;

-- Drop the symmetric key
DROP SYMMETRIC KEY TestSymmetricKey;

-- Drop the certificate
DROP CERTIFICATE TestCertificate;

-- Drop the DMK
DROP MASTER KEY;

-- Drop the temp table
DROP TABLE #TempNames;
```

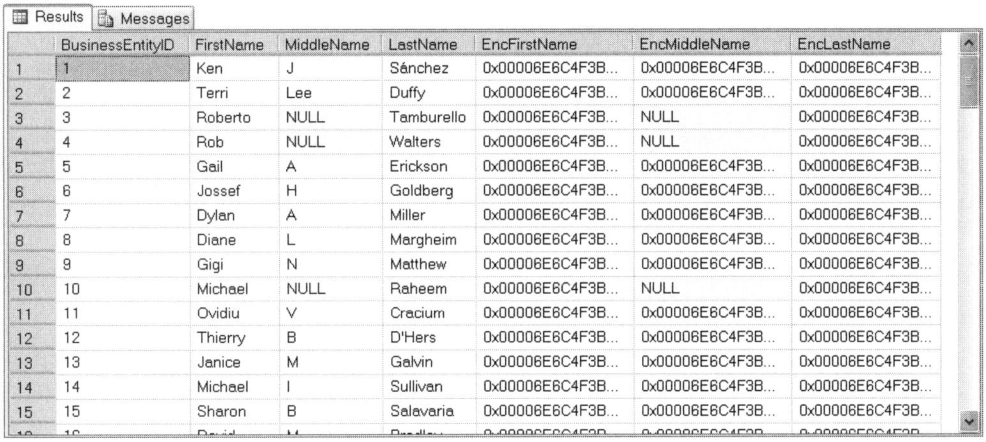

	BusinessEntityID	FirstName	MiddleName	LastName	EncFirstName	EncMiddleName	EncLastName
1	1	Ken	J	Sánchez	0x00006E6C4F3B...	0x00006E6C4F3B...	0x00006E6C4F3B...
2	2	Terri	Lee	Duffy	0x00006E6C4F3B...	0x00006E6C4F3B...	0x00006E6C4F3B...
3	3	Roberto	NULL	Tamburello	0x00006E6C4F3B...	NULL	0x00006E6C4F3B...
4	4	Rob	NULL	Walters	0x00006E6C4F3B...	NULL	0x00006E6C4F3B...
5	5	Gail	A	Erickson	0x00006E6C4F3B...	0x00006E6C4F3B...	0x00006E6C4F3B...
6	6	Jossef	H	Goldberg	0x00006E6C4F3B...	0x00006E6C4F3B...	0x00006E6C4F3B...
7	7	Dylan	A	Miller	0x00006E6C4F3B...	0x00006E6C4F3B...	0x00006E6C4F3B...
8	8	Diane	L	Margheim	0x00006E6C4F3B...	0x00006E6C4F3B...	0x00006E6C4F3B...
9	9	Gigi	N	Matthew	0x00006E6C4F3B...	0x00006E6C4F3B...	0x00006E6C4F3B...
10	10	Michael	NULL	Raheem	0x00006E6C4F3B...	NULL	0x00006E6C4F3B...
11	11	Ovidiu	V	Cracium	0x00006E6C4F3B...	0x00006E6C4F3B...	0x00006E6C4F3B...
12	12	Thierry	B	D'Hers	0x00006E6C4F3B...	0x00006E6C4F3B...	0x00006E6C4F3B...
13	13	Janice	M	Galvin	0x00006E6C4F3B...	0x00006E6C4F3B...	0x00006E6C4F3B...
14	14	Michael	I	Sullivan	0x00006E6C4F3B...	0x00006E6C4F3B...	0x00006E6C4F3B...
15	15	Sharon	B	Salavaria	0x00006E6C4F3B...	0x00006E6C4F3B...	0x00006E6C4F3B...

Figure 8-6. *Symmetric key encryption results (partial)*

Listing 8-14 first creates a temporary table to hold the encryption and decryption results:

```
-- Create a temporary table to hold results
CREATE TABLE #TempNames
(
  BusinessEntityID  int PRIMARY KEY,
  FirstName         nvarchar(50),
  MiddleName        nvarchar(50),
  LastName          nvarchar(50),
  EncFirstName      varbinary(200),
  EncMiddleName     varbinary(200),
  EncLastName       varbinary(200)
);
```

Then a DMK is created to protect the certificate that will be created next. The certificate that's created is then used to encrypt the symmetric key.

```
-- Create DMK
CREATE MASTER KEY
  ENCRYPTION BY PASSWORD = 'Test_P@ssw0rd';

-- Create certificate to protect symmetric key
CREATE CERTIFICATE TestCertificate
  WITH SUBJECT = 'AdventureWorks Test Certificate',
  EXPIRY_DATE = '2026-10-31';

-- Create symmetric key to encrypt data
CREATE SYMMETRIC KEY TestSymmetricKey
  WITH ALGORITHM = AES_128
  ENCRYPTION BY CERTIFICATE TestCertificate;
```

In order to encrypt data with the symmetric key, the sample must first execute the OPEN SYMMETRIC KEY statement to open the symmetric key. The DECRYPTION BY clause specifies the method to use to decrypt the symmetric key for use. In this example, the key is protected by certificate, so DECRYPTION BY CERTIFICATE is used. You can specify decryption by certificate, asymmetric key, symmetric key, or password. If the DMK was used to encrypt the certificate or asymmetric key, leave off the WITH PASSWORD clause.

```
-- Open symmetric key
OPEN SYMMETRIC KEY TestSymmetricKey
  DECRYPTION BY CERTIFICATE TestCertificate;
```

The next step is to use the EncryptByKey function to encrypt the data. In this example, the FirstName, MiddleName, and LastName for 100 rows from the Person.Person table are encrypted with EncryptByKey. The EncryptByKey function accepts a clear text char, varchar, binary, varbinary, nchar, or nvarchar constant, column, or T-SQL variable with a maximum length of 8000 bytes. The result returned is the encrypted data in varbinary format with a maximum length of 8000 bytes. In addition to clear text, EncryptByKey accepts a GUID identifying the symmetric key you wish to encrypt the clear text with. The Key_GUID function returns a symmetric key's GUID by name.

```
-- Populate temp table with 100 encrypted names from the Person.Person table
INSERT
INTO #TempNames
(
  BusinessEntityID,
  EncFirstName,
  EncMiddleName,
  EncLastName
)
```

```
SELECT TOP(100) BusinessEntityID,
  EncryptByKey(Key_GUID(N'TestSymmetricKey'), FirstName),
  EncryptByKey(Key_GUID(N'TestSymmetricKey'), MiddleName),
  EncryptByKey(Key_GUID(N'TestSymmetricKey'), LastName)
FROM Person.Person
ORDER BY BusinessEntityID;
```

The sample code then uses the DecryptByKey function to decrypt the previously encrypted cipher text in the temporary table. SQL Server stores the GUID of the symmetric key used to encrypt the data with the encrypted data, so you don't need to supply the symmetric key GUID to DecryptByKey. In the sample code, the varbinary encrypted cipher text is all that's passed to the EncryptByKey function.

```
-- Update the temp table with decrypted names
UPDATE #TempNames
SET FirstName = DecryptByKey(EncFirstName),
  MiddleName = DecryptByKey(EncMiddleName),
  LastName = DecryptByKey(EncLastName);
```

Finally, the results are shown and the symmetric key is closed with the CLOSE SYMMETRIC KEY statement:

```
-- Show the results
SELECT BusinessEntityID,
  FirstName,
  MiddleName,
  LastName,
  EncFirstName,
  EncMiddleName,
  EncLastName
FROM #TempNames;

-- Close the symmetric key
CLOSE SYMMETRIC KEY TestSymmetricKey;
```

The balance of the code drops the symmetric key, the certificate, the master key, and the temporary table:

```
-- Drop the symmetric key
DROP SYMMETRIC KEY TestSymmetricKey;

-- Drop the certificate
DROP CERTIFICATE TestCertificate;

-- Drop the DMK
DROP MASTER KEY;

-- Drop the temp table
DROP TABLE #TempNames;
```

> ■**Note** You can close a single symmetric key by name or use the `CLOSE ALL SYMMETRIC KEYS` statement to close all open symmetric keys. Opening and closing symmetric keys affects only the current session on the server. All open symmetric keys available to the current session are automatically closed when the current session ends.

SALT AND AUTHENTICATORS

The *initialization vector (IV)*, or *salt*, is an important aspect of encryption security. The IV is a block of bits that further obfuscates the result of an encryption. The idea is that the IV will help prevent the same data from generating the same cipher text if it is encrypted more than once by the same key and algorithm. SQL Server does not allow you to specify an IV when encrypting data with a symmetric key, however. Instead SQL Server generates a random IV automatically when you encrypt data with block ciphers like AES and DES. The obfuscation provided by the IV helps eliminate patterns from your encrypted data—patterns that cryptanalysts can use to their advantage when attempting to hack your encrypted data. The downside to SQL Server's randomly generated IVs is that they make indexing an encrypted column a true exercise in futility.

In addition to random IV generation, SQL Server's `EncryptByKey` and `DecryptByKey` functions provide another tool to help eliminate patterns in encrypted data. Both functions provide two options parameters: an add authenticator flag and an authenticator value. If the add authenticator flag is set to 1, SQL Server will derive an authenticator from the authenticator value passed in. The authenticator is then used to obfuscate your encrypted data further, preventing patterns that can reveal information to hackers through correlation analysis attacks. If you supply an authenticator value during encryption, the same authenticator value must be supplied during decryption.

When SQL Server encrypts your data with a symmetric key, it automatically adds metadata to the encrypted result, as well as padding, making the encrypted result larger (sometimes significantly larger) than the unencrypted plain text. The format for the encrypted result with metadata follows the following format:

- The first 16 bytes of the encrypted result represent the GUID of the symmetric key used to encrypt the data.

- The next 4 bytes represent a version number, currently hard-coded as 0x01000000.

- The next 8 bytes for DES encryption (16 bytes for AES encryption) represent the randomly generated IV.

- If an authenticator was used, the next 8 bytes contain header information with an additional 20-byte SHA1 hash of the authenticator, making the header information 28 bytes in length.

- The last part of the encrypted data is the actual padded data itself. For DES algorithms, the length of this encrypted data will be a multiple of 8 bytes. For AES algorithms, the length will be a multiple of 16 bytes.

In addition to `DecryptByKey`, SQL Server 2008 provides `DecryptByKeyAutoCert` and `DecryptByKeyAutoAsymKey` functions. Both functions combine the functionality of the `OPEN SYMMETRIC KEY` statement with the `DecryptByKey` function, meaning that you don't need to issue an `OPEN SYMMETRIC KEY` to decrypt your cipher text. The `DecryptByKeyAutoAsymKey` function automatically opens an asymmetric key protecting a symmetric key, while `DecryptByKeyAutoCert` automatically opens a certificate protecting a symmetric key. If a password is used to encrypt your asymmetric key or certificate, that same password must be passed to these functions. If the asymmetric key is encrypted with the DMK, you pass `NULL` as the password. You can also specify an authenticator with these functions if one was used during encryption. Decryption of data in bulk using these functions might cause a pretty severe performance penalty over using the `OPEN SYMMETRIC KEY` statement and the `DecryptByKey` function.

Encryption Without Keys

SQL Server 2008 provides additional functions for encryption and decryption without keys, and for one-way hashing. These functions are named `EncryptByPassPhrase`, `DecryptByPassPhrase`, and `HashBytes`, respectively.

The `EncryptByPassPhrase` function accepts a *passphrase* and clear text to encrypt. The passphrase is simply a plain text phrase from which SQL Server can derive an encryption key. The idea behind the passphrase is that users are more likely to remember a simple phrase than a complex encryption key. The function derives a temporary encryption key from the passphrase and uses it to encrypt the plain text. You can also pass an optional authenticator value to `EncryptByPassPhrase` if you wish. `EncryptByPassPhrase` always uses the triple DES algorithm to encrypt the clear text passed in.

`DecryptByPassPhrase` decrypts cipher text that was previously encrypted with `EncryptByPassPhrase`. To decrypt using this function, you must supply the same passphrase and authenticator options that you used when encrypting the clear text.

Hashing Data

The `HashBytes` function performs a one-way hash on the data passed to it and returns the hash value generated. `HashBytes` accepts two parameters: a hash algorithm name and the data to hash. The return value is a fixed-length `varbinary` hash value, which is analogous to a fingerprint for any given data. Table 8-2 lists the SQL Server–supported hash algorithms.

Table 8-2. *SQL Server–Supported Hash Algorithms*

Algorithm	Hash Length
MD2, MD4, MD5	128 bits (16 bytes)
SHA, SHA1	160 bits (20 bytes)

■**Caution** For highly secure applications, the MD2, MD4, and MD5 series of hashes should be avoided. Cryptanalysts have produced *meaningful hash collisions* with these algorithms over the past few years that have revealed vulnerabilities to hacker attacks. A *hash collision* is a string of bytes that produces a hash value that is identical to another string of bytes. A *meaningful* hash collision is one that can be produced with meaningful (or apparently meaningful) strings of bytes. Generating a hash collision by modifying the content of a certificate would be an example of a meaningful, and dangerous, hash collision.

Listing 8-15 demonstrates the EncryptByPassPhrase, DecryptByPassPhrase, and HashBytes functions. The results are shown in Figure 8-7.

Listing 8-15. *Encryption and Decryption by Passphrase and Byte Hashing*

```
DECLARE @cleartext nvarchar(256);
DECLARE @encrypted varbinary(512);
DECLARE @decrypted nvarchar(256);

SELECT @cleartext = N'To be, or not to be: that is the question: ' +
  N'Whether ''tis nobler in the mind to suffer ' +
  N'The slings and arrows of outrageous fortune, ' +
  N'Or to take arms against a sea of troubles';

SELECT @encrypted = EncryptByPassPhrase(N'Shakespeare''s Donkey', @cleartext);

SELECT @decrypted = CAST
(
  DecryptByPassPhrase(N'Shakespeare''s Donkey', @encrypted)
    AS nvarchar(128)
);

SELECT @cleartext AS ClearText;
SELECT @encrypted AS Encrypted;
SELECT @decrypted AS Decrypted;
SELECT HashBytes ('SHA1', @ClearText) AS Hashed;
```

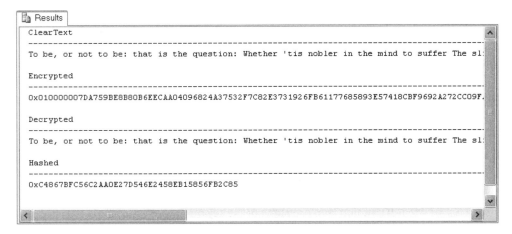

Figure 8-7. *Results of encryption by passphrase and hashing*

Extensible Key Management

SQL Server 2008 adds a new feature known as EKM, which allows you to encrypt your SQL Server asymmetric keys (and symmetric keys) with keys generated and stored on a third-party HSM. To use EKM, you must first turn on the EKM provider enabled option with sp_configure, as shown in Listing 8-16.

■**Note** EKM is available only on the Enterprise, Developer, and Evaluation editions of SQL Server 2008, and it requires a third-party HSM and supporting software.

Listing 8-16. *Enabling EKM Providers*

```
sp_configure 'show advanced', 1;
GO
RECONFIGURE;
GO

sp_configure 'EKM provider enabled', 1;
GO
RECONFIGURE;
GO
```

Once you have enabled EKM providers and have an HSM available, you must register a cryptographic provider with SQL Server. The cryptographic provider references a vendor-supplied DLL file installed on the server. Listing 8-17 gives an example of registering a cryptographic provider with SQL Server.

Listing 8-17. *Registering a Cryptographic Provider*

```
CREATE CRYPTOGRAPHIC PROVIDER Eagle_EKM_Provider
  FROM FILE = 'c:\Program Files\Eagle_EKM\SQLEKM.DLL';
GO
```

Once your EKM provider is registered with SQL Server, creating an asymmetric key that is encrypted by an existing key on the HSM is simply a matter of specifying the EKM provider, the CREATION_DISPOSITION option, and the name of the key on the EKM device via the PROVIDER_KEY_NAME option. Listing 8-18 gives an example.

Listing 8-18. *Creating an Asymmetric Key with HSM Protection*

```
CREATE ASYMMETRIC KEY AsymKeyEKMProtected
  FROM PROVIDER Eagle_EKM_Provider
  WITH PROVIDER_KEY_NAME = 'EKM_Key_1',
    CREATION_DISPOSITION = OPEN_EXISTING;
GO
```

EKM is designed to support enterprise-level encryption key management by providing additional encryption key security. It provides this additional security by physically separating the encryption keys from the data they encrypt. In addition to external storage of encryption keys, HSM vendors can also provide hardware-based bulk encryption and decryption functionality and external support for additional encryption options beyond what is supported natively by SQL Server 2008. Some of the additional options provided by HSM vendors include key aging and key rotation functionality.

Transparent Data Encryption

Up to this point, I've talked about the column-level encryption functionality available in SQL Server 2008. These functions are specifically designed to encrypt data stored in the columns of your database tables. SQL Server 2008 provides a new method of encryption, TDE, which allows you to encrypt your entire database at once.

TDE automatically encrypts every page in your database and decrypts pages as required when you access them. This new feature allows you to secure an entire database without worrying about all those little details that pop up when encrypting at the column level. TDE does not require extra storage space, and it allows the query optimizer to generate far more efficient query plans than it can when you search on encrypted columns. As an added bonus, TDE is easy to implement and allows you to secure the data in your databases with no changes to middle-tier or front-end code.

The first step to implement TDE in your database is to create a *server certificate* (see Listing 8-19). A server certificate is simply a certificate created in the master database for the purpose of encrypting databases with TDE.

Listing 8-19. *Creating a Server Certificate*

```
USE master;
GO

CREATE MASTER KEY
  ENCRYPTION BY PASSWORD = 'p@$$w0rd';
GO

CREATE CERTIFICATE ServerCert
  WITH SUBJECT = 'Server Certificate for TDE',
  EXPIRY_DATE = '2022-12-31';
GO
```

■**Tip** Remember to back up your server certificate immediately after you create it!

Once you've created a server certificate, you can create a database encryption key in the database to be encrypted (see Listing 8-20). The database encryption key is created with the CREATE DATABASE ENCRYPTION KEY statement. Using this statement, you can create a key using one of the four different algorithms listed in Table 8-3.

Table 8-3. *Database Encryption Key Algorithms*

Algorithm	Description
AES_128	AES, 128-bit key
AES_192	AES, 192-bit key
AES_256	AES, 256-bit key
TRIPLE_DES_3KEY	Three-key triple-DES, ~112-bit effective key

Listing 8-20. *Creating a Database Encryption Key and Securing the Database*

```
USE AdventureWorks;
GO

CREATE DATABASE ENCRYPTION KEY
  WITH ALGORITHM = AES_128
  ENCRYPTION BY SERVER CERTIFICATE ServerCert;
GO

ALTER DATABASE AdventureWorks
  SET ENCRYPTION ON;
GO
```

The obvious question at this point is, since TDE is so simple and secure, why not use it all the time? Well, the simplicity and security of TDE comes at a cost. When you encrypt a database with TDE, SQL Server also encrypts the database log file and the `tempdb` database. This is done to prevent leaked data that a hacker with the right tools might be able to access. Because `tempdb` is encrypted, the performance of every database on the same server takes a hit. Also, SQL Server incurs additional CPU overhead since it has to decrypt noncached data pages that are accessed by queries.

Summary

Back in the days of SQL Server 2000, database encryption functionality could be achieved only through third-party tools or by creating your own encryption and decryption functions. SQL Server 2008 continues the tradition of T-SQL column-level encryption and decryption functionality introduced in SQL Server 2005. The tight integration of Windows DPAPI encryption functionality with native T-SQL statements and functions makes database encryption easier and more secure than ever.

SQL Server 2008 also introduces new functionality, including TDE for quickly and easily encrypting entire databases transparently, and EKM for providing access to third-party HSMs to implement enterprise-level security solutions and bulk encryption functionality.

In this chapter, I discussed the SQL Server hierarchical encryption model, which defines the relationship between SMKs, DMKs, certificates, asymmetric keys, and symmetric keys. SQL Server provides a variety of T-SQL statements to create and manage encryption keys and certificates, which I demonstrated in code samples throughout the chapter. SQL Server also provides several functions for generating one-way hashes, generating data signatures, and encrypting data by certificate, asymmetric key, symmetric key, and passphrase.

In the next chapter, I'll cover the topics of SQL windowing functions and common table expressions (CTEs).

EXERCISES

1. [True/false] Symmetric keys can be used to encrypt other symmetric keys or data.

2. [Choose all that apply] SQL Server provides native support for which of the following built-in encryption algorithms?

    a.   DES

    b.   AES

    c.   Loki

    d.   Blowfish

    e.   RC4

3. [True/false] SQL Server 2008 T-SQL includes a `BACKUP ASYMMETRIC KEY` statement.

4. [Fill in the blank] You must set the ___ option to turn on EKM for your server.

5. [True/false] TDE automatically encrypts the `tempdb`, `model`, and `master` databases.

6. [True/false] SQL Server automatically generates random initialization vectors when you use symmetric encryption.

CHAPTER 9

■ ■ ■

Common Table Expressions and Windowing Functions

SQL Server 2008 continues support for the extremely useful common table expression (CTE), first introduced in SQL Server 2005. CTEs can simplify your queries to make them more readable and maintainable. SQL Server also supports self-referential CTEs, which make for very powerful recursive queries.

In addition, SQL Server supports windowing functions, which allow you to partition your results and apply numbering and ranking values to the rows in the result set partitions. This chapter begins with a discussion of the power and benefits of CTEs and finishes with a discussion of SQL Server windowing functions.

Common Table Expressions

CTEs are a powerful addition to SQL Server. A CTE generates a named result set that exists only during the life of a single query or DML statement. CTEs offer several benefits over derived tables and views, including the following:

- CTEs are transient, existing only for the life of a single query or DML statement. This means that you don't have create them as permanent database objects like views.

- A single CTE can be referenced multiple times by name in a single query or DML statement, making your code more manageable. Derived tables have to be rewritten in their entirety every place they are referenced.

- CTEs can be self-referencing, providing a powerful recursion mechanism.

CTEs can range in complexity from extremely simple to highly elaborate constructs. All CTEs begin with the WITH keyword followed by the name of the CTE and a list of the columns it returns. This is followed by the AS keyword and the body of the CTE. And every CTE is followed by an associated query or DML statement. Listing 9-1 is a very simple example of a CTE designed to show the basic syntax.

Listing 9-1. *Simple CTE*

```
WITH GetNamesCTE
(
  BusinessEntityID,
  FirstName,
  MiddleName,
  LastName
)
AS
(
  SELECT
    BusinessEntityID,
    FirstName,
    MiddleName,
    LastName
  FROM Person.Person
)
SELECT
  BusinessEntityID,
  FirstName,
  MiddleName,
  LastName
FROM GetNamesCTE;
```

In Listing 9-1, the CTE is defined with the name `GetNamesCTE` and returns columns named `BusinessEntityID`, `FirstName`, `MiddleName`, and `LastName`. The CTE body consists of a simple `SELECT` statement from the AdventureWorks 2008 `Person.Person` table. The CTE has an associated `SELECT` statement immediately following it. The `SELECT` statement references the CTE in its `FROM` clause.

WITH OVERLOADED

The `WITH` keyword is *overloaded* in SQL Server, meaning that it's used in many different ways for many different purposes in T-SQL. It's used to specify additional options in DDL `CREATE` statements, to add table hints to queries and DML statements, and to declare XML namespaces when used in the `WITH XMLNAMESPACES` clause, just to name a few. Now it's also used as the keyword that indicates the beginning of a CTE definition. Because of this, whenever a CTE is not the first statement in a batch, the statement preceding it must end with a semicolon. This is one reason I strongly recommend using the statement-terminating semicolon throughout your code.

Simple CTEs have some restrictions on their definition and declaration:

- All columns returned by a CTE must have a unique name. If all of the columns returned by the query in the CTE body have unique names, you can leave the column list out of the CTE declaration.

- A CTE can reference other previously defined CTEs in the same WITH clause, but cannot reference CTEs defined after the current CTE (known as a *forward reference*).

- You cannot use the following keywords, clauses, and options within a CTE: COMPUTE, COMPUTE BY, FOR BROWSE, INTO, and OPTION (query hint). Also, you cannot use ORDER BY unless you specify the TOP clause.

- As I mentioned in the "WITH Overloaded" sidebar, when a CTE is not the first statement in a batch, the preceding statement must end with a semicolon statement terminator.

Keep these restrictions in mind when you create CTEs.

Multiple Common Table Expressions

You can define multiple CTEs for a single query or DML statement by separating your CTE definitions with commas. The main reason for doing this is to simplify your code to make it easier to read and manage. CTEs provide a means of visually splitting your code into smaller functional blocks, making it easier to develop and debug. Listing 9-2 demonstrates a query with multiple CTEs, with the second CTE referencing the first. Results are shown in Figure 9-1.

Listing 9-2. *Multiple CTEs*

```
WITH GetNamesCTE
(
  BusinessEntityID,
  FirstName,
  MiddleName,
  LastName
)
AS
(
  SELECT
    BusinessEntityID,
    FirstName,
    MiddleName,
    LastName
  FROM Person.Person
),
GetContactCTE
(
  BusinessEntityID,
  FirstName,
```

```
    MiddleName,
    LastName,
    Email,
    HomePhoneNumber
)
AS
(
  SELECT
    gn.BusinessEntityID,
    gn.FirstName,
    gn.MiddleName,
    gn.LastName,
    ea.EmailAddress,
    pp.PhoneNumber
  FROM GetNamesCTE gn
  LEFT JOIN Person.EmailAddress ea
    ON gn.BusinessEntityID = ea.BusinessEntityID
  LEFT JOIN Person.PersonPhone pp
    ON gn.BusinessEntityID = pp.BusinessEntityID
      AND pp.PhoneNumberTypeID = 2
)
SELECT
  BusinessEntityID,
  FirstName,
  MiddleName,
  LastName,
  Email,
  HomePhoneNumber
FROM GetContactCTE;
```

	BusinessEntityID	FirstName	MiddleName	LastName	Email	HomePhoneNumber
135	7458	Ana	R	Alexander	ana17@adven...	1 (11) 500 555-0181
136	7678	Angela	NULL	Alexander	angela21@ad...	NULL
137	7161	Angelica	NULL	Alexander	angelica18@a...	214-555-0150
138	3683	Anna	NULL	Alexander	anna44@adve...	150-555-0156
139	13220	Antonio	NULL	Alexander	antonio19@ad...	NULL
140	7719	Arianna	NULL	Alexander	arianna17@ad...	140-555-0167
141	12597	Ashley	J	Alexander	ashley46@adv...	NULL
142	6266	Austin	NULL	Alexander	austin15@adv...	1 (11) 500 555-0140
143	6726	Benjamin	A	Alexander	benjamin20@...	240-555-0151
144	6919	Brandon	NULL	Alexander	brandon16@a...	780-555-0152
145	19276	Brianna	NULL	Alexander	brianna64@ad...	242-555-0137
146	7210	Brittany	NULL	Alexander	brittany17@ad...	804-555-0125
147	5561	Caleb	NULL	Alexander	caleb15@adv...	670-555-0141
148	6315	Cameron	NULL	Alexander	cameron14@a...	399-555-0196
149	6800	Caroline	NULL	Alexander	caroline20@a...	NULL

Figure 9-1. *Results of a query with multiple CTEs*

CTE READABILITY BENEFITS

You can use CTEs to make your queries more readable than equivalent query designs that utilize nested subqueries. To demonstrate, the following query uses nested subqueries to return the same result as the CTE-based query in Listing 9-2.

```
SELECT
  gn.BusinessEntityID,
  gn.FirstName,
  gn.MiddleName,
  gn.LastName,
  gn.Email,
  gn.HomePhoneNumber
FROM
(
  SELECT
    p.BusinessEntityID,
    p.FirstName,
    p.MiddleName,
    p.LastName,
    ea.Email,
    ea.HomePhoneNumber
  FROM Person.Person p
  LEFT JOIN
  (
    SELECT
      ea.BusinessEntityID,
      ea.Email,
      pp.HomePhoneNumber
    FROM Person.EmailAddress ea
    LEFT JOIN
    (
      SELECT
        pp.BusinessEntityID,
        pp.PhoneNumber AS HomePhoneNumber,
        pp.PhoneNumberTypeID
      FROM Person.PersonPhone pp
    ) pp
    ON ea.BusinessEntityID = pp.BusinessEntityID
      AND pp.PhoneNumberTypeID = 2
  ) ea
  ON p.BusinessEntityID = ea.BusinessEntityID
) gn
```

The CTE-based version of this query is much easier to read and understand than the nested subquery version, which makes it easier to debug and maintain in the long term.

The sample in Listing 9-2 contains two CTEs, named `GetNamesCTE` and `GetContactCTE`. The `GetNamesCTE` is borrowed from Listing 9-1; it simply retrieves the names from the `Person.Person` table.

```
WITH GetNamesCTE
(
  BusinessEntityID,
  FirstName,
  MiddleName,
  LastName
)
AS
(
  SELECT
    BusinessEntityID,
    FirstName,
    MiddleName,
    LastName
  FROM Person.Person
)
```

The second CTE, `GetContactCTE`, joins the results of `GetNamesCTE` to the `Person.EmailAddress` table and the `Person.PersonPhone` tables:

```
GetContactCTE
(
  BusinessEntityID,
  FirstName,
  MiddleName,
  LastName,
  Email,
  HomePhoneNumber
)
AS
(
  SELECT
    gn.BusinessEntityID,
    gn.FirstName,
    gn.MiddleName,
    gn.LastName,
    ea.EmailAddress,
    pp.PhoneNumber
  FROM GetNamesCTE gn
  LEFT JOIN Person.EmailAddress ea
    ON gn.BusinessEntityID = ea.BusinessEntityID
  LEFT JOIN Person.PersonPhone pp
    ON gn.BusinessEntityID = pp.BusinessEntityID
      AND pp.PhoneNumberTypeID = 2
)
```

Notice that the WITH keyword is only used once at the beginning of the entire statement. The second CTE declaration is separated from the first by a comma, and does not accept the WITH keyword. Finally, notice how simple and readable the SELECT query associated with the CTEs becomes when the joins are moved into CTEs.

```
SELECT
  BusinessEntityID,
  FirstName,
  MiddleName,
  LastName,
  Email,
  HomePhoneNumber
FROM GetContactCTE;
```

■ **Tip** You can reference a CTE from within the body of another CTE or from the associated query or DML statement. Both types of CTE references are shown in Listing 9-2—the GetNamesCTE is referenced by the GetContactCTE and the GetContactCTE is referenced in the query associated with the CTEs.

Recursive Common Table Expressions

CTEs can reference themselves in the body of the CTE, which is a powerful feature for querying hierarchical data stored in the adjacency list model. Recursive CTEs are similar to nonrecursive CTEs, except that the body of the CTE consists of two sets of queries that generate result sets unioned together with the UNION ALL set operator. At least one of the queries in the body of the recursive CTE must not reference the CTE; this query is known as the *anchor query*. Recursive CTEs also contain one or more *recursive queries* that reference the CTE. These recursive queries are unioned together with the anchor query (or queries) in the body of the CTE. Recursive CTEs require a top-level UNION ALL operator to union the recursive and nonrecursive queries together. Multiple anchor queries may be unioned together with INTERSECT, EXCEPT, or UNION operators, while multiple recursive queries can be unioned together with UNION ALL. Listing 9-3 is a simple recursive CTE that retrieves a result set consisting of the numbers 1 through 10.

Listing 9-3. *Simple Recursive CTE*

```
WITH Numbers (n)
AS
(
  SELECT 1 AS n

  UNION ALL

  SELECT n + 1
  FROM Numbers
  WHERE n < 10
)
```

```
SELECT n
FROM Numbers;
```

The CTE in Listing 9-3 begins with a declaration that defines the CTE name and the column returned:

```
WITH Numbers (n)
```

The CTE body contains a single anchor query that returns a single row with the number 1 in the n column:

```
SELECT 1 AS n
```

The anchor query is unioned together with the recursive query by the UNION ALL set operator. The recursive query contains a self-reference to the Numbers CTE, adding 1 to the n column with each recursive reference. The WHERE clause limits the results to the first 10 numbers.

```
SELECT n + 1
FROM Numbers
WHERE n < 10
```

Recursive CTEs have a maximum recursion level of 100 by default. This means that the recursive query in the CTE body can only call itself 100 times. You can use the MAXRECURSION option to increase the maximum recursion level of CTEs on an individual basis. Listing 9-4 modifies the CTE in Listing 9-3 to return the numbers 1 to 1000. The modified query uses the MAXRECURSION option to increase the maximum recursion level. Without the MAXRECURSION option, this CTE would error out after the first 100 levels of recursion.

Listing 9-4. *Recursive CTE with MAXRECURSION Option*

```
WITH Numbers (n)
AS
(
  SELECT 1 AS n

  UNION ALL

  SELECT n + 1
  FROM Numbers
  WHERE n < 1000
)
SELECT n
FROM Numbers
OPTION (MAXRECURSION 1000);
```

The MAXRECURSION value specified must be between 0 and 32767. SQL Server throws an exception if the MAXRECURSION limit is surpassed. A MAXRECURSION value of 0 indicates that no limit should be placed on recursion for the CTE. Be careful with this option—if you don't properly limit the results in the query with a WHERE clause, you can easily end up in an infinite loop.

■**Tip** Creating a permanent table of counting numbers can be more efficient than using a recursive CTE to generate numbers, particularly if you plan to execute the CTEs that generate numbers often.

Recursive CTEs are useful for querying data stored in a hierarchical adjacency list format. As I discussed in Chapter 2, the adjacency list provides a model for storing hierarchical data in relational databases. In the adjacency list model, each row of the table contains a pointer to its parent in the hierarchy. The `Production.BillOfMaterials` table in the AdventureWorks database is a practical example of the adjacency list model. This table contains two important columns, `ComponentID` and `ProductAssemblyID`, that reflect the hierarchical structure. The `ComponentID` is a unique number identifying every component that AdventureWorks uses to manufacture their products. The `ProductAssemblyID` is a parent component created from one or more AdventureWorks product components. Figure 9-2 demonstrates the relationship between components and product assemblies in the AdventureWorks database.

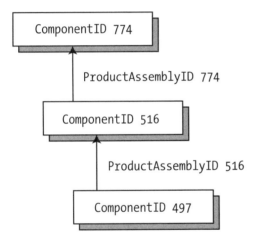

Figure 9-2. *Component/product assembly relationship*

The recursive CTE shown in Listing 9-5 retrieves the complete AdventureWorks hierarchical bill of materials (BOM) for a specified component. The component used in the example is the AdventureWorks silver Mountain-100 48-inch bike, `ComponentID` 774. Partial results are shown in Figure 9-3.

Listing 9-5. *Recursive BOM CTE*

```
DECLARE @ComponentID int = 774;

WITH BillOfMaterialsCTE
(
  BillOfMaterialsID,
  ProductAssemblyID,
```

```sql
      ComponentID,
      Quantity,
      Level
   )
   AS
   (
      SELECT
         bom.BillOfMaterialsID,
         bom.ProductAssemblyID,
         bom.ComponentID,
         bom.PerAssemblyQty AS Quantity,
         0 AS Level
      FROM Production.BillOfMaterials bom
      WHERE bom.ComponentID = @ComponentID

      UNION ALL

      SELECT
         bom.BillOfMaterialsID,
         bom.ProductAssemblyID,
         bom.ComponentID,
         bom.PerAssemblyQty,
         Level + 1
      FROM Production.BillOfMaterials bom
      INNER JOIN BillOfMaterialsCTE bomcte
         ON bom.ProductAssemblyID = bomcte.ComponentID
      WHERE bom.EndDate IS NULL
   )
   SELECT
      bomcte.ProductAssemblyID,
      p.ProductID,
      p.ProductNumber,
      p.Name,
      p.Color,
      bomcte.Quantity,
      bomcte.Level
   FROM BillOfMaterialsCTE bomcte
   INNER JOIN Production.Product p
      ON bomcte.ComponentID = p.ProductID;
```

	ProductAssemblyID	ProductID	ProductNumber	Name	Color	Quantity	Level
1	NULL	774	BK-M82S-48	Mountain-100 Silver, 48	Silver	1.00	0
2	774	516	SA-M687	HL Mountain Seat Assembly	NULL	1.00	1
3	774	741	FR-M94S-52	HL Mountain Frame - Silver, 48	Silver	1.00	1
4	774	807	HS-3479	HL Headset	NULL	1.00	1
5	774	810	HB-M918	HL Mountain Handlebars	NULL	1.00	1
6	774	817	FW-M928	HL Mountain Front Wheel	Black	1.00	1
7	774	825	RW-M928	HL Mountain Rear Wheel	Black	1.00	1
8	774	894	RD-2308	Rear Derailleur	Silver	1.00	1
9	774	907	RB-9231	Rear Brakes	Silver	1.00	1
10	774	937	PD-M562	HL Mountain Pedal	Silv...	1.00	1
11	774	945	FD-2342	Front Derailleur	Silver	1.00	1
12	774	948	FB-9873	Front Brakes	Silver	1.00	1
13	774	951	CS-9183	HL Crankset	Black	1.00	1
14	774	952	CH-0234	Chain	Silver	1.00	1
15	774	996	BB-9108	HL Bottom Bracket	NULL	1.00	1
16	996	3	BE-2349	BB Ball Bearing	NULL	10.00	2
17	996	526	SH-9312	HL Shell	NULL	1.00	2

Figure 9-3. *Partial results of the recursive BOM CTE*

Like the previous CTE examples, Listing 9-3 begins with the CTE name and column list declaration.

```
WITH BillOfMaterialsCTE
(
  BillOfMaterialsID,
  ProductAssemblyID,
  ComponentID,
  Quantity,
  Level
)
```

The anchor query simply retrieves the row from the table where the `ComponentID` matches the specified ID. This is the top-level component in the BOM, set to 774 in the example. Notice that the CTE can reference T-SQL variables like `@ComponentID` in the example.

```
SELECT
    bom.BillOfMaterialsID,
    bom.ProductAssemblyID,
    bom.ComponentID,
    bom.PerAssemblyQty AS Quantity,
    0 AS Level
FROM Production.BillOfMaterials bom
WHERE bom.ComponentID = @ComponentID
```

The recursive query retrieves successive levels of the BOM from the CTE where the ProductAssemblyID of each row matches the ComponentID of the higher-level rows. That is to say, the recursive query of the CTE retrieves lower-level rows in the hierarchy that match the hierarchical relationship previously illustrated in Figure 9-2.

```
SELECT
   bom.BillOfMaterialsID,
   bom.ProductAssemblyID,
   bom.ComponentID,
   bom.PerAssemblyQty,
   Level + 1
FROM Production.BillOfMaterials bom
INNER JOIN BillOfMaterialsCTE bomcte
   ON bom.ProductAssemblyID = bomcte.ComponentID
WHERE bom.EndDate IS NULL
```

The CTE has a SELECT statement associated with it that joins the results to the Production. Product table to retrieve product-specific information like the name and color of the component:

```
SELECT
   bomcte.ProductAssemblyID,
   p.ProductID,
   p.ProductNumber,
   p.Name,
   p.Color,
   bomcte.Quantity,
   bomcte.Level
FROM BillOfMaterialsCTE bomcte
INNER JOIN Production.Product p
   ON bomcte.ComponentID = p.ProductID;
```

The restrictions on simple CTEs that I described earlier in this chapter also apply to recursive CTEs. In addition, the following restrictions apply specifically to recursive CTEs:

- Recursive CTEs must have at least one anchor query and at least one recursive query specified in the body of the CTE. All anchor queries must appear before any recursive queries.

- All anchor queries must be unioned with the set operators UNION, UNION ALL, INTERSECT, or EXCEPT. When using multiple anchor queries and recursive queries, the last anchor query and the first recursive query must be unioned together with the UNION ALL operator. Additionally, all recursive queries must be unioned together with UNION ALL.

- The data types of all columns in the anchor queries and recursive queries must match.

- The recursive queries cannot contain the following operators and keywords: GROUP BY, HAVING, LEFT JOIN, RIGHT JOIN, OUTER JOIN, and SELECT DISTINCT. Recursive queries also cannot contain aggregate functions (like SUM and MAX), windowing functions, subqueries, or hints on the recursive CTE reference.

Windowing Functions

SQL Server 2008 supports windowing functions that partition results and can apply numbering, ranking, and aggregate functions to each partition. The key to windowing functions is the OVER clause, which allows you to define the partitions, and in some cases the ordering of rows in the partition, for your data. In this section, I'll discuss SQL Server 2008 windowing functions and the numbering, ranking, and aggregate functions that support the OVER clause.

The ROW_NUMBER Function

You can use ROW_NUMBER to make light work of paging applications, such as front-end web applications that need to retrieve a fixed number of rows of data at a time, and other applications that require numbered rows in result sets.

The ROW_NUMBER function takes the OVER clause with an ORDER BY clause and an optional PARTITION BY clause. Listing 9-6 retrieves names from the Person.Person table. The OVER clause is used to partition the rows by LastName and order the rows in each partition by LastName, FirstName, and MiddleName. The ROW_NUMBER function is used to assign a number to each row.

Listing 9-6. *ROW_NUMBER with Partitioning*

```
SELECT
  ROW_NUMBER() OVER
  (
    PARTITION BY
      LastName
    ORDER BY
      LastName,
      FirstName,
      MiddleName
  ) AS Number,
  LastName,
  FirstName,
  MiddleName
FROM Person.Person;
```

The partition created in Listing 9-6 acts as a window that slides over your result set (hence the name "windowing function"). The ORDER BY clause orders the rows of each partition by LastName, FirstName, and MiddleName. SQL Server applies the ROW_NUMBER function to each partition. The net result is that the ROW_NUMBER function numbers all rows in the result set, restarting the numbering at 1 every time it encounters a new LastName, as shown in Figure 9-4.

■**Note** When PARTITION BY is used, it must appear before ORDER BY inside of the OVER clause.

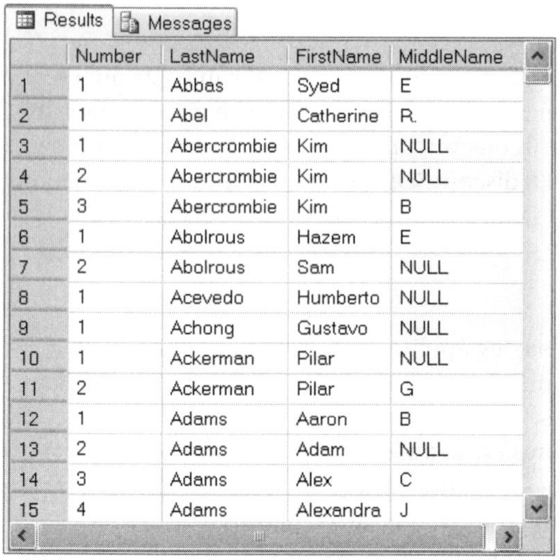

	Number	LastName	FirstName	MiddleName
1	1	Abbas	Syed	E
2	1	Abel	Catherine	R.
3	1	Abercrombie	Kim	NULL
4	2	Abercrombie	Kim	NULL
5	3	Abercrombie	Kim	B
6	1	Abolrous	Hazem	E
7	2	Abolrous	Sam	NULL
8	1	Acevedo	Humberto	NULL
9	1	Achong	Gustavo	NULL
10	1	Ackerman	Pilar	NULL
11	2	Ackerman	Pilar	G
12	1	Adams	Aaron	B
13	2	Adams	Adam	NULL
14	3	Adams	Alex	C
15	4	Adams	Alexandra	J

Figure 9-4. *Using ROW_NUMBER to number rows in partitions*

The `ROW_NUMBER` function can also be used without the `PARTITION BY` clause, in which case the entire result set is treated as one partition. This is useful for numbering entire result sets for applications like front-end paging of result sets on web pages. Listing 9-7 is a stored procedure that uses `ROW_NUMBER` to number all rows in the `Person.Person` table in `LastName`, `FirstName`, `MiddleName` order. The procedure accepts a starting row number and returns the ten names from the result set beginning at the row number specified.

Listing 9-7. *ROW_NUMBER Function Example*

```
CREATE PROCEDURE Person.GetTenContacts @RowNum int
AS
BEGIN
  WITH PageContacts AS
  (
    SELECT
      ROW_NUMBER() OVER
      (
        ORDER BY
          LastName,
          FirstName,
          MiddleName
      ) AS PosNo,
      LastName,
      FirstName,
      MiddleName
    FROM Person.Person
  )
```

```
SELECT
    PosNo,
    LastName,
    FirstName,
    MiddleName
  FROM PageContacts
  WHERE PosNo BETWEEN @RowNum AND @RowNum + 9;
END;
GO
```

```
EXEC Person.GetTenContacts 6100;
```

The procedure in Listing 9-7 consists of a CTE that uses the `ROW_NUMBER` function to number all rows in the `Person.Person` table in order by `LastName`, `FirstName`, and `MiddleName`:

```
SELECT
    ROW_NUMBER() OVER
    (
      ORDER BY
        LastName,
        FirstName,
        MiddleName
    ) AS PosNo,
    LastName,
    FirstName,
    MiddleName
  FROM Person.Person
```

The `SELECT` query associated with the CTE returns the ten rows from the CTE result set beginning with the row number specified by the `@RowNum` parameter in the procedure call:

```
SELECT
    PosNo,
    LastName,
    FirstName,
    MiddleName
  FROM PageContacts
  WHERE PosNo BETWEEN @RowNum AND @RowNum + 9;
```

The sample procedure call passes a `@RowNum` parameter value of `6100` to the procedure and returns the ten rows numbered 6100 to 6109, as shown in Figure 9-5.

	PosNo	LastName	FirstName	MiddleName
1	6100	Harding	Katherine	NULL
2	6101	Harnpadoungsataya	Sariya	E
3	6102	Harrington	Kimberly	Beth
4	6103	Harrington	Lucy	NULL
5	6104	Harrington	Mark	L
6	6105	Harris	Abigail	NULL
7	6106	Harris	Alexander	E
8	6107	Harris	Alexandra	NULL
9	6108	Harris	Alexis	NULL
10	6109	Harris	Alyssa	E

Figure 9-5. *Using ROW_NUMBER to implement client-side paging*

The RANK and DENSE_RANK Functions

The RANK and DENSE_RANK functions are SQL Server's ranking functions. They both assign a numeric rank value to each row in a partition. Suppose you want to figure out Adventure-Works's best one-day sales dates for the calendar year 2001. This scenario might be phrased with a business question like "What were the best one-day sales days in 2001?" RANK can easily give you that information, as shown in Listing 9-8. Partial results are shown in Figure 9-6.

Listing 9-8. *Ranking AdventureWorks Daily Sales Totals*

```
WITH TotalSalesBySalesDate
(
  DailySales,
  OrderDate
)
AS
(
  SELECT
    SUM(soh.SubTotal) AS DailySales,
    soh.OrderDate
  FROM Sales.SalesOrderHeader soh
  WHERE soh.OrderDate >= '20010101'
    AND soh.OrderDate < '20020101'
  GROUP BY soh.OrderDate
)
SELECT
  RANK() OVER
  (
    ORDER BY
      DailySales DESC
  ) AS Ranking,
  DailySales,
  OrderDate
```

```
FROM TotalSalesBySalesDate
ORDER BY Ranking;
```

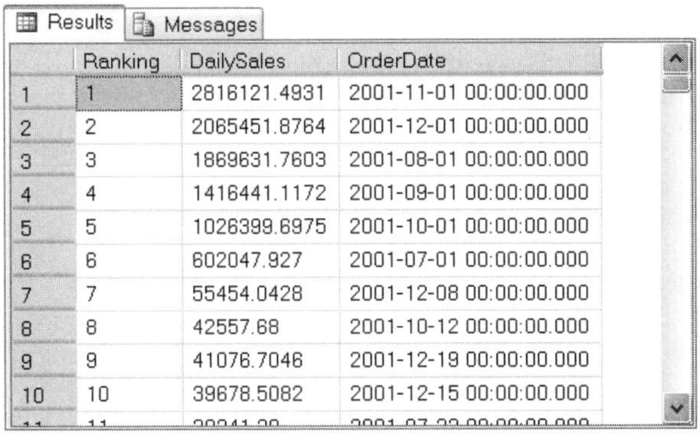

	Ranking	DailySales	OrderDate
1	1	2816121.4931	2001-11-01 00:00:00.000
2	2	2065451.8764	2001-12-01 00:00:00.000
3	3	1869631.7603	2001-08-01 00:00:00.000
4	4	1416441.1172	2001-09-01 00:00:00.000
5	5	1026399.6975	2001-10-01 00:00:00.000
6	6	602047.927	2001-07-01 00:00:00.000
7	7	55454.0428	2001-12-08 00:00:00.000
8	8	42557.68	2001-10-12 00:00:00.000
9	9	41076.7046	2001-12-19 00:00:00.000
10	10	39678.5082	2001-12-15 00:00:00.000

Figure 9-6. *Top ten AdventureWorks daily sales totals*

Listing 9-8 is a CTE that returns two columns, DailySales and OrderDate. The DailySales is the sum of all sales grouped by OrderDate. The results are limited by the WHERE clause to include only sales in the 2001 sales year.

```
WITH TotalSalesBySalesDate
(
  DailySales,
  OrderDate
)
AS
(
  SELECT
    SUM(soh.SubTotal) AS DailySales,
    soh.OrderDate
  FROM Sales.SalesOrderHeader soh
  WHERE soh.OrderDate >= '20010101'
    AND soh.OrderDate < '20020101'
  GROUP BY soh.OrderDate
)
```

The RANK function is used with the OVER clause to apply ranking values to the rows returned by the CTE in descending order (highest to lowest) by the DailySales column:

```
SELECT
  RANK() OVER
  (
    ORDER BY
      DailySales DESC
  ) AS Ranking,
  DailySales,
  OrderDate
```

```
FROM TotalSalesBySalesDate
ORDER BY Ranking;
```

Like the `ROW_NUMBER` function, `RANK` can accept the `PARTITION BY` clause in the `OVER` clause. Listing 9-9 builds on the previous example and uses the `PARTITION BY` clause to rank the daily sales for each month. This type of query can answer a business question like "What were AdventureWorks's best one-day sales days for each month of 2002?" Partial results are shown in Figure 9-7.

Listing 9-9. *Determining the Best Daily Sales per Month*

```
WITH TotalSalesBySalesDatePartitioned
(
  DailySales,
  OrderMonth,
  OrderDate
)
AS
(
  SELECT
    SUM(soh.SubTotal) AS DailySales,
    DATENAME(MONTH, soh.OrderDate) AS OrderMonth,
    soh.OrderDate
  FROM Sales.SalesOrderHeader soh
  WHERE soh.OrderDate >= '20020101'
    AND soh.OrderDate < '20030101'
  GROUP BY soh.OrderDate
)
SELECT
  RANK() OVER
  (
    PARTITION BY
      OrderMonth
    ORDER BY
      DailySales DESC
  ) AS Ranking,
  DailySales,
  OrderMonth,
  OrderDate
FROM TotalSalesBySalesDatePartitioned
ORDER BY OrderMonth,
  Ranking;
```

	Ranking	DailySales	OrderMonth	OrderDate
26	26	11230.6282	April	2002-04-24 00:00:00.000
27	26	11230.6282	April	2002-04-19 00:00:00.000
28	28	10734.81	April	2002-04-08 00:00:00.000
29	29	10556.53	April	2002-04-02 00:00:00.000
30	30	7855.6382	April	2002-04-14 00:00:00.000
31	1	4387553.2504	August	2002-08-01 00:00:00.000
32	2	26391.0766	August	2002-08-13 00:00:00.000
33	3	24183.3095	August	2002-08-06 00:00:00.000
34	4	23598.2839	August	2002-08-19 00:00:00.000
35	5	23309.8227	August	2002-08-31 00:00:00.000

Figure 9-7. *Partial results of daily one-day sales rankings, partitioned by month*

The query in Listing 9-9, like the previous listing, begins with a CTE to calculate one-day sales totals for the year. The main differences between this CTE and the previous example are that Listing 9-9 returns an additional OrderMonth column and the results are limited to the year 2002.

```
WITH TotalSalesBySalesDatePartitioned
(
  DailySales,
  OrderMonth,
  OrderDate
)
AS
(
  SELECT
    SUM(soh.SubTotal) AS DailySales,
    DATENAME(MONTH, soh.OrderDate) AS OrderMonth,
    soh.OrderDate
  FROM Sales.SalesOrderHeader soh
  WHERE soh.OrderDate >= '20020101'
    AND soh.OrderDate < '20030101'
  GROUP BY soh.OrderDate
)
```

The SELECT query associated with the CTE uses the RANK function to assign rankings to the results. The PARTITION BY clause is used to partition the results by OrderMonth so that the rankings restart at 1 for each new month.

```
SELECT
  RANK() OVER
  (
    PARTITION BY
      OrderMonth
```

```
      ORDER BY
         DailySales DESC
   ) AS Ranking,
   DailySales,
   OrderMonth,
   OrderDate
FROM TotalSalesBySalesDatePartitioned
ORDER BY OrderMonth,
   Ranking;
```

When the RANK function encounters two equal DailySales amounts in the same partition, it assigns the same rank number to both and skips the next number in the ranking. As shown in Figure 9-8, the DailySales total for two days in April 2002 was $11,230.6282, resulting in the RANK function assigning both days a Ranking value of 26. The RANK function then skips the Ranking value 27 and assigns the next row a Ranking of 28.

	Ranking	DailySales	OrderMonth	OrderDate
25	25	13931.52	April	2002-04-13 00:00:00.000
26	26	11230.6282	April	2002-04-24 00:00:00.000
27	26	11230.6282	April	2002-04-19 00:00:00.000
28	28	10734.81	April	2002-04-08 00:00:00.000

Figure 9-8. *The RANK function skips a value in the case of a tie.*

DENSE_RANK, like RANK, assigns duplicate values the same rank, but with one important difference: it does not skip the next ranking in the list. Listing 9-10 modifies Listing 9-9 to use the DENSE_RANK function in place of RANK. As you can see in Figure 9-9, DENSE_RANK still assigns the same Ranking to both rows in the result, but it doesn't skip the next Ranking value.

Listing 9-10. *Using DENSE_RANK to Rank Best Daily Sales Per Month*

```
WITH TotalSalesBySalesDatePartitioned
(
  DailySales,
  OrderMonth,
  OrderDate
)
AS
(
  SELECT
    SUM(soh.SubTotal) AS DailySales,
    DATENAME(MONTH, soh.OrderDate) AS OrderMonth,
    soh.OrderDate
  FROM Sales.SalesOrderHeader soh
  WHERE soh.OrderDate >= '20020101'
    AND soh.OrderDate < '20030101'
  GROUP BY soh.OrderDate
)
```

```
SELECT
  DENSE_RANK() OVER
  (
    PARTITION BY
      OrderMonth
    ORDER BY
      DailySales DESC
  ) AS Ranking,
  DailySales,
  OrderMonth,
  OrderDate
FROM TotalSalesBySalesDatePartitioned
ORDER BY OrderMonth,
  Ranking;
```

	Ranking	DailySales	OrderMonth	OrderDate
25	25	13931.52	April	2002-04-13 00:00:00.000
26	28	11230.6282	April	2002-04-24 00:00:00.000
27	26	11230.6282	April	2002-04-19 00:00:00.000
28	27	10734.81	April	2002-04-08 00:00:00.000

Figure 9-9. *DENSE_RANK does not skip ranking values after a tie.*

The NTILE Function

NTILE is another ranking function that fulfills a slightly different need. This function divides your result set into approximate n-tiles. An *n-tile* can be a quartile (1/4th, or 25 percent slices), a quintile (1/5th, or 20 percent slices), a percentile (1/100th, or 1 percent slices), or just about any other fractional slice you can imagine. The reason NTILE divides result sets into *approximate* n-tiles is that the number of rows returned might not be evenly divisible into the required number of groups. A table with 27 rows, for instance, is not evenly divisible into quartiles or quintiles. When you query a table with the NTILE function and the number of rows is not evenly divisible by the specified number of groups, NTILE creates groups of two different sizes. The larger groups will all be one row larger than the smaller groups, and the larger groups are numbered first. In the example of 27 rows divided into quintiles (1/5th), the first two groups will have six rows each, and the last three groups will have five rows each.

Like the ROW_NUMBER function, you can include both PARTITION BY and ORDER BY in the OVER clause. NTILE requires an additional parameter that specifies how many groups it should divide your results into.

NTILE is useful for answering business questions like "Which salespeople comprised the top 10 percent of the sales force in 2003?" Answers to questions like this can be used to determine things like which salespeople gets bonuses, which ones get additional training, and which ones get to collect unemployment benefits. Listing 9-11 uses NTILE to divide the AdventureWorks salespeople into ten groups, each one representing 10 percent of the total sales force. The ORDER BY clause is used to specify that rows are assigned to the groups in order of their total sales. The results are shown in Figure 9-10.

Listing 9-11. *Using NTILE to Group and Rank Salespeople*

```
WITH SalesTotalBySalesPerson
(
  SalesPersonID,
  SalesTotal
)
AS
(
  SELECT
    soh.SalesPersonID,
    SUM(soh.SubTotal) AS SalesTotal
  FROM Sales.SalesOrderHeader soh
  WHERE DATEPART(YEAR, soh.OrderDate) = 2003
  GROUP BY soh.SalesPersonID
)
SELECT
  NTILE(10) OVER
  (
    ORDER BY
      st.SalesTotal DESC
  ) AS Tile,
  p.LastName,
  p.FirstName,
  p.MiddleName,
  st.SalesPersonID,
  st.SalesTotal
FROM SalesTotalBySalesPerson st
INNER JOIN Person.Person p
  ON st.SalesPersonID = p.BusinessEntityID;
```

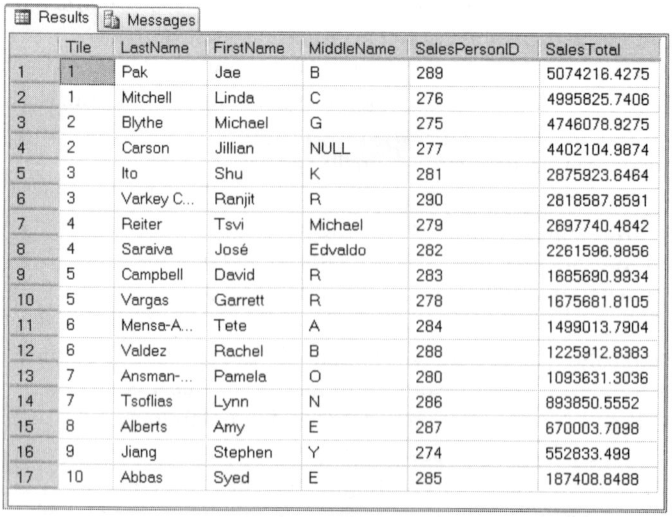

	Tile	LastName	FirstName	MiddleName	SalesPersonID	SalesTotal
1	1	Pak	Jae	B	289	5074216.4275
2	1	Mitchell	Linda	C	276	4995825.7406
3	2	Blythe	Michael	G	275	4746078.9275
4	2	Carson	Jillian	NULL	277	4402104.9874
5	3	Ito	Shu	K	281	2875923.6464
6	3	Varkey C...	Ranjit	R	290	2818587.8591
7	4	Reiter	Tsvi	Michael	279	2697740.4842
8	4	Saraiva	José	Edvaldo	282	2261596.9856
9	5	Campbell	David	R	283	1685690.9934
10	5	Vargas	Garrett	R	278	1675681.8105
11	6	Mensa-A...	Tete	A	284	1499013.7904
12	6	Valdez	Rachel	B	288	1225912.8383
13	7	Ansman-...	Pamela	O	280	1093631.3036
14	7	Tsoflias	Lynn	N	286	893850.5552
15	8	Alberts	Amy	E	287	670003.7098
16	9	Jiang	Stephen	Y	274	552833.499
17	10	Abbas	Syed	E	285	187408.8488

Figure 9-10. *AdventureWorks salespeople grouped and ranked by NTILE*

The code begins with a simple CTE that returns the SalesPersonID and sum of the order SubTotal values from the Sales.SalesOrderHeader table. The CTE limits its results to the sales that occurred in the year 2003.

```
WITH SalesTotalBySalesPerson
(
  SalesPersonID,
  SalesTotal
)
AS
(
  SELECT
    soh.SalesPersonID,
    SUM(soh.SubTotal) AS SalesTotal
  FROM Sales.SalesOrderHeader soh
  WHERE DATEPART(YEAR, soh.OrderDate) = 2003
  GROUP BY soh.SalesPersonID
)
```

The SELECT query associated with this CTE uses NTILE(10) to group the AdventureWorks salespeople into ten groups of approximately 10 percent each. The OVER clause specifies that the groups should be assigned based on the SalesTotal in descending order.

```
SELECT
  NTILE(10) OVER
  (
    ORDER BY
      st.SalesTotal DESC
  ) AS Tile,
  p.LastName,
  p.FirstName,
  p.MiddleName,
  st.SalesPersonID,
  st.SalesTotal
FROM SalesTotalBySalesPerson st
INNER JOIN Person.Person p
  ON st.SalesPersonID = p.BusinessEntityID;
```

Aggregate Functions and OVER

As previously discussed, the new numbering and ranking functions (ROW_NUMBER, RANK, etc.) all work with the OVER clause to define the order and partitioning of their input rows via the ORDER BY and PARTITION BY clauses. The OVER clause also provides windowing functionality to T-SQL aggregate functions such as SUM, COUNT, and SQL CLR user-defined aggregates. For instance, you can apply the OVER clause to the Purchasing.PurchaseOrderDetail table in the Adventure-Works database to retrieve the SUM of the quantities of products ordered, partitioned by ProductId, using the sample query in Listing 9-12. Partial results are shown in Figure 9-11.

Listing 9-12. *Using the OVER Clause with the SUM Aggregate Function*

```
SELECT
  PurchaseOrderID,
  ProductID,
  SUM(OrderQty) OVER
  (
    PARTITION BY
      ProductId
  ) AS TotalOrderQty
FROM Purchasing.PurchaseOrderDetail;
```

	PurchaseOrderID	ProductID	TotalOrderQty
1997	371	358	3000
1998	213	358	3000
1999	55	358	3000
2000	134	358	3000
2001	78	359	72
2002	2	359	72
2003	394	359	72
2004	397	359	72

Figure 9-11. *Partial results of SUM with the OVER clause*

As you can see in Figure 9-11, the result of the aggregate function with the OVER clause is returned on every row of the result set. You can achieve the same result via an inner join and a subquery, as shown in Listing 9-13.

Listing 9-13. *Using INNER JOIN to Duplicate Aggregate OVER Clause Results*

```
SELECT
  pod.PurchaseOrderID,
  pod.ProductID,
  pqty.TotalOrderQty
FROM Purchasing.PurchaseOrderDetail pod
INNER JOIN (
  SELECT
    ProductID,
    SUM(OrderQty) AS TotalOrderQty
  FROM Purchasing.PurchaseOrderDetail
  GROUP BY ProductID
) pqty
ON pod.ProductID = pqty.ProductID;
```

NO ORDER BY ALLOWED

When used with an aggregate function like SUM, COUNT, or AVG, or a user-defined aggregate, the OVER clause can only take a PARTITION BY clause—not an ORDER BY clause. This is a serious shortcoming in the SQL Server implementation of OVER for aggregate functions. ORDER BY in the OVER clause for aggregate functions allows you to easily perform single-statement running sum–type calculations. Running sum calculations without this feature require extensive joins, causing many people to fall back on cursors.

ORDER BY for the aggregate OVER clause, and other features related to windowing functions, has been submitted as a feature request to Microsoft. Hopefully, we'll see it implemented at some point in the near future.

Summary

CTEs are powerful SQL Server features that come in two varieties: recursive and nonrecursive. Nonrecursive CTEs allow you to write expressive T-SQL code that is easier to code, debug, and manage than complex queries that make extensive use of derived tables. Recursive CTEs simplify queries of hierarchical data and allow for easily generating result sets consisting of sequential numbers, which are very useful in themselves.

SQL Server's support for windowing functions and the OVER clause makes partitioning, row numbering, and ranking result sets simple. SQL Server supports several windowing functions, including the following:

- ROW_NUMBER: This function numbers the rows of a result set sequentially, beginning with 1.

- RANK *and* DENSE_RANK: These functions rank a result set, applying the same rank value in the case of a tie.

- NTILE: This function groups a result set into a user-specified number of groups.

You can also use the OVER clause to apply windowing functionality to built-in aggregate functions and SQL CLR user-defined aggregates.

Both CTEs and windowing functions provide useful functionality and extend the syntax of T-SQL, allowing you to write more powerful code than ever in a simpler syntax than was possible without them.

EXERCISES

1. [True/false] When a CTE is not the first statement in a batch, the statement preceding it must end with a semicolon statement terminator.

2. [Choose all that apply] A recursive CTE requires which of the following:

    a.   The WITH keyword

    b.   An anchor query

    c.   The EXPRESSION keyword

    d.   A recursive query

3. [Fill in the blank] The MAXRECURSION option can accept a value between 0 and ___.

4. [Choose one] SQL Server supports which of the following windowing functions:

    a.   ROW_NUMBER

    b.   RANK

    c.   DENSE_RANK

    d.   NTILE

    e.   All of the above

5. [True/false] You can use ORDER BY in the OVER clause when used with aggregate functions.

6. [True/false] When PARTITION BY and ORDER BY are both used in the OVER clause, PARTITION BY must appear first.

7. [Fill in the blank] The names of all columns returned by a CTE must be ___.

CHAPTER 10

■■■

Integrated Full-Text Search

Full-text search (FTS) provides the tools necessary to perform linguistic searches in a wide variety of languages against data and documents stored in SQL Server. Each new release of SQL Server has improved on FTS support since its initial introduction in SQL Server 7.0. SQL Server 2008 carries on with this tradition of continuous improvement in FTS functionality. The new integrated FTS (iFTS) model provides tighter integration with the SQL Server query engine, greater transparency with new dynamic management views and functions, improved support for more languages, and better T-SQL administration and management tools. In this chapter, I'll introduce the new generation of SQL Server iFTS functionality.

iFTS Architecture

The new iFTS differs from the FTS functionality available in previous versions of SQL Server in several ways. In previous releases of SQL Server, the full-text query engine was a completely separate service from the SQL Server service. In the classic architecture, the SQL Server query engine handed off full-text queries to the full-text query engine service for processing, and the full-text query engine passed results back to SQL Server. This interservice communication generated additional overhead. Because the full-text query engine was a separate service, the SQL Server query engine could not effectively estimate full-text query costs—a very important step in optimizing overall query performance when full-text queries are involved.

A major enhancement in iFTS is the tight integration with the SQL Server query engine. SQL Server 2008 integrates the full-text query engine into the SQL Server query processor, eliminating a lot of interprocess overhead and allowing for much more efficient full-text query processing and optimizations. A simplified view of the new full-text engine integration with the SQL Server query processor is shown in Figure 10-1.

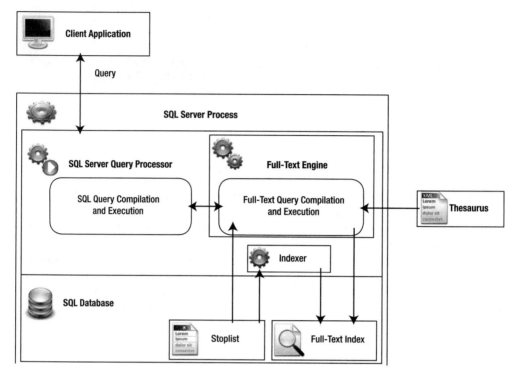

Figure 10-1. *New iFTS architecture (simplified)*

The new tighter integration of the full-text engine with the SQL Server query processor increases the efficiency, scalability, flexibility, and transparency of FTS, including the following:

- The full-text engine is hosted in the SQL Server process eliminating much of the overhead associated with interservice communications.

- SQL Server can use iFTS integration to better predict query performance through the use of new query operators.

- SQL Server can optimize access to full-text indexes because they are now stored in the database.

- New functionality is available for creating customized stoplists of words to ignore during FTS, adding flexibility to iFTS.

- SQL Server provides new dynamic management views and functions that provide greater transparency in understanding how iFTS queries are processed and executed.

Creating Full-Text Catalogs and Indexes

The first step to take advantage of SQL Server iFTS is to create full-text catalogs and full-text indexes. A full-text catalog can contain one or more full-text indexes, and each full-text index can only be assigned to one full-text catalog. You can create full-text catalogs and full-text indexes in SQL Server Management Studio (SSMS) using GUI (graphical user interface) wizards or T-SQL statements.

Creating Full-Text Catalogs

You can access the GUI full-text catalog wizard by right-clicking Full Text Catalogs in the SSMS Object Explorer. The New Full-Text Catalog option on the pop-up context menu starts the wizard (see Figure 10-2).

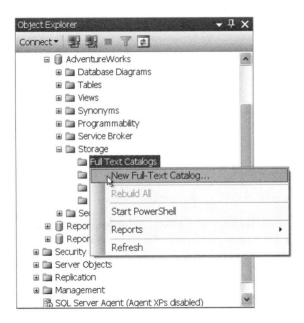

Figure 10-2. *New Full-Text Catalog context menu option*

After selecting New Full-Text Catalog, SSMS presents the wizard's New Full-Text Catalog window. This window allows you to define the name of your full-text catalog, the full-text catalog's owner, an accent sensitivity setting, and whether or not this full-text catalog is designated as the default for a database. The New Full-Text Catalog window is shown in Figure 10-3.

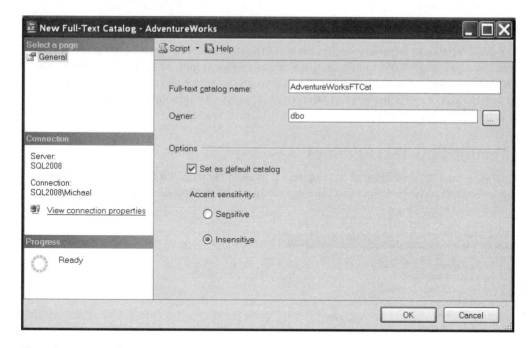

Figure 10-3. *New Full-Text Catalog window*

For this sample full-text catalog, I chose the following options:

- The full-text catalog is named AdventureWorksFTCat, and dbo is designated as the owner.

- The full-text catalog is designated the default full-text catalog for the database. When a new full-text index is created, if a full-text catalog is not specified, the default catalog is used.

- The accent sensitivity is set to Insensitive, meaning that words with accent marks are treated as equivalent to those without accent marks (e.g., for search purposes, *resumé* is the same as *resume*).

You can also create and manage full-text catalogs using T-SQL statements. Listing 10-1 shows how to create the same full-text catalog that I created previously in this section with the SSMS wizard.

Listing 10-1. *Creating a Full-Text Catalog with T-SQL*

```
CREATE FULLTEXT CATALOG AdventureWorksFTCat
WITH ACCENT_SENSITIVITY = OFF
AS DEFAULT
AUTHORIZATION dbo;
```

Once you've created your full-text catalog, the next step is to build full-text indexes. I describe full-text index creation in the next section. Maximum-performance full-text catalogs, particularly those you anticipate will become very large, should be created on filegroups that are located on their own physical drives. This is also useful for administrative functions such as performing filegroup backups and restores independent of data and log files.

Creating Full-Text Indexes

As with full-text catalogs, you have two options for creating full-text indexes—you can use the GUI wizard in SSMS or you can use T-SQL statements. Once you've created a full-text catalog, as described in the previous section, it's time to define your full-text indexes. Begin by right-clicking a table in the SSMS Object Explorer to pull up the table context menu. From the context menu, choose the Full-Text Index ➤ Define Full-Text Index option, shown in Figure 10-4.

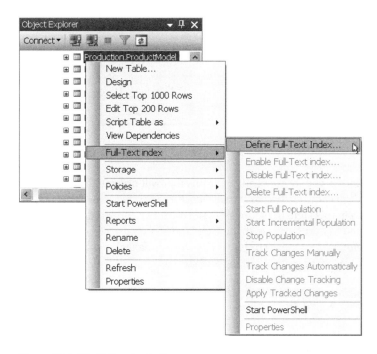

Figure 10-4. *"Full-Text index" context menu*

The full-text index wizard shows a splash screen the first time you access it. You can choose to turn off the splash screen or just ignore it. On the next screen, shown in Figure 10-5, the wizard allows you to select a single-column unique index on the table. Every full-text index requires a single-column unique index that allows the full-text index to reference individual rows in the table. If you don't have a single-column unique index defined on the table you're trying to create a full-text index on, the wizard will display an error message as soon as you try to run it. In this example, I've chosen to use the table's integer primary key for the full-text index.

■**Tip** It's recommended that you specify a single-column unique index defined on an integer column when creating a full-text index. This will help maximize performance and minimize full-text index storage requirements.

Figure 10-5. *Selecting a single-column unique index*

After you select a unique index, you'll choose the columns that will provide the searchable content for the full-text index. You can specify char, nchar, varchar, nvarchar, xml, varbinary, text, ntext, and image columns in this step. In Figure 10-6, the nvarchar and xml data type columns of the table are selected to participate in the full-text index. I've also selected English as the word-breaker language for each of these columns. The word-breaker language specification determines the language used for word-breaking and stemming.

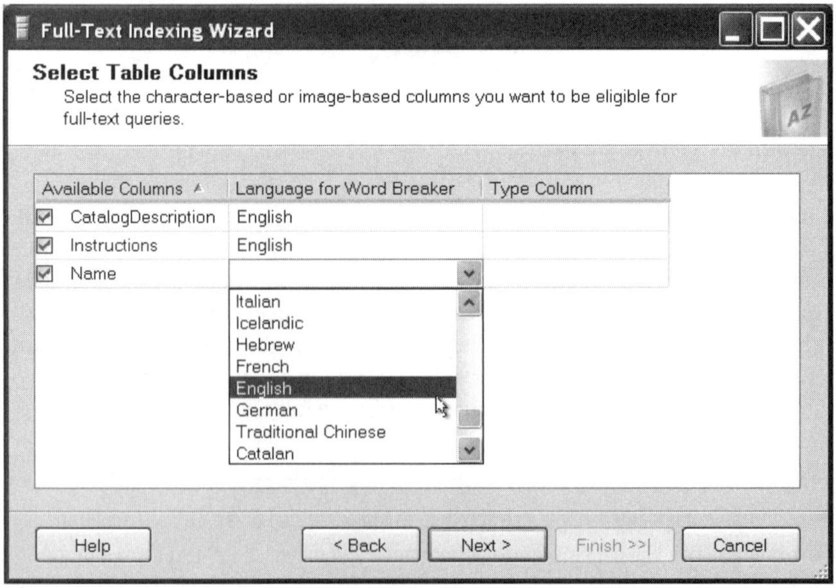

Figure 10-6. *Selecting columns to participate in full-text searches*

■**Note** The *type column*, not used in this example, is the name of a column indicating the document type (e.g., Microsoft Word, Excel, PowerPoint, Adobe PDF, and others) when you full-text index documents stored in varbinary(max) or image columns. Be aware that some document types require installation and configuration of additional IFilter components. More information is available on Microsoft TechNet at http://technet.microsoft.com/en-us/library/ms142499(SQL.100).aspx.

After you've selected the columns that will participate in full-text searches against a table, you must select the change-tracking option. *Change tracking* determines whether SQL Server maintains a change log for the full-text indexed columns, and how the log is used to update the full-text index. Figure 10-7 shows the change-tracking options available through the wizard.

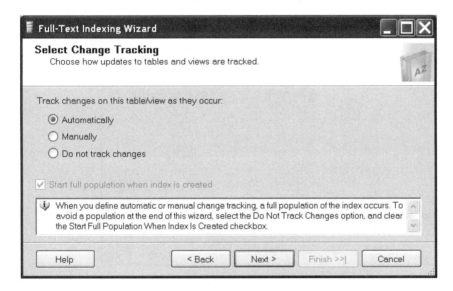

Figure 10-7. *Selecting a change-tracking option*

The change-tracking options available through the wizard include the following:

- *Automatically*: SQL Server updates the full-text index automatically when data is modified in the columns that participate in the full-text index. This is the default option.

- *Manually*: The change-tracking log is either used to update the full-text index via SQL Agent on a scheduled basis, or through manual intervention. This option is useful when automatic full-text index updates could slow down your server during business hours.

- *Do not track changes*: SQL Server does not track changes. Updating the full-text index requires you to issue an ALTER FULLTEXT INDEX statement with the START FULL or INCREMENTAL POPULATION clause to populate the entire full-text index.

■**Tip** Keep in mind that *automatic* updates to the full-text index are not necessarily *immediate* updates. When automatic change tracking is specified, there may be some lag time between changes in the table data and updates to the full-text index.

The next step in the wizard allows you to assign your full-text index to a full-text catalog. You can choose a preexisting full-text catalog, like the AdventureWorksFTCat shown in Figure 10-8, or you can create a new full-text catalog. You can also choose a filegroup and full-text stoplist for the full-text index in this step.

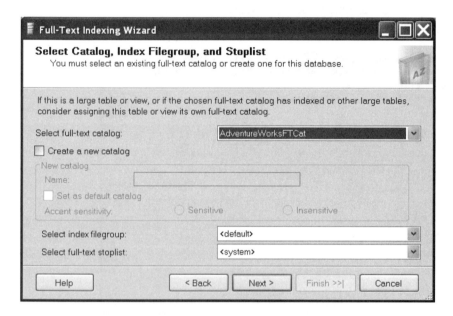

Figure 10-8. *Assigning a full-text index to a catalog*

The final steps of the wizard allow you to create a full-text index population schedule and review your previous wizard selections. Since automatic population is used in the example, no schedule is necessary. In the review window of the wizard, shown in Figure 10-9, you can look at the choices you've made in each step of the wizard and go back to previous steps to make changes if necessary. Once you click the Finish button, the full-text index is created in your database.

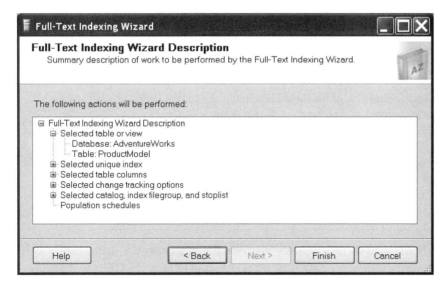

Figure 10-9. *Review wizard selections*

The SSMS full-text index wizard is very thorough, but you can also create and manage full-text indexes using T-SQL statements. Listing 10-2 shows the T-SQL statements required to create and enable a full-text index with the same options previously selected in the SSMS wizard example.

Listing 10-2. *Creating a Full-Text Index with T-SQL Statements*

```
CREATE FULLTEXT INDEX
ON Production.ProductModel
(
  CatalogDescription LANGUAGE English,
  Instructions LANGUAGE English,
  Name LANGUAGE English
)
KEY INDEX PK_ProductModel_ProductModelID
ON
(
  AdventureWorksFTCat
)
WITH
(
  CHANGE_TRACKING AUTO
);
GO

ALTER FULLTEXT INDEX
ON Production.ProductModel ENABLE;
GO
```

The CREATE FULLTEXT INDEX statement builds the full-text index on the Production. ProductModel table with the specified options. In this example, the CatalogDescription, Instructions, and Name columns are all participating in the full-text index. The LANGUAGE clause specifies that the English language word-breaker will be used to index the columns. The KEY INDEX clause specifies the primary key of the table, PK_ProductModel_ProductModelID, as the single-column unique index for the table. Finally, the CHANGE TRACKING AUTO option turns on automatic change tracking for the full-text index.

The ALTER FULLTEXT INDEX statement in the listing enables the full-text index and starts a full population. ALTER FULLTEXT INDEX is a flexible statement that can be used to add columns to, or remove columns from, a full-text index. You can also use it to enable or disable a full-text index, set the change-tracking options, start or stop a full-text index population, or change full-text index stoplist settings.

■**Note** *Stoplists* are lists of words that are considered unimportant for purposes of FTS. These words are known as *stopwords*, and are equivalent to the noise words in previous releases of SQL Server. Stopwords are language dependent, with the English system stoplist containing words like *a, an, and,* and *the* (and many others). SQL Server 2008 provides a system stoplist and allows you to create your own custom stoplists. I will discuss stoplists later in this chapter.

Full-Text Querying

After you create a full-text catalog and a full-text index, you can take advantage of iFTS with SQL Server's FTS predicates and functions. SQL Server provides four ways to query a full-text index. The FREETEXT and CONTAINS predicates retrieve rows from a table that match a given FTS criteria, in much the same way that the EXISTS predicate returns rows that meet given criteria. The FREETEXTTABLE and CONTAINSTABLE functions return rowsets with two columns: a key column, which is a row identifier (the unique index value specified when the full-text index was created) and a rank column, which is a relevance rating.

The FREETEXT Predicate

The FREETEXT predicate offers the simplest method of using iFTS to search character-based columns of a full-text index. FREETEXT searches for words that match inflectional forms and thesaurus expansions and replacements. The FREETEXT predicate accepts a column name or list of columns, a free-text search string, and an optional language identifier (a locale ID, or LCID).

Because it is a predicate, FREETEXT can be used in the WHERE clause of a SELECT query or DML statement. All rows for which the FREETEXT predicate returns true (a match) are returned. Listing 10-3 shows a simple FREETEXT query that uses the full-text index created on the Production. ProductModel table in the previous section. The results are shown in Figure 10-10. The wildcard character (*) passed as a parameter to the FREETEXT predicate indicates that all columns participating in the full-text index should be searched for a match. The second FREETEXT parameter is the word you want to match.

Listing 10-3. *Simple FREETEXT Full-Text Query*

```
SELECT
  ProductModelID,
  Name,
  CatalogDescription,
  Instructions
FROM Production.ProductModel
WHERE FREETEXT(*, N'sock');
```

	ProductModelID	Name	CatalogDescription	Instructions
1	18	Mountain Bike Socks	NULL	NULL
2	24	Racing Socks	NULL	NULL

Figure 10-10. *Using FREETEXT to find socks*

The FREETEXT predicate automatically stems words to find inflectional forms. The query in Listing 10-3 returns rows that contain an inflectional form of the word *sock*—in this case, iFTS finds two rows that contain the plural form of the word, *socks*. FREETEXT also performs iFTS thesaurus expansions and replacements automatically, if a thesaurus file is available.

The integration of iFTS with the SQL Server query engine results in a more efficient FTS experience than in previous versions of FTS. In SQL Server 2008, iFTS can take advantage of new optimized operators like the Table Valued Function [FulltextMatch] operator shown in Figure 10-11. The query plan shown is generated by the query in Listing 10-3.

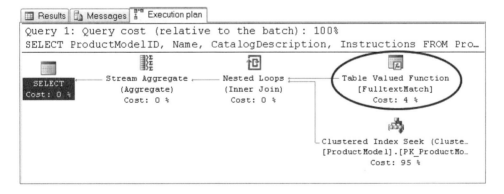

Figure 10-11. *FREETEXT query execution plan*

IFTS PERFORMANCE OPTIMIZATION

In previous releases of SQL Server, the FTS functionality was provided via an independent service known as MSFTESQL (Microsoft Full-Text Engine for SQL Server). Because it was completely separate from the SQL Server query engine, the MSFTESQL service could not take advantage of T-SQL operators to optimize performance. As an example, consider the following variation on the query in Listing 10-3:

```
SELECT
  ProductModelID,
  Name,
  CatalogDescription,
  Instructions
FROM Production.ProductModel
WHERE FREETEXT(*, N'sock')
AND ProductModelID < 100;
```

Imagine for a moment that the Production.ProductModel table has 1,000,000 rows that match the FREETEXT predicate. Prior versions of SQL Server were incapable of using the additional T-SQL ProductModelID < 100 predicate in the WHERE clause to limit the rows accessed by the FTS service. In SQL Server 2005, the MSFTESQL service had to return all 1,000,000 rows from the FREETEXT predicate and then narrow them down. With SQL Server 2008's new iFTS integration, the FTS engine can work in tandem with the SQL Server query engine to optimize the query plan and limit the number of rows touched by the FREETEXT predicate.

■**Tip** You'll see heavy use of the phrase *inflectional forms* throughout this section. Inflectional forms of words include verb conjugations like *go*, *goes*, *going*, *gone*, and *went*. Inflectional forms also include plural and singular noun variants of words, like *bike* and *bikes*. Searching for any word with FREETEXT automatically results in matches of all supported inflectional forms.

Listing 10-4 demonstrates a FREETEXT query that performs automatic stemming of the word *ride*. This query retrieves all rows that contain inflectional forms of the word *ride* in the CatalogDescription column. Inflectional forms that are matched in this query include the plural noun *riders* and the verb *riding*. In this FREETEXT query, the CatalogDescription column name is identified by name to restrict the search to a single column, and the LANGUAGE specifier is used to indicate LCID 1033, which is US English. The results are shown in Figure 10-12.

Listing 10-4. *FREETEXT Query with Automatic Word Stemming*

```
SELECT
  ProductModelID,
  Name,
  CatalogDescription,
  Instructions
FROM Production.ProductModel
WHERE FREETEXT(CatalogDescription, N'weld', LANGUAGE 1033);
```

	ProductModelID	Name	CatalogDescription	Instructions
1	7	HL Touring Frame	NULL	<root xmlns="http://sche...
2	10	LL Touring Frame	NULL	<root xmlns="http://sche...
3	19	Mountain-100	<?xml-stylesheet href="...	NULL
4	25	Road-150	<?xml-stylesheet href="...	NULL
5	47	LL Touring Handlebars	NULL	<root xmlns="http://sche...
6	48	HL Touring Handlebars	NULL	<root xmlns="http://sche...

Figure 10-12. *Automatic stemming with FREETEXT*

You can't see the words that matched in the xml type CatalogDescription and Instructions columns in Figure 10-2 (there's not enough space on the page to reproduce the entire result). Rest assured that FREETEXT has located valid matches in each row, though. To demonstrate, I've reproduced a portion of the matched content for each of the result rows in Figure 10-13. Notice that the word *weld*, used in the FREETEXT predicate, is automatically stemmed to match *Welding* and *welded* in the results.

ProductMode...	Name	CatalogDescription	Instructions
7	HL Touring Frame	NULL	...Work Center 20 - Frame Welding...
10	LL Touring Frame	NULL	...Work Center 20 - Frame Welding...
19	Mountain-100	...The heat-treated welded...	NULL
25	Road-150	...it is welded and...	NULL
47	LL Touring Handlebars	NULL	...Work Center 20 - Frame Welding...
48	HL Touring Handlebars	NULL	...Work Center 20 - Frame Welding...

Figure 10-13. *Partial matched contents for the FREETEXT query*

The CONTAINS Predicate

In addition to the FREETEXT predicate, SQL Server 2008 supports the CONTAINS predicate. CONTAINS allows more advanced full-text query options than the FREETEXT predicate. Just like FREETEXT, the CONTAINS predicate accepts a column name or list of columns, a search condition, and an optional language identifier as parameters. The CONTAINS predicate can search for simple strings like FREETEXT, but it also allows sophisticated search conditions that include word or phrase prefixes, words that are in close proximity to other words, inflectional word forms, thesaurus synonyms, and combinations of search criteria.

The simplest `CONTAINS` predicates are basic word searches, similar to `FREETEXT`. Unlike `FREETEXT`, however, the `CONTAINS` predicate does not automatically search for inflectional forms of words or thesaurus expansions and replacements. Listing 10-5 modifies Listing 10-4 to demonstrate a simple `CONTAINS` query. The results are shown in Figure 10-14. As you can see, a couple of rows that do not contain an exact match for the word *weld* are eliminated from the results.

Listing 10-5. *Simple CONTAINS Query*

```
SELECT
  ProductModelID,
  Name,
  CatalogDescription,
  Instructions
FROM Production.ProductModel
WHERE CONTAINS(*, N'weld');
```

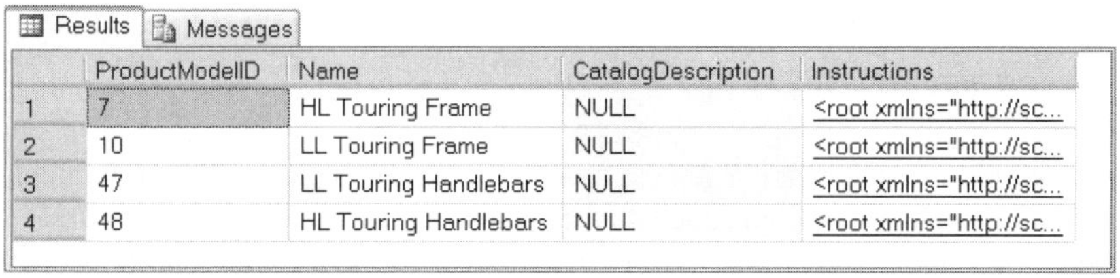

	ProductModelID	Name	CatalogDescription	Instructions
1	7	HL Touring Frame	NULL	<root xmlns="http://sc...
2	10	LL Touring Frame	NULL	<root xmlns="http://sc...
3	47	LL Touring Handlebars	NULL	<root xmlns="http://sc...
4	48	HL Touring Handlebars	NULL	<root xmlns="http://sc...

Figure 10-14. *Results of the simple CONTAINS query*

To use inflectional forms or thesaurus expansions and replacements with `CONTAINS`, use the `FORMSOF` generation term in your search condition. Listing 10-6 performs a `CONTAINS` search on the `Name` and `CatalogDescription` columns of the `Production.ProductModel` table. The results, which include matches for inflectional forms of the word *sport*, like *sports* and *sporting*, are shown in Figure 10-15.

Listing 10-6. *Sample CONTAINS Query with FORMSOF Inflectional Generation Term*

```
SELECT
  ProductModelID,
  Name,
  CatalogDescription
FROM Production.ProductModel
WHERE CONTAINS
(
  (
    Name,
    CatalogDescription
  ),
  N'FORMSOF(INFLECTIONAL, sport)'
);
```

	ProductModelID	Name	CatalogDescription
1	13	Men's Sports Shorts	NULL
2	28	Road-450	<?xml-stylesheet href="...
3	33	Sport-100	NULL

Figure 10-15. *Results of the CONTAINS query with inflectional FORMSOF term*

The CONTAINS predicate also allows you to combine simple search terms like these with the AND (&), AND NOT (&!), and OR (|) Boolean operators. Listing 10-7 demonstrates combining two search terms in a CONTAINS predicate. The results of this sample query, which retrieves all rows containing inflectional forms of the word *sport* (like *sports*) or the word *tube* in the Name or CatalogDescription columns, are shown in Figure 10-16.

Listing 10-7. *Compound CONTAINS Search Term*

```
SELECT
  ProductModelID,
  Name,
  CatalogDescription
FROM Production.ProductModel
WHERE CONTAINS
(
  (
    Name,
    CatalogDescription
  ),
  N'"tube" | FORMSOF(INFLECTIONAL, sport)'
);
```

	ProductModelID	Name	CatalogDescription
1	13	Men's Sports Shorts	NULL
2	19	Mountain-100	<?xml-stylesheet hr...
3	28	Road-450	<?xml-stylesheet hr...
4	33	Sport-100	NULL
5	34	Touring-1000	<?xml-stylesheet hr...
6	92	Mountain Tire Tube	NULL
7	93	Road Tire Tube	NULL
8	94	Touring Tire Tube	NULL

Figure 10-16. *Results of the CONTAINS query with a compound search term*

Listing 10-7 uses FORMSOF to return matches for inflectional forms. You can also use the FORMSOF (THESAURUS, . . .) format to return matches for expansions and replacements of words, as defined in your language-specific thesaurus files.

CONTAINS also supports prefix searches using the wildcard asterisk (*) character. Place the search word or phrase, immediately followed by the wildcard character, in double quotes to specify a prefix search. Listing 10-8 demonstrates a simple prefix search to retrieve all rows that have a word starting with the prefix *bot* in the Name column. The results are shown in Figure 10-17.

Listing 10-8. *CONTAINS Prefix Search*

```
SELECT
  ProductModelID,
  Name
FROM Production.ProductModel
WHERE CONTAINS(Name, N'"bot*"');
```

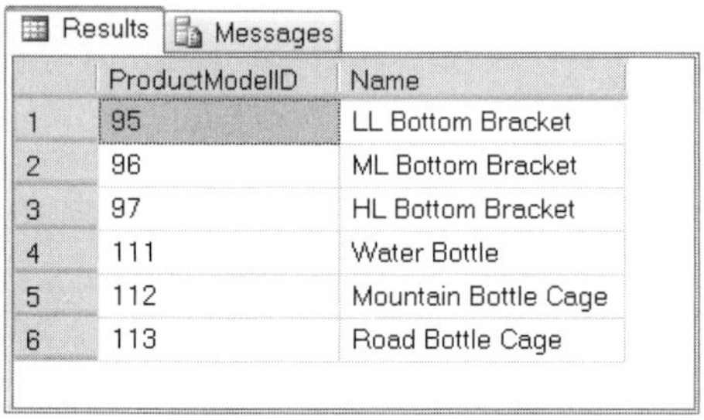

	ProductModelID	Name
1	95	LL Bottom Bracket
2	96	ML Bottom Bracket
3	97	HL Bottom Bracket
4	111	Water Bottle
5	112	Mountain Bottle Cage
6	113	Road Bottle Cage

Figure 10-17. *Results of the CONTAINS prefix search*

The CONTAINS predicate also supports the NEAR (~) keyword for proximity searches. NEAR will return matches for words that are close to one another in the source columns. Listing 10-9 demonstrates a NEAR proximity search that looks for instances of the word *aluminum* that occur in close proximity to the word *jig* in the Instructions column. The results are shown in Figure 10-18.

Tip The proximity search considers words that are within about 50 words of one another as close enough to be considered a match.

Listing 10-9. *CONTAINS Proximity Search*

```
SELECT
  ProductModelID,
  Name
FROM Production.ProductModel
WHERE CONTAINS(Instructions, N'aluminum NEAR jig');
```

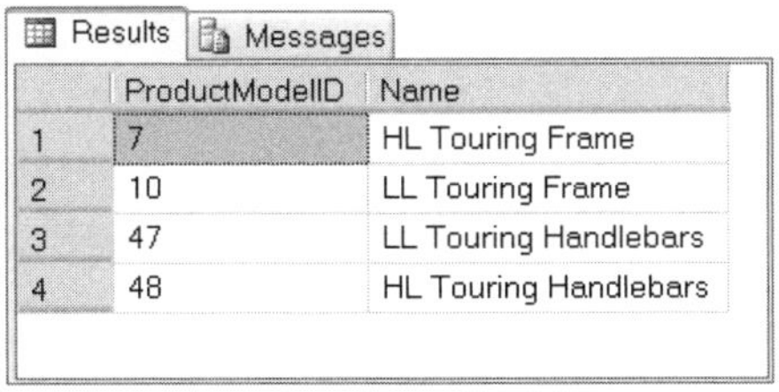

	ProductModelID	Name
1	7	HL Touring Frame
2	10	LL Touring Frame
3	47	LL Touring Handlebars
4	48	HL Touring Handlebars

Figure 10-18. *CONTAINS proximity query results*

The FREETEXTTABLE and CONTAINSTABLE Functions

SQL Server provides TVF-based counterparts to the FREETEXT and CONTAINSTABLE predicates, known as FREETEXTTABLE and CONTAINSTABLE. These functions operate like the similarly named predicates, but both functions return result sets consisting of a table with two columns, named KEY and RANK. The KEY column contains the key index values relating back to the unique index of matching rows in the source table, and the RANK column contains relevance rankings.

The FREETEXTTABLE function accepts the name of the table to search, a single column name or column list, a search string, and an optional language identifier just like the FREETEXT predicate. FREETEXTTABLE can also take an additional "top *n* by rank" parameter to limit the rows returned to a specific number of the highest-ranked rows. The results of FREETEXTTABLE are useful for joining back to the source table via the KEY column of the results. Listing 10-10 demonstrates a simple FREETEXTTABLE query that locates rows where the word *aluminum* appears in the Instructions column of the Production.ProductModel table. The results are joined back to the source table to return the ProductModelID and Name, as shown in Figure 10-19.

Listing 10-10. *FREETEXTTABLE Results Joined to Source Table*

```
SELECT
  ftt.[KEY],
  ftt.[RANK],
  pm.ProductModelID,
  pm.Name
FROM FREETEXTTABLE
(
  Production.ProductModel,
  Instructions,
  N'aluminum'
) ftt
INNER JOIN Production.ProductModel pm
  ON ftt.[KEY] = pm.ProductModelID;
```

	KEY	RANK	ProductModelID	Name
1	7	545	7	HL Touring Frame
2	10	545	10	LL Touring Frame
3	47	616	47	LL Touring Handlebars
4	48	616	48	HL Touring Handlebars

Figure 10-19. *Results of the FREETEXTTABLE query*

The CONTAINSTABLE function offers the advanced search capabilities of the CONTAINS predicate in a function form. The CONTAINSTABLE function accepts the name of the source table, a single column name or list of columns, and a CONTAINS-style search condition. Like FREETEXTTABLE, the CONTAINSTABLE function also accepts an optional language identifier and "top *n* by rank" parameter. Listing 10-11 demonstrates the CONTAINSTABLE function in a simple keyword search that retrieves KEY and RANK values for all rows containing inflectional forms of the word *tours*. The results are shown in Figure 10-20.

Listing 10-11. *Simple CONTAINSTABLE Query*

```
SELECT
  [KEY],
  [RANK]
FROM CONTAINSTABLE
(
  Production.ProductModel,
  [Name],
  N'FORMSOF(INFLECTIONAL, tours)'
);
```

	KEY	RANK
1	7	64
2	10	64
3	34	64
4	35	64
5	36	64
6	43	64
7	44	64
8	47	64
9	48	64
10	53	64
11	65	64
12	66	64
13	67	64
14	91	64
15	94	64
16	120	64

Figure 10-20. *Results of the CONTAINSTABLE query with inflectional forms*

CONTAINSTABLE supports all of the options supported by the CONTAINS predicate, including the ISABOUT term, which assigns weights to the matched words it locates. With ISABOUT, each search word is assigned a weight value between 0.0 and 1.0. CONTAINSTABLE applies the weight to the relevance rankings returned in the RANK column. Listing 10-12 shows two CONTAINSTABLE queries. The first query returns all products with the words *aluminum* or *polish* in their XML Instructions column. The second query uses ISABOUT to assign each of these words a weight between 0.0 and 1.0, which is then applied to the result RANK for each row. The results, shown in Figure 10-21, demonstrate how ISABOUT weights can rearrange the rankings of your CONTAINSTABLE query results.

Listing 10-12. *ISABOUT in a CONTAINSTABLE Query*

```
SELECT
  ct.[RANK],
  ct.[KEY],
  pm.[Name]
FROM CONTAINSTABLE
(
  Production.ProductModel,
  Instructions,
  N'aluminum OR polish'
) ct
INNER JOIN Production.ProductModel pm
  ON ct.[KEY] = pm.ProductModelID
ORDER BY ct.[RANK] DESC;

SELECT
  ct.[RANK],
  ct.[KEY],
  pm.[Name]
FROM CONTAINSTABLE
(
  Production.ProductModel,
  Instructions,
  N'ISABOUT(aluminum WEIGHT(1.0), polish WEIGHT(0.1))'
) ct
INNER JOIN Production.ProductModel pm
  ON ct.[KEY] = pm.ProductModelID
ORDER BY ct.[RANK] DESC;
```

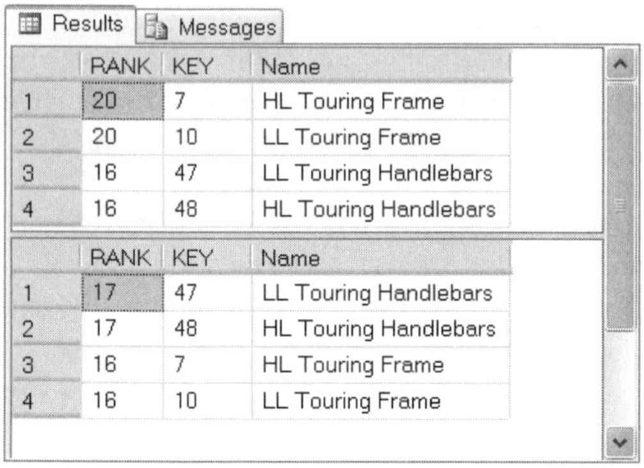

	RANK	KEY	Name
1	20	7	HL Touring Frame
2	20	10	LL Touring Frame
3	16	47	LL Touring Handlebars
4	16	48	HL Touring Handlebars

	RANK	KEY	Name
1	17	47	LL Touring Handlebars
2	17	48	HL Touring Handlebars
3	16	7	HL Touring Frame
4	16	10	LL Touring Frame

Figure 10-21. *Changing result set rankings with ISABOUT*

Thesauruses and Stoplists

The FREETEXT predicate and FREETEXTTABLE function automatically perform word stemming for inflectional forms and thesaurus expansions and replacements. The CONTAINS predicate and CONTAINSTABLE function require you to explicitly specify that you want inflectional forms and thesaurus expansions and replacements with the FORMSOF term. While inflectional forms include verb conjugations and plural forms of words, thesaurus functionality is based on user-managed XML files that define word replacement and expansion patterns.

Each language-specific thesaurus is located in an XML file in the MSSQL\FTDATA directory of your SQL Server installation. The thesaurus files are named using the format ts*nnn*.xml, where *nnn* is a three-letter code representing a specific language. The file name tsenu.xml, for instance, is the US English thesaurus. To demonstrate the iFTS thesaurus capabilities, I'll begin by creating a new full-text index on the Production.Product table using the code in Listing 10-13.

Listing 10-13. *Creating a Full-Text Index*

```
CREATE FULLTEXT INDEX ON Production.Product
(
  Name LANGUAGE English,
  Color LANGUAGE English
)
KEY INDEX PK_Product_ProductID
ON (AdventureWorksFTCat)
WITH
(
  CHANGE_TRACKING AUTO,
  STOPLIST = SYSTEM
);
GO
```

```
ALTER FULLTEXT INDEX ON Production.Product
ENABLE;
GO
```

You can edit the thesaurus XML files with a simple text editor or a more advanced XML editor. For this example, I opened the tsenu.xml thesaurus file in Notepad, made the appropriate changes, and saved the file back to the MSSQL\FTDATA directory. The contents of the tsenu.xml file, after my edits, are shown in Listing 10-14.

Listing 10-14. *tsenu.xml US English XML Thesaurus File*

```
<XML ID = "Microsoft Search Thesaurus">
  <thesaurus xmlns = "x-schema:tsSchema.xml">
    <diacritics_sensitive>0</diacritics_sensitive>
    <expansion>
      <sub>thin</sub>
      <sub>flat</sub>
    </expansion>
    <replacement>
      <pat>sapphire</pat>
      <pat>indigo</pat>
      <pat>navy</pat>
      <sub>blue</sub>
    </replacement>
  </thesaurus>
</XML>
```

After editing the XML thesaurus file, you can use the sys.sp_fulltext_load_thesaurus_file stored procedure (SP) to reload the thesaurus file. This procedure accepts an integer LCID parameter, as shown in Listing 10-15. The LCID used in the listing is 1033, which specifies US English.

■**Note** Unlike previous versions of SQL Server, reloading a thesaurus in SQL Server 2008 does not require a SQL Server service restart.

Listing 10-15. *Reloading US English XML Thesaurus*

```
EXEC sys.sp_fulltext_load_thesaurus_file 1033;
GO
```

The diacritics_sensitive element of the thesaurus file indicates whether accent marks are replaced during expansion and replacement. For instance, if diacritics_sensitive is set to 0, the words *cafe* and *café* are considered equivalent for purposes of the thesaurus. If diacritics_sensitive is set to 1, however, these two words would be considered different.

The `expansion` element indicates substitutions that should be applied during the full-text query. The word being searched is expanded to match the other words in the expansion set. In the example, if the user queries for the word *thin*, the search is automatically expanded to include matches for the word *flat*, and vice versa. An expansion set can include as many substitutions as you care to define, and the thesaurus can contain as many expansion sets as you need. The sample `FREETEXT` query in Listing 10-16 shows the expansion sets in action, with partial results shown in Figure 10-22.

Listing 10-16. *FREETEXT Query with Thesaurus Expansion Sets*

```
SELECT
  ProductID,
  Name
FROM Production.Product
WHERE FREETEXT(*, N'flat');
```

	ProductID	Name
4	344	Flat Washer 9
5	345	Flat Washer 4
6	346	Flat Washer 3
7	347	Flat Washer 8
8	348	Flat Washer 5
9	349	Flat Washer 7
10	359	Thin-Jam Hex Nut 9
11	360	Thin-Jam Hex Nut 10
12	361	Thin-Jam Hex Nut 1
13	362	Thin-Jam Hex Nut 2
14	363	Thin-Jam Hex Nut 15

Figure 10-22. *Partial results of the full-text query with expansion sets*

The `replacement` section of the thesaurus file indicates replacements for words that are used in a full-text query. In the example, I've defined patterns like *navy, sapphire,* and *indigo,* which will be replaced with the word *blue.* The result is that a full-text query for these replacement patterns will be converted internally to a search for *blue.* Listing 10-17 shows a `FREETEXT` query that uses the replacement patterns defined in the thesaurus. You can use any of the replacement patterns defined in the thesaurus file in the full-text query to get the same result. Figure 10-23 shows the results.

Listing 10-17. *FREETEXT Query with Thesaurus Replacement Patterns*

```
SELECT
  ProductID,
  Name,
  Color
FROM Production.Product
WHERE FREETEXT(*, N'navy');
```

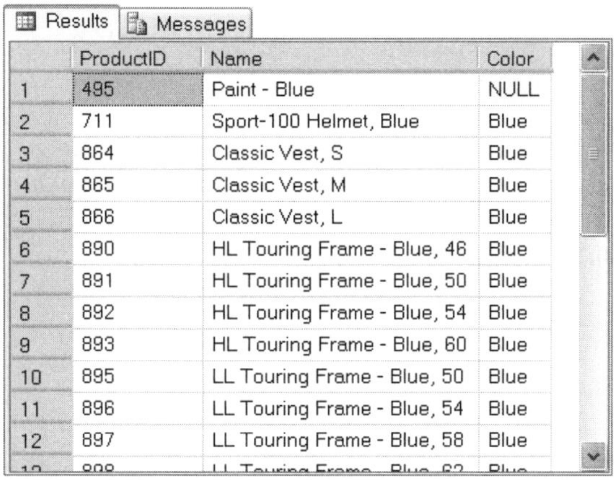

	ProductID	Name	Color
1	495	Paint - Blue	NULL
2	711	Sport-100 Helmet, Blue	Blue
3	864	Classic Vest, S	Blue
4	865	Classic Vest, M	Blue
5	866	Classic Vest, L	Blue
6	890	HL Touring Frame - Blue, 46	Blue
7	891	HL Touring Frame - Blue, 50	Blue
8	892	HL Touring Frame - Blue, 54	Blue
9	893	HL Touring Frame - Blue, 60	Blue
10	895	LL Touring Frame - Blue, 50	Blue
11	896	LL Touring Frame - Blue, 54	Blue
12	897	LL Touring Frame - Blue, 58	Blue

Figure 10-23. *Partial results of the full-text query with replacement sets*

Previous versions of FTS had system-defined lists of noise words, which provided a way to essentially ignore commonly occurring words that don't help the search. Commonly cited noise words included those like *the, a, an,* and others. The noise word implementation in previous versions stored the noise words in files in the file system.

In SQL Server 2008, there's a new implementation of the classic noise words, known in iFTS as stopwords. Stopwords are managed inside the SQL Server database using structures known as stoplists. You can use the system-supplied stoplists or create and manage your own language-specific stoplists with the `CREATE FULLTEXT STOPLIST`, `ALTER FULLTEXT STOPLIST`, and `DROP FULLTEXT STOPLIST` statements. The statement in Listing 10-18 creates a stoplist based on the system stoplist.

Listing 10-18. *Creating a Full-Text Stoplist*

```
CREATE FULLTEXT STOPLIST AWStoplist
FROM SYSTEM STOPLIST;
GO
```

Stoplists are more flexible than the old noise word lists since you can easily use T-SQL statements to add words to your stoplists. Consider AdventureWorks product model searches where the word *instructions* appears in several of the XML documents in the `Instructions` column. You can add the word *instructions* to the previously created stoplist with the `ALTER FULLTEXT STOPLIST` statement, and then associate the stoplist with the full-text index on the `Production.ProductModel` table via the `ALTER FULLTEXT INDEX` statement, as shown in Listing 10-19. This will effectively ignore the word *instructions* during full-text searches on this column.

Listing 10-19. *Adding the Word "instructions" to the Stoplist*

```
ALTER FULLTEXT STOPLIST AWStoplist
ADD N'instructions' LANGUAGE English;
GO
```

```
ALTER FULLTEXT INDEX ON Production.ProductModel
SET STOPLIST AWStoplist;
GO
```

After application of the newly created stoplist, a full-text query against the `Production.` `ProductModel` table for the word *instructions*, as shown in Listing 10-20, will return no results.

Listing 10-20. *Full-Text Query with Newly Created Stoplist*

```
SELECT
  ProductModelID,
  Name
FROM Production.ProductModel
WHERE FREETEXT(*, N'instructions');
```

Stored Procedures and Dynamic Management Views and Functions

SQL Server 2008 provides access to many of the legacy FTS SPs available in previous releases of SQL Server. Most of these procedures have been deprecated, however, and have been replaced by fully integrated T-SQL statements and dynamic management views and functions.

SQL Server 2008 does introduce two new SPs to aid in iFTS management. The first is the `sys.sp_fulltext_load_thesaurus_file` procedure that I introduced earlier in this chapter to load an XML thesaurus file. The second is the `sys.sp_fulltext_resetfdhostaccount` procedure that updates the Windows username and password that SQL Server uses to start the new filter daemon service.

A big issue for developers who used FTS in prior versions of SQL Server was the lack of transparency. Basically everything that FTS did was well hidden from view, and developers and administrators had to troubleshoot FTS issues in the dark. SQL Server 2008 introduces some new catalog views and dynamic management functions that make iFTS more transparent.

If you're experiencing iFTS query performance issues, the `sys.fulltext_index_fragments` catalog view can provide insight. This catalog view reports full-text index fragments and their status. You can use the information in this catalog view to decide if it's time to reorganize your full-text index.

The `sys.fulltext_stoplists` and `sys.fulltext_stopwords` catalog views let you see the user-defined stopwords and stoplists defined in the current database. The information returned by these catalog views is useful for troubleshooting issues with certain words being ignored (or not being ignored) in full-text queries. The `sys.fulltext_system_stopwords` catalog view returns a row for every stopword in the system stoplist, which is useful information to have if you want to use the system stoplist as the basis for your own stoplists.

The `sys.dm_fts_parser` function is a useful tool for troubleshooting full-text queries. This function accepts a full-text query string, an LCID, a stoplist ID, and an accent sensitivity setting. The result returned by the function shows the results produced by the word breaker and stemmer for any given full-text query. This information is very useful if you need to troubleshoot or just want to better understand exactly how the word breaker and stemmer affect your queries. Listing 10-21 is a simple demonstration of stemming the word *had* with the sys.dm_fts_parser function. Results are shown in Figure 10-24.

Listing 10-21. *Using sys.dm_fts_parser to See Word Breaking and Stemming*

```
SELECT
  keyword,
  group_id,
  phrase_id,
  occurrence,
  special_term,
  display_term,
  expansion_type,
  source_term
FROM sys.dm_fts_parser
(
  N'FORMSOF(FREETEXT, had)',
  1033,
  NULL,
  0
);
```

	keyword	group...	phrase...	occurre...	special_term	display_term	expan...	source_te...
1	0x0068006100760...	1	0	1	Exact Match	have	2	had
2	0x0068006100760...	1	0	1	Exact Match	having	2	had
3	0x006800610073	1	0	1	Exact Match	has	2	had
4	0x006800610064	1	0	1	Exact Match	had	0	had

Figure 10-24. *Results of word-breaking and stemming the word "had"*

Summary

SQL Server 2008 iFTS marks a big improvement in SQL Server FTS technology. The new iFTS functionality is better integrated with SQL Server than previous versions, providing more efficient full-text queries than ever before. Full-text indexes and stoplists are stored in the database, making iFTS more manageable, flexible, and scalable than in previous releases.

SQL Server provides the powerful FREETEXT and CONTAINS predicates, and FREETEXTTABLE and CONTAINSTABLE functions, to perform full-text searches. SQL Server also supports thesaurus and stoplist functionality to help customize iFTS. SQL Server 2008 also provides new dynamic management views and functions to make FTS more transparent and easier to troubleshoot than was the case in previous versions of SQL Server.

EXERCISES

1. [True/false] Stoplists and full-text indexes are stored in the database.

2. [Choose one] You can create a full-text index using which of the following methods:

    a.   Using a wizard in SSMS

    b.   Using the T-SQL CREATE FULLTEXT INDEX statement

    c.   Both (a) and (b)

    d.   None of the above

3. [Fill in the blanks] The `FREETEXT` predicate automatically performs word stemming and thesaurus ___ and ___.

4. [Fill in the blank] Stoplists contain stopwords, which are words that are ___ during full-text querying.

5. [True/false] The `sys.dm_fts_parser` dynamic management function shows the results produced by word breaking and stemming.

CHAPTER 11

∎∎∎

XML

SQL Server 2008 continues the standard for XML integration introduced with the SQL Server 2005 release. The new generation of XML support offers much tighter integration with T-SQL through the xml data type, support for the World Wide Web Consortium (W3C) XQuery and XML Schema recommendations, and improvements to legacy XML functionality.

SQL Server 2008's tight XML integration and the xml data type provide streamlined methods of performing several XML-related tasks that used to require clunky code to interface with COM objects and other tools external to the SQL Server engine. This chapter discusses the new xml data type and the XML tools built into T-SQL to take advantage of this new functionality.

Legacy XML

T-SQL support for XML was introduced with the release of SQL Server 2000 via the FOR XML clause of the SELECT statement, the OPENXML rowset provider, and the sp_xml_preparedocument and sp_xml_removedocument system SPs. In this section, I'll discuss the legacy OPENXML, sp_xml_preparedocument, and sp_xml_removedocument functionality. Though these tools still exist in SQL Server 2008 and can be used for backward-compatibility scripts, they are awkward and kludgy to use.

OPENXML

OPENXML is a legacy XML function that provides a rowset view of XML data. The process of converting XML data to relational form is known as *shredding*. OPENXML is technically a *rowset provider*, which means its contents can be queried and accessed like a table. The legacy SQL Server XML functionality requires the sp_xml_preparedocument and sp_xml_removedocument system SPs to parse text into an XML document and clean up afterward. These procedures are used in conjunction with the OPENXML function to move XML data from its textual representation into a parsed internal representation of an XML document, and from there into a tabular format.

This method is rather clunky compared to the newer methods first introduced by SQL Server 2005, but you might need it if you're writing code that needs to be backward compatible with SQL Server 2000. The OPENXML method has certain disadvantages based on its heritage, some of which are listed here:

- OPENXML relies on COM to invoke the Microsoft XML Core Services Library (MSXML) to perform XML manipulation and shredding.

- When it is invoked, MSXML assigns one-eighth of SQL Server's total memory to the task of parsing and manipulating XML data.

- If you fail to call sp_xml_removedocument after preparing an XML document with the sp_xml_preparedocument procedure, it won't be removed from memory until the SQL Server service is restarted.

■**Tip** I strongly recommend using xml data type methods like nodes(), value(), and query() to shred your XML data instead of using OPENXML. I'll discuss these xml data type methods later in this chapter, in the section titled "The xml Data Type Methods."

The sample query in Listing 11-1 is a simple demonstration of using OPENXML to shred XML data. The partial results of this query are shown in Figure 11-1.

Listing 11-1. *Simple OPENXML Query*

```
DECLARE @docHandle int;

DECLARE @xmlDocument nvarchar(max) = N'<Customers>
    <Customer CustomerID="1234" ContactName="Larry" CompanyName="APress">
        <Orders>
            <Order CustomerID="1234" OrderDate="2006-04-25T13:22:18"/>
            <Order CustomerID="1234" OrderDate="2006-05-10T12:35:49"/>
        </Orders>
    </Customer>
    <Customer CustomerID="4567" ContactName="Bill" CompanyName="Microsoft">
        <Orders>
            <Order CustomerID="4567" OrderDate="2006-03-12T18:32:39"/>
            <Order CustomerID="4567" OrderDate="2006-05-11T17:56:12"/>
        </Orders>
    </Customer>
</Customers>';

EXECUTE sp_xml_preparedocument @docHandle OUTPUT, @xmlDocument;

SELECT
    Id,
    ParentId,
    NodeType,
    LocalName,
```

```
    Prefix,
    NameSpaceUri,
    DataType,
    Prev,
    [Text]
FROM OPENXML(@docHandle, N'/Customers/Customer');

EXECUTE sp_xml_removedocument @docHandle;
GO
```

	Id	ParentId	NodeType	LocalName	Prefix	NameSpaceUri	DataType	Prev	Text
1	2	0	1	Customer	NULL	NULL	NULL	NULL	NULL
2	3	2	2	CustomerID	NULL	NULL	NULL	NULL	NULL
3	20	3	3	#text	NULL	NULL	NULL	NULL	1234
4	4	2	2	ContactName	NULL	NULL	NULL	NULL	NULL
5	21	4	3	#text	NULL	NULL	NULL	NULL	Larry
6	5	2	2	CompanyName	NULL	NULL	NULL	NULL	NULL
7	22	5	3	#text	NULL	NULL	NULL	NULL	APress
8	6	2	1	Orders	NULL	NULL	NULL	NULL	NULL
9	7	6	1	Order	NULL	NULL	NULL	NULL	NULL
10	8	7	2	OrderDate	NULL	NULL	NULL	NULL	NULL
11	23	8	3	#text	NULL	NULL	NULL	NULL	2006-04-25T13:22:18

Figure 11-1. *Results of the OPENXML query*

The first step in using OPENXML is to call the sp_xml_preparedocument SP to convert an XML-formatted string into an XML document:

```
DECLARE @docHandle int;

DECLARE @xmlDocument nvarchar(max) = N'<Customers>
    <Customer CustomerID="1234" ContactName="Larry" CompanyName="APress">
        <Orders>
            <Order CustomerID="1234" OrderDate="2006-04-25T13:22:18"/>
            <Order CustomerID="1234" OrderDate="2006-05-10T12:35:49"/>
        </Orders>
    </Customer>
    <Customer CustomerID="4567" ContactName="Bill" CompanyName="Microsoft">
        <Orders>
            <Order CustomerID="4567" OrderDate="2006-03-12T18:32:39"/>
            <Order CustomerID="4567"  OrderDate="2006-05-11T17:56:12"/>
        </Orders>
    </Customer>
</Customers>';

EXECUTE sp_xml_preparedocument @docHandle OUTPUT, @xmlDocument;
```

The `sp_xml_preparedocument` procedure invokes MSXML to parse your XML document into an internal Document Object Model (DOM) tree representation of the nodes. The `sp_xml_preparedocument` procedure accepts up to three parameters, as follows:

- The first parameter, called `hdoc`, is an output parameter that returns an `int` handle to the XML document created by the SP.

- The second parameter is the original XML document. This parameter is known as `xmltext`, and can be a `char`, `nchar`, `varchar`, `nvarchar`, `text`, `ntext`, or `xml` data type. If `NULL` is passed in or the `xmltext` parameter is omitted, an empty XML document is created. The default for this parameter is `NULL`.

- A third optional parameter, `xpath_namespaces`, specifies the namespace declarations used in `OPENXML` XPath expressions. Like `xmltext`, the `xpath_namespaces` parameter can be a `char`, `nchar`, `varchar`, `nvarchar`, `text`, `ntext`, or `xml` data type. The default `xpath_namespaces` value is `<root xmlns:mp="urn:schemas-microsoft-com:xml-metaprop">`.

The `OPENXML` rowset provider shreds the internal DOM representation of the XML document into relational format. The result of the rowset provider can be queried like a table or view, as shown following:

```
SELECT
    Id,
    ParentId,
    NodeType,
    LocalName,
    Prefix,
    NameSpaceUri,
    DataType,
    Prev,
    [Text]
FROM OPENXML(@docHandle, N'/Customers/Customer');
```

The `OPENXML` rowset provider accepts up to three parameters:

- The first parameter, `hdoc`, is the `int` document handle returned by the call to the `sp_xml_preparedocument` procedure.

- The second parameter, known as `rowpattern`, is an `nvarchar` XPath query pattern that determines which nodes of the XML document are returned as rows.

- The third parameter is an optional `flags` parameter. This `tinyint` value specifies the type of mapping to be used between the XML data and the relational rowset. If specified, `flags` can be a combination of the values listed in Table 11-1.

Table 11-1. *OPENXML Flags Parameter Options*

Value	Name	Description
0	DEFAULT	A flags value of 0 tells OPENXML to default to attribute-centric mapping. This is the default value if the flags parameter is not specified.
1	XML_ATTRIBUTES	A flags value of 1 indicates that OPENXML should use attribute-centric mapping.
2	XML_ELEMENTS	A flags value of 2 indicates that OPENXML should use element-centric mapping.
3	XML_ATTRIBUTES | XML_ELEMENTS	Combining the XML_ATTRIBUTES flag value with the XML_ELEMENTS flag value (logical OR) indicates that attribute-centric mapping should be applied first, and element-centric mapping should be applied to all columns not yet dealt with.
8		A flags value of 8 indicates that the consumed data should not be copied to the overflow property @mp:xmltext. This value can be combined (logical OR) with any of the other flags values.

The internal XML document generated by sp_xml_preparedocument is cached and will continue to take up SQL Server memory until it is explicitly removed with the sp_xml_removedocument procedure. The sp_xml_removedocument procedure accepts a single parameter, the int document handle initially generated by sp_xml_preparedocument:

```
EXECUTE sp_xml_removedocument @docHandle;
```

▪**Caution** Always call sp_xml_removedocument to free up memory used by XML documents created with sp_xml_createdocument. Any XML documents created with sp_xml_createdocument remain in memory until sp_xml_removedocument is called or the SQL Server service is restarted. Microsoft advises that not freeing up memory with sp_xml_removedocument could cause your server to run out of memory.

OPENXML Result Formats

The sample in Listing 11-1 returns a table in *edge table format*, which is the default OPENXML rowset format. According to BOL, "Edge tables represent the fine-grained XML document structure . . . in a single table" (http://msdn2.microsoft.com/en-us/library/ms186918(SQL.100).aspx). The columns returned by the edge table format are shown in Table 11-2.

Table 11-2. *Edge Table Format*

Column Name	Data Type	Description
id	bigint	The unique ID of the document node. The root element ID is 0.
parentid	bigint	The identifier of the parent of the node. If the node is a top-level node, the parentid is NULL.
nodetype	int	The column that indicates the type of the node. It can be 1 for an element node, 2 for an attribute node, or 3 for a text node.
localname	nvarchar	The local name of the element or attribute, or NULL if the DOM object does not have a name.
prefix	nvarchar	The namespace prefix of the node.
namespaceuri	nvarchar	The namespace URI of the node, or NULL if there's no namespace.
datatype	nvarchar	The data type of the element or attribute row, which is inferred from the inline DTD or inline schema.
prev	bigint	The XML ID of the previous sibling element, or NULL if there is no direct previous sibling.
text	ntext	The attribute value or element content.

OPENXML supports an optional WITH clause to specify a user-defined format for the returned rowset. The WITH clause lets you specify the name of an existing table or a schema declaration to define the rowset format. By adding a WITH clause to the OPENXML query in Listing 11-1, you can specify an explicit schema for the resulting rowset. This technique is demonstrated in Listing 11-2, with results shown in Figure 11-2. The differences between Listings 11-2 and 11-1 are shown in bold.

Listing 11-2. *OPENXML and WITH Clause, Explicit Schema*

```
DECLARE @docHandle int;

DECLARE @xmlDocument nvarchar(max) = N'<Customers>
    <Customer CustomerID="1234" ContactName="Larry" CompanyName="APress">
        <Orders>
            <Order CustomerID="1234" OrderDate="2006-04-25T13:22:18"/>
            <Order CustomerID="1234" OrderDate="2006-05-10T12:35:49"/>
        </Orders>
    </Customer>
    <Customer CustomerID="4567" ContactName="Bill" CompanyName="Microsoft">
        <Orders>
            <Order CustomerID="4567" OrderDate="2006-03-12T18:32:39"/>
            <Order CustomerID="4567"  OrderDate="2006-05-11T17:56:12"/>
        </Orders>
    </Customer>
</Customers>';
```

```
EXECUTE sp_xml_preparedocument @docHandle OUTPUT, @xmlDocument;

SELECT
  CustomerID,
    CustomerName,
    CompanyName,
    OrderDate
FROM OPENXML(@docHandle, N'/Customers/Customer/Orders/Order')
WITH
(
    CustomerID nchar(4) N'../../@CustomerID',
    CustomerName nvarchar(50) N'../../@ContactName',
    CompanyName nvarchar(50) N'../../@CompanyName',
    OrderDate datetime
);

EXECUTE sp_xml_removedocument @docHandle;
GO
```

	CustomerID	CustomerName	CompanyName	OrderDate
1	1234	Larry	APress	2006-04-25 13:22:18.000
2	1234	Larry	APress	2006-05-10 12:35:49.000
3	4567	Bill	Microsoft	2006-03-12 18:32:39.000
4	4567	Bill	Microsoft	2006-05-11 17:56:12.000

Figure 11-2. *Results of OPENXML with an explicit schema declaration*

The OPENXML WITH clause can also use the schema from an existing table to format the relational result set. This is demonstrated in Listing 11-3. The differences between Listing 11-3 and 11-2 are shown in bold.

Listing 11-3. *OPENXML with WITH Clause, Existing Table Schema*

```
DECLARE @docHandle int;

DECLARE @xmlDocument nvarchar(max) = N'<Customers>
    <Customer CustomerID="1234" ContactName="Larry" CompanyName="APress">
        <Orders>
            <Order CustomerID="1234" OrderDate="2006-04-25T13:22:18"/>
            <Order CustomerID="1234" OrderDate="2006-05-10T12:35:49"/>
        </Orders>
    </Customer>
```

```
        <Customer CustomerID="4567" ContactName="Bill" CompanyName="Microsoft">
          <Orders>
              <Order CustomerID="4567" OrderDate="2006-03-12T18:32:39"/>
              <Order CustomerID="4567" OrderDate="2006-05-11T17:56:12"/>
          </Orders>
        </Customer>
</Customers>';

EXECUTE sp_xml_preparedocument @docHandle OUTPUT, @xmlDocument;

CREATE TABLE #CustomerInfo
(
  CustomerID nchar(4) NOT NULL,
  ContactName nvarchar(50) NOT NULL,
  CompanyName nvarchar(50) NOT NULL
);

CREATE TABLE #OrderInfo
(
  CustomerID nchar(4) NOT NULL,
  OrderDate datetime NOT NULL
);

INSERT INTO #CustomerInfo
(
  CustomerID,
  ContactName,
  CompanyName
)
SELECT
  CustomerID,
  ContactName,
  CompanyName
FROM OPENXML(@docHandle, N'/Customers/Customer')
WITH #CustomerInfo;

INSERT INTO #OrderInfo
(
  CustomerID,
  OrderDate
)
SELECT
  CustomerID,
  OrderDate
FROM OPENXML(@docHandle, N'//Order')
WITH #OrderInfo;
```

```
SELECT
  c.CustomerID,
  c.ContactName,
  c.CompanyName,
  o.OrderDate
FROM #CustomerInfo c
INNER JOIN #OrderInfo o
  ON c.CustomerID = o.CustomerID;

DROP TABLE #OrderInfo;
DROP TABLE #CustomerInfo;

EXECUTE sp_xml_removedocument @docHandle;
GO
```

The WITH clause used by each OPENXML query in Listing 11-3 specifies a table name. OPENXML uses the table's schema to define the relational format of the result returned.

FOR XML Clause

SQL Server 2000 introduced the FOR XML clause for use with the SELECT statement to efficiently convert relational data to XML format. The FOR XML clause is highly flexible and provides a wide range of options that give you fine-grained control over your XML result.

FOR XML RAW

The FOR XML clause appears at the end of the SELECT statement and can specify one of five different modes and several mode-specific options. The first FOR XML mode is RAW mode, which returns data in XML format with each row represented as a node with attributes representing the columns. FOR XML RAW is useful for ad hoc FOR XML queries while debugging and testing. The FOR XML RAW clause allows you to specify the element name for each row returned in parentheses immediately following the RAW keyword (if you leave it off, the default name, row, is used). The query in Listing 11-4 demonstrates FOR XML RAW, with results shown in Figure 11-3.

Listing 11-4. *Sample FOR XML RAW Query*

```
SELECT
  ProductID,
  Name,
  ProductNumber
FROM Production.Product
WHERE ProductID = 770
  FOR XML RAW;
```

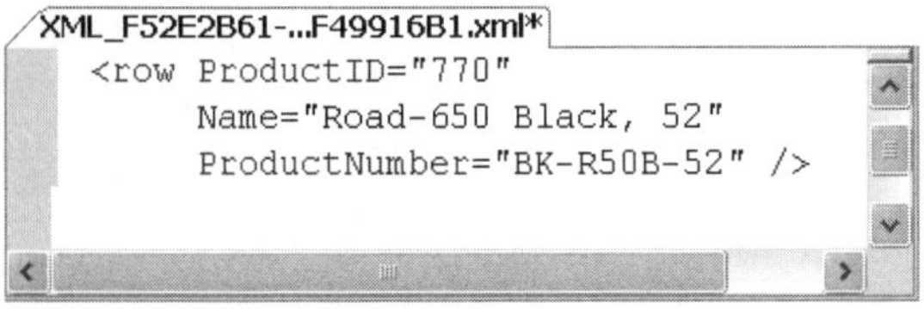

```
XML_F52E2B61-...F49916B1.xml*
    <row ProductID="770"
         Name="Road-650 Black, 52"
         ProductNumber="BK-R50B-52" />
```

Figure 11-3. *Results of the FOR XML RAW query*

The FOR XML clause modes support several additional options to control the resulting output. The options supported by all FOR XML modes are shown in Figure 11-4.

FOR XML Clause Options	XMLDATA*	XMLSCHEMA	ELEMENTS XSINIL	ELEMENTS ABSENT	BINARY BASE64	TYPE	ROOT	('ElementName')
FOR XML AUTO	●	●	●	●	●	●	●	
FOR XML RAW	●	●	●	●	●	●	●	●
FOR XML PATH			●	●	●	●	●	●
FOR XML EXPLICIT	●				●	●	●	

*The XMLDATA option is deprecated. Use XMLSCHEMA instead.

Figure 11-4. *FOR XML clause options*

The options supported by FOR XML RAW mode include the following:

- The TYPE option specifies that the result should be returned as an xml data type instance. This is particularly useful when you use FOR XML in nested subqueries. By default, without the TYPE option, all FOR XML modes return XML data as a character string.

- The ROOT option adds a single top-level root element to the XML result. Using the ROOT option guarantees a well-formed XML (single root element) result.

- The ELEMENTS option specifies that column data should be returned as subelements instead of attributes in the XML result. The ELEMENTS option can have the following additional options:

  - XSINIL specifies that columns with SQL nulls are included in the result with an xsi:nil attribute set to true.

  - ABSENT specifies that no elements are created for SQL nulls. ABSENT is the default action for handling nulls.

- The BINARY BASE64 option specifies that binary data returned by the query should be represented in Base64-encoded form in the XML result. If your result contains any binary data, the BINARY BASE64 option is required.

- XMLSCHEMA returns an inline XML schema definition (the W3C XML Schema Recommendation is available at www.w3.org/XML/Schema).

- XMLDATA appends an *XML-Data Reduced (XDR)* schema to the beginning of your XML result. This option is deprecated and should not be used for future development. If you currently use this option, Microsoft recommends changing your code to use the XMLSCHEMA option instead.

As I discuss the other FOR XML modes, I will point out the options supported by each.

FOR XML AUTO

For a query against a single table, the AUTO keyword retrieves data in a format similar to RAW mode, but the XML node name is the name of the table and not the generic label row. For queries that join multiple tables, however, each XML element is named for the tables from which the SELECT list columns are retrieved. The order of the column names in the SELECT list determine the XML element nesting in the result. The FOR XML AUTO clause is called similarly to the FOR XML RAW clause, as shown in Listing 11-5. The results are shown in Figure 11-5.

Listing 11-5. *FOR XML AUTO Query on a Single Table*

```
SELECT
  ProductID,
  Name,
  ProductNumber
FROM Production.Product
WHERE ProductID = 770
  FOR XML AUTO;
```

XML_F52E2B61-...F49916B2.xml*

```
<Production.Product ProductID="770"
                    Name="Road-650 Black, 52"
                    ProductNumber="BK-R50B-52" />
```

Figure 11-5. *Results of the FOR XML AUTO single-table query*

Listing 11-6 demonstrates using FOR XML AUTO in a SELECT query that joins two tables. The results are shown in Figure 11-6.

Listing 11-6. *FOR XML AUTO Query with a Join*

```
SELECT
  Product.ProductID,
  Product.Name,
  Product.ProductNumber,
  Inventory.Quantity
FROM Production.Product Product
INNER JOIN Production.ProductInventory Inventory
  ON Product.ProductID = Inventory.ProductID
WHERE Product.ProductID = 770
  FOR XML AUTO;
```

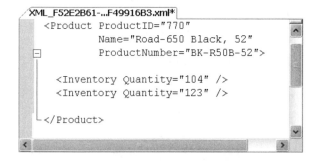

XML_F52E2B61-...F49916B3.xml*

```
<Product ProductID="770"
         Name="Road-650 Black, 52"
         ProductNumber="BK-R50B-52">

  <Inventory Quantity="104" />
  <Inventory Quantity="123" />

</Product>
```

Figure 11-6. *Results of the FOR XML AUTO query with a join*

The FOR XML AUTO statement can be further refined by adding the ELEMENTS option. Just as with the FOR XML RAW clause, the ELEMENTS option transforms the XML column attributes into subelements, as demonstrated in Listing 11-7, with results shown in Figure 11-7.

Listing 11-7. *FOR XML AUTO Query with ELEMENTS Option*

```
SELECT
  ProductID,
  Name,
  ProductNumber
FROM Production.Product
WHERE ProductID = 770
  FOR XML AUTO, ELEMENTS;
```

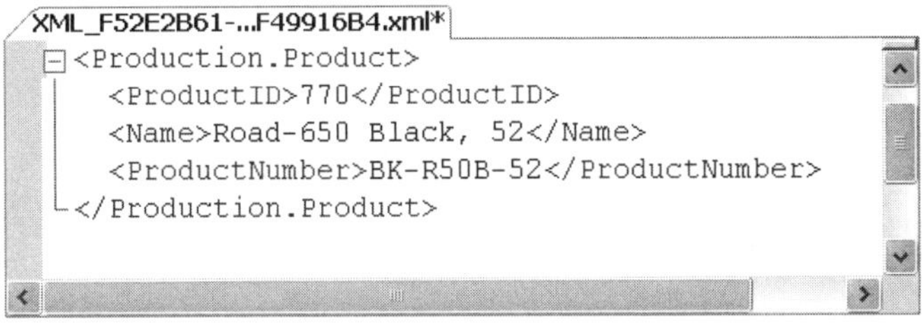

Figure 11-7. *Results of the FOR XML AUTO query with the ELEMENTS option*

The FOR XML AUTO clause can accept almost all of the same options as the FOR XML RAW clause. The only option that you can use with FOR XML RAW that's not available to FOR XML AUTO is the user-defined ElementName option, since AUTO mode generates row names based on the names of tables in the query.

FOR XML EXPLICIT

The FOR XML EXPLICIT clause is flexible but complex. This clause allows you to specify the exact hierarchy of XML elements and attributes in your XML result. This structure is specified in the SELECT statement itself using a special ElementName!TagNumber!AttributeName!Directive notation.

■**Tip** The FOR XML PATH clause, described in the next section, also allows you to explicitly define your XML result structure. The FOR XML PATH clause accepts XPath-style syntax to define the structure and node names, however, and is much easier to use than FOR XML EXPLICIT. As a general recommendation, I would advise using FOR XML PATH instead of FOR XML EXPLICIT for new development and converting old FOR XML EXPLICIT queries to FOR XML PATH when possible.

In order to get FOR XML EXPLICIT to convert your relational data to XML format, there's a strict requirement on the results of the SELECT query—it must return data in *universal table* format that includes a Tag column defining the level of the current tag and a Parent column with the parent level for the current tag. The remaining columns in the query are the actual data columns. Listing 11-8 demonstrates a FOR XML EXPLICIT query that returns information about a product, including all of its inventory quantities, as a nested XML result. The results are shown in Figure 11-8.

Listing 11-8. *FOR XML EXPLICIT Query*

```
SELECT
  1 AS Tag,
  NULL AS Parent,
  ProductID AS [Products!1!ProductID!element],
  Name AS [Products!1!ProductName],
  ProductNumber AS [Products!1!ProductNumber],
  NULL AS [Products!2!Quantity]
FROM Production.Product
WHERE ProductID = 770

UNION ALL

SELECT
  2 AS Tag,
  1 AS Parent,
  NULL,
  NULL,
  NULL,
  Quantity
FROM Production.ProductInventory
WHERE ProductID = 770
  FOR XML EXPLICIT;
```

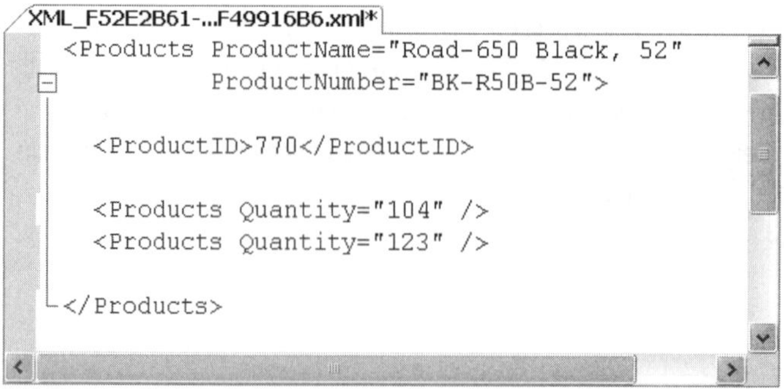

Figure 11-8. *Results of the FOR XML EXPLICIT query*

The FOR XML EXPLICIT query in Listing 11-8 defines the top-level elements with Tag = 1 and Parent = NULL. The next level is defined with Tag = 2 and Parent = 1, referencing back to the top level. Additional levels can be added by using the UNION keyword with additional queries that increment the Tag and Parent references for each additional level.

Each column of the query must be named with the ElementName!TagNumber!Attribute➡ Name!Directive format that I mentioned previously. As specified by this format, ElementName is the name of the XML element, in this case Products. TagNumber is the level of the element, which is 1 for top-level elements. AttributeName is the name of the attribute if you want the data in the column to be returned as an XML attribute. If you want the item to be returned as an XML element, use AttributeName to specify the name of the attribute, and set the Directive value to element. The Directive values that can be specified include the following:

- The hide directive value, which is useful when you want to retrieve values for sorting purposes but do not want the specified node included in the resulting XML.

- The element directive value, which generates an XML element instead of an attribute.

- The elementxsinil directive value, which generates an element for SQL null column values.

- The xml directive value, which generates an element instead of an attribute, but does not encode entity values.

- The cdata directive value, which wraps the data in a CDATA section and does not encode entities.

- The xmltext directive value, which wraps the column content in a single tag integrated with the document.

- The id, idref, and idrefs directive values, which allow you to create internal document links.

The additional options that the FOR XML EXPLICIT clause supports are BINARY BASE64, TYPE, ROOT, and XMLDATA. These options operate the same as they do in the FOR XML RAW and FOR XML AUTO clauses.

FOR XML PATH

The FOR XML PATH clause was first introduced in SQL Server 2005. It provides another way to convert relational data to XML format with a specific structure, but is much easier to use than the FOR XML EXPLICIT clause. Like FOR XML EXPLICIT, the FOR XML PATH clause makes you define the structure of the XML result. But the FOR XML PATH clause allows you to use a subset of the well-documented and much more intuitive XPath syntax to define your XML structure.

The FOR XML PATH clause uses column names to define the structure, as with FOR XML EXPLICIT. In keeping with the XML standard, column names in the SELECT statement with a FOR XML PATH clause are case sensitive. For instance, a column named Inventory is different from a column named INVENTORY. Any columns that do not have names are *inlined*, with their content inserted as XML content for xml data type columns or as a text node for other data types. This is useful for including the results of nameless computed columns or scalar sub-queries in your XML result.

FOR XML PATH uses XPath-style path expressions to define the structure and names of nodes in the XML result. Because path expressions can contain special characters like the forward slash (/) and at sign (@), you will usually want to use quoted column aliases as shown in Listing 11-9. The results of this sample FOR XML PATH query are shown in Figure 11-9.

Listing 11-9. *FOR XML PATH Query*

```
SELECT
  p.ProductID AS "Product/@ID",
  p.Name AS "Product/Name",
  p.ProductNumber AS "Product/Number",
  i.Quantity AS "Product/Quantity"
FROM Production.Product p
INNER JOIN Production.ProductInventory i
  ON p.ProductID = i.ProductID
WHERE p.ProductID = 770
  FOR XML PATH;
```

Figure 11-9. *Results of the FOR XML PATH query*

The FOR XML PATH clause imposes some rules on column naming, since the column names define not only the names of the XML nodes generated, but also the structure of the XML result. You can also use XPath node tests in your FOR XML PATH clauses. These rules and node tests are summarized in Table 11-3.

Table 11-3. *FOR XML PATH Column-Naming Conventions*

Column Name	Result
text()	The string value of the column is added as a text node.
comment()	The string value of the column is added as an XML comment.
node()	The string value of the column is inserted inline under the current element.
*	This is the same as node().
data()	The string value of the column is inserted as an atomic value. Spaces are inserted between atomic values in the resulting XML.
processing-instruction(*name*)	The string value of the column is inserted as an XML-processing instruction named *name*.
@name	The string value of the column is inserted as an attribute of the current element.
name	The string value of the column is inserted as a subelement of the current element.
elem/name	The string value of the column is inserted as a subelement of the specified element hierarchy, under the element specified by *elem*.
elem/@name	The string value of the column is inserted as an attribute of the last element in specified hierarchy, under the element specified by *elem*.

The FOR XML PATH clause supports the BINARY BASE64, TYPE, ROOT, and ELEMENTS options, and the user-defined *ElementName* options. The additional FOR XML PATH options operate the same as they do for the FOR XML AUTO and FOR XML RAW clauses.

The xml Data Type

SQL Server's legacy XML functionality can be cumbersome and clunky to use at times. Fortunately, SQL Server 2008 provides much tighter XML integration with its xml data type. The xml data type can be used anywhere that other SQL Server data types are used, including variable declarations, column declarations, SP parameters, and UDF parameters and return types. The T-SQL xml data type provides built-in methods that allow you to query and modify XML nodes. When you declare instances of the xml data type, you can create them as untyped (which is the default), or you can associate them with XML schemas to create typed xml instances. This section discusses both typed and untyped xml in T-SQL.

The xml data type can hold complete XML documents or XML fragments. An XML document must follow all the rules for well-formed XML, including the following:

- Well-formed XML must have at least one element.

- Every well-formed XML document has a single top-level, or root, element.

- Well-formed XML requires properly nested elements (tags cannot overlap).

- All tags must be properly closed in a well-formed XML document.

- Attribute values must be quoted in a well-formed XML document.

- Special characters in element content must be properly *entitized*, or converted to XML entities such as & for the ampersand character.

An XML fragment must conform to all the rules for well-formed XML, except that it may have more than one top-level element. The stored internal representation of an XML document or fragment stored in an xml variable or column maxes out at around 2.1 GB of storage.

Untyped xml

Untyped xml variables and columns are created by following them with the keyword xml in the declaration, as shown in Listing 11-10.

Listing 11-10. *Untyped xml Variable and Column Declarations*

```
DECLARE @x XML;
CREATE TABLE XmlPurchaseOrders
(
  PoNum int NOT NULL PRIMARY KEY,
  XmlPurchaseOrder xml
);
```

Populating an xml variable or column with an XML document or fragment requires a simple assignment statement. You can implicitly or explicitly convert char, varchar, nchar, nvarchar, varbinary, text, and ntext data to xml. There are some rules to consider when converting from these types to xml:

- The XML parser always treats nvarchar, nchar, and ntext data as a two-byte Unicode-encoded XML document or fragment.

- SQL Server treats char, varchar, and text data as a single-byte-encoded XML document or fragment. The code page of the source string, variable, or column is used for encoding by default.

- The content of varbinary data is passed directly to the XML parser, which accepts it as a stream. If the varbinary XML data is Unicode encoded, the byte-order mark/encoding information must be included in the varbinary data. If no byte-order mark/encoding information is included, the default of UTF-8 is used.

Note The binary data type can also be implicitly or explicitly converted to xml, but it must be the exact length of the data it contains. The extra padding applied to binary variables and columns when the data they contain is too short can cause errors in the XML-parsing process. Use the varbinary data type when you need to convert binary data to XML.

Listing 11-11 demonstrates implicit conversion from nvarchar to the xml data type. The CAST or CONVERT functions can be used when an explicit conversion is needed.

Listing 11-11. *Populating an Untyped xml Variable*

```
DECLARE @x xml = N'<?xml version="1.0" ?>
      <Address>
          <Latitude>47.642737</Latitude>
          <Longitude>-122.130395</Longitude>
          <Street>ONE MICROSOFT WAY</Street>
          <City>REDMOND</City>
          <State>WA</State>
          <Zip>98052</Zip>
          <Country>US</Country>
      </Address>';

SELECT @x;
```

Typed xml

To create a typed xml variable or column in SQL Server 2008, you must first create an XML schema collection with the CREATE XML SCHEMA COLLECTION statement. The CREATE XML SCHEMA COLLECTION statement allows you to specify a SQL Server name for your schema collection and an XML schema to add. Listing 11-12 shows how to create an XML schema collection.

Listing 11-12. *Creating a Typed xml Variable*

```
CREATE XML SCHEMA COLLECTION AddressSchemaCollection
    AS N'<?xml version="1.0" encoding="utf-16" ?>
    <xsd:schema xmlns:xsd="http://www.w3.org/2001/XMLSchema">
        <xsd:element name="Address">
            <xsd:complexType>
                <xsd:sequence>
                    <xsd:element name="Latitude" type="xsd:decimal" />
                    <xsd:element name="Longitude" type="xsd:decimal" />
                    <xsd:element name="Street" type="xsd:string" />
                    <xsd:element name="City" type="xsd:string" />
                    <xsd:element name="State" type="xsd:string" />
                    <xsd:element name="Zip" type="xsd:string" />
                    <xsd:element name="Country" type="xsd:string" />
                </xsd:sequence>
            </xsd:complexType>
        </xsd:element>
    </xsd:schema>';
GO
```

```
DECLARE @x XML (CONTENT AddressSchemaCollection);

SELECT @x =   N'<?xml version="1.0" ?>
        <Address>
            <Latitude>47.642737</Latitude>
            <Longitude>-122.130395</Longitude>
            <Street>ONE MICROSOFT WAY</Street>
            <City>REDMOND</City>
            <State>WA</State>
            <Zip>98052</Zip>
            <Country>US</Country>
        </Address>';

SELECT @x;

DROP XML SCHEMA COLLECTION AddressSchemaCollection;
GO
```

The first step in creating a typed xml instance is to create an XML schema collection, as I did in Listing 11-12:

```
CREATE XML SCHEMA COLLECTION AddressSchemaCollection
    AS N'<?xml version="1.0" encoding="utf-16" ?>
    <xsd:schema xmlns:xsd="http://www.w3.org/2001/XMLSchema">
        <xsd:element name="Address">
            <xsd:complexType>
                <xsd:sequence>
                    <xsd:element name="Latitude" type="xsd:decimal" />
                    <xsd:element name="Longitude" type="xsd:decimal" />
                    <xsd:element name="Street" type="xsd:string" />
                    <xsd:element name="City" type="xsd:string" />
                    <xsd:element name="State" type="xsd:string" />
                    <xsd:element name="Zip" type="xsd:string" />
                    <xsd:element name="Country" type="xsd:string" />
                </xsd:sequence>
            </xsd:complexType>
        </xsd:element>
    </xsd:schema>';
```

■**Tip** The World Wide Web Consortium (W3C) maintains the standards related to XML schemas. The official XML Schema recommendations are available at www.w3.org/TR/xmlschema-1/ and www.w3.org/TR/xmlschema-2/. These W3C recommendations are an excellent starting point for creating your own XML schemas.

The next step is to declare the variable as xml type, but with an XML schema collection specification included:

```
DECLARE @x XML (CONTENT AddressSchemaCollection);
```

In the example, I used the CONTENT keyword before the schema collection name in the xml variable declaration. SQL Server offers two keywords, DOCUMENT and CONTENT, that represent *facets* you can use to constrain typed xml instances. Using the DOCUMENT facet in your typed xml variable or column declaration constrains your typed XML data so that it must contain only one top-level root element. The CONTENT facet allows zero or more top-level elements. CONTENT is the default if neither is specified explicitly.

The next step in the example is the assignment of XML content to the typed xml variable. During the assignment, SQL Server validates the XML content against the XML schema collection.

```
SELECT @x =   N'<?xml version="1.0" ?>
      <Address>
          <Latitude>47.642737</Latitude>
          <Longitude>-122.130395</Longitude>
          <Street>ONE MICROSOFT WAY</Street>
          <City>REDMOND</City>
          <State>WA</State>
          <Zip>98052</Zip>
          <Country>US</Country>
      </Address>';

SELECT @x;
```

The DROP XML SCHEMA COLLECTION statement in the listing removes the XML schema collection from SQL Server.

```
DROP XML SCHEMA COLLECTION AddressSchemaCollection;
```

You can also add new XML schemas and XML schema components to XML schema collections with the ALTER XML SCHEMA COLLECTION statement.

The xml Data Type Methods

The xml data type has several methods for querying and modifying xml data. The built-in xml data type methods are summarized in Table 11-4.

Table 11-4. *xml Data Type Methods*

Method	Result
query(*xquery*)	Performs an XQuery query against an xml instance. The result returned is an untyped xml instance.
value(*xquery*, *sql_type*)	Performs an XQuery query against an xml instance and returns a scalar value of the specified SQL Server data type.
exist(*xquery*)	Performs an XQuery query against an xml instance and returns one of the following bit values: 1 if the *xquery* expression returns a nonempty result 0 if the *xquery* expression returns an empty result NULL if the xml instance is NULL
modify(*xml_dml*)	Performs an XML Data Modification Language (XML DML) statement to modify an xml instance.
nodes(*xquery*) as *table_name*(*column_name*)	Performs an XQuery query against an xml instance and returns matching nodes as a SQL result set. The *table_name* and *column_name* specify aliases for the virtual table and column to hold the nodes returned. These aliases are mandatory for the nodes() method.

This section introduces each of these xml data type methods.

The query Method

The xml data type query() method accepts an XQuery query string as its only parameter. This method returns all nodes matching the XQuery as a single untyped xml instance. Conveniently enough, Microsoft provides sample typed xml data in the Resume column of the HumanResources.JobCandidate table. Though all of its xml is well formed with a single root element, the Resume column is faceted with the default of CONTENT.

Listing 11-13 shows how to use the query() method to retrieve names from the resumes in the HumanResources.JobCandidate table.

Listing 11-13. *Using the query Method on the HumanResources.JobCandidate Resume XML*

```
SELECT Resume.query(N'declare namespace ns =
  "http://schemas.microsoft.com/sqlserver/2004/07/adventure-works/Resume";
  /ns:Resume/ns:Name') AS [NameXML]
FROM HumanResources.JobCandidate;
```

The first thing to notice is the namespace declaration inside the XQuery query via the declare namespace statement. This is done because the Resume column's xml data declares a namespace. In fact, the namespace declaration used in the XQuery is exactly the same as the declaration used in the xml data. The declaration section of the XQuery looks like this:

```
declare namespace ns =
  "http://schemas.microsoft.com/sqlserver/2004/07/adventure-works/Resume";
```

The actual query portion of the XQuery query is a simple path expression:

```
/ns:Resume/ns:Name
```

A sample of the results of Listing 11-13 are shown in Figure 11-10 (reformatted for easy reading).

```
NameXML2.xml*
  <ns:Name xmlns:ns =
  "http://schemas.microsoft.com/sqlserver/2004/07/adventure-works/Resume">
    <ns:Name.Prefix />
    <ns:Name.First>Shai</ns:Name.First>
    <ns:Name.Middle />
    <ns:Name.Last>Bassli</ns:Name.Last>
    <ns:Name.Suffix />
  </ns:Name>
  <ns:Name xmlns:ns =
  "http://schemas.microsoft.com/sqlserver/2004/07/adventure-works/Resume">
    <ns:Name.Prefix>Mr.</ns:Name.Prefix>
    <ns:Name.First>Max</ns:Name.First>
    <ns:Name.Middle />
    <ns:Name.Last>Benson</ns:Name.Last>
    <ns:Name.Suffix />
  </ns:Name>
  <ns:Name xmlns:ns =
  "http://schemas.microsoft.com/sqlserver/2004/07/adventure-works/Resume">
    <ns:Name.Prefix>Mr.</ns:Name.Prefix>
    <ns:Name.First>Krishna</ns:Name.First>
    <ns:Name.Middle />
```

Figure 11-10. *Retrieving job candidate names with the query method (partial results)*

■**Tip** SQL Server 2008 implements a subset of the W3C XQuery recommendation. Chapter 12 discusses SQL Server's XPath and XQuery implementations in detail. If you're just getting started with XQuery, additional resources include the W3C recommendation available at www.w3.org/TR/2004/WD-xquery-20040723/, and on BOL at http://msdn2.microsoft.com/en-us/library/ms189919(SQL.100).aspx.

The value Method

The xml data type's value() method performs an XQuery query against an xml instance and returns a scalar result. The scalar result of value() is automatically cast to the T-SQL data type specified in the call to value(). The sample code in Listing 11-14 uses the value() method to retrieve all last names from AdventureWorks job applicant resumes. The results are shown in Figure 11-11.

Listing 11-14. *xml Data Type value Method Sample*

```
SELECT Resume.value (N'declare namespace ns =
  "http://schemas.microsoft.com/sqlserver/2004/07/adventure-works/Resume";
  (/ns:Resume/ns:Name/ns:Name.Last)[1]',
  'nvarchar(100)') AS [LastName]
FROM HumanResources.JobCandidate;
```

	LastName
1	Bassli
2	Benson
3	Sunkammurali
4	Jiang
5	D'Hers
6	Kleinerman
7	Penuchot
8	Wu
9	Yang
10	Yee
11	คณาพล
12	เบญจศร
13	บางสุบศรี

Figure 11-11. *Using the value method to retrieve job candidate last names*

Like the `query()` method described previously, the `value()` method sample XQuery query begins by declaring a namespace:

```
declare namespace ns =
  "http://schemas.microsoft.com/sqlserver/2004/07/adventure-works/Resume";
```

The actual query portion of the XQuery query is a simple path expression:

```
(/ns:Resume/ns:Name/ns:Name.Last)[1]
```

Because `value()` returns a scalar value, the query is enclosed in parentheses with an XQuery numeric predicate [1] following it to force the return of a singleton atomic value. The second parameter passed into `value()` is the T-SQL data type that `value()` will cast the result to, in this case `nvarchar`. The `value()` method cannot cast its result to a SQL CLR user-defined type or an `xml`, `image`, `text`, `ntext`, or `sql_variant` data type.

The exist Method

The `xml` data type provides the `exist()` method for determining if an XML node exists in an `xml` instance, or if an existing XML node value meets a specific set of criteria. The example in Listing 11-15 uses the `exist()` method in a query to return all AdventureWorks job candidates that reported a bachelor's degree level of education. The results are shown in Figure 11-12.

Listing 11-15. *xml Data Type exist Method Example*

```
SELECT Resume.value (N'declare namespace ns =
  "http://schemas.microsoft.com/sqlserver/2004/07/adventure-works/Resume";
  (/ns:Resume/ns:Name/ns:Name.Last) [1]',
  'nvarchar(100)') AS [BachelorsCandidate]
FROM HumanResources.JobCandidate
WHERE Resume.exist (N'declare namespace ns =
  "http://schemas.microsoft.com/sqlserver/2004/07/adventure-works/Resume";
  /ns:Resume/ns:Education/ns:Edu.Level [ . = "Bachelor" ]') = 1;
```

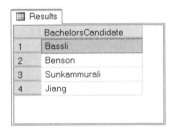

Figure 11-12. *Using the exist method to retrieve bachelor's degree job candidates*

The first part of the query borrows from the value() method example in Listing 11-13 to retrieve matching job candidate names:

```
SELECT Resume.value (N'declare namespace ns =
  "http://schemas.microsoft.com/sqlserver/2004/07/adventure-works/Resume";
  (/ns:Resume/ns:Name/ns:Name.Last) [1]',
  'nvarchar(100)') AS [BachelorsCandidate]
FROM HumanResources.JobCandidate
```

The exist() method in the WHERE clause specifies the xml match criteria. Like the previous sample queries, the exist() method XQuery query begins by declaring a namespace:

```
declare namespace ns =
  "http://schemas.microsoft.com/sqlserver/2004/07/adventure-works/Resume";
```

The query itself compares the Edu.Level node text to the string Bachelor:

```
/ns:Resume/ns:Education/ns:Edu.Level [ . = "Bachelor" ]
```

If there is a match, the query returns a result and the exist() method returns 1. If there is no match, there will be no nodes returned by the XQuery query, and the exist() method will return 0. If the xml is NULL, exist() returns NULL. The query limits the results to only matching resumes by returning only those where exist() returns 1.

The nodes Method

The nodes() method of the xml data type retrieves XML content in relational format—a process known as shredding. The nodes() method returns a rowset composed of the xml nodes that match a given XQuery expression. Listing 11-16 retrieves product names and IDs for those products with the word *Alloy* in the Material node of their CatalogDescription column. The table queried is Production.ProductModel. Notice that the CROSS APPLY operator is used to perform the nodes() method on all rows of the Production.ProductModel table.

Listing 11-16. *xml Data Type nodes Example*

```
SELECT
  ProductModelId,
  Name,
  Specs.query('.') AS Result
FROM Production.ProductModel
CROSS APPLY CatalogDescription.nodes('declare namespace ns =
"http://schemas.microsoft.com/sqlserver/2004/07/adventure-works/➥
  ProductModelDescription";
/ns:ProductDescription/ns:Specifications/Material/text()
  [ contains ( . , "Alloy" ) ]')
AS NodeTable(Specs);
```

The first part of the SELECT query retrieves the product model ID, the product name, and the results of the nodes() method via the query() method:

```
SELECT
  ProductModelId,
  Name,
  Specs.query('.') AS Result
FROM Production.ProductModel
```

One restriction of the nodes() method is that the relational results generated cannot be retrieved directly. They can only be accessed via the exist(), nodes(), query(), and value() methods of the xml data type, or checked with the IS NULL and IS NOT NULL operators.

The CROSS APPLY operator is used with the nodes() method to generate the final result set. The XQuery query used in the nodes() method begins by declaring a namespace:

```
CROSS APPLY CatalogDescription.nodes('declare namespace ns =
"http://schemas.microsoft.com/sqlserver/2004/07/adventure-works/➥
  ProductModelDescription";
```

The query portion is a path expression that retrieves XML nodes in which a Material node's text contains the word *Alloy*:

```
/ns:ProductDescription/ns:Specifications/Material/text()
  [ contains ( . , "Alloy" ) ]')
```

Notice that the nodes() method requires you to provide aliases for both the virtual table returned and the column that will contain the result rows. In this instance, I chose to alias the virtual table with the name NodeTable and the column with the name Specs.

```
AS NodeTable(Specs);
```

The modify Method

The xml data type modify() method can be used to modify the content of an xml variable or column. The modify() method allows you to insert, delete, or update xml content. The main restrictions on the modify() method is that it must be used in a variable SET statement or in the SET clause of an UPDATE statement. The example in Listing 11-17 demonstrates the modify() method on an untyped xml variable. The results are shown in Figure 11-13.

■**Tip** Although the SELECT and SET statements are similar in their functionality when applied to variables, the modify() method of the xml data type will not work in SELECT statements—even SELECT statements that assign values to variables. Use the SET statement as demonstrated in Listing 11-17 to use the modify() method on an xml variable.

Listing 11-17. *xml Data Type modify Method Example*

```
DECLARE @x xml = N'<?xml version="1.0" ?>
<Address>
  <Street>1 MICROSOFT WAY</Street>
  <City>REDMOND</City>
  <State>WA</State>
  <Zip>98052</Zip>
  <Country>US</Country>
  <Website>http://www.microsoft.com</Website>
</Address>';

SELECT @x;

SET @x.modify ('insert
(
  <CompanyName>Microsoft Corporation</CompanyName>,
  <Url>http://msdn.microsoft.com</Url>,
  <UrlDescription>Microsoft Developer Network</UrlDescription>
)
into (/Address)[1] ');

SET @x.modify('replace value of
  (/Address/Street/text())[1]
  with "ONE MICROSOFT WAY"
');

SET @x.modify('
  delete /Address/Website
');

SELECT @x;
```

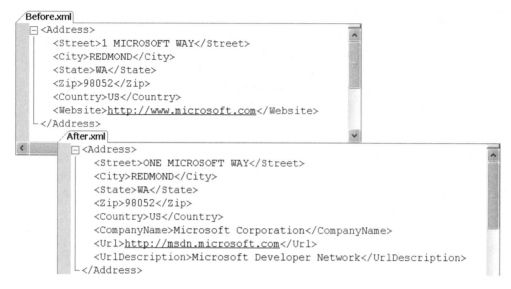

Figure 11-13. *Before-and-after results of the modify method*

The sample begins by creating an xml variable and assigning XML content to it:

```
DECLARE @x xml = N'<?xml version="1.0" ?>
<Address>
  <Street>1 MICROSOFT WAY</Street>
  <City>REDMOND</City>
  <State>WA</State>
  <Zip>98052</Zip>
  <Country>US</Country>
  <Website>http://www.microsoft.com</Website>
</Address>';
```

```
SELECT @x;
```

The XML DML insert statement inserts three new nodes into the xml variable, right below the top-level Address node:

```
SET @x.modify ('insert
(
  <CompanyName>Microsoft Corporation</CompanyName>,
  <Url>http://msdn.microsoft.com</Url>,
  <UrlDescription>Microsoft Developer&apos;s Network</UrlDescription>
)
into (/Address)[1] ');
```

The replace value of statement specified in the next modify() method updates the content of the Street node with the street address our good friends at Microsoft prefer: ONE MICROSOFT WAY, instead of 1 MICROSOFT WAY.

```
SET @x.modify('replace value of (/Address/Street/text())[1]
    with "ONE MICROSOFT WAY"
');
```

Finally, the XML DML method `delete` statement is used to remove the old `<Website>` tag from the `xml` variable's content:

```
SET @x.modify('
    delete /Address/Website
');

SELECT @x;
```

XML Indexes

SQL Server provides XML indexes to increase the efficiency of querying `xml` data type columns. XML indexes come in two flavors:

- *Primary XML index*: An XML column can have a single primary XML index declared on it. The primary XML index is different from the standard relational indexes most of us are used to. Rather, it is a persisted preshredded representation of your XML data. Basically, the XML data stored in a column with a primary XML index is converted to relational form and stored in the database. By persisting an `xml` data type column in relational form, you eliminate the implicit shredding that occurs with every query or manipulation of your XML data. In order to create a primary XML index on a table's `xml` column, a clustered index must be in place on the primary key columns for the table.

- *Secondary XML index*: Secondary XML indexes can also be created on a table's `xml` column. Secondary XML indexes are nonclustered relational indexes created on primary XML indexes. In order to create secondary XML indexes on an `xml` column, a primary XML index must already exist on that column. You can declare any of three different types of secondary XML index on your primary XML indexes:

  - The `PATH` index is a secondary XML index optimized for XPath and XQuery path expressions that rely heavily on path and node values. The `PATH` index creates an index on path and node values on the columns of the primary XML index. The path and node values are used as key columns for efficient path seek operations.

  - The `VALUE` index is optimized for queries by value where the path is not necessarily known. This type of index is the inverse of the `PATH` index, with the primary XML index node values indexed before the node paths.

  - The `PROPERTY` index is optimized for queries that retrieve data from other columns of a table based on the value of nodes or paths in the `xml` data type column. This type of secondary index is created on the primary key of the base table, node paths, and node values of the primary XML index.

Consider the example XQuery FLWOR (for, let, where, order by, return) expression in Listing 11-18 that retrieves the last, first, and middle names of all job applicants in the HumanResources.JobCandidate table with an education level of Bachelor. The results of this query are shown in Figure 11-14.

Listing 11-18. *Retrieving Job Candidates with Bachelor's Degrees*

```
SELECT Resume.query('declare namespace ns =
  "http://schemas.microsoft.com/sqlserver/2004/07/adventure-works/Resume";
for $m in /ns:Resume
where $m/ns:Education/ns:Edu.Level[. = "Bachelor" ]
return <Name>
  {
    data(($m/ns:Name/ns:Name.Last)[1]),
    data(($m/ns:Name/ns:Name.First)[1]),
    data(($m/ns:Name/ns:Name.Middle)[1])
  }
</Name>')
FROM HumanResources.JobCandidate;
GO
```

	(No column name)
1	<Name>Bassli Shai </Name>
2	<Name>Benson Max </Name>
3	<Name>Sunkammurali Krishna </Name>
4	<Name>Jiang Stephen Y </Name>
5	
6	
7	
8	
9	
10	
11	
12	
13	

Figure 11-14. *Retrieving candidate names with a FLWOR expression*

I'll describe FLWOR expressions in greater detail, with examples, in Chapter 12. For the purposes of this discussion, however, the results are not as important as what's going on under the hood. This FLWOR expression is returning the last, first, and middle names of all candidates for which the Edu.Level node contains the value Bachelor. As shown in Figure 11-15, the execution cost of this query is 41.2849.

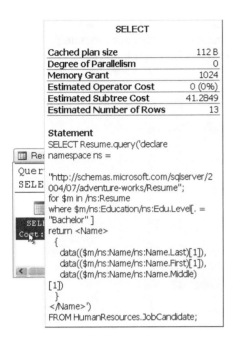

SELECT

Cached plan size	112 B
Degree of Parallelism	0
Memory Grant	1024
Estimated Operator Cost	0 (0%)
Estimated Subtree Cost	41.2849
Estimated Number of Rows	13

Statement
```
SELECT Resume.query('declare
namespace ns =
"http://schemas.microsoft.com/sqlserver/2
004/07/adventure-works/Resume";
for $m in /ns:Resume
where $m/ns:Education/ns:Edu.Level[. =
"Bachelor" ]
return <Name>
    {
      data(($m/ns:Name/ns:Name.Last)[1]),
      data(($m/ns:Name/ns:Name.First)[1]),
      data(($m/ns:Name/ns:Name.Middle)
[1])
    }
  </Name>')
FROM HumanResources.JobCandidate;
```

Figure 11-15. *The execution cost of the query*

By far the most expensive part of this query is contained in a step called *Table Valued Function [XML Reader with XPath Filter]*. This is the main operator SQL Server uses to shred XML data on the fly whenever you query XML data. In this query plan, it is invoked two times at a cost of 13.052 each, and three more times at a cost of 4.89054 each, accounting for over 98 percent of the query plan cost (see Figure 11-16).

Table Valued Function
Table valued function.

Physical Operation	Table Valued Function
Logical Operation	Table Valued Function
Actual Number of Rows	16
Estimated I/O Cost	0
Estimated CPU Cost	1.004
Estimated Operator Cost	13.052 (32%)
Estimated Subtree Cost	13.052
Estimated Number of Rows	200
Estimated Row Size	39 B
Actual Rebinds	13
Actual Rewinds	0
Node ID	20

Object
[XML Reader with XPath filter]
Output List
[XML Reader with XPath filter].id, [XML Reader with XPath filter].value

Figure 11-16. *Table Valued Function [XML Reader with XPath Filter] cost*

Adding XML indexes to this column of the HumanResources.JobCandidate table significantly improves XQuery query performance by eliminating on-the-fly XML shredding. Listing 11-19 adds a primary and secondary XML index to the Resume column.

Listing 11-19. *Adding XML Indexes to the Resume Column*

```
CREATE PRIMARY XML INDEX PXML_JobCandidate
ON HumanResources.JobCandidate (Resume);
GO

CREATE XML INDEX IXML_Education
ON HumanResources.JobCandidate (Resume)
USING XML INDEX PXML_JobCandidate
FOR PATH;
GO
```

With the primary and secondary XML indexes in place, the query execution cost drops significantly, from 41.2849 to 0.278555, as shown in Figure 11-17.

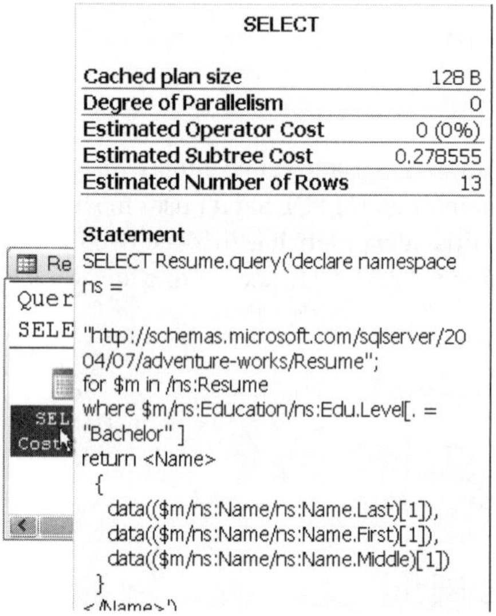

Figure 11-17. *The query execution cost with XML indexes*

The greater efficiency is brought about by the *XML Reader with XPath Filter* step being replaced with efficient index seek operators on both clustered and nonclustered indexes. The primary XML index eliminates the need to shred XML data at query time and the secondary XML index provides additional performance enhancement by providing a nonclustered index that can be used to efficiently fulfill the FLWOR expression where clause.

The CREATE PRIMARY XML INDEX statement in the example creates a primary XML index on the Resume column of the HumanResources.JobCandidate table. The primary XML index provides a significant performance increase by itself, since it eliminates on-the-fly XML shredding at query time.

```
CREATE PRIMARY XML INDEX PXML_JobCandidate
ON HumanResources.JobCandidate (Resume);
```

The primary XML index is a prerequisite for creating the secondary XML index that will provide additional performance enhancement for XQuery queries that specify both a path and a predicate based on node content. The CREATE XML INDEX statement in the example creates the secondary XML PATH index.

```
CREATE XML INDEX IXML_Education
ON HumanResources.JobCandidate (Resume)
USING XML INDEX PXML_JobCandidate
FOR PATH;
```

The USING XML INDEX clause of the CREATE XML INDEX statement specifies the name of the primary XML index on which to build the secondary XML index. The FOR clause determines the type of secondary XML index that will be created. You can specify a VALUE, PATH, or PROPERTY type as described previously.

The optional WITH clause of both of the XML index creation statements allows you to specify a variety of XML index creation options, as shown in Table 11-5.

Table 11-5. *XML Index Creation Options*

Option	Description
PAD_INDEX	This option specifies whether index padding is on or off. The default is OFF.
FILLFACTOR	This option indicates how full the leaf level index pages should be made during XML index creation or rebuild. Values of 0 and 100 are equivalent. The FILLFACTOR option is used in conjunction with the PAD_INDEX option.
SORT_IN_TEMPDB	This option specifies that intermediate sort results should be stored in tempdb. By default, SORT_IN_TEMPDB is set to OFF and intermediate sort results are stored in the local database.
STATISTICS_NORECOMPUTE	This option indicates whether distribution statistics are automatically recomputed. The default is OFF.
DROP_EXISTING	This option specifies that the preexisting XML index of the same name should be dropped before creating the index. The default is OFF.
ALLOW_ROW_LOCKS	This option allows SQL Server to use row locks when accessing the XML index. The default is ON.
ALLOW_PAGE_LOCKS	This option allows SQL Server to use page locks when accessing the XML index. The default is ON.
MAXDOP	This option determines the maximum degree of parallelism SQL Server can use during the XML index creation operation. MAXDOP can be one of the following values: 0: Uses up to the maximum number of processors available. 1: Uses only one processor; no parallel processing. 2 through 64: Restricts the number of processors used for parallel processing to the number specified or less.

XSL Transformations

One of the powerful features available to SQL Server 2008 is its ability to execute .NET Framework–based code via the SQL Common Language Runtime (SQL CLR). You can use standard .NET Framework classes to access XML-based functionality that is not supported directly within T-SQL. One useful feature that can be accessed via SQL CLR is the W3C *Extensible Stylesheet Language Transformations (XSLT)*. As defined by the W3C, XSLT is a language designed for the sole purpose of "transforming XML documents into other XML documents." SQL Server 2008 provides access to XSL transformations via a combination of the built-in xml data type and the .NET Framework XslCompiledTransform class.

■**Tip** The XSLT 1.0 standard is available at www.w3.org/TR/xslt.

You can access XSLT from SQL Server to perform server-side transformations of your relational data into other XML formats. I've chosen to use XHTML as the output format for this example, although some would argue that generating XHTML output is best done away from SQL Server, in the middle tier or presentation layer. Arguments can also be made for performing XSL transformations close to the data, for efficiency reasons. I'd like to put those arguments aside for the moment, and focus on the main purpose of this example: demonstrating that additional XML functionality is available to SQL Server via SQL CLR. Listing 11-20 demonstrates the first step in the process of performing server-side XSL transformations: using FOR XML to convert relational data to an xml variable.

Listing 11-20. *Using FOR XML to Convert Relational Data to Populate an xml Variable*

```
DECLARE @xml xml =
(
  SELECT
    p.ProductNumber AS "@Id",
    p.Name AS "Name",
    p.Color AS "Color",
    p.ListPrice AS "ListPrice",
    p.SizeUnitMeasureCode AS "Size/@UOM",
    p.Size AS "Size",
    p.WeightUnitMeasureCode AS "Weight/@UOM",
    p.Weight AS "Weight",
    (
      SELECT COALESCE(SUM(i.Quantity), 0)
      FROM Production.ProductInventory i
      WHERE i.ProductID = p.ProductID
    ) AS "QuantityOnHand"
  FROM Production.Product p
  WHERE p.FinishedGoodsFlag = 1
```

```
    ORDER BY p.Name
    FOR XML PATH ('Product'),
      ROOT ('Products')
);
```

The resulting xml document looks like Figure 11-18.

Figure 11-18. *Partial results of the FOR XML product query*

The next step is to create the XSLT style sheet to specify the transformation and assign it to an xml data type variable. Listing 11-21 demonstrates a simple XSLT style sheet to convert XML data to HTML.

Listing 11-21. *XSLT Style Sheet to Convert Data to HTML*

```
DECLARE @xslt xml = N'<?xml version="1.0" encoding="utf-16"?>
<xsl:stylesheet version="1.0"
    xmlns:xsl="http://www.w3.org/1999/XSL/Transform">
<xsl:template match="/Products">
<html>
    <head>
        <title>AdventureWorks Product Listing Report</title>
        <style type="text/css">
            tr.row-heading {
                background-color: 000099;
                color: ffffff;
                font-family: tahoma, arial, helvetica, sans-serif;
                font-size: 12px;
            }
```

```
            tr.row-light {
                background-color: ffffff;
                font-family: tahoma, arial, helvetica, sans-serif;
                font-size: 12px;
            }
            tr.row-dark {
                background-color: 00ffff;
                font-family: tahoma, arial, helvetica, sans-serif;
                font-size: 12px;
            }
            td.col-right {
                text-align: right;
            }
        </style>
    </head>
    <body>
        <table>
            <tr class="row-heading">
                <th>ID</th>
                <th>Product Name</th>
                <th>On Hand</th>
                <th>List Price</th>
                <th>Color</th>
                <th>Size</th>
                <th>Weight</th>
            </tr>
            <xsl:for-each select="Product">
                <xsl:element name="tr">
                    <xsl:choose>
                        <xsl:when test="position() mod 2 = 0">
                            <xsl:attribute name="class">row-light</xsl:attribute>
                        </xsl:when>
                        <xsl:otherwise>
                            <xsl:attribute name="class">row-dark</xsl:attribute>
                        </xsl:otherwise>
                    </xsl:choose>
                    <td><xsl:value-of select="@Id"/></td>
                    <td><xsl:value-of select="Name"/></td>
                    <td class="col-right">
                        <xsl:value-of select="QuantityOnHand"/>
                    </td>
                    <td class="col-right"><xsl:value-of select="ListPrice"/></td>
                    <td><xsl:value-of select="Color"/></td>
```

```
                    <td class="col-right">
                        <xsl:value-of select="Size"/>
                        <xsl:value-of select="Size/@UOM"/>
                    </td>
                    <td class="col-right">
                        <xsl:value-of select="Weight"/>
                        <xsl:value-of select="Weight/@UOM"/>
                    </td>
                </xsl:element>
            </xsl:for-each>
        </table>
    </body>
</html>
</xsl:template>
</xsl:stylesheet>';
```

■Tip I won't dive into the details of XSLT style sheet creation in this book, but information can be found at the official W3C XSLT 1.0 standard site, at www.w3.org/TR/xslt. My book *Pro SQL Server 2008 XML* (Apress, 2008) also offers a detailed discussion of XSLT on SQL Server.

The final step is to create a SQL CLR SP that accepts the raw XML data and the XSLT style sheet, performs the XSL transformation, and writes the results to an HTML file. The SQL CLR SP code is shown in Listing 11-22.

Listing 11-22. *SQL CLR SP for XSL Transformations*

```csharp
using System.Data.SqlTypes;
using System.Xml;
using System.Xml.Xsl;

namespace Apress.Samples
{
    public partial class XSLT
    {
        [Microsoft.SqlServer.Server.SqlProcedure]
        public static void XmlToHtml
        (
            SqlXml RawXml,
            SqlXml XslStyleSheet,
            SqlString OutputPage
        )
```

```
    {
        // Create and load the XslCompiledTransform object
        XslCompiledTransform xslt = new XslCompiledTransform();
        XmlDocument xmldoc1 = new XmlDocument();
        xmldoc1.LoadXml(XslStyleSheet.Value);
        xslt.Load(xmldoc1);

        // Create and load the Raw XML document
        XmlDocument xml = new XmlDocument();
        xml.LoadXml(RawXml.Value);

        // Create the XmlTextWriter for output to HTML document
        XmlTextWriter htmlout = new XmlTextWriter
        (
            OutputPage.Value,
            System.Text.Encoding.Unicode
        );

        // Perform the transformation
        xslt.Transform
        (
            xml,
            htmlout
        );

        // Close the XmlTextWriter
        htmlout.Close();
    }

    }
};
```

SQL CLR SECURITY SETTINGS

There are a few administrative details you need to take care of before you deploy SQL CLR code to SQL Server. The first thing to do is set the database to trustworthy mode with the `ALTER DATABASE` statement, as shown following:

```
ALTER DATABASE AdventureWorks
SET TRUSTWORTHY ON;
```

A better alternative to setting your database to trustworthy mode is to sign your assemblies with a certificate. While signing SQL CLR assemblies is beyond the scope of this book, authors Robin Dewson and Julian Skinner cover this topic in their book *Pro SQL Server 2005 Assemblies* (Apress, 2005).

For the example in Listing 11-22, which accesses the local file system, you also need to set the CLR assembly permission level to External. You can do this through Visual Studio, as shown in the following illustration, or you can use `WITH PERMISSION_SET` clause of the `CREATE ASSEMBLY` or `ALTER ASSEMBLY` statements in T-SQL.

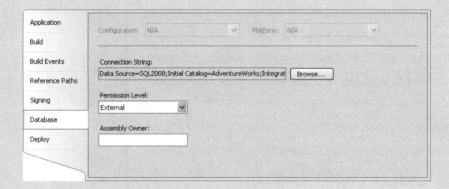

For SQL CLR code that doesn't require access to external resources or unmanaged code, a permission level of Safe is adequate. For SQL CLR assemblies that need access to external resources like hard drives or network resources, External permissions are the minimum required. Unsafe permissions are required for assemblies that access unsafe or unmanaged code. Always assign the minimum required permissions when deploying SQL CLR assemblies to SQL Server.

Finally, make sure the SQL Server service account has permissions to any required external resources. For this example, the service account needs permissions to write to the `c:\Documents and Settings\ All Users\Documents` directory.

After you have deployed the SQL CLR assembly to SQL Server and set the appropriate permissions, you can call the XmlToHtml procedure to perform the XSL transformation, as shown in Listing 11-23. The resulting HTML file is shown in Figure 11-19.

Listing 11-23. *Performing a SQL CLR XSL Transformation*

```
EXECUTE XmlToHtml @xml,
  @xslt,
  'c:\Documents and Settings\All Users\Documents\adventureworks-inventory.html';
```

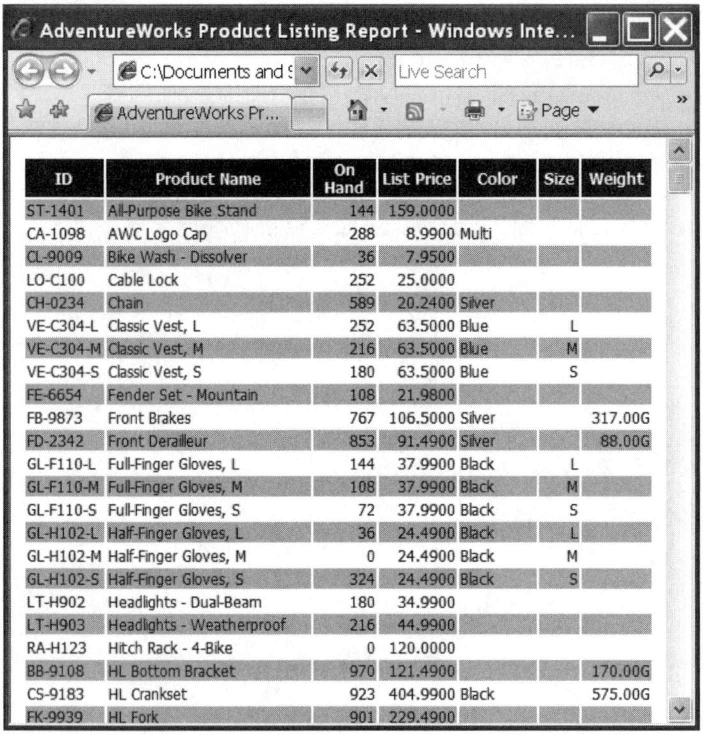

Figure 11-19. *Results of the XML-to-HTML transformation*

Summary

In this chapter, I discussed SQL Server 2008's integrated XML functionality. I began with a discussion of legacy XML functionality carried forward, and in some cases improved upon, from the days of SQL Server 2000. This legacy functionality includes the flexible FOR XML clause and the OPENXML rowset provider.

I then discussed the powerful xml data type and its many methods:

- The query() method allows you to retrieve XML nodes using XQuery queries.

- The value() method lets you retrieve singleton atomic values using XQuery path expressions to locate nodes.

- The exist() method determines whether a specific node exists in your XML data.

- The modify() method allows you to use XML DML to modify your XML data directly.

- The nodes() method makes shredding XML data simple.

I also presented SQL Server's primary and secondary XML indexes, which are designed to optimize XML query performance. Finally, I touched on SQL Server's SQL CLR integration and demonstrated how to use it to access .NET Framework XML functionality not directly available through the T-SQL language.

In the next chapter, I will continue the discussion of SQL Server XML by introducing XPath and XQuery support, including a more detailed discussion of the options, functions, operators, and expressions available for querying and manipulating XML on SQL Server.

EXERCISES

1. [Choose all that apply] SQL Server's FOR XML clause supports which of the following modes:

    a.   FOR XML RAW

    b.   FOR XML PATH

    c.   FOR XML AUTO

    d.   FOR XML EXPLICIT

    e.   FOR XML RECURSIVE

2. [Fill in the blank] By default, the OPENXML rowset provider returns data in ___ table format.

3. [True/false] The xml data type query() method returns its results as an untyped xml data type instance.

4. [Choose one] A SQL Server primary XML index performs which of the following functions:

    a.   It creates a nonclustered index on your xml data type column or variable.

    b.   It creates a clustered index on your xml data type column or variable.

    c.   It stores your xml data type columns in a preshredded relational format.

    d.   It stores your xml data type columns using an inverse index format.

5. [True/false] When you perform XQuery queries against an xml data type column with no primary XML index defined on it, SQL Server automatically shreds your XML data to relational format.

6. [True/false] You can access additional XML functionality on SQL Server through the .NET Framework via SQL Server's SQL CLR integration.

CHAPTER 12

■■■

XQuery and XPath

As I described in Chapter 11, SQL Server 2008 continues the high level of XML integration begun in SQL Server 2005. As part of that integration, SQL Server's xml data type provides built-in functionality for shredding XML data into relational format, querying XML nodes and singleton atomic values via XQuery, and modifying XML data via XML Data Modification Language (XML DML). This chapter focuses on how to get the most out of SQL Server's implementation of the powerful and flexible XPath and XQuery standards.

The XML data model represents a departure from the relational model SQL Server developers know so well. XML is not a replacement for the relational model, but it does nicely complement relational data. XML is very useful for sharing data with a wide variety of web services and disparate systems, and highly structured XML data from remote data sources is often shredded to relational format for easy storage and querying. The SQL Server 2008 xml data type and XML-specific query and conversion tools represent a marriage of some of the best features of relational database and XML technologies.

■**Note** This chapter is not meant to be a comprehensive guide to XPath and XQuery, but rather an introduction to SQL Server's XPath and XQuery implementations, which are both subsets of the W3C XPath 1.0 and XQuery 1.0 recommendations. In addition to the discussion in this chapter, Appendix B provides a reference to the XQuery Data Model (XDM) type system as implemented by SQL Server.

XPath and FOR XML PATH

The FOR XML PATH clause of the SELECT statement uses XPath 1.0–style path expressions to specify the structure of the XML result. Listing 12-1 demonstrates a simple FOR XML PATH query that returns the names and e-mail addresses of people in the AdventureWorks database. Partial results are shown in Figure 12-1.

Listing 12-1. *Retrieving Names and E-mail Addresses with FOR XML PATH*

```
SELECT
  p.BusinessEntityID AS "Person/ID",
  p.FirstName AS "Person/Name/First",
  p.MiddleName AS "Person/Name/Middle",
  p.LastName AS "Person/Name/Last",
  e.EmailAddress AS "Person/Email"
FROM Person.Person p
INNER JOIN Person.EmailAddress e
  ON p.BusinessEntityID = e.BusinessEntityID
FOR XML PATH;
```

```
XML_F52E2B61-...F49916B2.xml*
<row>
  <Person>
    <ID>285</ID>
    <Name>
      <First>Syed</First>
      <Middle>E</Middle>
      <Last>Abbas</Last>
    </Name>
    <Email>syed0@adventure-works.com</Email>
  </Person>
</row>
<row>
  <Person>
    <ID>293</ID>
    <Name>
      <First>Catherine</First>
      <Middle>R.</Middle>
      <Last>Abel</Last>
    </Name>
    <Email>catherine0@adventure-works.com</Email>
  </Person>
```

Figure 12-1. *Partial results of retrieving names and e-mail addresses with FOR XML PATH*

Because they are used specifically to define the structure of an XML result, FOR XML PATH XPath expressions are somewhat limited in their functionality. Specifically, you cannot use features that contain certain filter criteria or use absolute paths. Briefly, here are the restrictions:

- A FOR XML PATH XPath expression may not begin or end with the / step operator, and it may not begin with, end with, or contain //.

- FOR XML PATH XPath expressions cannot specify axis specifiers such as child:: or parent::.

- The . (context node) and .. (context node parent) axis specifiers are not allowed.

- The functions defined in Part 4 of the XPath specification, Core Function Library, are not allowed.

- Predicates, which are used to filter result sets, are not allowed. [position() = 4] is an example of a predicate.

Basically, the FOR XML PATH XPath subset allows you to specify the structure of the result-ing XML relative to the implicit root node. This means that advanced functionality of XPath expressions above and beyond defining a simple relative path expression is not allowed. In general, XPath 1.0 features that can be used to locate specific nodes, return sets of nodes, or filter result sets are not allowed with FOR XML PATH.

By default, FOR XML PATH uses the name row for the root node of each row it converts to XML format. The results of FOR XML PATH also default to an *element-centric* format, meaning that results are defined in terms of element nodes.

In Listing 12-1, I've aliased the column names using the XPath expressions that define the structure of the XML result. Because the XPath expressions often contain characters that are not allowed in SQL identifiers, you will probably want to use quoted identifiers.

```
SELECT
  p.BusinessEntityID AS "Person/ID",
  p.FirstName AS "Person/Name/First",
  p.MiddleName AS "Person/Name/Middle",
  p.LastName AS "Person/Name/Last",
  e.EmailAddress AS "Person/Email"
```

XPath expressions are defined as a path separated by *step operators*. The step operator (/) indicates that a node is a child of the preceding node. For instance, the XPath expression Person/ID in the example indicates that a node named ID will be created as a child of the node named Person in a hierarchical XML structure.

XPath Attributes

Alternatively, you can define a relational column as an attribute of a node. Listing 12-2 modifies Listing 12-1 slightly to demonstrates this. I've shown the differences between the two listings in bold print. Partial results are shown in Figure 12-2, reformatted slightly for easier reading.

Listing 12-2. *FOR XML PATH Creating XML Attributes*

```
SELECT
  p.BusinessEntityID AS "Person/@ID",
  e.EmailAddress AS "Person/@Email",
  p.FirstName AS "Person/Name/First",
  p.MiddleName AS "Person/Name/Middle",
  p.LastName AS "Person/Name/Last"
FROM Person.Person p
INNER JOIN Person.EmailAddress e
  ON p.BusinessEntityID = e.BusinessEntityID
FOR XML PATH;
```

```
XML_F52E2B61-...F49916B3.xml*
  ☐<row>
     <Person ID="285"
             Email="syed0@adventure-works.com">
       <Name>
         <First>Syed</First>
         <Middle>E</Middle>
         <Last>Abbas</Last>
       </Name>
     </Person>
   </row>
  ☐<row>
     <Person ID="293"
             Email="catherine0@adventure-works.com">
       <Name>
         <First>Catherine</First>
         <Middle>R.</Middle>
         <Last>Abel</Last>
       </Name>
     </Person>
   </row>
  ☐<row>
```

Figure 12-2. *Creating attributes with FOR XML PATH*

The bold portion of the SELECT statement in Listing 12-2 generates XML attributes of the ID and Email nodes by preceding their names in the XPath expression with the @ symbol. The result is that ID and Email become attributes of the Person element in the result:

```
p.BusinessEntityID AS "Person/@ID",
e.EmailAddress AS "Person/@Email",
```

Columns Without Names and Wildcards

Some of the other XPath expression features you can use with FOR XML PATH include columns without names and wildcard expressions, which are turned into inline content. The sample in Listing 12-3 demonstrates this.

Listing 12-3. *Using Columns Without Names and Wildcards with FOR XML PATH*

```
SELECT
  p.BusinessEntityID AS "*",
  ',' + e.EmailAddress,
  p.FirstName AS "Person/Name/First",
  p.MiddleName AS "Person/Name/Middle",
  p.LastName AS "Person/Name/Last"
FROM Person.Person p
INNER JOIN Person.EmailAddress e
  ON p.BusinessEntityID = e.BusinessEntityID
FOR XML PATH;
```

In this example, the XPath expression for BusinessEntityID is the wildcard character, *. The second column is defined as ',' + EmailAddress and the column is not given a name. Both of these columns are turned into inline content immediately below the row element, as shown in Figure 12-3. This is particularly useful functionality when creating lists within your XML data, or when your XML data conforms to a schema that looks for combined, concatenated, or list data in XML text nodes.

Figure 12-3. *Columns without names and wildcard expressions in FOR XML PATH*

Element Grouping

As you saw in the previous examples, FOR XML PATH groups together nodes that have the same parent elements. For instance, the First, Middle, and Last elements are all children of the Name element. They are grouped together in all of the examples because of this. However, as shown in Listing 12-4, this is not the case when these elements are separated by an element with a different parent element.

Listing 12-4. *Two Elements with a Common Parent Element Separated*

```
SELECT
  p.BusinessEntityID AS "@ID",
  e.EmailAddress AS "@EmailAddress",
  p.FirstName AS "Person/Name/First",
  pp.PhoneNumber AS "Phone/BusinessPhone",
  p.MiddleName AS "Person/Name/Middle",
  p.LastName AS "Person/Name/Last"
```

```
FROM Person.Person p
INNER JOIN Person.EmailAddress e
  ON p.BusinessEntityID = e.BusinessEntityID
INNER JOIN Person.PersonPhone pp
  ON p.BusinessEntityID = pp.BusinessEntityID
  AND pp.PhoneNumberTypeID = 3
FOR XML PATH;
```

The results of this query include a new Phone element as a direct child of the Person element. Because this new element is positioned between the Person/Name/First and Person/Name/Middle elements, FOR XML PATH creates two separate Person/Name elements: one to encapsulate the First element, and another to encapsulate the Middle and Last elements, as shown in Figure 12-4.

Figure 12-4. *Breaking Element Grouping with FOR XML PATH*

The data Function

The FOR XML PATH XPath expression provides support for a function called data(). If the column name is specified as data(), the value is treated as an atomic value in the generated XML. If the next item generated is also an atomic value, FOR XML PATH appends a space to the end of the data returned. This is useful for using subqueries to create lists of items, as in Listing 12-5, which demonstrates use of the data() function.

Listing 12-5. *The FOR XML PATH XPath data Node Test*

```
SELECT DISTINCT
  soh.SalesPersonID AS "SalesPerson/@ID",
  (
    SELECT soh2.SalesOrderID AS "data()"
    FROM Sales.SalesOrderHeader soh2
    WHERE soh2.SalesPersonID = soh.SalesPersonID
    FOR XML PATH ('')
  ) AS "SalesPerson/@Orders",
  p.FirstName AS "SalesPerson/Name/First",
  p.MiddleName AS "SalesPerson/Name/Middle",
  p.LastName AS "SalesPerson/Name/Last",
  e.EmailAddress AS "SalesPerson/Email"
FROM Sales.SalesOrderHeader soh
INNER JOIN Person.Person p
  ON p.BusinessEntityID = soh.SalesPersonID
INNER JOIN Person.EmailAddress e
  ON p.BusinessEntityID = e.BusinessEntityID
WHERE soh.SalesPersonID IS NOT NULL
FOR XML PATH;
```

This sample retrieves all `SalesPerson` ID numbers from the `Sales.SalesOrderHeader` table (eliminating `NULL`s for simplicity) and retrieves their names in the main query. The subquery uses the `data()` function to retrieve a list of each salesperson's sales order numbers and places them in a space-separated list in the `Orders` attribute of the `SalesPerson` element. A sample of the results is shown in Figure 12-5.

Figure 12-5. *Creating lists with the data node test*

NODE TESTS AND FUNCTIONS

The SQL Server 2008 FOR XML PATH expression provides access to both the text() function and the data() node test. In terms of FOR XML PATH, the text() function returns the data in the text node as inline text with no separator. The data() node test returns the data in the XML text node as a space-separated concatenated list.

In XQuery expressions, the data() node test, the text() function, and the related string() function all return slightly different results. The following code snippet demonstrates their differences:

```
DECLARE @x xml;
SET @x = N'<a>123<b>456</b><c>789</c></a><a>987<b>654</b><c>321</c></a>';

SELECT @x.query('/a/text()');

SELECT @x.query('data(/a)');

SELECT @x.query('string(/a[1])');
```

The text() function in this example returns the concatenated text nodes of the <a> elements; in this example, it returns 123987.

The data() node test returns the concatenated XML text nodes of the <a> elements and all their child elements. In this example, data() returns 123456789 987654321, the concatenation of the <a> elements and the <b> and <c> subelements they contain. The data() node test puts a space separator between the <a> elements during the concatenation.

The string() function is similar to the data() node test in that it concatenates the data contained in the specified element and all child elements. The string() function requires a singleton node instance, which is why I specified string(/a[1]) in the example. The result of the string() function used in the example is 123456789. I'll discuss the text() and string() functions in greater detail later in this chapter.

XPath and NULL

In all of the previous examples, FOR XML PATH maps SQL NULL to a missing element or attribute. Consider the results of Listing 12-1 for Kim Abercrombie, shown in Figure 12-6. Because her MiddleName in the table is NULL, the Name/Middle element is missing from the results.

```
XML_F52E2B61-...F49916B7.xml*
<row>
  <Person>
    <ID>295</ID>
    <Name>
      <First>Kim</First>
      <Last>Abercrombie</Last>
    </Name>
    <Email>kim2@adventure-works.com</Email>
  </Person>
</row>
```

Figure 12-6. *NULL middle name eliminated from the FOR XML PATH results*

If you want SQL NULL-valued elements and attributes to appear in the final results, use the ELEMENTS XSINIL option of the FOR XML clause, as shown in Listing 12-6.

Listing 12-6. *FOR XML with the ELEMENTS XSINIL Option*

```
SELECT
  p.BusinessEntityID AS "Person/ID",
  p.FirstName AS "Person/Name/First",
  p.MiddleName AS "Person/Name/Middle",
  p.LastName AS "Person/Name/Last",
  e.EmailAddress AS "Person/Email"
FROM Person.Person p
INNER JOIN Person.EmailAddress e
  ON p.BusinessEntityID = e.BusinessEntityID
FOR XML PATH,
  ELEMENTS XSINIL;
```

With the ELEMENTS XSINIL option, Kim's results now look like the results shown in Figure 12-7. The FOR XML PATH clause adds a reference to the xsi namespace, and elements containing SQL NULL are included but marked with the xsi:nil="true" attribute.

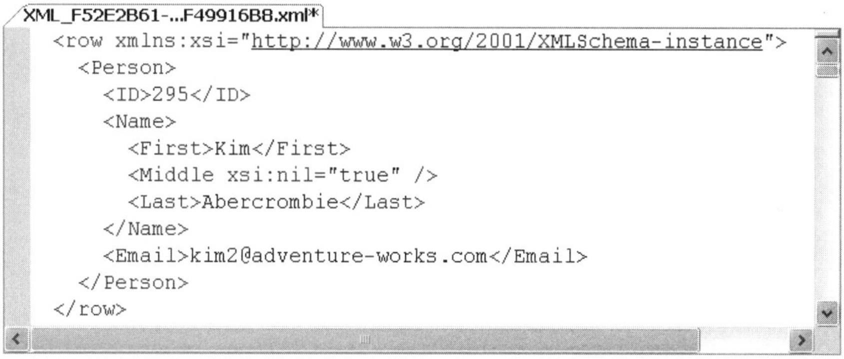

```
XML_F52E2B61-...F49916B8.xml*
    <row xmlns:xsi="http://www.w3.org/2001/XMLSchema-instance">
      <Person>
        <ID>295</ID>
        <Name>
          <First>Kim</First>
          <Middle xsi:nil="true" />
          <Last>Abercrombie</Last>
        </Name>
        <Email>kim2@adventure-works.com</Email>
      </Person>
    </row>
```

Figure 12-7. *NULL marked with the xsi:nil attribute*

The WITH XMLNAMESPACES Clause

Namespace support is provided for FOR XML clauses and other XML functions by the WITH XMLNAMESPACES clause. The WITH XMLNAMESPACES clause is added to the front of your SELECT queries to specify XML namespaces to be used by FOR XML clauses or xml data type methods. Listing 12-7 demonstrates the use of the WITH XMLNAMESPACES clause with FOR XML PATH.

Listing 12-7. *Using WITH XMLNAMESPACES to Specify Namespaces*

```
WITH XMLNAMESPACES('http://www.apress.com/xml/sampleSqlXmlNameSpace' as ns)
SELECT
  p.BusinessEntityID AS "ns:Person/ID",
  p.FirstName AS "ns:Person/Name/First",
```

```
    p.MiddleName AS "ns:Person/Name/Middle",
    p.LastName AS "ns:Person/Name/Last",
    e.EmailAddress AS "ns:Person/Email"
FROM Person.Person p
INNER JOIN Person.EmailAddress e
  ON p.BusinessEntityID = e.BusinessEntityID
FOR XML PATH;
```

The WITH XMLNAMESPACES clause in this example declares a namespace called ns with the URI http://www.apress.com/xml/sampleSqlXmlNameSpace. The FOR XML PATH clause adds this namespace prefix to the Person element, as indicated in the XPath expressions used to define the structure of the result. A sample of the results is shown in Figure 12-8.

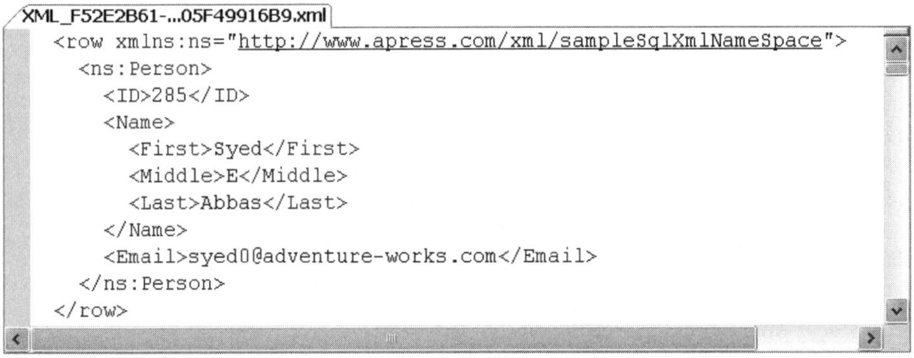

```
XML_F52E2B61-...05F49916B9.xml
    <row xmlns:ns="http://www.apress.com/xml/sampleSqlXmlNameSpace">
      <ns:Person>
        <ID>285</ID>
        <Name>
          <First>Syed</First>
          <Middle>E</Middle>
          <Last>Abbas</Last>
        </Name>
        <Email>syed0@adventure-works.com</Email>
      </ns:Person>
    </row>
```

Figure 12-8. *Adding an XML namespace to the FOR XML PATH results*

Node Tests

In addition to the previous options, the FOR XML PATH XPath implementation supports four node tests, including the following:

- The text() node test turns the string value of a column into a text node.

- The comment() node test turns the string value of a column into an XML comment.

- The node() node test turns the string value of a column into inline XML content; it is the same as using the wildcard * as the name.

- The processing-instruction(*name*) node test turns the string value of a column into an XML-processing instruction with the specified name.

Listing 12-8 demonstrates use of XPath node tests as column names in a FOR XML PATH query. The results are shown in Figure 12-9.

Listing 12-8. *FOR XML PATH Using XPath Node Tests*

```
SELECT
  p.NameStyle AS "processing-instruction(nameStyle)",
  p.BusinessEntityID AS "Person/@ID",
  p.ModifiedDate AS "comment()",
  pp.PhoneNumber AS "text()",
  FirstName AS "Person/Name/First",
  MiddleName AS "Person/Name/Middle",
  LastName AS "Person/Name/Last",
  EmailAddress AS "Person/Email"
FROM Person.Person p
INNER JOIN Person.EmailAddress e
  ON p.BusinessEntityID = e.BusinessEntityID
INNER JOIN Person.PersonPhone pp
  ON p.BusinessEntityID = pp.BusinessEntityID
FOR XML PATH;
```

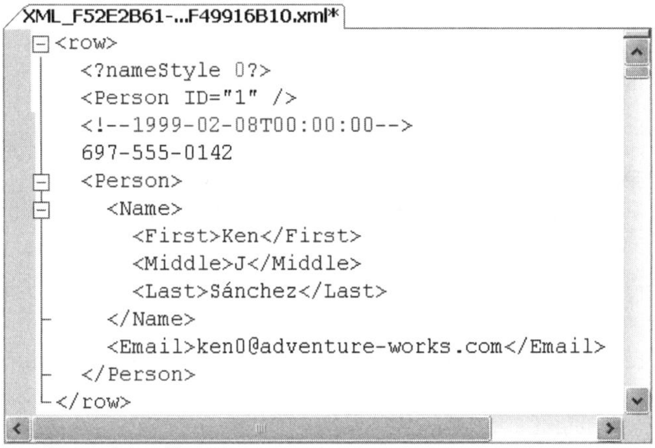

Figure 12-9. *Using node tests with FOR XML PATH*

In this example, the NameStyle column value is turned into an XML-processing instruction called nameStyle, the ModifiedDate column is turned into an XML comment, and the contact PhoneNumber is turned into a text node for each person in the AdventureWorks database.

XQuery and the xml Data Type

XQuery represents the most advanced standardized XML querying language to date. Designed as an extension to the W3C XPath 2.0 standard, XQuery is a case-sensitive, declarative, functional language with a rich type system based on the XDM. The SQL Server 2008 xml data type supports querying of XML data using a subset of XQuery via the query() method. Before diving into the details of the SQL Server implementation, I'm going to start this section with a discussion of XQuery basics.

Expressions and Sequences

XQuery introduces several advances on the concepts introduced by XPath and other previous XML query tools and languages. Two of the most important concepts in XQuery are *expressions* and *sequences*. A sequence is an ordered collection of items—either nodes or atomic values. The word *ordered*, as it applies to sequences, does not necessarily mean numeric or alphabetic order. Sequences are generally in *document order* (the order in which their contents appear in the raw XML document or data) by default, unless you specify a different ordering. The roughly analogous XPath 1.0 structure was known as a *node set*, a name that implies ordering was unimportant. Unlike the relational model, however, the order of nodes is extremely important to XML. In XML, the ordering of nodes and content provides additional context and can be just as important as the data itself. The XQuery sequence was redefined to ensure that the importance of proper ordering is recognized. There are also some other differences that I will cover later in this section.

Sequences can be returned by XQuery expressions or created by enclosing one of the following in parentheses:

- Lists of items separated by the comma operator (,)

- Range expressions

- Filter expressions

■**Tip** Range expressions and the range expression keyword `to` are not supported in SQL Server 2008 XQuery. If you are converting an XQuery with range expressions like (`1 to 10`), you will have to modify it to run on SQL Server 2008.

A sequence created as a list of items separated by the comma operator might look like the following:

```
(1, 2, 3, 4, (5, 6), 7, 8, (), 9, 10)
```

The comma operator evaluates each of the items in the sequence and concatenates the result. Sequences cannot be nested, so any sequences within sequences are "flattened out." Also, the empty sequence (a sequence containing no items, denoted by empty parentheses: ()) is eliminated. Evaluation of the previous sample sequence results in the following sequence of ten items:

```
(1, 2, 3, 4, 5, 6, 7, 8, 9, 10)
```

Notice that the nested sequence (`5, 6`) has been flattened out, and the empty sequence () is removed during evaluation.

■**Tip** SQL Server 2008 XQuery does not support the W3C-specified sequence operators `union`, `intersect`, and `except`. If you are porting XQuery code that uses these operators, it will have to be modified to run on SQL Server 2008.

Another method of generating a sequence is with a filter expression. A *filter expression* is a primary expression followed by zero or more predicates. An example of a filter expression to generate a sequence might look like the following:

```
(//Coordinates/*/text())
```

An important property of sequences is that a sequence of one item is indistinguishable from a singleton atomic value. So the sequence (1.0) is equivalent to the singleton atomic value 1.0.

Sequences come in three flavors: empty sequences, homogeneous sequences, and heterogeneous sequences. *Empty sequences* are sequences that contain no items. As mentioned before, the empty sequence is annotated with a set of empty parentheses: ( ).

Homogeneous sequences are sequences of one or more items of the same or compatible types. The examples already given are all examples of homogenous sequences.

Heterogeneous sequences are sequences of two or more items of incompatible types, or singleton atomic types and nodes. The following is an example of a heterogeneous sequence:

```
("Harry", 299792458, xs:date("2006-12-29Z"))
```

SQL Server does not allow heterogeneous sequences that mix nodes with singleton atomic values. Trying to declare the following sequence results in an error:

```
(<tag/>, "you are it!")
```

■**Note** *Singleton atomic values* are defined as values that are in the value space of the atomic types. The *value space* is the complete set of values that can be expressed with a given type. For instance, the complete value space for the xs:boolean type is true and false. Singleton atomic values are indivisible for purposes of the XDM standard (although you can extract portions of their content in some situations). Values that fall into this space are decimals, integers, dates, strings, and other primitive data types.

Primary expressions are the building blocks of XQuery. An expression in XQuery evaluates to a singleton atomic value or a sequence. Primary expressions can be any of several different items, including the following:

- *Literals*: These include string and numeric data type literals. String literals can be enclosed in either single or double quotes and may contain the XML-defined entity references >, <, &, ", and ', or Unicode character references such as €, which represents the euro symbol (€).

- *Variable references*: These are XML-qualified names (QNames) preceded by a $ sign. A variable reference is defined by its local name. Note that SQL Server 2008 does not support variable references with namespace URI prefixes, which are allowed under the W3C recommendation. An example of a variable reference is $count.

- *Parenthesized expressions*: These are expressions enclosed in parentheses. Parenthe-sized expressions are often used to force a specific order of operator evaluation. For instance, in the expression (3 + 4) * 2, the parentheses force the addition to be per-formed before the multiplication.

- *Context item expressions*: These are expressions that evaluate to the context item. The context item is the node or atomic value currently being referenced by the XQuery query engine.

- *Function calls*: These are composed of a QName followed by a list of arguments in parentheses. Function calls can reference built-in functions. SQL Server 2008 does not support XQuery user-defined functions.

The query Method

The query() method can be used to query and retrieve XML nodes from xml variables or xml-typed columns in tables, as demonstrated in Listing 12-9, with partial results shown in Figure 12-10.

Listing 12-9. *Retrieving Job Candidates with the query Method*

```
SELECT Resume.query
(
  N'//*:Name.First,
  //*:Name.Middle,
  //*:Name.Last,
  //*:Edu.Level'
)
FROM HumanResources.JobCandidate;
```

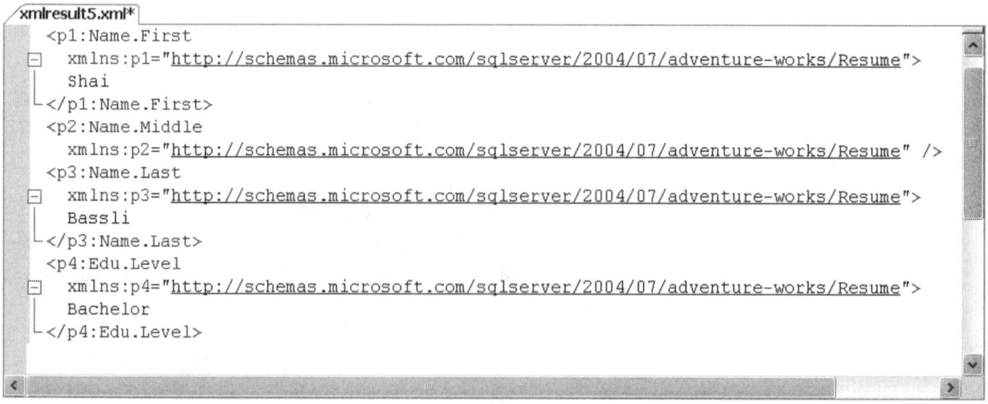

Figure 12-10. *Sample job candidate returned by the query method*

The simple XQuery query retrieves all first names, middle names, last names, and education levels for all AdventureWorks job candidates. The XQuery path expressions in the example demonstrate some key XQuery concepts, including the following:

- The first item of note is the `//` axis at the beginning of each path expression. This axis notation is defined as shorthand for the `descendant-or-self::node()`, which I'll describe in more detail in the next section. This particular axis retrieves all nodes with a name matching the location step, regardless of where it occurs in the XML being queried.

- In the example, the four node tests specified are `Name.First`, `Name.Middle`, `Name.Last`, and `Edu.Level`. All nodes with the names that match the node tests are returned no matter where they occur in the XML.

- The `*` namespace qualifier is a wildcard that matches any namespace occurring in the XML. Each node in the result node sequence includes an `xmlns` namespace declaration.

- This XQuery query is composed of four different paths denoting the four different node sequences to be returned. They are separated from one another by commas.

Location Paths

The *location path* determines which nodes should be accessed by XQuery. Following a location path from left to right is generally analogous to moving down and to the right in your XML node tree (there are exceptions, of course, which I discuss in the section on axis specifiers). If the first character of the path expression is a single forward slash (`/`), then the path expression is an absolute location path, meaning that it starts at the root of the XML. Listing 12-10 demonstrates the use of an XQuery absolute location path. The results are shown in Figure 12-11.

■Tip The left-hand forward slash actually stands for a conceptual root node that encompasses your XML input. The conceptual root node doesn't actually exist, and can neither be viewed in your XML input nor accessed or manipulated directly. It's this conceptual root node that allows XQuery to properly process XML fragments that are not well formed (i.e., XML with multiple root nodes) as input. Using a path expression that consists of only a single forward slash returns every node below the conceptual root node in your XML document or fragment.

Listing 12-10. *Querying with an Absolute Location Path*

```
DECLARE @x xml = N'<?xml version = "1.0"?>
<Geocode>
    <Info ID = "1">
        <Coordinates Resolution = "High">
            <Latitude>37.859609</Latitude>
            <Longitude>-122.291673</Longitude>
        </Coordinates>
```

```
        <Location Type = "Business">
            <Name>APress, Inc.</Name>
        </Location>
    </Info>
    <Info ID = "2">
        <Coordinates Resolution = "High">
            <Latitude>37.423268</Latitude>
            <Longitude>-122.086345</Longitude>
        </Coordinates>
        <Location Type = "Business">
            <Name>Google, Inc.</Name>
        </Location>
    </Info>
</Geocode>';

SELECT @x.query(N'/Geocode/Info/Coordinates');
```

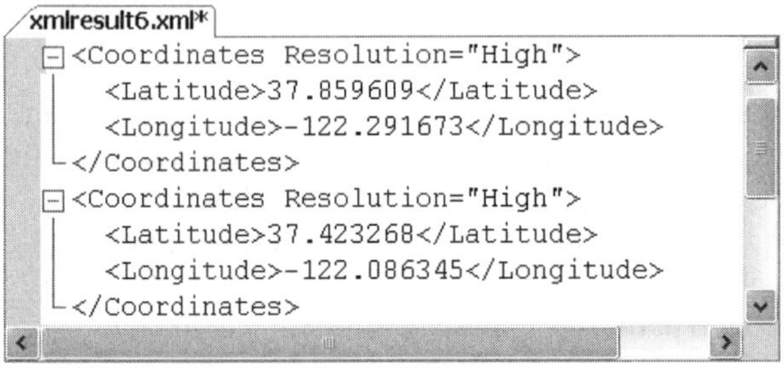

Figure 12-11. *Absolute location path query result*

Listing 12-10 defines an xml variable and populates it with an XML document containing geocoding data for a couple of businesses. I've used an absolute location path in the query to retrieve a node sequence of the latitude and longitude coordinates for the entire XML document.

A relative location path indicates a path relative to the current context node. The *context node* is the current node being accessed by the XQuery engine at a given point when the query is executed. The context node changes during execution of the query. Relative location paths are specified by excluding the leading forward slash, as in the following modification to Listing 12-10:

```
SELECT @x.query(N'Geocode/Info/Coordinates');
```

And, as previously mentioned, using a double forward slash (//) in the lead position returns nodes that match the node test anywhere they occur in the document. The following modification to Listing 12-10 demonstrates this:

```
SELECT @x.query(N'//Coordinates');
```

In addition, the wildcard character (*) can be used to match any node by name. The following example retrieves the root node, all of the nodes on the next level, and all `Coordinates` nodes below that:

```
SELECT @x.query(N'//*/*/Coordinates');
```

Because the XML document in the example is a simple one, all the variations of Listing 12-10 return the same result. For more complex XML documents or fragments, the results of different relative location paths could return completely different results.

Node Tests

The *node tests* in the previous example are simple *name node tests*. For a name node test to return a match, the nodes must have the same names as those specified in the node tests. In addition to name node tests, SQL Server 2008 XQuery supports four node *kind* tests, as listed in Table 12-1.

Table 12-1. *Supported Node Tests*

Node Kind Test	Description
comment()	Returns true for a comment node only.
node()	Returns true for any kind of node.
processing-instruction("*name*")	Returns true for a processing instruction node. The *name* paramenter is an optional string literal. If it is included, only processing instruction nodes with that name are returned; if not included, all processing instructions are returned.
text()	Returns true for a text node only.

■**Tip** Keep in mind that XQuery, like XML, is case sensitive. This means your node tests and other identifiers must all be of the proper case. The identifier `PersonalID`, for instance, does not match `personalid` in XML or XQuery. Also note that your database collation case sensitivity settings do not affect XQuery queries.

Listing 12-11 demonstrates use of the `processing-instruction()` node test to retrieve the processing instruction from the root level of a document for one product model. The results are shown in Figure 12-12.

Listing 12-11. *Sample processing-instruction Node Test*

```
SELECT CatalogDescription.query(N'/processing-instruction()') AS Processing_Instr
FROM Production.ProductModel
WHERE ProductModelID = 19;
```

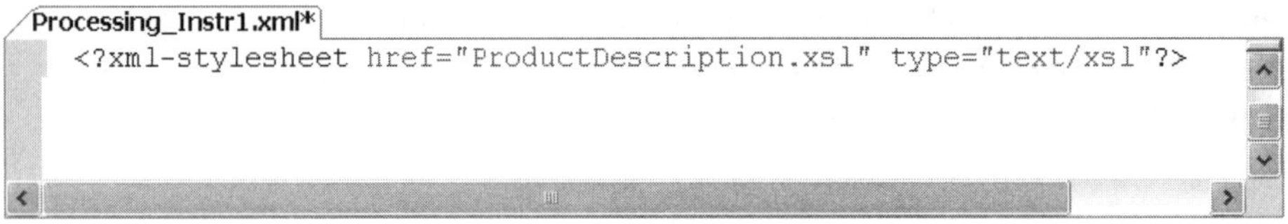

```
/Processing_Instr1.xml*
    <?xml-stylesheet href="ProductDescription.xsl" type="text/xsl"?>
```

Figure 12-12. *Results of the processing-instruction node test query*

The sample can be modified to retrieve all XML comments from the source by using the comment() node test, as in Listing 12-12. The results are shown in Figure 12-13.

Listing 12-12. *Sample comment Node Test*

```
SELECT CatalogDescription.query(N'//comment()') AS Comments
FROM Production.ProductModel
WHERE ProductModelID = 19;
```

```
/Comments1.xml*
  <!-- add one or more of these elements... one for
        each specific product in this product model -->
  <!-- add any tags in <specifications> -->
```

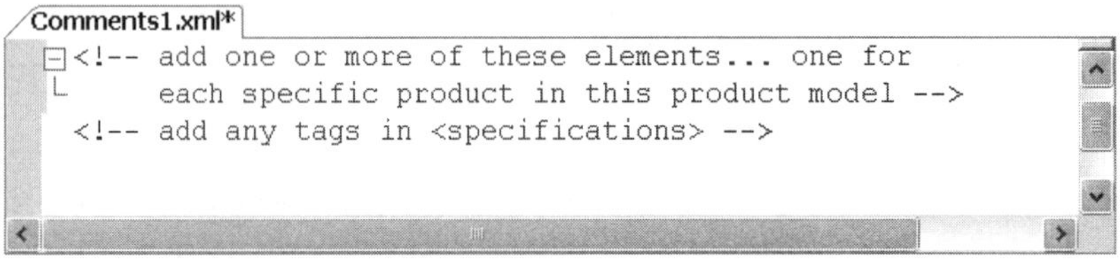

Figure 12-13. *Results of the comment node test query*

Listing 12-13 demonstrates use of another node test, node(), to retrieve the specifications for product model 19. Results are shown in Figure 12-14.

Listing 12-13. *Sample node Node Test*

```
SELECT CatalogDescription.query(N'//*:Specifications/node()') AS Specifications
FROM Production.ProductModel
WHERE ProductModelID = 19;
```

```
/Specifications1.xml*
    These are the product specifications.
    <Material>Almuminum Alloy</Material>
    <Color>Available in most colors</Color>
    <ProductLine>Mountain bike</ProductLine>
    <Style>Unisex</Style>
    <RiderExperience>Advanced to Professional riders</RiderExperience>
```

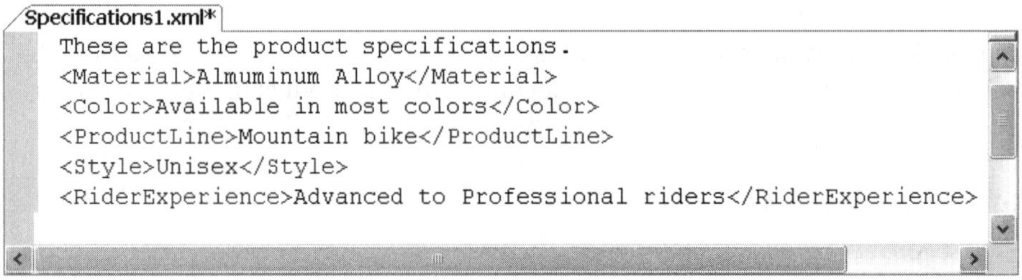

Figure 12-14. *Results of the node node test query*

SQL Server 2008 XQuery does not support other node kind tests specified in the XQuery recommendation. Specifically, the `schema-element()`, `element()`, `attribute()`, and `document-node()` kind tests are not implemented. SQL Server 2008 also doesn't provide support for *type tests*, which are node tests that let you query nodes based on their associated type information.

Namespaces

You might notice that the first node of the result shown in Figure 12-14 is not enclosed in XML tags. This node is a text node located in the `Specifications` node being queried. You might also notice that the * namespace wildcard mentioned previously is used in this query. This is because namespaces are declared in the XML of the `CatalogDescription` column. Specifically, the root node declaration looks like this:

```
<p1:ProductDescription xmlns:p1="http://schemas.microsoft.com/sqlserver/2004/➥
    07/adventure-works/ProductModelDescription"
    xmlns:wm="http://schemas.microsoft.com/sqlserver/2004/07/➥
    adventure-works/ProductModelWarrAndMain"
    xmlns:wf="http://www.adventure-works.com/schemas/OtherFeatures"
    xmlns:html="http://www.w3.org/1999/xhtml"
    ProductModelID="19"
    ProductModelName="Mountain 100">
```

The `Specifications` node of the XML document is declared with the `p1` namespace in the document. Not using a namespace in the query at all, as shown in Listing 12-14, results in an empty sequence being returned (no matching nodes).

Listing 12-14. *Querying CatalogDescription with No Namespaces*

```
SELECT CatalogDescription.query(N'//Specifications/node()') AS Specifications
FROM Production.ProductModel
WHERE ProductModelID = 19;
```

In addition to the wildcard namespace specifier, you can use the XQuery prolog to define namespaces for use in your query. Listing 12-15 shows how the previous example can be modified to include the `p1` namespace with a namespace declaration in the prolog.

Listing 12-15. *Prolog Namespace Declaration*

```
SELECT CatalogDescription.query
(
  N'declare namespace
  p1 = "http://schemas.microsoft.com/sqlserver/2004/07/adventure-works/➥
    ProductModelDescription";
  //p1:Specifications/node()'
)
FROM Production.ProductModel
WHERE ProductModelID = 19;
```

The keywords declare namespace allow you to declare specific namespaces that will be used in the query. You can also use the declare default element namespace keywords to declare a default namespace, as in Listing 12-16.

Listing 12-16. *Prolog Default Namespace Declaration*

```
SELECT CatalogDescription.query
(
  N'declare default element namespace
  "http://schemas.microsoft.com/sqlserver/2004/07/adventure-works/➥
    ProductModelDescription";
  //Specifications/node()'
)
FROM Production.ProductModel
WHERE ProductModelID = 19;
```

Declaring a default namespace with the declare default element namespace keywords allows you to eliminate namespace prefixes in your location paths (for steps that fall within the scope of the default namespace, of course). Listings 12-15 and 12-16 both generate the same result as the query in Listing 12-13.

■**Tip** You can also use the T-SQL WITH XMLNAMESPACES clause, described previously in this chapter, to declare namespaces for use by xml data type methods.

SQL Server defines an assortment of predeclared namespaces that can be used in your queries. With the exception of the xml namespace, you can redeclare these namespaces in your queries using the URIs of your choice. The predeclared namespaces are listed in Table 12-2.

Table 12-2. *SQL Server Predeclared XQuery Namespaces*

Namespace	URI	Description
fn	http://www.w3.org/2005/xpath-functions	XQuery 1.0, XPath 2.0, XSLT 2.0 functions and operators namespace
sqltypes	http://schemas.microsoft.com/sqlserver/2004/sqltypes	This namespace provides SQL Server 2005 to base type mapping
xdt	http://www.w3.org/2005/xpath-datatypes/	XQuery 1.0/XPath 2.0 data types namespace
xml	http://www.w3.org/XML/1998/namespace	Default XML namespace
xs	http://www.w3.org/2001/XMLSchema	XML schema namespace
xsi	http://www.w3.org/2001/	XML schema instance namespace XMLSchema-instance

■**Tip** The W3C-specified local functions namespace, `local` (`http://www.w3.org/2005/xquery-local-functions`), is not predeclared in SQL Server. SQL Server 2008 does not support XQuery user-defined functions.

Another useful namespace is `http://www.w3.org/2005/xqt-errors`, which is the namespace for XPath and XQuery function and operator error codes. In the XQuery documentation, this URI is bound to the namespace `err`, though this is not considered normative.

Axis Specifiers

Axis specifiers define the direction of movement of a location path step relative to the current context node. The XQuery standard defines several axis specifiers, which can be defined as *forward axes* or *reverse axes*. SQL Server 2005 supports a subset of these axis specifiers, as listed in Table 12-3.

Table 12-3. *SQL 2005 Supported Axis Specifiers*

Axis Name	Direction	Description
`child::`	Forward	Retrieves the children of the current context node.
`descendant::`	Forward	Retrieves all descendents of the current context node, recursive style. This includes children of the current node, children of the children, and so on.
`self::`	Forward	Contains just the current context node.
`descendant-or-self::`	Forward	Contains the context node and children of the current context node.
`attribute::`	Forward	Returns the specified attribute(s) of the current context node. This axis specifier may be abbreviated using an at sign (@).
`parent::`	Reverse	Returns the parent of the current context node. This axis specifier may be abbreviated as two periods (`..`).

In addition, the *context-item expression*, indicated by a single period (`.`), returns the current context item (which can be either a node or an atomic value). The current context item is the current node or atomic value being processed by the XQuery engine at any given point during query execution.

■**Note** The following axes, defined as *optional axes* by the XQuery 1.0 specification, are not supported by SQL Server 2008: `following-sibling::`, `following::`, `ancestor::`, `preceding-sibling::`, `preceding::`, `ancestor-or-self::`, and the deprecated `namespace::`. If you are porting XQuery queries from other sources, they may have to be modified to avoid these axis specifiers.

In all of the examples so far, the axis has been omitted, and the default axis of child::
is assumed by XQuery in each step. Because child:: is the default axis, the two queries in
Listing 12-17 are equivalent.

Listing 12-17. *Query with and Without Default Axes*

```
SELECT CatalogDescription.query(N'//*:Specifications/node()') AS Specifications
FROM Production.ProductModel
WHERE ProductModelID = 19;
```

```
SELECT CatalogDescription.query(N'//child::*:Specifications/child::node()')
    AS Specifications
FROM Production.ProductModel
WHERE ProductModelID = 19;
```

Listing 12-18 demonstrates the use of the parent:: axis to retrieve Coordinates nodes
from the sample XML.

Listing 12-18. *Sample Using the parent:: Axis*

```
DECLARE @x xml = N'<?xml version = "1.0"?>
<Geocode>
    <Info ID = "1">
        <Coordinates Resolution = "High">
            <Latitude>37.859609</Latitude>
            <Longitude>-122.291673</Longitude>
        </Coordinates>
        <Location Type = "Business">
            <Name>APress, Inc.</Name>
        </Location>
    </Info>
    <Info ID = "2">
        <Coordinates Resolution = "High">
            <Latitude>37.423268</Latitude>
            <Longitude>-122.086345</Longitude>
        </Coordinates>
        <Location Type = "Business">
            <Name>Google, Inc.</Name>
        </Location>
    </Info>
</Geocode>';
```

```
SELECT @x.query(N'//Location/parent::node()/Coordinates');
```

This particular query locates all Location nodes, then uses the parent:: axis to retrieve
their parent nodes (Info nodes), and finally returns the Coordinates nodes, which are children
of the Info nodes. The end result is shown in Figure 12-15.

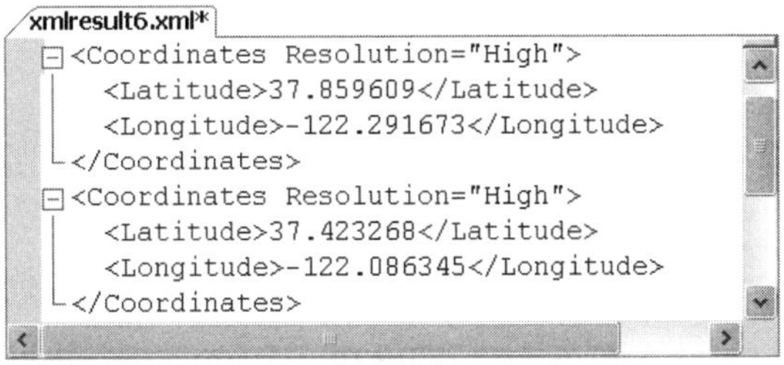

```
xmlresult6.xml*
  <Coordinates Resolution="High">
     <Latitude>37.859609</Latitude>
     <Longitude>-122.291673</Longitude>
  </Coordinates>
  <Coordinates Resolution="High">
     <Latitude>37.423268</Latitude>
     <Longitude>-122.086345</Longitude>
  </Coordinates>
```

Figure 12-15. *Retrieving Coordinates nodes with the parent:: axis*

Dynamic XML Construction

The XQuery 1.0 recommendation is based on XPath 2.0, which is in turn based largely on XPath 1.0. The XPath 1.0 recommendation was designed to consolidate many of the best features of both the W3C XSLT and XPointer recommendations. One of the benefits of XQuery's lineage is its ability to query XML and dynamically construct well-formed XML documents from the results. Consider the example in Listing 12-19, which uses an XQuery *direct constructor* to create an XML document. Figure 12-16 shows the results.

Listing 12-19. *XQuery Dynamic XML Construction*

```
DECLARE @x xml = N'<?xml version = "1.0"?>
<Geocode>
    <Info ID = "1">
        <Location Type = "Business">
            <Name>APress, Inc.</Name>
        </Location>
    </Info>
    <Info ID = "2">
        <Location Type = "Business">
            <Name>Google, Inc.</Name>
        </Location>
    </Info>
</Geocode>';
SELECT @x.query(N'<Companies>
    {
        //Info/Location/Name
    }
</Companies>');
```

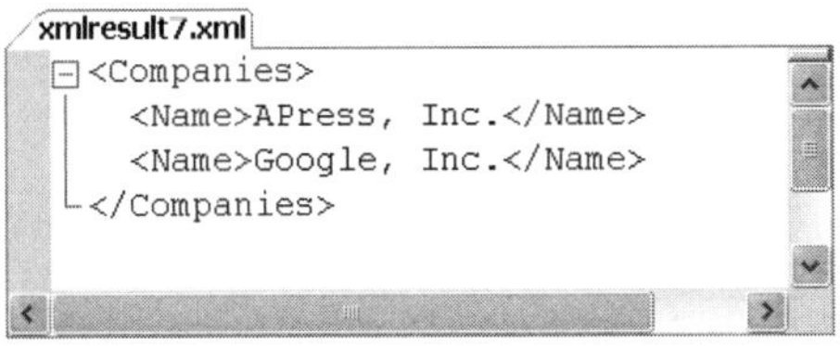

```
xmlresult7.xml
  <Companies>
     <Name>APress, Inc.</Name>
     <Name>Google, Inc.</Name>
  </Companies>
```

Figure 12-16. *Dynamic construction of XML with XQuery*

The direct constructor in the XQuery example looks like this:

```
<Companies>
    {
        //Info/Location/Name
    }
</Companies>
```

The `<Companies>` and `</Companies>` opening and closing tags in the direct constructor act as the root tag for the XML result. The opening and closing tags contain the *content expression,* which consists of the location path used to retrieve the nodes. The content expression is wrapped in curly braces between the `<Companies>` and `</Companies>` tags:

```
    {
        //Info/Location/Name
    }
```

■Tip If you need to output curly braces in your constructed XML result, you can escape them by doubling them up in your query using {{ and }}.

You can also use the `element`, `attribute`, and `text` computed constructors to build your XML result, as demonstrated in Listing 12-20, with the result shown in Figure 12-17.

Listing 12-20. *Element and Attribute Dynamic Constructors*

```
DECLARE @x xml = N'<?xml version = "1.0"?>
<Geocode>
    <Info ID = "1">
        <Location Type = "Business">
            <Name>APress, Inc.</Name>
            <Address>
                <Street>2560 Ninth St, Ste 219</Street>
                <City>Berkeley</City>
                <State>CA</State>
                <Zip>94710-2500</Zip>
                <Country>US</Country>
            </Address>
        </Location>
    </Info>
</Geocode>';

SELECT @x.query
(
  N'element Companies
  {
    element FirstCompany
```

```
    {
      attribute CompanyID
      {
        (//Info/@ID)[1]
      },
      (//Info/Location/Name)[1]
    }
  }'
);
```

Figure 12-17. *Results of the XQuery computed element construction*

The element `Companies` computed element constructor creates the root `Companies` node. The `FirstCompany` node is constructed as a child node using another element constructor:

```
element Companies
{
  element FirstCompany
  {
    ...
  }
}
```

The content expressions of the `FirstCompany` elements are where the real action takes place:

```
element FirstCompany
{
  attribute CompanyID
  {
      (//Info/@ID)[1]
  },
  (//Info/Location/Name)[1]
}
```

The `CompanyID` dynamic attribute constructor retrieves the `ID` attribute from the first `Info` node. The predicate [1] in the path ensures that only the first `//Info/@ID` is returned. This path location could also be written like this:

```
//Info[1]/@ID
```

The second path location retrieves the first Name node for the first Location node of the first Info node. Again, the [1] predicate ensures that only the first matching node is returned. The path is equivalent to the following:

```
//Info[1]/Location[1]/Name[1]
```

To retrieve the second node, change the predicate to [2], and so on.

Tip By definition, a predicate that evaluates to a numeric singleton value (such as the integer constant 1) is referred to as a *numeric predicate*. The effective Boolean value is true only when the context position is equal to the numeric predicate expression. When the numeric predicate is 3, for instance, the predicate truth value is true only for the third context position. This is a handy way to limit the results of an XQuery query to a single specific node.

XQuery Comments

XQuery comments (not to be confused with *XML comment nodes*) are used to document your queries inline. You can include them in XQuery expressions by enclosing them with the (: and :) symbols (just like the smiley face emoticon). Comments can be used in your XQuery expressions anywhere ignorable whitespace is allowed, and they can be nested. XQuery comments have no effect on query processing. The following example modifies the query in Listing 12-19 to include XQuery comments:

```
SELECT @x.query
(
  N'<Companies>  (: This is the root node :)
    {
      //Info/Location/Name (: Retrieves all company names (: ALL of them :) :)
    }
  </Companies>'
);
```

You will see XQuery comments used in some of the examples later in this chapter.

Data Types

XQuery maintains the string value and typed value for all nodes in the referenced XML. XQuery defines the string value of an element node as the concatenated string values of the element node and all its child element nodes. The type of a node is defined in the XML schema collection associated with the xml variable or column. As an example, the built-in AdventureWorks Production.ManuInstructionsSchemaCollection XML schema collection defines the LocationID attribute of the Location element as an xsd:integer:

```
<xsd:attribute name="LocationID" type="xsd:integer" use="required" />
```

Every instance of this attribute in the XML of the `Instructions` column of the `Production.ProductModel` table must conform to the requirements of this data type. Typed data can also be manipulated according to the functions and operators defined for this type. For untyped XML, the typed data is defined as `xdt:untypedAtomic`. A listing of XDM data types available to SQL Server via XQuery is given in Appendix B.

Predicates

An XQuery *predicate* is an expression that evaluates to one of the `xs:boolean` values `true` or `false`. In XQuery, predicates are used to filter the results of a node sequence, discarding nodes that don't meet the specified criteria from the results. Predicates limit the results by converting the result of the predicate expression into an `xs:boolean` value, referred to as the *predicate truth value*. The predicate truth value is determined for each item of the input sequence according to the following rules:

1. If the type of the expression is numeric, the predicate truth value is `true` if the value of the predicate expression is equal to the context position; otherwise for a numeric predicate, the predicate truth value is `false`.

2. If the type of the expression is a string, the predicate is `false` if the length of the expression is 0. For a string type expression with a length greater than 0, the predicate truth value is `true`.

3. If the type of the expression is `xs:boolean`, the predicate truth value is the value of the expression.

4. If the expression results in an empty sequence, the predicate truth value is `false`.

5. If the value of the predicate expression is a node sequence, the predicate truth value is `true` if the sequence contains at least one node; otherwise it is `false`.

Queries that include a predicate return only nodes in a sequence for which the predicate truth value evaluates to `true`. Predicates are composed of expressions, conveniently referred to as *predicate expressions*, enclosed in square brackets ([ ]). You can specify multiple predicates in a path, and they are evaluated in order of occurrence from left to right.

▌**Note** The XQuery specification says that multiple predicates are evaluated from left to right, but it also gives some wiggle room for vendors to perform predicate evaluations in other orders, allowing them to take advantage of vendor-specific features such as indexes and other optimizations. You don't have to worry too much about the internal evaluation order of predicates, though. No matter what order predicates are actually evaluated in, the end results have to be the same as if the predicates were evaluated left to right.

Value Comparison Operators

As I mentioned, the basic function of predicates is to filter results. Results are filtered by specified comparisons, and XQuery offers a rich set of comparison operators. These operators fall into three main categories: value comparison operators, general comparison operators, and node comparison operators. Value comparison operators compare singleton atomic values only. Trying to compare sequences with value comparison operators results in an error. The value comparison operators are listed in Table 12-4.

Table 12-4. *Value Comparison Operators*

Operator	Description
eq	Equal
ne	Not equal
lt	Less than
le	Less than or equal to
gt	Greater than
ge	Greater than or equal to

Value comparisons follow a specific set of rules:

1. The operands on the left and right sides of the operator are atomized.

2. If either atomized operand is an empty sequence, the result is an empty sequence.

3. If either atomized operand is a sequence with a length greater than 1, an error is raised.

4. If either atomized operand is of type xs:untypedAtomic, it is cast to xs:string.

5. If the operands have compatible types, they are compared using the appropriate operator. If the comparison of the two operands using the chosen operator evaluates to true, the result is true; otherwise the result is false. If the operands have incompatible types, an error is thrown.

Consider the value comparison examples in Listing 12-21, with results shown in Figure 12-18.

Listing 12-21. *Value Comparison Examples*

```
DECLARE @x xml = N'<?xml version = "1.0" ?>
<Animal>
    Cat
</Animal>';

SELECT @x.query(N'9 eq 9.0                    (: 9 is equal to 9.0 :)');
SELECT @x.query(N'4 gt 3                       (: 4 is greater than 3 :)');
SELECT @x.query(N'(/Animal/text())[1] lt "Dog" (: Cat is less than Dog :)') ;
```

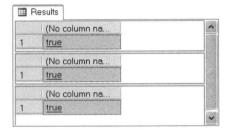

Figure 12-18. *Results of the XQuery value comparisons*

Listing 12-22 attempts to compare two values of incompatible types, namely an xs:decimal type value and an xs:string value. The result is the error message shown in the results following.

Listing 12-22. *Incompatible Type Value Comparison*

```
DECLARE @x xml = N'';

SELECT @x.query(N'3.141592 eq "Pi"') ;
```

```
Msg 2234, Level 16, State 1, Line 3
XQuery [query()]: The operator "eq" cannot be applied to "xs:decimal"
and "xs:string" operands.
```

General Comparison Operators

General comparisons are existential comparisons that work on operand sequences of any length. *Existential* simply means that if one atomized value from the first operand sequence fulfills a value comparison with at least one atomized value from the second operand sequence, the result is true. The general comparison operators will look familiar to programmers who are versed in other computer languages, particularly C-style languages. The general comparison operators are listed in Table 12-5.

Table 12-5. *General Comparison Operators*

Operator	Description
=	Equal
!=	Not equal
<	Less than
>	Greater than
<=	Less than or equal to
>=	Greater than or equal to

Listing 12-23 demonstrates comparisons using general comparisons on XQuery sequences. The results are shown in Figure 12-19.

Listing 12-23. *General Comparison Examples*

```
DECLARE @x xml = '';

SELECT @x.query('(3.141592, 1) = (2, 3.141592)                    (: true :) ');
SELECT @x.query('(1.0, 2.0, 3.0) = 1                              (: true :) ');
SELECT @x.query('("Joe", "Harold") < "Adam"                       (: false :) ');
SELECT @x.query('xs:date("1999-01-01") < xs:date("2006-01-01")    (: true :)');
```

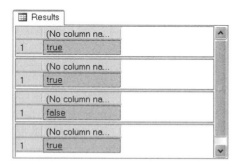

Figure 12-19. *General XQuery comparison results*

Here's how the general comparison operators work. The first query compares the sequences (3.141592, 1) and (2, 3.141592) using the = operator. The comparison atomizes the two operand sequences and compares them using the rules for the equivalent value comparison operators. Since the atomic value 3.141592 exists in both sequences, the equality test result is true.

The second example compares the sequence (1.0, 2.0, 3.0) to the atomic value 1. The atomic values 1.0 and 1 are compatible types and are equal, so the equality test result is true. The third query returns false because neither of the atomic values Joe or Harold are lexically less than the atomic value Adam.

The final example compares two xs:date values. Since the date 1999-01-01 is less than the date 2006-01-01, the result is true.

XQUERY DATE FORMAT

The XQuery implementation in SQL Server 2005 had a special requirement concerning xs:date, xs:time, xs:dateTime, and derived types. According to a subset of the ISO 8601 standard that SQL Server 2005 uses, date and time values had to include a mandatory time offset specifier. SQL Server 2008 does not strictly enforce this rule. When you leave the time offset information off an XQuery date or time value, SQL Server 2008 defaults to the zero meridian (Z specifier).

SQL Server 2008 also differs from SQL Server 2005 in how it handles time offset information. In SQL Server 2005, all dates were automatically *normalized* to coordinated universal time (UTC). SQL Server 2008 stores the time offset information you indicate when specifying a date or time value. If a time zone is provided, it must follow the date or time value, and can be either of the following:

- The capital letter *Z*, which stands for the *zero meridian*, or UTC. The zero meridian runs through Greenwich, England.

- An offset from the zero meridian in the format [+/–]hh:mm. For instance, the US Eastern Time zone would be indicated as –05:00.

Here are a few sample ISO 8601 formatted dates and times acceptable to SQL Server, with descriptions:

- *1999-05-16*: May 16, 1999, no time, UTC

- *09:15:00-05:00*: No date, 9:15 AM, US and Canada Eastern time

- *2003-12-25T20:00:00-08:00*: December 25, 2003, 8:00 PM, US and Canada Pacific time

- *2004-07-06T23:59:59.987+01:00*: July 6, 2004, 11:59:59.987 PM (.987 is fractional seconds), Central European time

Unlike the homogenous sequences in Listing 12-23, a heterogeneous sequence is one that combines nodes and atomic values, or atomic values of incompatible types (such as xs:string and xs:decimal). Trying to perform a general comparison with a heterogeneous sequence causes an error in SQL Server, as demonstrated by Listing 12-24.

Listing 12-24. *General Comparison with Heterogeneous Sequence*

```
DECLARE @x xml = '';

SELECT @x.query('(xs:date("2006-10-09"), 6.02E23) > xs:date("2007-01-01")');
```

The error generated by Listing 12-24 looks like the following:

```
Msg 9311, Level 16, State 1, Line 3
XQuery [query()]: Heterogeneous sequences are not allowed in '>', found
'xs:date' and 'xs:double'.
```

SQL Server also disallows heterogeneous sequences that mix nodes and atomic values, as demonstrated by Listing 12-25.

Listing 12-25. *Mixing Nodes and Atomic Values in Sequences*

```
DECLARE @x xml = '';

SELECT @x.query('(1, <myNode>Testing</myNode>)');
```

Trying to mix and match nodes and atomic values in a sequence like this results in an error message indicating that you tried to create a sequence consisting of atomic values and nodes, similar to the following:

```
Msg 2210, Level 16, State 1, Line 3
XQuery [query()]: Heterogeneous sequences are not allowed: found
'xs:integer' and 'element(myNode,xdt:untyped)'
```

Node Comparisons

The third type of comparison that XQuery allows is a *node comparison*. Node comparisons allow you to compare XML nodes in document order. The node comparison operators are listed in Table 12-6.

Table 12-6. *Node Comparison Operators*

Operator	Description
is	Node identity equality
<<	Left node precedes right node
>>	Left node follows right node

The is operator compares two nodes to each other and returns true if the left node is the same node as the right node. Note that this is not a test of the equality of node content but rather of the actual nodes themselves based on an internally generated node ID. Consider the sample node comparisons in Listing 12-26 with results shown in Figure 12-20.

Listing 12-26. *Node Comparison Samples*

```
DECLARE @x xml = N'<?xml version = "1.0"?>
<Root>
    <NodeA>Test Node</NodeA>
    <NodeA>Test Node</NodeA>
    <NodeB>Test Node</NodeB>
</Root>';

SELECT @x.query('((/Root/NodeA)[1] is (//NodeA)[1])           (: true :)');
SELECT @x.query('((/Root/NodeA)[1] is (/Root/NodeA)[2])       (: false :)');
SELECT @x.query('((/Root/NodeA)[2] << (/Root/NodeB)[1])       (: true :)');
```

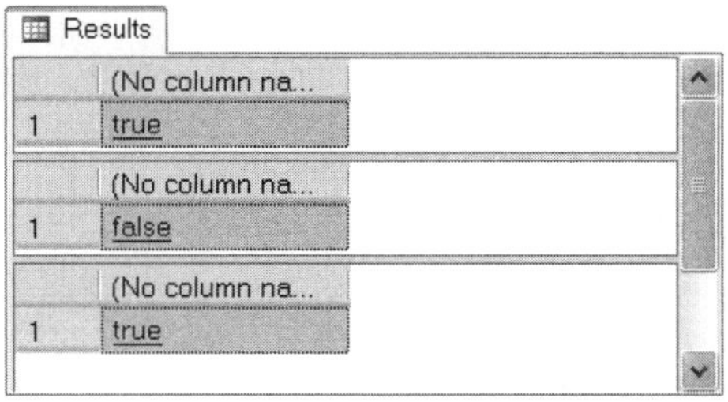

Figure 12-20. *Results of the XQuery node comparisons*

The first query uses the is operator to compare (/Root/NodeA)[1] to itself. The [1] numeric predicate at the end of the path ensures that only a single node is returned for comparison. The right-hand and left-hand expressions must both evaluate to a singleton or empty sequence. The result of this comparison is true only because (/Root/NodeA)[1] is the same node returned by the (//NodeA)[1] path on the right-hand side of the operator.

The second query compares (/Root/NodeA)[1] with (/Root/NodeA)[2]. Even though the two nodes have the same name and content, they are in fact different nodes. Because they are different nodes, the is operator returns false.

The final query retrieves the second NodeA node with the path (/Root/NodeA)[2]. Then it uses the << operator to determine if this node precedes the NodeB node from the path (/Root/NodeB)[1]. Since the second NodeA precedes NodeB in document order, the result of this comparison is true.

A node comparison results in an xs:boolean value or evaluates to an empty sequence if one of the operands results in an empty sequence. This is demonstrated in Listing 12-27.

Listing 12-27. *Node Comparison That Evaluates to an Empty Sequence*

```
DECLARE @x xml = N'<?xml version = "1.0"?>
<Root>
    <NodeA>Test Node</NodeA>
</Root>';

SELECT @x.query('((/Root/NodeA)[1] << (/Root/NodeZ)[1])   (: empty sequence :)');
```

The result of the node comparison is an empty sequence because the right-hand path expression evaluates to an empty sequence (because no node named NodeZ exists in the XML document).

Conditional Expressions (if...then...else)

As shown in the previous examples, XQuery returns xs:boolean values or empty sequences as the result of comparisons. XQuery also provides support for the conditional if...then...else expression. The if...then...else construct returns an expression based on the xs:boolean value of another expression. The format for the XQuery conditional expression is shown following:

```
if (test-expression)
then then-expression
else else-expression
```

In this syntax, *test-expression* represents the conditional expression that is evaluated, the result of which will determine the returned result. When evaluating *test-expression*, XQuery applies the following rules:

1. If *test-expression* results in an empty sequence, the result is false.

2. If *test-expression* results in an xs:boolean value, the result is the xs:boolean value of the expression.

3. If *test-expression* results in a sequence of one or more nodes, the result is true.

4. If these steps fail, a static error is raised.

If *test-expression* evaluates to true, *then-expression* is returned. If *test-expression* evaluates to false, *else-expression* is returned.

The XQuery conditional is a declarative expression. Unlike the C# if...else statement and Visual Basic's If...Then...Else construct, XQuery's conditional if...then...else doesn't represent a branch in procedural logic or a change in program flow. It acts like a function that accepts a conditional expression as input and returns an expression as a result. In this respect, XQuery's if...then...else has more in common with the SQL CASE expression and the C# ?: operator than the if statement in procedural languages. In the XQuery if...then...else, syntax parentheses are required around *test-expression*, and the else clause is mandatory.

Arithmetic Expressions

XQuery arithmetic expressions provide support for the usual suspects—standard mathematical operators found in most modern programming languages, including the following:

- Multiplication (*)

- Division (div)

- Addition (+)

- Subtraction (-)

- Modulo (mod)

INTEGER DIVISION IN XQUERY

SQL Server 2008 XQuery does not support the idiv integer division operator. Fortunately, the W3C XQuery recommendation defines the idiv operator as equivalent to the following div expression:

```
($arg1 div $arg2) cast as xs:integer?
```

If you need to convert XQuery code that uses idiv to SQL Server, you can use the div and cast operators as shown to duplicate idiv functionality.

XQuery also supports the unary plus (+) and unary minus (-) operators. Because the forward slash character is used as a path separator in XQuery, the division operator is specified using the keyword `div`. The modulo operator, `mod`, returns the remainder of division.

Of the supported operators, unary plus and unary minus have the highest precedence. Multiplication, division, and modulo are next. Binary addition and subtraction have the lowest precedence. Parentheses can be used to force the evaluation order of mathematical operations.

XQuery Functions

XQuery provides several built-in functions defined in the XQuery Functions and Operators specification (sometimes referred to as F&O), which is available at `www.w3.org/TR/xquery-operators/`. Built-in XQuery functions are in the predeclared namespace `fn`.

■**Tip** The `fn` namespace does not have to be specified when calling a built-in function. Some people leave it off to improve readability of their code.

I've listed the XQuery functions that SQL Server 2008 supports in Table 12-7.

Table 12-7. *Supported Built-In XQuery Functions*

Function	Description
`fn:avg(x)`	Returns the average of the sequence of numbers *x*. For example, `fn:avg( (10, 20, 30, 40, 50) )` returns 30.
`fn:ceiling(n)`	Returns the smallest number without a fractional part that is not less than *n*. For example, `fn:ceiling(1.1)` returns 2.
`fn:concat(s_1, s_2, ...)`	Concatenates zero or more strings and returns the concatenated string as a result. For example, `fn:concat("hi", ",", "how are you?")` returns "hi, how are you?".
`fn:contains(s_1, s_2)`	Returns true if the string s_1 contains the string s_2. For example, `fn:contains("fish", "is")` returns true.
`fn:count(x)`	Returns the number of items in the sequence *x*. For example, `fn:count( (1, 2, 4, 8, 16) )` returns 5.
`fn:data(a)`	Returns the typed value of each item specified by the argument *a*. For example, `fn:data( (3.141592, "hello") )` returns "3.141592 hello".
`fn:distinct-values(x)`	Returns the sequence *x* with duplicate values removed. For example, `fn:distinct-values( (1, 2, 3, 4, 5, 4, 5) )` returns "1 2 3 4 5".
`fn:empty(i)`	Returns true if *i* is an empty sequence; returns false otherwise. For example, `fn:empty( (1, 2, 3) )` returns false.
`fn:expanded-QName(u, l)`	Returns an `xs:QName`. The arguments *u* and *l* represent the `xs:QName`'s namespace URI and local name, respectively.
`fn:false()`	Returns the `xs:boolean` value false. For example, `fn:false()` returns false.

Continued

Table 12-7. *Continued*

Function	Description
fn:floor(*n*)	Returns the largest number without a fractional part that is not greater than *n*. For example, fn:floor(1.1) returns 1.
fn:id(*x*)	Returns the sequence of element nodes with ID values that match one or more of the IDREF values supplied in *x*. The parameter *x* is treated as a whitespace-separated sequence of tokens.
fn:last()	Returns the index number of the last item in the sequence being processed. The first index in the sequence has an index of 1.
fn:local-name(*n*)	Returns the local name, without the namespace URI, of the specified node *n*.
fn:local-name-from-QName(*q*)	Returns the local name part of the xs:QName argument *q*. The value returned is an xs:NCName.
fn:max(*x*)	Returns the item with the highest value from the sequence *x*. For example, fn:max((1.0, 2.5, 9.3, 0.3, -4.2)) returns 9.3.
fn:min(*x*)	Returns the item with the lowest value from the sequence *x*. For example, fn:min(("x", "q", "u", "e", "r", "y")) returns "e".
fn:namespace-uri(*n*)	Returns the namespace URI of the specified node *n*.
fn:namespace-uri-from-QName(*q*)	Returns the namespace URI part of the xs:QName argument *q*. The value returned is an xs:NCName.
fn:not(*b*)	Returns true if the effective Boolean value of *b* is false; returns false if the effective Boolean value is true. For example, fn:not(xs:boolean("true")) returns false.
fn:number(*n*)	Returns the numeric value of the node indicated by *n*. For example, fn:number("/Root/NodeA[1]").
fn:position()	Returns the index number of the context item in the sequence currently being processed.
fn:round(*n*)	Returns the number closest to *n* that does not have a fractional part. For example, fn:round(10.5) returns 11.
fn:string(*a*)	Returns the value of the argument *a*, expressed as an xs:string. For example, fn:string(3.141592) returns "3.141592".
fn:string-length(*s*)	Returns the length of the string *s*. For example, fn:string-length("abcdefghij") returns 10.
fn:substring(*s*, *m*, *n*)	Returns *n* characters from the string *s*, beginning at position *m*. If *n* is not specified, all characters from position *m* to the end of the string are returned. The first character in the string is position 1. For example, fn:substring("Money", 2, 3) returns "one".
fn:sum(*x*)	Returns the sum of the sequence of numbers in *x*. For example, fn:sum((1, 4, 9, 16, 25)) returns 55.
fn:true()	Returns the xs:boolean value true. For example, fn:true() returns true.

In addition, two functions from the `sql:` namespace are supported. The `sql:column` function allows you to expose and bind SQL Server relational column data in XQuery queries. This function accepts the name of a SQL column and exposes its values to your XQuery expressions. Listing 12-28 demonstrates the `sql:column` function.

Listing 12-28. *The sql:column Function*

```
DECLARE @x xml = N'';

SELECT @x.query(N'<Name>
    <ID>
      {
        sql:column("p.BusinessEntityID")
      }
    </ID>
    <FullName>
      {
        sql:column("p.FirstName"),
        sql:column("p.MiddleName"),
        sql:column("p.LastName")
      }
    </FullName>
</Name>')
FROM Person.Person p
WHERE p.BusinessEntityID <= 5
ORDER BY p.BusinessEntityID;
```

The result of this example, shown in Figure 12-21, is a set of XML documents containing the `BusinessEntityID` and full name of the first five contacts from the `Person.Person` table.

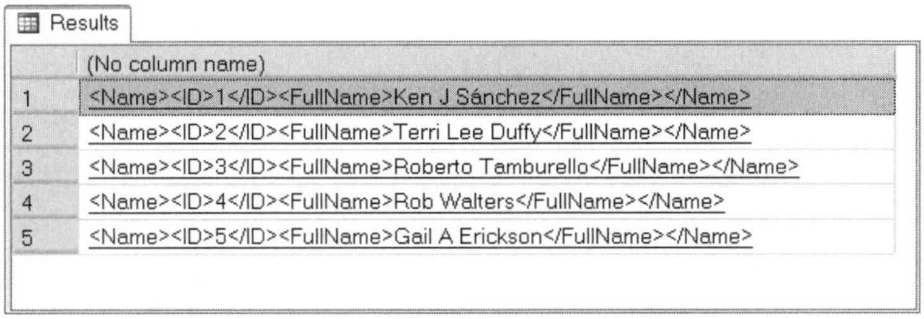

	(No column name)
1	`<Name><ID>1</ID><FullName>Ken J Sánchez</FullName></Name>`
2	`<Name><ID>2</ID><FullName>Terri Lee Duffy</FullName></Name>`
3	`<Name><ID>3</ID><FullName>Roberto Tamburello</FullName></Name>`
4	`<Name><ID>4</ID><FullName>Rob Walters</FullName></Name>`
5	`<Name><ID>5</ID><FullName>Gail A Erickson</FullName></Name>`

Figure 12-21. *Results of the sql:column function query*

The `sql:variable` function goes another step, allowing you to expose T-SQL variables to XQuery. This function accepts the name of a T-SQL variable and allows you to access its value in your XQuery expressions. Listing 12-29 is an example that combines the `sql:column` and `sql:variable` functions in a single XQuery query.

Listing 12-29. *XQuery sql:column and sql:variable Functions Example*

```
/* 10% discount */
DECLARE @discount NUMERIC(3, 2);
SELECT @discount = 0.10;
DECLARE @x xml;
SELECT @x = '';
SELECT @x.query('<Product>
    <Model-ID> { sql:column("ProductModelID") }</Model-ID>
        <Name> { sql:column("Name") }</Name>
        <Price> { sql:column("ListPrice") } </Price>
        <DiscountPrice>
            { sql:column("ListPrice") -
            (sql:column("ListPrice") * sql:variable("@discount") ) }
        </DiscountPrice>
</Product>
')
FROM Production.Product p
WHERE ProductModelID = 30;
```

The XQuery generates XML documents using the sql:column function to retrieve the ListPrice from the Production.Product table. It also uses the sql:variable function to calculate a discount price for the items retrieved. Figure 12-22 shows partial results of this query (formatted for easier reading):

Figure 12-22. *Partial results of the query with the sql:column and sql:variable functions*

Constructors and Casting

The XDM provides constructor functions to dynamically create instances of several supported types. The constructor functions are all in the format xs:TYP(*value*), where TYP is the XDM type name. Most of the XDM data types have constructor functions; however, the following types do not have constructors in SQL Server XQuery: xs:yearMonthDuration, xs:dayTimeDuration, xs:QName, xs:NMTOKEN, and xs:NOTATION.

The following are examples of XQuery constructor functions:

```
xs:boolean("1")        (: returns true :)
xs:integer(1234)       (: returns 1234 :)
xs:float(9.8723E+3)    (: returns 9872.3 :)
xs:NCName("my-id")     (: returns the NCName "my-id" :)
```

Numeric types can be implicitly cast to their base types (or other numeric types) by XQuery to ensure proper results of calculations. The process of implicit casting is known as *type promotion*. For instance, in the following sample expression, the xs:integer type value is promoted to a xs:decimal to complete the calculation:

```
xs:integer(100) + xs:decimal(100.99)
```

■**Note** Only numeric types can be implicitly cast. String and other types cannot be implicitly cast by XQuery.

Explicit casting is performed using the cast as keywords. Examples of explicit casting include the following:

```
xs:string("98d3f4") cast as xs:hexBinary?  (: 98d3f4 :)
100 cast as xs:double?                     (: 1.0E+2 :)
"0" cast as xs:boolean?                     (: true :)
```

The ? after the target data type is the *optional occurrence indicator*. It is used to indicate that an empty sequence is allowed. SQL Server XQuery requires the ? after the cast as expression. SQL Server BOL provides a detailed description of the XQuery type casting rules at http://msdn2.microsoft.com/en-us/library/ms191231(SQL.100).aspx.

The instance of Boolean operator allows you to determine the type of a singleton value. This operator takes a singleton value on its left side and a type on its right. The xs:boolean value true is returned if the atomic value represents an instance of the specified type. The following examples demonstrate the instance of operator:

```
10 instance of xs:integer        (: returns true :)
100 instance of xs:decimal       (: returns true :)
"hello" instance of xs:bytes     (: returns false :)
```

The ? optional occurrence indicator can be appended after the data type to indicate that the empty sequence is allowable (though it is not mandatory, as with the cast as operator), as in this example:

```
9.8273 instance of xs:double?  (: returns true :)
```

FLWOR Expressions

FLWOR expressions provide a way to iterate over a sequence and bind intermediate results to variables. *FLWOR* is an acronym for the keywords that define this type of expression: for, let, where, order by, and return. This section discusses XQuery's powerful FLWOR expressions.

The for and return Keywords

The for and return keywords have long been a part of XPath, though in not nearly so powerful a form as the XQuery FLWOR expression. The for keyword specifies that a variable is iteratively bound to the results of the specified path expression. The result of this iterative binding process is known as a *tuple stream*. The XQuery for expression is roughly analogous to the T-SQL SELECT statement. The for keyword must, at a minimum, have a matching return clause after it. The sample in Listing 12-30 demonstrates a basic for expression.

Listing 12-30. *Basic XQuery for...return Expression*

```
SELECT CatalogDescription.query(N'declare namespace ns =
  "http://schemas.microsoft.com/sqlserver/2004/07/adventure-➥
    works/ProductModelDescription";
  for $spec in //ns:ProductDescription/ns:Specifications/*
  return fn:string($spec)') AS Description
FROM Production.ProductModel
WHERE ProductModelID = 19;
```

The for clause iterates through all elements returned by the path expression. It then binds the elements to the $spec variable. The tuple stream that is bound to $spec consists of the following nodes in document order:

```
$spec = <Material>Almuminum Alloy</Material>
$spec = <Color>Available in most colors</Color>
$spec = <ProductLine>Mountain bike</ProductLine>
$spec = <Style>Unisex</Style>
$spec = <RiderExperience>Advanced to Professional riders</RiderExperience>
```

The return clause applies the fn:string function to the $spec variable to return the string value of each node as it is bound. The results look like the following:

```
Almuminum Alloy Available in most colors Mountain bike Unisex
Advanced to Professional riders
```

The sample can be modified to return an XML result, using the techniques described previously in the "Dynamic XML Construction" section. Listing 12-31 demonstrates with results shown in Figure 12-23.

Listing 12-31. *XQuery for...return Expression with XML Result*

```
SELECT CatalogDescription.query
(
```

```
N'declare namespace ns =
"http://schemas.microsoft.com/sqlserver/2004/07/adventure-➥
  works/ProductModelDescription";
for $spec in //ns:ProductDescription/ns:Specifications/*
return <detail>
  {
    $spec/text()
  }
</detail>'
) AS Description
FROM Production.ProductModel
WHERE ProductModelID = 19;
```

```
Description4.xml*
    <detail>Almuminum Alloy</detail>
    <detail>Available in most colors</detail>
    <detail>Mountain bike</detail>
    <detail>Unisex</detail>
    <detail>Advanced to Professional riders</detail>
```

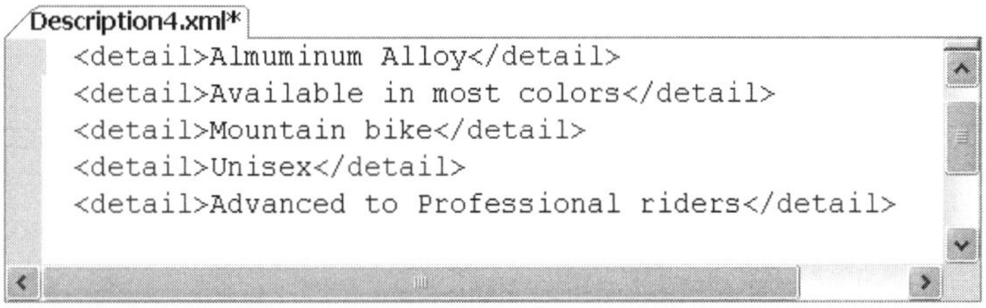

Figure 12-23. *Results of the for...return expression with XML construction*

XQuery allows you to bind multiple variables in the for clause. When you bind multiple variables, the result is the Cartesian product of all possible values of the variables. SQL Server programmers will recognize the Cartesian product as being equivalent to the SQL CROSS JOIN operator. Listing 12-32 modifies the previous example further to generate the Cartesian product of the Specifications and Warranty child node text.

Listing 12-32. *XQuery Cartesian Product with for Expression*

```
SELECT CatalogDescription.query(N'declare namespace ns =
  "http://schemas.microsoft.com/sqlserver/2004/07/adventure-➥
    works/ProductModelDescription";
  for $spec in //ns:ProductDescription/ns:Specifications/*,
      $feat in //ns:ProductDescription/*:Features/*:Warranty/node()
  return <detail>
    {
      $spec/text()
    } +
    {
      fn:string($feat/.)
    }
  </detail>'
) AS Description
FROM Production.ProductModel
WHERE ProductModelID = 19;
```

The $spec variable is bound to the same nodes shown previously. A second variable binding, for the variable $feat, is added to the for clause in this example. Specifically, this second variable is bound to the child nodes of the Warranty element, as shown following:

```
<p1:WarrantyPeriod>3 years</p1:WarrantyPeriod>
<p1:Description>parts and labor</p1:Description>
```

The Cartesian product of the text nodes of these two tuple streams consists of ten possible combinations. The final result of the XQuery expression is shown in Figure 12-24 (formatted for easier reading).

```
Description6.xml*
    <detail>Almuminum Alloy + 3 years</detail>
    <detail>Almuminum Alloy + parts and labor</detail>
    <detail>Available in most colors + 3 years</detail>
    <detail>Available in most colors + parts and labor</detail>
    <detail>Mountain bike + 3 years</detail>
    <detail>Mountain bike + parts and labor</detail>
    <detail>Unisex + 3 years</detail>
    <detail>Unisex + parts and labor</detail>
    <detail>Advanced to Professional riders + 3 years</detail>
    <detail>Advanced to Professional riders + parts and labor</detail>
```

Figure 12-24. *Cartesian product XQuery*

A bound variable can be used immediately after it is bound, even in the same for clause. Listing 12-33 demonstrates this.

Listing 12-33. *Using a Bound Variable in the for Clause*

```
SELECT CatalogDescription.query
(
  N'declare namespace ns =
  "http://schemas.microsoft.com/sqlserver/2004/07/adventure-➥
    works/ProductModelDescription";
  for $spec in //ns:ProductDescription/ns:Specifications,
      $color in $spec/Color
  return <color>
    {
      $color/text()
    }
  </color>'
) AS Color
FROM Production.ProductModel
WHERE ProductModelID = 19;
```

In this example, the $spec variable is bound to the Specifications node. It is then used in the same for clause to bind a value to the variable $color. The result is shown in Figure 12-25.

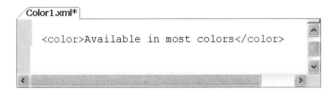

Figure 12-25. *Binding a variable to another bound variable in the for clause*

The where Keyword

The where keyword specifies an optional clause to filter tuples generated by the for clause. The expression in the where clause is evaluated for each tuple, and those for which the effective Boolean value evaluates to false are discarded from the final result. Listing 12-34 demonstrates use of the where clause to limit the results to only those tuples that contain the letter *A*. The results are shown in Figure 12-26.

Listing 12-34. *where Clause Demonstration*

```
SELECT CatalogDescription.query
(
  N'declare namespace ns =
  "http://schemas.microsoft.com/sqlserver/2004/07/adventure-➡
    works/ProductModelDescription";
  for $spec in //ns:ProductDescription/ns:Specifications/*
  where $spec[ contains( . , "A" ) ]
  return <detail>
    {
      $spec/text()
    }
  </detail>'
) AS Detail
FROM Production.ProductModel
WHERE ProductModelID = 19;
```

```
Detail1.xml*
    <detail>Almuminum Alloy</detail>
    <detail>Available in most colors</detail>
    <detail>Advanced to Professional riders</detail>
```

Figure 12-26. *Results of a FLWOR expression with the where clause*

The functions and operators described previously in this chapter (such as the contains function used in the example) can be used in the where clause expression to limit results as required by your application.

The order by Keywords

The order by clause is an optional clause of the FLWOR statement. The order by clause reorders the tuple stream generated by the for clause, using criteria that you specify. The order by criteria consists of one or more ordering specifications that are made up of an expression and an optional order modifier. Ordering specifications are evaluated from left to right.

The optional order modifier is either ascending or descending to indicate the direction of ordering. The default is ascending, as shown in Listing 12-35. The sample uses the order by clause to sort the results in descending (reverse) order. The results are shown in Figure 12-27.

Listing 12-35. *order by Clause*

```
SELECT CatalogDescription.query(N'declare namespace ns =
    "http://schemas.microsoft.com/sqlserver/2004/07/adventure-works/➥
        ProductModelDescription";
    for $spec in //ns:ProductDescription/ns:Specifications/*
    order by $spec/. descending
    return <detail> { $spec/text() } </detail>') AS Detail
FROM Production.ProductModel
WHERE ProductModelID = 19;
```

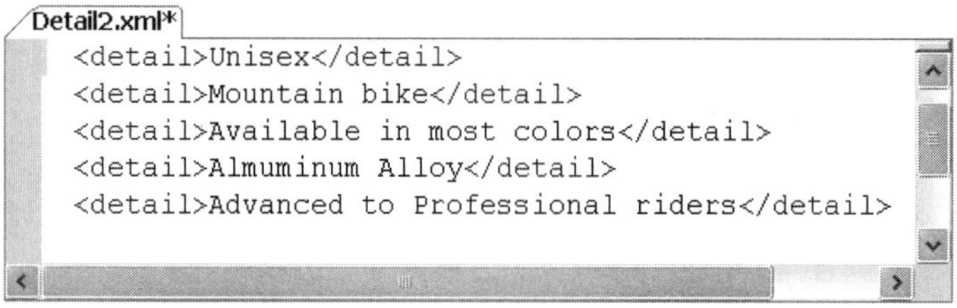

```
Detail2.xml*
    <detail>Unisex</detail>
    <detail>Mountain bike</detail>
    <detail>Available in most colors</detail>
    <detail>Almuminum Alloy</detail>
    <detail>Advanced to Professional riders</detail>
```

Figure 12-27. *Results of a FLWOR expression with the order by clause*

The let Keyword

SQL Server 2008 adds support for the FLWOR expression let clause. The let clause allows you to bind tuple streams to variables inside the body of the FLWOR expression. You can use the let clause to name repeating expressions. SQL Server XQuery inserts the expression assigned to the bound variable everywhere the variable is referenced in the FLWOR expression. Listing 12-36 demonstrates the let clause in a FLWOR expression, with results shown in Figure 12-28.

Listing 12-36. *let Clause*

```
SELECT CatalogDescription.query
(
  N'declare namespace ns =
  "http://schemas.microsoft.com/sqlserver/2004/07/adventure-➥
    works/ProductModelDescription";
  for $spec in //ns:ProductDescription/ns:Specifications/*
  let $val := $spec/text()
  order by fn:string($val[1]) ascending
  return <spec>
    {
      $val
    }
  </spec>'
) AS Detail
FROM Production.ProductModel
WHERE ProductModelID = 19;
```

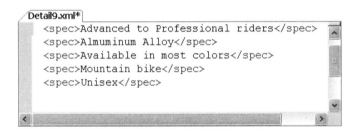

Figure 12-28. *Results of a FLWOR expression with the let clause*

Summary

This chapter has expanded the discussion of SQL Server XML functionality that I began in Chapter 11. In particular, I focused on the SQL Server implementations of XPath and XQuery. I provided a more detailed discussion of the SQL Server FOR XML PATH clause XPath implementation, including XPath expression syntax, axis specifiers, and supported node tests. I also discussed SQL Server support for XML namespaces via the WITH XMLNAMESPACES clause.

I used the majority of this chapter to detail SQL Server support for XQuery, which provides a powerful set of expression types, functions, operators, and support for the rich XDM data type system. SQL Server support for XQuery has improved with the release of SQL Server 2008, including new options like the FLWOR expression let clause and support for date and time literals without specifying explicit time offsets.

The next chapter discusses SQL Server 2008 catalog views and dynamic management views and functions that provide a way to look under the hood of your databases and server instances.

EXERCISES

1. [True/false] The FOR XML PATH clause supports a subset of the W3C XPath recommendation.

2. [Choose one] Which of the following symbols is used in XQuery and XPath as an axis specifier to identify XML attributes:

    a.   An at sign (@)

    b.   An exclamation point (!)

    c.   A period (.)

    d.   Two periods (..)

3. [Fill in the blanks] The context item, indicated by a single period (.) in XPath and XQuery, specifies the current ___ or scalar ___ being accessed at any given point in time during query execution.

4. [Choose all that apply] You can declare namespaces for XQuery expressions in SQL Server using which of the following methods:

    a.   The T-SQL WITH XMLNAMESPACES clause

    b.   The XQuery declare default element namespace statement

    c.   The T-SQL CREATE XML NAMESPACE statement

    d.   The XQuery declare namespace statement

5. [Fill in the blanks] In XQuery, you can dynamically construct XML via ___ constructors or ___ constructors.

6. [True/false] SQL Server 2008 supports the for, let, where, order by, and return clauses of XQuery FLWOR expressions.

7. [Choose all that apply] SQL Server supports the following types of XQuery comparison operators:

    a.   Array comparison operators

    b.   General comparison operators

    c.   Node comparison operators

    d.   Value comparison operators

■ ■ ■

CHAPTER 13

Catalog Views and Dynamic Management Views

SQL Server has always offered access to metadata describing your databases, tables, views, and other database objects. Prior to the introduction of catalog views in SQL Server 2005, the primary methods of accessing this metadata included system tables, system SPs, INFORMATION_SCHEMA views, and SQL Distributed Management Objects (SQL-DMO). Catalog views provide access to a richer set of detailed information than any one of these options provided in previous SQL Server releases. SQL Server even includes catalog views that allow you to access server-wide configuration metadata.

■Note *Metadata* is simply data that describes data. SQL Server 2008 databases are largely "self-describing." The data describing the objects, structures, and relationships that comprise a database are stored within the database itself. This data describing the database structure and objects is what we refer to as metadata.

SQL Server 2008 also provides dynamic management views (DMVs) and dynamic management functions (DMFs) that allow you to access server state information. The SQL Server DMVs and DMFs provide a relational tabular view of internal SQL Server data structures that would be otherwise inaccessible. Examples of metadata that can be accessed include information about the state of internal memory structures, the contents of caches and buffers, and statuses of processes and components. You can use the information returned by DMVs and DMFs to diagnose server problems, monitor server health, and tune performance. In this chapter, I'll discuss catalog views, DMVs, and DMFs.

Catalog Views

Catalog views provide insight into database objects and server-wide configuration options in much the same way that system tables, system SPs, and INFORMATION_SCHEMA views did in previous releases of SQL Server. Catalog views offer advantages over these older methods of accessing database and server metadata, including the following:

- Catalog views, unlike system SPs, can be used in queries with results joined to other catalog views or tables. You can also limit the results returned by catalog views with a WHERE clause.

- Catalog views offer SQL Server–specific information not available through the INFORMATION_SCHEMA views.

- Catalog views provide richer information than system tables. There are also more catalog views available than legacy system tables.

Tip SQL Server 2008 includes support for the old-style INFORMATION_SCHEMA views, compatibility views, and even some system SPs. Microsoft recommends that you use catalog views to access SQL Server metadata instead of these other methods. Many of the system SPs, for instance, have been deprecated and will be removed in a future version of SQL Server.

Many catalog views follow an inheritance model in which some catalog views are defined as extensions to other catalog views. The sys.tables catalog view, for instance, inherits columns from the sys.objects catalog view. Some catalog views, such as sys.all_columns, are defined as the union of two other catalog views. In this example, the sys.all_columns catalog view is defined as the union of the sys.columns and sys.system_columns catalog views.

SQL Server supplies a wide range of catalog views that return metadata about all different types of database objects and server configuration options, SQL CLR assemblies, XML schema collections, the SQL Server resource governor, change tracking, and more. Rather than give a complete list of all the available catalog views, I'm going to use this section to provide some usage examples and descriptions of the functionality available through catalog views.

Tip BOL details the complete list of available catalog views (there are over 100 of them) at http://msdn.microsoft.com/en-us/library/ms174365(SQL.100).aspx.

Table and Column Metadata

Way back in the pre–SQL Server Integration Services (SSIS) days, I spent a good deal of my time creating custom ETL (extract, transform, and load) solutions. One of the problems I faced was the quirky nature of the various bulk copy APIs available. Unlike SQL Server DML statements like INSERT, which specify columns to populate by name, the available bulk copy APIs require you to specify columns to populate by their ordinal position. This can lead to all kinds of problems if the table structure changes (e.g., if new columns are added, columns are removed, or the order of existing columns is changed). One way to deal with this type of disconnect is to create your own column name-to-ordinal position-mapping function. You can use catalog views to access exactly this type of functionality. In Listing 13-1, I join the sys.schemas, sys.tables, sys.columns, and sys.types catalog views to return column-level metadata about the AdventureWorks Person.Address table. The results are shown in Figure 13-1.

Listing 13-1. *Retrieving Column-Level Metadata with Catalog Views*

```
SELECT
  s.name AS schema_name,
  t.name AS table_name,
  t.type_desc AS table_type,
  c.name AS column_name,
  c.column_id,
  ty.name AS data_type_name,
  c.max_length,
  c.precision,
  c.scale,
  c.is_nullable
FROM sys.schemas s
INNER JOIN sys.tables t
  ON s.schema_id = t.schema_id
INNER JOIN sys.columns c
  ON t.object_id = c.object_id
INNER JOIN sys.types ty
  ON c.system_type_id = ty.system_type_id
    AND c.user_type_id = ty.user_type_id
WHERE s.name = 'Person'
  AND t.name = 'Address';
```

Results

	schema_name	table_name	table_type	column_name	column_id	data_type_name	max_length	precision	scale	is_nullable
1	Person	Address	USER_TABLE	AddressID	1	int	4	10	0	0
2	Person	Address	USER_TABLE	AddressLine1	2	nvarchar	120	0	0	0
3	Person	Address	USER_TABLE	AddressLine2	3	nvarchar	120	0	0	1
4	Person	Address	USER_TABLE	City	4	nvarchar	60	0	0	0
5	Person	Address	USER_TABLE	StateProvinceID	5	int	4	10	0	0
6	Person	Address	USER_TABLE	PostalCode	6	nvarchar	30	0	0	0
7	Person	Address	USER_TABLE	SpatialLocation	7	geography	-1	0	0	1
8	Person	Address	USER_TABLE	rowguid	8	uniqueidentifier	16	0	0	0
9	Person	Address	USER_TABLE	ModifiedDate	9	datetime	8	23	3	0

Figure 13-1. *Retrieving column-level metadata*

This type of metadata is also useful for administrative applications or dynamic queries that need to run against several different tables for which you don't necessarily know the structure in advance.

Whether it's for administrative applications, bulk loading, or dynamic queries that need to run against several different tables, SQL Server catalog views can provide structure and attribute information for database objects. SQL Server 2008 provides several methods of retrieving metadata.

Index Metadata

SQL Server metadata is useful for performing tedious administrative tasks, like identifying potential performance issues, updating statistics, and rebuilding indexes. Listing 13-2 uses catalog views to identify all tables in the AdventureWorks database with clustered or nonclustered indexes defined on them. The procedure then generates T-SQL ALTER INDEX statements to rebuild all the indexes defined on these tables. I've kept this example fairly simple, although it can be used as a basis for more complex index-rebuilding procedures that make decisions based on various factors like the current levels of index fragmentation and density. Figure 13-2 shows the ALTER INDEX statements created by the procedure.

Listing 13-2. *Stored Procedure to Rebuild Table Indexes*

```
CREATE PROCEDURE dbo.RebuildIndexes
AS
BEGIN
  SET NOCOUNT ON;

  CREATE TABLE #table_list
  (
    id int NOT NULL IDENTITY (1, 1) PRIMARY KEY,
    [schema_name] sysname,
    [table_name] sysname
  );

  INSERT INTO #table_list
  (
    [schema_name],
    [table_name]
  )
  SELECT DISTINCT
    SCHEMA_NAME(t.schema_id) AS [schema_name],
    t.name AS [table_name]
  FROM sys.tables t
  INNER JOIN sys.indexes i
    ON t.object_id = i.object_id
  WHERE t.type_desc = 'USER_TABLE'
    AND i.type_desc IN ('CLUSTERED', 'NONCLUSTERED');

  DECLARE @id int =
  (
    SELECT MIN(id)
    FROM #table_list
  );

  DECLARE @sqlcmd nvarchar(max);
```

```
WHILE (@id IS NOT NULL)
BEGIN

    SELECT @sqlcmd = 'ALTER INDEX ALL ON [' + [schema_name] + '].[' +
      [table_name] + '] REBUILD;'
    FROM #table_list
    WHERE id = @id;

    PRINT @sqlcmd;

    EXEC (@sqlcmd);

    SELECT @id = MIN(id)
    FROM #table_list
    WHERE id > @id;

  END;

  SELECT
    id,
    [schema_name],
    [table_name]
  FROM #table_list;

  DROP TABLE #table_list;
END
GO

EXEC dbo.RebuildIndexes;
GO
```

```
 Messages
ALTER INDEX ALL ON [HumanResources].[EmployeeDepartmentHistory] REBUILD;
ALTER INDEX ALL ON [HumanResources].[EmployeePayHistory] REBUILD;
ALTER INDEX ALL ON [HumanResources].[JobCandidate] REBUILD;
ALTER INDEX ALL ON [HumanResources].[Shift] REBUILD;
ALTER INDEX ALL ON [Person].[Address] REBUILD;
ALTER INDEX ALL ON [Person].[AddressType] REBUILD;
ALTER INDEX ALL ON [Person].[BusinessEntity] REBUILD;
ALTER INDEX ALL ON [Person].[BusinessEntityAddress] REBUILD;
ALTER INDEX ALL ON [Person].[BusinessEntityContact] REBUILD;
ALTER INDEX ALL ON [Person].[ContactType] REBUILD;
ALTER INDEX ALL ON [Person].[CountryRegion] REBUILD;
ALTER INDEX ALL ON [Person].[EmailAddress] REBUILD;
ALTER INDEX ALL ON [Person].[Password] REBUILD;
ALTER INDEX ALL ON [Person].[Person] REBUILD;
ALTER INDEX ALL ON [Person].[PersonPhone] REBUILD;
```

Figure 13-2. *ALTER INDEX statements to rebuild indexes on AdventureWorks tables*

The procedure in Listing 13-2 uses the sys.tables and sys.indexes catalog views to retrieve a list of all tables in the database that have a clustered or nonclustered index defined on them:

```
INSERT INTO #table_list
(
  [schema_name],
  [table_name]
)
SELECT DISTINCT
  SCHEMA_NAME(t.schema_id) AS [schema_name],
  t.name AS [table_name]
FROM sys.tables t
INNER JOIN sys.indexes i
  ON t.object_id = i.object_id
WHERE t.type_desc = 'USER_TABLE'
  AND i.type_desc IN ('CLUSTERED', 'NONCLUSTERED');

DECLARE @id int =
(
  SELECT MIN(id)
  FROM #table_list
);
```

The procedure then uses a simple WHILE loop to iterate through the table names and dynamically generate and execute ALTER INDEX ALL statements for each table:

```
WHILE (@id IS NOT NULL)
BEGIN

  SELECT @sqlcmd = 'ALTER INDEX ALL ON [' + [schema_name] + '].[' +
    [table_name] + '] REBUILD;'
  FROM #table_list
  WHERE id = @id;

  PRINT @sqlcmd;

  EXEC (@sqlcmd);

  SELECT @id = MIN(id)
  FROM #table_list
  WHERE id > @id;

END;
```

Querying Permissions

Another administrative task that can be performed through catalog views is querying and scripting database object permissions. Listing 13-3 begins this demonstration by creating a couple of new users named `jack` and `jill` in the AdventureWorks database. The `jill` user is assigned permissions to human resources–related objects, while `jack` is assigned permissions to production objects.

Listing 13-3. *Creating the jack and jill Users*

```
CREATE USER jill
WITHOUT LOGIN;

CREATE USER jack
WITHOUT LOGIN;

GRANT SELECT, INSERT
ON Schema::HumanResources TO jill;

GRANT SELECT
ON dbo.ufnGetContactInformation TO jill;

GRANT EXECUTE
ON HumanResources.uspUpdateEmployeeLogin TO jill;

DENY SELECT
ON Schema::Sales TO jill;

DENY SELECT
ON HumanResources.Shift (ModifiedDate) TO jill;

GRANT SELECT, UPDATE, INSERT, DELETE
ON Schema::Production TO jack WITH GRANT OPTION;
```

I've granted and denied permissions to these users on a wide selection of objects for demonstration purposes. The query in Listing 13-4 is a modified version of an example first published by SQL Server MVP Louis Davidson. The code uses the `sys.database_permissions`, `sys.database_principals`, and `sys.objects` catalog views to query the permissions granted and denied to database principals within the database. The results are shown in Figure 13-3.

Listing 13-4. *Querying Permissions on AdventureWorks Objects*

```
WITH Permissions
(
  permission,
  type,
  obj_name,
  db_principal,
  grant_type,
  schema_name
)
AS
```

```
(
  SELECT dp.permission_name,
    CASE dp.class_desc
      WHEN 'OBJECT_OR_COLUMN' THEN
        CASE
          WHEN minor_id > 0 THEN 'COLUMN'
          ELSE o.type_desc
        END
        ELSE dp.class_desc
      END,
    CASE dp.class_desc
      WHEN 'SCHEMA' THEN SCHEMA_NAME(dp.major_id)
      WHEN 'OBJECT_OR_COLUMN' THEN
        CASE
          WHEN dp.minor_id = 0 THEN object_name(dp.major_id)
          ELSE
            (
              SELECT object_name(o.object_id) + '.'+ c.name
              FROM sys.columns c
              WHERE c.object_id = dp.major_id
                AND c.column_id = dp.minor_id
            )
        END
        ELSE '**UNKNOWN**'
      END,
    dpr.name,
    dp.state_desc,
    SCHEMA_NAME(o.schema_id)
  FROM sys.database_permissions dp
  INNER JOIN sys.database_principals dpr
    ON dp.grantee_principal_id = dpr.principal_id
  LEFT JOIN sys.objects o
    ON o.object_id = dp.major_id
  WHERE dp.major_id > 0
)
SELECT
  p.permission,
  CASE type
    WHEN 'SCHEMA' THEN 'Schema::' + obj_name
    ELSE schema_name + '.' + obj_name
  END AS name,
  p.type,
  p.db_principal,
  p.grant_type
FROM Permissions p
```

```
ORDER BY
  p.db_principal,
  p.permission;
GO
```

	permission	name	type	db_princi...	grant_type
1	DELETE	Schema::Production	SCHEMA	jack	GRANT_WITH_GRANT_...
2	INSERT	Schema::Production	SCHEMA	jack	GRANT_WITH_GRANT_...
3	SELECT	Schema::Production	SCHEMA	jack	GRANT_WITH_GRANT_...
4	UPDATE	Schema::Production	SCHEMA	jack	GRANT_WITH_GRANT_...
5	EXECUTE	HumanResources.uspUpdateEmployeeLogin	SQL_STORED_PROCEDURE	jill	GRANT
6	INSERT	Schema::HumanResources	SCHEMA	jill	GRANT
7	SELECT	Schema::HumanResources	SCHEMA	jill	GRANT
8	SELECT	HumanResources.Shift.ModifiedDate	COLUMN	jill	DENY
9	SELECT	dbo.ufnGetContactInformation	SQL_TABLE_VALUED_FU...	jill	GRANT
10	SELECT	Schema::Sales	SCHEMA	jill	DENY

Figure 13-3. *Results of the permissions query*

As you can see in Figure 13-3, the query retrieves the explicit permissions granted and denied to the jack and jill database principals. These permissions are shown for each object along with information about the objects themselves. This simple example can be expanded to perform additional tasks, such as scripting object permissions.

■**Tip** *Explicit permissions* are permissions explicitly granted or denied through T-SQL GRANT, DENY, and REVOKE statements. The effective permissions of a principal are a combination of the principal's explicit permissions, permissions inherited from the roles or groups to which the principal belongs, and permissions implied by other permissions. You can use the sys.fn_my_permissions system function to view your effective permissions.

Dynamic Management Views and Functions

In addition to catalog views, SQL Server provides over 80 DMVs and DMFs that give you access to internal server state information. DMVs and DMFs are designed specifically for the benefit of database administrators (DBAs), but they can provide developers with extremely useful insights into the internal workings of SQL Server as well. Having access to this server state information can enhance the server management and administration experience, and help to identify potential problems and performance issues (for which developers are increasingly sharing responsibility).

SQL Server provides DMVs and DMFs that are scoped at the database level and at the server level. All DMVs and DMFs are in the sys schema, and their names all start with dm_*. There are several categories of DMVs and DMFs, with most being grouped together using standard name prefixes. I've listed some of the most commonly used categories in Table 13-1.

Table 13-1. *Commonly Used DMV and DMF Categories*

Names	Description
sys.dm_cdc_*	Contains information about Change Data Capture (CDC) transactions and log sessions
sys.dm_exec_*	Returns information related to user code execution
sys.dm_fts_*	Retrieves information about integrated Full-Text Search (iFTS) functionality
sys.dm_os_*	Displays low-level details such as locks, memory usage, and scheduling
sys.dm_trans_*	Provides information about current transactions and lock resources
sys.dm_io_*	Allows you to monitor network and disk I/O
sys.dm_db_*	Returns information about databases and database-level objects

I gave an example of DMV and DMF usage in Chapter 6 with an SP that extracts information from the SQL Server query plan cache, and again in Chapter 10 with examples of iFTS-specific DMVs and DMFs. In this section, I'll explore more uses for DMVs and DMFs.

Session Information

The sys.dm_exec_sessions DMV returns one row per session on the server. The information returned is similar to that returned by the sp_who2 system SP. You can use this DMV to retrieve information that includes the session ID, login name, client program name, CPU time and memory usage, and session settings like ANSI_NULLS and ANSI_PADDING. Listing 13-5 is a simple query against the sys.dm_exec_sessions DMV. Partial results are shown in Figure 13-4.

Listing 13-5. *Retrieving Session Information*

```
SELECT
  session_id,
  host_name,
  program_name,
  client_interface_name,
  login_name,
  cpu_time,
  ansi_nulls,
  ansi_padding
FROM sys.dm_exec_sessions;
```

	session_id	host_na...	program_name	client_interface_na...	login_name	cpu_time	ansi_nulls	ansi_padding	
27	52	SQL2008	Microsoft SQL S...	.Net SqlClient Data...	SQL2008\Michael	0	1	1	
28	53	SQL2008	Microsoft SQL S...	.Net SqlClient Data...	SQL2008\Michael	0	1	1	
29	54	SQL2008	Microsoft SQL S...	.Net SqlClient Data...	SQL2008\Michael	0	1	1	
30	55	SQL2008	Microsoft SQL S...	.Net SqlClient Data...	SQL2008\Michael	0	1	1	
31	56	SQL2008	Microsoft SQL S...	.Net SqlClient Data...	SQL2008\Michael	0	1	1	
32	57	SQL2008	Microsoft SQL S...	.Net SqlClient Data...	SQL2008\Michael	0	1	1	
33	58	SQL2008	Microsoft SQL S...	.Net SqlClient Data...	SQL2008\Michael	60	1	1	
34	59	SQL2008	Microsoft SQL S...	.Net SqlClient Data...	SQL2008\Michael	290	1	1	
35	60	SQL2008	Microsoft SQL S...	.Net SqlClient Data...	SQL2008\Michael	10	1	1	
36	61	SQL2008	Microsoft SQL S...	.Net SqlClient Data...	SQL2008\Michael	0	1	1	
37	62	SQL2008	Microsoft SQL S...	.Net SqlClient Data...	SQL2008\Michael	401	1	1	

Figure 13-4. *Retrieving session information with sys.dm_exec_sessions*

You can also use `sys.dm_exec_sessions` to retrieve summarized information about sessions. Listing 13-6 presents summary information for every current session on the server. The results are shown in Figure 13-5.

Listing 13-6. *Retrieving Summarized Session Information*

```
SELECT
    login_name,
    SUM(cpu_time) AS tot_cpu_time,
    SUM(memory_usage) AS tot_memory_usage,
    AVG(total_elapsed_time) AS avg_elapsed_time,
    SUM(reads) AS tot_reads,
    SUM(writes) AS tot_writes,
    SUM(logical_reads) AS tot_logical_reads,
    COUNT(session_id) as tot_sessions
FROM sys.dm_exec_sessions
WHERE session_id > 50
GROUP BY login_name;
```

	login_name	tot_cpu_time	tot_memory_usage	avg_elapsed_time	tot_reads	tot_writes	tot_logical_reads	tot_sessions
1	sa	0	2	11	0	0	4	1
2	SQL2008\Michael	2726	26	2116	90	10	74267	14

Figure 13-5. *Summary session information*

Connection Information

In addition to session information, you can retrieve connection information via the `sys.dm_exec_connections` DMV. The `sys.dm_exec_connections` DMV returns connection information for every session with a `session_id` greater than 50 (50 and below are used exclusively by the server). Listing 13-7 uses the DMV to retrieve connection information; the results are shown in Figure 13-6. Notice that this DMV also returns client network address, port, and authentication scheme information with no fuss.

Listing 13-7. *Retrieving Connection Information*

```
SELECT
    session_id,
    client_net_address,
    auth_scheme,
    net_transport,
    client_tcp_port,
    local_tcp_port,
    connection_id
FROM sys.dm_exec_connections;
```

	session_id	client_net_address	auth_scheme	net_transport	client_tcp_port	local_tcp_port	connection_id
9	56	\<local machine\>	NTLM	Shared memory	NULL	NULL	97419B34-5DF2-468A-97D...
10	60	\<local machine\>	NTLM	Shared memory	NULL	NULL	4681E03E-9D31-4E1F-A89...
11	61	\<local machine\>	NTLM	Shared memory	NULL	NULL	B5040F51-C2AF-444A-A56...
12	62	\<local machine\>	NTLM	Shared memory	NULL	NULL	8536B388-5ABA-46CF-988...
13	63	\<local machine\>	NTLM	Shared memory	NULL	NULL	C073720E-7E8A-4C89-ADC...
14	64	192.168.10.6	SQL	TCP	4233	1433	3F1BE303-AD0A-4692-90F...
15	65	127.0.0.1	NTLM	TCP	4234	1433	C2A42757-3BD6-40B9-B2E...

Figure 13-6. *Connection information retrieved via DMV*

Currently Executing SQL

The `sys.dm_exec_requests` DMV allows you to see all currently executing requests on SQL Server. You can use this DMV in conjunction with the `sys.dm_exec_sql_text` DMF to view the text of currently executing SQL statements, as shown in Listing 13-8. Results are shown in Figure 13-7.

■**Tip** The `sys.dm_exec_requests` DMV can be used to retrieve additional information for currently executing requests like request CPU time, reads, writes, and the amount of granted memory, among others. The information returned is similar to what is returned by the `sys.dm_exec_sessions` DMV I described previously in this section, but on a per-request basis instead of a per-session basis.

Listing 13-8. *Querying Currently Executing SQL Statements*

```
SELECT
  r.session_id,
  r.command,
  t.text
FROM sys.dm_exec_requests r
CROSS APPLY sys.dm_exec_sql_text(r.sql_handle) t;
```

	session_id	command	text
1	58	SELECT	SELECT r.session_id, r.command, t.text F...
2	62	SELECT	SELECT * FROM Person.Person;

Figure 13-7. *Currently executing SQL statements*

Notice that I used the CROSS APPLY operator in this example to submit the sql_handle returned by sys.dm_exec_requests to sys.dm_exec_sql_text. As you can see, on my server I was running a SELECT query in a separate session when I ran this example. The results show the text of both queries, which were executing at the same time. If you have more simultaneous requests on your server, this query will report them all.

Tempdb Space

The tempdb system database holds a position of prominence for DBAs. The tempdb database constitutes a global server-wide resource shared by all sessions, connections, and databases for temporary storage on a single SQL Server instance. An improperly managed tempdb can bring a SQL Server instance to its knees. The tempdb system database is so important, in fact, that SQL Server 2008 includes the sys.dm_db_file_space_usage DMV to report specifically on tempdb space usage. Listing 13-9 demonstrates a simple usage of sys.dm_db_file_space_usage to report free and used space in tempdb. The results are shown in Figure 13-8.

Listing 13-9. *Querying Free and Used Space in tempdb*

```
SELECT
  'tempdb' AS database_name,
  SUM(unallocated_extent_page_count) AS free_pages,
  SUM(unallocated_extent_page_count) * 8.0 AS free_KB,
  SUM(user_object_reserved_page_count) AS user_object_pages,
  SUM(user_object_reserved_page_count) * 8.0 AS user_object_KB,
  SUM(internal_object_reserved_page_count) AS internal_object_pages,
  SUM(internal_object_reserved_page_count) * 8.0 AS internal_object_KB
FROM sys.dm_db_file_space_usage;
```

	database_name	free_pages	free_KB	user_object_pages	user_object_KB	internal_object_pages	internal_object_KB
1	tempdb	3040	24320.0	40	320.0	32	256.0

Figure 13-8. *Free and used space in tempdb*

In addition to the `sys.dm_db_file_space_usage` DMV, SQL Server 2008 provides the `sys.dm_db_partition_stats`, `sys.dm_db_session_space_usage`, and `sys.dm_db_task_space_usage` DMVs to return information about `tempdb` usage. This type of information can be useful when trying to troubleshoot `tempdb`-related performance issues.

Server Resources

The `sys.dm_os_*` DMVs and functions allow you to query detailed low-level information about your server and resources. This is useful for retrieving resource usage or low-level server configuration details. Listing 13-10 retrieves low-level server configuration information, including the number of logical CPUs on the server, the ratio of logical to physical CPUs, and physical and virtual memory available to the server. The results are shown in Figure 13-9.

Listing 13-10. *Retrieving Low-Level Configuration Information*

```
SELECT
  cpu_count AS logical_CPUs,
  hyperthread_ratio,
  physical_memory_in_bytes / 1048576.00 AS physical_MB,
  virtual_memory_in_bytes / 1048576.00 AS virtual_MB,
  sqlserver_start_time
FROM sys.dm_os_sys_info;
```

	logical_CPUs	hyperthread_ratio	physical_MB	virtual_MB	sqlserver_start_time
1	1	1	767.4843750000	2047.8750000000	2008-04-30 03:33:07.483

Figure 13-9. *Low-level configuration details*

Unused Indexes

Another important aspect to managing a database is determining which indexes are used and which ones aren't. SQL Server provides the `sys.dm_db_index_usage_stats` DMV to report which indexes have been used since the SQL Server service was last started. Listing 13-11 demonstrates a simple query that lists all indexes that have not been used since the service was last restarted. Partial results are shown in Figure 13-10.

Listing 13-11. *Listing Unused Indexes*

```
DECLARE @database_name sysname = 'AdventureWorks';

WITH IndexOps
(
  schema_name,
  table_name,
  index_name,
  user_ops
)
AS
(
  SELECT
    OBJECT_SCHEMA_NAME(i.object_id),
    OBJECT_NAME(i.object_id),
    i.name,
    COALESCE(s.user_updates + s.user_seeks +
      s.user_scans + s.user_lookups, 0)
  FROM sys.indexes i
  LEFT JOIN sys.dm_db_index_usage_stats s
    ON s.object_id = i.object_id
    AND i.index_id = s.index_id
  WHERE s.database_id = DB_ID(@database_name)
)
SELECT
  schema_name,
  table_name,
  index_name,
  user_ops
FROM IndexOps
WHERE user_ops = 0
ORDER BY
  schema_name,
  table_name;
```

	schema_name	table_name	index_name	user_ops
4	HumanResources	Department	AK_Department_Name	0
5	HumanResources	Employee	PK_Employee_BusinessEntityID	0
6	HumanResources	Employee	AK_Employee_OrganizationNode	0
7	HumanResources	Employee	AK_Employee_OrganizationLevel_OrganizationNode	0
8	HumanResources	Employee	AK_Employee_LoginID	0
9	HumanResources	Employee	AK_Employee_NationalIDNumber	0
10	HumanResources	Employee	AK_Employee_rowguid	0
11	HumanResources	EmployeeDep...	PK_EmployeeDepartmentHistory_BusinessEntityID...	0

Figure 13-10. *Indexes that have not been used recently*

While the indexes listed by this function have not been used recently, that's no guarantee that they will not be used in the future. If you gather index usage information like this on a regular basis, however, you can develop a picture of index usage patterns. You can use this information to optimize existing indexes and redesign or drop irrelevant indexes.

INFORMATION_SCHEMA Views

INFORMATION_SCHEMA views provide yet another method of retrieving metadata in SQL Server 2008. Defined by the SQL-92 standard, INFORMATION_SCHEMA views provide the advantage of being cross-platform compatible with other SQL-92–compliant database platforms. One of the major disadvantages is that they leave out a lot of platform-specific metadata like detailed SQL CLR assembly information. Also, unlike some of the catalog views that are server wide, all INFORMATION_SCHEMA views are database specific. The INFORMATION_SCHEMA views are listed in Table 13-2.

Table 13-2. *INFORMATION_SCHEMA Views List*

Name	Description
CHECK_CONSTRAINTS	Returns a row of descriptive information for each check constraint in the current database.
COLUMN_DOMAIN_USAGE	Returns a row of metadata for each column in the current database that has an alias data type.
COLUMN_PRIVILEGES	Returns a row of information for each column in the current database with a privilege that has been granted by, or granted to, the current user of the database.
COLUMNS	Returns descriptive information for each column that can be accessed by the current user in the current database.
CONSTRAINT_COLUMN_USAGE	Returns one row of metadata for each column in the current database that has a constraint defined on it, on each table-type object for which the current user has permissions.
CONSTRAINT_TABLE_USAGE	Returns one row of information for each table in the current database that has a constraint defined on it for which the current user has permissions.
DOMAIN_CONSTRAINTS	Returns a row of descriptive information for each alias data type in the current database that the current user can access and that has a rule bound to it.
DOMAINS	Returns a row of descriptive metadata for each alias data type in the current database that the current user can access.
KEY_COLUMN_USAGE	Returns a row of metadata for each column that is constrained by a key for which the current user has permissions in the current database.
PARAMETERS	Returns a row of descriptive information for each parameter for all user-defined functions (UDFs) and SPs that can be accessed by the current user in the current database. For UDFs, the results also contain a row with return value information.
REFERENTIAL_CONSTRAINTS	Returns a row of metadata for each FOREIGN KEY constraint defined in the current database, on objects for which the current user has permissions.

Name	Description
ROUTINE_COLUMNS	Returns a row of descriptive information for each column returned by table-valued functions (TVFs) defined in the current database. This INFORMATION_SCHEMA view only returns information about TVFs for which the current user has access.
ROUTINES	Returns a row of metadata for each SP and function in the current database that is accessible to the current user.
SCHEMATA	Returns a row of information for each schema defined in the current database.
TABLE_CONSTRAINTS	Returns a row of metadata for each table constraint in the current database on table-type objects for which the current user has permissions.
TABLE_PRIVILEGES	Returns a row of descriptive metadata for each table privilege that is either granted by, or granted to, the current user in the current database.
TABLES	Returns a row of metadata for each table in the current database for which the current user has permissions.
VIEW_COLUMN_USAGE	Returns a row of information for each column in the current database that is used in a view definition, on objects for which the current user has permissions.
VIEW_TABLE_USAGE	Returns a row of information for each table that the current user has permissions for in the current database. The tables returned are those for which the current user has permissions.
VIEWS	Returns a row of metadata for each view that can be accessed by the current user in the current database.

■**Note** Some of the changes in SQL Server 2008 can break backward compatibility with SQL Server 2005, 2000, or 7.0 INFORMATION_SCHEMA views and applications that rely on them. Also note that SQL Server 6.5 and earlier do not implement INFORMATION_SCHEMA views. Check BOL for specific change information if your application uses INFORMATION_SCHEMA and requires backward compatibility.

Retrieving column information with the INFORMATION_SCHEMA.COLUMNS view is similar to using the sys.columns catalog view. Listing 13-12 demonstrates this, with results shown in Figure 13-11.

Listing 13-12. *Retrieving Column Data with INFORMATION_SCHEMA.COLUMNS*

```
SELECT
  c.COLUMN_NAME,
  c.ORDINAL_POSITION
FROM INFORMATION_SCHEMA.COLUMNS c
WHERE c.TABLE_SCHEMA = 'Person'
  AND c.TABLE_NAME = 'Person'
ORDER BY c.ORDINAL_POSITION;
```

Results

	COLUMN_NAME	ORDINAL_POSITION
1	BusinessEntityID	1
2	PersonType	2
3	NameStyle	3
4	Title	4
5	FirstName	5
6	MiddleName	6
7	LastName	7
8	Suffix	8
9	EmailPromotion	9
10	AdditionalContactInfo	10
11	Demographics	11
12	rowguid	12
13	ModifiedDate	13

Figure 13-11. *Column metadata retrieved via INFORMATION_SCHEMA*

INFORMATION_SCHEMA views are useful for applications that require cross-platform or high levels of ISO compatibility. Because they are ISO compliant, INFORMATION_SCHEMA views do not report a lot of platform-specific metadata. The ISO standard has also not kept up with the demand for access to server-wide metadata, so there is no standard server-scoped equivalent to INFORMATION_SCHEMA.

Summary

In this chapter, I discussed catalog views, which allow you to query database and server-wide metadata. Catalog views allow you to retrieve comprehensive information about databases, database objects, and configuration information. I provided some scenarios for catalog view usage and gave code examples to demonstrate their utility.

I also introduced DMVs and DMFs, which provide an amazing level of detailed insight into the inner workings of SQL Server. SQL Server 2008 supports the DMVs and DMFs introduced in SQL Server 2005 and introduces several more to support new SQL Server functionality like CDC and iFTS. While DMVs and DMFs are targeted to fulfill the needs of DBAs, the information they provide can be valuable to developers who are troubleshooting performance problems or other issues.

Finally, I briefly discussed the ISO standard INFORMATION_SCHEMA metadata views. The INFORMATION_SCHEMA views provide less detail than catalog views, and are scoped at the database level only, but they do provide the advantage of cross-platform portability when that is a requirement. Because they have to conform to the ISO SQL standard, however, they leave out a lot of useful platform-specific metadata.

In the next chapter, I will discusses SQL CLR programming and the improvements that Server 2008 provides over the previous release.

EXERCISES

1. [Fill in the blank] "Metadata" is defined as "data that describes ___."

2. [Fill in the blanks] ___ ___ provide insight into database objects and server-wide configuration options.

3. [Choose one] Many catalog views are defined using what model:

    a.   European model

    b.   Inheritance model

    c.   First In, First Out model

    d.   Procedural model

4. [True/false] Dynamic management views and functions provide access to internal SQL Server data structures that would be otherwise inaccessible.

5. [Choose all that apply] The advantages provided by INFORMATION_SCHEMA views include

    a.   ISO SQL standard compatibility

    b.   Access to server-scoped metadata

    c.   Cross-platform compatibility

    d.   Operating system configuration metadata

CHAPTER 14

■ ■ ■

SQL CLR Programming

One of the most prominent enhancements to SQL Server 2005 was the introduction of the integrated SQL Common Language Runtime (SQL CLR). SQL CLR is a SQL Server–specific version of the .NET Common Language Runtime, which allows you to run .NET managed code in the database. SQL CLR programming is a broad subject that could easily fill an entire book, and in fact it does—*Pro SQL Server 2005 Assemblies*, by Robin Dewson and Julian Skinner (Apress, 2005), is an excellent resource for in-depth coverage of SQL CLR programming. In this chapter, I'll discuss the methods used to extend SQL Server functionality in the past, and explain the basics of the SQL CLR programming model and the improvements made to SQL CLR in SQL Server 2008.

The Old Way

In versions of SQL Server prior to the 2005 release, developers could extend SQL Server functionality by writing extended stored procedures (XPs). Writing high-quality XPs required a strong knowledge of the Open Data Services (ODS) library and the poorly documented C-style Extended Stored Procedure API. Anyone who attempted the old style of XP programming can tell you it was a complex undertaking, where a single misstep could easily result in memory leaks and corruption of the SQL Server process space. Additionally, the threading model used by XPs required SQL Server to rely on the operating system to control threading within the XP. This could lead to many issues, such as unresponsiveness of XP code.

■**Caution** XPs have been deprecated since SQL Server 2005. Use SQL CLR instead of XPs for SQL Server 2008 development.

Earlier SQL Server releases also allowed you to create OLE Automation server objects via the sp_OACreate SP. Creating OLE Automation servers can be complex and kludgy as well. OLE Automation servers created with sp_OACreate can result in memory leaks and in some instances corruption of the SQL Server process space.

Another option in previous versions of SQL Server was to code all business logic exclusively in physically separate business objects. While this method is preferred by many developers and administrators, it can result in extra network traffic and a less robust security model than can be achieved through tight integration with the SQL Server security model.

The SQL CLR Way

The introduction of the SQL CLR programming model in SQL Server 2005 provided several advantages over older methods of extending SQL Server functionality via XPs, OLE Automation, or external business objects. These advantages included the following:

- A managed code base that runs on the SQL CLR .NET Framework is managed by the SQL Server Operating System (SQL OS). This means that SQL Server can properly manage threading, memory usage, and other resources accessed via SQL CLR code.

- Tight integration of SQL CLR into SQL Server means that SQL Server can provide a robust security model for running code, and maintain stricter control over database objects and external resources accessed by SQL CLR code.

- SQL CLR is more thoroughly documented in more places than the Extended Stored Procedure API ever was (or presumably ever will be).

- SQL CLR does not tie you to the C language–based Extended Stored Procedure API. In theory, the SQL CLR programming model does not tie you to any one specific language (although Microsoft currently supports only Visual Basic 2005, C#, and C++ SQL CLR programming).

- SQL CLR allows access to the familiar .NET namespaces, data types, and managed objects, easing development.

- SQL CLR introduces SQL Server–specific namespaces that allow direct access to the underlying SQL Server databases and resources, which can be used to limit or reduce network traffic generated by using external business objects.

There's a misperception expressed by some that SQL CLR is a replacement for T-SQL altogether. I can't speak with authority about Microsoft's plans for the future, but as it stands now, SQL CLR is not a replacement for T-SQL, but rather a supplement that works hand in hand with T-SQL to make SQL Server 2008 more powerful than ever. So when should you use SQL CLR code in your database? There are no hard and fast rules concerning this, but here are some general guidelines:

- Existing XPs on older versions of SQL Server are excellent candidates for conversion to SQL Server 2008 SQL CLR assemblies—that is, if the functionality provided isn't already part of SQL Server 2008 T-SQL (e.g., encryption).

- Code that accesses external server resources, such as calls to xp_cmdshell, are also excellent candidates for conversion to more secure and robust SQL CLR assemblies.

- T-SQL code that performs lots of complex calculations and string manipulations can make strong candidates for conversion to SQL CLR assemblies.

- Highly procedural code with lots of processing steps might be considered for conversion.

- External business objects that pull a lot of data across the wire and perform a lot of processing on that data might be considered for conversion. You might first consider these business objects for conversion to T-SQL SPs, especially if they don't perform a lot of processing on the data in question.

On the flip side, here are some general guidelines for items that should not be converted to SQL CLR assemblies:

- External business objects that pull relatively little data across the wire, or that pull a lot of data across the wire but perform little processing on that data, are good candidates for conversion to T-SQL SPs instead of SQL CLR assemblies.

- T-SQL code and SPs that do not perform many complex calculations or string manipulations generally won't benefit from conversion to SQL CLR assemblies.

- T-SQL can be expected to always be faster for set-based operations on data stored in the database than SQL CLR.

As with T-SQL SPs, the decision on whether and to what extent SQL CLR will be used in your databases depends on your needs, including organizational policies and procedures. The recommendations I presented here are guidelines of instances that can make good business cases for conversion of existing code and creation of new code.

SQL CLR Assemblies

SQL CLR exposes .NET managed code to SQL Server via *assemblies*. An assembly is a compiled .NET managed code library that can be registered with SQL Server using the CREATE ASSEMBLY statement. Publicly accessible members of classes within the assemblies are then referenced in the appropriate CREATE statements, which I will describe later in this chapter.

Creating a SQL CLR assembly requires

1. Designing and programming .NET classes that publicly expose the appropriate members.

2. Compiling the .NET classes into managed code DLL manifest files containing the assembly.

3. Registering the assemblies with SQL Server via the CREATE ASSEMBLY statement.

4. Registering the appropriate assembly members via the appropriate CREATE FUNCTION, CREATE PROCEDURE, CREATE TYPE, CREATE TRIGGER, or CREATE AGGREGATE statements.

SQL CLR provides additional SQL Server–specific namespaces, classes, and attributes to facilitate development of assemblies. Visual Studio 2008 also includes a new SQL Server Project project type that assists in quickly creating assemblies. Perform the following steps to create a new assembly using Visual Studio 2008:

1. Select File ➤ New Project from the menu.

2. Select your .NET language of choice (currently supported languages are Visual Basic, C#, and Visual C++) and choose the SQL Server Project installed template from the Databases submenu of the New Project dialog, as shown in Figure 14-1.

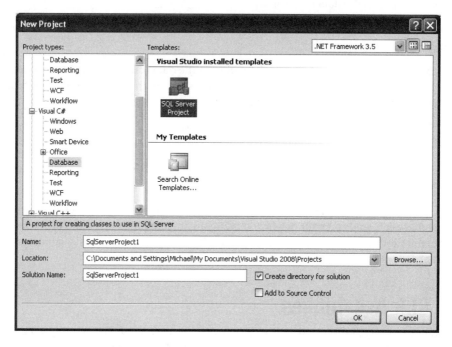

Figure 14-1. *Visual Studio 2008 New Project dialog*

3. You will be prompted with a dialog to select a database connection for the project, as shown in Figure 14-2. You may be prompted to turn on SQL CLR debugging for the connection. This is required if you want to test your assemblies in Debug mode.

Figure 14-2. *The Add Database Reference dialog*

4. Next, highlight the project name in the Solution Explorer and right-click. Then choose a type of SQL CLR item to add to the solution (User-Defined Function, Stored Procedure, etc.), as shown in Figure 14-3.

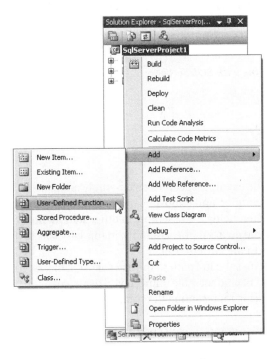

Figure 14-3. *Adding a new SQL CLR class to your project*

5. Visual Studio will automatically generate a template for the item you select in the language of your choice, complete with the appropriate Imports statements (using in C#).

In addition to the standard .NET namespaces and classes, SQL CLR implements some SQL Server–specific namespaces and classes to simplify interfacing your code with SQL Server. Some of the most commonly used namespaces include the following:

- The System namespace, which includes the base .NET data types and the Object class from which all .NET classes inherit.

- The System.Data namespace, which contains the DataSet class and other classes for ADO.NET data management.

- The System.Data.SqlClient namespace, which contains the SQL Server–specific ADO.NET data provider.

- The Microsoft.SqlServer.Server namespace, which contains the SqlContext and SqlPipe classes that allow assemblies to communicate with SQL Server.

- The System.Data.SqlTypes namespace, which contains SQL Server data types. This is important because (unlike the standard .NET data types) these types can be set to SQL NULL and are defined to conform to the same operator rules, behaviors, precision, and scale as their SQL Server type counterparts.

Once the assembly is created and compiled, it is registered with SQL Server via the CREATE ASSEMBLY statement. Listing 14-1 demonstrates a CREATE ASSEMBLY statement that registers a SQL CLR assembly with SQL Server from an external DLL file. The DLL file used in the example is not supplied in precompiled form in the sample downloads for this book, but you can compile it yourself from the code I will introduce in Listing 14-2. Source code is included in the sample downloads available on the Apress web site.

Listing 14-1. *Registering a SQL CLR Assembly with SQL Server*

```
CREATE ASSEMBLY EmailUDF
AUTHORIZATION dbo
FROM N'C:\MyApplication\EmailUDF.DLL'
WITH PERMISSION_SET = SAFE;
GO
```

The CREATE ASSEMBLY statement in the example specifies an assembly name of EmailUDF. This name must be a valid SQL Server identifier, and it must be unique within the database. You will use this assembly name when referencing the assembly in other statements.

The AUTHORIZATION clause specifies the owner of the assembly, in this case dbo. If you leave out the AUTHORIZATION clause, it defaults to the current user.

The FROM clause in this example specifies the full path to the external DLL file. Alternatively, you can specify a varbinary value instead of character file name. If you use a varbinary value, SQL Server uses it, as it is a long binary string representing the compiled assembly code, and no external file needs to be specified.

Finally, the WITH PERMISSION_SET clause grants a set of code access permissions to the assembly. Valid permission sets include the following:

- The SAFE permission set is the most restrictive, and prevents the assembly from accessing system resources outside of SQL Server. SAFE is the default.

- EXTERNAL_ACCESS allows assemblies to access some external resources, such as files, network, the registry, and environment variables.

- UNSAFE permission allows assemblies unlimited access to external resources, including the ability to execute unmanaged code.

After the assembly is installed, you can use variations of the T-SQL database object creation statements (e.g., CREATE FUNCTION, CREATE PROCEDURE) to access the methods exposed by the assembly classes. I will demonstrate these statements individually in the following sections.

User-Defined Functions

SQL CLR UDFs can return scalar values or tabular result sets. SQL CLR UDFs that return scalar values are similar to standard .NET functions. The primary differences are that the SqlFunction attribute must be applied to the main function if you are using Visual Studio to deploy your function or if you need to set additional attribute values like IsDeterministic and DataAccess. Listing 14-2 demonstrates a scalar UDF that accepts an input string value and a regular expression pattern, and returns a bit value indicating a match (1) or no match (0).

Listing 14-2. *Regular Expression Match UDF*

```
using System.Data.SqlTypes;
using System.Text.RegularExpressions;

namespace Apress.Examples
{
  public static class UDFExample
  {
    private static readonly Regex email_pattern = new Regex
    (
      // Everything before the @ sign (the "local part")
      "^[a-z0-9!#$%&'*+/=?^_`{|}~-]+(?:\\.[a-z0-9!#$%&'*+/=?^_`{|}~-]+)*" +

      // Subdomains after the @ sign
      "@(?:[a-z0-9](?:[a-z0-9-]*[a-z0-9])?\\.)+" +

      // Top-level domains
      "(?:[a-z]{2}|com|org|net|gov|mil|biz|info|mobi|name|aero|jobs|museum)\\b$"
    );

    [Microsoft.SqlServer.Server.SqlFunction
    (
        IsDeterministic = true
    )]
    public static SqlBoolean EmailMatch(SqlString input)
    {
      SqlBoolean result = new SqlBoolean();
      if (input.IsNull)
        result = SqlBoolean.Null;
      else
        result = (email_pattern.IsMatch(input.Value.ToLower()) == true)
          ? SqlBoolean.True : SqlBoolean.False;
      return result;
    }
  }
}
```

The first part of the listing is standard SQL CLR boilerplate code. It specifies the required namespaces to import. This UDF uses the System.Data.SqlTypes and System.Text. RegularExpressions namespaces.

```
using System.Data.SqlTypes;
using System.Text.RegularExpressions;
```

The UDFExample class and the EmailMatch function it exposes are both declared static. The function is decorated with the Microsoft.SqlServer.Server.SqlFunction attribute with the IsDeterministic property set to true to indicate the function is a deterministic SQL CLR method. The function body is relatively simple. It accepts a SqlString input string value. If the input string is NULL, the function returns NULL; otherwise the function uses the .NET Regex.IsMatch function to perform a regular expression match. If the result is a match, the function returns a bit value of 1; otherwise it returns 0.

```
public static class UDFExample
{
  private static readonly Regex email_pattern = new Regex(
    // Everything before the @ sign (the "local part")
    "^[a-z0-9!#$%&'*+/=?^_`{|}~-]+(?:\\.[a-z0-9!#$%&'*+/=?^_`{|}~-]+)*" +

    // Subdomains after the @ sign
    "@(?:[a-z0-9](?:[a-z0-9-]*[a-z0-9])?\\.)+" +

    // Top-level domains
    "(?:[a-z]{2}|com|org|net|gov|mil|biz|info|mobi|name|aero|jobs|museum)\\b$"
  );

  [Microsoft.SqlServer.Server.SqlFunction
  (
    IsDeterministic = true
  )]
  public static SqlBoolean EmailMatch(SqlString input)
  {
    SqlBoolean result = new SqlBoolean();
    if (input.IsNull)
      result = SqlBoolean.Null;
    else
      result = (email_pattern.IsMatch(input.Value.ToLower()) == true)
        ? SqlBoolean.True : SqlBoolean.False;
    return result;
  }
}
```

The regular expression pattern used in Listing 14-2 was created by Jan Goyvaerts of Regular-Expressions.info (www.regular-expressions.info). Jan's regular expression validates e-mail addresses according to RFC 2822, the standard for e-mail address formats. While not perfect, Jan estimates that this regular expression matches over 99 percent of "e-mail addresses in actual use today." Performing this type of e-mail address validation using only T-SQL statements would be cumbersome, complex, and inefficient.

■Tip It's considered good practice to use the SQL Server data types for parameters and return values to SQL CLR methods (SqlString, SqlBoolean, SqlInt32, etc.). Standard .NET data types have no concept of SQL NULL and will error out if NULL is passed in as a parameter, calculated within the function, or returned from the function.

After the assembly is installed via the CREATE ASSEMBLY statement, the function is created with the CREATE FUNCTION statement using the EXTERNAL NAME clause, as shown in Listing 14-3.

Listing 14-3. *Creating SQL CLR UDF from Assembly Method*

```
CREATE FUNCTION dbo.EmailMatch (@input nvarchar(4000))
RETURNS bit
WITH EXECUTE AS CALLER
AS
EXTERNAL NAME RegexUDF.[Apress.Examples.UDFExample].EmailMatch
GO
```

After this, the SQL CLR function can be called like any other T-SQL UDF, as shown in Listing 14-4. The results are shown in Figure 14-4.

Listing 14-4. *Validating E-mail Addresses with Regular Expressions*

```
SELECT 'nospam-123@yahoo.com' AS Email,
  dbo.EmailMatch (N'nospam-123@yahoo.com') AS Valid
UNION
SELECT '123@456789',
  dbo.EmailMatch('123@456789')
UNION
SELECT 'BillyG@HOTMAIL.COM',
  dbo.EmailMatch('BillyG@HOTMAIL.COM');
```

	Email	Valid
1	123@456789	0
2	BillyG@HOTMAIL.COM	1
3	nospam-123@yahoo.com	1

Figure 14-4. *Results of e-mail address validation with regular expressions*

■**Tip** You can automate the process of compiling your assembly, registering it with SQL Server, and installing the SQL CLR UDF with Visual Studio's Build ➤ Deploy option. You can also test the SQL CLR UDF with the Visual Studio Debug ➤ Start Debugging option.

As I mentioned previously, SQL CLR UDFs also allow tabular results to be returned to the caller. This example demonstrates another situation in which SQL CLR can be a useful supplement to T-SQL functionality—accessing external resources such as the file system, network resources, or even the Internet. Listing 14-5 uses SQL CLR to retrieve the Yahoo Top News Stories RSS feed and return the results as a table. Table-valued SQL CLR UDFs are a little more complex than scalar functions.

Listing 14-5. *Retrieving Yahoo RSS Feed Top News Stories*

```
using System;
using System.Collections;
using System.Data.SqlTypes;
using Microsoft.SqlServer.Server;
using System.Xml;

namespace Apress.Examples
{
  public partial class YahooRSS
  {
    [Microsoft.SqlServer.Server.SqlFunction
    (
      IsDeterministic = false,
      DataAccess = DataAccessKind.None,
      TableDefinition = "title nvarchar(256)," +
        "link nvarchar(256), " +
        "pubdate datetime, " +
        "description nvarchar(max)",
      FillRowMethodName = "GetRow"
    )]
    public static IEnumerable GetYahooNews()
    {
      XmlTextReader xmlsource =
        new XmlTextReader("http://rss.news.yahoo.com/rss/topstories");
      XmlDocument newsxml = new XmlDocument();
      newsxml.Load(xmlsource);
      xmlsource.Close();
      return newsxml.SelectNodes("//rss/channel/item");
    }

    private static void GetRow
    (
      Object o,
      out SqlString title,
      out SqlString link,
      out SqlDateTime pubdate,
      out SqlString description
    )
    {
      XmlElement element = (XmlElement)o;
      title = element.SelectSingleNode("./title").InnerText;
```

```
      link = element.SelectSingleNode("./link").InnerText;
      pubdate = DateTime.Parse(element.SelectSingleNode("./pubDate").InnerText);
      description = element.SelectSingleNode("./description").InnerText;
    }
  }
}
```

Before I step through the source listing, I need to address security since this function accesses the Internet. Because the function needs to access an external resource, it requires EXTERNAL_ACCESS permissions. In order to deploy a non-SAFE assembly, one of two sets of conditions must be met:

- The database must be marked TRUSTWORTHY and the user installing the assembly must have EXTERNAL_ACCESS ASSEMBLY or UNSAFE ASSEMBLY permission; or

- The assembly must be signed with an asymmetric key or certificate associated with a login that has proper permissions.

To meet the first set of requirements

1. Execute the ALTER DATABASE AdventureWorks SET TRUSTWORTHY ON; statement.

2. In Visual Studio, select Project Properties ➤ Database and change the permission level to External.

As I mentioned previously, signing assemblies is beyond the scope of this book. Additional information on signing assemblies is available in the book *Expert SQL Server 2005 Development*, coauthored by Hugo Kornelis, Lara Rubbelke, and one of my favorite SQL Server authors, the gifted Adam Machanic (Apress, 2007).

The code listing begins with the using statements. This function requires the addition of the System.Xml namespace in order to parse the RSS feed, the System.Collections namespace to use the IEnumerable interface, and a few others.

```
using System;
using System.Collections;
using System.Data.SqlTypes;
using Microsoft.SqlServer.Server;
using System.Xml;
```

The primary public function again requires the SqlFunction attribute be declared. This time there are several additional attributes that need to be declared with it:

```
[Microsoft.SqlServer.Server.SqlFunction
    (
        IsDeterministic = false,
        DataAccess = DataAccessKind.None,
        TableDefinition = "title nvarchar(256)," +
            "link nvarchar(256), " +
            "pubdate datetime, " +
            "description nvarchar(max)",
        FillRowMethodName = "GetRow"
    )]
```

```
public static IEnumerable GetYahooNews()
{
  XmlTextReader xmlsource =
    new XmlTextReader("http://rss.news.yahoo.com/rss/topstories");
  XmlDocument newsxml = new XmlDocument();
  newsxml.Load(xmlsource);
  xmlsource.Close();
  return newsxml.SelectNodes("//rss/channel/item");
}
```

I specifically set the IsDeterministic attribute to false this time to indicate that the contents of an RSS feed can change between calls, making this UDF nondeterministic. Since the function does not read data from system tables using the in-process data provider, the DataAccess attribute is set to DataAccessKind.None. This SQL CLR TVF also sets the additional TableDefinition attribute defining the structure of the result set for Visual Studio. It also needs the FillRowMethodName attribute to designate the fill-row method. The *fill-row method* is a user method that converts each element of an IEnumerable object into a SQL Server result set row.

The public function is declared to return an IEnumerable result. This particular function opens an XmlTextReader that retrieves the Yahoo Top News Stories RSS feed and stores it in an XmlDocument. The function then uses the SelectNodes method to retrieve news story summaries from the RSS feed. The SelectNodes method, used to return results from the function, generates an XmlNodeList. The XmlNodeList class implements the IEnumerable interface. This is important since the fill-row method is fired once for each object returned by the IEnumerable collection returned (in this case the XmlNodeList).

The GetRow method is declared as a C# void function. The method communicates with SQL Server via its out parameters. The first parameter is an Object passed by value—in this case an XmlElement. The remaining parameters correspond to the columns of the result set. The GetRow method casts the first parameter to an XmlElement. It then uses the SelectSingleNode method and InnerText property to retrieve the proper text from individual child nodes of the XmlElement, assigning each to the proper columns of the result set along the way.

```
private static void GetRow
(
  Object o,
  out SqlString title,
  out SqlString link,
  out SqlDateTime pubdate,
  out SqlString description
)
{
  XmlElement element = (XmlElement)o;
  title = element.SelectSingleNode("./title").InnerText;
  link = element.SelectSingleNode("./link").InnerText;
  pubdate = DateTime.Parse(element.SelectSingleNode("./pubDate").InnerText);
  description = element.SelectSingleNode("./description").InnerText;
}
```

The SQL CLR TVF can be called with a SELECT query, as shown in Listing 14-6. The results are shown in Figure 14-5.

Listing 14-6. *Querying a SQL CLR TVF*

```
SELECT
  title,
  link,
  pubdate,
  description
FROM dbo.GetYahooNews();
```

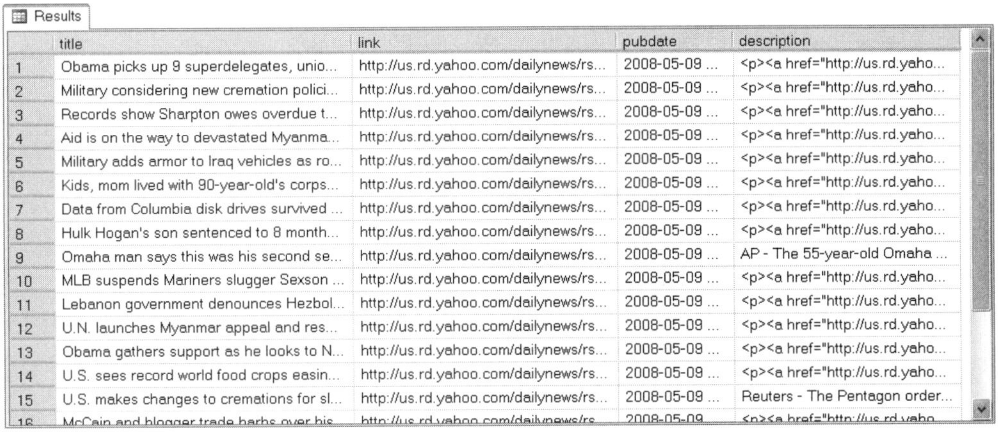

	title	link	pubdate	description
1	Obama picks up 9 superdelegates, unio...	http://us.rd.yahoo.com/dailynews/rs...	2008-05-09 ...	<p><a href="http://us.rd.yaho...
2	Military considering new cremation polici...	http://us.rd.yahoo.com/dailynews/rs...	2008-05-09 ...	<p><a href="http://us.rd.yaho...
3	Records show Sharpton owes overdue t...	http://us.rd.yahoo.com/dailynews/rs...	2008-05-09 ...	<p><a href="http://us.rd.yaho...
4	Aid is on the way to devastated Myanma...	http://us.rd.yahoo.com/dailynews/rs...	2008-05-09 ...	<p><a href="http://us.rd.yaho...
5	Military adds armor to Iraq vehicles as ro...	http://us.rd.yahoo.com/dailynews/rs...	2008-05-09 ...	<p><a href="http://us.rd.yaho...
6	Kids, mom lived with 90-year-old's corps...	http://us.rd.yahoo.com/dailynews/rs...	2008-05-09 ...	<p><a href="http://us.rd.yaho...
7	Data from Columbia disk drives survived ...	http://us.rd.yahoo.com/dailynews/rs...	2008-05-09 ...	<p><a href="http://us.rd.yaho...
8	Hulk Hogan's son sentenced to 8 month...	http://us.rd.yahoo.com/dailynews/rs...	2008-05-09 ...	<p><a href="http://us.rd.yaho...
9	Omaha man says this was his second se...	http://us.rd.yahoo.com/dailynews/rs...	2008-05-09 ...	AP - The 55-year-old Omaha ...
10	MLB suspends Mariners slugger Sexson ...	http://us.rd.yahoo.com/dailynews/rs...	2008-05-09 ...	<p><a href="http://us.rd.yaho...
11	Lebanon government denounces Hezbol...	http://us.rd.yahoo.com/dailynews/rs...	2008-05-09 ...	<p><a href="http://us.rd.yaho...
12	U.N. launches Myanmar appeal and res...	http://us.rd.yahoo.com/dailynews/rs...	2008-05-09 ...	<p><a href="http://us.rd.yaho...
13	Obama gathers support as he looks to N...	http://us.rd.yahoo.com/dailynews/rs...	2008-05-09 ...	<p><a href="http://us.rd.yaho...
14	U.S. sees record world food crops easin...	http://us.rd.yahoo.com/dailynews/rs...	2008-05-09 ...	<p><a href="http://us.rd.yaho...
15	U.S. makes changes to cremations for sl...	http://us.rd.yahoo.com/dailynews/rs...	2008-05-09 ...	Reuters - The Pentagon order...
16	McCain and blogger trade barbs over his...	http://us.rd.yahoo.com/dailynews/rs...	2008-05-09 ...	<p><a href="http://us.rd.yaho...

Figure 14-5. *Retrieving the Yahoo RSS feed with the GetYahooNews function*

Stored Procedures

SQL CLR SPs provide an alternative to extend SQL Server functionality when T-SQL SPs just won't do. Of course, like other SQL CLR functionality, there is a certain amount of overhead involved with SQL CLR SPs, and you can expect them to be less efficient than comparable T-SQL code for set-based operations. On the other hand, if you need to access .NET functionality or external resources, or if you have code that is computationally intensive, SQL CLR SPs can provide an excellent alternative to straight T-SQL code.

Listing 14-7 shows how to use SQL CLR to retrieve operating system environment variables and return them as a recordset via an SP.

Listing 14-7. *Retrieving Environment Variables with a SQL CLR SP*

```
using System;
using System.Collections;
using System.Data;
```

```csharp
using System.Data.SqlClient;
using System.Data.SqlTypes;
using Microsoft.SqlServer.Server;

namespace Apress.Examples
{
  public partial class SampleProc
  {
    [Microsoft.SqlServer.Server.SqlProcedure()]
    public static void GetEnvironmentVars()
    {
      try
      {
        SortedList environment_list = new SortedList();
        foreach (DictionaryEntry de in Environment.GetEnvironmentVariables())
        {
          environment_list[de.Key] = de.Value;
        }
        SqlDataRecord record = new SqlDataRecord
          (
            new SqlMetaData("VarName", SqlDbType.NVarChar, 1024),
            new SqlMetaData("VarValue", SqlDbType.NVarChar, 4000)
          );
        SqlContext.Pipe.SendResultsStart(record);
        foreach (DictionaryEntry de in environment_list)
        {
          record.SetValue(0, de.Key);
          record.SetValue(1, de.Value);
          SqlContext.Pipe.SendResultsRow(record);
        }
        SqlContext.Pipe.SendResultsEnd();
      }
      catch (Exception ex)
      {
        SqlContext.Pipe.Send(ex.Message);
      }
    }
  }
};
```

As with the previous SQL CLR examples, appropriate namespaces are imported at the top:

```csharp
using System;
using System.Collections;
using System.Data;
using System.Data.SqlClient;
using System.Data.SqlTypes;
using Microsoft.SqlServer.Server;
```

The GetEnvironmentVars method is declared as a public void function. The SqlProcedure() attribute is applied to the function in this code to indicate to Visual Studio that this is a SQL CLR SP. The body of the SP is wrapped in a try...catch block to capture any .NET exceptions, which are returned to SQL Server. If an exception occurs in the .NET code, it's sent back to SQL Server via the SqlContext.Pipe.Send method.

```
public partial class SampleProc
{
  [Microsoft.SqlServer.Server.SqlProcedure()]
  public static void GetEnvironmentVars()
  {
    try
    {
      ...
    }
    catch (Exception ex)
    {
      SqlContext.Pipe.Send(ex.Message);
    }
  }
}
```

THROWING READABLE EXCEPTIONS

When you need to raise an exception in a SQL CLR SP, you have two options. For code readability reasons, I've chosen the simpler option of just allowing exceptions to bubble up through the call stack. This results in .NET Framework exceptions being returned to SQL Server. The .NET Framework exceptions return a lot of extra information, like call stack data, however.

If you want to raise a nice, simple SQL Server–style error without all the extra .NET Framework exception information, you can use a method introduced in the book *Pro SQL Server 2005*, by Thomas Rizzo et al. (Apress, 2005). This second method involves using the ExecuteAndSend method of the SqlContext.Pipe to execute a T-SQL RAISERROR statement. This method is shown in the following C# code snippet:

```
try
{
  SqlContext.Pipe.ExecuteAndSend("RAISERROR ('This is a T-SQL Error', 16, 1);");
}
catch
{
  // do nothing
}
```

The ExecuteAndSend method call executes the RAISERROR statement on the current context connection. The try...catch block surrounding the call simply prevents the .NET exception that got you here in the first place from being bubbled up the call stack. Keep this method in mind if you want to raise SQL Server–style errors instead of returning the verbose .NET Framework exception information to SQL Server.

As the procedure begins, all of the environment variable names and their values are copied from the .NET `Hashtable` returned by the `Environment.GetEnvironmentVariables()` functions to a .NET `SortedList`. In this procedure, I chose to use the `SortedList` to ensure that the results are returned in order by key. I added the `SortedList` just for display purposes, but it's not required. Greater efficiency can be gained by iterating the `HashTable` directly without a `SortedList`.

```
SortedList environment_list = new SortedList();
foreach (DictionaryEntry de in Environment.GetEnvironmentVariables())
{
  environment_list[de.Key] = de.Value;
}
```

The procedure uses the `SqlContext.Pipe` to return results to SQL Server as a result set. The first step to using the `SqlContext.Pipe` to send results back is to set up a `SqlRecord` with the structure that you wish the result set to take. For this example, the result set consists of two `nvarchar` columns: `VarName`, which contains the environment variable names, and `VarValue`, which contains their corresponding values.

```
SqlDataRecord record = new SqlDataRecord
  (
    new SqlMetaData("VarName", SqlDbType.NVarChar, 1024),
    new SqlMetaData("VarValue", SqlDbType.NVarChar, 4000)
  );
```

Next, the function calls the `SendResultsStart` method with the `SqlDataRecord` to initialize the result set:

```
SqlContext.Pipe.SendResultsStart(record);
```

Then it's a simple matter of looping through the `SortedList` of environment variable key/value pairs and sending them to the server via the `SendResultsRow` method:

```
foreach (DictionaryEntry de in environment_list)
{
  record.SetValue(0, de.Key);
  record.SetValue(1, de.Value);
  SqlContext.Pipe.SendResultsRow(record);
}
```

The `SetValue` method is called for each column of the `SqlRecord` to properly set the results, and then `SendResultsRow` is called for each row. After all results have been sent to the client, the `SendResultsEnd` method of the `SqlContext.Pipe` is called to complete the result set and return the `SqlContext.Pipe` to its initial state.

```
SqlContext.Pipe.SendResultsEnd();
```

The `GetEnvironmentVars` SQL CLR SP can be called using the T-SQL `EXEC` statement, shown in Listing 14-8. The results are shown in Figure 14-6.

Listing 14-8. *Executing the GetEnvironmentVars SQL CLR Procedure*

```
EXEC dbo.GetEnvironmentVars;
```

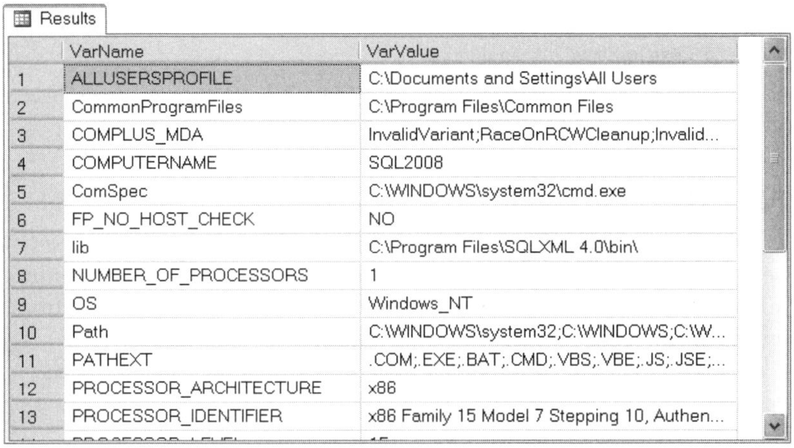

	VarName	VarValue
1	ALLUSERSPROFILE	C:\Documents and Settings\All Users
2	CommonProgramFiles	C:\Program Files\Common Files
3	COMPLUS_MDA	InvalidVariant;RaceOnRCWCleanup;Invalid...
4	COMPUTERNAME	SQL2008
5	ComSpec	C:\WINDOWS\system32\cmd.exe
6	FP_NO_HOST_CHECK	NO
7	lib	C:\Program Files\SQLXML 4.0\bin\
8	NUMBER_OF_PROCESSORS	1
9	OS	Windows_NT
10	Path	C:\WINDOWS\system32;C:\WINDOWS;C:\W...
11	PATHEXT	.COM;.EXE;.BAT;.CMD;.VBS;.VBE;.JS;.JSE;...
12	PROCESSOR_ARCHITECTURE	x86
13	PROCESSOR_IDENTIFIER	x86 Family 15 Model 7 Stepping 10, Authen...

Figure 14-6. *Retrieving environment variables with SQL CLR*

User-Defined Aggregates

User-defined aggregates (UDAs) are an exciting addition to SQL Server's functionality. UDAs are similar to the built-in SQL aggregate functions (`SUM`, `AVG`, etc.) in that they can act on entire sets of data at once, as opposed to one item at a time. A SQL CLR UDA has access to .NET functionality and can operate on numeric, character, date/time, or even user-defined data types. A basic UDA has four required methods:

- The UDA calls its `Init` method when the SQL Server engine prepares to aggregate. The code in this method can reset member variables to their start state, initialize buffers, and perform other initialization functions.
- The `Accumulate` method is called as each row is processed, allowing you to aggregate the data passed in. The `Accumulate` method might increment a counter, add a row's value to a running total, or possibly perform other more complex processing on a row's data.
- The `Merge` method is invoked when SQL Server decides to use parallel processing to complete an aggregate. If the query engine decides to use parallel processing, it will create multiple instances of your UDA and call the `Merge` method to join the results into a single aggregation.
- The `Terminate` method is the final method of the UDA. It is called after all rows have been processed and any aggregates created in parallel have been merged. The `Terminate` method returns the final result of the aggregation to the query engine.

Tip In SQL Server 2005, there was a serialization limit of 8000 bytes for an instance of a SQL CLR UDA, making certain tasks harder to perform using a UDA. For instance, creating an array, hash table, or other structure to hold intermediate results during an aggregation (like aggregates that calculate statistical mode or median) could cause a UDA to very quickly run up against the 8000-byte limit and throw an exception for large datasets. SQL Server 2008 does not have this limitation.

Creating a Simple UDA

The sample UDA in Listing 14-9 determines the statistical range for a set of numbers. The statistical range for a given set of numbers is the difference between the minimum and maximum values for the set. The UDA determines the minimum and maximum values of the set of numbers passed in and returns the difference.

Listing 14-9. *Sample Statistical Range UDA*

```
using System;
using System.Data;
using System.Data.SqlClient;
using System.Data.SqlTypes;
using Microsoft.SqlServer.Server;

namespace Apress.Examples
{
  [Serializable]
  [Microsoft.SqlServer.Server.SqlUserDefinedAggregate(Format.Native)]
  public struct Range
  {

    SqlDouble min, max;

    public void Init()
    {
      min = SqlDouble.Null;
      max = SqlDouble.Null;
    }

    public void Accumulate(SqlDouble value)
    {
      if (!value.IsNull)
      {
        if (min.IsNull || value < min)
        {
          min = value;
        }
```

```
      if (max.IsNull || value > max)
      {
        max = value;
      }
    }
  }

  public void Merge(Range group)
  {
    if (min.IsNull || (!group.min.IsNull && group.min < min))
    {
      min = group.min;
    }
    if (max.IsNull || (!group.max.IsNull && group.max > max))
    {
      max = group.max;
    }
  }

  public SqlDouble Terminate()
  {
    SqlDouble result = SqlDouble.Null;
    if (!min.IsNull && !max.IsNull)
    {
      result = max - min;
    }
    return result;
  }
 }
}
```

This UDA begins, like the previous SQL CLR assemblies, by importing the proper namespaces:

```
using System;
using System.Data;
using System.Data.SqlClient;
using System.Data.SqlTypes;
using Microsoft.SqlServer.Server;
```

Next, the code declares the struct that represents the UDA. The attributes Serializable and SqlUserDefinedAggregate are applied to the struct. I used the Format.Native serialization format for this UDA. Because this is a simple UDA, Format.Native will provide the best performance and will be the easiest to implement. More complex UDAs that use reference types require Format.UserDefined serialization and must implement the IBinarySerialize interface.

```
[Serializable]
[Microsoft.SqlServer.Server.SqlUserDefinedAggregate(Format.Native)]
public struct Range
{
  ...
}
```

The struct declares two member variables, min and max, which will hold the minimum and maximum values encountered during the aggregation process:

```
SqlDouble min, max;
```

The mandatory Init method in the aggregate body initializes the min and max member variables to SqlDouble.Null:

```
public void Init()
{
  min = SqlDouble.Null;
  max = SqlDouble.Null;
}
```

The Accumulate method accepts a SqlDouble parameter. This method first checks that the value is not NULL (NULL is ignored during aggregation). Then it checks to see if the value passed in is less than the min variable (or if min is NULL), and if so, assigns the parameter value to min. The method also checks max and updates it if the parameter value is greater than max (or if max is NULL). In this way, the min and max values are determined on the fly as the query engine feeds values into the Accumulate method.

```
public void Accumulate(SqlDouble value)
{
  if (!value.IsNull)
  {
    if (min.IsNull || value < min)
    {
      min = value;
    }
    if (max.IsNull || value > max)
    {
      max = value;
    }
  }
}
```

The Merge method merges a Range structure that was created in parallel with the current structure. The method accepts a Range structure and compares its min and max variables to those of the current Range structure. It then adjusts the current structure's min and max variables based on the Range structure passed into the method, effectively merging the two results.

```
public void Merge(Range group)
{
  if (min.IsNull || (!group.min.IsNull && group.min < min))
  {
    min = group.min;
  }
  if (max.IsNull || (!group.max.IsNull && group.max > max))
  {
    max = group.max;
  }
}
```

The final method of the UDA is the Terminate function, which returns a SqlDouble result. This function checks for min or max results that are NULL. The UDA returns NULL if either min or max is NULL. If neither min nor max are NULL, the result is the difference between the max and min values.

```
public SqlDouble Terminate()
{
  SqlDouble result = SqlDouble.Null;
  if (!min.IsNull && !max.IsNull)
  {
    result = max - min;
  }
  return result;
}
```

■ **Note** The Terminate method must return the same data type that the Accumulate method accepts. If these data types do not match, an error will occur. Also, as mentioned previously, it is best practice to use the SQL Server–specific data types, since the standard .NET types will choke on NULL.

Listing 14-10 is a simple test of this UDA. The test determines the statistical range of unit prices that customers have paid for AdventureWorks products. Information like this, on a per-product or per-model basis, can be paired with additional information to help the AdventureWorks sales teams set optimal price points for their products. The results are shown in Figure 14-7.

Listing 14-10. *Retrieving Statistical Ranges with UDA*

```
SELECT
  ProductID,
  dbo.Range(UnitPrice) AS UnitPriceRange
FROM Sales.SalesOrderDetail
WHERE UnitPrice > 0
GROUP BY ProductID;
```

Results

	ProductID	UnitPriceRange
1	707	19.2445
2	708	19.2445
3	709	0.95
4	710	0
5	711	19.2445
6	712	4.6679
7	713	0
8	714	22.4955
9	715	25.9563
10	716	22.111
11	717	100.8241
12	718	100.8241
13	719	78.0817999999999

Figure 14-7. *Results of the Range aggregate applied to unit prices*

Creating an Advanced UDA

You can create more advanced SQL CLR aggregates that use reference data types and user-defined serialization. When creating a UDA that uses reference (nonvalue) data types such as `ArrayLists`, `SortedLists`, and `Objects`, SQL CLR imposes the additional restriction that you cannot mark the UDA for `Format.Native` serialization. Instead these aggregates have to be marked for `Format.UserDefined` serialization, which means that the UDA must implement the `IBinarySerialize` interface, including both the `Read` and `Write` methods. Basically, you have to tell SQL Server how to serialize your data when using reference types. There is a performance impact associated with `Format.UserDefined` serialization as opposed to `Format.Native`.

Listing 14-11 is a UDA that calculates the statistical median of a set of numbers. The statistical median is the middle number of an ordered group of numbers. If there is an even number of numbers in the set, the statistical median is the average (mean) of the middle two numbers in the set.

Listing 14-11. *UDA to Calculate Statistical Median*

```
using System;
using System.Collections.Generic;
using System.Data;
using System.Data.SqlTypes;
using System.Runtime.InteropServices;
using Microsoft.SqlServer.Server;
```

```
namespace Apress.Examples
{
  [Serializable]
  [Microsoft.SqlServer.Server.SqlUserDefinedAggregate
    (
      Format.UserDefined,
      IsNullIfEmpty = true,
      MaxByteSize = -1
    )]
  [StructLayout(LayoutKind.Sequential)]
  public struct Median : IBinarySerialize
  {

    List<double> temp; // List of numbers

    public void Init()
    {
      // Create new list of double numbers
      this.temp = new List<double>();
    }

    public void Accumulate(SqlDouble number)
    {
      if (!number.IsNull) // Skip over NULLs
      {
        this.temp.Add(number.Value); // If number is not NULL, add it to list
      }
    }

    public void Merge(Median group)
    {
      // Merge two sets of numbers
      this.temp.InsertRange(this.temp.Count, group.temp);
    }

    public SqlDouble Terminate()
    {

      SqlDouble result = SqlDouble.Null; // Default result to NULL

      this.temp.Sort(); // Sort list of numbers

      int first, second; // Indexes to middle two numbers
```

```
    if (this.temp.Count % 2 == 1)
    {
      // If there is an odd number of values get the middle number twice
      first = this.temp.Count / 2;
      second = first;
    }
    else
    {
      // If there is an even number of values get the middle two numbers
      first = this.temp.Count / 2 - 1;
      second = first + 1;
    }

    if (this.temp.Count > 0) // If there are numbers, calculate median
    {
      // Calculate median as average of middle number(s)
      result = (SqlDouble)( this.temp[first] + this.temp[second] ) / 2.0;
    }

    return result;
  }

  #region IBinarySerialize Members

  // Custom serialization read method
  public void Read(System.IO.BinaryReader r)
  {

    // Create a new list of double values
    this.temp = new List<double>();

    // Get the number of values that were serialized
    int j = r.ReadInt32();

    // Loop and add each serialized value to the list
    for (int i = 0; i < j; i++)
    {
      this.temp.Add(r.ReadDouble());
    }
  }

  // Custom serialization write method
  public void Write(System.IO.BinaryWriter w)
  {
    // Write the number of values in the list
    w.Write(this.temp.Count);
```

```
      // Write out each value in the list
      foreach (double d in this.temp)
      {
        w.Write(d);
      }
    }

    #endregion
  }
}
```

This UDA begins, like the other SQL CLR examples, with namespace imports. I've added the System.Collections.Generic namespace this time so I can use the .NET List<T> strongly typed list.

```
using System;
using System.Collections.Generic;
using System.Data;
using System.Data.SqlTypes;
using System.Runtime.InteropServices;
using Microsoft.SqlServer.Server;
```

The Median structure in the example is declared with the Serializable attribute to indicate that it can be serialized, and the StructLayout attribute with the LayoutKind.Sequential property to force the structure to be serialized in sequential fashion. The LayoutKind.Sequential property is actually optional for structures since .NET applies LayoutKind.Sequential to structures by default. You do have to declare LayoutKind.Sequential for classes, however. The SqlUserDefinedAggregate attribute declares three properties, as follows:

- The Format.UserDefined property indicates that the UDA will implement user-defined serialization methods through the IBinarySerialize interface. This is required since the List<T> reference type is being used in the UDA.

- The IsNullIfEmpty property is set to true, indicating that NULL will be returned if no rows are passed to the UDA.

- The MaxByteSize property is set to -1 so that the UDA can be serialized if it is greater than 8000 bytes. (The 8000-byte serialization limit was a strict limit in SQL Server 2005 that prevented serialization of large objects, like large ArrayList objects, in the UDA.)

Because Format.UserDefined was specified on the Median structure, it must implement the IBinarySerialize interface. Inside the body of the struct, I've defined a List<double> named temp that will hold an intermediate temporary list of numbers passed into the UDA.

```
[Serializable]
[Microsoft.SqlServer.Server.SqlUserDefinedAggregate
  (
    Format.UserDefined,
    IsNullIfEmpty = true,
    MaxByteSize = -1
  )]
```

```
[StructLayout(LayoutKind.Sequential)]
public struct Median : IBinarySerialize
{

  List<double> temp; // List of numbers


  ...
}
```

The Read and Write methods of the IBinarySerialize interface are used to deserialize and serialize the list, respectively:

```
#region IBinarySerialize Members

// Custom serialization read method
public void Read(System.IO.BinaryReader r)
{

  // Create a new list of double values
  this.temp = new List<double>();

  // Get the number of values that were serialized
  int j = r.ReadInt32();

  // Loop and add each serialized value to the list
  for (int i = 0; i < j; i++)
  {
    this.temp.Add(r.ReadDouble());
  }
}

// Custom serialization write method
public void Write(System.IO.BinaryWriter w)
{
  // Write the number of values in the list
  w.Write(this.temp.Count);

  // Write out each value in the list
  foreach (double d in this.temp)
  {
    w.Write(d);
  }
}

#endregion
```

The Init method of the UDA initializes the temp list by creating a new List<double> instance:

```
public void Init()
{
  // Create new list of double numbers
  this.temp = new List<double>();
}
```

The `Accumulate` method accepts a `SqlDouble` number and adds all non-`NULL` values to the `temp` list. Although you can include `NULL`s in your aggregate results, keep in mind that T-SQL developers are used to the `NULL` handling of built-in aggregate functions like `SUM` and `AVG`. In particular, developers are used to their aggregate functions discarding `NULL`. This is the main reason I eliminate `NULL` in this UDA.

```
public void Accumulate(SqlDouble number)
{
  if (!number.IsNull) // Skip over NULLs
  {
    this.temp.Add(number.Value); // If number is not NULL, add it to list
  }
}
```

The `Merge` method in the example merges two lists of numbers if SQL Server decides to calculate the aggregate in parallel. If so, the server will pass a list of numbers into the `Merge` method. This list of numbers must then be appended to the current list. For efficiency, I use the `InsertRange` method of `List<T>` to combine the lists.

```
public void Merge(Median group)
{
  // Merge two sets of numbers
  this.temp.InsertRange(this.temp.Count, group.temp);
}
```

The `Terminate` method of the UDA sorts the list of values and then determines the indexes of the middle numbers. If there is an odd number of values in the list, there is only a single middle number; if there is an even number of values in the list, the median is the average of the middle two numbers. If the list contains no values (which can occur if every value passed to the aggregate is `NULL`), the result is `NULL`; otherwise the `Terminate` method calculates and returns the median.

```
public SqlDouble Terminate()
{

  SqlDouble result = SqlDouble.Null; // Default result to NULL

  this.temp.Sort(); // Sort list of numbers

  int first, second; // Indexes to middle two numbers
```

```
    if (this.temp.Count % 2 == 1)
    {
      // If there is an odd number of values get the middle number twice
      first = this.temp.Count / 2;
      second = first;
    }
    else
    {
      // If there is an even number of values get the middle two numbers
      first = this.temp.Count / 2 - 1;
      second = first + 1;
    }

    if (this.temp.Count > 0) // If there are numbers, calculate median
    {
      // Calculate median as average of middle number(s)
      result = (SqlDouble)( this.temp[first] + this.temp[second] ) / 2.0;
    }

    return result;
  }
```

Listing 14-12 demonstrates the use of this UDA to calculate the median UnitPrice from the Sales.SalesOrderDetail table on a per-product basis. The results are shown in Figure 14-8.

Listing 14-12. *Calculating Median Unit Price with a UDA*

```
SELECT
  ProductID,
  dbo.Median(UnitPrice) AS MedianUnitPrice
FROM Sales.SalesOrderDetail
GROUP BY ProductID;
```

	ProductID	MedianUnitPrice
1	707	34.99
2	708	34.99
3	709	5.7
4	710	5.7
5	711	34.99
6	712	8.99
7	713	49.99
8	714	29.994
9	715	29.994
10	716	29.994
11	717	780.8182
12	718	780.8182
13	719	858.9

Figure 14-8. *Median unit price for each product*

SQL CLR User-Defined Types

SQL Server 2000 had built-in support for user-defined data types, but they were limited in scope and functionality. The old-style user-defined data types had the following restrictions and capabilities:

- They had to be derived from built-in data types.

- Their format and/or range could only be restricted through T-SQL rules.

- They could be assigned a default value.

- They could be declared as NULL or NOT NULL.

SQL Server 2008 provides support for old style user-defined data types and rules, presumably for backward compatibility with existing applications. The AdventureWorks database contains examples of old-style user-defined data types, like the dbo.Phone data type, which is an alias for the VARCHAR(25) data type.

■**Caution** Rules have been deprecated since SQL Server 2005 and will be removed from a future version. T-SQL user-defined data types are now often referred to as alias types.

SQL Server 2008 supports a far more flexible solution to your custom data type needs in the form of SQL CLR user-defined types. *SQL CLR user-defined types (UDTs)* allow you to access the power of the .NET Framework to meet your custom data type needs. Common examples of SQL CLR UDTs include mathematical concepts like points, vectors, complex numbers, and other types not built into the SQL Server type system. In fact, SQL CLR UDTs are so powerful that Microsoft has begun including some as standard in SQL Server. These new SQL CLR UDTs include the spatial data types geography and geometry, and the hierarchyid data type.

SQL CLR UDTs are useful for implementing data types that require special handling and that implement their own special methods and functions. Complex numbers, which are a superset of real numbers, are one example. Complex numbers are represented with a "real" part and an "imaginary" part in the format "$a+bi$," where a is a real number representing the real part of the value, b is a real number representing the imaginary part, and the literal letter i after the imaginary part stands for the imaginary number i, which is the square root of -1. Complex numbers are often used in math, science, and engineering to solve difficult abstract problems. Some examples of complex numbers include 101.9+3.7i, 98+12i, −19i, and 12+0i (which can also be represented as 12). Because their format is different from real numbers and calculations with them require special functionality, complex numbers are a good candidate for SQL CLR. The example in Listing 14-13 implements a complex number SQL CLR UDT.

■**Note** The sample download file includes an expanded version of this SQL CLR UDT that includes additional documentation and implementations of many more mathematical operators and trigonometric functions.

Listing 14-13. *Complex Numbers UDT*

```csharp
using System;
using System.Data.SqlTypes;
using Microsoft.SqlServer.Server;
using System.Text.RegularExpressions;

namespace Apress.Examples
{
  [Serializable]
  [Microsoft.SqlServer.Server.SqlUserDefinedType
    (
      Format.Native,
      IsByteOrdered = true
    )]
  public struct Complex : INullable
  {

    #region "Complex Number UDT Fields/Components"

    private bool m_Null;    public Double real;
    public Double imaginary;

    #endregion

    #region "Complex Number Parsing, Constructor, and Methods/Properties"

    private static readonly Regex rx = new Regex(
      "^(?<Imaginary>[+-]?([0-9]+|[0-9]*\\.[0-9]+))[i|I]$|" +
      "^(?<Real>[+-]?([0-9]+|[0-9]*\\.[0-9]+))$|" +
      "^(?<Real>[+-]?([0-9]+|[0-9]*\\.[0-9]+))" +
      "(?<Imaginary>[+-]?([0-9]+|[0-9]*\\.[0-9]+))[i|I]$");

    public static Complex Parse(SqlString s)
    {
      Complex u = new Complex();
      if (s.IsNull)
        u = Null;
      else
      {
        MatchCollection m = rx.Matches(s.Value);
        if (m.Count == 0)
          throw (new FormatException("Invalid Complex Number Format."));
        String real_str = m[0].Groups["Real"].Value;
        String imaginary_str = m[0].Groups["Imaginary"].Value;
```

```csharp
      if (real_str == "" && imaginary_str == "")
        throw (new FormatException("Invalid Complex Number Format."));
      if (real_str == "")
        u.real = 0.0;
      else
        u.real = Convert.ToDouble(real_str);
      if (imaginary_str == "")
        u.imaginary = 0.0;
      else
        u.imaginary = Convert.ToDouble(imaginary_str);
  }
  return u;
}

public override String ToString()
{
  String sign = "";
  if (this.imaginary >= 0.0)
    sign = "+";
  return this.real.ToString() + sign + this.imaginary.ToString() + "i";
}

public bool IsNull
{
  get
  {
    return m_Null;
  }
}

public static Complex Null
{
  get
  {
    Complex h = new Complex();
    h.m_Null = true;
    return h;
  }
}

public Complex(Double r, Double i)
{
  this.real = r;
  this.imaginary = i;
  this.m_Null = false;
}
```

```csharp
#endregion

#region "Useful Complex Number Constants"

// The property "i" is the Complex number 0 + 1i. Defined here because
// it is useful in some calculations

public static Complex i
{
  get
  {
    return new Complex(0, 1);
  }
}

// The property "Pi" is the Complex representation of the number
// Pi (3.141592... + 0i)

public static Complex Pi
{
  get
  {
    return new Complex(Math.PI, 0);
  }
}

// The property "One" is the Complex number representation of the
// number 1 (1 + 0i)

public static Complex One
{
  get
  {
    return new Complex(1, 0);
  }
}

#endregion

#region "Complex Number Basic Operators"

// Complex number addition

public static Complex operator +(Complex n1, Complex n2)
{
  Complex u;
```

```
  if (n1.IsNull || n2.IsNull)
    u = Null;
  else
    u = new Complex(n1.real + n2.real, n1.imaginary + n2.imaginary);
  return u;
}

// Complex number subtraction

public static Complex operator -(Complex n1, Complex n2)
{
  Complex u;
  if (n1.IsNull || n2.IsNull)
    u = Null;
  else
    u = new Complex(n1.real - n2.real, n1.imaginary - n2.imaginary);
  return u;
}

// Complex number multiplication

public static Complex operator *(Complex n1, Complex n2)
{
  Complex u;
  if (n1.IsNull || n2.IsNull)
    u = Null;
  else
    u = new Complex((n1.real * n2.real) - (n1.imaginary * n2.imaginary),
      (n1.real * n2.imaginary) + (n2.real * n1.imaginary));
  return u;
}

// Complex number division

public static Complex operator /(Complex n1, Complex n2)
{
  Complex u;
  if (n1.IsNull || n2.IsNull)
    u = Null;
  else
  {
    if (n2.real == 0.0 && n2.imaginary == 0.0)
      throw new DivideByZeroException
        ("Complex Number Division By Zero Exception.");
```

```csharp
      u = new Complex(((n1.real * n2.real) +
        (n1.imaginary * n2.imaginary)) /
        ((Math.Pow(n2.real, 2) + Math.Pow(n2.imaginary, 2))),
        ((n1.imaginary * n2.real) - (n1.real * n2.imaginary)) /
        ((Math.Pow(n2.real, 2) + Math.Pow(n2.imaginary, 2))));
    }
    return u;
}

// Unary minus operator

public static Complex operator -(Complex n1)
{
  Complex u;
  if (n1.IsNull)
    u = Null;
  else
    u = new Complex(-n1.real, -n1.imaginary);
  return u;
}

#endregion

#region "Exposed Mathematical Basic Operator Methods"

// Add complex number n2 to n1

public static Complex CAdd(Complex n1, Complex n2)
{
  return n1 + n2;
}

// Subtract complex number n2 from n1

public static Complex Sub(Complex n1, Complex n2)
{
  return n1 - n2;
}

// Multiply complex number n1 * n2

public static Complex Mult(Complex n1, Complex n2)
{
  return n1 * n2;
}
```

```
// Divide complex number n1 by n2

public static Complex Div(Complex n1, Complex n2)
{
  return n1 / n2;
}

// Returns negated complex number

public static Complex Neg(Complex n1)
{
  return -n1;
}

#endregion

  }
}
```

The code begins with the required namespace imports and the namespace declaration for the sample:

```
using System;
using System.Data.SqlTypes;
using Microsoft.SqlServer.Server;
using System.Text.RegularExpressions;
```

Next is the declaration of the structure that represents an instance of the UDT. The Serializable, Format.Native, and IsByteOrdered=true attributes and attribute properties are all set on the UDT. In addition, all SQL CLR UDTs must implement the INullable interface. INullable requires that the IsNull and Null properties be defined.

```
[Serializable]
[Microsoft.SqlServer.Server.SqlUserDefinedType
  (
    Format.Native,
    IsByteOrdered = true
  )]
public struct Complex : INullable
{
  ...
}
```

Table 14-1 shows a few of the common attributes that are used in SQL CLR UDT definitions.

Table 14-1. *Common SQL CLR UDT Attributes*

Attribute	Property	Value	Description
Serializable	n/a	n/a	Indicates that the UDT can be serialized and deserialized.
SqlUserDefinedType	Format.Native	n/a	Specifies that the UDT uses native format for serialization. The native format is the most efficient format for serialization/deserialization, but it imposes some limitations. You can only expose .NET value data types (Char, Integer, etc.) as the fields. You cannot expose reference data types (Strings, Arrays, etc.).
SqlUserDefinedType	Format. UserDefined	n/a	Specifies that the UDT uses a user-defined format for serialization. When this is specified, your UDT must implement the IBinarySerialize interface, and you are responsible for supplying the Write() and Read() methods that serialize and deserialize your UDT.
SqlUserDefinedType	IsByteOrdered	true/false	Allows comparisons and sorting of UDT values based on their binary representation. This is also required if you intend to create indexes on columns defined as a SQL CLR UDT type.
SqlUserDefinedType	IsFixedLength	true/false	Should be set to true if the serialized instance of your UDT is a fixed length.
SqlUserDefinedType	MaxByteSize	<= 8000 or -1	The maximum size of your serialized UDT instances in bytes. This value must be between 1 and 8000; or it can be -1 for a maximum size of 2.1 GB.

The public and private fields are declared inside the body of the Complex structure. The real and imaginary public fields represent the real and imaginary parts of the complex number, respectively. The m_Null field is a bool value that is set to true if the current instance of the complex type is NULL, and is set to false otherwise.

```
#region "Complex Number UDT Fields/Components"

private bool m_Null;
public Double real;
public Double imaginary;

#endregion
```

The first method declared in the UDT is the `Parse` method (required by all UDTs), which takes a string value from SQL Server and parses it into a complex number. The `Parse` method uses a .NET regular expression to simplify parsing a bit.

```
private static readonly Regex rx = new Regex(
  "^(?<Imaginary>[+-]?([0-9]+|[0-9]*\\.[0-9]+))[i|I]$|" +
  "^(?<Real>[+-]?([0-9]+|[0-9]*\\.[0-9]+))$|" +
  "^(?<Real>[+-]?([0-9]+|[0-9]*\\.[0-9]+))" +
  "(?<Imaginary>[+-]?([0-9]+|[0-9]*\\.[0-9]+))[i|I]$");

public static Complex Parse(SqlString s)
{
  Complex u = new Complex();
  if (s.IsNull)
    u = Null;
  else
  {
    MatchCollection m = rx.Matches(s.Value);
    if (m.Count == 0)
      throw (new FormatException("Invalid Complex Number Format."));
    String real_str = m[0].Groups["Real"].Value;
    String imaginary_str = m[0].Groups["Imaginary"].Value;
    if (real_str == "" && imaginary_str == "")
      throw (new FormatException("Invalid Complex Number Format."));
    if (real_str == "")
      u.real = 0.0;
    else
      u.real = Convert.ToDouble(real_str);
    if (imaginary_str == "")
      u.imaginary = 0.0;
    else
      u.imaginary = Convert.ToDouble(imaginary_str);
  }
  return u;
}
```

The regular expression (a.k.a. regex) uses *named groups* to parse the input string into `Real` and/or `Imaginary` named groups. If the regex is successful, at least one (if not both) of these named groups will be populated. If unsuccessful, both named groups will be empty and an exception of type `FormatException` will be thrown. If at least one of the named groups is properly set, the string representations are converted to `Double` type and assigned to the appropriate UDT fields. Table 14-2 shows some sample input strings and the values assigned to the UDT fields when they are parsed.

Table 14-2. *Complex Number Parsing Samples*

Complex Number	Real	Imaginary	m_Null
100+11i	100.0	11.0	false
99.9	99.9	0.0	false
3.7-9.8i	3.7	-9.8	false
2.1i	0.0	2.1	false
-9-8.2i	-9.0	-8.2	false
NULL			true

The ToString method is required for all UDTs as well. This method converts the internal UDT data to its string representation. In the case of complex numbers, ToString needs to perform the following steps:

1. Convert the real part to a string.

2. Append a plus sign (+) if the imaginary part is 0 or positive.

3. Append the imaginary part.

4. Append the letter i to indicate that it does in fact represent a complex number.

Notice that if the imaginary part is negative, no sign is appended between the real and imaginary parts, since the sign is already included in the imaginary part:

```
public override String ToString()
{
  String sign = "";
  if (this.imaginary >= 0.0)
    sign = "+";
  return this.real.ToString() + sign + this.imaginary.ToString() + "i";
}
```

The IsNull and Null properties are both required by all UDTs. IsNull is a bool property that indicates whether a UDT instance is NULL or not. The Null property returns a NULL instance of the UDT type. One thing you need to be aware of any time you invoke a UDT (or any SQL CLR object) from T-SQL is SQL NULL. For purposes of the Complex UDT, I take a cue from T-SQL and return a NULL result any time a NULL is passed in as a parameter to any UDT method. So a Complex value plus NULL returns NULL, as does a Complex value divided by NULL, and so on. You will notice a lot of code in the complete Complex UDT listing that is specifically designed to deal with NULL.

```
public bool IsNull
{
  get
  {
    return m_Null;
  }
}
```

```
public static Complex Null
{
  get
  {
    Complex h = new Complex();
    h.m_Null = true;
    return h;
  }
}
```

This particular UDT includes a constructor function that accepts two Double type values and creates a UDT instance from them:

```
public Complex(Double r, Double i)
{
  this.real = r;
  this.imaginary = i;
  this.m_Null = false;
}
```

■ **Tip** For a UDT designed as a .NET structure, a constructor method is not required. In fact, a default constructor (that takes no parameters) is not even allowed. To keep later code simple, I added a constructor method to this example.

In the next region, I defined a few useful complex number constants and exposed them as static properties of the Complex UDT:

```
#region "Useful Complex Number Constants"

// The property "i" is the Complex number 0 + 1i. Defined here because
// it is useful in some calculations

public static Complex i
{
  get
  {
    return new Complex(0, 1);
  }
}

...

#endregion
```

To keep this listing short but highlight the important points, the sample UDT supports only the basic math operators for complex numbers. The UDT overrides the + and / math operators (addition and division). Redefining these operators makes it easier to write and debug additional UDT methods. These overridden .NET math operators are not available to T-SQL code, so the standard T-SQL math operators will not work on the UDT.

```
#region "Complex Number Basic Operators"

// Complex number addition

public static Complex operator +(Complex n1, Complex n2)
{
  Complex u;
  if (n1.IsNull || n2.IsNull)
    u = Null;
  else
    u = new Complex(n1.real + n2.real, n1.imaginary + n2.imaginary);
  return u;
}

// Complex number subtraction

public static Complex operator -(Complex n1, Complex n2)
{
  Complex u;
  if (n1.IsNull || n2.IsNull)
    u = Null;
  else
    u = new Complex(n1.real - n2.real, n1.imaginary - n2.imaginary);
  return u;
}
...

#endregion
```

Performing mathematical operations on UDT values from T-SQL must be done via explicitly exposed methods of the UDT. These methods in the Complex UDT are CAdd and Div, for complex number addition and division, respectively. Note that I chose CAdd (which stands for "complex number add") as a method name to avoid conflicts with the T-SQL reserved word ADD. I won't go too deeply into the inner workings of complex numbers, but I chose to implement the basic operators in this listing because some (like complex number addition) are straightforward operations, while others (like division) are a bit more complicated. The math operator methods are declared as static, so they can be invoked on the UDT data type itself from SQL Server instead of on an instance of the UDT.

```
#region "Exposed Mathematical Basic Operator Methods"

// Add complex number n2 to n1
```

```
public static Complex CAdd(Complex n1, Complex n2)
{
  return n1 + n2;
}

// Subtract complex number n2 from n1

public static Complex Sub(Complex n1, Complex n2)
{
  return n1 - n2;
}

...

#endregion
```

■Note Static methods of a UDT (declared with the `static` keyword in C# or the `Shared` keyword in Visual Basic) are invoked from SQL Server using a format like this:

`Complex::CAdd(@n1, @n2)`

Nonshared, or instance, methods of a UDT are invoked from SQL Server using a format similar to this:

`@n1.CAdd(@n2)`

The style of method you use (shared or instance) is a determination you'll need to make on a case-by-case basis.

Listing 14-14 demonstrates how the `Complex` UDT can be used, and the results are shown in Figure 14-9.

Listing 14-14. *Complex Number UDT Demonstration*

```
DECLARE @c complex = '+100-10i',
  @d complex = '5i';
SELECT 'ADD: ' + @c.ToString() + ' , ' + @d.ToString() AS Op,
  complex::CAdd(@c, @d).ToString() AS Result
UNION
SELECT 'DIV: ' + @c.ToString() + ' , ' + @d.ToString(),
  complex::Div(@c, @d).ToString()
UNION
SELECT 'SUB: ' + @c.ToString() + ' , ' + @d.ToString(),
  complex::Sub(@c, @d).ToString()
```

```
UNION
SELECT 'MULT: ' + @c.ToString() + ' , ' + @d.ToString(),
  complex::Mult(@c, @d).ToString()
UNION
SELECT 'PI:  ',
  complex::Pi.ToString();
GO
```

	Op	Result
1	ADD: 100-10i , 0+5i	100-5i
2	DIV: 100-10i , 0+5i	-2-20i
3	MULT: 100-10i , 0+5i	50+500i
4	PI:	3.14159265358979+0i
5	SUB: 100-10i , 0+5i	100-15i

Figure 14-9. *Performing operations with the Complex UDT*

In addition to the basic operations, the Complex class can be easily extended to support several more advanced complex number operators and functions. The code sample download file contains a full listing of an expanded Complex UDT, including all the basic math operators, as well as logarithmic and exponential functions (Log(), Power(), etc.) and trigonometric and hyperbolic functions (Sin(), Cos(), Tanh(), etc.) for complex numbers.

Summary

SQL Server 2005 introduced SQL CLR integration, allowing you to create UDFs, UDAs, SPs, and UDTs in managed .NET code. SQL Server 2008 improves on SQL CLR functionality by allowing UDTs and UDAs to have a maximum size of 2.1 GB.

In this chapter, I talked about SQL CLR usage considerations, and scenarios when SQL CLR code might be considered a good alternative to strict T-SQL. I also discussed assemblies and security, including the SAFE, EXTERNAL_ACCESS, and UNSAFE permission sets that can be applied on a per-assembly basis.

Finally, I provided several examples of SQL CLR code that cover a wide range of possible uses, including the following:

- SQL CLR can be invaluable when access to external resources is required from the server.

- SQL CLR can be useful when non-table specific aggregations are required.

- SQL CLR simplifies complex data validations that would be complex and difficult to perform in T-SQL.

- SQL CLR allows you to supplement SQL Server's data typing system with your own specialized data types that define their own built-in methods and properties.

This chapter has served as an introduction to SQL CLR programming. For in-depth SQL CLR programming information, I highly recommend *Pro SQL Server 2005 Assemblies*, by Robin Dewson and Julian Skinner (Apress, 2005). Though written for SQL Server 2005, much of the information it contains is still relevant to SQL Server 2008. In the next chapter, I will introduce client-side .NET connectivity to SQL Server 2008.

EXERCISES

1. [Choose all that apply] SQL Server 2008 provides support for which of the following SQL CLR objects:

    a. UDFs

    b. UDAs

    c. UDTs

    d. SPs

    e. User-defined catalogs

2. [True/false] SQL Server 2008 limits SQL CLR UDAs and UDTs to a maximum size of 8000 bytes.

3. [Choose one] SAFE permissions allow your SQL CLR code to

    a. Write to the file system

    b. Access network resources

    c. Read the computer's registry

    d. Execute managed .NET code

    e. All of the above

4. [True/false] SQL CLR UDAs and UDTs must be defined with the Serializable attribute.

5. [Fill in the blank] A SQL CLR UDA that is declared as Format.UserDefined must implement the ___ interface.

6. [Choose all that apply] A SQL CLR UDA must implement which of the following methods:

    a. Init

    b. Aggregate

    c. Terminate

    d. Merge

    e. Accumulate

CHAPTER 15

.NET Client Programming

Which is more important, an efficient database or a well-designed client application that connects to the database? In my estimation, they are both equally important. After all, your database can be very well designed and extremely efficient, but that won't matter to the end user if the client application they use to connect to your database is slow and unresponsive. While this book focuses on SQL Server server-side development functionality, I've decided to take a moment to introduce some of the tools available to create efficient SQL Server client applications. The .NET Framework, in particular, offers several options to make SQL Server 2008 client connectivity simple and efficient. In this chapter, I will discuss using ADO.NET and the .NET SqlClient as a basis for building your own easy-to-use, cutting-edge SQL Server client applications.

ADO.NET

The System.Data.* namespaces consist of classes and enumerations that comprise the ADO.NET architecture, the .NET Framework's primary tool for database access. You can use the classes in the System.Data.* namespaces to connect to your databases and access them in real time, or in a disconnected fashion via the DataSet, DataTable, and DataAdapter classes. The following are some of the more commonly used namespaces for SQL Server data access:

- The System.Data namespace provides access to classes that implement the ADO.NET architecture, such as DataSet and DataTable.

- The System.Data.Common namespace provides access to classes that are shared by .NET Framework data access providers, such as the DbProviderFactory class.

- The primary namespace for native SQL Server connectivity is System.Data.SqlClient. This namespace includes classes that provide optimized access to SQL Server (version 7.0 and higher) via SQL Server Native Client. The classes in this namespace are designed specifically to take advantage of SQL Server–specific features and won't work with other data sources.

- Microsoft also provides the System.Data.OleDb namespace, which can connect to a variety of data sources, including SQL Server. OLE DB is not as efficient as the native SQL client for SQL Server access, but it is a good option for applications that need to access data on multiple platforms, such as both SQL Server and Microsoft Access.

- The System.Data.Odbc namespace provides managed access to old-fashioned ODBC drivers. ODBC was developed in the early 1990s as a one-size-fits-all standard for connecting to a wide array of varied data sources. Because of its mission of standardizing data access across a wide variety of data sources, ODBC provides a generally "plain vanilla" interface that often does not take advantage of SQL Server or other database management system (DBMS) platform-specific features. This means that ODBC is not as efficient as the SQL client or OleDb clients, but it still provides a useful option for connecting to legacy database systems. It is also a proven interface for connecting to a wide variety of data sources such as Excel spreadsheets or other DBMSs.

- The System.Data.SqlTypes namespace provides .NET classes representing native, nullable SQL Server data types. These .NET SQL Server–specific data types for the most part use the same internal representation as the equivalent SQL Server native data types, helping to reduce precision loss problems. Using these types can also help speed up SQL Server connectivity, since it helps eliminate implicit conversions. And these data types, unlike the standard .NET value types, have built-in NULL-handling capability. Table 15-1 lists the .NET SqlTypes types and their corresponding native T-SQL data types.

Table 15-1. *System.Data.SqlTypes Conversions*

System.Data.SqlTypes Class	Native T-SQL Data Type
SqlBinary	binary, image, timestamp, varbinary
SqlBoolean	bit
SqlByte	tinyint
SqlDateTime	datetime, smalldatetime
SqlDecimal	decimal, numeric
SqlDouble	float
SqlGuid	uniqueidentifier
SqlInt16	smallint
SqlInt32	int
SqlInt64	bigint
SqlMoney	money, smallmoney
SqlSingle	real
SqlString	char, nchar, ntext, nvarchar, text, varchar
SqlXml	xml

Note At the time of this writing, there are no .NET SqlTypes types corresponding to the new SQL Server data types introduced in SQL Server 2008 (e.g., date, time, datetimeoffset, and datetime2).

The .NET SQL Client

The .NET native SQL client is the most efficient way to connect to SQL Server from a client application. With the possible exceptions of upgrading legacy code or designing code that must access non-SQL Server data sources, the native SQL client is the client connectivity method of choice. The main classes for establishing a connection, sending SQL commands, and retrieving results with `SqlClient` are listed in Table 15-2.

Table 15-2. *Commonly Used Native SQL Client Classes*

System.Data.SqlClient Class	Description
SqlCommand	The `SqlCommand` object represents a SQL statement or SP to execute.
SqlCommandBuilder	The `SqlCommandBuilder` automatically generates single-table commands to reconcile changes made to an ADO.NET `DataSet`.
SqlConnection	The `SqlConnection` establishes and opens a connection to a SQL Server database.
SqlConnectionStringBuilder	The `SqlConnectionStringBuilder` builds connection strings for use by `SqlConnection` objects.
SqlDataAdapter	The `SqlDataAdapter` wraps a set of `SqlCommand` objects and a `SqlConnection` that can be used to fill an ADO.NET `DataSet` and update a SQL Server database.
SqlDataReader	The `SqlDataReader` provides methods to read a forward-only stream of rows from a SQL Server database.
SqlException	The `SqlException` class provides access to SQL Server–specific exceptions. This class can be used to capture a SQL Server error or warning.
SqlParameter	The `SqlParameter` represents a parameter to a `SqlCommand`.
SqlParameterCollection	The `SqlParameter` collection is a collection of `SqlParameter` objects associated with a `SqlCommand`.
SqlTransaction	The `SqlTransaction` class enables a SQL Server transaction to be initiated and managed from a client.

Connected Data Access

Listing 15-1 demonstrates `SqlClient` data access via a `SqlDataReader` instance. This is the type of access you might use in an ASP.NET page to quickly retrieve values for a drop-down list, for example. This sample is written to run as a C# console application. The SQL Server connection string defined in the `sqlconnect` variable should be modified to suit your local SQL Server environment and security.

Listing 15-1. *SqlDataReader Sample*

```
using System;
using System.Data.SqlClient;
```

```csharp
namespace Apress.Examples
{
  class Listing15_1
  {
    static void Main(string[] args)
    {
      string sqlconnect = "DATA SOURCE=SQL2008;" +
        "INITIAL CATALOG=AdventureWorks;" +
        "INTEGRATED SECURITY=SSPI;";

      string sqlcommand = "SELECT " +
        "  DepartmentId, " +
        "  Name, " +
        "  GroupName " +
        " FROM HumanResources.Department " +
        " ORDER BY DepartmentId";

      SqlConnection connection = null;
      SqlCommand command = null;
      SqlDataReader datareader = null;

      try
      {
        connection = new SqlConnection(sqlconnect);
        connection.Open();
        command = new SqlCommand(sqlcommand, connection);
        datareader = command.ExecuteReader();

        while (datareader.Read())
        {
          Console.WriteLine
            (
              "{0}\t{1}\t{2}",
              datareader["DepartmentId"].ToString(),
              datareader["Name"].ToString(),
              datareader["GroupName"].ToString()
            );
        }
      }
      catch (SqlException ex)
      {
        Console.WriteLine(ex.Message);
      }
      finally
      {
        if (datareader != null)
          datareader.Dispose();
```

```
      if (command != null)
        command.Dispose();
      if (connection != null)
        connection.Dispose();
    }
    Console.Write("Press a Key to Continue...");
    Console.ReadKey();
  }
 }
}
```

This example is a very simple console application that retrieves the list of departments from the HumanResources.Department table of the AdventureWorks database and writes the data to the display. The example begins by importing the System and System.Data.SqlClient namespaces. Though not required, importing the namespaces saves some keystrokes and helps make code more readable by eliminating the need to prefix the classes and enumerations used with their associated namespaces.

```
using System;
using System.Data.SqlClient;
```

The body of the class defines the SQL Server connection string and the T-SQL command that will retrieve the department data. The SqlConnection, SqlCommand, and SqlDataReader objects are also declared and set to null.

```
      string sqlconnect = "DATA SOURCE=SQL2008;" +
        "INITIAL CATALOG=AdventureWorks;" +
        "INTEGRATED SECURITY=SSPI;";

      string sqlcommand = "SELECT " +
        "   DepartmentId, " +
        "   Name, " +
        "   GroupName " +
        " FROM HumanResources.Department " +
        " ORDER BY DepartmentId";

      SqlConnection connection = null;
      SqlCommand command = null;
      SqlDataReader datareader = null;
```

The SqlConnection connection string is composed of a series of key/value pairs separated by semicolons, as shown following:

```
DATA SOURCE=SQL2008;INITIAL CATALOG=AdventureWorks;INTEGRATED SECURITY=SSPI;
```

Some of the commonly used SqlConnection connection string keys are listed in Table 15-3.

Table 15-3. *SqlConnection Connection String Keys*

Connection String Keys	Description
AttachDBFileName	This is the name of the full path to an attachable primary database file (MDF file).
Connection Timeout	This is the length of time (in seconds) to wait for a server connection before stopping the attempt.
Data Source	This is the name or IP address of a SQL Server instance to connect to. Use the *server\instance* format for named instances. A port number can be added to the end of the name or network address by appending the port number with a comma.
Encrypt	This indicates that SSL encryption will be used to communicate with SQL Server.
Initial Catalog	This is the name of the database to connect to once a server connection is established.
Integrated Security	When set to true, yes, or sspi, Windows integrated security is used to connect. When false or no, SQL Server security is used.
MultipleActiveResultSets	When true, a connection can enable Multiple Active Result Sets (MARS). When false, all result sets from a batch must be processed before any other batch can be executed on the connection.
Password	This is the password for the SQL Server account used to log in. Using integrated security is recommended over SQL Server account security.
Persist Security Info	When set to false or no, sensitive security information (like a password) is not returned as part of the connection if the connection has been opened. The recommended setting is false.
User ID	This is the SQL Server account user ID used to log in. Integrated security is recommended over SQL Server account security.

The next section of code is enclosed in a try...catch block because of the possibility that a database connection or other error might occur. If an error does occur, control is passed to the catch block and the error message is displayed. The try...catch block includes the finally block, which cleans up the database connection whether an exception is thrown or not.

```
try
{
  ...
}
catch (SqlException ex)
{
  Console.WriteLine(ex.Message);
}
finally
```

```
  {
    if (datareader != null)
      datareader.Dispose();
    if (command != null)
      command.Dispose();
    if (connection != null)
      connection.Dispose();
  }
```

When connecting to SQL Server from a client application, it's a very good idea to code defensively with try...catch blocks. Defensive coding simply means trying to anticipate the problems that might occur and making sure that your code handles them. Following this practice in database client applications can save you a lot of headaches down the road. Some of the possible errors you might encounter in SQL Server client applications include problems connecting to SQL Server, trying to access tables and other database objects that have been changed or no longer exist, and returning NULL when you expect other values.

Within the example's try...catch block, the SqlConnection is instantiated and opened using the connection string defined previously. Then a SqlCommand is created on the open connection and executed with the ExecuteReader method. The ExecuteReader method returns a SqlDataReader instance, which allows you to retrieve result set rows in an efficient forward-only fashion. In this example, I use the SqlDataReader in a while loop to quickly retrieve all rows and display them on the console.

```
try
{
  connection = new SqlConnection(sqlconnect);
  connection.Open();
  command = new SqlCommand(sqlcommand, connection);
  datareader = command.ExecuteReader();

  while (datareader.Read())
  {
    Console.WriteLine
      (
        "{0}\t{1}\t{2}",
        datareader["DepartmentId"].ToString(),
        datareader["Name"].ToString(),
        datareader["GroupName"].ToString()
      );
  }
}
```

The results of the simple client utility from Listing 15-1 are shown in Figure 15-1.

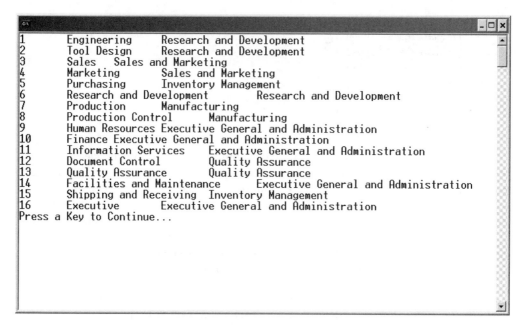

Figure 15-1. *Querying the database table and iterating the result set*

Disconnected Datasets

The example in Listing 15-1 demonstrated the forward-only read-only SqlDataReader, which provides an efficient interface for data retrieval but is far less flexible than ADO.NET disconnected datasets. A disconnected dataset is an in-memory cache of a dataset. It provides flexibility because you do not need a constant connection to the database in order to query and manipulate the data. Listing 15-2 demonstrates how to use the SqlDataAdapter to fill a DataSet and print the results. The differences between Listing 15-2 and Listing 15-1 are shown in bold.

Listing 15-2. *Using SqlDataReader to Fill a DataSet*

```
using System;
using System.Data;
using System.Data.SqlClient;

namespace Apress.Examples
{
  class Listing15_2
  {
    static void Main(string[] args)
    {
      string sqlconnect = "DATA SOURCE=SQL2008;" +
        "INITIAL CATALOG=AdventureWorks;" +
        "INTEGRATED SECURITY=SSPI;";
```

```
    string sqlcommand = "SELECT " +
      "   DepartmentId, " +
      "   Name, " +
      "   GroupName " +
      " FROM HumanResources.Department " +
      " ORDER BY DepartmentId";

    SqlDataAdapter adapter = null;
    DataSet dataset = null;

    try
    {
      adapter = new SqlDataAdapter(sqlcommand, sqlconnect);
      dataset = new DataSet();
      adapter.Fill(dataset);

      foreach (DataRow row in dataset.Tables[0].Rows)
      {
        Console.WriteLine
          (
            "{0}\t{1}\t{2}",
            row["DepartmentId"].ToString(),
            row["Name"].ToString(),
            row["GroupName"].ToString()
          );
      }
    }
    catch (SqlException ex)
    {
      Console.WriteLine(ex.Message);
    }
    finally
    {
      if (dataset != null)
        dataset.Dispose();
      if (adapter != null)
        adapter.Dispose();
    }
    Console.Write("Press a Key to Continue...");
    Console.ReadKey();
  }
 }
}
```

The second version of the application, in Listing 15-2, generates the same results as Listing 15-1. The first difference is that this sample imports the System.Data namespace, because the DataSet class is a member of System.Data. Again, this is not required, but it does save wear and tear on your fingers by eliminating the need to prefix System.Data classes and enumerations with the namespace.

```
using System;
using System.Data;
using System.Data.SqlClient;
```

The SQL connection string and query string definitions are the same in both examples. Listing 15-2 departs from Listing 15-1 by declaring a SqlDataAdapter and a DataSet instead of a SqlConnection, SqlCommand, and SqlDataReader.

```
SqlDataAdapter adapter = null;
DataSet dataset = null;
```

The code to retrieve the data creates a new SqlDataAdapter and DataSet, and then populates the DataSet via the Fill method of the SqlDataAdpater.

```
adapter = new SqlDataAdapter(sqlcommand, sqlconnect);
dataset = new DataSet();
adapter.Fill(dataset);
```

The main loop iterates through each DataRow in the single table returned by the DataSet and writes the results to the console:

```
foreach (DataRow row in dataset.Tables[0].Rows)
{
  Console.WriteLine
    (
      "{0}\t{1}\t{2}",
      row["DepartmentId"].ToString(),
      row["Name"].ToString(),
      row["GroupName"].ToString()
    );
}
```

The balance of the code handles exceptions, performs cleanup by disposing of the DataSet and SqlDataAdapter, and waits for a key press before exiting:

```
if (dataset != null)
  dataset.Dispose();
if (adapter != null)
  adapter.Dispose();
```

Parameterized Queries

ADO.NET provides a safe method for passing parameters to an SP or SQL statement, known as *parameterization*. The "classic" Visual Basic 6/VBScript method of concatenating parameter values directly into a long SQL query string is inefficient and potentially unsafe (see the "SQL Injection and Performance" sidebar later in this chapter for more information). A concatenated string query might look like this:

```
string sqlstatement = "SELECT " +
  "  BusinessEntityID, " +
  "  LastName, " +
  "  FirstName, " +
  "  MiddleName " +
  "FROM Person.Person " +
  "WHERE LastName = N'" + name + "';";
```

The value of the name variable can contain additional SQL statements, leaving SQL Server wide open to SQL injection attacks, as in the following:

```
string name = "'; DELETE FROM Person.Person; --";
```

This value for the name variable results in the following dangerous SQL statements being executed on the server:

```
SELECT
  BusinessEntityID,
  LastName,
  FirstName,
  MiddleName
FROM Person.Person
WHERE LastName = N'';
DELETE FROM Person.Person; -- ';
```

Parameterized queries avoid SQL injection by sending the parameter values to the server separately from the SQL statement. Listing 15-3 demonstrates a simple parameterized query. (The results are shown in Figure 15-2.)

Listing 15-3. *Parameterized SQL Query*

```
using System;
using System.Data;
using System.Data.SqlClient;

namespace Apress.Examples
{
  class Listing15_3
  {
    static void Main(string[] args)
    {

      string name = "SMITH";
      string sqlconnection = "SERVER=SQL2008; " +
        "INITIAL CATALOG=AdventureWorks; " +
        "INTEGRATED SECURITY=SSPI;";

      string sqlcommand = "SELECT " +
        "  BusinessEntityID, " +
        "  FirstName, " +
        "  MiddleName, " +
```

```
            "  LastName " +
            "FROM Person.Person " +
            "WHERE LastName = @name";

        SqlConnection connection = null;
        SqlCommand command = null;
        SqlDataReader datareader = null;

        try
        {
            connection = new SqlConnection(sqlconnection);
            connection.Open();
            command = new SqlCommand(sqlcommand, connection);
            SqlParameter par = command.Parameters.Add("@name", SqlDbType.NVarChar,
                50);
            par.Value = name;
            datareader = command.ExecuteReader();
            while (datareader.Read())
            {
                Console.WriteLine
                    (
                        "{0}\t{1}\t{2}\t{3}",
                        datareader["BusinessEntityID"].ToString(),
                        datareader["LastName"].ToString(),
                        datareader["FirstName"].ToString(),
                        datareader["MiddleName"].ToString()
                    );
            }
        }
        catch (Exception ex)
        {
            Console.WriteLine(ex.Message);
        }
        finally
        {
            if (datareader != null)
                datareader.Close();
            if (command != null)
                command.Dispose();
            if (connection != null)
                connection.Dispose();
        }
        Console.WriteLine("Press any key...");
        Console.ReadKey();
    }
  }
}
```

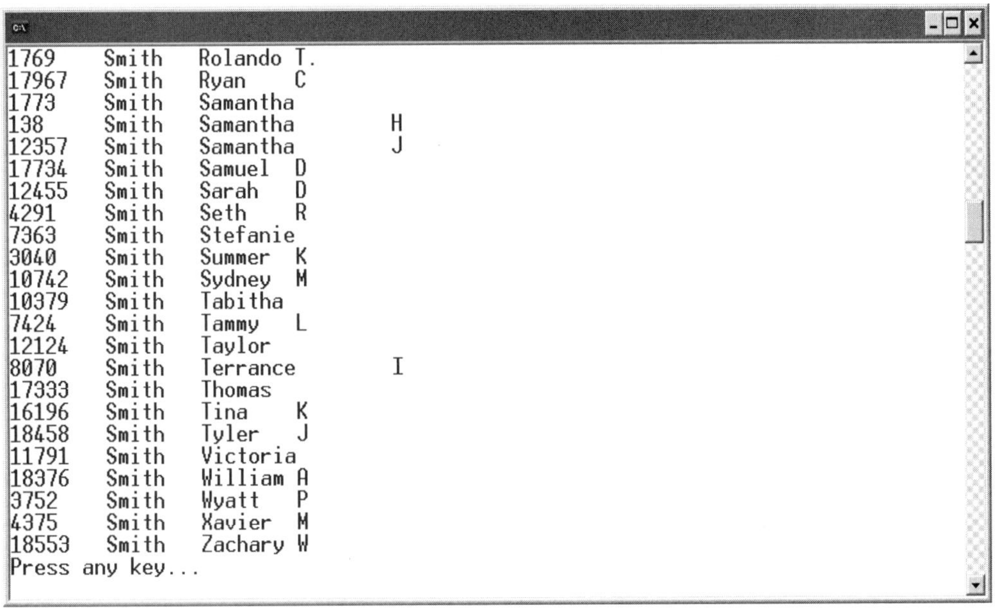

Figure 15-2. *Results of the parameterized query*

Listing 15-3 retrieves and prints the contact information for all people in the Adventure-Works `Person.Person` table whose last name is Smith. The sample begins by importing the appropriate namespaces. The `System.Data` namespace is referenced here because it contains the `SqlDbType` enumeration that is used to declare parameter data types.

```
using System;
using System.Data;
using System.Data.SqlClient;
```

The program begins by declaring a variable to hold the parameter value, the `SqlClient` connection string, a parameterized SQL `SELECT` statement, and the `SqlConnection`, `SqlCommand`, and `SqlDataReader` objects.

```
string name = "SMITH";
string sqlconnection = "SERVER=SQL2008; " +
  "INITIAL CATALOG=AdventureWorks; " +
  "INTEGRATED SECURITY=SSPI;";

string sqlcommand = "SELECT " +
  "  BusinessEntityID, " +
  "  FirstName, " +
  "  MiddleName, " +
  "  LastName " +
  "FROM Person.Person " +
  "WHERE LastName = @name";
```

```
SqlConnection connection = null;
SqlCommand command = null;
SqlDataReader datareader = null;
```

As with the previous examples, try...catch is used to capture runtime exceptions. The parameterized SQL SELECT statement contains a reference to a SQL Server parameter named @name. Next, a connection is established to the AdventureWorks database:

```
connection = new SqlConnection(sqlconnection);
connection.Open();
```

A SqlCommand is created using the previously defined query string, and a value is assigned to the @name parameter. Every SqlCommand exposes a SqlParameterCollection property called Parameters. The Add method of the Parameters collection allows you to add parameters to the SqlCommand. In this sample, the parameter added is named @name; it is an nvarchar type parameter, and its length is 50. The parameters in the Parameters collection are passed along to SQL Server with the SQL statement when the ExecuteReader, ExecuteScalar, ExecuteNonQuery, or ExecuteXmlReader method of the SqlCommand is called. The addition of a Parameter object to the SqlCommand is critical; this is the portion of the code that inhibits SQL injection attacks.

```
command = new SqlCommand(sqlcommand, connection);
SqlParameter par = command.Parameters.Add("@name", SqlDbType.NVarChar,
    50);
par.Value = name;
```

In this instance, the ExecuteReader method is called to return the results via SqlDataReader instance, and a while loop is used to iterate over and display the results.

```
datareader = command.ExecuteReader();
while (datareader.Read())
{
  Console.WriteLine
    (
      "{0}\t{1}\t{2}\t{3}",
      datareader["BusinessEntityID"].ToString(),
      datareader["LastName"].ToString(),
      datareader["FirstName"].ToString(),
      datareader["MiddleName"].ToString()
    );
}
```

SQL INJECTION AND PERFORMANCE

SQL developers and DBAs have long known of the potential security risks that SQL injection attacks can pose. Even as I write this chapter, I've received several e-mail newsletters and security advisories indicating that over half a million web pages have been attacked using SQL injection techniques. Even the United Nations web site has been compromised. So if developers and DBAs have known all about the evils of SQL injection for years, why are so many databases getting compromised?

The problem is not that people don't know what SQL injection is. Most DBAs and developers instinctively shudder at the sound of those two little words. Instead it appears that many developers either don't know how, or are just not motivated, to properly code to defend against this vicious attack. A lot of injection-susceptible code was written on the Visual Basic 6 and classic ASP platforms, where query parameterization was a bit of a hassle. A lot of programmers have carried their bad coding habits over to .NET, despite the fact that query parameterization with `SqlClient` is easier than ever.

As an added benefit, when you properly parameterize your queries, you can get a performance boost. When SQL Server receives a parameterized query, it automatically caches the query plan generated by the optimizer. On subsequent executions of the same parameterized query, SQL Server can use the cached query plan. Concatenated string queries without parameterization generally cannot take advantage of cached query plan reuse, so SQL Server must regenerate the query plan every time the query is executed. Keep these benefits in mind when developing SQL Server client code.

Nonquery, Scalar, and XML Querying

The examples covered so far in this chapter have all been SQL SELECT queries that return rows. SQL statements that do not return result sets are classified by .NET as nonqueries. Examples of nonqueries include UPDATE, INSERT, and DELETE statements, as well as DDL statements like CREATE INDEX and ALTER TABLE. The .NET Framework provides the ExecuteNonQuery method of the SqlCommand class to execute statements such as these. Listing 15-4 is a code snippet that shows how to execute a nonquery using the ExecuteNonQuery method of the SqlCommand.

Listing 15-4. *Executing a Nonquery*

```
SqlCommand command = new SqlCommand
  (
    "CREATE TABLE #temp " +
    "  ( " +
    "    Id INT NOT NULL PRIMARY KEY, " +
    "    Name NVARCHAR(50) " +
    "  );", connection
  );
command.ExecuteNonQuery();
```

The example creates a temporary table named #temp with two columns. Because the statement is a DDL statement that returns no result set, the ExecuteNonQuery method is used. In addition to queries that return no result sets, some queries return a result set consisting of a single row and a single column. For these queries, .NET provides a shortcut method of retrieving the value. The ExecuteScalar method retrieves the single value returned as a scalar value as a .NET Object. Using this method, you can avoid the hassle of creating a SqlDataReader instance and iterating it to retrieve a single value. Listing 15-5 is a code snippet that demonstrates the ExecuteScalar method.

Listing 15-5. *Using ExecuteScalar to Retrieve a Row Count*

```
SqlCommand command = new SqlCommand
  (
    "SELECT COUNT(*) " +
    "FROM Person.Person;", sqlcon
  );
Object count = command.ExecuteScalar();
```

If you call `ExecuteScalar` on a `SqlCommand` that returns more than one row or column, only the first row of the first column is retrieved. Your best bet is to make sure you only call `ExecuteScalar` on queries that return a single scalar value (one row, one column) to avoid possible confusion and problems down the road.

■**Tip** You may find that using the `ExecuteNonQuery` method with scalar OUTPUT parameters is more efficient than the `ExecuteScalar` method for servers under heavy workload.

An additional method of retrieving results in .NET is the `ExecuteXmlReader` method. This method of the `SqlCommand` object uses an `XmlReader` to retrieve XML results, such as those generated by a `SELECT` query with the `FOR XML` clause. Listing 15-6 demonstrates a modified version of the code in Listing 15-3 that uses the `ExecuteXmlReader` method. Differences between this listing and Listing 15-3 are in bold.

Listing 15-6. *Reading XML Data with ExecuteXmlReader*

```
using System;
using System.Data;
using System.Data.SqlClient;
using System.Xml;

namespace Apress.Examples
{
  class Listing15_6
  {
    static void Main(string[] args)
    {
      string name = "SMITH";
      string sqlconnection = "SERVER=SQL2008; " +
        "INITIAL CATALOG=AdventureWorks2008; " +
        "INTEGRATED SECURITY=SSPI;";

      string sqlcommand = "SELECT " +
        " BusinessEntityID, " +
        " FirstName, " +
        " COALESCE(MiddleName, '') AS MiddleName, " +
        " LastName " +
```

```
    "FROM Person.Person " +
    "WHERE LastName = @name " +
    "FOR XML AUTO;";

  SqlConnection connection = null;
  SqlCommand command = null;
  XmlReader xmlreader = null;

  try
  {
    connection = new SqlConnection(sqlconnection);
    connection.Open();
    command = new SqlCommand(sqlcommand, connection);
    SqlParameter par = command.Parameters.Add("@name", SqlDbType.NVarChar,
      50);
    par.Value = name;
    xmlreader = command.ExecuteXmlReader();
    while (xmlreader.Read())
    {
      Console.WriteLine
      (
        "{0}\t{1}\t{2}\t{3}",
        xmlreader["BusinessEntityID"].ToString(),
        xmlreader["LastName"].ToString(),
        xmlreader["FirstName"].ToString(),
        xmlreader["MiddleName"].ToString()
      );
    }
  }
  catch (Exception ex)
  {
    Console.WriteLine(ex.Message);
  }
  finally
  {
    if (xmlreader != null)
      xmlreader.Close();
    if (command != null)
      command.Dispose();
    if (connection != null)
      connection.Dispose();
  }
  Console.WriteLine("Press any key...");
  Console.ReadKey();
    }
  }
}
```

The first difference between this listing and Listing 15-3 is the addition of the System.Xml namespace, since the XmlReader class is being used:

```
using System;
using System.Data;
using System.Data.SqlClient;
using System.Xml;
```

The SQL SELECT statement is also slightly different. For one thing, the COALESCE function is used on the MiddleName column to replace NULL middle names with empty strings. The FOR XML clause leaves NULL attributes out of the generated XML by default. Missing attributes would generate exceptions when trying to display the results. The FOR XML AUTO clause was used in the SELECT query to inform SQL Server that it needs to generate an XML result.

```
string sqlcommand = "SELECT " +
  " BusinessEntityID, " +
  " FirstName, " +
  " COALESCE(MiddleName, '') AS MiddleName, " +
  " LastName " +
  "FROM Person.Person " +
  "WHERE LastName = @name " +
  "FOR XML AUTO;";
```

Inside the try...catch block, I've used the ExecuteXmlReader method instead of the ExecuteReader method. The loop that displays the results is very similar to Listing 15-3 as well. The main difference in this listing is that an XmlReader is used in place of a SqlDataReader.

```
xmlreader = command.ExecuteXmlReader();
while (xmlreader.Read())
{
  Console.WriteLine
  (
    "{0}\t{1}\t{2}\t{3}",
    xmlreader["BusinessEntityID"].ToString(),
    xmlreader["LastName"].ToString(),
    xmlreader["FirstName"].ToString(),
    xmlreader["MiddleName"].ToString()
  );
}
}
```

The remaining code in the sample performs exception handling and proper cleanup, as do the other example listings.

SqlBulkCopy

SQL Server provides tools, such as SQL Server Integration Services (SSIS) and the Bulk Copy Program (BCP), to help populate your databases from external data sources. Some applications can benefit built-in .NET bulk load functionality. The .NET Framework (versions 2.0 and higher) SqlClient implements the SqlBulkCopy class to make efficient bulk loading easy. SqlBulkCopy can be used to load data from a database table, an XML table, a flat file, or any other type of data source you choose. The SqlBulkCopy example in Listing 15-7 loads US Postal Service ZIP code data from a tab-delimited flat file into a SQL Server table. A sample of the source text file is shown in Table 15-4.

Table 15-4. *Sample Tab-Delimited ZIP Code Data*

ZIP Code	Latitude	Longitude	City	State
99546	54.2402	−176.7874	ADAK	AK
99551	60.3147	−163.1189	AKIACHAK	AK
99552	60.3147	−163.1189	AKIAK	AK
99553	55.4306	−162.5581	AKUTAN	AK
99554	62.1172	−163.2376	ALAKANUK	AK
99555	58.9621	−163.1189	ALEKNAGIK	AK

The complete sample ZIP code file is included with the downloadable source code for this book. The target table is built with the CREATE TABLE statement in Listing 15-7. You need to execute this statement to create the target table in the AdventureWorks database (or another target database if you choose).

Listing 15-7. *Creating the ZipCodes Target Table*

```
CREATE TABLE dbo.ZipCodes
(
  ZIP CHAR(5) NOT NULL PRIMARY KEY,
  Latitude NUMERIC(8, 4) NOT NULL,
  Longitude NUMERIC(8, 4) NOT NULL,
  City NVARCHAR(50) NOT NULL,
  State CHAR(2) NOT NULL
)
GO
```

The code presented in Listing 15-8 uses the SqlBulkCopy class to bulk copy the data from the flat file into the destination table.

Listing 15-8. *SqlBulkCopy Class Example*

```
using System;
using System.Data;
using System.Data.SqlClient;
using System.Diagnostics;
using System.IO;
```

```csharp
namespace Apress.Example
{
  class Listing15_8
  {
    static string sqlconnection = "DATA SOURCE=SQL2008; " +
      "INITIAL CATALOG=AdventureWorks; " +
      "INTEGRATED SECURITY=SSPI;";

    static string sourcefile = "c:\\ZIPCodes.txt";

    static DataTable loadtable = null;

    static void Main(string[] args)
    {
      Stopwatch clock = new Stopwatch();
      clock.Start();
      int rowcount = DoImport();
      clock.Stop();
      Console.WriteLine("{0} Rows Imported in {1} Seconds.",
        rowcount, (clock.ElapsedMilliseconds / 1000.0));
      Console.WriteLine("Press a Key...");
      Console.ReadKey();
    }

    static int DoImport()
    {
      using (SqlBulkCopy bulkcopier = new SqlBulkCopy(sqlconnection))
      {
        bulkcopier.DestinationTableName = "dbo.ZIPCodes";
        try
        {
          LoadSourceFile();
          bulkcopier.WriteToServer(loadtable);
        }
        catch (SqlException ex)
        {
          Console.WriteLine(ex.Message);
        }
      }
      return loadtable.Rows.Count;
    }

    static void LoadSourceFile()
    {
      loadtable = new DataTable();
      DataColumn loadcolumn = new DataColumn();
      DataRow loadrow = null;
```

```
loadcolumn.DataType = typeof(System.String);
loadcolumn.ColumnName = "ZIP";
loadcolumn.Unique = true;
loadtable.Columns.Add(loadcolumn);

loadcolumn = new DataColumn();
loadcolumn.DataType = typeof(System.Double);
loadcolumn.ColumnName = "Latitude";
loadcolumn.Unique = false;
loadtable.Columns.Add(loadcolumn);

loadcolumn = new DataColumn();
loadcolumn.DataType = typeof(System.Double);
loadcolumn.ColumnName = "Longitude";
loadcolumn.Unique = false;
loadtable.Columns.Add(loadcolumn);

loadcolumn = new DataColumn();
loadcolumn.DataType = typeof(System.String);
loadcolumn.ColumnName = "City";
loadcolumn.Unique = false;
loadtable.Columns.Add(loadcolumn);

loadcolumn = new DataColumn();
loadcolumn.DataType = typeof(System.String);
loadcolumn.ColumnName = "State";
loadcolumn.Unique = false;
loadtable.Columns.Add(loadcolumn);

using (StreamReader stream = new StreamReader(sourcefile))
{
  string record = stream.ReadLine();
  while (record != null)
  {
    string[] cols = record.Split('\t');
    loadrow = loadtable.NewRow();
    loadrow["ZIP"] = cols[0];
    loadrow["Latitude"] = cols[1];
    loadrow["Longitude"] = cols[2];
    loadrow["City"] = cols[3];
    loadrow["State"] = cols[4];
    loadtable.Rows.Add(loadrow);
    record = stream.ReadLine();
  }
}
      }
     }
    }
}
```

The code begins by importing required namespaces, declaring the Apress.Samples namespace, and declaring the module name. The System.IO namespace is imported for the StreamReader, and the System.Diagnostics namespace is imported for the Stopwatch class so that the program can report the import time.

```
using System;
using System.Data;
using System.Data.SqlClient;
using System.Diagnostics;
using System.IO;
```

The class defines a SQL connection string, the source file name, and a DataTable:

```
static string sqlconnection = "DATA SOURCE=SQL2008; " +
  "INITIAL CATALOG=AdventureWorks; " +
  "INTEGRATED SECURITY=SSPI;";

static string sourcefile = "c:\\ZIPCodes.txt";

static DataTable loadtable = null;
```

The class contains three functions: Main, DoImport, and LoadSourceFile. The Main function begins by starting a Stopwatch to time the import process. Then it invokes the DoImport function that performs the actual import and reports back the number of rows. Finally, the Stopwatch is stopped and the number of rows imported and number of seconds elapsed are displayed.

```
static void Main(string[] args)
{
  Stopwatch clock = new Stopwatch();
  clock.Start();
  int rowcount = DoImport();
  clock.Stop();
  Console.WriteLine("{0} Rows Imported in {1} Seconds.",
    rowcount, (clock.ElapsedMilliseconds / 1000.0));
  Console.WriteLine("Press a Key...");
  Console.ReadKey();
}
```

The second function, DoImport, initializes an instance of the SqlBulkCopy class. It then calls the LoadSourceFile function to populate the DataTable with data from the source flat file. The populated DataTable is passed into the WriteToServer method of the SqlBulkCopy object. This method performs a bulk copy of all the rows in the DataTable to the destination table. The DoImport function ends by returning the number of rows loaded into the DataTable.

```
static int DoImport()
{
  using (SqlBulkCopy bulkcopier = new SqlBulkCopy(sqlconnection))
  {
    bulkcopier.DestinationTableName = "dbo.ZIPCodes";
    try
```

```
      {
        LoadSourceFile();
        bulkcopier.WriteToServer(loadtable);
      }
      catch (SqlException ex)
      {
        Console.WriteLine(ex.Message);
      }
    }
    return loadtable.Rows.Count;
  }
```

The third and final function, LoadSourceFile, initializes the structure of the DataTable and loads the source file data into it:

```
static void LoadSourceFile()
{
  loadtable = new DataTable();
  DataColumn loadcolumn = new DataColumn();
  DataRow loadrow = null;

  loadcolumn.DataType = typeof(System.String);
  loadcolumn.ColumnName = "ZIP";
  loadcolumn.Unique = true;
  loadtable.Columns.Add(loadcolumn);

  loadcolumn = new DataColumn();
  loadcolumn.DataType = typeof(System.Double);
  loadcolumn.ColumnName = "Latitude";
  loadcolumn.Unique = false;
  loadtable.Columns.Add(loadcolumn);
  ...
  using (StreamReader stream = new StreamReader(sourcefile))
  {
    string record = stream.ReadLine();
    while (record != null)
    {
      string[] cols = record.Split('\t');
      loadrow = loadtable.NewRow();
      loadrow["ZIP"] = cols[0];
      loadrow["Latitude"] = cols[1];
      ...
      loadtable.Rows.Add(loadrow);
      record = stream.ReadLine();
    }
  }
}
    }
  }
}
```

After it completes, Listing 15-8 reports the number of rows bulk loaded and the amount of time required, as shown in Figure 15-3.

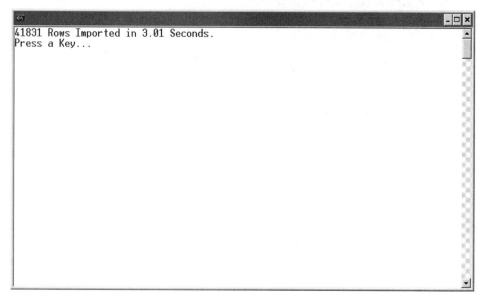

Figure 15-3. *Report of bulk copy rows imported and time required*

You can perform a simple SELECT statement like the one shown in Listing 15-9 to verify that the destination table was properly populated. Partial results are shown in Figure 15-4.

Listing 15-9. *Verifying Bulk Copy Results*

```
SELECT ZIP,
  Latitude,
  Longitude,
  City,
  State
FROM ZipCodes;
```

	ZIP	Latitude	Longitu...	City	State
1	00501	40.9223	-72.6371	HOLTSVILLE	NY
2	00544	40.9223	-72.6371	HOLTSVILLE	NY
3	01001	42.1405	-72.7887	AGAWAM	MA
4	01002	42.3671	-72.4646	AMHERST	MA
5	01003	42.3695	-72.6359	AMHERST	MA
6	01004	42.3845	-72.5131	AMHERST	MA
7	01005	42.3292	-72.1394	BARRE	MA
8	01007	42.2802	-72.4021	BELCHERTOWN	MA
9	01008	42.1777	-72.9583	BLANDFORD	MA
10	01009	42.2060	-72.3405	BONDSVILLE	MA
11	01010	42.1086	-72.2044	BRIMFIELD	MA
12	01011	42.2943	-72.8527	CHESTER	MA

Figure 15-4. *ZIP codes bulk loaded into the database*

Multiple Active Result Sets

Prior to SQL Server 2005, client-side applications were limited to one open result set per connection to SQL Server. The workaround was to fully process or cancel all open result sets on a single connection before retrieving a new result set, or to open multiple connections, each with its own single open result.

SQL Server 2008, like SQL Server 2005, allows you to use MARS functionality. MARS allows you to process multiple open result sets over a single connection. Listing 15-10 demonstrates how to use MARS to perform the following tasks over a single connection:

1. Open a result set and begin reading it.

2. Stop reading the result set after a few rows.

3. Open a second result set and read it to completion.

4. Resume reading the first result set.

■**Note** This is a very simple example that doesn't necessarily represent a best use case for MARS. Christian Kleinerman describes real-world MARS use cases on TechNet at http://technet.microsoft.com/en-us/library/ms345109.aspx.

Listing 15-10. *Opening Two Result Sets Over a Single Connection*

```
using System;
using System.Data;
using System.Data.SqlClient;

namespace Apress.Examples
{
  class MARS
  {
    static string sqlconnection = "SERVER=SQL2008; " +
      "INITIAL CATALOG=AdventureWorks; " +
      "INTEGRATED SECURITY=SSPI; " +
      "MULTIPLEACTIVERESULTSETS=true; ";

    static string sqlcommand1 = "SELECT " +
      "  DepartmentID, " +
      "  Name, " +
      "  GroupName " +
      "FROM HumanResources.Department; ";

    static string sqlcommand2 = "SELECT " +
      "  ShiftID, " +
```

```
          "  Name, " +
          "  StartTime, " +
          "  EndTime " +
          "FROM HumanResources.Shift; ";

      static SqlConnection connection = null;
      static SqlCommand command1 = null;
      static SqlCommand command2 = null;
      static SqlDataReader datareader1 = null;
      static SqlDataReader datareader2 = null;

      static void Main(string[] args)
      {
        try
        {
          connection = new SqlConnection(sqlconnection);
          connection.Open();
          command1 = new SqlCommand(sqlcommand1, connection);
          command2 = new SqlCommand(sqlcommand2, connection);
          datareader1 = command1.ExecuteReader();
          datareader2 = command2.ExecuteReader();
          int i = 0;

          Console.WriteLine("===========");
          Console.WriteLine("Departments");
          Console.WriteLine("===========");
          while (datareader1.Read() && i++ < 3)
          {
            Console.WriteLine
            (
              "{0}\t{1}\t{2}",
              datareader1["DepartmentID"].ToString(),
              datareader1["Name"].ToString(),
              datareader1["GroupName"].ToString()
            );
          }

          Console.WriteLine("======");
          Console.WriteLine("Shifts");
          Console.WriteLine("======");
          while (datareader2.Read())
          {
            Console.WriteLine
            (
              "{0}\t{1}\t{2}\t{3}",
              datareader2["ShiftID"].ToString(),
              datareader2["Name"].ToString(),
```

```
          datareader2["StartTime"].ToString(),
          datareader2["EndTime"].ToString()
        );
      }


    Console.WriteLine("======================");
    Console.WriteLine("Departments, Continued");
    Console.WriteLine("======================");
    while (datareader1.Read())
    {
      Console.WriteLine
      (
        "{0}\t{1}\t{2}",
        datareader1["DepartmentID"].ToString(),
        datareader1["Name"].ToString(),
        datareader1["GroupName"].ToString()
      );
    }
  }
  catch (SqlException ex)
  {
    Console.WriteLine(ex.Message);
  }
  finally
  {
    if (datareader1 != null)
      datareader1.Dispose();
    if (datareader2 != null)
      datareader2.Dispose();
    if (command1 != null)
      command1.Dispose();
    if (command2 != null)
      command2.Dispose();
    if (connection != null)
      connection.Dispose();
  }
  Console.WriteLine("Press a key to end...");
  Console.ReadKey();
  }
 }
}
```

Listing 15-10 begins by importing the necessary namespaces:

```
using System;
using System.Data;
using System.Data.SqlClient;
```

The class begins by declaring a SQL connection string and two SQL query strings. It also declares a SqlConnection, two SqlCommand objects, and two SqlDataReader objects. The connection is then opened, and two SqlCommands are created on the single connection to retrieve the two result sets:

```
static string sqlconnection = "SERVER=SQL2008; " +
   "INITIAL CATALOG=AdventureWorks2008; " +
   "INTEGRATED SECURITY=SSPI; " +
   "MULTIPLEACTIVERESULTSETS=true; ";

static string sqlcommand1 = "SELECT " +
   "  DepartmentID, " +
   "  Name, " +
   "  GroupName " +
   "FROM HumanResources.Department; ";

static string sqlcommand2 = "SELECT " +
   "  ShiftID, " +
   "  Name, " +
   "  StartTime, " +
   "  EndTime " +
   "FROM HumanResources.Shift; ";

static SqlConnection connection = null;
static SqlCommand command1 = null;
static SqlCommand command2 = null;
static SqlDataReader datareader1 = null;
static SqlDataReader datareader2 = null;
```

The key to enabling MARS is the MULTIPLEACTIVERESULTSETS=true key/value pair in the connection string. The Main function creates and opens the SqlConnection, the SqlCommand objects, and the SqlDataReader objects required to create two active result sets over one connection.

```
connection = new SqlConnection(sqlconnection);
connection.Open();
command1 = new SqlCommand(sqlcommand1, connection);
command2 = new SqlCommand(sqlcommand2, connection);
datareader1 = command1.ExecuteReader();
datareader2 = command2.ExecuteReader();
```

The balance of the code loops through the result sets displaying the data on the console. The code interrupts the first result set after three rows are consumed, consumes the second result set in its entirety, and then finishes up the first result set, all over a single connection. The results are shown in Figure 15-5.

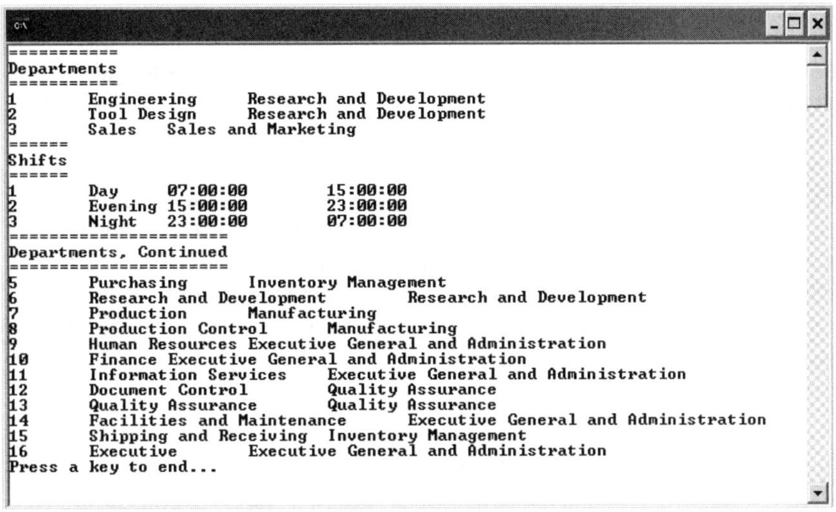

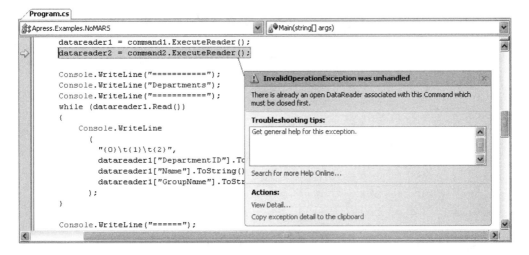

Figure 15-5. *Results of iterating two active result sets over one connection*

Removing the MULTIPLEACTIVERESULTSETS=true option from the connection string, as shown in the code snippet in Listing 15-11, results in the invalid operation exception in Figure 15-6 being thrown.

Listing 15-11. *SQL Connection String Without MARS Enabled*

```
static string sqlconnection = "SERVER=SQL2008; " +
  "INITIAL CATALOG=AdventureWorks2008; " +
  "INTEGRATED SECURITY=SSPI; ";
```

Figure 15-6. *Trying to open two result sets on one connection without MARS*

LINQ to SQL

Language Integrated Query (LINQ) is a set of technologies built into Visual Studio and the .NET Framework that allow you to query data from any data source. LINQ ships with standard libraries that support querying SQL databases, XML, and objects. Additional LINQ-enabled data providers have already been created to query Amazon.com, NHibernate, and LDAP, among others. LINQ to SQL encapsulates LINQ's built-in support for SQL database querying.

LINQ to SQL provides an object/relational mapping (O/RM) implementation for the .NET Framework. LINQ to SQL allows you to create .NET classes that model your database, allowing you to query and manipulate data using object-oriented methodologies. In this section, I'll introduce LINQ to SQL. For an in-depth introduction, I recommend the book *LINQ for Visual C# 2008*, by Fabio Claudio Ferracchiati (Apress, 2008).

■**Tip** In addition to Fabio's *LINQ for Visual C#* books, Apress publishes several books on LINQ. You can view the list at www.apress.com/book/search?searchterm=linq&act=search. The MSDN web site (http://msdn.microsoft.com) also has several LINQ resources available.

Using the O/RM Designer

Visual Studio includes a LINQ to SQL designer that makes .NET O/RM a relatively painless process. The LINQ to SQL designer can be accessed from within Visual Studio by adding a new LINQ to SQL Classes item to your .NET project, as shown in Figure 15-7. Note that there is some importance placed on the file name you choose, as the .NET data context class created will be based on the name you choose (without the .dbml extension). In this case, I chose the name AdventureWorks.dbml.

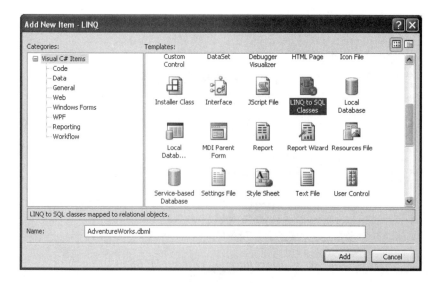

Figure 15-7. *Adding a LINQ to SQL Classes item to a project*

Once the LINQ to SQL Classes item has been added, you need to create a Microsoft SQL Server SqlClient connection that points to your server and database. You can add a data connection through the Visual Studio Server Explorer, as shown in Figure 15-8.

Figure 15-8. *Adding a connection through the Server Explorer*

Once you've added the connection to your database, the Server Explorer displays the tables and other objects contained within the database. You can select tables and SPs and drag them from the Server Explorer onto the O/RM designer surface. Figure 15-9 shows the selection of two tables, Person.Person and Person.EmailAddress, in the Server Explorer.

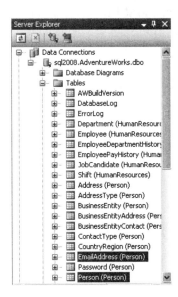

Figure 15-9. *Viewing and selecting tables in the Server Explorer*

Once the tables have been dragged onto the O/RM designer surface, Visual Studio provides a visual representation of the classes it created to model the database and the relationships between them. Figure 15-10 shows the designer surface with the Person.Person and Person.EmailAddress tables added to it.

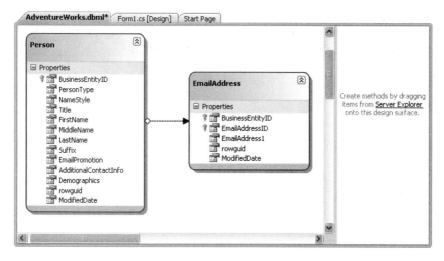

Figure 15-10. *O/RM designer surface with tables added to it*

Querying with LINQ to SQL

Once you've created your LINQ to SQL O/RM classes with the designer, it's time to write queries. LINQ not only allows you to query any data source including SQL, it is also integrated directly into Visual Basic and C# via brand new keywords. These new LINQ-specific keywords include from, select, where, and others that will seem eerily familiar to SQL developers. These new keywords, combined with some other new features, provide a powerful mechanism for performing declarative queries directly in your procedural code.

Basic LINQ to SQL Querying

My first LINQ to SQL query example, in Listing 15-12, queries the Persons property of the AdventureWorksDataContext class.

Listing 15-12. *Querying Persons with LINQ to SQL*

```
using System;
using System.Linq;

namespace Apress.Examples
{
  class Listing15_12
  {
    static void Main(string[] args)
    {
      AdventureWorksDataContext db = new AdventureWorksDataContext();
      db.Log = Console.Out;
```

```
    var query = from p in db.Persons
                select p;

    foreach (Person p in query)
    {
      Console.WriteLine
        (
          "{0}\t{1}\t{2}",
          p.FirstName,
          p.MiddleName,
          p.LastName
        );
    }
    Console.WriteLine("Press a key to continue...");
    Console.ReadKey();
  }
 }
}
```

The first thing to notice about this example is the namespace declarations. Since I am using LINQ to SQL, I had to import the System.Linq namespace. This namespace provides access to the LINQ IQueryable interface, which will be used later.

```
using System;
using System.Linq;
```

The Main method of the program begins by creating an instance of the AdventureWorksDataContext, which I will query against. Notice that I've set the Log property of the AdventureWorksDataContext instance to Console.Out. This will display the actual SQL query that LINQ to SQL generates on the console.

```
    AdventureWorksDataContext db = new AdventureWorksDataContext();
    db.Log = Console.Out;
```

After the AdventureWorksDataContext class is instantiated, querying with the new C# keywords is as simple as assigning a query to a variable. For this example, I've taken advantage of the new .NET *anonymous types* feature. Anonymous types allow you to declare variables without an explicit type through use of the var keyword. When you declare a variable using anonymous types, the compiler automatically infers the type at compile time. This is an important distinction from Object and variant data types, which represent general-purpose types that are determined at runtime. The query is simple, using the from...in clause to indicate the source of the data and the select keyword to return objects.

```
    var query = from p in db.Persons
                select p;
```

The final part of this example uses a foreach loop to iterate over all the Person objects returned by the query and prints the names to the display. Partial results of this query are shown in Figure 15-11.

```
foreach (Person p in query)
{
  Console.WriteLine
    (
      "{0}\t{1}\t{2}",
      p.FirstName,
      p.MiddleName,
      p.LastName
    );
}
```

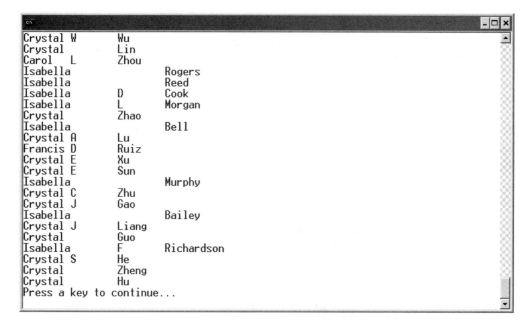

Figure 15-11. *Querying Persons with LINQ to SQL*

As I mentioned previously, you can use the Log attribute of your data context class to output the SQL code generated by LINQ to SQL. This is useful for debugging or just finding out more about how LINQ to SQL works internally. The SQL query generated by Listing 15-12 is shown in Listing 15-13 (reformatted for readability).

Listing 15-13. *LINQ to SQL–Generated SQL Query*

```
SELECT
  [t0].[BusinessEntityID],
  [t0].[PersonType],
  [t0].[NameStyle],
  [t0].[Title],
```

```
       [to].[FirstName],
       [to].[MiddleName],
       [to].[LastName],
       [to].[Suffix],
       [to].[EmailPromotion],
       [to].[AdditionalContactInfo],
       [to].[Demographics],
       [to].[rowguid],
       [to].[ModifiedDate]
FROM [Person].[Person] AS [to]
```

LINQ to SQL provides several clauses in addition to from and select. Table 15-5 is a summary of some commonly used LINQ to SQL query operators. I will continue the discussion of LINQ to SQL query operators in the sections that follow.

Table 15-5. *Useful LINQ Standard Query Operators*

Function	Keyword	Description
Restriction	where	The restriction operator restricts/filters the results returned by a query, returning only the items that match the where predicate condition. You can think of this as equivalent to the WHERE clause in SQL.
Projection	select	The projection operator is used to define/restrict the attributes that should be returned in the result collection. The select keyword approximates the SQL SELECT clause.
Join	join	The join operator performs an inner join of two sequences based on matching keys from both sequences. This is equivalent to the SQL INNER JOIN clause.
Join	join...into	The join operator can accept an into clause to perform a left outer join. This form of the join keyword is equivalent to the SQL LEFT OUTER JOIN clause.
Ordering	orderby	The orderby keyword accepts a comma-separated list of keys to sort your query results. Each key can be followed by the ascending or descending keyword. The ascending keyword is the default. This is equivalent to the SQL ORDER BY clause.
Grouping	group	The group keyword allows you to group your results by a specified set of key values. You can use the group...into syntax if you want to perform additional query operations on the grouped results. The behavior of this keyword approximates the SQL GROUP BY clause.
Subexpressions	let	The let keyword in a query allows you to store subexpressions in a variable during the query. You can use the variable in subsequent query clauses. SQL doesn't have an equivalent for this statement, although subqueries can approximate the behavior in some instances. The best equivalent for this keyword is the XQuery FLWOR expression let clause.

The where Clause

The where clause allows you to restrict the results returned by the query, as shown in Listing 15-14. Replacing the query in Listing 15-12 with this query restricts the Person objects returned to only those with the letters *smi* in their last name.

Listing 15-14. *Querying Persons with "smi" in Their Last Names*

```
var query = from p in db.Persons
            where p.LastName.Contains("SMI")
            select p;
```

The SQL code generated by this LINQ to SQL query is slightly different from the previous SQL query, as shown in Listing 15-15.

Listing 15-15. *LINQ to SQL–Generated SQL Query with WHERE Clause*

```
SELECT
  [t0].[BusinessEntityID],
  [t0].[PersonType],
  [t0].[NameStyle],
  [t0].[Title],
  [t0].[FirstName],
  [t0].[MiddleName],
  [t0].[LastName],
  [t0].[Suffix],
  [t0].[EmailPromotion],
  [t0].[AdditionalContactInfo],
  [t0].[Demographics],
  [t0].[rowguid],
  [t0].[ModifiedDate]
FROM [Person].[Person] AS [t0]
WHERE [t0].[LastName] LIKE @p0
```

One interesting aspect to this query is that LINQ to SQL converts the Contains method of the Person object's LastName property to a SQL LIKE predicate. This is important because it means that LINQ to SQL is smart enough to realize that it doesn't have to retrieve an entire table, instantiate objects for every row of the table, and then use .NET methods to limit the results on the client. This can be a significant performance enhancement over the alternative.

Another interesting feature that LINQ to SQL provides is query parameterization. In this instance, the generated SQL query includes a parameter named @p0 that is defined as an nvarchar(5) parameter and assigned a value of %SMI%.

The orderby Clause

LINQ to SQL also provides result ordering via the orderby clause. You can use the orderby keyword in your query to specify the attributes to sort by. Listing 15-16 builds on the query in Listing 15-14 by adding an orderby clause that sorts results by the LastName and FirstName attributes of the Person object.

Listing 15-16. *Ordering LINQ to SQL Query Results*

```
var query = from p in db.Persons
            where p.LastName.Contains("SMI")
            orderby p.LastName, p.FirstName
            select p;
```

Replacing the query in Listing 15-12 with this query returns all Person objects whose last names contain the letters *smi*, and sorts the objects by their last and first names. The generated SQL query is shown in Listing 15-17. It's similar to the previous query except that LINQ to SQL has added a SQL ORDER BY clause.

Listing 15-17. *LINQ to SQL–Generated SQL Query with ORDER BY Clause*

```
SELECT
  [t0].[BusinessEntityID],
  [t0].[PersonType],
  [t0].[NameStyle],
  [t0].[Title],
  [t0].[FirstName],
  [t0].[MiddleName],
  [t0].[LastName],
  [t0].[Suffix],
  [t0].[EmailPromotion],
  [t0].[AdditionalContactInfo],
  [t0].[Demographics],
  [t0].[rowguid],
  [t0].[ModifiedDate]
FROM [Person].[Person] AS [t0]
WHERE [t0].[LastName] LIKE @p0
ORDER BY
  [t0].LastName,
  [t0].FirstName
```

The join Clause

LINQ to SQL also provides the join clause, which allows you to perform inner joins in your queries. An inner join relates two entities, like Person and EmailAddress in the example, based on common values of an attribute. The LINQ to SQL join operator essentially works the same way as the SQL INNER JOIN operator. Listing 15-18 demonstrates a LINQ to SQL join query.

Listing 15-18. *Retrieving Persons and Related E-mail Addresses*

```
using System;
using System.Linq;

namespace Apress.Examples
{
  class Listing15_18
```

```
{
  static void Main(string[] args)
  {
    AdventureWorksDataContext db = new AdventureWorksDataContext();
    db.Log = Console.Out;

    var query = from p in db.Persons
                join e in db.EmailAddresses
                on p.BusinessEntityID equals e.BusinessEntityID
                where p.LastName.Contains("SMI")
                orderby p.LastName, p.FirstName
                select new
                {
                  LastName = p.LastName,
                  FirstName = p.FirstName,
                  MiddleName = p.MiddleName,
                  EmailAddress = e.EmailAddress1
                };

    foreach (var q in query)
    {
      Console.WriteLine
        (
          "{0}\t{1}\t{2}\t{3}",
          q.FirstName,
          q.MiddleName,
          q.LastName,
          q.EmailAddress
        );
    }
    Console.WriteLine("Press a key to continue...");
    Console.ReadKey();
  }
}
}
```

THE EQUALS OPERATOR AND NON-EQUIJOINS

C# uses the equals keyword in the LINQ join...on clause instead of the familiar == operator. This is done for clarity. The LINQ from...join pattern maps directly to the Enumerable.Join() LINQ query operator, which requires two delegates that are used to compute values for comparison. The delegate/key on the left side of the operator consumes the outer sequence and the right delegate/key consumes the inner sequence. The decision was made to use the equals keyword to clarify this concept primarily because implementing a full query processor for LINQ would have resulted in significant overhead. In order to perform other types of non-equijoins in LINQ, you can use a combination of the LINQ GroupJoin operator and the where clause.

The LINQ to SQL query in Listing 15-18 uses the `join` operator to identify the entities to join and the `on` clause specify the join criteria. In this example, the `Person` and `EmailAddress` entities are joined based on their `BusinessEntityID` attributes. Because the query needs to return some attributes of both entities, the `select` clause creates a new anonymous type on the fly. Partial results of the join query are shown in Figure 15-12.

```
var query = from p in db.Persons
            join e in db.EmailAddresses
            on p.BusinessEntityID equals e.BusinessEntityID
            where p.LastName.Contains("SMI")
            orderby p.LastName, p.FirstName
            select new
            {
              LastName = p.LastName,
              FirstName = p.FirstName,
              MiddleName = p.MiddleName,
              EmailAddress = e.EmailAddress1
            };
```

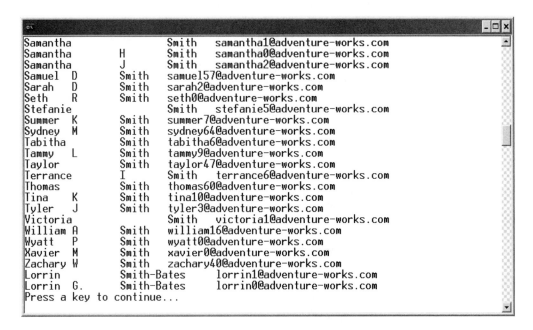

Figure 15-12. *Retrieving Person names and related e-mail addresses*

The SQL query generated by LINQ to SQL includes a SQL `INNER JOIN` clause, and only retrieves the columns required by the query, as shown in Listing 15-19.

Listing 15-19. *LINQ to SQL–Generated SQL Query with INNER JOIN Clause*

```
SELECT
  [t0].[LastName],
  [t0].[FirstName],
  [t0].[MiddleName],
  [t1].[EmailAddress]
FROM [Person].[Person] AS [t0]
INNER JOIN [Person].[EmailAddress] AS [t1]
  ON [t0].[BusinessEntityID] = [t1].[BusinessEntityID]
WHERE [t0].[LastName] LIKE @p0
ORDER BY
  [t0].[LastName],
  [t0].[FirstName]
```

Deferred Query Execution

LINQ to SQL uses a query execution pattern known as *deferred query execution*. When you declare a LINQ to SQL query, .NET creates an *expression tree*. The expression tree is essentially a data structure that acts as a guide that LINQ to SQL can use to execute your query. The expression tree does not contain the actual data retrieved by the query, but rather the information required to execute the query. Deferred query execution causes the execution of the query to be delayed until the data returned by the query is actually needed—when you iterate the results in a foreach loop, for instance. You can view deferred query execution in action by placing breakpoints on the foreach loops of the code samples in the previous sections. LINQ to SQL will not generate and output its SQL code until after the foreach loop iteration begins. This is shown in Figure 15-13.

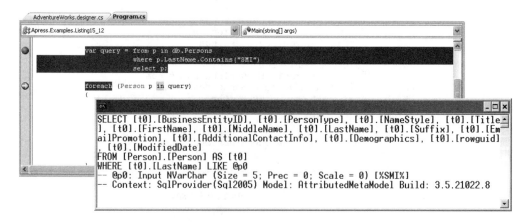

Figure 15-13. *Deferred query execution test*

Deferred query execution is an important concept that every LINQ to SQL developer needs to be familiar with. If the value of a variable that the query depends on changes between the time the query is declared and the time it is executed, the query can return unexpected results.

Inspecting the O/RM Classes

When you drag tables and SPs onto the O/RM design surface, which I discussed previously in this section, Visual Studio automatically generates .NET classes that model your database objects and their relationships. You can view the full code for the classes that Visual Studio creates by opening the newly added file with the .designer.cs or .designer.vb extension.

Here I'll discuss some of the highlights of the classes generated in the AdventureWorks example introduced in the previous section. The first things to notice are the comments generated at the top of the class file. As they state, be aware that changes to the code in the file can cause problems.

```
//------------------------------------------------------------------------------
// <auto-generated>
//     This code was generated by a tool.
//     Runtime Version:2.0.50727.1433
//
//     Changes to this file may cause incorrect behavior and will be lost if
//     the code is regenerated.
// </auto-generated>
//------------------------------------------------------------------------------
```

The next point of interest is the inclusion of the LINQ-specific namespaces in the file. These namespaces provide support for LINQ to SQL.

```
using System.Data.Linq;
using System.Data.Linq.Mapping;
using System.Linq;
using System.Linq.Expressions;
...
```

The O/RM class generated by Visual Studio is called AdventureWorksDataContext in this instance. The Name property of the System.Data.Linq.Mapping.DatabaseAttribute is set to the name of the database for the class, and the AdventureWorksDataContext class itself inherits from the System.Data.Linq.DataContext class.

```
[System.Data.Linq.Mapping.DatabaseAttribute(Name="AdventureWorks")]
public partial class AdventureWorksDataContext : System.Data.Linq.DataContext
{
  ...
}
```

The AdventureWorksDataContext class has two main public properties, representing a table of Persons and a table of EmailAddresses:

```
public System.Data.Linq.Table<Person> Persons
{
  ...
}
```

```
public System.Data.Linq.Table<EmailAddress> EmailAddresses
{
  ...
}
```

These properties each expose a generic System.Data.Linq.Table<TEntity> class based on the Person and EmailAddress classes, which model rows of their respective tables. The Person class has the Name property of the Table attribute set to the source table's name—in this case Person.Person. The Person class also implements the INotifyPropertyChanging and INotifyPropertyChanged interfaces.

```
[Table(Name="Person.Person")]
public partial class Person : INotifyPropertyChanging, INotifyPropertyChanged
{
  ...
}
```

The Person class declares several private variables representing the different columns of the source database table. For instance, _BusinessEntityID represents the BusinessEntityID column and _PersonType represents the PersonType column from the Person.Person table in the database. Another interesting feature is the EntitySet<EmailAddress> declaration. This declaration identifies that EmailAddress represents the "many" side of the one-to-many relationship that exists between the Person and EmailAddress objects.

```
    private int _BusinessEntityID;
    private string _PersonType;
    private bool _NameStyle;
    private string _Title;
    private string _FirstName;
    private string _MiddleName;
    private string _LastName;
    private string _Suffix;
    private int _EmailPromotion;
    private EntitySet<EmailAddress> _EmailAddresses;
    ...
```

The Person class exposes these private members via properties with the Column attribute defined on them. The get method of these properties simply provides access to the private member variables. The put method surrounds the private member assignment statement with firing events indicating the property is changing or has been changed.

```
[Column(Storage="_BusinessEntityID", DbType="Int NOT NULL", IsPrimaryKey=true)]
public int BusinessEntityID
{
  get
  {
    return this._BusinessEntityID;
  }
```

```
  set
  {
    if ((this._BusinessEntityID != value))
    {
      this.OnBusinessEntityIDChanging(value);
      this.SendPropertyChanging();
      this._BusinessEntityID = value;
      this.SendPropertyChanged("BusinessEntityID");
      this.OnBusinessEntityIDChanged();
    }
  }
}
...
```

The EmailAddress class nearly mirrors the Person class in structure. The main differences are that the EmailAddress class maps to a different table, has different names for both private member variables and the public properties that expose them, and has an EntityRef<Person> declaration where the Person class declares an EntitySet<EmailAddress>. The EntityRef<Person> declaration defines the Person object as the "one" side of the one-to-many relationship between Person and EmailAddress.

Summary

Although the focus of this book is on server-side development, a good database is only useful if the end users can access the data contained within it efficiently. That's where an efficient and well-designed client-side application comes in. In this chapter, I discussed several options available for connecting to SQL Server 2008 from .NET.

I began the chapter with a discussion of the ADO.NET namespaces and the .NET SQL Server Native Client (SqlClient), including connected data access, which requires constant database connectivity, and disconnected datasets, which allow users to cache data locally and connect to a database as needed. Although .NET offers other options for connecting to SQL Server, including OLE DB and ODBC, the primary method of connecting to SQL Server (version 7.0 and higher) is encapsulated in ADO.NET and the System.Data.SqlClient namespace.

I also discussed parameterized queries, including the topics of security and SQL injection. Other topics I covered included the various methods and options that .NET provides to query SQL Server, bulk copy data into SQL Server, and open multiple result sets over a single active database connection.

I rounded this chapter out with a discussion of the new LINQ to SQL and O/RM functionality provided by .NET and Visual Studio. Visual Studio's built-in visual designer and automated class generation can make light work of many O/RM applications. The ability to write declarative LINQ to SQL queries directly in procedural code elevates data querying to the level of a first-class programming concept.

In the next chapter, I will introduce SQL Server HTTP endpoints.

EXERCISES

1. [True/false] The `System.Data.SqlClient` namespace provides optimized access to SQL Server via the SQL Server Native Client library.

2. [Choose one] Which of the following concepts allows for local caching of data, with establishment of database connections on an as-needed basis:

    a.   Connected data access

    b.   Disconnected datasets

    c.   Casual data access

    d.   Partial datasets

3. [Choose all that apply] Which of the following are benefits of query parameterization:

    a.   Protection against SQL injection attacks

    b.   Conversion of lead to gold

    c.   Increased efficiency through query plan reuse

    d.   Decreased power consumption by at least 25 percent

4. [True/false] Turning on MARS by setting `MULTIPLEACTIVERESULTSETS=true` in your connection string allows you to open two result sets, but requires at least two open connections.

5. [True/false] Visual Studio includes a drag-and-drop visual O/RM designer.

6. [Choose one] LINQ to SQL uses which of the following query execution patterns:

    a.   Instant query execution

    b.   Fast-forward query execution

    c.   Random query execution

    d.   Deferred query execution

CHAPTER 16

Data Services

Back in the days of SQL Server 2000 Simple Object Access Protocol (SOAP), web service support was provided primarily through SQLXML. The SQL Server 2000 model relied on a loose coupling of SQL Server and Internet Information Services (IIS), making setup and configuration a bit of a hassle. The end result was that a lot of developers found that creating web services in the middle tier was a far more flexible and easier-to-use solution than the SQL Server 2000/SQLXML/IIS model.

SQL Server 2005 introduced native HTTP endpoints to expose SPs and UDFs as web methods directly from SQL Server, via SOAP. HTTP endpoints were easy to create and administer, and the SQL Server HTTP endpoints model used SQL Server to provide security.

Beginning with SQL Server 2008, HTTP endpoints, though still available, are deprecated. Now that HTTP endpoints are slated for removal from SQL Server, developers will need to start looking for technologies that enable data access over the Internet and enterprise intranets. IIS-powered .NET web services in the middle tier are a viable alternative, but Microsoft has another new technology in store: ADO.NET Data Services. ADO.NET Data Services promises to support representational state transfer (REST)–style data querying and updates over HTTP, support for the standard Atom XML format, and truly data source–independent queries. At the time of this writing, ADO.NET Data Services requires installation of two beta service packs: Visual Studio 2008 SP 1 Beta and the .NET Framework 3.5 SP 1 Beta. I will be introducing all of these methods of exposing your data over the Internet and intranets in this chapter.

■**Caution** At the time of this writing, Visual Studio 2008 SP 1 and the .NET Framework 3.5 Beta 1 were both still in beta release. It's strongly recommended that you not introduce beta software into production environments.

Introducing HTTP Endpoints

The W3C, in its Web Services Glossary (www.w3.org/TR/ws-gloss/#defs), defines an endpoint as the following:

> *An association between a binding and a network address, specified by a URI, that may be used to communicate with an instance of a service. An endpoint indicates a specific location for accessing a service using a specific protocol and data format.*

My primary reason for describing HTTP endpoints in this section is to provide a frame of reference for those who must support or update applications that currently use HTTP endpoints.

■**Note** SQL Server HTTP endpoints are supported on Windows Server 2003, Windows Vista, Windows XP SP 2, and Windows Server 2008.

SQL Server 2008 provides the full complement of DDL statements to manage HTTP endpoints. As the names suggest, the CREATE ENDPOINT statement creates endpoints, ALTER ENDPOINT modifies existing endpoints, and DROP ENDPOINT deletes endpoints from the server. Though they are tied to specific objects in specific databases, HTTP endpoints are in fact server-level objects. Listing 16-1 creates an SP and exposes it as a web service method using an HTTP endpoint on SQL Server 2008.

■**Note** SQL Server 2008 also supports creating TCP endpoints for Service Broker and database mirroring applications. I am focusing on HTTP SOAP endpoint creation in this section, but the full syntax for the CREATE ENDPOINT statement is available in BOL. The full syntax includes all TCP, T-SQL, Service Broker, and database mirroring options.

Listing 16-1. *Exposing a Stored Procedure via HTTP Endpoint*

```
CREATE PROCEDURE Person.SearchByLastName
(
  @LastName nvarchar(50)
)
AS
BEGIN
  SELECT
    LastName,
    FirstName,
    MiddleName
  FROM Person.Person
  WHERE LastName LIKE @LastName + N'%'
END
GO

EXEC dbo.sp_reserve_http_namespace N'http://SQL2008:2008/AdvPersonSearch'
GO

CREATE ENDPOINT AdvPersonSearch
  STATE = STARTED
```

```
AS HTTP
(
  PATH = N'/AdvPersonSearch',
  AUTHENTICATION = (INTEGRATED),
  PORTS = (CLEAR),
  CLEAR_PORT = 2008,
  SITE = N'SQL2008'
)
FOR SOAP
(
  WEBMETHOD N'SearchByLastName'
  (
    NAME = N'AdventureWorks.Person.SearchByLastName',
    FORMAT = ROWSETS_ONLY
  ),
  WSDL = DEFAULT,
  DATABASE = N'AdventureWorks',
  SCHEMA = STANDARD
);
GO
```

The first step to exposing an SP via HTTP endpoint is to choose an SP. In Listing 16-1, I've created an SP named Person.SearchByLastName that will be exposed. This SP accepts a single nvarchar(50) parameter that it uses to narrow the results of a SELECT query.

```
CREATE PROCEDURE Person.SearchByLastName
(
  @LastName nvarchar(50)
)
AS
BEGIN
  SELECT
    LastName,
    FirstName,
    MiddleName
  FROM Person.Person
  WHERE LastName LIKE @LastName + N'%'
END
GO
```

I use the sp_reserve_http_namespace system SP to reserve the URI that I will expose as a web method. In this case, the full URI will be http://SQL2008:2008/AdvPersonSearch, where the name of the server is SQL2008, the port number specified for the endpoint is 2008, and the name of the web method is AdvPersonSearch. You will need to replace the server name and port number in this example with your own.

```
EXEC sp_reserve_http_namespace N'http://SQL2008:2008/AdvPersonSearch'
GO
```

The final step is to use CREATE ENDPOINT to expose the Person.SearchByLastName SP as a web service method. Again, you will need to replace the server name and port number with your own.

```
CREATE ENDPOINT AdvPersonSearch
  STATE = STARTED
AS HTTP
(
  PATH = N'/AdvPersonSearch',
  AUTHENTICATION = (INTEGRATED),
  PORTS = (CLEAR),
  CLEAR_PORT = 2008,
  SITE = N'SQL2008'
)
FOR SOAP
(
  WEBMETHOD N'SearchByLastName'
  (
    NAME = N'AdventureWorks.Person.SearchByLastName',
    FORMAT = ROWSETS_ONLY
  ),
  WSDL = DEFAULT,
  DATABASE = N'AdventureWorks',
  SCHEMA = STANDARD
);
GO
```

The CREATE ENDPOINT statement consists of three parts: the CREATE ENDPOINT clause, the HTTP protocol–specific arguments, and the SOAP-specific arguments. The CREATE ENDPOINT clause in the example defines the name of the HTTP endpoint and sets its creation state to STARTED. The STARTED state configures the HTTP endpoint to actively listen for connections and respond to requests.

The HTTP protocol–specific arguments of the CREATE ENDPOINT statement begin with the AS HTTP clause. This clause defines the HTTP endpoint service path, setting it to /AdvPersonSearch in the example. It also sets the authentication method to Windows integrated security, the web request site name to SQL2008, and the HTTP port to 2008 using clear (nonencrypted) communications. With these options set, the HTTP endpoint will respond to requests sent to the http://SQL2008:2008/AdvPersonSearch URI.

The third and final part of the CREATE ENDPOINT statement is the FOR SOAP clause, which includes the SOAP-specific arguments. These arguments include the WEBMETHOD clause, which exposes an SP or scalar UDF and assigns it a web method name. The WEBMETHOD clause also defines the data return format, which should be set to ROWSETS_ONLY for an SP or ALL_RESULTS for a scalar UDF.

The FOR SOAP clause in the example also specifies that the HTTP endpoint should use the default Web Services Description Language (WSDL) format to describe the web service methods it supports. Finally, the default database for the HTTP endpoint is set to AdventureWorks, and results include an inline XML schema definition (XSD).

Once you have created the HTTP endpoint on SQL Server 2008, you can use Internet Explorer to test it. Simply type in the URI of your HTTP endpoint web service method with the ?wsdl parameter appended to it. For the example in Listing 16-1, the full address would be http://SQL2008:2008/AdvPersonSearch?wsdl. The WSDL document for your web service method is returned and displayed in your web browser, as shown in Figure 16-1. WSDL document details are available from the W3C Web Services Description Working Group home page, at www.w3.org/2002/ws/desc/.

Figure 16-1. *Partial WSDL document in Internet Explorer*

Consuming HTTP Endpoints

Once you've created an HTTP endpoint, it's a relatively simple matter to consume it with a .NET application. In this section, I'll create a simple .NET console application to consume the /AdvPersonSearch web service method exposed in Listing 16-1. The first step to creating a web service method consumer is to create a Visual Studio 2008 project. For this example, I've created a C# console application named EndPointClient. Once the project is created, you need to add a service reference by right-clicking References in the Solution Explorer, as shown in Figure 16-2.

Figure 16-2. *Adding a service reference to a Visual Studio project*

When you add a service reference, the Add Service Reference window pops up. Enter the web service method address with the ?wsdl parameter appended. You can also change the namespace—in this case, I've changed it to AdvPersonSearchService to make the application source code a bit more readable. The Add Service Reference window is shown in Figure 16-3.

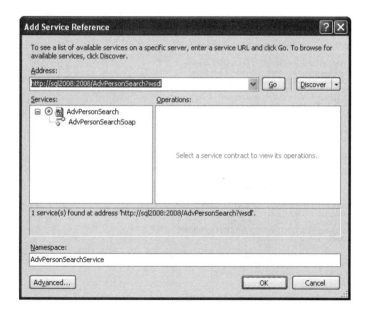

Figure 16-3. *The Add Service Reference window*

Adding a service reference automatically generates the service information files, configuration files, and .NET class files necessary to connect to the web service method. After adding the service reference, it's time to write the code that consumes the web service method. Listing 16-2 is a simple C# program that consumes the service reference added in previous steps.

Listing 16-2. *Consuming a Web Service Method*

```
using System;
using System.Data;
using System.Data.SqlTypes;
```

```
namespace Apress.Examples
{
  class EndpointClient
  {
    static void Main(string[] args)
    {
      Console.Write("Enter a last name prefix: ");
      string nameprefix = Console.ReadLine();

      AdvPersonSearchService.AdvPersonSearchSoapClient client =
        new AdvPersonSearchService.AdvPersonSearchSoapClient();

      client.ClientCredentials.Windows.ClientCredential =
        System.Net.CredentialCache.DefaultNetworkCredentials;

      client.Open();
      DataSet result = client.SearchByLastName(new SqlString(nameprefix));

      foreach (DataRow row in result.Tables[0].Rows)
      {
        Console.WriteLine
        (
          "{0}\t{1}\t{2}",
          row["LastName"].ToString(),
          row["FirstName"].ToString(),
          row["MiddleName"].ToString()
        );
      }

      client.Close();

      Console.WriteLine("Press a key to continue...");
      Console.ReadKey();
    }
  }
}
```

Listing 16-2 begins with some namespace imports, including System.Data because the web service method returns a DataSet, and System.Data.SqlTypes because the web service method accepts a SqlString parameter:

```
using System;
using System.Data;
using System.Data.SqlTypes;
```

The Main function begins by asking the user to enter a last name prefix:

```
Console.Write("Enter a last name prefix: ");
string nameprefix = Console.ReadLine();
```

The program creates an instance of the web service method client and sets the security credentials to the default network credentials:

```
AdvPersonSearchService.AdvPersonSearchSoapClient client =
    new AdvPersonSearchService.AdvPersonSearchSoapClient();

client.ClientCredentials.Windows.ClientCredential =
    System.Net.CredentialCache.DefaultNetworkCredentials;
```

The next step is to open the client and execute the SearchByLastName method. The SearchByLastName method accepts a single SqlString parameter (the name prefix that the user entered previously) and returns an ADO.NET DataSet result.

```
client.Open();
DataSet result = client.SearchByLastName(new SqlString(nameprefix));
```

Once the web service method completes, the program iterates the results using a foreach loop, displaying the names returned in the DataSet:

```
foreach (DataRow row in result.Tables[0].Rows)
{
    Console.WriteLine
    (
        "{0}\t{1}\t{2}",
        row["LastName"].ToString(),
        row["FirstName"].ToString(),
        row["MiddleName"].ToString()
    );
}
```

The program ends by closing the client connection:

```
client.Close();

Console.WriteLine("Press a key to continue...");
Console.ReadKey();
```

Before you run the application, you'll need to edit some settings in the project's app.config file. I've highlighted the settings you'll need to change in Figure 16-4.

```
<binding name="AdvPersonSearchSoap" closeTimeout="00:01:00" openTimeout="00:01:00"
    receiveTimeout="00:10:00" sendTimeout="00:01:00" allowCookies="false"
    bypassProxyOnLocal="false" hostNameComparisonMode="StrongWildcard"
    maxBufferSize="1000000" maxBufferPoolSize="524288"
    maxReceivedMessageSize="1000000" messageEncoding="Text"
    textEncoding="utf-8" transferMode="Buffered"
    useDefaultWebProxy="true">
    <readerQuotas maxDepth="32" maxStringContentLength="8192" maxArrayLength="16384"
        maxBytesPerRead="4096" maxNameTableCharCount="16384" />
    <security mode="TransportCredentialOnly">
        <transport clientCredentialType="Windows" proxyCredentialType="Windows"
            realm="" />
        <message clientCredentialType="UserName" algorithmSuite="Default" />
    </security>
</binding>
```

Figure 16-4. *Changing settings in the app.config file*

The following settings in the `app.config` file need to be modified:

- The `maxBufferSize` and `maxReceivedMessageSize` attributes of the `binding` element both need to be changed to a larger number than the default 65536. I changed them to 1000000 in this example. These two values need to be the same. In SQL Server 2005, there was no need to change these options; .NET 3.5 and the Windows Communication Foundation (WCF), however, restrict large transfers. This is why this new requirement has been added for SQL Server 2008.

- The `mode` attribute of the `security` element should be set to `TransportCredentialOnly` for Windows integrated security.

- The `clientCredentialType` and `proxyCredentialType` of the `transport` element should both be set to Windows when using Windows integrated security.

Once you've completed the changes to `app.config`, the web service method consumer application is ready to run. Figure 16-5 shows the result of calling the web service method with a last name prefix of *bur*.

```
Enter a last name prefix: bur
Burke    Brian
Burke    Megan    E.
Burkhardt        Ingrid  K.
Burkhardt        Karren  K.
Burlacu Ovidiu
Burnell Dana     H.
Burnett Linda    E.
Burnett Timothy B.
Burton   Stephen R.
Press a key to continue...
```

Figure 16-5. *Results of the web service method consumer application*

HTTP endpoints also expose additional security features like Kerberos authentication and support for encrypted communications. As you can see from this simple example, HTTP endpoints make it relatively easy to expose SPs as web service methods, and .NET makes creating a consumer application fairly painless. HTTP endpoints are deprecated, however, so I'll discuss some of the other technologies you can use to access your data over the Internet in the following sections.

Web Services

You can use a web server like IIS and ASP.NET to create web services that expose your data and database functionality to authorized users and applications. Note that you're not limited to this choice of web server and web application framework when you design web services, but these are the tools I've selected to demonstrate web service functionality in this section. Creating web services with ASP.NET requires a properly installed and configured IIS server, Visual Studio 2008, and the .NET Framework.

> ■**Note** The installation and configuration of these tools is beyond the scope of this book. Instructions for installing and configuring IIS, Visual Studio, and the .NET Framework are all available on Microsoft's TechNet web site at `http://technet.microsoft.com`.

Creating an ASP.NET web service is relatively simple. The first step is to create a new ASP.NET Web Service web site in Visual Studio, as shown in Figure 16-6.

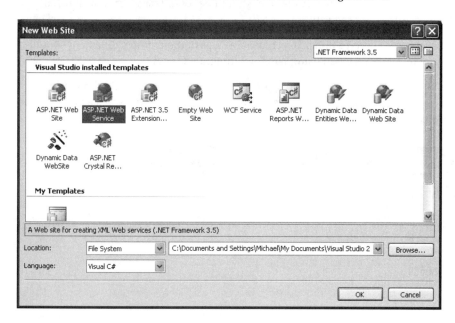

Figure 16-6. *Creating an ASP.NET Web Service web site*

Once the web site is created, you can edit the contents of the `Service.cs` file to expose your web service's methods. In Listing 16-3, I've created a web service based on the `Person.SearchByLastName` SP previously created in Listing 16-1. I'm using this SP as the basis for a web method named `AdvPersonSearch` exposed by the web service.

Listing 16-3. *Web Service Exposing a Single Web Method*

```
using System;
using System.Data;
using System.Data.SqlClient;
using System.Web.Services;

[WebService(Namespace = "apress:examples:webservices")]
[WebServiceBinding(ConformsTo = WsiProfiles.BasicProfile1_1)]
public class Service : System.Web.Services.WebService
```

```csharp
{
  public Service ()
  {
    //InitializeComponent();
  }

  [WebMethod]
  public DataSet AdvPersonSearch(string LastName)
  {
    string sqlconnection = "SERVER=SQL2008;" +
      "INITIAL CATALOG=AdventureWorks;" +
      "INTEGRATED SECURITY=SSPI;";

    DataSet result = new DataSet();
    SqlDataAdapter adapter = null;

    try
    {
      adapter = new SqlDataAdapter
        (
          "Person.SearchByLastName",
          sqlconnection
        );

      adapter.SelectCommand.CommandType = CommandType.StoredProcedure;

      adapter.SelectCommand.Parameters.Add
        (
          "@LastName",
          SqlDbType.VarChar,
          50
        ).Value = LastName;

      adapter.Fill(result);
    }
    catch (Exception ex)
    {
      throw (ex);
    }
    finally
    {
      if (adapter != null)
        adpater.Dispose();
    }

    return result;
  }
}
```

The sample web service begins by importing the required namespaces. The System.Data and System.Data.SqlClient namespaces provide SQL Server connectivity and database functionality. The System.Web.Services namespace provides web service support classes and functionality.

```
using System;
using System.Data;
using System.Data.SqlClient;
using System.Web.Services;
```

The web service is created as a .NET class decorated with the WebService and WebServiceBinding attributes. The WebService attribute sets the Namespace property, defining the namespace URI for the web service. The default is http://tempuri.org/, but it's strongly recommended that you change this as I've done in the listing.

The WebServiceBinding attribute sets the ConformsTo property to indicate that the web service conforms to the Basic Profile, version 1.1, of the Web Services Interoperability Organization (WS-I) specification.

The Service class inherits from the System.Web.WebServices.WebService base class. This base class provides the classes, methods, and functionality that turn your .NET class into a real web service.

```
[WebService(Namespace = "apress:examples:webservices")]
[WebServiceBinding(ConformsTo = WsiProfiles.BasicProfile1_1)]
public class Service : System.Web.Services.WebService
{
  ...
}
```

■**Note** WS-I is an industry consortium that defines specifications and best practices for web services interoperability across platforms. The official WS-I web site is at www.ws-i.org.

The constructor for the Service class has a single line, commented out. This line is a call to the InitializeComponent method. The InitializeComponent method is a private method that supports visual designer components. You don't need to add this method or call it in the constructor function if your web service does not use designer components.

```
public Service ()
{
  //InitializeComponent();
}
```

The web method that the sample web service exposes is called AdvPersonSearch. It's declared just like any other .NET function, with public scope, parameters (if any), and a return value. The AdvPersonSearch function, like all .NET web methods, is decorated with the WebMethod attribute.

```
[WebMethod]
public DataSet AdvPersonSearch(string LastName)
{
   ...
}
```

The body of the method connects to the AdventureWorks database on my SQL Server 2008 instance (you'll need to change the connection string to match your settings). When you call the web method, it creates a SqlDataAdapter that calls the Person.SearchByLastName SP. The web method populates a DataSet with the results returned by the SqlDataAdapter, and returns the results to the caller. I've wrapped the code in a try...catch block that simply rethrows any exceptions.

```
string sqlconnection = "SERVER=SQL2008;" +
  "INITIAL CATALOG=AdventureWorks;" +
  "INTEGRATED SECURITY=SSPI;";

DataSet result = new DataSet();
SqlDataAdapter adapter = null;

try
{
  adapter = new SqlDataAdapter
    (
      "Person.SearchByLastName",
      sqlconnection
    );

  adapter.SelectCommand.CommandType = CommandType.StoredProcedure;

  adapter.SelectCommand.Parameters.Add
    (
      "@LastName",
      SqlDbType.VarChar,
      50
    ).Value = LastName;

  adapter.Fill(result);
}
catch (Exception ex)
```

```
    {
      throw (ex);
    }
    finally
    {
      if (adapter != null)
        adapter.Dispose();
    }
    return result;
}
```

You can run the web service in Debug mode through Visual Studio. When you start debugging in Visual Studio, your web browser window will open up to the web service launch page. From this page, you can select the AdvPersonSearch web method, which opens another page. The web method page, shown in Figure 16-7, allows you to enter any parameter values and invoke the method.

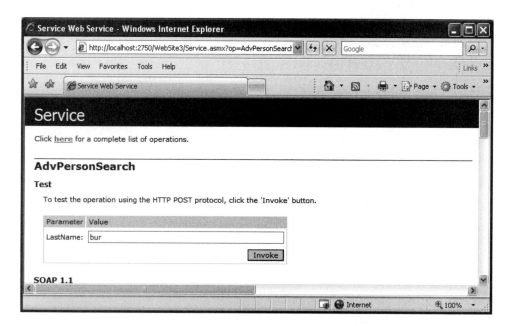

Figure 16-7. *Executing a web service method while debugging*

After you enter a value for the LastName parameter and press the Invoke button, the web method returns a result similar to the one shown in Figure 16-8.

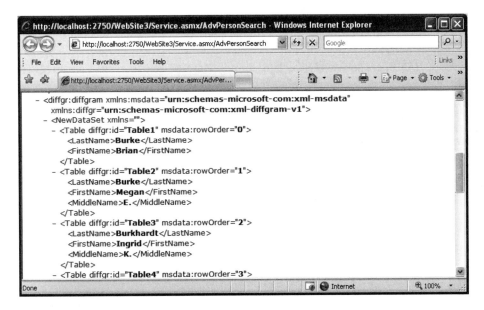

Figure 16-8. *Partial results of the web method call*

As with SQL Server HTTP endpoints, you can access web services from .NET Windows applications, ASP.NET web applications, or any other platform that can submit HTTP POST requests to a web server. Adding a service reference for a web service is very similar to adding a service reference for an HTTP endpoint, after which you can create instances of the web service class and use it like any other .NET class. Beginning with the .NET Framework 3.5 SP 1, Microsoft has introduced yet another method of querying and updating data over the Internet: ADO.NET Data Services. I'll discuss this new technology in the next section.

ADO.NET Data Services

Beginning with the .NET Framework 3.5 SP1 and Visual Studio 2008 SP1, Microsoft has added support for a new method of querying and updating your data remotely over the Internet.

■Caution The information provided in this section is based on a prerelease beta of ADO.NET Data Services (code-named Astoria). The information contained in this section is subject to change as future versions are released. Please bear this in mind as the Astoria team moves toward their final release.

ADO.NET Data Services supports the concept of REST services for accessing your data remotely. REST-style services provide simple URI-based querying, a simpler mechanism than the SOAP protocol. ADO.NET Data Services translates regular HTTP requests into *create, read, update, delete (CRUD)* operations against a data source. ADO.NET Data Services uses an HTTP request-to-CRUD operation mapping, as shown in Table 16-1.

Table 16-1. *HTTP Requests to ADO.NET Data Services Operations*

HTTP Request	ADO.NET Data Services Operation
GET	Query the data source; retrieve data
POST	Create a new entity and insert it into the data source
PUT	Update an entity in the data source
DELETE	Delete an entity from the data source

Creating an ADO.NET Data Service

As with a web service, the first step to creating an ADO.NET data service is to create a new web site project. A standard ASP.NET web site project, as shown in Figure 16-9, works well.

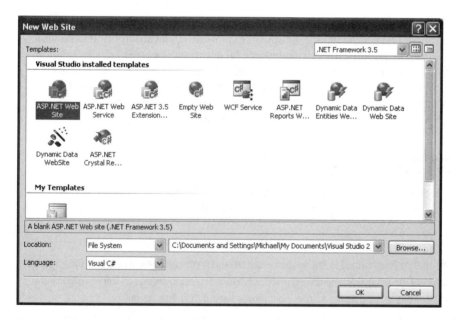

Figure 16-9. *Creating an ASP.NET web site*

Defining the Data Source

Once you have created a web site, you need to add a source for your data. The easiest way is to add an ADO.NET entity data model (EDM) through the File ➤ New ➤ File menu option in Visual Studio. Selecting the ADO.NET Entity Data Model template in the Add New Item window, as shown in Figure 16-10, launches the ADO.NET Entity Data Model wizard.

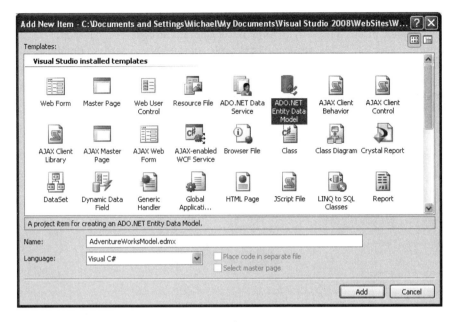

Figure 16-10. *Adding an ADO.NET EDM item to your web site*

The ADO.NET Entity Data Model wizard starts with two choices: you can generate an EDM from an existing database or generate an empty EDM. For this example, I've chosen to generate an EDM based on tables in the AdventureWorks database. The second screen of the wizard, which allows you to select a data source, is shown in Figure 16-11.

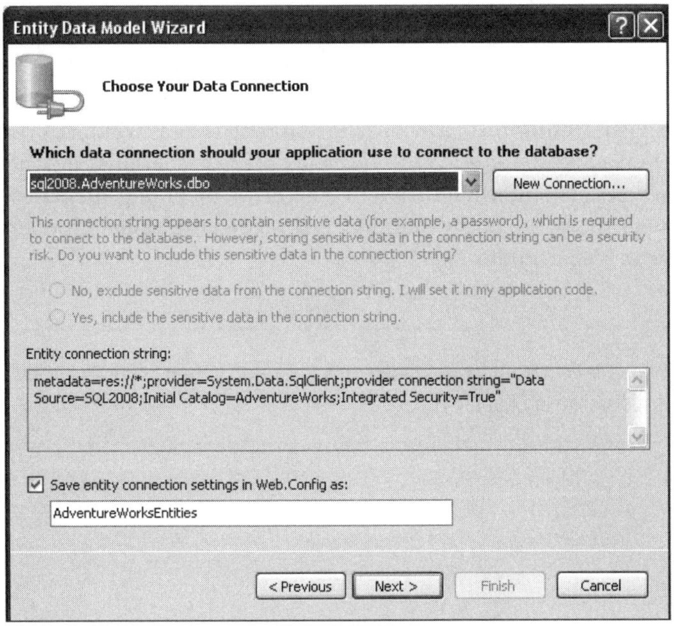

Figure 16-11. *Selecting an EDM data source*

The third and final screen of the wizard allows you to select the tables and SPs to include in your EDM. For this example, I chose to include the Production.Product, Production.ProductPhoto, and Production.ProductProductPhoto tables of the AdventureWorks database, as shown in Figure 16-12.

Figure 16-12. *Adding tables to the EDM*

Once you've added tables to your EDM, you can view them in the Entity Data Model designer. The designer window shows you the tables you've added to your EDM and the relationships (if any) between them. Visual Studio also provides the Mapping Details window, which shows you the mappings between your entity attributes and database columns, and the Model Browser, which lets you see detailed information about your EDM, including attributes, keys, and associations. Figure 16-13 shows the Entity Data Model designer, the Model Browser, and the Mapping Details window in Visual Studio.

■Tip ADO.NET Data Services also supports data sources that implement the IQueryable interface, including LINQ data sources. LINQ to SQL is discussed in Chapter 15.

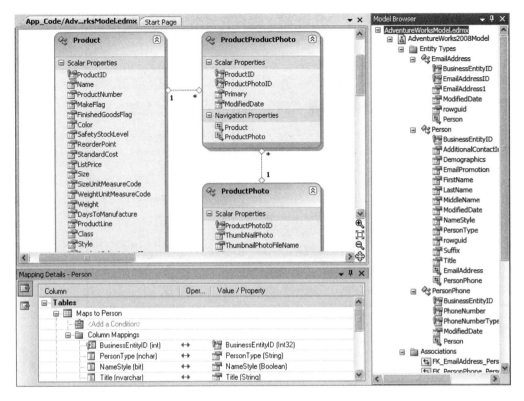

Figure 16-13. *ADO.NET Entity Data Model designer*

Creating the Data Service

The next step after you've defined your EDM is to add an ADO.NET Data Service item to your project through the File ➤ New ➤ File menu option. The Add New Item window is shown in Figure 16-14 with the ADO.NET Data Service template highlighted.

The ADO.NET Data Service template automatically generates two files. The first file is the service landing page, named `AdventureWorksDataService.svc` in this example. This is the page you need to call to request the service. The second file generated is named `AdventureWorksDataService.cs` in this example. This second file contains a class definition for the service that defines access rules for entity sets and service operations. The class defined by this file requires some modification by hand; at minimum you must set the entity access rules, as I've done in Listing 16-4.

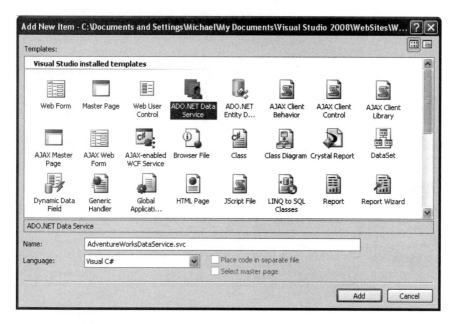

Figure 16-14. *Adding an ADO.NET data service*

Listing 16-4. *AdventureWorksDataService Class Definition*

```csharp
using System.Data.Services;

public class AdventureWorksDataService
  : DataService<AdventureWorksModel.AdventureWorksEntities>
{
  // This method is called only once to initialize service-wide policies.
  public static void InitializeService(IDataServiceConfiguration config)
  {
    config.SetEntitySetAccessRule("Product", EntitySetRights.AllRead);
    config.SetEntitySetAccessRule("ProductPhoto", EntitySetRights.AllRead);
    config.SetEntitySetAccessRule("ProductProductPhoto",
      EntitySetRights.AllRead);

    // Example for service operations
    // config.SetServiceOperationAccessRule("*", ServiceOperationRights.All);
  }
}
```

■**Caution** You can use the wildcard character (*) to set rights for all entities and service operations at once, but Microsoft strongly recommends against this. Although it's useful for testing purposes, in a production environment this can lead to serious security problems.

In Listing 16-4, I've set the access rules to AllRead, meaning that the service allows queries by key or queries for all contents of the entity set. The rights allowed are shown in Table 16-2.

Table 16-2. *Service Entity and Operation Access Rights*

Access Rights	Entity/Operation	Description
All	Both	Allows full read/write access to the entity and full read access to operations.
AllRead	Both	Allows full read access to the entity or operation. It is shorthand for ReadSingle and ReadMultiple access rights combined with a logical OR (|) operation.
AllWrite	Entity	Allows full write access to the entity. It is shorthand for WriteAppend, WriteUpdate, WriteDelete access rights combined with a logical OR (|) operation.
None	Both	Allows no read or write access, and will not appear in the services metadata document.
ReadSingle	Both	Allows for queries by key against an entity set.
ReadMultiple	Both	Allows for queries for the entire contents of the set.
WriteAppend	Entity	Allows new resources to be appended to the set.
WriteDelete	Entity	Allows existing resources to be deleted from the set.
WriteUpdate	Entity	Allows existing resources to be updated in the set.

The final step to setting up your ADO.NET data service—and this is an important one—is to set the service page (.svc extension) as the project start page. In fact, you can delete the Default.aspx page in this project since it's not needed.

You can test your ADO.NET data service by running it in Debug mode from Visual Studio. Visual Studio will open a browser window with the address set to the start page for your project. In my example, the default start page address is http://localhost:1428/AdvSearchService/ AdventureWorksDataService.svc. Your start address and port number will most likely be different. The ADO.NET data service will respond to your request with a listing of entities for which you have access, as shown in Figure 16-15.

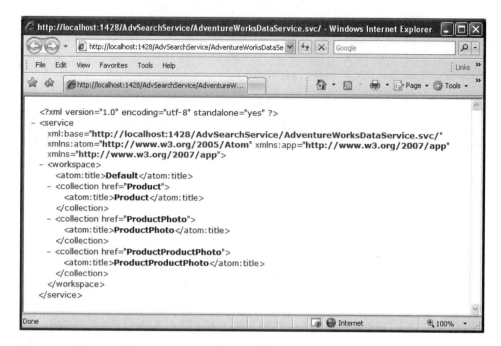

Figure 16-15. *Calling the default start page for the ADO.NET data service*

■**Tip** ADO.NET Data Services currently supports two payload types. The *payload type* is the standard format for incoming request data and outgoing results data. ADO.NET Data Services supports both JavaScript Object Notation (JSON) and the Atom Publishing Protocol for payloads. If you call the default start page for your ADO.NET Data Service and the results look like a nonsensical syndication feed instead of standard XML, you will need to turn off the feed-reading view in your browser. In Internet Explorer 7, you can uncheck the Tools ➤ Internet Options ➤ Content ➤ Settings ➤ Turn On Feed Reading View option.

Once you've confirmed that the ADO.NET data service is up and running, you can query the service using a combination of path expression–style syntax in the URI to locate entities and query string parameters to further restrict and control output. The following are some examples of ADO.NET data service queries:

- `http://localhost:1428/AdvSearchService/AdventureWorksDataService.svc/Product`: This query retrieves all `Product` entities.

- `http://localhost:1428/AdvSearchService/AdventureWorksDataService.svc/Product(749)`: This query retrieves the `Product` entities with a primary key value of 749. The primary key of the `Product` entity is `ProductID`.

- `http://localhost:1428/AdvSearchService/AdventureWorksDataService.svc/Product?$skip=10&$top=10`: This query skips the first ten `Product` entities and retrieves the following ten (items 11 through 20) in key order.

- `http://localhost:1428/AdvSearchService/AdventureWorksDataService.svc/Product?$top=20&$orderby=Name`: This query retrieves the first 20 `Product` entities ordered (sorted) by the `Name` attribute.

- `http://localhost:1428/AdvSearchService/AdventureWorksDataService.svc/Product?$filter=ListPrice gt 1000&$expand=ProductProductPhoto/ProductPhoto`: This query retrieves all the `Product` entities with a `ListPrice` attribute that is greater than 1000. The results include related `ProductProductPhoto` and `ProductPhoto` entities expanded inline.

This is just a small sampling of the types of REST-style queries you can create using ADO.NET Data Services. In fact, ADO.NET Data Services supports several query string options, as shown in Table 16-3.

Table 16-3. *Query String Options*

Option	Description
`$expand`	Expands results to include one or more related entities inline in the results.
`$filter`	Restricts the results returned by applying an expression to the last entity set identified in the URI path. The `$filter` option supports a simple expression language that includes logical, arithmetic, and grouping operators, and an assortment of string, date, and math functions.
`$orderby`	Orders (sorts) results by the attributes specified. You can specify multiple attributes separated by commas, and each attribute can be followed by an optional `asc` or `desc` modifier indicating ascending or descending sort order, respectively.
`$skip`	Skips a given number of rows when returning results.
`$top`	Restricts the number of entities returned to the specified number.

Creating an ADO.NET Data Service Consumer

Once you have an ADO.NET data service up and running, creating a consumer application is relatively simple. For this example, I've created a simple .NET application that calls the service to display the image and details of products selected from a drop-down list.

The first step in building a consumer application is to create classes based on your EDM. Fortunately, the ADO.NET Data Services team has supplied a utility to automate this process. The `DataSvcUtil.exe` program, located in the `Windows\Microsoft.NET\Framework\v3.5` directory, automatically generates C# or Visual Basic classes for use in client applications. Listing 16-5 shows the command line I used to generate C# classes based on the `AdventureWorksModel` EDM in the previous examples.

Tip As mentioned previously in this section, ADO.NET Data Services is currently a prerelease beta. One example of the constant state of change is that `DataSvcUtil.exe` was previously named `WebDataGen.exe`. In fact, you may find blogs and tutorials online referencing this handy tool by the old name. The name and location may change again by the time ADO.NET Data Services is released to production.

Listing 16-5. *Generating C# Classes from an EDM*

```
DataSvcUtil /in:"AdventureWorksModel.edmx" /out:"AdventureWorksModel.cs"
```

The next step, once you've created EDM-based classes, is to create a new application and add your classes to that project. In this case, I chose to create an ASP.NET application, so I created a new ASP.NET web site application and added the classes file to it.

Step three of the process is to create the Default.aspx page of the client application. This page will perform the necessary calls to the service. You are not tied to a web application, however; you can just as easily call ADO.NET Data Services from Windows applications, Silverlight applications, or any other platform that can initiate HTTP requests (although object deserialization on platforms that don't support .NET classes could pose a bit of a challenge). For this client application, I simply added a drop-down list, an image control, and a table to the web form. Then I wired up the page load and drop-down list selection change events. The code is shown in Listing 16-6, with results shown in Figure 16-16.

Listing 16-6. *ASP.NET Client Application Default.aspx Page*

```
using System;
using System.Web.UI.WebControls;
using System.Data.Services.Client;
using AdventureWorksModel;

public partial class _Default : System.Web.UI.Page
{
  protected void Page_Load(object sender, EventArgs e)
  {
    PopulateDropDown();
  }

  private void PopulateDropDown()
  {
    DataServiceContext ctx = new DataServiceContext
    (
      new Uri
        ("http://localhost:1428/AdvSearchService/AdventureWorksDataService.svc")
    );

    DataServiceQuery<Product> qry =
      ctx.CreateQuery<Product>
        (
          "/Product?$filter=FinishedGoodsFlag eq true&$orderby=Name asc"
        );
```

```
      foreach (Product p in qry.Execute())
      {
        ProductDropDown.Items.Add(new ListItem(p.Name, p.ProductID.ToString()));
      }

      string id = ProductDropDown.SelectedValue;
      UpdateImage(id);
    }

    private void UpdateImage(string id)
    {
      ProductImage.ImageUrl = string.Format("GetImage.aspx?id={0}", id);
    }

    protected void ProductDropDownList_SelectedIndexChanged(object sender,
      EventArgs e)
    {
      string id = ProductDropDown.SelectedValue;
      DataServiceContext ctx = new DataServiceContext
      (
        new Uri
          ("http://localhost:1428/AdvSearchService/AdventureWorksDataService.svc")
      );

      DataServiceQuery<Product> qry =
        ctx.CreateQuery<Product>(string.Format("/Product({0})", id));

      foreach (Product p in qry.Execute())
      {
        Table1.Rows[0].Cells[1].Text = p.Class;
        Table1.Rows[1].Cells[1].Text = p.Color;
        Table1.Rows[2].Cells[1].Text = p.Size + " " + p.SizeUnitMeasureCode;
        Table1.Rows[3].Cells[1].Text = p.Weight + " " + p.WeightUnitMeasureCode;
        Table1.Rows[4].Cells[1].Text = p.ListPrice.ToString();
        Table1.Rows[5].Cells[1].Text = p.ProductNumber;
      }
      UpdateImage(id);
    }
}
```

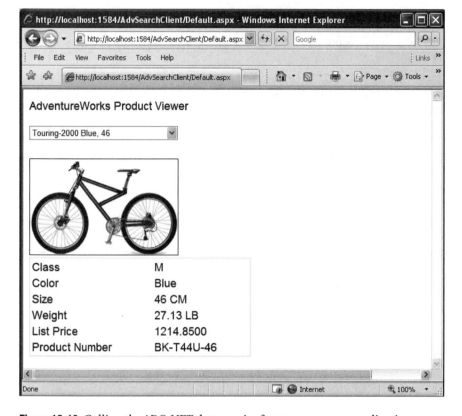

Figure 16-16. *Calling the ADO.NET data service from a consumer application*

The first part of the code imports the necessary namespaces. The System.Data.Services. Client namespace is required to create ADO.NET Data Services client queries. You will need to add a reference to the System.Data.Services.Client component library to your project. The AdventureWorksModel namespace is a reference to my EDM classes namespace.

```
using System;
using System.Web.UI.WebControls;
using System.Data.Services.Client;
using AdventureWorksModel;
```

The Page_Load event of the Default.aspx page simply calls a little function called PopulateDropDown that populates the drop-down list with the names and IDs of all "finished goods" products that AdventureWorks keeps in its database:

```
PopulateDropDown();
```

The PopulateDropDown function begins by creating a DataServiceContext that points to the URI of the ADO.NET data service:

```
DataServiceContext ctx = new DataServiceContext
(
  new Uri
    ("http://localhost:1428/AdvSearchService/AdventureWorksDataService.svc")
);
```

Next, this function uses the DataServiceContext to create a DataServiceQuery that retrieves only the Product entities whose FinishedGoodsFlag attributes are set to true. Results are sorted by the Name attribute.

```
DataServiceQuery<Product> qry =
  ctx.CreateQuery<Product>
    (
      "/Product?$filter=FinishedGoodsFlag eq true&$orderby=Name asc"
    );
```

The query is executed synchronously with the Execute method, which returns an IEnumerable result that can be iterated using foreach. In this example, the Name and ProductID attributes are iterated and added to the drop-down list.

```
foreach (Product p in qry.Execute())
{
  ProductDropDown.Items.Add(new ListItem(p.Name, p.ProductID.ToString()));
}
```

Finally, the product image is updated based on the selected value of the drop-down list:

```
string id = ProductDropDown.SelectedValue;
UpdateImage(id);
```

I've also wired the SelectedIndexChanged event of the drop-down list so that the image and other data being displayed are updated when the user selects a new product. The first thing this function does is retrieve the currently selected value from the drop-down list.

```
string id = ProductDropDown.SelectedValue;
```

Then, as with the PopulateDropDown function, this function must create a DataServiceContext that points to the ADO.NET data service:

```
DataServiceContext ctx = new DataServiceContext
(
  new Uri
    ("http://localhost:1428/AdvSearchService/AdventureWorksDataService.svc")
);
```

Once the DataServiceContext is created, a query is created on it. In this case, the query returns the Product entity with the key value (ProductID) of the product selected from the drop-down list.

```
DataServiceQuery<Product> qry =
  ctx.CreateQuery<Product>(string.Format("/Product({0})", id));
```

This function also executes its query. After the query executes, the function iterates the results and updates the display, including the summary information table and the product image.

```
foreach (Product p in qry.Execute())
{
  Table1.Rows[0].Cells[1].Text = p.Class;
  Table1.Rows[1].Cells[1].Text = p.Color;
  Table1.Rows[2].Cells[1].Text = p.Size + " " + p.SizeUnitMeasureCode;
  Table1.Rows[3].Cells[1].Text = p.Weight + " " + p.WeightUnitMeasureCode;
  Table1.Rows[4].Cells[1].Text = p.ListPrice.ToString();
  Table1.Rows[5].Cells[1].Text = p.ProductNumber;
}
UpdateImage(id);
```

The UpdateImage function, called by two of the event handlers in this example, consists of a single line that changes the URL of the product image:

```
ProductImage.ImageUrl = string.Format("GetImage.aspx?id={0}", id);
```

Note In order to actually show the images on a web page, I had to resort to an old ASP.NET trick. Because the images are stored in the database, I had to create a second page in the project called GetImage.aspx to retrieve the appropriate image. This method calls the ADO.NET data service and returns the binary product photo image as a JPEG image. I won't go into the details here because they're not essential to understanding ADO.NET Data Services, but the source code is available in the downloadable sample files for the curious.

Summary

In SQL Server 2005, Microsoft introduced HTTP SOAP endpoints, which allowed developers to expose SPs and UDFs within the database as web service methods. While this provided a potentially useful tool to developers, it has been deprecated beginning with SQL Server 2008. Because it has been available as an option since the last release of SQL Server, you may run into situations in which you need to support applications that use it, so I began this chapter with a discussion of HTTP SOAP endpoints on SQL Server 2008.

Because HTTP SOAP endpoints are deprecated (and will be removed from a future version of SQL Server), I spent the remainder of the chapter discussing technologies that provide similar functionality and might be considered replacement technologies for HTTP SOAP endpoints.

I talked about ASP.NET web services, which provide SOAP-based web services and can provide a layer of abstraction and security for accessing your data remotely over the Internet. Web services provide fine-grained control over database access and a standardized format over HTTP.

I closed the chapter out with an introduction to ADO.NET Data Services. As I write this, ADO.NET Data Services is currently in prerelease beta form, but it looks promising. With built-in support for entity data models and the powerful ASP.NET EDM designer, REST-style querying, and both the JSON and Atom payload formats, ADO.NET Data Services can provide a lightweight alternative to SOAP-based web services.

EXERCISES

1. [True/false] HTTP SOAP endpoints are deprecated in SQL Server 2008.

2. [Choose one] SQL Server can generate which of the following metadata documents for HTTP endpoints:

    a.   WSDL documents

    b.   JSON files

    c.   C# classes

    d.   Object-oriented Perl code

3. [Fill in the blanks] Visual Studio 2008 provides a ___ ___ ___ project template to create new web services.

4. [True/false] Visual Studio 2008 SP 1 includes a graphical EDM designer.

5. [Choose one] ADO.NET Data Services accepts which type of query requests:

    a.   SQL queries

    b.   XSLT queries

    c.   REST-style queries

    d.   English language queries

CHAPTER 17

■■■

New T-SQL Features

SQL Server 2005 introduced several new built-in T-SQL functions, operators, and clauses, including the INTERSECT and EXCEPT operators and the DML statement OUTPUT clause. SQL Server 2008 supports these prior enhancements and adds some of its own. In this chapter, I will cover the developer-centric T-SQL features that I haven't discussed in previous chapters.

Set Operators

SQL Server has long supported the UNION and UNION ALL set-based operators to combine the results of multiple queries into a single result set. SQL Server 2008 also supports the INTERSECT and EXCEPT set-based operators, which allow you to use entire result sets to restrict the results returned by queries. The INTERSECT operator takes two queries, one on either side of the INTERSECT keyword, just like the UNION operator. INTERSECT compares the result set generated by the first query with the result set generated by the second query, returning only those rows that are the same in both queries. The INTERSECT operator also removes duplicate rows from the final result set, just like the UNION operator. Listing 17-1 uses INTERSECT to retrieve the IDs of all AdventureWorks salespeople who made a sale during the month of June 2002.

Listing 17-1. *Retrieving Salespeople with Sales After a Specified Date*

```
SELECT
  BusinessEntityID
FROM Sales.SalesPerson

INTERSECT

SELECT
  DISTINCT SalesPersonID
FROM Sales.SalesOrderHeader
WHERE OrderDate BETWEEN '2002-06-01' AND '2002-06-30';
```

The top query retrieves the IDs of all salespeople in the Sales.SalesPerson table. The bottom query retrieves the IDs of all salespeople who made a sale in the month of June 2002. The INTERSECT operator restricts the results to only those rows that match in each query. This operator also removes all duplicates. The final results are the ten rows shown Figure 17-1.

Results

	BusinessEntityID
1	274
2	275
3	276
4	277
5	278
6	279
7	280
8	281
9	282
10	283

Figure 17-1. *IDs of salespeople with sales in June 2002*

The EXCEPT operator also accepts two queries, with one on either side of the EXCEPT keyword. The EXCEPT operator takes the results of the top query and eliminates all rows that have a match in the bottom query. Like the INTERSECT operator, EXCEPT eliminates duplicates from the final result set. Listing 17-2 modifies Listing 17-1 to return the IDs of all salespeople who did not sell anything during June 2002. The results are the seven rows shown in Figure 17-2.

Listing 17-2. *Retrieving Salespeople with No Sales After a Specified Date*

```
SELECT
  BusinessEntityID
FROM Sales.SalesPerson

EXCEPT

SELECT
  SalesPersonID
FROM Sales.SalesOrderHeader
WHERE OrderDate BETWEEN '2002-06-01' AND '2002-06-30';
```

Results

	BusinessEntityID
1	284
2	285
3	286
4	287
5	288
6	289
7	290

Figure 17-2. *IDs of salespeople who didn't make a sale in June 2002*

The functionality provided by the INTERSECT and EXCEPT operators can be achieved using the EXISTS and NOT EXISTS predicates, but INTERSECT and EXCEPT can simplify complex set-based operations considerably when large numbers of columns are involved. As an example, Listing 17-3 uses NOT EXISTS to return the same result as the EXCEPT operator in Listing 17-2.

Listing 17-3. *Using NOT EXISTS to Simulate the EXCEPT Operator*

```
SELECT
  sp.BusinessEntityID
FROM Sales.SalesPerson sp
WHERE NOT EXISTS
(
  SELECT
    soh.SalesPersonID
  FROM Sales.SalesOrderHeader soh
  WHERE soh.SalesPersonID = sp.BusinessEntityID
    AND soh.OrderDate BETWEEN '2002-06-01' AND '2002-06-30'
);
```

As you add more column comparisons to the query in the NOT EXISTS clause, the query grows significantly in complexity. Using set-based operators like INTERSECT and EXCEPT simplifies development and maintenance.

INTERSECT and EXCEPT follow a specific set of rules when performing row comparisons. These rules will be familiar to those who have used the UNION and UNION ALL operators, and I've given a summary, as follows:

- When comparing rows for distinct values, NULLs are considered equal. Usually (and for most SQL operations), NULLs are not considered equal to anything, even other NULLs.

- The number and order of all columns on both sides of the expression have to be the same. The data types of matching columns on both sides of the expression do not have to be the same, but they must be compatible. In other words, they must be able to be compared via implicit conversion.

- The columns on either side of the expression cannot be text, ntext, image, xml, or non–byte ordered SQL CLR user-defined types.

- The column names returned by the operator are taken from the left side of the operator.

- Just like the UNION and UNION ALL operators, you can use an ORDER BY clause only on the final result of the INTERSECT and EXCEPT operators. The ORDER BY clause must reference column names from the left side of the operator.

- You cannot use GROUP BY and HAVING clauses on the final result of the INTERSECT or EXCEPT queries. You can use them on the individual queries on either side of the operator, though.

The OUTPUT Clause

The OUTPUT clause, added to T-SQL in SQL Server 2005, is also supported in SQL Server 2008. You can use the OUTPUT clause with the INSERT, UPDATE, DELETE, and MERGE DML statements.

The OUTPUT clause returns information about the rows affected by DML statements that can be useful in comparing preupdate and postupdate data, or for troubleshooting and logging purposes. The OUTPUT clause uses inserted and deleted virtual tables to access data from rows that were inserted and deleted by the DML statement.

You can use the OUTPUT clause to output a SQL result set like that returned by a SELECT statement, or you can combine OUTPUT with the INTO clause to output rows to a table or table variable. The simple example shown in Listing 17-4 inserts and deletes a new work shift into the HumanResources.Shift table. These INSERT and DELETE statements use the OUTPUT clause to return information about the changes made. The results are shown in Figure 17-3.

Listing 17-4. *OUTPUT Clause Example*

```
INSERT INTO HumanResources.Shift
(
  [Name],
  StartTime,
  EndTime
)
OUTPUT
  'INSERTED',
  CURRENT_USER,
  inserted.ShiftID
SELECT
  N'Swing Shift',
  '12:00:00 PM',
  '8:00:00 PM';

DELETE FROM HumanResources.Shift
OUTPUT
  'DELETED',
  CURRENT_USER,
  deleted.ShiftID
WHERE [Name] = N'Swing Shift';
```

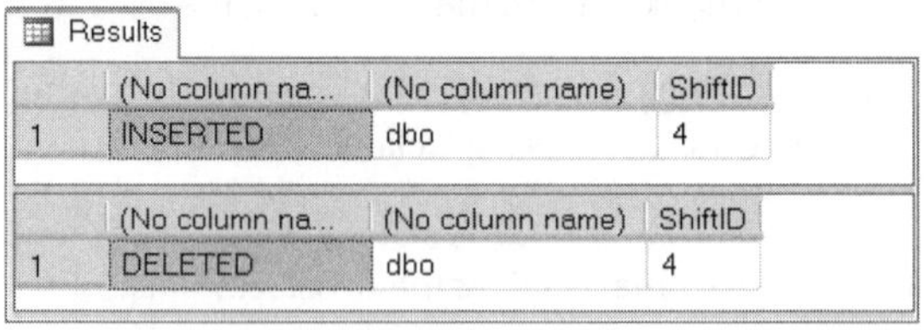

Results			
	(No column na…	(No column name)	ShiftID
1	INSERTED	dbo	4

	(No column na…	(No column name)	ShiftID
1	DELETED	dbo	4

Figure 17-3. *The OUTPUT clause returns data about rows affected by DML statements.*

■**Note** If you use the OUTPUT clause in a trigger, you must alias the trigger's inserted and deleted virtual tables to prevent conflicts with the OUTPUT clause's inserted and deleted virtual tables.

The OUTPUT clause functionality in SQL Server 2008 has been extended through a new feature known as composable DML. The *composable DML* feature allows you to use a DML statement with an OUTPUT clause as a subquery for an INSERT statement. Listing 17-5 demonstrates a composable DML statement that increases the list prices of all AdventureWorks products by 20 percent and then logs only those rows where the new list price is greater than $500.00. Partial results are shown in Figure 17-4.

Listing 17-5. *Using Composable DML to Log Specified Updates*

```
CREATE TABLE #AuditPriceChange
(
  ProductID int NOT NULL PRIMARY KEY,
  OldListPrice money NOT NULL,
  NewListPrice money NOT NULL
);

INSERT INTO #AuditPriceChange
(
  ProductID,
  OldListPrice,
  NewListPrice
)
SELECT
  s.ProductID,
  s.OldListPrice,
  s.NewListPrice
FROM
(
  UPDATE Production.Product
  SET ListPrice = ListPrice + (ListPrice * 0.20)
  OUTPUT
    inserted.ProductID AS ProductID,
    deleted.ListPrice AS OldListPrice,
    inserted.ListPrice AS NewListPrice
) s
WHERE s.NewListPrice > 500.0;

SELECT
  ProductID,
  OldListPrice,
  NewListPrice
FROM #AuditPriceChange
ORDER BY NewListPrice;

DROP TABLE #AuditPriceChange;
```

Results

	ProductID	OldListPrice	NewListPrice
63	797	1120.49	1344.588
64	798	1120.49	1344.588
65	799	1120.49	1344.588
66	800	1120.49	1344.588
67	801	1120.49	1344.588
68	970	1214.85	1457.82
69	971	1214.85	1457.82
70	972	1214.85	1457.82
71	953	1214.85	1457.82
72	743	1349.60	1619.52
73	744	1349.60	1619.52
74	745	1349.60	1619.52
75	746	1349.60	1619.52

Figure 17-4. *Results of the composable DML statement*

The example in Listing 17-5 begins by creating a temporary table to hold the logged entry results, including the `ProductID`, `OldListPrice`, and `NewListPrice`:

```
CREATE TABLE #AuditPriceChange
(
  ProductID int NOT NULL PRIMARY KEY,
  OldListPrice money NOT NULL,
  NewListPrice money NOT NULL
);
```

The composable DML statement contains an `UPDATE` statement with an `OUTPUT` clause that acts as a subquery. This `UPDATE` statement increases all list prices in the `Production.Product` table by 20 percent across the board.

```
(
  UPDATE Production.Product
  SET ListPrice = ListPrice + (ListPrice * 0.20)
  OUTPUT
    inserted.ProductID AS ProductID,
    deleted.ListPrice AS OldListPrice,
    inserted.ListPrice AS NewListPrice
) s
```

The `UPDATE` statement uses the `OUTPUT` clause to return the `ProductID` and new list price from the `inserted` virtual table and the old list price from the `deleted` virtual table. The outer `INSERT` statement is fed by a `SELECT` query. The `SELECT` query, in turn, uses the results of the `UPDATE` statement as a source subquery. The `SELECT` query also has a `WHERE` clause that limits the results to only those where the new list price is greater than $500.00.

```
INSERT INTO #AuditPriceChange
(
  ProductID,
  OldListPrice,
  NewListPrice
)
SELECT
  s.ProductID,
  s.OldListPrice,
  s.NewListPrice
FROM
(
  ...
) s
WHERE s.NewListPrice > 500.0;
```

The net effect is that every single product has its ListPrice increased by 20 percent, but only those items where the new list price is more than $500.00 are logged to the temp table. The balance of the code queries the temp table to show the results, and then drops the temp table.

■Note Currently, the only statement that can use composable DML as a source is the INSERT statement.

The TOP Keyword

The TOP keyword has long been a staple of SQL SELECT statements. Beginning with SQL Server 2005, TOP has been considerably improved. In SQL Server 2008, you can use a T-SQL variable to specify the number of rows to return. You can apply this to percentages or actual row counts, as shown in Listing 17-6, with partial results shown in Figure 17-5.

Listing 17-6. *Selecting TOP Rows with a Variable*

```
DECLARE @i int = 20;
SELECT TOP (@i) PERCENT
  FirstName,
  MiddleName,
  LastName
FROM Person.Person
ORDER BY
  FirstName,
  MiddleName,
  LastName;
```

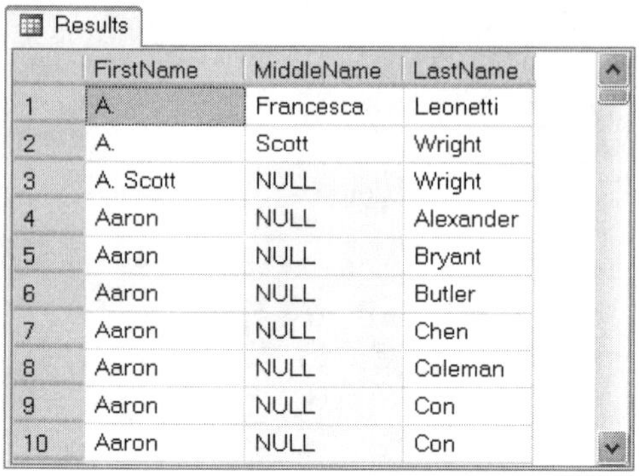
Results

	FirstName	MiddleName	LastName
1	A.	Francesca	Leonetti
2	A.	Scott	Wright
3	A. Scott	NULL	Wright
4	Aaron	NULL	Alexander
5	Aaron	NULL	Bryant
6	Aaron	NULL	Butler
7	Aaron	NULL	Chen
8	Aaron	NULL	Coleman
9	Aaron	NULL	Con
10	Aaron	NULL	Con

Figure 17-5. *Retrieving the top 20 percent of Person.Person names with a variable*

Doing something this simple in SQL Server prior to the 2005 release required kludging ugly dynamic SQL or using the `SET ROWCOUNT` statement. Additionally, you can use a subquery to specify the number of rows to return. Listing 17-7 returns one-fifth of the rows from the `Person.Person` table.

Listing 17-7. *Selecting TOP Rows with a Subquery*

```
SELECT TOP
(
  SELECT COUNT(*) / 5
  FROM Person.Person
)
  FirstName,
  MiddleName,
  LastName
FROM Person.Person
ORDER BY
  FirstName,
  MiddleName,
  LastName;
```

You can also use the `TOP` keyword with a constant value just like in prior versions of SQL Server. Although you can leave the parentheses off when using `SELECT TOP`, don't rely on this backward-compatibility feature. With new T-SQL scripts, always use parentheses around the expression to specify the number of rows to return.

Note When you use a variable or subquery with `SELECT TOP`, you must enclose it in parentheses. For compatibility with SQL Server 2000 and 2005 scripts, the parentheses aren't required if you specify a constant value with `SELECT TOP`. This backward-compatibility feature might be removed in a future version of SQL Server, and Microsoft now recommends always using parentheses with `TOP`.

The TOP keyword was not introduced in T-SQL until SQL Server 7.0. And in SQL Server 7.0 and 2000, the TOP keyword was allowed only in SELECT statements. SQL Server 2008 also allows the TOP keyword with the INSERT, UPDATE, DELETE, and MERGE DML statements. When used with DML statements, the order of rows affected cannot be specified explicitly. For all intents and purposes, you can consider a DELETE TOP statement as a "random" deletion of the specified number of rows from your table. This limits the usefulness of this particular feature unless you are modifying rows in a table and don't particularly care which rows are affected.

CROSS APPLY and OUTER APPLY

Probably one of the most frequently asked questions on the SQL Server newsgroups (news://microsoft.public.sqlserver.programming) concerns passing columns as parameters to TVFs. In SQL Server 2000, this required resorting to procedural code or cursors. SQL Server 2008 supports the CROSS APPLY and OUTER APPLY operators to resolve this problem.

Like the JOIN operators, APPLY operators take tables on both sides of the operator. The APPLY operators allow columns from the left-hand table to be used as parameters for a TVF on the right side of the operator. As a simple example, Listing 17-8 creates a simple inline TVF that returns the square (n^2) and cube (n^3) of a number passed to it. The CROSS APPLY operator in the example applies the numbers in a table to the TVF. The results are shown in Figure 17-6.

Listing 17-8. *Using CROSS APPLY to Apply Result Set Rows to a Function*

```
CREATE FUNCTION dbo.fnPowers (@Num INT)
RETURNS TABLE
AS
RETURN
(
  SELECT
    @Num * @Num AS Squared_Result,
    @Num * @Num * @Num AS Cubed_Result
);
GO

WITH Numbers (Number)
AS
(
  SELECT 1

  UNION

  SELECT 2

  UNION

  SELECT 3
)
```

```
SELECT n.Number,
  s.Squared_Result,
  s.Cubed_Result
FROM Numbers n
CROSS APPLY dbo.fnPowers (n.Number) s;
GO


DROP FUNCTION dbo.fnPowers;
GO
```

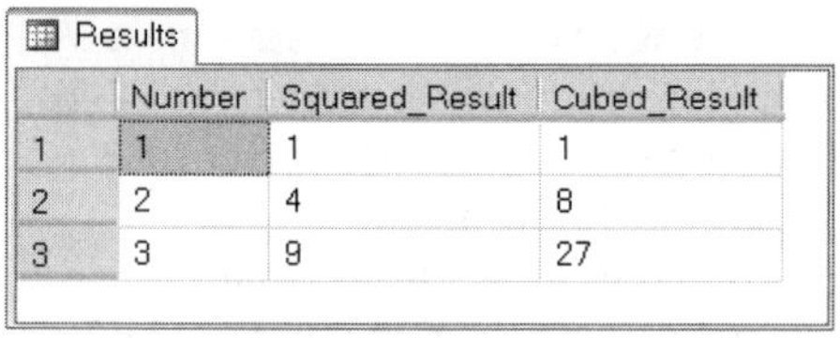

	Number	Squared_Result	Cubed_Result
1	1	1	1
2	2	4	8
3	3	9	27

Figure 17-6. *Using CROSS APPLY to pass rows to a function*

The sample first creates an inline TVF that returns the square and cube of an integer passed to it:

```
CREATE FUNCTION dbo.fnPowers (@Num INT)
RETURNS TABLE
AS
RETURN
(
  SELECT
    @Num * @Num AS Squared_Result,
    @Num * @Num * @Num AS Cubed_Result
);
GO
```

The CROSS APPLY sample query starts with a CTE that simply returns a set of numbers as a result set. In this example, it just returns the numbers 1, 2, and 3.

```
WITH Numbers (Number)
AS
(
  SELECT 1

  UNION

  SELECT 2

  UNION

  SELECT 3
)
```

The CROSS APPLY operator used in the SELECT statement takes every row from the Numbers CTE and passes the integer Number column to the inline TVF. The columns of the CTE and the columns returned by the inline TVF are all available to the SELECT statement:

```
SELECT
  n.Number,
  s.Squared_Result,
  s.Cubed_Result
FROM Numbers n
CROSS APPLY dbo.fnPowers (n.Number) s;
```

You've encountered the CROSS APPLY operator in examples in previous chapters. Some common uses of CROSS APPLY are to shred XML data into relational results using the xml data type nodes method, and to pass rows of data to DMFs for further processing.

While the CROSS APPLY operator returns every row for which the TVF returns results for the left table, OUTER APPLY returns all rows, NULL-extended—even those for which the function returns no results. In this respect, CROSS APPLY has the behavioral characteristics of an inner join while OUTER APPLY behaves more like an outer join. If no results are returned by the TVF for a given input row, OUTER APPLY returns NULL values for the TVF columns.

The TABLESAMPLE Clause

Occasionally, it's necessary to select a random sample of data from a table. Many people have come up with inventive solutions for this on the SQL Server 2000 platform, including methods based on pregenerated random numbers, procedural code, or globally unique identifiers (GUIDs). SQL Server 2008 supports the TABLESAMPLE clause for the SELECT statement to make the task of random sampling easier. The TABLESAMPLE clause follows the table name in the WHERE clause.

The TABLESAMPLE clause accepts a *sample_number* parameter that specifies a percent or number of rows to return in the sample. The sample method actually samples a percentage of pages randomly, so the number of rows specified might not be the exact number or percent requested.

■Note When you specify an exact number of rows, TABLESAMPLE converts the number to a percentage of rows before executing. So even if you specify an exact number of rows, you will still get an approximate number of rows in the result set. TABLESAMPLE always returns an approximate number of rows because of the way it samples data. The required percentage is the number of data pages SQL Server retrieves in full to fulfill your TABLESAMPLE request. The number of rows returned by TABLESAMPLE will often be slightly lower or higher than the specified amount.

You can use the TOP clause in the SELECT statement to further limit rows to the exact number required. The SYSTEM keyword specifies a system-dependent random sampling method. Since SQL Server 2008 offers only one random sampling method, the SYSTEM keyword has no effect. The random sampling method used by SQL Server 2005 involves retrieving a random number of complete physical pages that make up the specified table. This means that the number of rows returned will always be approximate and that tables occupying more storage space and containing more rows will more closely approximate the specified TABLESAMPLE percentage. A small table that takes up only one physical page, for instance, will return either all rows or none.

If you need to repeat the same random sampling multiple times, specify REPEATABLE with *repeat_seed*, which is a random seed generation number. Specifying the same *repeat_seed* with the same SELECT statement on the same data produces the same results.

■**Note** The REPEATABLE keyword, even with the same *repeat_seed*, will produce different results from query to query if the data stored in the table or the structure of the table change.

The SELECT statement shown in Listing 17-9 randomly selects approximately 10 percent of the rows from the Person.Person table.

Listing 17-9. *Randomly Selecting 10 Percent of Table Data with TABLESAMPLE*

```
SELECT
  FirstName,
  MiddleName,
  LastName
FROM Person.Contact
TABLESAMPLE (10 PERCENT);
```

You can use the TABLESAMPLE clause only when querying local tables and locally defined temporary tables. You cannot use it on views, derived tables from subqueries, result sets from TVFs and rowset functions, linked server tables, OPENXML, or table variables. If you need to retrieve a random sampling of rows from a view, derived table, or linked server table, consider using a method like that shown in Listing 17-10, popularized by SQL Server MVP Erland Sommarskog.

Listing 17-10. *Alternate Method of Retrieving Random Rows*

```
SELECT TOP (10) PERCENT
  FirstName,
  MiddleName,
  LastName
FROM HumanResources.vEmployee
ORDER BY NEWID();
```

This method works by generating a GUID for each row, sorting based on the value generated, and selecting the top 10 percent from that result. The result is a random sample of rows from your table. Although not a true statistical sampling, these random sampling methods are adequate for most development and testing purposes.

The NEWSEQUENTIALID Function

The new NEWSEQUENTIALID function generates GUIDs represented in T-SQL with the data type uniqueidentifier. This function generates sequential GUIDs in increasing order. You can use the NEWSEQUENTIALID function only as a DEFAULT for a uniqueidentifier-type column of a table, as demonstrated in Listing 17-11. Results are shown in Figure 17-7; notice that the GUID digits are displayed in groups in reverse order. In the results, the first byte of each GUID represents the sequentially increasing values generated by NEWSEQUENTIALID with each row inserted.

Listing 17-11. *Generating Sequential GUIDs*

```
CREATE TABLE #TestSeqID
(
  [ID] uniqueidentifier DEFAULT NEWSEQUENTIALID() PRIMARY KEY NOT NULL,
  Num int NOT NULL
);

INSERT INTO #TestSeqID
(
  Num
)
VALUES
  (1),
  (2),
  (3);

SELECT
  [ID],
  Num
FROM #TestSeqID;

DROP TABLE #TestSeqID;
```

	ID	Num
1	306F6EA8-3029-DD11-803F-0003FF410BC3	1
2	316F6EA8-3029-DD11-803F-0003FF410BC3	2
3	326F6EA8-3029-DD11-803F-0003FF410BC3	3

Figure 17-7. *Results generated by the NEWSEQUENTIALID function*

The NEWSEQUENTIALID function is useful when you are using a uniqueidentifier as the clustered index on a table. Because it generates GUIDs in increasing order, the NEWSEQUENTIALID function eliminates costly page splits and their associated overhead.

Date and Time Functions

Back in Chapter 2, I covered the new SQL Server date and time data types, which bring a new level of precision and accuracy to time-based data in the database. In addition to these new data types—date, time, datetimeoffset, and datetime2—SQL Server 2008 provides new built-in date- and time-related functions.

The SYSDATETIME function returns the system date and time, as reported by the server's local operating system, as a datetime2 value without time offset information. The value returned by SYSDATETIME is the date and time reported by Windows on the computer where your SQL Server instance is installed.

The SYSUTCDATETIME function returns the system date and time information converted to UTC as a datetime2 value. As with the SYSDATETIME function, the value returned does not contain additional time offset information.

The SYSDATETIMEOFFSET function returns the system date and time as a datetimeoffset value, including the time offset information. Listing 17-12 uses these functions to display the current system date and time in various formats. The results are shown in Figure 17-8.

Listing 17-12. *Using the New Date and Time Functions*

```
SELECT SYSDATETIME() AS "SYSDATETIME";

SELECT SYSUTCDATETIME() AS "SYSUTCDATETIME";

SELECT SYSDATETIMEOFFSET() AS "SYSDATETIMEOFFSET";
```

	SYSDATETIME
1	2008-05-23 22:14:31.828

	SYSUTCDATETIME
1	2008-05-24 02:14:31.828

	SYSDATETIMEOFFSET
1	5/23/2008 10:14:31 PM -04:00

Figure 17-8. *The current system date and time in a variety of formats*

SQL Server 2008's new time offset support, enabled by the datetimeoffset data type, introduces the need for new time offset–enabled functions for conversions and calculations. The TODATETIMEOFFSET function allows you to add time offset information to date and time data without time offset information. You can use TODATETIMEOFFSET to add time offset information to a date, time, datetime, datetime2, or datetimeoffset value. The result returned by the function is a datetimeoffset value with time offset information added. Listing 17-13 demonstrates by adding time offset information to a datetime value. The results are shown in Figure 17-9.

Listing 17-13. *Adding an Offset to a datetime Value*

```
DECLARE @current datetime = '2008-02-14 10:00:00';
SELECT @current AS "No_Offset";
SELECT TODATETIMEOFFSET(@current, '-04:00') AS "With_Offset";
```

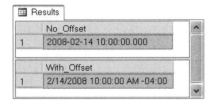

Figure 17-9. *Converting a datetime value to a datetimeoffset*

The SWITCHOFFSET function adjusts a given datetimeoffset value to another given time offset. This is useful when you need to convert a date and time to another time offset. In Listing 17-14, I use the SWITCHOFFSET function to convert a datetimeoffset value in Los Angeles to several other regional time offsets. The results are shown in Figure 17-10.

■**Tip** You can use the Z time offset in datetimeoffset literals as an abbreviation for UTC (+00:00 offset). You cannot, however, specify Z as the time offset parameter with the TODATETIMEOFFSET and SWITCHOFFSET functions.

Listing 17-14. *Converting a datetimeoffset to Several Time Offsets*

```
DECLARE @current datetimeoffset = '2008-05-23 19:30:00 -07:00';

SELECT
  'Los Angeles' AS "Location",
  @current AS "Current Time"

UNION

SELECT
  'New York',
  SWITCHOFFSET(@current, '-04:00')

UNION

SELECT
  'Bermuda',
  SWITCHOFFSET(@current, '-03:00')
```

```
UNION

SELECT
  'London',
  SWITCHOFFSET(@current, '+01:00');
```

	Location	Current Time
1	Bermuda	5/23/2008 11:30:00 PM -03:00
2	London	5/24/2008 3:30:00 AM +01:00
3	Los Angeles	5/23/2008 7:30:00 PM -07:00
4	New York	5/23/2008 10:30:00 PM -04:00

Figure 17-10. *Date and time information in several different time offsets*

TIME ZONES AND OFFSETS

Time offsets are not the same thing as time zones. A time offset is relatively easy to calculate—it's simply a plus or minus offset in hours and minutes from the UTC offset (+00:00), as defined by the ISO 8601 standard. A time zone, however, is an identifier for a specific location or region and is defined by regional laws and regulations. Time zones can have very complex sets of rules that include such oddities as Daylight Savings Time (DST). SQL Server uses time offsets in calculations, not time zones. If you want to perform date and time calculations involving actual time zones, you will have to write custom code. Just keep in mind that time zone calculations are fairly involved, especially since calculations like DST can change over time. Case in point— the start and end dates for DST were extended in the United States beginning in 2007.

In addition to the new date and time functions, SQL Server 2008 enhances the classic DATEPART function, which returns an int value representing a specific part of a given date. SQL Server 2008 supports all of the existing DATEPART options (e.g., year, month, and day), but it also allows you to retrieve the microsecond, nanosecond, time offset, and ISO standard week parts of a given date. Table 17-1 lists the new options supported by DATEPART.

Table 17-1. *New DATEPART Options*

Date Part	Abbreviation
microsecond	mcs
nanosecond	ns
TZoffset	tz
ISO_WEEK	isowk, isoww

The TZoffset option returns the time offset in minutes. For a date with a time offset of –04:00, DATEPART with the TZoffset option returns –240. The ISO_WEEK option returns the week number for a date, as defined by the ISO 8601 standard. In the ISO week numbering system, weeks begin on Monday, and week 1 of the year is defined as the week containing the first Thursday of that year. This means that in the ISO system, years can have either 52 or 53 weeks, and some days in a given year can end up being attributed to weeks in the previous or next year. While the ISO calculation is a bit more complicated than the simple week number calculation common in the United States, the ISO version is commonly used by governments and international agencies.

The max Data Types

In the heady days of SQL Server 2000, large object (LOB) data storage and manipulation required use of the old style text, ntext, and image data types. If you've ever tried to use the text, ntext, and image data types, you'll be happy to hear they've been deprecated and replaced with new, easier-to-use types. SQL Server 2008 supports the max data types, varchar(max), nvarchar(max), and varbinary(max), which were first introduced in SQL Server 2005.

The max data types are complete replacements for the older LOB data types. Like the older types, each of these new data types can hold over 2.1 billion bytes of character or binary data. Unlike the legacy LOB types, however, the max data types operate similarly to the standard varchar, nvarchar, and varbinary data types. Standard string manipulation functions such as LEN and CHARINDEX, which didn't work well with the older LOB data types, work as expected with the new max data types. The new data types also eliminate the need for kludgy solutions involving the TEXTPTR, READTEXT, and WRITETEXT statements to manipulate LOB data.

■**Note** The varchar(max), nvarchar(max), and varbinary(max) data types are complete replacements for the SQL Server 2000 text, ntext, and image data types. The text, ntext, and image data types and their support functions will be removed in a future version of SQL Server. Because they are deprecated, Microsoft recommends you avoid these older data types for new development.

The new max data types support a .WRITE clause extension to the UPDATE statement to perform optimized minimally logged updates and appends to varchar(max), varbinary(max), and nvarchar(max) types. You can use the .WRITE clause by appending it to the end of the column name in your UPDATE statement. The example in Listing 17-15 compares performance of the .WRITE clause to a simple string concatenation when updating a column. The results of this simple comparison are shown in Figure 17-11.

Listing 17-15. *Comparison of .WRITE Clause and String Append*

```
-- Turn off messages that can affect performance
SET NOCOUNT ON;

-- Create and initially populate a test table
CREATE TABLE #test
```

```
(
  Id int NOT NULL PRIMARY KEY,
  String varchar(max) NOT NULL
);

INSERT INTO #test
(
  Id,
  String
)
VALUES
(
  1,
  ''
),
(
  2,
  ''
);

-- Initialize variables and get start time
DECLARE @i int = 1;
DECLARE @quote varchar(50) = 'Four score and seven years ago...';
DECLARE @start_time datetime2(7) = SYSDATETIME();

-- Loop 2500 times and use .WRITE to append to a varchar(max) column
WHILE @i < 2500
BEGIN
  UPDATE #test
  SET string.WRITE(@quote, LEN(string), LEN(@quote))
  WHERE Id = 1;

  SET @i += 1;
END;

SELECT '.WRITE Clause', DATEDIFF(ms, @start_time, SYSDATETIME()), 'ms';

-- Reset variables and get new start time
SET @i = 1;
SET @start_time = SYSDATETIME();

-- Loop 2500 times and use string append to a varchar(max) column
WHILE @i < 2500
BEGIN
  UPDATE #test
  SET string += @quote
  WHERE Id = 2;
```

```
  SET @i += 1;
END;

SELECT 'Append Method', DATEDIFF(ms, @start_time, SYSDATETIME()), 'ms';

SELECT
  Id,
  String,
  LEN(String)
FROM #test;

DROP TABLE #test;
```

Results			
	(No column na...	(No column na...	(No column na...
1	.WRITE Clause	1572	ms

	(No column na...	(No column na...	(No column na...
1	Append Method	7972	ms

	Id	String	(No column na...
1	1	Four score and seven years ago...Four score and ...	82467
2	2	Four score and seven years ago...Four score and ...	82467

Figure 17-11. *Testing the .WRITE clause against simple string concatenation*

As you can see in this example, the `.WRITE` clause is appreciably more efficient than a simple string concatenation when updating a `max` data type column. Note that these times were achieved on one of my development machines, and your results may vary significantly depending on your specific configuration. You can expect the `.WRITE` method to perform more efficiently than simple string concatenation when updating `max` data type columns, however.

You should note the following about the `.WRITE` clause:

- The second `.WRITE` parameter, `@offset`, is a zero-based `bigint` and cannot be negative. The first character of the target string is at offset `0`.

- If the `@offset` parameter is `NULL`, the expression is appended to the end of the target string. `@length` is ignored in this case.

- If the third parameter, `@length`, is `NULL`, SQL Server truncates anything past the end of the string expression (the first `.WRITE` parameter) after the target string is updated. The `@length` parameter is a `bigint` and cannot be negative.

Synonyms

Synonyms provide a handy way to alias database objects. This can help make code easier to read and reduce the number of keystrokes while coding. Synonyms are particularly useful for aliasing three- and four-part names. You can create synonyms for a variety of database objects, including tables, views, procedures, functions, and aggregates. The CREATE SYNONYM statement creates a synonym, as demonstrated in Listing 17-16.

Listing 17-16. *Creating a Synonym for a Table*

```
CREATE SYNONYM Folks
FOR AdventureWorks.Person.Person;

SELECT
  LastName,
  FirstName,
  MiddleName
FROM Folks;
```

Listing 17-16 creates the synonym Folks for the AdventureWorks.Person.Person table. You can use the synonym to reference the base object as I did with the SELECT query in the sample listing. You can drop synonyms with the DROP SYNONYM statement, shown in Listing 17-17.

Listing 17-17. *Dropping a Synonym*

```
DROP SYNONYM Folks;
```

■**Tip** Synonyms use late binding, so the object a synonym references does not have to exist at the time you create the synonym.

FILESTREAM Support

SQL Server is optimized for dealing with highly structured relational data, but SQL developers have long had to deal with heterogeneous unstructured data. The varbinary(max) LOB data type provides a useful method of storing arbitrary binary data directly in database tables; however, it still has some limitations, including the following:

- There is a hard 2.1 GB limit on the size of binary data that can be stored in a varbinary(max) column, which can be an issue if the documents you need to store are larger.

- Storing and managing large varbinary(max) data in SQL Server can have a negative impact on performance, owing largely to the fact that the SQL Server engine must maintain proper locking and isolation levels to ensure data integrity in the database.

Many developers and administrators have come up with clever solutions to work around this problem. Most of these solutions are focused on storing binary large object (BLOB) data as files in the file system and storing file paths pointing to those files in the database. This introduces additional complexities to the system since you must maintain the links between database entries and physical files in the file system. You also must manage BLOB data stored in the file system using external tools, outside of the scope of database transactions. Finally, this type of solution can double the amount of work required to properly secure your data, since you must manage security in the database and separately in the file system.

SQL Server 2008 provides a third option: integrated FILESTREAM support. SQL Server can store FILESTREAM-enabled varbinary(max) data as files in the file system. SQL Server can manage the contents of the FILESTREAM containers on the file system for you and control access to the files, while the NT File System (NTFS) provides efficient file streaming and file system transaction support. This combination of SQL Server and NTFS functionality provides several advantages when dealing with LOB data, including increased efficiency, manageability, and concurrency. Microsoft provides some general guidelines for use of FILESTREAM over regular LOB data types, including the following:

- When the average size of your BLOBs is greater than 1 MB

- When you have to store any BLOBs that are larger than 2.1 GB

- When fast read access is a priority

- When you want to access BLOB data from middle-tier code

■**Tip** For smaller BLOB data, storing the data directly in the database might make more sense than using FILESTREAM.

Enabling FILESTREAM Support

The first step to using FILESTREAM functionality in SQL Server is enabling it. You can enable FILESTREAM support through the SQL Server Configuration Manager. You can set FILESTREAM access in the SQL Server service Properties ➤ FILESTREAM page. Once you've enabled FILESTREAM support, you can set the level of access for the SQL Server instance with sp_configure. Listing 17-18 enables FILESTREAM support on the SQL Server instance for the maximum allowable access.

Listing 17-18. *Enabling FILESTREAM Support on the Server*

```
EXEC sp_ configure 'filestream access level', 2;
GO
RECONFIGURE;
GO
```

Currently, when you change the FILESTREAM support level on a SQL Server instance, you receive a message that you need to restart the server. The SQL Server team is working to eliminate this requirement. The configuration value defines the access level for FILESTREAM support. The levels supported are listed in Table 17-2.

Table 17-2. *FILESTREAM Access Levels*

Configuration Value	Description
0	Disabled (default)
1	Access via T-SQL only
2	Access via T-SQL and file system

You can use the query in Listing 17-19 to see the FILESTREAM configuration information at any time. Sample results from my local server are shown in Figure 17-12.

Listing 17-19. *Viewing FILESTREAM Configuration Information*

```
SELECT
  SERVERPROPERTY('ServerName') AS Server_Name,
  SERVERPROPERTY('FilestreamSharename') AS Share_Name,
  CASE SERVERPROPERTY('FilestreamEffectiveLevel')
    WHEN 0 THEN 'Disabled'
    WHEN 1 THEN 'T-SQL Access Only'
    WHEN 2 THEN 'Local T-SQL/File System Access Only'
    WHEN 3 THEN 'Local T-SQL/File System and Remote File System Access'
    END AS Effective_Level,
  CASE SERVERPROPERTY('FilestreamConfiguredLevel')
    WHEN 0 THEN 'Disabled'
    WHEN 1 THEN 'T-SQL Access Only'
    WHEN 2 THEN 'Local T-SQL/File System Access Only'
    WHEN 3 THEN 'Local T-SQL/File System and Remote File System Access'
    END AS Configured_Level;
```

	Server_Name	Share_Name	Effective_Level	Configured_Level
1	SQL2008	MSSQLSERVER	Local T-SQL/File System and Remote ...	Local T-SQL/File System and Remote...

Figure 17-12. *Viewing FILESTREAM configuration information*

Creating FILESTREAM Filegroups

Once you've enabled FILESTREAM support on your SQL Server instance, you have to create a SQL Server filegroup with the CONTAINS FILESTREAM option. This filegroup is where SQL Server will store FILESTREAM BLOB files. The AdventureWorks 2008 sample database already contains a FILESTREAM filegroup, which is shown in the CREATE DATABASE statement in Listing 17-20. The FILEGROUP clause of the statement that creates the FILESTREAM filegroup is shown in bold.

Listing 17-20. *CREATE DATABASE for AdventureWorks 2008 Database*

```
CREATE DATABASE AdventureWorks
(
  NAME = N'AdventureWorks2008_Data',
  FILENAME = N'C:\Program Files\Microsoft SQL Server\MSSQL10.MSSQLSERVER\➥
    MSSQL\DATA\AdventureWorks2008.mdf'
),
FILEGROUP DocumentFileStreamGroup CONTAINS FILESTREAM
DEFAULT
(
  NAME = N'FileStreamDocuments',
  FILENAME = N'C:\Program Files\Microsoft SQL Server\MSSQL10.MSSQLSERVER\➥
    MSSQL\DATA\AdventureWorks2008_2.Documents'
)
LOG ON
(
  NAME = N'AdventureWorks2008_Log',
  FILENAME = N'C:\Program Files\Microsoft SQL Server\MSSQL10.MSSQLSERVER\➥
    MSSQL\DATA\AdventureWorks2008_1.ldf'
);
GO
```

Alternatively, if your existing database doesn't contain a FILESTREAM filegroup, but you would like to add one, you can use the ALTER DATABASE statement as shown in Listing 17-21.

Listing 17-21. *Adding a FILESTREAM Filegroup to an Existing Database*

```
ALTER DATABASE AdventureWorks
ADD FILEGROUP DocumentFileStreamGroup CONTAINS FILESTREAM;
GO

ALTER DATABASE AdventureWorks
ADD FILE
(
  NAME = N'FileStreamDocuments',
  FILENAME = N'C:\Program Files\Microsoft SQL Server\MSSQL10.MSSQLSERVER\➥
    MSSQL\DATA\AdventureWorks2008_2.Documents'
)
TO FILEGROUP DocumentFileStreamGroup;
GO
```

FILESTREAM-Enabling Tables

Once you've enabled FILESTREAM on the server instance and created a FILESTREAM filegroup, you're ready to create FILESTREAM-enabled tables. FILESTREAM storage is accessed by creating a varbinary(max) column in a table with the FILESTREAM attribute. The FILESTREAM-enabled table must also have a uniqueidentifier column with a ROWGUIDCOL attribute. The Production. Document table in the AdventureWorks sample database is FILESTREAM-enabled. The Document column is declared as a varbinary(max) with the FILESTREAM attribute, and the rowguid column is declared as a uniqueidentifier with the ROWGUIDCOL attribute. Listing 17-22 shows the CREATE TABLE statement for the Production.Document table, with the Document and rowguid columns shown in bold.

Listing 17-22. *Production.Document FILESTREAM-Enabled Table*

```
CREATE TABLE Production.Document
(
  DocumentNode    hierarchyid NOT NULL PRIMARY KEY,
  DocumentLevel   AS (DocumentNode.GetLevel()),
  Title           nvarchar(50) NOT NULL,
  Owner           int NOT NULL,
  FolderFlag      bit NOT NULL,
  FileName        nvarchar(400) NOT NULL,
  FileExtension   nvarchar(8) NOT NULL,
  Revision        nchar(5) NOT NULL,
  ChangeNumber    int NOT NULL,
  Status          tinyint NOT NULL,
  DocumentSummary nvarchar(max) NULL,
  Document        varbinary(max) FILESTREAM  NULL,
  rowguid         uniqueidentifier ROWGUIDCOL  NOT NULL,
  ModifiedDate    datetime NOT NULL
);
GO
```

The AdventureWorks database also comes standard with sample files stored in the FILESTREAM filegroup accessible through the Document column of the Production.Document table. You can view these files in Windows Explorer, as shown in Figure 17-13. The file names appear as a jumble of grouped digits that don't offer up much information about the BLOB files' contents.

■**Caution** SQL Server also creates a file named filestream.hdr. This file is used by SQL Server to manage FILESTREAM data. Do not open or modify this file.

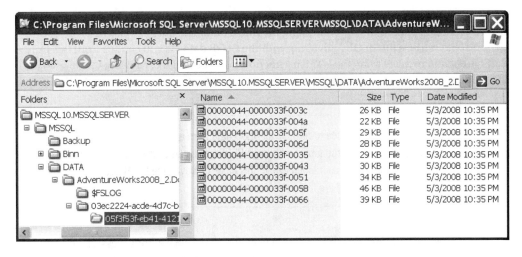

Figure 17-13. *BLOB files stored in the FILESTREAM filegroup*

Accessing FILESTREAM Data

You can access and manipulate your FILESTREAM-enabled varbinary(max) columns using standard SQL Server SELECT queries and DML statements like INSERT and DELETE. Listing 17-23 demonstrates querying the varbinary(max) column of the Production.Document table. The results are shown in Figure 17-14.

Listing 17-23. *Querying a FILESTREAM-Enabled Table*

```
SELECT
  d.Title,
  d.Document.PathName() AS BLOB_Path,
  d.Document AS BLOB_Data
FROM Production.Document d
WHERE d.Document IS NOT NULL;
```

	Title	BLOB_Path	BLOB_Data
1	Introduction 1	\\SQL2008\MSSQLSERVER\v1\AdventureWorks\Pro...	0xD0CF11E0A1B11AE1000000000...
2	Repair and Service Guidelin...	\\SQL2008\MSSQLSERVER\v1\AdventureWorks\Pro...	0xD0CF11E0A1B11AE1000000000...
3	Crank Arm and Tire Mainten...	\\SQL2008\MSSQLSERVER\v1\AdventureWorks\Pro...	0xD0CF11E0A1B11AE1000000000...
4	Lubrication Maintenance	\\SQL2008\MSSQLSERVER\v1\AdventureWorks\Pro...	0xD0CF11E0A1B11AE1000000000...
5	Front Reflector Bracket and ...	\\SQL2008\MSSQLSERVER\v1\AdventureWorks\Pro...	0xD0CF11E0A1B11AE1000000000...
6	Front Reflector Bracket Inst...	\\SQL2008\MSSQLSERVER\v1\AdventureWorks\Pro...	0xD0CF11E0A1B11AE1000000000...
7	Installing Replacement Pedals	\\SQL2008\MSSQLSERVER\v1\AdventureWorks\Pro...	0xD0CF11E0A1B11AE1000000000...
8	Seat Assembly	\\SQL2008\MSSQLSERVER\v1\AdventureWorks\Pro...	0xD0CF11E0A1B11AE1000000000...
9	Training Wheels 2	\\SQL2008\MSSQLSERVER\v1\AdventureWorks\Pro...	0xD0CF11E0A1B11AE1000000000...

Figure 17-14. *Results of querying the FILESTREAM-enabled table*

A property called PathName() is exposed on FILESTREAM-enabled varbinary(max) columns to retrieve the full path to the file containing the BLOB data. The query in Listing 17-23 uses PathName() to retrieve the BLOB path along with the BLOB data. As you can see from this example, SQL Server abstracts away the NTFS interaction to a large degree, allowing you to query and manipulate FILESTREAM data as if it were relational data stored directly in the database.

■**Tip** In most cases, it's not a good idea to retrieve all BLOB data from a FILESTREAM-enabled table in a single query as in this example. For large tables with large BLOBs, this can cause severe performance problems and make client applications unresponsive. In this case, however, the BLOB data being queried is actually very small in size, and there are few rows in the table.

SQL Server 2008 provides support for the OpenSqlFilestream API for accessing and manipulating FILESTREAM data in client applications. A full description of the OpenSqlFilestream API is beyond the scope of this book, but *Accelerated SQL Server 2008*, by Rob Walters et al. (Apress, 2008), provides a description of the OpenSqlFilestream API with source code for a detailed client application.

Summary

In this chapter, I've taken a step back to discuss functionality supported by SQL Server 2008 that was first introduced in SQL Server 2005. Synonyms, for example, provide a means of aliasing database objects, simplifying coding, management, and administration. The SQL Server max data types greatly simplify the task of querying, managing, and manipulating LOB data inside the database. New set-based operators like INTERSECT and EXCEPT provide a simplified way to use a result set to restrict the results produced by another result set.

Additional features like the OUTPUT clause provide real-time feedback about rows affected by the INSERT, UPDATE, DELETE, and MERGE DML statements. The TOP keyword has been enhanced with options to use a variable or subquery to specify the number of rows to return. TOP functionality has also been extended to DML statements like UPDATE and DELETE in addition to SELECT queries.

The NEWSEQUENTIALID function allows you to generate sequential GUIDs to minimize page splitting caused by clustered indexes. CROSS APPLY and OUTER APPLY allow you to invoke functions on query result set rows using a set-based syntax. The TABLESAMPLE clause allows you to quickly and easily retrieve random rows from a table.

I also continued the exploration of new SQL Server 2008 features like the new date and time manipulation functions in support of the new SQL Server 2008 date and time data types. I also discussed SQL Server 2008's FILESTREAM support, which allows SQL Server to store BLOB data in the file system, increasing BLOB data retrieval efficiency, increasing scalability, and simplifying management and administration.

EXERCISES

1. [Choose all that apply] SQL Server 2008 supports which of the following set-based operators:

   a.   INTERSECT

   b.   EXCEPT

   c.   COMPLEMENT

   d.   INCLUDED

2. [True/false] The OUTPUT clause provides real-time feedback about rows affected by DML statements like DELETE and INSERT.

3. [Fill in the blank] The TABLESAMPLE clause returns a ___ sample of rows from a table.

4. [Choose one] Which of the following functions adjusts a given datetimeoffset value to another specified time offset:

   a.   TODATETIMEOFFSET

   b.   SWITCHOFFSET

   c.   CHANGEOFFSET

   d.   CALCULATEOFFSET

5. [Choose all that apply] Which of the following LOB data types are deprecated:

   a.   image

   b.   varchar(max)

   c.   text

   d.   ntext

   e.   All of the above

6. [True/false] The FILESTREAM functionality in SQL Server 2008 uses NTFS to provide streaming BLOB data support.

■ ■ ■

CHAPTER 18

Error Handling and Dynamic SQL

Prior to SQL Server 2005, error handling was limited almost exclusively to the @@error system function and the RAISERROR statement, or through client-side exception handling. T-SQL in SQL Server 2008 still provides access to these tools, but also supports modern structured error handling similar to that offered by other high-level languages such as C++, C#, and Visual Basic. In this chapter, I will discuss legacy T-SQL error-handling functionality and the newer structured error-handling model in T-SQL. This chapter introduces tools useful for debugging server-side code, including T-SQL statements and the Visual Studio IDE.

I will also discuss dynamic SQL in this chapter, which is often more difficult to debug and manage than standard (nondynamic) T-SQL statements. Dynamic SQL, while a useful tool, also has security implications, which I will address.

Error Handling

SQL Server 2008 provides improvements in error handling over SQL Server 2000 and prior releases. In this section, I'll discuss legacy error handling and SQL Server 2008 improved TRY...CATCH structured error handling.

Legacy Error Handling

In SQL Server 2000, the primary method of handling exceptions was through the @@error system function. This function returns an int value representing the current error code. An @@error value of 0 means no error occurred. One of the major limitations of this function is that it is automatically reset to 0 after every successful statement. This means you cannot have any statements between the code that you expect might produce an exception and the code that checks the value of @@error. This also means that after @@error is checked, it is automatically reset to 0, so you can't both check the value of @@error and return @@error from within a SP. Listing 18-1 demonstrates an SP that generates an error, and attempts to print the error code from within the procedure and return the value of @@error to the caller.

Listing 18-1. *Incorrect Error Handling with @@error*

```
CREATE PROCEDURE dbo.TestError (@e int OUTPUT)
AS
```

```
BEGIN
  INSERT INTO Person.Person(BusinessEntityID)
  VALUES (1);

  PRINT N'Error code in procedure = ' + CAST(@@error AS nvarchar(10));

  SET @e = @@error;
END
GO

DECLARE @ret int,
  @e int;
EXEC @ret = dbo.TestError @e OUTPUT;
PRINT N'Returned error code = ' + CAST(@e AS nvarchar(10));
PRINT N'Return value = ' + CAST(@ret AS nvarchar(10));
```

The TestError procedure in Listing 18-1 demonstrates one problem with @@error. The result of executing the procedure should be similar to the following:

```
Msg 515, Level 16, State 2, Procedure TestError, Line 4
Cannot insert the value NULL into column 'PersonType', table
'AdventureWorks.Person.Person'; column does not allow nulls. INSERT fails.
The statement has been terminated.
Error code in procedure = 515
Returned error code = 0
Return value = -6
```

As you can see, the error code generated by the failed INSERT statement is 515 when printed inside the SP, but a value of 0 (no error) is returned to the caller via the OUTPUT parameter. The problem is with the following line in the SP:

```
PRINT N'Error code in procedure = ' + CAST(@@error AS nvarchar(10));
```

The PRINT statement automatically resets the value of @@error after it executes, meaning you can't test or retrieve the same value of @@error afterward (it will be 0 every time). The workaround is to store the value of @@error in a local variable immediately after the statement you suspect might fail (in this case the INSERT statement). Listing 18-2 demonstrates this method of using @@error.

Listing 18-2. *Corrected Error Handling with @@error*

```
CREATE PROCEDURE dbo.TestError2 (@e int OUTPUT)
AS
BEGIN
  INSERT INTO Person.Person(BusinessEntityID)
  VALUES (1);

  SET @e = @@error;
```

```
    PRINT N'Error code in procedure = ' + CAST(@e AS nvarchar(10));
END
GO

DECLARE @ret int,
  @e int;
EXEC @ret = dbo.TestError2 @e OUTPUT;
PRINT N'Returned error code = ' + CAST(@e AS nvarchar(10));
PRINT N'Return value = ' + CAST(@ret AS nvarchar(10));
```

By storing the value of @@error immediately after the statement you suspect might cause an error, you can test or retrieve the value as often as you like for further processing. The following is the result of the new procedure:

```
Msg 515, Level 16, State 2, Procedure TestError2, Line 4
Cannot insert the value NULL into column 'PersonType', table
'AdventureWorks.Person.Person'; column does not allow nulls. INSERT fails.
The statement has been terminated.
Error code in procedure = 515
Returned error code = 515
Return value = -6
```

In this case, the proper @@error code is both printed and returned to the caller by the SP. Also of note is that the SP return value is automatically set to a nonzero value when the error occurs.

Try...Catch Exception Handling

SQL Server 2008 supports the TRY...CATCH model of exception handling common in other modern programming languages. In the T-SQL TRY...CATCH model, you wrap the code you suspect could cause an exception in a BEGIN TRY...END TRY block. This block is immediately followed by a BEGIN CATCH...END CATCH block that will be invoked only if the statements in the TRY block cause an error. Listing 18-3 demonstrates TRY...CATCH exception handling with a simple SP.

Listing 18-3. *Sample TRY...CATCH Error Handling*

```
CREATE PROCEDURE dbo.TestError3 (@e int OUTPUT)
AS
BEGIN

  SET @e = 0;

  BEGIN TRY
    INSERT INTO Person.Address (AddressID)
    VALUES (1);
  END TRY
```

```
  BEGIN CATCH
    SET @e = ERROR_NUMBER();

    PRINT N'Error Code = ' + CAST(@e AS nvarchar(10));
    PRINT N'Error Procedure = ' + ERROR_PROCEDURE();
    PRINT N'Error Message = ' + ERROR_MESSAGE();
  END CATCH

END
GO

DECLARE @ret int,
  @e int;
EXEC @ret = dbo.TestError3 @e OUTPUT;
PRINT N'Error code = ' + CAST(@e AS nvarchar(10));
PRINT N'Return value = ' + CAST(@ret AS nvarchar(10));
```

The result is similar to Listing 18-2, but SQL Server's TRY...CATCH support gives you more control and flexibility over the output, as shown here:

```
(0 row(s) affected)
Error Code = 544
Error Procedure = TestError3
Error Message = Cannot insert explicit value for identity column in table
'Address' when IDENTITY_INSERT is set to OFF.
Returned error code = 544
Return value = -6
```

The T-SQL statements in the BEGIN TRY...END TRY block execute normally. If the block completes without error, the T-SQL statements between the BEGIN CATCH...END CATCH block are skipped. If an exception is thrown by the statements in the TRY block, control transfers to the statements in the BEGIN CATCH...END CATCH block.

The CATCH block exposes several functions for determining exactly what error occurred and where it occurred. I used some of these functions in Listing 18-3 to return additional information about the exception thrown. These functions are available only between the BEGIN CATCH...END CATCH keywords, and only during error handling when control has been transferred to it by an exception thrown in a TRY block. If used outside of a CATCH block, all of these functions return NULL. The functions available are listed in Table 18-1.

Table 18-1. *CATCH Block Functions*

Function Name	Description
ERROR_LINE()	Returns the line number on which the exception occurred
ERROR_MESSAGE()	Returns the complete text of the generated error message
ERROR_PROCEDURE()	Returns the name of the SP or trigger where the error occurred
ERROR_NUMBER()	Returns the number of the error that occurred

Function Name	Description
ERROR_SEVERITY()	Returns the severity level of the error that occurred
ERROR_STATE()	Returns the state number of the error that occurred

TRY...CATCH blocks can be nested. You can have TRY...CATCH blocks within other TRY blocks or CATCH blocks to handle errors that might be generated within your exception-handling code.

You can also test the state of transactions within a CATCH block by using the XACT_STATE function. I strongly recommend testing your transaction state before issuing a COMMIT TRANSACTION or ROLLBACK TRANSACTION statement in your CATCH block to ensure consistency. Table 18-2 lists the return values for XACT_STATE and how you should handle each in your CATCH block.

Table 18-2. *XACT_STATE Function Return Values*

XACT_STATE	Meaning
-1	There is an uncommittable transaction pending. Issue a ROLLBACK TRANSACTION statement.
0	There is no transaction pending. No action is necessary.
1	There is a committable transaction pending. Issue a COMMIT TRANSACTION statement.

The T-SQL TRY...CATCH method of error handling has certain limitations attached to it. For one, TRY...CATCH can only capture errors that have a severity greater than 10 that do not close the database connection. The following errors are not caught:

- Errors with a severity of 10 or lower (*informational messages*) are not caught.

- Errors with a severity level of 20 or higher (*connection-termination errors*) are not caught, because they close the database connection immediately.

- Most compile-time errors, such as syntax errors, are not caught by TRY...CATCH, although there are exceptions (e.g., when using dynamic SQL).

- Statement-level recompilation errors, such as object-name resolution errors, are not caught, due to SQL Server's deferred-name resolution.

Also keep in mind that errors captured by a TRY...CATCH block are not returned to the caller. You can, however, use the RAISERROR statement (described in the next section) to return error information to the caller.

The RAISERROR Statement

The RAISERROR statement is a T-SQL statement that allows you to throw an exception at runtime. It is similar to the throw statement, used to throw and rethrow exceptions in languages such as C++ and C#. The RAISERROR statement accepts a message ID number or message string, severity level, state information, and optional argument parameters for special formatting codes in error messages. Listing 18-4 uses RAISERROR to throw an exception with a custom error message, a severity level of 17, and a state of 127.

Listing 18-4. *Raising a Custom Exception with RAISERROR*

```
RAISERROR ('This is an exception.', 17, 127);
```

When you pass a string error message to the RAISERROR statement, as in Listing 18-4, a default error code of 50000 is raised. If you specify a message ID number instead, the number must be between 13000 and 2147483647, and it cannot be 50000. The severity level is a number between 0 and 25, with each level representing the seriousness of the error. Table 18-3 lists the severity levels recognized by SQL Server.

Table 18-3. *SQL Server Error Severity Levels*

Range	Description
0–10	Informational messages
11–18	Errors
19–25	Fatal errors

■**Tip** Only members of the sysadmin fixed server role of users with ALTER TRACE permissions can specify severity levels greater than 18 with RAISERROR, and the WITH LOG option must be used.

The state value passed to RAISERROR is a user-defined informational value between 1 and 127. The state information can be used to help locate specific errors within your code when using RAISERROR. For instance, you can use a state of 1 for the first RAISERROR statement in a given SP and a state of 2 for the second RAISERROR statement in the same SP. The state information provided by RAISERROR isn't as necessary in SQL Server 2008 since you can retrieve much more descriptive and precise information from the functions available in CATCH blocks.

The RAISERROR statement supports an optional WITH clause for specifying additional options. The WITH LOG option logs the error raised to the application log and the SQL error log, the WITH NOWAIT option sends the error message to the client immediately, and the WITH SETERROR option sets the @@error system function (in a CATCH block) to an indicated message ID number. This should be used with a severity of 10 or less to set @@error without causing other side effects (e.g., batch termination).

RAISERROR can be used within a TRY or CATCH block to generate errors. Within the TRY block, if RAISERROR generates an error with severity between 11 and 19, control passes to the CATCH block. For errors with severity of 10 or lower, processing continues in the TRY block. For errors with severity of 20 or higher, the client connection is terminated and control does not pass to the CATCH block. For these high-severity errors, the error is returned to the caller.

Debugging Tools

In procedural languages like C#, debugging code is somewhat easier than in declarative languages like T-SQL. In procedural languages, you can easily follow the flow of a program, setting breakpoints at each atomic step of execution. In declarative languages, however, a single statement can perform dozens or hundreds of steps in the background, most of which you will probably not even be aware of at execution time. The good news is that the SQL Server team did not leave us without tools to debug and troubleshoot T-SQL code. The unpretentious PRINT statement provides a very simple and effective method of debugging.

PRINT Statement Debugging

The PRINT statement, as demonstrated in Listing 18-3, is a simple and useful server-side debugging tool. Simply printing constants and variable values to standard output during script or SP execution often provides enough information to quickly locate problem code. PRINT works from within SPs and batches, but does not work inside of UDFs, because of the built-in restrictions on functions causing side effects. Consider the sample code in Listing 18-5, in which I am trying to achieve an end result where @i is equal to 10. Because the end result of the code is not @i = 10, I've added a couple of simple PRINT statements to uncover the reason.

Listing 18-5. *Debugging Script with PRINT*

```
DECLARE @i int;
PRINT N'Initial value of @i = ' + COALESCE(CAST(@i AS nvarchar(10)), N'NULL');
SET @i += 10;
PRINT N'Final value of @i = ' + COALESCE(CAST(@i AS nvarchar(10)), N'NULL');
```

The result, shown in Figure 18-1, shows that the desired end result is not occurring because I failed to initialize the variable @i to 0 at the beginning of my script. Because the initial value of @i is NULL, my end result is NULL. Once I've identified the issue, fixing it is a relatively simple matter in this example.

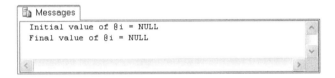

Figure 18-1. *Results of PRINT statement debugging*

In addition to the simple PRINT statement, you can use the RAISERROR statement with NOWAIT clause to send a message or status indication immediately to the client. While the PRINT statement waits for the buffer to flush, RAISERROR with the NOWAIT clause sends the message immediately.

Trace Flags

SQL Server 2008 provides several trace flags that can help with debugging, particularly when you suspect you have a problem with SQL Server settings. Trace flags can turn on or off specific SQL Server behavior, or change other server characteristics temporarily for a server or session. As an example, trace flag 1204 returns the resources and types of locks participating in a deadlock, and the current command affected.

■**Tip** Many trace flags are undocumented, and may only be revealed to you by Microsoft Product Support Services when you report a specific issue; but those that are documented can provide very useful information. BOL provides a complete list of documented SQL Server 2008 trace flags under the title of "Trace Flags."

Turning on or off a trace flag is as simple as using the DBCC TRACEON and DBCC TRACEOFF statements, as shown in Listing 18-6.

Listing 18-6. *Turning Trace Flag 1204 On and Off*

```
DBCC TRACEON (1204, -1);
GO

DBCC TRACEOFF (1204, -1);
GO
```

Trace flags may report information via standard output, the SQL Server log, or additional log files created just for that specific trace flag. Check BOL for specific information about the methods that specific trace flags report back to you.

SSMS Integrated Debugger

SQL Server 2005 did away with the integrated user interface debugger in SSMS, although it was previously a part of Query Analyzer (QA). Apparently, the thought was that Visual Studio would be the debugging tool of choice for stepping through T-SQL code and setting breakpoints in SPs. Now, in SQL Server 2008, integrated SSMS debugging is back by popular demand. The SSMS main menu contains several debugging actions accessible through the new Debug menu, as shown in Figure 18-2.

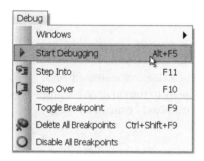

Figure 18-2. *The SSMS Debug menu*

The options are similar to the options available when debugging Visual Studio projects. From this menu, you can start debugging, step into/over your code one statement at a time, and manage breakpoints. Figure 18-3 shows an SSMS debugging session that has just hit a breakpoint inside the body of a SP.

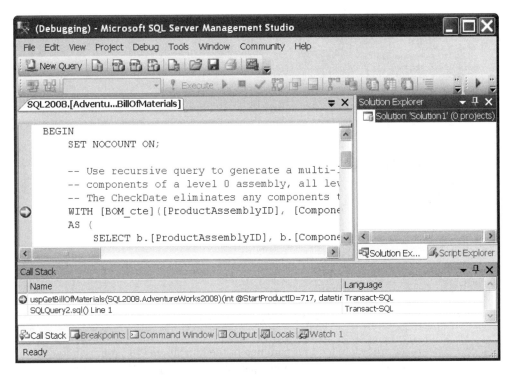

Figure 18-3. *Stepping into code with the SSMS debugger*

The SSMS debugger provides several windows that provide additional debugging information, including the Call Stack, Breakpoints, Command, Output, Locals, and Watch windows.

Visual Studio T-SQL Debugger

Visual Studio 2008 Pro and Team editions also offer an excellent facility for stepping through SPs and UDFs just like any Visual Basic or C# application. You can access Visual Studio's T-SQL debugger through the Server Explorer window. Simply expand the data connection pointing at your SQL Server instance and the SP or function you wish to debug under the appropriate database. Then right-click the procedure or function and select either the Step Into Procedure or Step Into Function option from the pop-up context menu. Figure 18-4 demonstrates by selecting to step into the dbo.uspGetBillOfMaterials SP in the AdventureWorks 2008 database.

■**Tip** It's much easier to configure Visual Studio T-SQL debugging on a locally installed instance of SQL Server than to set up remote debugging. BOL offers information about setting up both local and remote SQL Server debugging in the article "Debugging SQL" (http://msdn.microsoft.com/en-us/library/zefbf0t6.aspx).

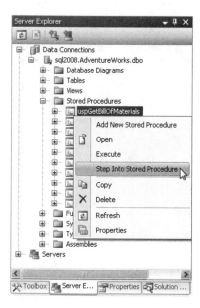

Figure 18-4. *Stepping into the dbo.uspGetBillOfMaterials procedure*

If your function or procedure requires parameters, the Run Stored Procedure window will open and ask you to enter values for the required parameters (see Figure 18-5). For this example, I've entered 770 for the @StartProductID parameter and 7/10/2001 for the @CheckDate parameter required by the dbo.uspGetBillOfMaterials procedure.

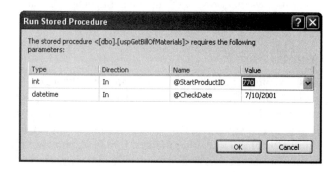

Figure 18-5. *Entering parameter values in the Run Stored Procedure window*

After you enter the parameters, the procedure will begin running in Debug mode in Visual Studio. Visual Studio shows the script and highlights each line in yellow as you step through it, as shown in Figure 18-6.

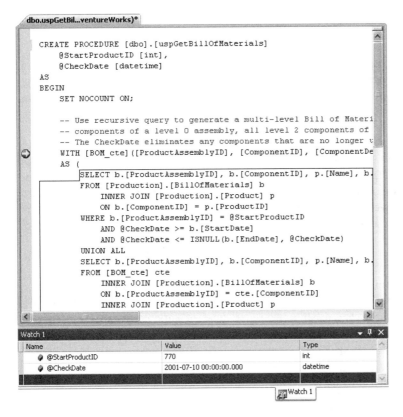

Figure 18-6. *Stepping through an SP in Debug mode*

In Debug mode, you can set breakpoints by clicking the left border and using the Continue (F5), Stop Debugging (Shift+F5), Step Over (F10), Step Into (F11), and Step Out (Shift+F11) commands, just like when you debug C# or Visual Basic programs. You can also add watches and view locals to inspect parameter and variable values as your code executes. Any result sets and return values from the SP are shown in the Visual Studio Output window, as in Figure 18-7.

```
Output                                                                  ▾ ⇧ ✕
Show output from: Debug                        ▾  📄  📄 📄  📑  🔄

ProductAssemblyID ComponentID ComponentDesc                          TotalQuantity    S↑▲
----------------- ----------- ------------------------------------   -------------   --
770               517         LL Road Seat Assembly                  1                9
770               738         LL Road Frame - Black, 52              1                2
770               806         ML Headset                             1                4.
770               811         LL Road Handlebars                     1                1
770               818         LL Road Front Wheel                    1                3
770               826         LL Road Rear Wheel                     1                4 ▼
◄                                         │││                              ►
🔲 Error List 📄 Output
```

Figure 18-7. *The Visual Studio Output window*

Dynamic SQL

SQL Server MVP Erland Sommarskog said it best: dynamic SQL is a curse and a blessing. Put simply, dynamic SQL is a means of constructing SQL statements as strings in your server-side (or even client-side) applications and executing them dynamically, on the fly. When used properly, dynamic SQL can be used to generate complex queries at runtime, in some cases improve performance, and do tasks that just aren't possible (or are extremely difficult) in standard, non-dynamic T-SQL.

The downside is that there are numerous ways to shoot yourself in the foot with dynamic SQL. If not used properly, dynamic SQL can open up security holes in your system big enough to drive a truck through. Even as I began writing this book, I received a newsletter highlighting a recent spate of SQL injection attacks against over half a million web pages, including some United Nations–owned web sites. In this section, I will discuss the various methods of executing dynamic SQL, as well as some of the risks and rewards that Erland alludes to.

The EXECUTE Statement

The most basic form of server-side dynamic SQL is achieved by simply passing a SQL query or other instruction as a string to the EXECUTE statement (often abbreviated EXEC). The EXECUTE statement accepts a char, varchar, nchar, or nvarchar constant, variable, or expression that contains valid T-SQL statements. Listing 18-7 shows the most basic form of dynamic SQL with an EXECUTE statement and a string constant.

Listing 18-7. *Basic EXECUTE Statement*

```
EXECUTE (N'SELECT ProductID FROM Production.Product');
```

As you can see, there is no real advantage to performing dynamic SQL on a string constant. A simple SELECT statement without the EXECUTE would perform the same function and return the same result. The true power of dynamic SQL is that you can build a SQL statement or query dynamically and execute it. Listing 18-8 demonstrates how this can be done.

Listing 18-8. *More Complex Dynamic SQL Example*

```
DECLARE @min_product_id int = 500;
DECLARE @sql_stmt nvarchar(128) =
  N'SELECT ProductID ' +
  N'FROM Production.Product ' +
  N'WHERE ProductID >= ' + CAST(@min_product_id AS nvarchar(10));
EXECUTE (@sql_stmt);
```

Now that I've given you this simple code sample, let's explore all the things that are wrong with it.

SQL Injection and Dynamic SQL

In Listing 18 -9, the variable @sql_stmt contains the dynamic SQL query. The query is built dynamically by appending the minimum product ID to the WHERE clause. This is not the recommended method of performing this type of query, and I show it here to make a point.

One of the problems with this method is that you lose some of the benefits of cached query plan execution. SQL Server 2008 has some great features that can help in this area, including parameter sniffing and the ability to turn on forced parameterization, but there are many exceptions to SQL Server's ability to automatically parameterize queries or clauses. To guarantee efficient reuse of cached query execution plans as the text of your query changes, you should parameterize queries yourself.

But the big problem here is SQL injection. Although not really a problem when appending an integer value to the end of a dynamic query (as in Listing 18-8), SQL injection can provide a back door for hackers trying to access or destroy your data when you concatenate strings to create dynamic SQL queries. Take a look at the innocent-looking dynamic SQL query in Listing 18-9. I will discuss how a hacker could wreak havoc with this query after the listing.

Listing 18-9. *Basic Dynamic SQL Query with a String Appended*

```
DECLARE @product_name nvarchar(50) = N'Mountain';
DECLARE @sql_stmt NVARCHAR(128) = N'SELECT ProductID, Name ' +
    N'FROM Production.Product ' +
    N'WHERE Name LIKE ''' +
    @product_name + N'%''';
EXECUTE (@sql_stmt);
```

This query simply returns all product IDs and names of all products that begin with the word *Mountain*. The problem is with how SQL Server interprets the concatenated string. The EXECUTE statement sees the following concatenated string (the bold portion reflects the value of the variable that was concatenated into the query).

```
SELECT ProductID, Name
FROM Production.Product
WHERE Name LIKE 'Mountain%'
```

A simple substitution for @product_name can execute other unwanted statements on your server. This is especially true with data coming from an external source (e.g., from the front end or application layer). Consider the following change to Listing 18-9:

```
DECLARE @product_name nvarchar(50) =
  N'''; DROP TABLE Production.Product; --'
```

The EXECUTE statement now executes the following string (again, the portion provided by the variable is shown in bold):

```
SELECT ProductID, Name
FROM Production.Product
WHERE Name LIKE '';
DROP TABLE Production.Product; --%'
```

The simple dynamic SQL query is now *two* queries, the second of which will drop the Production.Product table from the database! Now consider if the value of the @product_name variable had been retrieved from a user interface, like a web page. A malicious hacker could easily issue arbitrary INSERT, UPDATE, DELETE, DROP TABLE, TRUNCATE TABLE, or other statements to destroy data or open a back door into your system. Depending on how secure your server is, a hacker may be able to use SQL injection to grant himself administrator rights, retrieve and modify data stored in your server's file system, take control of your server, or access network resources.

The only justification for using the string concatenation method with EXECUTE is if you have to dynamically name the tables or columns in your statements. And this is far rarer than many people think. In fact, the only time this is usually necessary is if you need to dynamically generate SQL statements around database, table, or column names—if you are creating a dynamic pivot table–type query or coding an administration tool for SQL Server, for instance.

If you must use string concatenation with the EXECUTE method, be sure to take the following precautions with the strings being passed in from the user interface:

- Don't ever trust data from the front end. Always validate the data. If you are expecting only the letters A through Z and the numbers 0 through 9, reject all other characters in the input data.

- Disallow apostrophes, semicolons, parentheses, and double hyphens (--) in the input if possible. These characters have special significance to SQL Server and should be avoided. If you must allow these characters, scrutinize the input thoroughly before using it.

- If you absolutely must allow apostrophes in your data, escape them (double them up) before accepting the input.

- Reject strings that contain binary data, escape sequences, and multiline comment markers (/* and */).

- Validate XML input data against an XML schema when possible.

- Take extra special care when input data contains xp_ or sp_, as it may indicate an attempt to run procedures or XPs on your server.

■**Tip** If you are concatenating one-part table and object names into SQL statements on the server side, you can use the QUOTENAME function to safely quote them. The QUOTENAME function does not work for two-, three-, and four-part names, however.

Usually, data validations like the ones listed previously are performed on the client side, on the front end, in the application layer, or in the middle tiers of multitier systems. In highly secure and critical applications, it may be important to also perform server-side validations or some combination of client- and server-side validations. Triggers and check constraints can perform this type of validation on data before it's inserted into a table, and you can create UDFs or SPs to perform validations on dynamic SQL before executing it. Listing 18-10 shows a simple UDF that uses the Numbers table created in Chapter 5 to perform basic validation on a string, ensuring that it contains only the letters A through Z, the digits 0 through 9, and the underscore character (_), which is a common validation used on usernames, passwords, and other simple data.

Listing 18-10. *Simple T-SQL String Validation Function*

```
CREATE FUNCTION dbo.ValidateString (@string nvarchar(4000))
RETURNS int
AS
BEGIN
  DECLARE @result int = 0;
  WITH Numbers (Num)
  AS
  (
    SELECT 1
    UNION ALL
    SELECT Num + 1
    FROM Numbers
    WHERE Num <= LEN(@string)
  )
  SELECT @result = SUM
  (
    CASE
      WHEN SUBSTRING(@string, n.Num, 1) LIKE N'[A-Z0-9\_]' ESCAPE '\'
        THEN 0
        ELSE 1
        END
  )
  FROM Numbers n
  WHERE n.Num <= LEN(@string)
  OPTION (MAXRECURSION 0);
  RETURN @result;
END
GO
```

The function in Listing 18-10 uses a CTE to validate each character in the given string. The result is the total number of invalid characters in the string: a value of 0 indicates that all the characters in the string are valid. More complex validations can be performed with the LIKE operator or procedural code to ensure that data is in a prescribed format as well.

Troubleshooting Dynamic SQL

A big disadvantage to using dynamic SQL is in debugging and troubleshooting code. Complex dynamic SQL queries can be difficult to troubleshoot, and very simple syntax or other errors can be hard to locate. Fortunately, there is a fairly simple fix for that: write your troublesome query directly in T-SQL, replacing parameters with potential values. Highlight the code, and parse—or execute—it. Any syntax errors will be detected and described by SQL Server immediately. Fix the errors and repeat until all errors have been fixed. Then and only then revert the values back to their parameter names and put the statement back in dynamic SQL. Another handy method of troubleshooting is to print the dynamic SQL statement before executing it. Highlight, copy, and attempt to parse or run it in SSMS. You should be able to quickly and easily locate any problems and fix them as necessary.

One of the restrictions on dynamic SQL is that it cannot be executed in a UDF. This restriction is in place because UDFs cannot produce side effects that change the database. Dynamic SQL offers infinite opportunities to circumvent this restriction, so it is simply not allowed.

The sp_executesql Stored Procedure

The sp_executesql SP provides a second method of executing dynamic SQL. When used correctly, it is safer than the simple EXECUTE method for concatenating strings and executing them. Like EXECUTE, sp_executesql takes a string constant or variable as a SQL statement to execute. Unlike EXECUTE, the SQL statement parameter must be an nchar or nvarchar.

The sp_executesql procedure offers a distinct advantage over the EXECUTE method: you can specify your parameters separately from the SQL statement. When you specify the parameters separately instead of concatenating them into one large string, SQL Server passes the parameters to sp_executesql separately. SQL Server then substitutes the values of the parameters in the parameterized SQL statement. Because the parameter values are not concatenated into the SQL statement, sp_executesql protects against SQL injection attacks. sp_executesql parameterization also improves query execution plan cache reuse, which helps with performance.

A limitation to this approach is that you cannot use the parameters in your SQL statement in place of table, column, or other object names. Listing 18-11 shows how to parameterize the previous example.

Listing 18-11. *Dynamic SQL sp_executesql Parameterized*

```
DECLARE @product_name NVARCHAR(50) = N'Mountain%';
DECLARE @sql_stmt NVARCHAR(128) = N'SELECT ProductID, Name ' +
    N'FROM Production.Product ' +
    N'WHERE Name LIKE @name';
EXECUTE  sp_executesql @sql_stmt,
    N'@name NVARCHAR(50)',
    @name = @product_name;
```

■**Tip** It's strongly recommended that you use parameterized queries whenever possible when using dynamic SQL. If you can't parameterize (e.g., you need to dynamically change the table name in a query), be sure to thoroughly validate the incoming data.

Dynamic SQL and Scope

Dynamic SQL executes in its own batch. What this means is that variables and temporary tables created in a dynamic SQL statement or statement batch are not directly available to the calling routine. Consider the example in Listing 18-12.

Listing 18-12. *Limited Scope of Dynamic SQL*

```
DECLARE @sql_stmt NVARCHAR(512) = N'CREATE TABLE #Temp_ProductIDs ' +
  N'(' +
  N'  ProductID int NOT NULL PRIMARY KEY' +
  N'); ' +
  N'INSERT INTO #Temp_ProductIDs (ProductID) ' +
  N'SELECT ProductID ' +
  N'FROM Production.Product;' ;

EXECUTE (@sql_stmt);

SELECT ProductID
FROM #Temp_ProductIDs;
```

The #Temp_ProductIDs temporary table is created in a dynamic SQL batch, so it is not available outside of the batch. This causes the following error message to be generated:

```
(504 row(s) affected)
Msg 208, Level 16, State 0, Line 9
Invalid object name '#Temp_ProductIDs'.
```

The message (504 row(s) affected) indicates that the temporary table creation and INSERT INTO statement of the dynamic SQL executed properly and without error. The problem is with the SELECT statement after EXECUTE. Since the #Temp_ProductIDs table was created within the scope of the dynamic SQL statement, the temporary table is dropped immediately once the dynamic SQL statement completes. This means that once SQL Server reaches the SELECT statement, the #Temp_ProductIDs table no longer exists. One way to work around this issue is to create the temporary table before the dynamic SQL executes. The dynamic SQL is able to access and update the temporary table created by the caller, as shown in Listing 18-13.

Listing 18-13. *Creating a Temp Table Accessible to Dynamic SQL*

```
CREATE TABLE #Temp_ProductIDs
(
  ProductID int NOT NULL PRIMARY KEY
);

DECLARE @sql_stmt NVARCHAR(512) = N'INSERT INTO #Temp_ProductIDs (ProductID) ' +
    N'SELECT ProductID ' +
    N'FROM Production.Product;' ;

EXECUTE (@sql_stmt);

SELECT ProductID
FROM #Temp_ProductIDs;
```

Table variables and other variables declared by the caller are not accessible to dynamic SQL, however. Variables and table variables have well-defined scope. They are only available to the batch, function, or procedure in which they are created, and are not available to dynamic SQL or other called routines.

Client-Side Parameterization

Parameterization of dynamic SQL queries is not just a good idea on the server side; it's also a great idea to parameterize queries instead of building dynamic SQL strings on the client side. Apart from the security implications, query parameterization provides cached query execution plan reuse, making queries more efficient than their concatenated string counterparts. Microsoft .NET languages provide the tools necessary to parameterize queries from the application layer in the System.Data.SqlClient and System.Data namespaces. I discussed parameterization on the client side in Chapter 15.

Summary

SQL Server has long supported simple error handling using the @@error system function to retrieve error information and the RAISERROR statement to throw exceptions. SQL Server 2008 continues to support these methods of handling errors, but also provides modern, structured TRY...CATCH exception handling similar to other modern languages. T-SQL TRY...CATCH exception handling includes several functions that expose error-specific information in the CATCH block.

In addition to the SSMS integrated debugger, which can be accessed through the Debug menu, SQL Server itself and Visual Studio provide tools that are useful for troubleshooting and debugging your T-SQL code. These include simple tools like the PRINT statement and trace flags, and even more powerful tools like Visual Studio debugging, which lets you set breakpoints, step into code, and use much of the same functionality that is useful in debugging C# and Visual Basic programs.

Also in this chapter, I discussed dynamic SQL, a very useful and powerful tool in its own right, but often incorrectly used. Misuse of dynamic SQL can expose your databases, servers, and other network resources, leaving your IT infrastructure vulnerable to SQL injection attacks. Improper use of dynamic SQL can also impact application performance. SQL injection and query performance are the two most compelling reasons to take extra precautions when using dynamic SQL.

In the next chapter, I will given an overview of SQL Server 2008 query performance tuning.

EXERCISES

1. [Fill in the blank] The ____ system function automatically resets to 0 after every successful statement execution.

2. [Choose one] Which of the following functions, available only in the CATCH block in SQL Server, returns the severity level of the error that occurred:

   a. ERR_LEVEL()

   b. EXCEPTION_SEVERITY()

   c. EXCEPTION_LEVEL()

   d. ERROR_SEVERITY()

3. [True/false] The `RAISERROR` statement allows you to raise errors in SQL Server.

4. [True/false] Visual Studio provides integrated debugging, which allows you to step into T-SQL functions and SPs and set breakpoints.

5. [Choose all that apply] The potential problems with dynamic SQL include which of the following:

    a.   Potential performance issues

    b.   SQL injection attacks

    c.   General exception errors caused by interference with graphics drivers

    d.   All of the above

CHAPTER 19

∎∎∎

Performance Tuning

In most production environments, database and server optimization has long been the domain of DBAs. This includes server settings, hardware optimizations, index creation and maintenance, and many other responsibilities. SQL developers, however, are responsible for ensuring that their queries perform optimally. SQL Server is truly a developer's DBMS, and as a result the developer responsibilities can overlap with those of the DBA. This overlap includes recommending database design and indexing strategies, troubleshooting poorly performing queries, and making other performance enhancement recommendations. In this chapter, I'll discuss various tools and strategies for query optimization and performance enhancement.

SQL Server Storage

SQL Server is designed to abstract away many of the logical and physical aspects of storage and data retrieval. In a perfect world, you wouldn't have to worry about such things—you would be able to just "set it and forget it." Unfortunately, the world is not perfect, and how SQL Server stores data can have a noticeable impact on query performance. Understanding SQL Server storage mechanisms is essential to properly troubleshooting performance issues. With that in mind, I'm going to give a brief overview of how SQL Server stores your data.

∎Tip This section will give only a summarized description of how SQL Server stores data. The best detailed description of the SQL Server storage engine internals is in the book *Inside Microsoft SQL Server 2005: The Storage Engine*, by Kalen Delaney et al. (Microsoft Press, 2006).

Files and Filegroups

SQL Server stores your databases in files. Each database consists of at least two files, a database file with an `.mdf` extension and a log file with an `.ldf` extension. You can also add additional files to a SQL Server database, normally with an `.ndf` extension.

Filegroups are logical groupings of files for administration and allocation purposes. By default, SQL Server creates all database files in a single primary filegroup. You can add additional filegroups to an existing database or specify additional filegroups at creation time. One of the big performance benefits of using multiple filegroups comes from placing the different filegroups on different physical drives. It's common practice to increase performance by placing data files on a separate filegroup and physical drive from nonclustered indexes. It's also common to place log files on a separate physical drive from both data and nonclustered indexes.

Understanding how physical separation of files improves performance requires an explanation of the read/write patterns involved with each type of information that SQL Server stores. Your actual database data will generally utilize a random access read/write pattern. The hard drive head is constantly repositioning itself to read and write user data to the database. Nonclustered indexes, likewise, are also usually random access in nature. The hard drive head repositions itself all over the place to traverse the nonclustered index. Once nodes that match the query criteria are found in the nonclustered index, if columns must be accessed that are not in the nonclustered index, the hard drive must again reposition itself to locate the actual data stored in the data file. The transaction log file has a completely different access pattern from both data and nonclustered indexes. SQL Server writes to the transaction log in a serial fashion. These conflicting access patterns can result in "head thrashing," or constant repositioning of the hard drive head to read and write these different types of information.

Dividing your files by type and placing them on separate physical drives helps improve performance by reducing head thrashing and allowing SQL Server to perform I/O activities in parallel.

You can also place multiple data files in a single filegroup. When you create a database with multiple files in a single filegroup, SQL Server uses a proportional fill strategy across the files as data is added to the database. This means that SQL Server tries to fill all files in a filegroup at approximately the same time. Log files, which are not part of a filegroup, are filled using a serial strategy. If you add additional log files to a database, they will not be used until the current log file is filled.

■**Tip** You can move a table from its current filegroup to a new filegroup by dropping the current clustered index on the table and creating a new clustered index, specifying the new filegroup in the CREATE CLUSTERED INDEX statement.

Space Allocation

SQL Server allocates space in the database in units called *extents* and *pages*. A page is an 8 KB block of contiguous storage. An extent consists of 8 logically contiguous pages, or 64 KB of storage. SQL Server has two types of extents: *uniform extents*, which are owned completely by a single database object, and *mixed extents*, which can be shared by up to eight different database objects.

This physical limitation on the size of pages is the reason for the historic limitations on data types such as varchar and nvarchar (up to 8,000 and 4,000 characters, respectively) and row size (8060 bytes). It's also why special handling is required internally for LOB data types such as varbinary(max) and xml, since the data they contain can span many pages.

SQL Server keeps track of allocated extents with special types of pages known as *global allocation map (GAM)* pages and *shared global allocation map (SGAM)* pages. GAM pages use bits to track all extents that have been allocated. SGAM pages use bits to track mixed extents with one or more free pages available. The combination of the GAM and SGAM pages allows SQL Server to quickly locate free extents, uniform/full mixed extents, and mixed extents with free pages as necessary.

The behavior of the SQL Server storage engine can have a direct bearing on performance. For instance, consider the code in Listing 19-1, which creates a table with narrow rows. Note that SQL Server can optimize storage for variable-length data types like varchar and nvarchar, so I've forced the issue by using fixed-length char data types for this example.

Listing 19-1. *Creating a Narrow Table*

```
CREATE TABLE dbo.SmallRows
(
  Id int NOT NULL,
  LastName nchar(50) NOT NULL,
  FirstName nchar(50) NOT NULL,
  MiddleName nchar(50) NULL
);

INSERT INTO dbo.SmallRows
(
  Id,
  LastName,
  FirstName,
  MiddleName
)
SELECT
  BusinessEntityID,
  LastName,
  FirstName,
  MiddleName
FROM Person.Person;
```

The rows in the dbo.SmallRows table are 304 bytes wide. This means that SQL Server can fit about 25 rows on a single 8 KB page. You can verify this with the undocumented sys.fn_PhysLocFormatter function, as shown in Listing 19-2. Partial results are shown in Figure 19-1. The sys.fn_PhysLocFormatter function returns the physical locator in the form (*file*:*page*:*slot*). As you can see in the figure, SQL Server fits 25 rows on each page (rows are numbered 0 to 24).

■**Note** The sys.fn_PhysLocFormatter function is undocumented and not supported by Microsoft. I've used it here for demonstration purposes, as it's handy for looking at row allocations on pages; but don't use it in production code.

Listing 19-2. *Looking at Data Allocations for the SmallRows Table*

```
SELECT
  sys.fn_PhysLocFormatter(%%physloc%%) AS [Row_Locator],
  Id
FROM dbo.SmallRows;
```

	Row_Locator	Id
22	(1:9062:21)	1770
23	(1:9062:22)	4194
24	(1:9062:23)	305
25	(1:9062:24)	16691
26	(1:21880:0)	4891
27	(1:21880:1)	10251
28	(1:21880:2)	16872
29	(1:21880:3)	10293
30	(1:21880:4)	4503
31	(1:21880:5)	4970

Figure 19-1. *SQL Server fits 25 rows per page for the dbo.SmallRows table.*

By way of comparison, the code in Listing 19-3 creates a table with wide rows—3,604 bytes wide to be exact. The final SELECT query in Listing 19-3 retrieves the row locator information, demonstrating that SQL Server can only fit two rows per page for the dbo.LargeRows table. The results are shown in Figure 19-2.

Listing 19-3. *Creating a Table with Wide Rows*

```
CREATE TABLE dbo.LargeRows
(
  Id int NOT NULL,
  LastName nchar(600) NOT NULL,
  FirstName nchar(600) NOT NULL,
  MiddleName nchar(600) NULL
);

INSERT INTO dbo.LargeRows
(
  Id,
  LastName,
  FirstName,
  MiddleName
)
```

```
SELECT
  BusinessEntityID,
  LastName,
  FirstName,
  MiddleName
FROM Person.Person;

SELECT
  sys.fn_PhysLocFormatter(%%physloc%%) AS [Row_Locator],
  Id
FROM dbo.SmallRows;
```

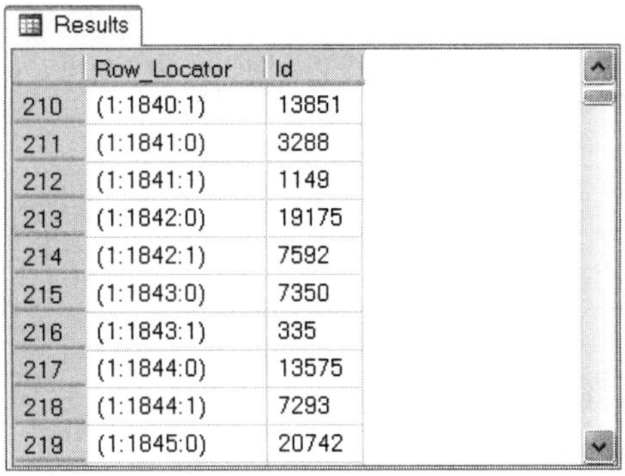

	Row_Locator	Id
210	(1:1840:1)	13851
211	(1:1841:0)	3288
212	(1:1841:1)	1149
213	(1:1842:0)	19175
214	(1:1842:1)	7592
215	(1:1843:0)	7350
216	(1:1843:1)	335
217	(1:1844:0)	13575
218	(1:1844:1)	7293
219	(1:1845:0)	20742

Figure 19-2. *SQL Server fits only two rows per page for the dbo.LargeRows table.*

Now that I have created two tables with different row widths, the query in Listing 19-4 queries both tables with STATISTICS IO turned on to demonstrate the difference this makes to your I/O.

Listing 19-4. *I/O Comparison of Narrow and Wide Tables*

```
SET STATISTICS IO ON;

SELECT
  Id,
  LastName,
  FirstName,
  MiddleName
FROM dbo.SmallRows;

SELECT
  Id,
  LastName,
  FirstName,
  MiddleName
FROM dbo.LargeRows;
```

The results returned, as shown following, demonstrate a significant difference in both logical reads and read-ahead reads:

```
(19972 row(s) affected)
Table 'SmallRows'. Scan count 1, logical reads 799, physical reads 0,
read-ahead reads 43, lob logical reads 0, lob physical reads 0,
lob read-ahead reads 0.

(19972 row(s) affected)
Table 'LargeRows'. Scan count 1, logical reads 9986, physical reads 0,
read-ahead reads 10013, lob logical reads 0, lob physical reads 0,
lob read-ahead reads 0.
```

The extra I/Os incurred by the query on the dbo.LargeRows table significantly affect the query plan estimated I/O cost. The query plan for the dbo.SmallRows query is shown in Figure 19-3, with an estimated I/O cost of 0.594315.

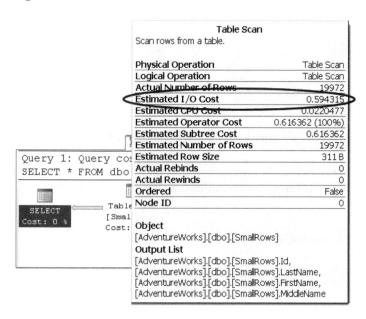

Figure 19-3. *Estimated I/O cost for the dbo.SmallRows query*

The query against the dbo.LargeRows table is significantly costlier with an estimated I/O cost of 7.39942—nearly 12.5 times greater than the dbo.SmallRows query. Figure 19-4 shows the higher cost for the dbo.LargeRows query.

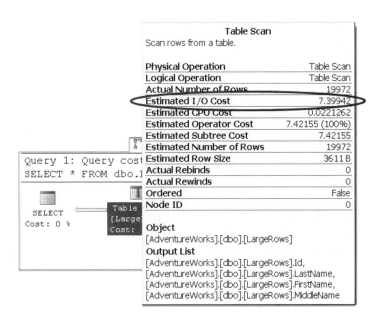

Figure 19-4. *Estimated I/O cost for the dbo.LargeRows query*

As you can see from these simple examples, SQL Server has to read significantly more pages when a table is defined with wide rows. This increased I/O cost can cause a significant performance drain when performing SQL Server queries, even those queries that are otherwise highly optimized. One way to minimize the cost of I/O is to minimize the width of columns where possible, and always use the appropriate data type for the job. In the examples given, a variable-width character data type (varchar) would have significantly reduced the storage requirements of the sample tables. Although I/O cost is often a secondary consideration for developers and DBAs, and is often only addressed after slow queries begin to cause drag on a system, it's a good idea to keep the cost of I/O in mind when initially designing your tables.

Data Compression

In addition to minimizing the width of columns by using the appropriate data type for the job, SQL Server 2008 provides built-in data compression functionality. By compressing your data directly in the database, SQL Server can reduce I/O contention and minimize storage requirements. There is some overhead associated with compression and decompression of data during queries and DML activities, but data compression is particularly useful for historical data storage where access and manipulation demands are not as high as they might be for the most recent data. I'll discuss the types of compression that SQL Server supports as well as the associated overhead and recommended usage of each.

Row Compression

SQL Server 2005 introduced an optimization to the storage format for the decimal data type in SP 2. The vardecimal type provided optimized variable-length storage for decimal data, which often resulted in significant space savings—particularly when your decimal columns contained a lot of zeros. This optimization is internal to the storage engine, so it's completely transparent to developers and end users. In SQL Server 2008, this optimization has been expanded to include all fixed-length numeric, date/time, and character data types in a feature known as row compression.

■**Note** The `vardecimal` compression options and SPs to manage this feature, including `sp_db_vardecimal_storage_format` and `sp_estimated_rowsize_reduction_for_vardecimal`, are deprecated, since SQL Server 2008 rolls this functionality up into the new row compression feature.

SQL Server 2008 provides the useful `sp_estimate_data_compression_savings` procedure to estimate the savings you'll get from applying compression to a table. Listing 19-5 estimates the space you'll save by applying row compression to the `Production.TransactionHistory` table. This particular table contains fixed-length `int`, `datetime`, and `money` columns. The results are shown in Figure 19-5.

Listing 19-5. *Estimating Row Compression Space Savings*

```
EXEC sp_estimate_data_compression_savings 'Production',
  'TransactionHistory',
  NULL,
  NULL,
  'ROW';
```

	object_name	schema_...	index_id	partition...	size_cur_cmp	size_req_cmp	size_sample_cur_cmp	size_sample_req_cmp
1	TransactionHistory	Production	1	1	6336	4168	6336	4168
2	TransactionHistory	Production	2	1	1256	1144	1256	1144
3	TransactionHistory	Production	3	1	1704	1488	2152	1888

Figure 19-5. *Row compression space savings estimate for a table*

■**Note** I changed the names of the last four columns in this example so they would fit in the image. The abbreviations are `size_cur_cmp` for Size with current compression setting (KB), `size_req_cmp` for Size with requested compression setting (KB), `size_sample_cur_cmp` for Sample size with current compression setting (KB), and `size_sample_req_cmp` for Sample size with requested compression setting (KB).

The results shown in Figure 19-5 indicate the current size of the clustered index (`index_id` = 1) is about 6.1 MB, while the two nonclustered indexes (`index_id` = 1 and 2) total about 2.9 MB. SQL Server estimates that it can compress this table down to a size of about 4.0 MB for the clustered index and 2.6 MB for the nonclustered indexes.

■**Tip** If your table does not have a clustered index, the heap is indicated in the results with an `index_id` of 0.

You can turn row compression on for a table with the `DATA_COMPRESSION = ROW` option of the `CREATE TABLE` and `ALTER TABLE` DDL statements. Listing 19-6 turns on row compression for the `Production.TransactionHistory` table.

Listing 19-6. *Turning On Row Compression for a Table*

```
ALTER TABLE Production.TransactionHistory REBUILD
WITH (DATA_COMPRESSION = ROW);
```

You can verify that the `ALTER TABLE` statement has applied row compression to your table with the `sp_spaceused` procedure, as shown in Listing 19-7. The results are shown in Figure 19-6.

Listing 19-7. *Viewing Space Used by a Table After Applying Row Compression*

```
EXEC sp_spaceused N'Production.TransactionHistory';
```

	name	rows	reserved	data	index_size	unused
1	TransactionHistory	113443	7384 KB	4152 KB	2976 KB	256 KB

Figure 19-6. *Space used by the table after applying row compression*

As you can see in the figure, the size of the data used by the `Production.TransactionHistory` table has dropped to about 4.0 MB. You can also see that the nonclustered indexes are not automatically compressed by the `ALTER TABLE` statement. To compress the nonclustered indexes, you need to issue `ALTER INDEX` statements with the `DATA_COMPRESSION = ROW` option. You can use the `DATA_COMPRESSION = NONE` option to turn off row compression for a table or index.

Row compression uses variable-length formats to store your fixed-length data, and SQL Server stores an offset value in each record for every variable-length value it stores. Prior to SQL Server 2008, this offset value was fixed at 2 bytes of overhead per variable-length value. SQL Server 2008 introduces a new record format that uses a 4-bit offset for variable-length columns that are 8 bytes in length or less.

Page Compression

SQL Server 2008 also has the capability to compress data at the page level using two methods: *column-prefix compression* and *page-dictionary compression*. Where row compression is good for minimizing the storage requirements for highly unique fixed-length data at the row level, page compression helps minimize the storage space required by duplicated data stored in pages.

The column-prefix compression method looks for repeated prefixes in columns of data stored on a page. Figure 19-7 shows a sample page from a table with repeated prefixes in columns underlined.

BusinessEntityID	FirstName	LastName
18069 (0x00004695)	Alexander	Smith
15854 (0x00003DEE)	Alexandra	Smith
16058 (0x00003EBA)	Alexis	Smith
18863 (0x000049AF)	Andrew	Smith
18118 (0x000046C6)	Austin	Smith

Figure 19-7. *Page with repeated column prefixes identified*

To compress the column prefixes identified in Figure 19-7, SQL Server creates an *anchor record*. This is a row in the table just like any other row, except that it serves the special purpose of storing the longest value in the column containing a duplicated column prefix. The anchor record is later used by the storage engine to re-create the full representations of the compressed column values when they are accessed. This special type of record is accessible only internally by the storage engine and cannot be retrieved or modified directly by normal queries or DML operations. Figure 19-8 shows the column prefix–compressed version of the page in Figure 19-7.

	BusinessEntityID	FirstName	LastName
Anchor Record	18069 (0x00004695)	Alexander	Smith
	[NULL] ([NULL])	[NULL]	[NULL]
	[2]15854 ([2]3DEE)	[7]ra	[NULL]
	[2]16058 ([2]3EBA)	[4]is	[NULL]
	[2]18863 ([2]49AF)	[1]ndrew	[NULL]
	[3]198 ([3]C6)	[1]ustin	[NULL]

Figure 19-8. *Page with column-prefix compression applied*

There are several items of note in the column prefix–compressed page shown in Figure 19-8. First is that the anchor record has been added to the page. Column-prefix compression uses byte patterns to indicate prefixes, making the column-prefix method data type–agnostic. In this instance, the BusinessEntityID column is an int data type, but as you can see it takes advantage of data type compression as well. I've shown the BusinessEntityID column values in both int and varbinary format to demonstrate that they are compressed as well.

The next interesting feature of column-prefix compression is that SQL Server replaces the prefix of each column with an indicator of how many bytes need to be prepended from the anchor record value to re-create the original value. NULL is used to indicate that the value in the table is actually the full anchor record value.

■**Note** The storage engine uses metadata associated with each value to indicate the difference between an actual NULL in the column and a NULL indicating a placeholder for the anchor record value.

In the example given, each column of the first row is replaced with NULLs that act as placeholders for the full anchor record values. The second row's BusinessEntityID column indicates that the first two bytes of the value should be replaced with the first two bytes of the BusinessEntityID anchor record column. The FirstName column of this row indicates that the first seven bytes of the value should be replaced with the first seven bytes of the FirstName anchor record column, and so on.

Page-dictionary compression is the second type of compression that SQL Server uses to compress pages. Page-dictionary compression creates an on-page dictionary of values that occur multiple times across any columns and rows on the page. It then replaces those duplicate values with indexes into the dictionary. Consider Figure 19-9, which shows a data page with duplicate values.

BusinessEntityID	FirstName	LastName
1585 (0x00003DEB)	Maurizio	Macagno
3150 (0x00000C4E)	Adriana	Arthur
17387 (0x000043EB)	Austin	Martin
10935 (0x00002AB7)	Arthur	Martin
16756 (0x00004174)	Martin	Fernandez

Figure 19-9. *Uncompressed page with duplicate values across columns and rows*

The duplicate values Arthur and Martin are added to the dictionary and replaced in the data page with indexes into the dictionary. The value Martin is replaced with the index value (0) everywhere it occurs in the data page, and the value Arthur is replaced with the index value (1). This is demonstrated in Figure 19-10.

	BusinessEntityID	FirstName	LastName
Dictionary	(0)=Martin, (1)=Arthur		
	1585 (0x00003DEB)	Maurizio	Macagno
	3150 (0x00000C4E)	Adriana	(1)
	17387 (0x000043EB)	Austin	(0)
	10935 (0x00002AB7)	(1)	(0)
	16756 (0x00004174)	(0)	Fernandez

Figure 19-10. *Page compressed with page-dictionary compression*

When SQL Server performs page compression on data pages and leaf index pages, it first applies row compression, and then it applies page-dictionary compression.

■**Note** For performance reasons, SQL Server does not apply page-dictionary compression to non–leaf index pages.

You can estimate the savings you'll get through page compression with the sp_estimate_data_compression_savings procedure, as shown in Listing 19-8. The results are shown in Figure 19-11.

Listing 19-8. *Estimating Data Compression Savings with Page Compression*

```
EXEC sp_estimate_data_compression_savings 'Person',
  'Person',
  NULL,
  NULL,
  'PAGE';
```

	object_name	schema_...	index_id	partition...	size_cur_cmp	size_req_cmp	size_sample_cur_cmp	size_sample_req_cmp
1	Person	Person	1	1	30528	18656	30528	18656
2	Person	Person	2	1	840	456	840	456
3	Person	Person	3	1	472	560	552	664

Figure 19-11. *Page compression space savings estimate*

As you can see in Figure 19-11, SQL Server estimates that it can use page compression to compress the Person.Person table from 29.8 MB in size down to about 18.2 MB, a considerable savings. You can apply page compression to a table with the ALTER TABLE statement, as shown in Listing 19-9.

Listing 19-9. *Applying Page Compression to the Person.Person Table*

```
ALTER TABLE Person.Person REBUILD
WITH (DATA_COMPRESSION = PAGE);
```

As with row compression, you can use the sp_spaceused procedure to verify how much space page compression saved you.

Page compression is great for saving space, but it does not come without a cost. Specifically, you pay for the space savings with increased CPU overhead for SELECT queries and DML statements. So when should you use page compression? Microsoft makes the following recommendations:

- If the table or index is small in size, then the overhead you incur from compression will probably not be worth the extra CPU overhead.

- If the table or index is heavily accessed for queries and DML actions, the extra CPU overhead can significantly impact your performance. It's important to identify usage patterns when deciding whether or not to compress the table or index.

- Use the sp_estimate_data_compression_savings procedure to estimate the space savings. If the estimated space savings is insignificant (or nonexistent), then the extra CPU overhead will probably outweigh the benefits.

Sparse Columns

In addition to row compression and page compression, SQL Server provides *sparse columns,* which let you optimize NULL value storage in columns. The trade-off (and you knew there would be one) is that the cost of storing non-NULL values goes up by 4 bytes for each value. Microsoft recommends using sparse columns when it will result in at least 20 to 40 percent space savings. For an int column, for instance, at least 64 percent of the values must be NULL to achieve a 40 percent space savings with sparse columns.

To demonstrate sparse columns in action, I'll use a query that generates columns with a lot of NULLs in them. The query shown in Listing 19-10 creates a pivot-style report that lists the CustomerID numbers associated with every sales order down the right-hand side of the results, and a selection of product names from the sales orders. The intersection of each CustomerID and product name contains the number of each item ordered by each customer. A NULL indicates that a customer did not order an item. Partial results of this query are shown in Figure 19-12.

Listing 19-10. *Pivot Query That Generates Columns with Many NULLs*

```
SELECT
  CustomerID,
  "HL Road Frame - Black, 58",
  "HL Road Frame - Red, 58",
  "HL Road Frame - Red, 62",
  "HL Road Frame - Red, 44",
  "HL Road Frame - Red, 48",
  "HL Road Frame - Red, 52",
  "HL Road Frame - Red, 56",
  "LL Road Frame - Black, 58"
FROM
(
  SELECT soh.CustomerID, p.Name AS ProductName,
    COUNT
    (
      CASE WHEN sod.LineTotal IS NULL THEN NULL
      ELSE 1
      END
    ) AS NumberOfItems
    FROM Sales.SalesOrderHeader soh
    INNER JOIN Sales.SalesOrderDetail sod
      ON soh.SalesOrderID = sod.SalesOrderID
    INNER JOIN Production.Product p
      ON sod.ProductID = p.ProductID
    GROUP BY
      soh.CustomerID,
      sod.ProductID,
      p.Name
) src
```

```
PIVOT
(
  SUM(NumberOfItems) FOR ProductName
  IN
  (
    "HL Road Frame - Black, 58",
    "HL Road Frame - Red, 58",
    "HL Road Frame - Red, 62",
    "HL Road Frame - Red, 44",
    "HL Road Frame - Red, 48",
    "HL Road Frame - Red, 52",
    "HL Road Frame - Red, 56",
    "LL Road Frame - Black, 58"
  )
) AS pvt;
```

	CustomerID	HL Road Frame - Black, 58	HL Road Frame - Red, 58	HL Road Frame - Red, 62	HL Road Frame - Red, 44
19112	30111	NULL	NULL	NULL	NULL
19113	30112	NULL	NULL	1	2
19114	30113	NULL	NULL	NULL	NULL
19115	30114	NULL	NULL	NULL	NULL
19116	30115	NULL	NULL	NULL	NULL
19117	30116	NULL	NULL	NULL	NULL
19118	30117	NULL	NULL	2	2
19119	30118	NULL	NULL	NULL	NULL

Figure 19-12. *Pivot query that returns the number of each item ordered by each customer*

Listing 19-11 creates two similar tables to hold the results generated by the query in Listing 19-10. The tables generated by the CREATE TABLE statements in Listing 19-11 have the same structure, except that the SparseTable includes the keyword SPARSE in its column declarations, indicating that these are sparse columns.

Listing 19-11. *Creating Sparse and Nonsparse Tables*

```
CREATE TABLE NonSparseTable
(
  CustomerID int NOT NULL PRIMARY KEY,
  "HL Road Frame - Black, 58" int NULL,
  "HL Road Frame - Red, 58" int NULL,
  "HL Road Frame - Red, 62" int NULL,
  "HL Road Frame - Red, 44" int NULL,
  "HL Road Frame - Red, 48" int NULL,
  "HL Road Frame - Red, 52" int NULL,
  "HL Road Frame - Red, 56" int NULL,
  "LL Road Frame - Black, 58" int NULL
);
```

```
CREATE TABLE SparseTable
(
  CustomerID int NOT NULL PRIMARY KEY,
  "HL Road Frame - Black, 58" int SPARSE NULL,
  "HL Road Frame - Red, 58" int SPARSE NULL,
  "HL Road Frame - Red, 62" int SPARSE NULL,
  "HL Road Frame - Red, 44" int SPARSE NULL,
  "HL Road Frame - Red, 48" int SPARSE NULL,
  "HL Road Frame - Red, 52" int SPARSE NULL,
  "HL Road Frame - Red, 56" int SPARSE NULL,
  "LL Road Frame - Black, 58" int SPARSE NULL
);
```

After using the query in Listing 19-10 to populate these two tables, you can use the sp_spaceused procedure to see the space savings that sparse columns provide. Listing 19-12 executes sp_spaceused on these two tables, both of which contain identical data. The results shown in Figure 19-13 demonstrate that the SparseTable takes up only about 25 percent of the space used by the NonSparseTable since NULL values in sparse columns take up no storage space.

Listing 19-12. *Calculating the Space Savings of Sparse Columns*

```
EXEC sp_spaceused N'NonSparseTable';
EXEC sp_spaceused N'SparseTable';
```

Results

name	rows	reserved	data	index_size	unused
1	NonSparseTable	19119	904 KB	872 KB	16 KB	16 KB

name	rows	reserved	data	index_size	unused
1	SparseTable	19119	328 KB	256 KB	16 KB	56 KB

Figure 19-13. *Space savings provided by sparse columns*

Sparse Column Sets

In addition to sparse columns, SQL Server provides support for XML sparse column sets. An XML column set is defined as an xml data type column, and it contains non-NULL sparse column data from the table. An XML sparse column set is declared using the COLUMN_SET FOR ALL_SPARSE_COLUMNS option on an xml column. As a simple example, the AdventureWorks Production.Product table contains several products that do not have associated size, color, or other descriptive information. Listing 19-13 creates a table called Production.SparseProduct that defines several sparse columns and a sparse column set.

Listing 19-13. *Creating and Populating a Table with a Sparse Column Set*

```
CREATE TABLE Production.SparseProduct
(
  ProductID int NOT NULL PRIMARY KEY,
  Name dbo.Name NOT NULL,
```

```
  ProductNumber nvarchar(25) NOT NULL,
  Color nvarchar(15) SPARSE NULL,
  Size nvarchar(5) SPARSE NULL,
  SizeUnitMeasureCode nchar(3) SPARSE NULL,
  WeightUnitMeasureCode nchar(3) SPARSE NULL,
  Weight decimal(8, 2) SPARSE NULL,
  Class nchar(2) SPARSE NULL,
  Style nchar(2) SPARSE NULL,
  SellStartDate datetime NOT NULL,
  SellEndDate datetime SPARSE NULL,
  DiscontinuedDate datetime SPARSE NULL,
  SparseColumnSet xml COLUMN_SET FOR ALL_SPARSE_COLUMNS
);
GO

INSERT INTO Production.SparseProduct
(
  ProductID,
  Name,
  ProductNumber,
  Color,
  Size,
  SizeUnitMeasureCode,
  WeightUnitMeasureCode,
  Weight,
  Class,
  Style,
  SellStartDate,
  SellEndDate,
  DiscontinuedDate
)
SELECT
  ProductID,
  Name,
  ProductNumber,
  Color,
  Size,
  SizeUnitMeasureCode,
  WeightUnitMeasureCode,
  Weight,
  Class,
  Style,
  SellStartDate,
  SellEndDate,
  DiscontinuedDate
FROM Production.Product;
GO
```

You can view the sparse column set in XML form with a query like the one in Listing 19-14. The results in Figure 19-14 show that the first five products do not have any sparse column data associated with them, so the sparse column data takes up no space. By contrast, products 317 and 318 both have Color and Class data associated with them.

Listing 19-14. *Querying XML Sparse Column Set As XML*

```
SELECT TOP(7)
  ProductID,
  SparseColumnSet
FROM Production.SparseProduct;
```

	ProductID	SparseColumnSet
1	1	NULL
2	2	NULL
3	3	NULL
4	4	NULL
5	316	NULL
6	317	<Color>Black</Color><Class>L </Class>
7	318	<Color>Black</Color><Class>M </Class>

Figure 19-14. *Viewing sparse column sets in XML format*

Although SQL Server manages sparse column sets using XML, you don't need to know XML to access sparse column set data. In fact, you can access the columns defined in sparse column sets using the same query and DML statements you've always used, as shown in Listing 19-15. The results of this query are shown in Figure 19-15.

Listing 19-15. *Querying Sparse Column Sets by Name*

```
SELECT
  ProductID,
  Name,
  ProductNumber,
  SellStartDate,
  Color,
  Class
FROM Production.SparseProduct
WHERE ProductID IN (1, 317);
```

	ProductID	Name	ProductNum...	SellStartDate	Color	Class
1	1	Adjustable Race	AR-5381	1998-06-01 00:00:00.000	NULL	NULL
2	317	LL Crankarm	CA-5965	1998-06-01 00:00:00.000	Black	L

Figure 19-15. *Querying sparse column sets with SELECT queries*

Sparse column sets provide the benefits of sparse columns, with NULLs taking up no storage space at all. However, the downside is that non-NULL sparse columns that are a part of a column set are stored in XML format, adding some storage overhead as compared with their nonsparse, non-NULL counterparts.

Indexes

Your query performance may begin to lag over time for several reasons. It may be that database usage patterns have changed significantly over time, or the amount of data stored in the database has increased significantly over time, or the database has fallen out of maintenance. Whatever the reason, the knee-jerk reaction of many developers and DBAs is to throw indexes at the problem. While indexes are indeed useful for increasing performance, they do consume resources, both in storage and maintenance. Before creating new indexes all over database, it's important to understand how they work. In this section, I'll give an overview of SQL Server's indexing mechanisms.

Heaps

In SQL Server parlance, a heap is simply an unordered collection of data pages with no clustered index. SQL Server uses *index allocation map (IAM)* pages to track *allocation units* of the following types:

- Heap or B-tree (a.k.a. "hobt") allocation units, which track storage allocation for tables and indexes

- LOB allocation units, which track storage allocation for LOB data

- Small LOB (SLOB) allocation units, which track storage allocation for row overflow data

As any DBA will tell you, a *table scan*, which is SQL Server's "brute force" data retrieval method, is a bad thing (though not necessarily the worst thing that can happen). In a table scan, SQL Server literally scans every data page that was allocated by the heap. Any query against the heap causes a table scan operation. To determine which pages have been allocated for the heap, SQL Server must refer back to the IAM. A table scan is known as an *allocation order scan* since it uses the IAM to scan the data pages in the order in which they were allocated by SQL Server.

Heaps are also subject to fragmentation, and the only way to eliminate fragmentation from the heap is to copy the heap to a new table or create a clustered index on the table. Forward pointers introduce another performance-related issue to heaps. When SQL Server must move a row in a heap to a new location, it leaves a forward pointer to the new location at the old location. If the row is moved again, SQL Server leaves another forward pointer, and so on. Forward pointers result in additional I/Os, making table scans even less efficient (and you thought it wasn't possible!).

■**Tip** Querying a heap with no clustered or nonclustered indexes always results in a costly table scan.

Clustered Indexes

If a heap is an unordered collection of data pages, how do you impose order on the heap? The answer is a clustered index. A clustered index turns an unordered heap into a collection of data pages ordered by the specified clustered index columns. Clustered indexes are managed in the database as B-tree structures.

The top level of the clustered index B-tree is known as the root node, the bottom level nodes are known as leaf nodes, and all nodes in between the root node and leaf nodes are collectively referred to as intermediate nodes. In a clustered index, the leaf nodes contain the actual data rows for a table, and all leaf nodes point to the next and previous leaf nodes, forming a doubly linked list. The clustered index holds a special position in SQL Server indexing: because its leaf nodes contain the actual table data, there can only be one clustered index defined per table. The clustered index B-tree structure is shown in Figure 19-16.

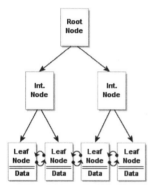

Figure 19-16. *Clustered index B-tree structure*

GUARANTEED ORDER

Despite the fact that the data pages in a clustered index are ordered by the clustered index columns, you cannot depend on table rows being returned in clustered index order unless you specify an ORDER BY clause in your queries. There are a couple of reasons for this, including the following:

- Your query may join multiple tables and the optimizer may choose to return results in another order based on indexes on another table.

- The optimizer may use an allocation order scan of your clustered index, which will return results in the order in which data pages were allocated.

The bottom line is that the SQL query optimizer may decide that, for whatever reason, it is more efficient to return results unordered or in an order other than clustered index order. Because of this, you can't depend on results always being returned in the same order without an explicit ORDER BY clause. I've seen many cases of developers being bitten because their client-side code expected results in a specific order, and after months of receiving results in the correct order, the optimizer decided that returning results in a different order would be more efficient. Don't fall victim to this false optimism—use ORDER BY when ordered results are important.

Many are under the impression that a clustered index scan is the same thing as a table scan. In one sense they are correct—when SQL Server performs an *unordered clustered index scan*, it refers back to the IAM to scan the data pages of the clustered index using an allocation order scan, just like a table scan.

However, SQL Server has another option for clustered indexes, the *ordered clustered index scan*. In an ordered clustered index scan, or leaf-level scan, SQL Server can follow the doubly linked list at the leaf node level instead of referring back to the IAM. The leaf-level scan has the benefit of scanning in clustered index order. Table scans do not have the option of a leaf-level scan since the leaf-level pages are not ordered or linked. Clustered indexes also eliminate the performance problems associated with forward pointers in the heap, although you do have to pay attention to fragmentation and page splits when you have a clustered index on your table.

So when should you use a clustered index? As a general rule, I like to put a clustered index on nearly every table I create. Although you will have to decide on which columns you wish to create your clustered indexes, here are some general recommendations for columns to consider in your clustered index design:

- Columns that provide a high degree of uniqueness. Monotonically increasing columns, such as IDENTITY columns, are ideal as they also reduce the overhead associated with page splits that result from insert and update operations.

- Columns that return a range of values using operators like >=, <, and BETWEEN. When you use a range query on clustered index columns, after the first match is found, the remaining values are guaranteed to be linked/adjacent in the B-tree.

- Columns that are used in queries that return large result sets.

- Columns that are used in the ON clause of a JOIN. Usually, these are primary key or foreign key columns.

- Columns that are used in GROUP BY or ORDER BY clauses. A clustered index on these columns can help SQL Server improve performance when ordering query result sets.

You should also make your clustered indexes as narrow as possible (often a single int or uniqueidentifier column), since they are automatically appended to all nonclustered indexes on the same table as row locators.

Nonclustered Indexes

Nonclustered indexes provide another tool for indexing relational data in SQL Server. Like clustered indexes, SQL Server stores nonclustered indexes as B-tree structures. Unlike clustered indexes, however, each leaf node in a nonclustered index contains the nonclustered key value and a row locator. The table rows are stored apart from the nonclustered index—in the clustered index if there is one defined on the table or in a heap if the table has no clustered index. Figure 19-17 shows the nonclustered index B-tree structure.

If a table has a clustered index, all nonclustered indexes defined on the table automatically include the clustered index columns as the row locator. If the table is a heap, SQL Server creates row locators to the rows from the combination of the file identifier, page number, and slot on the page.

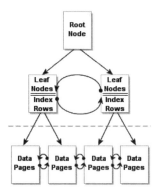

Figure 19-17. *Nonclustered index B-tree structure*

Nonclustered indexes are associated with the RID lookup and key lookup operations. *RID lookups* are bookmark lookups into the heap using row identifiers (RIDs), while *key lookups* are bookmark lookups on tables with clustered indexes. Once SQL Server locates the index rows that fulfill a query, if the query requires more columns than the nonclustered index covers, then the query engine must use the row locator to find the rows in the clustered index or the heap to retrieve necessary data. These are the operations referred to as a RID and key lookups, and they are costly operations—so costly, in fact, that many performance-tuning operations are based on eliminating them.

■**Note** In prior versions of SQL Server, we had the bookmark lookup operation. In SQL Server 2008, this operation has been split into two distinct operations, the RID lookup and the key lookup, to differentiate between bookmark lookups against heaps and clustered indexes.

On method of dealing with RID and key lookups is to create *covering indexes*. A covering index is a nonclustered index that contains all of the columns necessary to fulfill a given query or set of queries. When you define a covering index, the query engine can determine that all the information it needs to fulfill the query is stored in the nonclustered index rows, so it does not need to perform a lookup operation.

■**Tip** Prolific author and SQL Server MVP Adam Machanic defines a clustered index as a covering index for every possible query against a table. This definition provides a good tool for demonstrating that there's not much difference between clustered and nonclustered indexes, and it helps to reinforce the concept of index covering.

The sample query in Listing 19-16 shows a simple query against the Person.Person table that requires a bookmark lookup, which is itself shown in the query plan in Figure 19-18.

Listing 19-16. *Query Requiring a Bookmark Lookup*

```
SELECT
  BusinessEntityID,
  LastName,
  FirstName,
  MiddleName,
  Title
FROM Person.Person
WHERE LastName = N'Duffy';
```

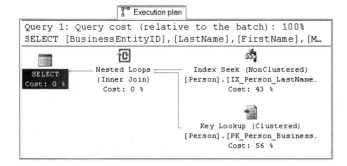

Figure 19-18. *Bookmark lookup in the query plan*

So why is there a bookmark lookup (referenced as a key lookup operator in the query plan)? The answer lies in the query. This particular query uses the LastName column in the WHERE clause to limit results, so the query engine decides to use the IX_Person_LastName_FirstName_MiddleName nonclustered index to fulfill the query. This nonclustered index contains the LastName, FirstName, and MiddleName columns, as well as the BusinessEntityID column, which is defined as the clustered index. The lookup operation is required because the SELECT clause also specifies that the Title column needs to be returned in the result set. Since the Title column is not included in the covering index, SQL Server has to refer back to the table's data pages to retrieve it.

Eliminating the Title column from the query, as shown in Listing 19-17, removes the lookup operation from the query plan. As shown in Figure 19-19, the IX_Person_LastName_FirstName_MiddleName index covers the query.

Tip Another alternative to eliminate this costly lookup operation is to modify the nonclustered index used in the example to include the Title column, which would create a covering index for the query.

Listing 19-17. *Query Using a Covering Index*

```
SELECT
  BusinessEntityID,
  LastName,
```

```
   FirstName,
   MiddleName
FROM Person.Person
WHERE LastName = N'Duffy';
```

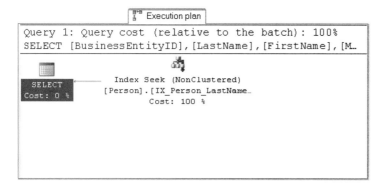

Figure 19-19. *The covering index eliminates the lookup operation.*

You can define up to 999 nonclustered indexes per table. You should carefully plan your indexing strategy and try to minimize the number of indexes you define on a single table. Nonclustered indexes can require a substantial amount of additional storage, and there is a definite overhead involved in automatically updating them whenever the table data changes. When deciding how many indexes to add to a table, consider the usage patterns carefully. Tables with data that does not change—or rarely changes—may derive greater benefit from having lots of indexes defined on them than tables whose data is modified often.

■**Note** If you happen to define more than 500 nonclustered indexes on a single table, please send me an e-mail. I would love to hear about that requirement!

Nonclustered indexes are useful for the following types of queries:

- Queries that return one row, or few rows, which would otherwise result in a clustered index or table scan. These types of queries often use simple equality predicates (=) in the WHERE clause.

- Queries that can use an index with high selectivity (generally above 95 percent). Selectivity is a measure of the unique key values in an index. SQL Server will often ignore indexes with low selectivity.

- Queries that return small ranges of data that would otherwise result in a clustered index or table scan.

- Queries that are completely covered by the nonclustered index.

Filtered Indexes

In SQL Server 2008, filtered indexes provide a way to create more targeted indexes that require less storage and can support more efficient queries. Filtered indexes allow you to easily add filtering criteria to restrict the rows included in the index with a WHERE clause. Listing 19-18 creates a filtered index on the Size column of the Production.Product table that excludes NULL.

Listing 19-18. *Creating and Testing a Filtered Index on the Production.Product Table*

```
CREATE NONCLUSTERED INDEX IX_Product_Size
ON Production.Product
(
  Size,
  SizeUnitMeasureCode
)
WHERE Size IS NOT NULL;
GO

SELECT
  ProductID,
  Size,
  SizeUnitMeasureCode
FROM Production.Product
WHERE Size = 'L';
GO
```

■**Tip** Filtered indexes are particularly well suited for indexing non-NULL values of sparse columns.

Optimizing Queries

One of the more interesting tasks that SQL developers and DBAs must perform is optimizing queries. To borrow an old cliché, query optimization is as much art as science. There are a lot of moving parts within the SQL query engine, and your task is to give the optimizer as much good information as you can so that it can make good decisions at runtime.

Performance is generally measured in terms of *response time* and *throughput*, defined as follows:

- Response time is the time that it takes for SQL Server to complete a task, such as a query.

- Throughput is a measure of the volume of work that SQL Server can complete in a fixed period of time, such as the number of transactions per minute.

There are several other factors that affect your overall system performance but are outside the scope of this book. Application responsiveness, for instance, depends on several additional factors like network latency and UI architecture, both of which are beyond SQL Server's control. In this section, I will talk about how to use query plans to diagnose performance issues.

Reading Query Plans

When you submit a T-SQL script or statement to the SQL Server query engine, SQL Server compiles your code into a query plan. The query plan is composed of a series of physical and logical operators that the optimizer has chosen to complete your query. The optimizer bases its choice of operators on a wide array of factors like data distribution statistics, cardinality of tables, and availability of useful indexes.

SQL Server can return query plans in a variety of formats. My personal preference is the graphical query execution plan, which I've used in examples throughout the book. Figure 19-20 shows a query plan for a simple query that joins two tables.

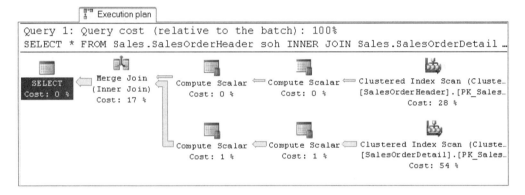

Figure 19-20. *Query execution plan for an inner join query*

You can generate a graphical query plan for a given query by selecting the Query ➤ Include Actual Execution Plan option from the SSMS menu, and then running your SQL statements. Alternatively, you can select Query ➤ Display Estimated Execution Plan without running the query.

A graphical query plan is read from right to left and top to bottom. It contains arrows indicating the flow of data through the query plan. The arrows show the relative amount of data being moved from one operator to the next, with wider arrows indicating larger numbers of rows, as shown in Figure 19-20. You can position the mouse pointer on top of any operator or arrow in the graphical query plan to display a pop-up with additional information about the operator or data flow between operators, such as the number of rows being acted upon and the estimated row size. You can also right-click an operator or arrow and select Properties from the pop-up menu to view even more descriptive information.

You can also right-click in the Execution Plan window and select Save Execution Plan As to save your graphical execution plan as an XML query plan. Query plans are saved with a .sqlplan file extension, and can be viewed in graphical format in SSMS by double-clicking the file. This is particularly useful for troubleshooting queries remotely, since your users or other developers can save the graphical query plan and e-mail it to you, and you can open it up in a local instance of SSMS for further investigation.

ACTUAL OR ESTIMATED?

Estimated execution plans are useful in determining the optimizer's intent. The word *estimated* in the name can be a bit misleading since all query plans are based on the optimizer's estimates of your data distribution, table cardinality, and more.

There are some differences between estimated and actual query plans, however. Since an actual query plan is generated as your T-SQL statements are executed, the optimizer can add additional information to the query plan as it runs. This additional information includes items like actual rebinds, rewinds, and actual number of rows. When dealing with temporary objects, actual query plans have better information available concerning which operators are being used as well. Consider the following simple script that creates, populates, and queries a temporary table:

```
CREATE TABLE #t1
(
  Id int NOT NULL,
  LastName nvarchar(50),
  FirstName nvarchar(50),
  MiddleName nvarchar(50)
);

CREATE INDEX t1_LastName
ON #t1 (LastName);

INSERT INTO #t1
(
  Id,
  LastName,
  FirstName,
  MiddleName
)
SELECT
  BusinessEntityID,
  LastName,
  FirstName,
  MiddleName
FROM Person.Person;

SELECT
  BusinessEntityID,
  LastName,
  FirstName,
  MiddleName
FROM #t1
WHERE LastName = N'Duffy';

DROP TABLE #t1;
```

In the estimated query plan for this code, the optimizer indicates that it will use a table scan, as shown following, to fulfill the SELECT query at the end of the script:

```
Table Scan
  [#t1]
Cost: 100 %
```

The actual query plan, however, uses a much more efficient nonclustered index seek with a bookmark lookup operation to retrieve the two relevant rows from the table, as shown here:

```
Index Seek (NonClustered)
   [#t1].[t1_LastName]
        Cost: 44 %


   RID Lookup (Heap)
        [#t1]
      Cost: 56 %
```

The difference between the estimated and actual query plans in this case is the information available at the time the query plan is generated. When the estimated query plan is created, there is no temporary table and no index on the temporary table, so the optimizer guesses that a table scan will be required. When the actual query plan is generated, the temporary table and its nonclustered index both exist, so the optimizer comes up with a better query plan.

In addition to graphical query plans, SQL Server supports XML query plans and text query plans, and can report additional runtime statistics. This additional information can be accessed using the statements shown in Table 19-1.

Table 19-1. *Query Plan Generation Statements*

Statement	Description
SET SHOWPLAN_ALL ON/OFF	Returns a text-based estimated execution plan without executing the query
SET SHOWPLAN_TEXT ON/OFF	Returns a text-based estimated execution plan without executing the query
SET SHOWPLAN_XML ON/OFF	Returns an XML-based estimated execution plan without executing the query
SET STATISTICS IO ON/OFF	Returns statistics information about logical I/O operations during execution of a query
SET STATISTICS PROFILE ON/OFF	Returns actual query execution plans in result sets following the result set generated by each query executed
SET STATISTICS TIME ON/OFF	Returns statistics about the time required to parse, compile, and execute statements at runtime

Methodology

The methodology that has served me well when troubleshooting performance issues involves the following seven steps:

1. *Recognize the issue*: Before you can troubleshoot a performance issue, you must first determine that there is an actual issue. The recognition of an issue can begin with something as simple as end users complaining that their applications are running slowly.

2. *Identify the source*: Once you've recognized that there is an issue, you need to identify the problem as a SQL Server–related problem. For instance, if you receive reports of database-enabled applications running slowly, it's important to narrow down the source of the problem. If the issue is a network bandwidth or latency issue, for instance, it can't be resolved through simple query optimizations. If it's a T-SQL issue, you can use tools like SQL Profiler and query plans to identify the problematic code.

3. *Analyze the code*: Once you've identified T-SQL code as the source of the problem, it's time to dig deeper and analyze the root cause of the problem. The operators returned in graphical query plans provide an excellent indicator of the source of many problems. For example, you may spot a costly clustered index scan operator where you expected a more efficient nonclustered index seek.

4. *Define possible solutions*: After the issues have been identified in the code, it's time to come up with potential solutions. If bookmark lookup operations are slowing down your query performance, for instance, you may determine that adding a new nonclustered index or modifying an existing one is a possible fix for the issue. Another possible solution might be changing the query to return fewer columns that are already covered by an index.

5. *Evaluate the solutions*: A critical step after defining your possible solutions is to evaluate the practicality of those solutions. Many things affect whether or not a solution is practical. For instance, you may be forbidden to change indexes on the production servers, in which case adding or modifying indexes to solve an issue may be impractical. On the other hand, your client applications may depend on all of the columns currently being returned in the query's result sets, so changing the query to return fewer columns may not be a workable solution.

   During this step of the process, you also need to determine the impact of your solutions on other parts of the system. Adding or modifying an index on the server to solve a query performance problem might fix the problem for a single query, but it might introduce new performance problems for other queries or DML statements. These conflicting needs should be evaluated.

6. *Implement the solution*: This step of the process is where you actually apply your solution. You will most likely have a subprocess here, in which you apply the solution first to a development environment, and then to a quality assurance (QA) environment, and finally promote it to the production environment.

7. *Examine the impact of the solution*: After implementing your solution, you should revisit it to ensure that it actually fixes the problem. This is a very important step that many people largely ignore, only revisiting their solutions when another issue occurs. By scheduling to revisit your solution, you can take a proactive approach and head off problems before they affect your end users.

Scalability is another important factor to consider when writing T-SQL. Scalability is a measure of how well your code works under increasing demands. For instance, a query may provide acceptable performance when the source table contains 100,000 rows and 10 end users simultaneously querying. However, the same query may suffer performance problems when the table grows to 1,000,000 rows and the number of end users grows to 100. Increasing stress on a system tends to uncover scalability and performance issues that weren't previously apparent in your code base. As pressure on your database grows, it's important to monitor changing access patterns and increasing demands on the system to proactively handle issues before they affect end users.

It's important to also understand when an issue is not really a problem, or at least not one that requires a great deal of attention. As a general rule, I like to apply the 80/20 rule when optimizing queries. That is to say, as a rule of thumb, focus your efforts on optimizing the 20 percent of code that is executed 80 percent of the time. If you have an SP that takes a long time to execute but is only run once a day, and a second procedure that takes a significant amount of time but is run 10,000 times a day, you'd be well served to focus your efforts on the latter procedure.

Summary

SQL Server stores data in 8 KB pages that it allocates in contiguous groups of 8 pages each, known as extents. In a perfect world, SQL Server's logical and physical storage mechanisms would not make a difference to you as a developer. In the real world, however, an understanding of storage engine operation is important to maximizing performance. I began this chapter with an overview of the SQL Server storage engine and how it affects performance.

Indexes are the primary means of increasing query performance on SQL Server. I continued the discussion by addressing the concepts of heaps, clustered indexes, and nonclustered indexes, with details of how each affects the overall performance of your queries and DML statements.

Optimizing queries depends on maximizing two critical aspects: response time and throughput. SQL Server provides query plans and statistics, in addition to other external tools, to help diagnose performance issues. I wrapped up this chapter with a suggested methodology for dealing with performance issues. Using a methodology like the seven-step process described here will help you quickly narrow down the source of performance issues; define, evaluate, and implement solutions; and take a proactive approach in addressing future performance-related issues.

I hope that you've enjoyed reading this book as much as I've enjoyed bringing it to you. I wish you all the best in your T-SQL development efforts, and I hope you find this book helpful in your development endeavors.

EXERCISES

1. [Choose all that apply] SQL Server 2008 uses which of the following types of files to store database information:

    a. Data files (.mdf extension)

    b. Transaction log files (.ldf extension)

    c. Additional data files (.ndf extension)

    d. Rich text files (.rtf extension)

2. [True/false] SQL Server stores data in 8 KB storage units known as pages.

3. [Choose one] Eight contiguous 8 KB pages of storage in SQL Server are known as which of the following:

    a. A filegroup

    b. A chunk

    c. An extent

    d. A file

4. [Fill in the blank] A heap is an ___ collection of data pages.

5. [Fill in the blank] Clustered indexes and nonclustered indexes are managed by SQL Server as ___ structures.

6. [Choose all that apply] SQL Server performance is measured using which of the following terms:

    a. Throughput

    b. Luminescence

    c. Response time

    d. All of the above

APPENDIX A

■■■

Exercise Answers

This appendix contains the answers to the exercises at the end of each chapter. The answers are grouped by chapter and numbered to match the associated exercises in the corresponding chapter.

Chapter 1

1. Imperative languages require you to provide the computer with step-by-step directions to perform a task—essentially, you tell the computer *how* to achieve the end result. Declarative languages allow you to tell the computer what the end result should be and trust the computer to take appropriate action to achieve it. Instead of telling the computer how to achieve the result, in declarative languages you tell the computer *what* the end result should be.

2. *ACID* stands for "atomicity, consistency, isolation, durability." These represent the basic properties of a database that guarantee reliability of data storage, processing, and manipulations.

3. The five index types that SQL Server supports are clustered indexes, nonclustered indexes, XML indexes, spatial indexes, and full-text indexes.

4. All of the following are restrictions on all SQL Server UDFs: (1) they cannot perform DML or DDL statements, (2) they cannot change the state of the database (no side effects), (3) they cannot use dynamic SQL, and (4) they cannot utilize certain nondeterministic functions.

5. False. All newly declared variables are set to NULL on creation. You should always initialize newly created variables immediately after creation.

Chapter 2

1. The correct answers are A, B, and D. SQL Server 2008 includes single-statement variable declaration and initialization, C-style assignment operators, and row constructors. Multitable TRUNCATE TABLE statements are not allowed in SQL Server 2008.

2. False. The SQL Server 2008 date data type does not store time zone information. Use the datetimeoffset data type if you need to store time zone information with your date/time data.

3. The hierarchyid data type uses the materialized path model to represent hierarchies in the database.

4. The *geometry* data type stores flat-earth spatial data, while the *geography* data type stores round-earth spatial data.

5. The correct answer is B. The geography data type requires Polygon objects to have a counterclockwise orientation. Also, spatial objects created with the geography data type must be contained in a single hemisphere.

6. True. The new grouping sets can be used to perform the same tasks that were previously performed with CUBE and ROLLUP. Grouping sets also allow you to create powerful customized summary groupings.

7. The correct answer is D. SQL Server 2008 creates spatial indexes as four-level B-tree-based grid hierarchies.

8. Your existing T-SQL scripts should run with minimal changes, so long as you followed *best practices* when writing them.

Chapter 3

1. SSMS replaces the SQL Server 2000 Enterprise Manager and Query Analyzer (QA) tools.

2. The correct answers are A, B, and C. SQL Server 2008 SSMS provides color-coding of scripts, integrated Object Explorer, and Intellisense. PDF and PostScript query plans are not SSMS features. SSMS supports generation and display of plain text, XML, and graphical query plans.

3. SSIS is considered an ETL (extract, transform, load) tool.

4. True. SQLCMD scripting variables can be set via command-line options and environment variables, and in script via the SQLCMD :setvar command.

5. The correct answer is D, all of the above. BCP can generate format files that can be used with the SSIS Bulk Insert task, with the T-SQL BULK INSERT statement, or with BCP itself. BCP can also import data into tables without a format file and export data from a table to a file.

6. After selecting the events you wish to trace, SQL Profiler allows you to further narrow your results by adding filters to your trace.

7. BIDS allows you to create Analysis Services (SSAS) projects, Reporting Services (SSRS) projects, and Integration Services (SSIS) projects.

Chapter 4

1. True. SQL 3VL supports the three Boolean results true, false, and unknown.

2. The correct answer is A. In SQL, NULL represents an unknown or missing value. NULL does not represent a numeric value of 0 or a zero-length string.

3. False. SQL's BEGIN...END construct defines a statement block, but does not limit the scope of variables declared within the statement block. This is contrary to the behavior of C#'s curly braces ({ }).

4. The *BREAK* statement forces a WHILE loop to terminate immediately.

5. False. TRY...CATCH can't capture syntax errors, errors that cause a broken connection, or errors with severity of 10 or less, among others.

6. SQL CASE expressions come in both *simple* and *searched* CASE expression forms.

7. The correct answers are A and B. T-SQL provides support for read-only cursors and forward-only cursors. There is no such thing as a backward-only cursor or a write-only cursor.

8. The following code modifies the example in Listing 4-13 to return the total sales (TotalDue) by region in pivot table format. The required change to the code is shown in bold.

```
-- Declare variables
DECLARE @sql nvarchar(4000);

DECLARE @temp_pivot table (TerritoryID int NOT NULL PRIMARY KEY,
  CountryRegion nvarchar(20) NOT NULL,
  CountryRegionCode nvarchar(3) NOT NULL);

-- Get column names from source table rows
INSERT INTO @temp_pivot (TerritoryID,
  CountryRegion,
  CountryRegionCode)
SELECT TerritoryID,
  Name,
  CountryRegionCode
FROM Sales.SalesTerritory
GROUP BY TerritoryID, Name, CountryRegionCode;

-- Generate dynamic SQL query
SET @sql = N'SELECT' +
  SUBSTRING(
```

```
(
  SELECT N', SUM(CASE WHEN t.TerritoryID = ' +
    CAST(TerritoryID AS NVARCHAR(3)) +
    N' THEN soh.TotalDue ELSE 0 END) AS ' + QUOTENAME(CountryRegion) AS "*"
  FROM @temp_pivot
  FOR XML PATH('')
), 2, 4000) +
N' FROM Sales.SalesOrderHeader soh ' +
N' INNER JOIN Sales.SalesTerritory t ' +
N' ON soh.TerritoryID = t.TerritoryID; ' ;

-- Print and execute dynamic SQL
PRINT @sql;

EXEC (@sql);
```

Chapter 5

1. SQL Server supports three types of T-SQL UDFs: *scalar UDFs, multistatement TVFs,* and *inline TVFs.*

2. True. The `RETURNS NULL ON NULL INPUT` option is a performance-enhancing option that automatically returns `NULL` if any of the parameters passed into a scalar UDF are `NULL`.

3. False. The `ENCRYPTION` option performs a simple code obfuscation that is easily reverse-engineered. In fact, there are several programs and scripts available online that allow anyone to decrypt your code with the push of a button.

4. The correct answers are A, B, and D. Multistatement TVFs (as well as all other TVFs) do not allow you to execute `PRINT` statements, call `RAISERROR`, or create temporary tables. In multistatement TVFs, you can declare table variables.

5. The following code creates a deterministic scalar UDF that accepts a `float` parameter, converts it from degrees Fahrenheit to degrees Celsius, and returns a `float` result. Notice that the `WITH SCHEMABINDING` option is required to make this scalar UDF deterministic.

```
CREATE FUNCTION dbo.FahrenheitToCelsius (@Degrees float)
RETURNS float
WITH SCHEMABINDING
AS
BEGIN
  RETURN (@Degrees - 32.0) * (5.0 / 9.0);
END;
```

Chapter 6

1. False. The SP RETURN statement can return only an int scalar value.

2. One method of proving that two SPs that call each other recursively are limited to 32 levels of recursion in total is shown following. Differences from the code in the original listing are shown in bold.

```
CREATE PROCEDURE dbo.FirstProc (@i int)
AS
BEGIN
  PRINT @i;
  SET @i += 1;
  EXEC dbo.SecondProc @i;
END;
GO

CREATE PROCEDURE dbo.SecondProc (@i int)
AS
BEGIN
  PRINT @i;
  SET @i += 1;
  EXEC dbo.FirstProc @i;
END;
GO


EXEC dbo.FirstProc 1;
```

3. The correct answer is D. Table-valued parameters must be declared READONLY.

4. The correct answers are A and B. You can use the sp_recompile system SP or the WITH RECOMPILE option to force SQL Server to recompile an SP. FORCE RECOMPILE and DBCC RECOMPILE_ALL_SPS are not valid options/statements.

Chapter 7

1. True. In DDL triggers, the EVENTDATA function returns information about the DDL event that fired the trigger.

2. True. In a DML trigger, an UPDATE event is treated as a DELETE followed by an INSERT, so both the deleted and inserted virtual tables are populated for UPDATE events.

3. The correct answers are A, C, and E. SQL Server 2008 supports logon triggers, DDL triggers, and DML triggers.

4. The SET NOCOUNT ON statement prevents extraneous rows affected messages.

5. The correct answer is A. The COLUMNS_UPDATED function returns a varbinary string with bits set to represent affected columns.

6. True. @@ROWCOUNT at the beginning of a trigger returns the number of rows affected by the DML statement that fired the trigger.

7. False. You cannot create any AFTER triggers on a view.

Chapter 8

1. True. Symmetric keys can be used to encrypt data or other symmetric keys.

2. The correct answers are A, B, and E. SQL Server 2008 provides native support for DES, AES, and RC4 encryption. Although the Loki and Blowfish algorithms are real encryption algorithms, SQL Server does not provide native support for them.

3. False. SQL Server 2008 T-SQL provides no BACKUP ASYMMETRIC KEY statement.

4. You must turn on the *EKM provider enabled* option with sp_configure to activate EKM on your server.

5. False. TDE automatically encrypts the tempdb database, but it does not encrypt the model and master databases.

6. True. SQL Server automatically generates random initialization vectors when you encrypt data with symmetric encryption.

Chapter 9

1. True. When a CTE is not the first statement in a batch, the statement preceding it must end with a semicolon statement terminator.

2. The correct answers are A, B, and D. Recursive CTEs require the WITH keyword, an anchor query, and a recursive query. SQL Server does not support an EXPRESSION keyword.

3. The MAXRECURSION option can accept a value between 0 and *32767*.

4. The correct answer is E, all of the above. SQL Server supports the ROW_NUMBER, RANK, DENSE_RANK, and NTILE functions.

5. False. You cannot use ORDER BY with the OVER clause when used with aggregate functions.

6. True. When PARTITION BY and ORDER BY are both used in the OVER clause, PARTITION BY must appear first.

7. The names of all columns returned by a CTE must be *unique*.

Chapter 10

1. True. Stoplists and full-text indexes are stored in the database.

2. The correct answer is C. You can create a full-text index using the wizard in SSMS or the T-SQL `CREATE FULLTEXT INDEX` statement.

3. The `FREETEXT` predicate automatically performs word stemming and thesaurus *replacements* and *expansions*.

4. Stoplists contain stopwords, which are words that are *ignored* during full-text querying.

5. True. The `sys.dm_fts_parser` dynamic management function shows the results produced by word breaking and stemming.

Chapter 11

1. The correct answers are A, B, C, and D. The SQL Server `FOR XML` clause supports the `FOR XML RAW`, `FOR XML PATH`, `FOR XML AUTO`, and `FOR XML EXPLICIT` modes. `FOR XML RECURSIVE` is not a valid `FOR XML` mode.

2. `OPENXML` returns results in *edge* table format by default.

3. True. The `xml` data type `query()` method returns results as untyped `xml` instances.

4. The correct answer is C. A SQL Server primary XML index stores your `xml` data type columns in a preshredded relational format.

5. True. When you haven't defined a primary XML index on an `xml` data type column, performing XQuery queries against the column causes SQL Server to perform on-the-fly shredding of your XML data. This can result in a severe performance penalty.

6. True. Additional XML functionality, available through the .NET Framework, can be accessed via SQL Server's SQL CLR integration.

Chapter 12

1. True. The `FOR XML PATH` clause supports a subset of the W3C XPath recommendation for explicitly specifying your XML result structure.

2. The correct answer is A. The at sign (@) is used to identify attribute nodes in both XPath and XQuery.

3. The context item (indicated by a single period) specifies the current *node* or scalar *value* being accessed at any given point in time during query execution.

4. The correct answers are A, B, and D. You can declare XML namespaces for SQL Server XQuery expressions with the `WITH XMLNAMESPACES` clause, the `declare default element namespace` statement, or the `declare namespace` statement. There is no `CREATE XML NAMESPACE` statement.

5. In XQuery, you can dynamically construct XML via *direct* constructors or *computed* constructors.

6. True. SQL Server 2008 supports all five clauses of FLWOR expressions: `for`, `let`, `where`, `order by`, and `return`. Note that SQL Server 2005 did not support the `let` clause.

7. The correct answers are B, C, and D. XQuery provides three types of comparison operators: general comparison operators, node comparison operators, and value comparison operators.

Chapter 13

1. "Metadata" is "data that describes *data*."

2. *Catalog views* provide insight into database objects and server-wide configuration options.

3. The correct answer is B. Many catalog views are defined using an inheritance model. In the inheritance model, catalog views inherit columns from other catalog views. Some catalog views are also defined as the union of two other catalog views.

4. True. Dynamic management views and functions provide access to internal SQL Server data structures that would be otherwise inaccessible. DMVs and DMFs present these internal data structures in relational tabular format.

5. The correct answers are A and C. `INFORMATION_SCHEMA` views provide the advantages of ISO SQL standard compatibility and, as a consequence, cross-platform compatibility.

Chapter 14

1. The correct answers are A, B, C, and D. SQL Server 2008 provides support for SQL CLR UDFs, UDAs, UDTs, and SPs.

2. False. SQL Server 2008 expands the limit on `MaxByteSize` for UDAs and UDTs to over 2 billion bytes. In SQL Server 2005, there was an 8000 byte limit on the size of UDAs and UDTs.

3. The correct answer is D. `SAFE` permissions allow SQL CLR code to execute managed .NET code. `EXTERNAL_ACCESS` permissions are required to write to the file system, access network resources, and read the computer's registry.

4. True. SQL CLR UDAs and UDTs must be declared with the `Serializable` attribute.

5. A SQL CLR UDA that is declared as `Format.UserDefined` must implement the *IBinarySerialize* interface.

6. The correct answers are A, C, D, and E. A SQL CLR UDA is required to implement the following methods: `Init`, `Terminate`, `Merge`, and `Accumulate`. The `Aggregate` method is not a required method for UDAs.

Chapter 15

1. True. The `System.Data.SqlClient` namespace provides support for the SQL Server Native Client library, which provides optimized access to SQL Server.

2. The correct answer is B. Disconnected datasets cache required data locally and allow you to connect to a database only as needed.

3. The correct answers are A and C. The benefits of query parameterization include protection against SQL injection attacks and increased efficiency through query plan reuse.

4. False. When you turn on MARS, you can open two or more result sets over a single open connection. MARS requires only one open connection.

5. True. Visual Studio provides a visual O/RM designer with a drag-and-drop interface.

6. The correct answer is D. LINQ to SQL uses deferred query execution, meaning that it does not execute your query until the data returned by the query is actually needed.

Chapter 16

1. True. HTTP SOAP endpoints are deprecated in SQL Server 2008.

2. The correct answer is A. SQL Server can generate WSDL documents for SOAP HTTP endpoints.

3. Visual Studio 2008 provides the *ASP.NET Web Service* template for creating new web services.

4. True. Visual Studio 2008 includes a built-in graphical EDM designer beginning with SP 1.

5. The correct answer is C. ADO.NET Data Services accepts REST-style queries in requests.

Chapter 17

1. The correct answers are A and B. SQL Server 2008 supports the `INTERSECT` and `EXCEPT` set-based operators. SQL Server also supports the `UNION` and `UNION ALL` set-based operators.

2. True. The `OUTPUT` clause provides real-time feedback about rows affected by DML statements like `DELETE` and `INSERT`.

3. The TABLESAMPLE clause returns a *random* sample of rows from a table.

4. The correct answer is B. The SWITCHOFFSET function adjusts a given datetimeoffset value to another specified time offset.

5. The correct answers are A, C, and D. The image, text, and ntext LOB data types are deprecated and will be removed from a future version of SQL Server. None of the max data types are deprecated.

6. True. SQL Server 2008's FILESTREAM functionality utilizes NTFS functionality to provide streaming BLOB data support.

Chapter 18

1. The @@error system function automatically resets to 0 after every successful statement execution.

2. The correct answer is D. The ERROR_SEVERITY() function, available only in the CATCH block in SQL Server, returns the severity level of the error that occurred.

3. True. The RAISERROR statement allows you to raise errors in SQL Server.

4. True. Visual Studio provides integrated debugging of T-SQL functions and SPs. Using Visual Studio, you can step into T-SQL code and set breakpoints.

5. The correct answers are A and B. The potential problems with dynamic SQL include performance issues caused by lack of query plan reuse, and exposure to SQL injection attacks.

Chapter 19

1. The correct answers are A, B, and C. SQL Server 2008 uses data files with an .mdf extension, transaction log files with an .ldf extension, and additional data files with an .ndf extension.

2. True. SQL Server stores data in 8 KB storage units known as pages.

3. The correct answer is C. Eight contiguous 8 KB pages of storage in SQL Server are known as an extent.

4. A heap is an *unordered* collection of data pages.

5. Clustered indexes and nonclustered indexes are managed by SQL Server as *B-tree* structures.

6. The correct answers are A and C. SQL Server performance is measured in terms of throughput and response time.

APPENDIX B

■■■

XQuery Data Types

SQL Server 2008 supports the data types defined in the XQuery Data Model (XDM). The supported data types are listed with their definitions in Table B-1. The diagram in Figure B-1 is a quick reference showing the relationships between the XDM data types.

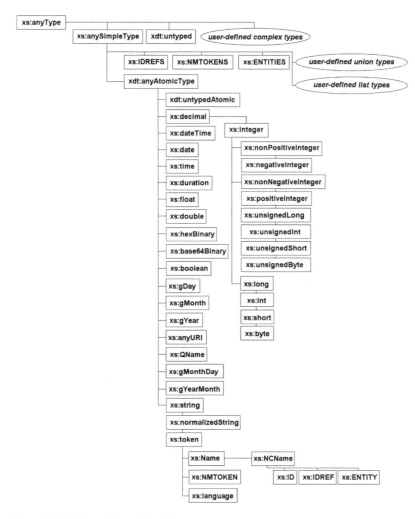

Figure B-1. *XQuery Data Type System*

Table B-1. *XQuery Data Types*

Type	Description
Base Types	
xs:anySimpleType	This is the base type for all simple built-in types.
xs:anyType	This is the base type for xs:anySimpleType and complex built-in types.
Date/Time Types	
xs:date	This type represents a Gregorian calendar–based date value exactly one day in length, represented in the format yyyy-mm-dd[*time_offset*]. *time_offset* can be a capital Z for *zero-meridian* (UTC), or in the format +/-hh:mm to represent a UTC offset. An example of a valid xs:date is 2006-12-25Z, which represents December 25, 2006, UTC time.
xs:dateTime	This type represents a Gregorian calendar–based date and time value with precision to 1/1000th of a second. The format is yyyy-mm-ddThh:mm:ss.sss[*time_offset*]. Time is specified using a 24-hour clock. As with xs:date, *time_offset* can be a capital Z (UTC) or a UTC offset in the format +/-hh:mm. A valid xs:dateTime value is 2006-10-30T13:00:59.500-05:00, which represents October 30, 2006, 1:00:59.5 PM, US Eastern Standard time. Unlike SQL Server 2005, in SQL Server 2008 the xs:dateTime type maintains the time zone information you assign instead of automatically converting all date/time values to a single time zone. The time zone is also not mandatory in SQL Server 2008.
xs:duration	This type represents a Gregorian calendar–based temporal (time-based) duration, represented as PyyyyYmmMddDThhHmmMss.sssS. P0010Y03M12DT00H00M00.000S, for instance, represents 10 years, 3 months, 12 days.
xs:gDay	This type represents a Gregorian calendar–based day. The format is ---dd[*time_offset*] (notice the three preceding hyphen [-] characters). The *time_offset* is optional. A valid xs:gDay value is ---09Z, which stands for the ninth day of the month, UTC time.
xs:gMonth	This type represents a Gregorian calendar–based month. The format is --mm[*time_offset*] (notice the two preceding hyphen characters). *time_offset* is optional. A valid xs:gMonth value is -12, which stands for December.
xs:gMonthDay	This type represents a Gregorian calendar–based month and day. The format is --mm-dd[*time_offset*] (notice the two preceding hyphens). The *time_offset* for this data type is optional. A valid xs:gMonthDay value is --02-29 for February 29.
xs:gYear	This type represents a Gregorian calendar–based year. The format is yyyy[*time_offset*]. The *time_offset* is optional. The year can also have a preceding hyphen character indicating a negative (BCE—"before the Christian Era") year as opposed to a positive (CE—"Christian Era") date. A valid xs:gYear value is -0044 for 44 BCE. Notice that all four digits are required in the year representation, even for years that can be normally represented with less than four digits.
xs:gYearMonth	This type represents a Gregorian calendar–based year and month. The format is yyyy-mm[*time_offset*]. The *time_offset* for this data type is optional and can be Z or a UTC offset. A valid xs:gYearMonth value is 2001-01 for January 2001.

Type	Description
xs:time	This type represents a time value with precision to 1/1000th of a second, using a 24-hour clock representation. The format is hh:mm:ss.sss [time_offset]. As with other temporal data types, time_offset can be Z (UTC) or a UTC offset in the format +/-hh:mm. A valid xs:time value is 23:59:59.000-06:00, which represents 11:59:59 PM, US Central Standard time. The canonical representation of midnight in 24-hour format is 00:00:00.

Binary Types

Type	Description
xs:base64Binary	This type represents Base64-encoded binary data. Base64-encoding symbols are defined in RFC 2045 (www.ietf.org/rfc/rfc2045.txt) as A through Z, a through z, 0 through 9, +, /, and the trailing = sign. Whitespace characters are also allowed, and lowercase letters are considered distinct from uppercase letters. An example of a valid xs:base64Binary value is QVByZXNzIEJvb2tzIEFuZCBTUUwwgU2V➥ ydmVyIDIwMDU=.
xs:hexBinary	This type represents hexadecimal-encoded binary data. The symbols defined for encoding data in hexadecimal format are 0 through 9, A through F, and a through f. Upper- and lowercase letters A through F are considered equivalent by this data type. An example of a valid xs:hexBinary value is 6170726573732E636F6D.

Boolean Type

Type	Description
xs:boolean	This type represents a Boolean binary truth value. The values supported are true (1) and false (0). An example of a valid xs:boolean value is true.

Numeric Types

Type	Description
xs:byte	This type represents an 8-bit signed integer in the range -128 to +127.
xs:decimal	This type represents an exact decimal value up to 38 digits in length. These numbers can have up to 28 digits before the decimal point and up to 10 digits after the decimal point. A valid xs:decimal value is 8372.9381.
xs:double	This type represents a double-precision floating point value patterned after the IEEE standard for floating point types. The representation of values is similar to xs:float values nE[+/-]e, where n is the mantissa followed by the letter E or e and an exponent e. The range of valid values for xs:double are approximately -1.79E+308 to -2.23E-308 for negative numbers, 0, and +2.23E-308 to +1.79E+308 for positive numbers.
xs:float	This type represents an approximate single-precision floating point value per the IEEE 754-1985 standard. The format for values of this type is nEe, where n is a decimal mantissa followed by the letter E or e and an exponent. The value represents $n \cdot 10^e$. The range for xs:float values is approximately -3.4028e+38 to -1.401298E-45 for negative numbers, 0, and +1.401298E-45 to +3.4028e+38 for positive numbers. The special values -INF and +INF represent negative and positive infinity. SQL Server does not support the XQuery-specified special value NaN, which stands for "not a number." A valid xs:float value is 1.98E+2.
xs:int	This type represents a 32-bit signed integer in the range -2147483648 to +2147483647.
xs:integer	This type represents an integer value up to 28 digits in length. A valid xs:integer value is 76372.

Continued

Table B-1. *Continued*

Type	Description
xs:long	This type represents a 64-bit signed integer in the range -9223372036854775808 to +9223372036854775807.
xs:negativeInteger	This type represents a negative nonzero integer value derived from the xs:integer type. It can be up to 28 digits in length.
xs:nonNegativeInteger	This type represents a positive or zero integer value derived from the xs:integer type. It can be up to 28 digits in length.
xs:nonPositiveInteger	This type represents a negative or zero integer value derived from the xs:integer type. It can be up to 28 digits in length.
xs:positiveInteger	This type represents a positive nonzero integer value derived from the xs:integer type. It can be up to 28 digits in length.
xs:short	This type represents a 16-bit signed integer in the range -37268 to +32767.
xs:unsignedByte	This type represents an unsigned 8-bit integer in the range 0 to 255.
xs:unsignedInt	This type represents an unsigned 32-bit integer in the range 0 to +4294967295.
xs:unsignedLong	This type represents an unsigned 64-bit integer in the range 0 to +18446744073709551615.
xs:unsignedShort	This type represents an unsigned 16-bit integer in the range 0 to +65535.
String Types	
xs:ENTITIES	This type is a space-separated list of ENTITY types.
xs:ENTITY	This type is equivalent to the ENTITY type from the XML 1.0 standard. The lexical space has the same construction as an xs:NCName.
xs:ID	This type is equivalent to the ID attribute type from the XML 1.0 standard. An xs:ID value has the same lexical construction as an xs:NCName.
xs:IDREF	This type represents the IDREF attribute type from the XML 1.0 standard. The lexical space has the same construction as an xs:NCName.
xs:IDREFS	This type is a space-separated list of IDREF attribute types.
xs:language	This type is a language identifier string representing natural language identifiers as specified by RFC 3066 (www.ietf.org/rfc/rfc3066.txt). A complete list of language codes is maintained by the IANA registry at www.iana.org/assignments/language-subtag-registry. Language identifiers must conform to the regular expression pattern [a-zA-Z]{1,8}(-[a-zA-Z0-9]{1,8})*. An example of a valid language identifier is tlh, which is the identifier for the Klingon language.
xs:Name	This type is an XML name string. A name string must match the XML-specified production for Name. Per the standard, a Name must begin with a letter, an underscore, or a colon, and may then contain a combination of letters, numbers, underscores, colons, periods, hyphens, and various other characters designated in the XML standard as *combining characters* and *extenders*. Refer to the XML standard at www.w3.org/TR/2000/WD-xml-2e-20000814#NT-Name for specific information about these additional allowable Name characters.
xs:NCName	This type is a noncolonized name. The format for an xs:NCName is the same as for xs:Name, but without colon characters.

Type	Description
xs:NMTOKEN	This type is an NMTOKEN type from the XML 1.0 standard. An xs:NMTOKEN value is composed of any combination of letters, numbers, underscores, colons, periods, hyphens, and XML combining characters and extenders.
xs:NMTOKENS	This type is a space-separated list of xs:NMTOKEN values.
xs:normalizedString	This type is an XML whitespace-normalized string. A *whitespace-normalized* string is one that does not contain the whitespace characters #x9 (tab), #xA (line feed), or #xD (carriage return).
xs:string	This type is an XML character string.
xs:token	This type is an XML whitespace-normalized string with the following additional restrictions on #x20 (space) characters: (1) it can have no leading or trailing spaces, and (2) it cannot contain any sequences of two space characters in a row.

Glossary

ACID

This is an acronym for *atomicity, consistency, isolation, durability*. These four concepts of transactional data stores, including SQL databases, ensure data integrity.

Adjacency list model

This is the representation of all arcs or edges of a graph as a list. In SQL, this is often implemented as a self-referential table in which each row maintains a pointer to its parent node in the graph.

ADO.NET Data Services

Also known as "Project Astoria," ADO.NET Data Services provides middle-tier support for accessing SQL Server databases through REST-style queries and entity data models (EDMs).

Anchor query

This is the nonrecursive query specified in the body of a CTE.

Application programming interface (API)

This is a well-defined interface provided by an application or service to support requests and communications from other applications.

Assembly

In SQL Server, a .NET assembly is a compiled SQL CLR executable or DLL.

Asymmetric encryption

Asymmetric encryption is encryption that requires two different keys: one to encrypt data and another to decrypt it. The most common form of asymmetric encryption is public key encryption, in which the two keys are mathematically related.

Atomic data types, list data types, and union data types

Atomic data types are indivisible data types that derive from the `xs:anyAtomicType` type. Examples include `xs:boolean`, `xs:date`, and `xs:integer`. List data types are types that are constructed of sequences of other types. Union data types are constructed from the *ordered union* of two or more data types, or a restricted subset of a data type. The XML

Schema 1.1 Part 2: Datatypes specification working draft (`www.w3.org/TR/xmlschema11-2/#ordinary-built-ins`) defines no built-in union data types.

Axis

An axis specifier indicates the relationship between the nodes selected by the location step and the context node. Examples of axis specifiers include `child`, `parent`, and `ancestor`.

Bulk Copy Program (BCP)

This is a command-line utility supplied with SQL Server for the purpose of quickly loading large datasets into tables.

Business Intelligence Development Studio (BIDS)

BIDS consists of the Visual Studio shell IDE and extensions and project types specifically for developing business intelligence projects.

Catalog view

A catalog view returns a SQL Server database and server-specific metadata.

Certificate

A certificate is an electronic document consisting of an asymmetric key with additional metadata such as an expiration date and a digital signature that allows it to be verified by a third-party like a certificate authority (CA).

Check constraint

A check constraint is a condition placed on a table that restricts the range of valid values for one or more columns.

Closed-world assumption (CWA)

The CWA is a logic formalism that states what is not known to be true is false. SQL databases violate the CWA through the introduction of `NULL`s.

Clustered index

This is an index that contains a table's row data in its leaf-level nodes.

Comment

XQuery comments are denoted by the (: and :) delimiters in XQuery queries. XQuery comments are ignored during processing. They should not be confused with XML *comment nodes*, which are designated with `<!--` and `-->` delimiters.

T-SQL allows single-line comments that begin with `--` or multiline comments enclosed in `/*` and `*/` delimiters.

Computed constructor

Computed constructors provide an alternative way to create XML nodes by specifying the type of node to be created through the use of special keywords.

Content expression

A content expression is part of a computed constructor, enclosed in braces, that generates XML node content.

Context item expression

This expression evaluates to the context node.

Context node

The context node is the node currently being processed. Each node of each set/sequence returned by a step in a location path is used in turn as a context node. Subsequent steps define their axes in relation to the current context node. For instance, with the sample XPath expression `/Root/Person/Address`, the `Root` node is the first context node. All `Person` nodes returned below `Root` become the context node in turn, and the `Address` nodes are retrieved relative to these context nodes.

Database encryption key

This is an encryption key used by TDE to encrypt entire SQL Server databases.

Database master key

This is a database-level encryption key used to secure other keys in the database.

Data domain

The data domain for a column includes all valid values that may be stored in that column. The data domain can be restricted through the use of data types, check constraints, referential integrity/foreign key constraints, and triggers.

Data page

A data page is the smallest unit of storage that SQL Server can allocate. The data page consists of 8 KB of logically contiguous storage.

Datum

A geodetic datum is a set of reference points against which position can be measured. A datum is often associated with a model of the shape of the earth to define a geographic coordinate system.

Empty sequence

This is an XPath 2.0/XQuery 1.0 sequence containing zero items.

Entity data model (EDM)

An EDM is an abstract logical representation of a physical database, used to implement database connectivity in the middle or client tiers.

Extensible key management (EKM)

EKM is a SQL Server 2008 encryption option that allows you to physically store encryption keys on third-party hardware security modules (HSMs).

Extent

An extent is SQL Server's basic allocation unit of storage. An extent is 64 KB in size and consists of eight logically contiguous data pages, each page being 8 KB in size.

Extract, Transform, Load (ETL)

ETL processes involve pulling data from disparate data sources, cleaning and scrubbing the data, manipulating it (transform), and storing it in the database.

Facet

A facet is a schema component used to constrain data types. A couple of commonly used facets are whiteSpace, which controls how whitespace in string values is handled, and length, which restricts values to a specific number of units in length.

Filter expression

This is a primary expression followed by zero or more predicates.

FLWOR expression

FLWOR is an acronym for the XQuery keywords for, let, where, order by, and return. FLWOR expressions support iteration and binding variables.

Foreign key constraint

A foreign key constraint is a logical coupling of two SQL tables through the values of specified columns.

Full-text catalog

A full-text catalog is a logical grouping of SQL Server full-text indexes for management purposes.

Full-text index

A full-text index enables advanced text-based searches to be performed against a database table.

Functions and Operators (F&O)

This is XQuery 1.0 and XPath 2.0 Functions and Operators specification, available at www.w3.org/TR/xquery-operators/.

General comparison

This is an existentially quantified XQuery comparison that may be applied to operand sequences of any length. In general comparisons, the nodes are atomized and the atomic values of both operands are compared using value comparisons. If any of the value comparisons evaluate to true, the result is true.

Geography Markup Language (GML)

GML is a standard for the representation of geographic data using XML.

Grouping set

A grouping set is a SQL Server 2008 feature that allows you to define sets of grouping columns in your queries.

Hash

A hash is the result of applying a mathematical function or transformation on data to generate a smaller "fingerprint" of the data. Generally, the most useful hash functions are one-way collision-free hashes that guarantee a high level of uniqueness in their results.

Heap

A heap is an unordered collection of data pages. Any table without a clustered index is a heap.

Heterogeneous sequence

A heterogeneous sequence is an XQuery sequence of atomic values of different types and/or XML nodes. SQL Server XQuery does not support heterogeneous sequences consisting of atomic values and nodes.

Homogenous sequence

A homogeneous sequence is an XQuery sequence consisting entirely of nodes or entirely of singleton atomic values of compatible data types.

Indirect recursion

Indirect recursion is recursion by a trigger that occurs when a trigger fires, causing another trigger of the same type to fire, which causes the first trigger to fire again.

Inflectional form

SQL Server integrated full-text search (FTS) can search for inflectional forms of a word, including verb tenses and plural forms of nouns.

Initialization vector (IV)

An IV is a block of bits that is used to obfuscate the first block of data during the encryption process.

Integrated full-text search (iFTS)

iFTS is the SQL Server 2008 implementation of SQL Server full-text search (FTS). iFTS features integration of the full-text search engine with the SQL Server query engine.

Language Integrated Query (LINQ)

LINQ adds native data source–agnostic querying capabilities to .NET languages using a declarative syntax.

Location path

A *path* is an XPath or XQuery expression that addresses a specific subset of nodes in an XML document. A location path is a series of *steps* separated by the solidus (forward slash) character, evaluated from left to right. Each step generates a sequence of items. Location paths can be relative or absolute. *Absolute* location paths begin with a single solidus character; *relative* location paths do not.

Logon triggers

Logon triggers fire in response to a server LOGON event.

Materialized path model

In the materialized path model for storing hierarchical data, the entire path to the root node is stored with each node in the hierarchy.

Multiple Active Result Sets (MARS)

MARS allows you to simultaneously open multiple result sets on a single open connection.

Nested sets model

In the nested sets model, hierarchical data is represented as a collection of sets containing other sets. The lower and upper bounds of each set define the contents of the set.

Node

XPath 2.0 and XQuery 1.0 treat XML data as a hierarchical tree structure, similar to (but not exactly the same as) the Document Object Model (DOM) that web programmers often use to manipulate HTML and XML. XPath and XQuery XML trees are composed of the seven types of nodes defined in the W3C XQuery 1.0 and XPath 2.0 Data Model (XDM), full descriptions of which are available at www.w3.org/TR/xpath-datamodel/#node-identity. These node types include the following:

- Attribute nodes, which represent XML attributes

- Comment nodes, which encapsulate XML comments

- Document nodes, which encapsulate XML documents

- Element nodes, which encapsulate XML elements

- Namespace nodes, which represent the binding of a namespace URI to a namespace prefix (or the default namespace)

- Processing instruction nodes, which encapsulate processing instructions

- Text nodes, which encapsulate XML character content

XPath 1.0 defines the node types it uses in Part 5 of the XPath 1.0 specification. The main difference between XPath 1.0 nodes and XDM nodes is that XPath 1.0 defines the *root node* of a document in place of the *document nodes* of the XDM. Another major difference is that in the XDM, element nodes are either explicitly or implicitly (based on content) assigned type information.

Node comparison

A node comparison in XQuery compares nodes by their document order or identity.

Node test

A node test is a condition that must be true for each node generated by a step. A node test can be based on the name of the node, the kind of node, or the type of node.

Nonclustered index

A nonclustered index is an index that stores the clustering key or row ID to the row data in its leaf nodes, depending on whether the table is a clustered table or a heap.

Optional occurrence indicator

The ? character, when used in conjunction with the cast as keywords, is referred to as the optional occurrence indicator. It indicates that the empty sequence is allowed.

Object-relational mapping (O/RM)

O/RM is a technique for mapping data between relational databases and object-oriented programming languages.

Open-world assumption (OWA)

The OWA is a logic formalism that states that the truth of a statement is independent of whether it is known to be true.

Parameterization

Parameterization is the act of using named or positional markers in place of constant values in a T-SQL query or statement. The actual values are passed to SQL Server independently of the actual query.

Path expression

See *location path*.

Predicate

A T-SQL predicate is an expression that evaluates to a SQL truth value. Predicates are used to control program flow and to limit the results of queries and the effect of statements.

An XQuery predicate is an expression enclosed in brackets ([ ]) that is used to filter a sequence. The predicate expressions are generally comparison expressions of some sort (equality, inequality, etc.).

Predicate truth value

In XQuery, a predicate truth value is a Boolean value derived from the result of an expression through a set of rules defined in the XQuery recommendation.

Primary expression

This is the basic *primitive* of the XQuery language. A primary expression can be a literal, a variable reference, a context item expression, a data type constructor, or a function call.

Query plan

A query plan is a sequence of logical and physical operators and data flows that the SQL query optimizer returns for use by the query processor to retrieve or modify data.

Recompilation

Recompilation is the process of compiling a new query plan for a given query, statement, or stored procedure (SP) when a plan already exists in the query plan cache. Recompilation can be triggered by SQL Server due to changes that have occurred since the prior query plan was generated for the statement, or it can be forced by user actions and T-SQL options.

Recursion

Recursion is a method of defining functions, CTEs, procedures, or triggers in such a way that they call themselves or cause themselves to be called multiple times.

Row constructor

A row constructor is a SQL Server 2008 feature that allows you to specify multiple rows in a single VALUES clause of the INSERT statement.

Scalar function

A scalar function returns a single atomic value as its result.

Searched CASE expression

A searched CASE expression allows you to specify one or more SQL predicates in WHEN clauses.

Sequence

XPath 2.0 and XQuery 1.0 define a sequence as an ordered collection of zero or more items. The term *ordered* is important here, as it differentiates a sequence from a *set*, which, as most T-SQL programmers know (or quickly come to realize), is unordered. XPath 1.0 defined its results in terms of *node sets*, which are unordered and cannot contain duplicates. XQuery changes this terminology to *node sequences*, which recognize the importance of node order in XML and can contain duplicates.

Server certificate

A server certificate is a certificate created in the master database for purposes of encrypting an entire database via transparent data encryption (TDE).

Service master key (SMK)

The SMK is an encryption key managed at the SQL Server service level. The SMK is used to encrypt all other keys in the SQL Server encryption key hierarchy.

Shredding

This is the process of converting XML data to relational style rows and columns.

Simple CASE expression

A simple CASE expression is defined with constants or value expressions in its WHEN clauses. The simple CASE evaluates to a series of simple equality expressions.

SOAP

SOAP, the Simple Object Access Protocol, is an XML-based protocol designed for exchanging structured information in distributed, decentralized environments.

Spatial data

Spatial data is used to represent objects and points on the earth.

Spatial index

A spatial index is a mechanism for increasing the efficiency of geographic calculations like the distance between points, or whether an object contains another point or object.

SQL injection

SQL injection is a technique that exploits security vulnerabilities in the application layer and middle tier, allowing users to execute arbitrary SQL statements on a server.

Step

A step in XQuery is composed of an axis, a node test, and zero or more predicates. Each step is a part of a path expression that generates a sequence of items and then filters the sequence.

Table type

This is an alias type that defines a table structure for use with table-valued parameters.

Three-valued logic (3VL)

The SQL language supports 3VL with three truth values: true, false, and unknown.

Transparent data encryption (TDE)

TDE is a SQL Server 2008 feature that allows you to encrypt an entire database at once.

Untyped XML

This is an XML data instance that is not associated with an XML schema collection.

User-defined aggregate (UDA)

A UDA is a SQL CLR routine that applies a function or calculation to an entire set of values.

User-defined type (UDT)

A UDT is a SQL CLR–based data type.

Value comparison

This is a comparison of single values in XQuery.

Well-formed XML

This is XML data that follows the W3C XML recommendation for well-formed data. It includes a single root element and properly nested elements, and is properly entitized.

Well-known text (WKT)

WKT format is a plain-text format for defining geospatial data.

Windowing functions

Windowing functions are functions that can partition and possibly order datasets before they are applied to the dataset partitions.

World Wide Web Consortium (W3C)

The W3C is a standards body with the stated mission of "developing interoperable technologies . . . to lead the Web to its full potential."

XML

XML is the acronym for Extensible Markup Language, a restricted form of SGML (Standardized General Markup Language) designed to be easily served, received, and processed on the Web.

XML Schema

Part 2 of the XML Schema 1.1 standard defines XML Schema data types, which are the basic data types utilized by XQuery.

XPath

XPath, or XML Path Language, is an expression language designed to allow processing of values that conform to the XPath Data Model (XDM).

XQuery

XQuery, or XML Query Language, is an XML query language designed to retrieve and interpret data from diverse XML sources.

XQuery/XPath Data Model (XDM)

The XQuery 1.0 and XPath 2.0 Data Model is defined by the W3C at www.w3.org/TR/2006/PR-xpath-datamodel-20061121/. See *XQuery*.

XSL

XSL, or Extensible Stylesheet Language, is a language for expressing style sheets, consisting of a language for transforming XML documents and an XML vocabulary for specifying formatting semantics. See *XSLT*.

XSLT

XSLT, or XSL Transformations, is a language for transforming XML documents into other XML documents. For instance, XSLT can be used to transform an XML document into an XHTML document. See *XSL*.

SQLCMD Quick Reference

SQLCMD is the standard text-based tool for executing batches of T-SQL on SQL Server. As a text-based tool, SQLCMD provides a lightweight but powerful tool for automating T-SQL batches. This appendix is designed as a quick reference to SQLCMD. The descriptions of many of the features and the functionality given here differ from BOL in some instances. The descriptions I give in this appendix are based on extensive testing of SQLCMD.

Command-Line Options

SQLCMD provides several command-line options to provide flexibility in connecting to SQL Server and executing T-SQL batches in a database. The full format for SQLCMD is shown here:

```
sqlcmd [ [-U login_id ] [-P password ] | [-E] ]
  [-S server [\instance] ] [-d db_name] [-H workstation]
  [-l timeout] [-t timeout] [-h headers] [-s column_separator] [-w column_width]
  [-a packet_size] [-I] [-L[c] ] [-W] [-r[0|1]]
  [-q "query"] [-Q "query"] [-c batch_term] [-e]
  [-m error_level] [-V severity_level] [-b]
  [-i input_file [,input_file₂ [, ...] ] ] ] [-o output_file] [-u]
  [-v var = "value" [,var₂ = "value₂"] [,...] ] [-X[1] ] [-x] [-?]
  [-z new_password] [-Z new_password]
  [-f codepage | i:in_codepage [,o:out_codepage] ]
  [-k[1|2] ] [-y display_width] [-Y display_width] [-p[1] ] [-R] [-A]
```

The available command-line options are listed in Table D-1. The SQLCMD command-line options are case sensitive, so, for example, -v is a different option from -V.

Table D-1. *SQLCMD Command-Line Options*

Option	Description
-?	The -? option displays the SQLCMD help/syntax screen.
-A	The -A option tells SQLCMD to log into SQL Server with a dedicated administrator connection. This type of connection is usually used for troubleshooting.
-a packet_size	The -a option requests communications with a specific packet size. The default is 4096. packet_size must be within the range 512 to 32767.

Continued

Table D-1. *Continued*

Option	Description
-b	The -b option specifies that SQLCMD exits on an error and returns an ERRORLEVEL value to the operating system. When this option is set, a SQL error of severity 11 or greater will return an ERRORLEVEL of 1; an error or message of severity 10 or less will return an ERRORLEVEL of 0. If the -V option is also used, SQLCMD will report only the errors with a severity greater than or equal to the severity_level (level 11 or greater) specified with the -V option.
-c batch_term	The -c option specifies the batch terminator. By default, it is the GO keyword. Avoid using special characters and reserved words as the batch terminator.
-d db_name	The -d option specifies the database to use after SQLCMD connects to SQL Server. Alternatively, you can set this option via the SQLCMDDBNAME environment variable. If the database specified does not exist, SQLCMD exits with an error.
-E	The -E option uses a trusted connection (Windows authentication mode) to connect to SQL Server. This option ignores the SQLCMDUSER and SQLCMDPASSWORD environment variables, and you cannot use it with the -U and -P options.
-e	The -e option prints (echoes) input scripts to the standard output device (usually the screen by default).
-f codepage | i:in_codepage [,oout_codepage]	The -f option specifies the code pages for input and output. If i: is specified, in_codepage is the input code page. If o: is specified, out_codepage is the output code page. If i: and o: are not specified, the codepage supplied is the code page for both input and output. To specify a code page, use its numeric identifier. The following code pages are supported by SQL Server 2005:

Code Page Number	Code Page Name
437	MS-DOS US English
850	Multilingual (MS-DOS Latin1)
874	Thai
932	Japanese
936	Chinese (Simplified)
949	Korean
950	Chinese(Traditional)
1250	Central European
1251	Cyrillic
1252	Latin1 (ANSI)
1253	Greek
1254	Turkish
1255	Hebrew
1256	Arabic
1257	Baltic
1258	Vietnamese

Option	Description
-H workstation	The -H option sets the workstation name. You can use -H to differentiate between sessions with commands such as sp_who.
-h headers	The -h option specifies the number of rows of data to print before a new column header is generated. The value must be from -1 (no headers) to 2147483647. The default value of 0 prints headings once for each set of results.

Option	Description
-I	The -I option sets the connection QUOTED_IDENTIFIER option to ON. Turning the QUOTED_IDENTIFIER option on makes SQL Server follow the ANSI SQL-92 rules for quoted identifiers. This option is set to OFF by default.
-i input_file [,input_file2] [,...]	The -i option specifies that SQLCMD should use files that contain batches of T-SQL statements for input. The files are processed in order from left to right. If any of the files don't exist, SQLCMD exits with an error. You can use the GO batch terminator inside your SQL script files.
-k [1|2]	The -k option removes control characters from the output. If 1 is specified, control characters are replaced one for one with spaces. If 2 is specified, consecutive control characters are replaced with a single space.
-L [c]	The -L option returns a listing of available SQL Server machines on the network and local computer. If the -Lc format is used, a "clean" listing is returned without heading information. The listing is limited to a maximum of 3,000 servers. Note that because of the way SQL Server broadcasts to gather server information, any servers that don't respond in a timely manner will not be included in the list. You cannot use the -L option with other options.
-l timeout	The -l option specifies the login timeout. The timeout value must be from 0 to 65534. The default value is 8 seconds, and a value of 0 is no timeout (infinite).
-m error_level	The -m option defines an error message customization level. Only errors with a severity greater than the specified level are displayed. If error_level is -1, all messages are returned, even informational messages.
-o output_file	The -o option specifies the file to which SQLCMD should direct output. If -o is not specified, SQLCMD defaults to standard output (usually the screen).
-P password	The -P option specifies a password to log into SQL Server when using SQL authentication mode. If -P is omitted, SQLCMD looks for the SQLCMDPASSWORD environment variable to get the password to log in. If the SQLCMDPASSWORD environment variable isn't found, SQLCMD will prompt you for the password to log in using SQL authentication mode. If neither -P nor -U is specified and the corresponding environment variables aren't set, SQLCMD will attempt to log in using Windows authentication mode.
-p [1]	The -p option prints performance statistics for each result set. Specifying 1 produces colon-separated output.
-Q "query" and -q "query"	The -Q and -q options both execute a SQL query/command from the command line. -q remains in SQLCMD after query completion. -Q exits SQLCMD after completion.
-R	The -R option specifies client regional settings for currency and date/time formatting.
-r [0|1]	The -r option redirects error message output to the standard error output device—the monitor by default. If 1 is specified, all error messages and informational messages are redirected. If 0 or no number is specified, only error messages with a severity of 11 or greater are redirected. The redirection does not work with the -o option; it does work if standard output is redirected with the Windows command-line redirector (>).

Continued

Table D-1. *Continued*

Option	Description
-S server [\instance]	The -S option specifies the SQL Server server or named instance to which SQLCMD should connect. If this option is not specified, SQLCMD connects to the default SQL Server instance on the local machine.
-s column_separator	The -s option sets the column separator character. By default, the column separator is a space character. separator can be enclosed in quotes, which is useful if you want to use a character that the operating system recognizes as a special character, such as the greater-than sign (>).
-t timeout	The -t option specifies the SQL query/command timeout in seconds. The timeout value must be in the range 0 to 65535. If -t is not specified, or if it is set to 0, queries/commands do not time out.
-U login_id	The -U option specifies the user login ID to log into SQL Server using SQL authentication mode. If the -U option is omitted, SQLCMD looks for the SQLCMDUSER environment variable to get the login password. If the -U option is omitted, SQLCMD attempts to use the current user's Windows login name to log in.
-u	The -u option specifies that the output of SQLCMD will be in Unicode format. Use this option with the -o option.
-V severity_level	The -V option specifies the lowest severity level that SQLCMD reports back. Errors and messages of severity less than severity_level are reported as 0. severity_level must be in the range 1 to 25. In a command-line batch file, -V returns the severity level of any SQL Server errors encountered via the ERRORLEVEL so that your batch file can take appropriate action.
-v var = "value" [,var2 = "value2"] [,...]	The -v option sets scripting variables that SQLCMD can use in your scripts to the specified values. I describe scripting variables later in this appendix.
-W	The -W option removes trailing spaces from a column. You can use this option with the -s option when preparing data that is to be exported to another application. You cannot use -W in conjunction with the -Y or -y options.
-w column_width	The -w option specifies screen width for output. The width value must be in the range 9 to 65535. The default of 0 is equivalent to the width of the output device. For screen output, the default is the width of the screen. For files, the default width is unlimited.
-X [1]	The -X option disables options that can compromise security in batch files. Specifically, the -X option does the following: • Disables the SQLCMD :!! and :ED commands. • Prevents SQLCMD from using operating system environment variables. • Disables the SQLCMD startup script. If a disabled command is encountered, SQLCMD issues a warning and continues processing. If the optional 1 is specified with the -X option, SQLCMD exits with an error when a disabled command is encountered. I describe SQLCMD commands, script variables, environment variables, and the startup script in more detail later in this appendix.

Option	Description
-x	The -x option forces SQLCMD to ignore scripting variables.
-Y display_width	The -Y option limits the number of characters returned for the char, nchar, varchar (8000 bytes or less), nvarchar (4000 bytes or less), and sql_variant data types.
-y display_width	The -y option limits the number of characters returned for variable-length data types such as varchar(max), varbinary(max), xml, text, and fixed-length or variable-length user-defined types (UDTs).
-Z new_password and -z new_password	When used with SQL authentication (the -U and -P options), the -Z and -z options change the SQL login password. If the -P option is not specified, SQLCMD will prompt you for the current password. -z changes the password and enters interactive mode. -Z exits SQLCMD immediately after the password is changed.

Scripting Variables

SQLCMD supports scripting variables, which allow you to dynamically replace script content at execution time. This allows you to use a single script in multiple scenarios. Using scripting variables you can, for instance, execute a single script against different servers or databases without modification. SQLCMD allows you to set your own custom scripting variables with the -v command-line option. If more than one scripting variable is specified with the same name, the variable with the highest precedence (according to the following list) is used:

1. System-level environment variables have the highest precedence.

2. User-level environment variables are next.

3. Variables set via the command shell SET option are next.

4. Variables set via the SQLCMD -v command-line option are next.

5. Variables set inside a SQLCMD batch via the :SETVAR command have the lowest precedence.

■**Note** The -X and -x options disable startup script execution and environment variable access, respectively. -x also prevents SQLCMD from dynamically replacing scripting variable references in your code with the appropriate values. This is a feature designed for secure environments where scripting variable usage could compromise security.

SQLCMD also provides several predefined scripting variables, which are listed in Table D-2. You can set the predefined read-only SQLCMD scripting variables via the command shell SET option or through SQLCMD command-line options; you cannot alter them from within a SQLCMD script with :SETVAR.

Table D-2. *SQLCMD Scripting Variables*

Name	Default	Read/Write	Description
SQLCMDCOLSEP		Read/write	Column separator character. See the -s command-line switch (in Table D-1).
SQLCMDCOLWIDTH	0	Read/write	Output column width. See the -w command-line switch.
SQLCMDDBNAME		Read-only	Default database name. See the -d command-line switch.
SQLCMDERRORLEVEL	0	Read/write	Level of error message customization. See the -m command-line switch.
SQLCMDHEADERS	0	Read/write	Number of lines to print between result set headers. See the -h command-line switch.
SQLCMDINI		Read-only	SQLCMD startup script.
SQLCMDLOGINTIMEOUT	8	Read/write	Login timeout setting (in seconds). See the -l command-line switch.
SQLCMDMAXFIXEDTYPEWIDTH	256	Read/write	Fixed-width data type display limit. See the -Y command-line switch.
SQLCMDMAXVARTYPEWIDTH	0	Read/write	Variable-length data type display limit. See the -y command-line switch.
SQLCMDPACKETSIZE	4096	Read-only	Packet size being used for SQL communications. See the -a command-line switch.
SQLCMDPASSWORD		N/A	SQL Server login password. See the -P command-line switch.
SQLCMDSERVER	server name	Read-only	SQL Server/instance name. See the -S command-line switch.
SQLCMDSTATTIMEOUT	0	Read/write	Query/command timeout setting (in seconds). See the -t command-line switch.
SQLCMDUSER		Read-only	SQL Server login username. See the -U command-line switch.
SQLCMDWORKSTATION		Read-only	SQL Server workstation name. See the -H command-line switch.

Commands

SQLCMD recognizes a set of commands that are not part of T-SQL. These SQLCMD commands are not recognized by other query tools; they're not even recognized by SSMS (except when running it in SQLCMD mode). SQLCMD commands all begin on a line with a colon (:) to identify them as different from T-SQL statements. You can intersperse SQLCMD commands within your T-SQL scripts. Table D-3 lists the SQLCMD commands available.

Tip For backward compatibility with older `osql` scripts, you can enter the following commands without a colon prefix: `!!`, `ED`, `RESET`, `EXIT`, and `QUIT`. Also, SQLCMD commands are case insensitive, they must appear at the beginning of a line, and they must be on their own line. A SQLCMD command cannot be followed on the same line by a T-SQL statement or another SQLCMD command.

Table D-3. *SQLCMD Commands*

Command	Description
`:!! command`	The `:!!` command invokes the command shell. It executes the specified operating system command in the command shell.
`:CONNECT server [\instance]` `[-l timeout] [-U user [-P password]]`	The `:CONNECT` command connects to a SQL Server instance. The server name (`server`) and instance name (`\instance`) are specified in the command. When `:CONNECT` is executed, the current connection is closed. You can use the following options with the `:CONNECT` command: the `-l` option specifies the login timeout (specified in seconds; 0 equals no timeout); the `-U` option specifies the SQL authentication username; the `-P` option specifies the SQL authentication password.
`:ED`	The `:ED` command starts the text editor to edit the current batch or the last executed batch. The `SQLCMDEDITOR` environment variable defines the application used as the SQLCMD editor. The default is the Windows `EDIT` utility.
`:ERROR destination`	The `:ERROR` command redirects error messages to the specified `destination`. `destination` can be a file name, `STDOUT` for standard output, or `STDERR` for standard error output.
`:EXIT [()|(query)]`	The `:EXIT` command has three forms: `:EXIT` alone immediately exits without executing the batch and with no return code. `:EXIT()` executes the current batch and exits with no return code. `:EXIT(query)` executes the batch, including the query specified, and returns the first value of the first result row of the query as a 4-byte integer to the operating system.
`GO [n]`	`GO` is the batch terminator. The `GO` batch terminator executes the statements in the cache. If n is specified, `GO` will execute the statement *n* times.
`:HELP`	The `:HELP` command displays a list of SQLCMD commands.
`:LIST`	The `:LIST` list command lists the contents of the current batch of statements in the statement cache.
`:LISTVAR`	The `:LISTVAR` command lists all the SQLCMD scripting variables (that have been set) and their current values.
`:ON ERROR action`	The `:ON ERROR` command specifies the action SQLCMD should take when an error is encountered. `action` can be one of two values: `EXIT` stops processing and exits, returning the appropriate error code. `IGNORE` disregards the error and continues processing.

Continued

Table D-3. *Continued*

Command	Description
`:OUT destination`	The `:OUT` command redirects output to the specified destination. `destination` can be a file name, `STDOUT` for standard output, or `STDERR` for standard error output. Output is sent to `STDOUT` by default.
`:PERFTRACE destination`	The `:PERFTRACE` command redirects performance trace/timing information to the specified `destination`. `destination` can be a file name, `STDOUT` for standard output, or `STDERR` for standard error output. Trace information is sent to `STDOUT` by default.
`:QUIT`	The `:QUIT` command quits SQLCMD immediately.
`:R filename`	The `:R` command reads in the contents of the specified file and appends it to the statement cache.
`:RESET`	The `:RESET` command resets/clears the statement cache.
`:SERVERLIST`	The `:SERVERLIST` command lists all SQL Server instances on the local machine and any servers broadcasting on the local network. If SQLCMD doesn't receive timely responses from a server on the network, it may not be listed.
`:SETVAR var [value]`	The `:SETVAR` command allows you to set or remove SQLCMD scripting variables. To remove a SQLCMD scripting variable, use the `:SETVAR var` format. To set a SQLCMD scripting variable to a value, use the `:SETVAR var value` format.
`:XML ON|OFF`	The `:XML` command indicates to SQLCMD that you expect XML output from SQL Server (i.e., the `SELECT` statement's `FOR XML` clause). Use `:XML ON` before your SQL batch is run and `:XML OFF` after the batch has executed (after the `GO` batch terminator).

Index

You Need the Companion eBook

Your purchase of this book entitles you to buy the companion PDF-version eBook for only $10. Take the weightless companion with you anywhere.

We believe this Apress title will prove so indispensable that you'll want to carry it with you everywhere, which is why we are offering the companion eBook (in PDF format) for $10 to customers who purchase this book now. Convenient and fully searchable, the PDF version of any content-rich, page-heavy Apress book makes a valuable addition to your programming library. You can easily find and copy code—or perform examples by quickly toggling between instructions and the application. Even simultaneously tackling a donut, diet soda, and complex code becomes simplified with hands-free eBooks!

Once you purchase your book, getting the $10 companion eBook is simple:

❶ Visit **www.apress.com/promo/tendollars/**.

❷ Complete a basic registration form to receive a randomly generated question about this title.

❸ Answer the question correctly in 60 seconds, and you will receive a promotional code to redeem for the $10.00 eBook.

Offer valid through 2/09.